The Complexity of Boolean Functions

Wiley-Teubner Series in Computer Science

The Complexity of Boolean Functions

Ingo Wegener
Johann Wolfgang Goethe-Universität

B. G. TEUBNER
Stuttgart

JOHN WILEY & SONS
Chichester · New York · Brisbane · Toronto · Singapore

Library of Congress Cataloguing in Publication Data:
Wegener, Ingo
  The complexity of Boolean functions.
  (Wiley–Teubner series in computer science)
  Bibliography: p.
  Inlcudes index.
  1. Algebra, Boolean. 2. Computational complexity.
I. Title. II. Series.
AQ10.3.W44 1987 511.3'24 87-10388

ISBN 0 471 91555 6 (Wiley)

British Library Cataloguing in Publication Data:

Wegener, Ingo
  The complexity of Boolean functions.—(Wiley–Teubner series in computer science).
  1. Electronic data processing—Mathematics 2. Algebra, Boolean
  I.Title II. Teubner, B. G.
004.01'511324   QA76.9.M3

ISBN 0 471 91555 6

CIP- Kurztitelaufnahme der Deutschen Bibliothek

Wegener, Ingo
The complexity of Boolean functions/Ingo Wegener.—Stuttgart: Teubner; Chichester;
New York; Brisbane; Toronto; Singapore: Wiley, 1987
  (Wiley–Teubner series in computer science)
  ISBN 3 519 02107 2 (Teubner)
  ISBN 0 471 91555 6 (Wiley)

Printed and bound in Great Britain

Preface

When Goethe had fundamentally rewritten his IPHIGENIE AUF TAURIS eight years after its first publication, he stated (with resignation, or perhaps as an excuse or just an explanation) that, "Such a work is never actually finished: one has to declare it finished when one has done all that time and circumstances will allow." This is also my feeling after working on a book in a field of science which is so much in flux as the complexity of Boolean functions. On the one hand it is time to set down in a monograph the multiplicity of important new results; on the other hand new results are constantly being added.

I have tried to describe the latest state of research concerning results and methods. Apart from the classical circuit model and the parameters of complexity, circuit size and depth, providing the basis for sequential and for parallel computations, numerous other models have been analysed, among them monotone circuits, Boolean formulas, synchronous circuits, probabilistic circuits, programmable (universal) circuits, bounded depth circuits, parallel random access machines and branching programs. Relationships between various parameters of complexity and various models are studied, and also the relationships to the theory of complexity and uniform computation models.

The book may be used as the basis for lectures and, due to the inclusion of a multitude of new findings, also for seminar purposes. Numerous exercises provide the opportunity of practising the acquired methods. The book is essentially complete in itself, requiring only basic knowledge of computer science and mathematics.

This book I feel should not just be read with interest but should encourage the reader to do further research. I do hope, therefore, to have written a book in accordance with Voltaire's statement, "The most useful books are those that make the reader want to add to vi

them."

I should like to express my thanks to Annemarie Fellmann, who set up the manuscript, to Linda Stapleton for the careful reading of the text, and to Christa, whose complexity (in its extended definition, as the sum of all features and qualities) far exceeds the complexity of all Boolean functions.

Frankfurt a.M./Bielefeld, November 1986   Ingo Wegener

Contents

1.   Introduction to the theory of Boolean functions and
   circuits   1
1.1   Introduction   1
1.2   Boolean functions, laws of computation, normal forms   3
1.3   Circuits and complexity measures   6
1.4   Circuits with bounded fan-out   10
1.5   Discussion   15
    Exercises   19

2.   The minimization of Boolean functions   22
2.1   Basic definitions   22
2.2   The computation of all prime implicants and reductions
   of the table of prime implicants   25
2.3   The minimization method of Karnaugh   29
2.4   The minimization of monotone functions   31
2.5   The complexity of minimizing   33
2.6   Discussion   35
    Exercises   36

3.   The design of efficient circuits for some fundamental
   functions   39
3.1   Addition and subtraction   39
3.2   Multiplication   51
3.3   Division   67
3.4   Symmetric functions   74
3.5   Storage access   76
3.6   Matrix product   78
3.7   Determinant   81
    Exercises   83

4.   Asymptotic results and universal circuits   87
4.1   The Shannon effect   87
4.2   Circuits over complete bases   88
4.3   Formulas over complete bases   93
4.4   The depth over complete bases   96
4.5   Monotone functions   98
4.6   The weak Shannon effect   106
4.7   Boolean sums and quadratic functions   107
4.8   Universal circuits   110
      Exercises   117

5.   Lower bounds on circuit complexity   119
5.1   Discussion on methods   119
5.2   2 n - bounds by the elimination method   122
5.3   Lower bounds for some particular bases   125
5.4   2.5 n - bounds for symmetric functions   127
5.5   A 3n - bound   133
5.6   Complexity theory and lower bounds on circuit
      complexity   138
      Exercises   142

6.   Monotone circuits   145
6.1   Introduction   145
6.2   Design of circuits for sorting and threshold functions   148
6.3   Lower bounds for threshold functions   154
6.4   Lower bounds for sorting and merging   158
6.5   Replacement rules   160
6.6   Boolean sums   163
6.7   Boolean convolution   168
6.8   Boolean matrix product   170
6.9   A generalized Boolean matrix product   173
6.10 Razborov's method   180
6.11 An exponential lower bound for clique functions   184
6.12 Other applications of Razborov's method   192

6.13 Negation is powerless for slice functions   195
6.14 Hard slices of NP-complete functions   203
6.15 Set circuits - a new model for proving lower bounds   207
      Exercises   214

7.   Relations between circuit size, formula size and depth   218
7.1   Formula size vs. depth   218
7.2   Circuit size vs. formula size and depth   221
7.3   Joint minimization of depth and circuit size, trade-offs 225
7.4   A trade-off result   229
      Exercises   233

8.   Formula size   235
8.1   Threshold - 2   235
8.2   Design of efficient formulas for threshold - k   239
8.3   Efficient formulas for all threshold functions   243
8.4   The depth of symmetric functions   247
8.5   The Hodes and Specker method   249
8.6   The Fischer, Meyer and Paterson method   251
8.7   The Nechiporuk method   253
8.8   The Krapchenko method   258
      Exercises   263

9.   Circuits and other non uniform computation methods vs.
      Turing machines and other uniform computation models   267
9.1   Introduction   267
9.2   The simulation of Turing machines by circuits: time and
      size   271
9.3   The simulation of Turing machines by circuits: space and
      depth   277
9.4   The simulation of circuits by Turing machines with
      oracles   279
9.5   A characterization of languages with polynomial circuits 282
9.6   Circuits and probabilistic Turing machines   285

9.7	May NP-complete problems have polynomial circuits ?	288
9.8	Uniform circuits	292
	Exercises	294
10.	Hierarchies, mass production and reductions	296
10.1	Hierarchies	296
10.2	Mass production	301
10.3	Reductions	306
	Exercises	318
11.	Bounded-depth circuits	320
11.1	Introduction	320
11.2	The design of bounded-depth circuits	321
11.3	An exponential lower bound for the parity function	325
11.4	The complexity of symmetric functions	332
11.5	Hierarchy results	337
	Exercises	338
12.	Synchronous, planar and probabilistic circuits	340
12.1	Synchronous circuits	340
12.2	Planar and VLSI - circuits	344
12.3	Probabilistic circuits	352
	Exercises	359
13.	PRAMs and WRAMs: Parallel random access machines	361
13.1	Introduction	361
13.2	Upper bounds by simulations	363
13.3	Lower bounds by simulations	368
13.4	The complexity of PRAMs	373
13.5	The complexity of PRAMs and WRAMs with small communication width	380
13.6	The complexity of WRAMs with polynomial resources	387
13.7	Properties of complexity measures for PRAMs and WRAMs	396
	Exercises	411

14.	Branching programs	414
14.1	The comparison of branching programs with other models of computation	414
14.2	The depth of branching programs	418
14.3	The size of branching programs	421
14.4	Read-once-only branching programs	423
14.5	Bounded-width branching programs	431
14.6	Hierarchies	436
	Exercises	439
	References	442
	Index	455

1. INTRODUCTION TO THE THEORY OF BOOLEAN FUNCTIONS AND CIRCUITS

1.1 Introduction

Which of the following problems is easier to solve - the addition or the multiplication of two n-bit numbers ? In general, people feel that adds are easier to perform and indeed, people as well as our computers perform additions faster than multiplications. But this is not a satisfying answer to our question. Perhaps our multiplication method is not optimal. For a satisfying answer we have to present an algorithm for addition which is more efficient than any possible algorithm for multiplication. We are interested in efficient algorithms (leading to upper bounds on the complexity of the problem) and also in arguments that certain problems cannot be solved efficiently (leading to lower bounds). If upper and lower bound for a problem coincide then we know the complexity of the problem.

Of course we have to agree on the measures of efficiency. Comparing two algorithms by examining the time someone spends on the two procedures is obviously not the right way. We only learn which algorithm is more adequat for the person in question at this time. Even different computers may lead to different results. We need fair criterions for the comparison of algorithms and problems. One criterion is usually not enough to take into account all the relevant aspects. For example, we have to understand that we are able to work only sequentially, i.e. one step at a time, while the hardware of computers has arbitrary degree of parallelism. Nowadays one even constructs parallel computers consisting of many processors. So we distinguish between sequential and parallel algorithms.

The problems we consider are Boolean functions $f : \{0,1\}^n \rightarrow \{0,1\}^m$. There is no loss in generality if we encode all information by the binary alphabet $\{0,1\}$. But we point out that we investigate finite functions, the number of possible inputs as well as the number of possible outputs is finite. Obviously, all these functions are computable. In § 2 we introduce a rather general computation model, namely circuits. Circuits build a model for sequential computations as well as for parallel computations. Furthermore, this model is rather robust. For several other models we show that the complexity of Boolean functions in these models does not differ significantly from the circuit complexity. Considering circuits we do not take into account the specific technical and organizational details of a computer. Instead of that, we concentrate on the essential subjects.

The time we require for the computation of a particular function can be reduced in two entirely different ways, either using better computers or better algorithms. We like to determine the complexity of a function independently from the stage of the development of technology. We only mention a universal time bound for electronic computers. For any basic step at least $5.6 \cdot 10^{-33}$ seconds are needed (Simon (77)).

Boolean functions and their complexity have been investigated since a long time, at least since Shannon's (49) pioneering paper. The earlier papers of Shannon (38) and Riordan and Shannon (42) should also be cited. I tried to mention the most relevant papers on the complexity of Boolean functions. In particular, I attempted to present also results of papers written in Russian. Because of a lack of exchange several results have been discovered independently in both "parts of the world".

There is large number of textbooks on "logical design" and "switching circuits" like Caldwell (64), Edwards (73), Gumm and Poguntke (81), Hill and Peterson (81), Lee (78), Mendelson (82), Miller (79), Muroga (79), and Weyh (72). These books are essentially concerned with the minimization of Boolean functions in circuits with only two logical levels. We only deal with this problem in Ch.2 briefly. The algebraical starting-point of Hotz (72) will not be continued here. We develop the theory of the complexity of Boolean functions in the sense of the book by Savage (76) and the survey papers by

Fischer (74), Harper and Savage (73), Paterson (76), and Wegener (84 a). As almost 60% of our more than 300 cited papers were published later than Savage's book, many results are presented for the first time in a textbook. The fact that more than 40% of the relevant papers on the complexity of Boolean functions are published in the eighties is a statistical argument for the claim that the importance of this subject has increased during the last years.

Most of the book is self-contained. Fundamental concepts of linear algebra, analysis, combinatorics, the theory of efficient algorithms (see Aho, Hopcroft and Ullman (74) or Knuth (81)) and the complexity theory (see Garey and Johnson (79) or Paul (78)) will be applied.

1.2 Boolean functions, laws of computation, normal forms

By $B_{n,m}$ we denote the set of Boolean functions $f : \{0,1\}^n \rightarrow \{0,1\}^m$. B_n also stands for $B_{n,1}$. Furthermore we define the most important subclass of $B_{n,m}$, the class of monotone functions $M_{n,m}$. Again $M_n = M_{n,1}$.

DEFINITION 2.1 : Let $a = (a_1, \ldots, a_n)$, $b = (b_1, \ldots, b_n) \in \{0,1\}^n$. We use the canonical ordering, i.e. $a \leq b$ iff $a_i \leq b_i$ for all i where $0 \leq 1$. A Boolean function is called monotone iff $a \leq b$ implies $f(a) \leq f(b)$.

For functions $f \in B_n$ we have 2^n different inputs, each of them can be mapped to 0 or 1.

PROPOSITION 2.1. : There exist 2^{2^n} functions in B_n.

Because of the large number of Boolean functions we avoid proofs by case inspection at least if $n \geq 3$. Since we use the 16 functions of B_2 as basic operations, we discuss these functions. We have the two constant functions also denoted by 0 and 1. Similarly, we use x_i to denote not only a variable but also to denote the i-th projection. Two projections, x_1 and x_2, are contained in B_2 as there are two negations, $\bar{x}_1$ and $\bar{x}_2$ ($\bar{x} = 1$ iff $x = 0$). The logical conjunction $x \wedge y$ computes 1 iff $x = y = 1$, and the logical disjunction $x \vee y$ computes 1 iff $x = 1$ or $y = 1$. Let $x^1 = x$ and $x^0 = \bar{x}$. For $a,b,c \in \{0,1\}$ we get 8 different functions of type $-\wedge$, namely $(x^a \wedge y^b)^c$. Obviously $x \vee y = \neg(\bar{x} \wedge \bar{y})$ is of type $-\wedge$. The same holds for $\mathrm{NAND}(x,y) = \neg(x \wedge y)$ and $\mathrm{NOR}(x,y) = \neg(x \vee y) = \bar{x} \wedge \bar{y}$. The EXCLUSIVE - OR (XOR)-function also called parity is denoted by $x \oplus y$ and computes 1 iff exactly one of the variables equals 1. The last 2 functions in B_2 are XOR and its negation $x \equiv y = \neg(x \oplus y)$ called EQUIVALENCE. $\oplus$ and $\equiv$ are type $-\oplus$ functions. We list some simple laws of computation.

PROPOSITION 2.2 : Let x,y and z be Boolean variables.

i)   (Calculations with constants): $x \vee 0 = x$, $x \vee 1 = 1$, $x \wedge 0 = 0$, $x \wedge 1 = x$, $x \oplus 0 = x$, $x \oplus 1 = \bar{x}$.

ii) $\vee$, $\wedge$ and $\oplus$ are associative and commutative.

iii) $(\vee,\wedge)$, $(\wedge,\vee)$ and $(\oplus,\wedge)$ are distributive, e.g. $x \wedge (y \oplus z) = (x \wedge y) \oplus (x \wedge z)$.

iv) (Laws of simplification): $x \vee x = x$, $x \vee \bar{x} = 1$, $x \wedge x = x$, $x \wedge \bar{x} = 0$, $x \oplus x = 0$, $x \oplus \bar{x} = 1$, $x \vee (x \wedge y) = x$, $x \wedge (x \vee y) = x$.

v)   (Laws of deMorgan): $\neg(x \vee y) = \bar{x} \wedge \bar{y}$, $\neg(x \wedge y) = \bar{x} \vee \bar{y}$.

These laws of computation remain correct if we replace Boolean variables by Boolean functions. By induction we may generalize the laws of deMorgan to n variables. We remark that $(\{0,1\},\oplus,\wedge)$ is the Galois field $\mathbb{Z}_2$. Instead of $x \wedge y$ we often write only xy. In case of doubt we perform conjunctions at first, so $x \wedge y \vee z$ stands for $(x \wedge y) \vee z$. Similarly to the iterated sum Σ and the iterated product

Π, we use $\wedge, \vee$ and $\oplus$ for iterated $\wedge, \vee, \oplus$.

Before presenting computation models for Boolean functions we want to discuss how we can define and describe Boolean functions. Because we consider finite functions $f \in B_{n,m}$ we can describe them by a complete table $x \to f(x)$ whose length is 2^n. If $f \in B_n$ it is sufficient to specify $f^{-1}(1)$ or $f^{-1}(0)$. In general it is easier to describe a function by its behavior, e.g. $f \in B_n$ computes 1 iff the number of ones in the input is larger than the number of zeros.

As a second step we describe Boolean functions by Boolean operations. The disjunctive and conjunctive normal form (DNF and CNF) are based on $f^{-1}(1)$ and $f^{-1}(0)$ resp.

DEFINITION 2.2 : The minterm m_a for $a = (a(1),...,a(n)) \in \{0,1\}^n$ is defined by $m_a(x) = x_1^{a(1)} \wedge \cdots \wedge x_n^{a(n)}$.
The appropriate maxterm is $s_a(x) = x_1^{\neg a(1)} \vee \cdots \vee x_n^{\neg a(n)}$.

THEOREM 2.1 : $f(x) = \bigvee_{a \in f^{-1}(1)} m_a(x) = \bigwedge_{b \in f^{-1}(0)} s_b(x)$.

The first and second representation are called disjunctive and conjunctive normal form resp. (DNF and CNF).

Proof : By definition, $m_a(x) = 1$ iff $x = a$ and $s_a(x)=0$ iff $x = a$. $f(x)$ equals 1 iff $x \in f^{-1}(1)$ iff one of the minterms $m_a(x)$ for $a \in f^{-1}(1)$ computes 1. Similar arguments work for the CNF of f.

$\square$

Since $(f \wedge g)^{-1}(1) = f^{-1}(1) \cap g^{-1}(1)$ and $(f \vee g)^{-1}(1) = f^{-1}(1) \cup g^{-1}(1)$, it is easy to compute the DNF (or CNF) of $f \wedge g$ or $f \vee g$. Both representations are not convenient for the solution of Boolean equations. We are not able to subtract terms, because neither $(\{0,1\}, \wedge)$ nor $(\{0,1\}, \vee)$ is a group as $(\{0,1\}, \oplus)$ is.

THEOREM 2.2 : (Ring sum expansion (RSE) of f)

For each Boolean function $f \in B_n$ there is exactly one 0-1 - vector $a = (a_A)_{A \subseteq \{1,\ldots,n\}}$ such that

$$f(x) = \bigoplus_{A \subseteq \{1,\ldots,n\}} a_A \wedge \bigwedge_{i \in A} x_i \, . \qquad (2.1)$$

Proof : The existence of the vector a is proved constructively. We start with the CNF of f. Using the laws of deMorgan, we replace disjunctions by conjunctions and negations, in particular, the maxterm $s_b(x)$ is replaced by $\neg\, (x_1^{b(1)} \wedge \cdots \wedge x_n^{b(n)})$. Afterwards we replace negations $\bar{x}$ by $x \oplus 1$. Since we obtain a representation of f by $\wedge$ and $\oplus$, we may apply the law of distributivity to get a $\oplus$ -sum of $\wedge$ -products and constants. Since $t \oplus t = 0$, we set $a_A = 1$ iff the number of terms $\wedge\, x_i$ $(i \in A)$ in our sum is odd.

For different functions f and g we obviously require different vectors $a(f)$ and $a(g)$. Since the number of different vectors $a = (a_A)_{A \subseteq \{1,\ldots,n\}}$ equals the number of functions $f \in B_n$, there cannot be two different vectors a and a' for f . $\qquad\qquad\qquad \square$

The RSE of f is appropriate for the solution of Boolean equations. Since $t \oplus t = 0$, we may subtract t by $\oplus$ -adding t .

1.3 Circuits and complexity measures

We may use the normal forms of § 2 for the computation of Boolean functions. But intuitively simple functions may have exponential length for all normal forms. Consider for example $f \in B_n$ where $f(x) = 1$ iff $x_1 + \cdots + x_n \equiv 0 \mod 3$.

In order to develop an appropriate computation model we try to simulate the way in which we perform calculations with long numbers. We only use a small set of well-known operations, the addition of digits, the application of multiplication tables, comparison of digits, and if - tests. All our calculations are based on these basic operations only. Here we choose a finite set Ω of one - output Boolean functions as basis. Inputs of our calculations are the variables $x_1, \ldots, x_n$ and w.l.o.g. also the constants 0 and 1. We do neither distinguish between constants and constant functions nor between variables and projections $x \to x_i$. One computation step is the application of one of the basic operations $\omega \in \Omega$ to some inputs and/or already computed data. In the following we give a correct description of such a computation called circuit.

DEFINITION 3.1 : An Ω - circuit works for a fixed number n of Boolean input variables $x_1, \ldots, x_n$. It consists of a finite number b of gates $G(1),\ldots,G(b)$. Gate $G(i)$ is defined by its type $\omega_i \in \Omega$ and, if $\omega_i \in B_{n(i)}$, some $n(i)$ - tuple $(P(1),\ldots,P(n(i)))$ of predecessors. $P(j)$ may be some element from $\{0,1,x_1,\ldots,x_n, G(1),\ldots,G(i-1)\}$. By $res_{G(i)}$ we denote the Boolean function computed at $G(i)$. res is defined inductively. For an input I res_I is equal to I.
If $G(i) = (\omega_i, P(1),\ldots, P(n(i)))$,

$$res_{G(i)}(x) = \omega_i(res_{P(1)}(x),\ldots, res_{P(n(i))}(x)) . \tag{3.1}$$

Finally the output vector $y = (y_1, \ldots, y_m)$, where y_i is some input or gate, describes what the circuit computes, namely $f \in B_{n,m}$, where $f = (f_1, \ldots, f_m)$ and f_i is the function computed at y_i .

It is often convenient to use the representation of a circuit by a directed acyclic graph. The inputs are the sources of the graph, the vertex for the gate $G(i)$ is labelled by the type ω_i of $G(i)$ and has $n(i)$ numbered incoming edges from the predecessors of $G(i)$. If ω_i is commutative, we may withdraw the numbering of edges.

Our definition will be illustrated by a circuit for a fulladder $f(x_1,x_2,x_3) = (y_1,y_0)$. Here (y_1,y_0) is the binary representation of $x_1 + x_2 + x_3$, i.e. $x_1 + x_2 + x_3 = y_0 + 2y_1$. We design a B_2- circuit in the following way. y_1, the carry bit, equals 1 iff $x_1 + x_2 + x_3$ is at least 2, and y_0, the sum bit, equals 1 iff $x_1 + x_2 + x_3$ is odd. In particular, $y_0 = x_1 \oplus x_2 \oplus x_3$ can be computed by 2 gates. Since $x_1 \oplus x_2$ is already computed, it is efficient to use this result for y_1. It is easy to check that

$$y_1 = [(x_1 \oplus x_2) \wedge x_3] \vee [x_1 \wedge x_2] . \tag{3.2}$$

We obtain the following circuit where all edges are directed top - down.

$$G_1 = (\oplus, x_1, x_2) \quad G_2 = (\oplus, G_1, x_3) \quad G_3 = (\wedge, x_1, x_2)$$
$$G_4 = (\wedge, G_1, x_3) \quad G_5 = (\vee, G_3, G_4) \quad (y_1, y_0) = (G_5, G_2)$$

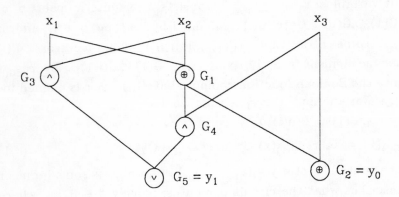

Fig. 3.1

In the following we define circuits in a more informal way.

Many circuits are computing the same function. So we look for optimal circuits, i.e. we need criterions to compare the efficiency of circuits. If a circuit is used for a sequential computation the number of gates measures the time for the computation. In order to ease the discussion we assume that the necessary time is for all basic operations the same. Circuits (or chips) in the hardware of computers have arbitrary degree of parallelism. In our example G_1 and G_3 may be evaluated in parallel at the same time, afterwards the inputs of G_2 and G_4 are computed and we may evaluate these two gates in parallel, and finally G_5. We need only 3 instead of 5 computation steps.

DEFINITION 3.2 : The size or complexity $C(S)$ of a circuit S equals the number of its gates. The circuit complexity of f with respect to the basis Ω, $C_\Omega(f)$, is the smallest number of gates in an Ω - circuit computing f. The depth $D(S)$ of S is the length (number of gates) of the longest path in S. The depth of f with respect to Ω, $D_\Omega(f)$, is the minimal depth of an Ω - circuit computing f.

For sequential computations the circuit complexity (or briefly just complexity) corresponds to the computation time. In Ch. 9 we derive connections between depth and storage space for sequential computations. For parallel computations the size measures the cost for the construction of the circuit, and depth corresponds to computation time. In either case we should try to minimize simultaneously size and depth. It does not seem to be possible to realize this for all functions (see Ch. 7).

We want to show that the circuit model is robust. The complexity measures do not really depend on the underlying basis if the basis is large enough. In § 4 we show that the complexity of functions does not increase significantly by the necessary (from the technical point of view) restrictions on the number of edges (or wires) leaving a gate.

DEFINITION 3.3 : A basis Ω is complete if any Boolean function can be computed in an Ω - circuit.

The normal forms in § 2 have shown that $\{\wedge,\vee,\neg\}$ and $\{\oplus,\wedge\}$ are complete bases. By the laws of deMorgan even the smaller bases $\{\wedge,\neg\}$ and $\{\vee,\neg\}$ are complete, whereas $\{\wedge,\vee\}$ is incomplete. Complexity and depth of Boolean functions can increase only by a constant factor if we switch from one complete basis to another. Therefore we may restrict ourselves to the basis B_2 and denote by $C(f)$

and $D(f)$ the circuit complexity and depth resp. of f with respect to B_2 . In Ch.6 we prove that $C_{\{\wedge,\vee\}}(f) / C(f)$ can become arbitrarily large for functions computable over $\{\wedge,\vee\}$.

THEOREM 3.1 : Let Ω and Ω' be complete bases, $c = \max \{ C_\Omega(g) \mid g \in \Omega'\}$ and $d = \max \{ D_\Omega(g) \mid g \in \Omega' \}$.
Then $C_\Omega(f) \le c \; C_{\Omega'}(f)$ and $D_\Omega(f) \le d \; D_{\Omega'}(f)$ for all $f \in B_n$.

Proof : We make use of the idea that subcircuits may be replaced by equivalent subcircuits. Here we replace gates for $g \in \Omega'$, which are small subcircuits, by optimal (with respect to size or depth) Ω - circuits for g . Starting with an Ω' - circuit computing f we obtain an Ω - circuit with the required properties.

$\square$

1.4 Circuits with bounded fan - out

From the technical point of view it may be necessary to bound the fan-out of gates by some constant s , i.e. the result of a gate may be used only s times. The appropriate complexity measures are denoted by $C_{s,\Omega}$ and $D_{s,\Omega}$. By definition

$$C_\Omega \le \; \cdots \; \le C_{s+1,\Omega} \le C_{s,\Omega} \le \; \cdots \; \le C_{1,\Omega} \; . \tag{4.1}$$

Any function computable by an Ω - circuit may be computed by an Ω-circuit with fan-out 1 . This can be proved by induction on $c = C_\Omega(f)$. Nothing has to be proved for $c = 0$. For $c > 0$ we consider an Ω - circuit for f with c gates. Let $g_1, \ldots, g_r$ be the functions computed at the predecessors of the last gate. Since $C_\Omega(g_i) < c$, g_i can be computed by an Ω - circuit with fan-out 1 . We take disjoint Ω - circuits with fan-out 1 for $g_1, \ldots, g_r$ and combine them to an Ω - circuit with fan-out 1 for f . The depth of the new circuit is not larger than that of the old one, thus $D_\Omega(f) = D_{s,\Omega}(f)$ for all s . In future we do not investigate $D_{s,\Omega}$ anymore. With the above procedure the size of the circuit may increase rapidly. For $s \geq 2$, we can bound the increase of size by the following algorithm of Johnson, Savage and Welch (72). We also bound the fan-out of the variables by s .

If some gate G (or some variable) has fan-out $r > s$ we use $s-1$ outgoing wires in the same way as before and the last outgoing wire to save the information of G . We build a subcircuit in which again res_G is computed. We still have to simulate $r-(s-1)$ outgoing wires of G . If $s \geq 2$, the number of unsimulated wires decreases with each step by $s-1$. How can we save the information of gate G ? By computing the identity $x \to x$. Let $l(\Omega)$ be the smallest number of gates in order to compute a function $g = res_G$ at some gate given g as input. We claim that $l(\Omega) \in \{1,2\}$. Let $\omega \in \Omega$ be a nonconstant basic operation. Let $\omega \in B_m$. Since ω is not constant, input vectors exist differing only at one position (w.l.o.g. the last one) such that $\omega(a_1, \ldots, a_{m-1}, 1) \ne \omega(a_1, \ldots, a_{m-1}, 0)$. We need only one wire out of G to compute $\omega(a_1, \ldots, a_{m-1}, res_G)$ which equals res_G , implying $l(\Omega) = 1$, or $\neg\, res_G$. In the second case we repeat the procedure and compute $\neg\, (\neg\, res_G) = res_G$ implying $l(\Omega) = 2$. At the end we obtain a circuit for f in which the fan-out is bounded by s .

THEOREM 4.1 : Let k be the fan-in of the basis Ω , i.e. the largest number of inputs for a function of Ω . If $f \in B_n$ may be computed by an Ω - circuit and if $s \geq 2$ then

$$C_{s,\Omega}(f) \leq (1 + l(\Omega)(k-1)/(s-1))\, C_\Omega(f) .$$

(4.2)

Proof : If the fan-out of some gate is large, we need many gates of fan-out s for the simulation of this gate. But the average fan-out of the gates cannot be large. Since the fan-in is bounded by k the average fan-out cannot be larger than k . We explain these ideas in detail.

Let r be the fan-out of some gate or variable. If $p \geq 0$ is the smallest number such that $s + p(s-1) \geq r$, then it is sufficient to save the information of the gate p times. For this, $l(\Omega)$ p gates are sufficient. With the definition of p we conclude that

$$s + (p-1)(s-1) < r \quad \text{if} \quad r \geq 1 . \tag{4.3}$$

Therefore p is bounded by $(r-1)/(s-1)$ if $r \geq 1$. In an optimal circuit for $f \in B_n$ at most n-1 variables and at most one gate have fan-out 0. Let $c = C_\Omega(f)$ and let r_i be the fan-out of the i-th gate and r_{j+c} the fan-out of x_j. We have to sum up all r_i - 1 where $r_i \geq 1$. The sum of all r_i (where $r_i \geq 1$) equals the number of wires. Since the fan-in of the basis is k, the number of wires is bounded by ck. As at most n parameters r_i are equal to 0 the sum of all $r_i - 1$ where $r_i \geq 1$ is not larger than ck - c. Thus the number of new gates is bounded by $l(\Omega)(ck-c)/(s-1)$. Altogether we proved that

$$C_{s,\Omega}(f) \leq c + c\, l(\Omega)(k-1)/(s-1)$$
$$= (1 + l(\Omega)(k-1)/(s-1))\, C_\Omega(f) . \tag{4.4}$$

$\square$

For each basis Ω the number of gates is increased by a constant factor only. $l(\Omega) = 1$ and $k = 2$, if $\Omega = B_2$. For all $s \geq 2$ we only have to double the number of gates. For $s = 1$ our algorithm does not work. The situation for $s = 1$ indeed is essentially different. In Ch.8 we present examples in which $C_{1,\Omega}(f) / C_\Omega(f)$ becomes arbitrarily large.

DEFINITION 4.1 : The circuits whose fan-out of gates is bounded by 1 are called (Boolean) formulas. $L_\Omega(f) = C_{1,\Omega}(f)$ is called the formula size of f .

We have motivated circuits with bounded fan-out by technical restrictions. These restrictions are not so strong that the fan-out is restricted to 1 . Nevertheless we investigate Boolean formulas in Ch.7 and 8 . One reason for this is that we obtain a strong connection between formula size and depth (see Ch.7). Another reason is that Boolean formulas correspond to those expressions we usually call formulas. Given a formula we may also bound the fan-out of the inputs by 1 by using many copies of the inputs. From our graph representation we obtain a tree where the root is the last gate. Basically this is the representation of arithmetical expressions by trees.

We could be satisfied. Bounding the fan-out does not increase the depth of the circuit and the size has to be increased only by a small constant factor, if $s \geq 2$. But with both algorithms discussed we cannot bound the increase of size and depth simultaneously. This was achieved at first by an algorithm of Hoover, Klawe and Pippenger (84). Size and depth will increase only by a constant factor. Perhaps the breadth is still increasing (see Schnorr (77) for a discussion of the importance of breadth).

We present the algorithm only for the case $l(\Omega) = 1$. We saw that p identity gates are sufficient to simulate a gate of fan-out r where p is the smallest integer such that $r \leq s + p(s-1)$. For $s = 3$ we show in Fig. 4.1 a how Johnson, Savage and Welch replaced a gate of fan-out 12. In general, we obtain a tree consisting of a chain of p+1 nodes whose fan-out is bounded by s. Any other tree with p+1 nodes, r leaves and fan-out bounded by s (as shown in Fig. 4.1 b) will also do the job. The root is the gate that has to be simulated, and the other p nodes are identity gates. The r outgoing wires can be used to simulate the r outgoing wires of the gate we simulate. The number of gates behaves as in the algorithm of Johnson et al. We have some influence on the increase in depth of the circuit by choosing appropriate trees.

In a given circuit S with b gates $G_1, \ldots, G_b$ we work bottom-up. Let $S_b = S$. We construct S_{i-1} from S_i by replacing gate G_i by an appropriate tree. Then $S' = S_0$ is a circuit of fan-out s equivalent to S. The best thing we could do in each step is to replace G_i by a tree T_i such that the longest path in S_{i-1}, starting at the root of T_i, is kept as short as possible. In the following we describe an efficient algorithm for the choice of T_i.

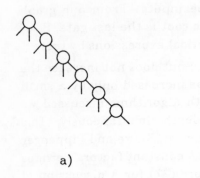 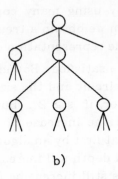

a)   b)

Fig. 4.1

We define a weight function on the nodes of all trees T with r leaves, fan-out bounded by s and $p+1$ inner nodes. Here r is the fan-out of G_i and p is the proper parameter. Let $S(T)$ be the circuit produced by the replacement of G_i by T in S_i. Then the weight of a node $u \in T$ should be the length of the longest path in $S(T)$ starting in u. The weight of the r leaves of T is given and the weight of the inner nodes is recursively defined by

$$w(u) = 1 + \max\{ w(u') \mid u' \text{ is son of } u \} . \tag{4.5}$$

In order to choose a tree whose root has minimal weight, we use a so-called Huffman algorithm (for a discussion of this class of algorithms see Ahlswede and Wegener (86), Glassey and Karp (72) or Picard (65)).

It is easier to handle trees where all inner nodes have fan-out exactly s. For that reason we add $s + p(s-1) - r$ dummy leaves whose weight is $-\infty$. Altogether we now have exactly $s + p(s-1)$ leaves.

ALGORITHM 4.1 :

Input : V, a set of $s + p(s-1)$ nodes, and a weight function w on V.
Output : T a tree with $p+1$ inner nodes of fan-out s. The leaves correspond uniquely to the nodes in V.
Let $W = V$. If $|W| = 1$, T is constructed. While $|W| > 1$, we choose

those s nodes $v_1, \ldots, v_s \in W$ which have the smallest weight. These nodes become the sons of a new node v' whose weight is defined by (4.5). We remove $v_1, \ldots, v_s$ from W and add v' to W.

We would stray too much from the subject, if we presented those results on Huffman algorithms which lead to the following estimation of the depth of S'. For the size of S' we obtain the same bound as in Theorem 4.1.

THEOREM 4.2: Let S be an Ω - circuit with one output and let k be the fan-in of Ω. For $s \geq 2$, we can efficiently construct an equivalent circuit S' whose fan-out is bounded by s such that

$$C(S') \leq (1 + l(\Omega)(k-1)/(s-1)) C(S) \tag{4.6}$$

and

$$D(S') \leq (1 + l(\Omega) \log_s k) D(S). \tag{4.7}$$

In § 5 we summarize the conclusions drawn from the results of § 3 and § 4.

1.5 Discussion

It turned out that circuits build an excellent model for the computation of Boolean functions. Certainly circuit complexity and depth of a Boolean function cannot be measured unambigously. These complexity measures depend on

- the costs and the computation time of the different types of gates
- the underlying basis and

the fan-out restriction.

This effect is unpleasant. How can we find out whether f is easier than g ? The results of § 3 and § 4 showed that the effect of the above mentioned criterions on circuit complexity and depth of a Boolean function can be estimated by a constant factor (with the only exceptions of incomplete bases' and the fan-out restriction 1) . If we ignore constant factors, we can limit ourselves to a fixed circuit model. The basis is B_2 , all gates cause the same cost, and the fan-out is not restricted. Comparing two functions f and g not only $C(f)$ and $C(g)$ but also $D(f)$ and $D(g)$ differ "by a constant factor". In fact we do not consider some definite function f but natural sequences of functions f_n. Instead of the addition of two 7-bit numbers, a function $f \in B_{14,8}$, we investigate the sequence of functions $f_n \in B_{2n,n+1}$ where f_n is the addition of two n-bit numbers.

Let (f_n) and (g_n) be sequences of functions. If $C(f_n) = 11 n$ and $C(g_n) = n^2$, $C(f_n) \leq C(g_n)$ for $n \leq 11$ but $C(f_n)/C(g_n)$ is bounded by 11 and converges to 0 . We state that (g_n) is more complex than (f_n) , since for all circuit models the quotient of the complexity of f_n and the complexity of g_n converges to 0 . We ignore that g_n may be computed more efficiently than f_n for small n . We are more interested in the asymptotic behavior of $C(f_n)$ and $C(g_n)$.

Certainly, it would be best to know $C(f_n)$ exactly. If it is too difficult to achieve this knowledge, then, in general, the asymptotic behavior describes the complexity of f_n quite good. Sometimes the concentration on asymptotics may lead to absurd results.
If $C(f_n) = 15 n^{34816}$ and $C(g_n) = 2^{n/100}$, $C(f_n)/ C(g_n)$ converges to 0 , but for all relevant n the complexity of f_n is larger than the complexity of g_n . But this is an unrealistic example that probably would not occur. In the following we introduce the "big-oh" notation.

DEFINITION 5.1 : Let $f,g : \mathbb{N} \to \mathbb{R}$ such that $f(n), g(n) > 0$ for large n.

i) $f = O(g)$ (f does not grow faster than g) if $f(n)/g(n) \le c$ for some constant c and large n.

ii) $f = \Omega(g)$ if $g = O(f)$.

iii) $f = \Theta(g)$ (f and g have the same asymptotic behavior) if $f = O(g)$ and $g = O(f)$.

iv) $f = o(g)$ (f grows slower than g) if $f(n)/g(n)$ tends to 0.

v) $f = \omega(g)$ if $g = o(f)$.

vi) f grows polynomially if $f = O(p)$ for some polynomial p. Notation: $f = n^{O(1)}$.

vii) f grows exponentially if $f = \Omega(2^{n^{\varepsilon}})$ for some $\varepsilon > 0$.

We try to estimate $C(f_n)$ and $C(g_n)$ as accurately as possible. Often we have to be satisfied with assertions like the following. The number of gates of the circuits S_n for f_n has the same asymptotic behavior as n, $n \log n$, n^2, n^3 or even 2^n. We want to emphasize the structural difference of algorithms with n, $n \log n$, n^2, n^3 or 2^n computation steps. In Table 5.1 we compute the maximal input size of a problem which can be solved in a given time if one computation step can be performed within 0.001 seconds. The reader should extend this table by multiplying the running times $T(n)$ by factors not too large and by adding numbers not too large.

The next table shows how much we gain if we perform 10 computation steps in the same time as we did 1 computation step before. Constant factors for $T(n)$ do not play any role in this table.

For the polynomially growing functions the maximal possible input length is increased by a constant factor which depends on the degree of the polynomial. But for exponentially growing functions the maximal possible input length is only increased by an additive term. Therefore functions whose circuit size is polynomially bounded are called efficiently computable while the other functions are called

T(n)	Maximal input length which can be processed within		
	1 sec.	1 min.	1 h.
n	1000	60000	3600000
$n \log_2 n$	140	4893	200000
n^2	31	244	1897
n^3	10	39	153
2^n	9	15	21

Tab. 5.1

T(n)	Maximal input length which can be processed		Remarks
	before	afterwards	
n	m	10 m	
$n \log n$	m	(nearly) 10 m	
n^2	m	3.16 m	$10 \approx 3.16^2$
n^3	m	2.15 m	$10 \approx 2.15^3$
2^n	m	m + 3.3	$10 \approx 2^{3.3}$

Tab. 5.2

intractable. This notation is based on the experience that algorithms whose running time is a polynomial of very large degree or whose running time is of size 2^{n^ε} for a very small ε are exceptions.

At the end of our discussion we refer to a property distinguishing circuits and programs for computers. A program for the sorting problem or the multiplication of matrices or any other reasonable problem should work for instances of arbitrary length. A circuit can work only for inputs of a given length. For problems like the ones mentioned above, we have to construct sequences of circuits S_n such that S_n solves the problem for instances of length n . The design of S_n and the design of S_m are independent if $n \neq m$. Therefore we say that circuits build a non uniform computation model while software models like Turing machines build a uniform model. Non uniform models are adequate for the hardware of computers. Designing circuits we do not have if-tests to our disposal, but we can do different things for different input lengths. Hence it happens that any sequence of Boolean functions $f_n \in B_n$ may be computed by (a sequence of) circuits while not all sequences $f_n \in B_n$ can be computed by a computer or a Turing machine. Furthermore, it is not astonishing that Turing machine programs may be simulated efficiently by circuits (see Ch.9). Because of our way of thinking most of the sequences of circuits we design may be described uniformly and therefore can be simulated efficiently by Turing machines.

EXERCISES

1. What is the cardinality of $B_{n,m}$?

2. Let $f(x_1,x_2,x_3) = (y_1,y_0)$ be the fulladder of § 3 . y_1 is monotone but y_0 is not. Design an $\{\wedge,\vee\}$ - circuit for y_1 .

3. f is called non degenerated if f depends essentially on all its variables, i.e. the subfunctions of f for $x_i = 0$ and $x_i = 1$ are different. Let N_k be the number of non degenerated functions $f \in B_k$ and $N_0 = 2$.

Then $\sum_{0\leq k\leq n} \binom{n}{k} N_k = |B_n|$.

4. The fraction of degenerated functions $f \in B_n$ tends to 0 as $n \to \infty$.

5. How many functions have the property that we cannot obtain a constant subfunction even if we replace $n-1$ variables by constants ?

6. Let $f,g \in M_n$, $t = x_1 \cdots x_n$, $t' = x_1 \vee \cdots \vee x_n$.

   a) $t \leq f \vee g \implies t \leq f$ or $t \leq g$.

   b) $f \wedge g \leq t' \implies f \leq t'$ or $g \leq t'$.

7. Let different functions $f,g \in B_n$ be given by their RSE. How can one construct an input a where $f(a) \neq g(a)$ without testing all inputs ?

8. Design circuits of small size or depth for the following functions :

   a) $f_n(x_1, \ldots, x_n, y_1, \ldots, y_n) = 1$ iff $x_i \neq y_i$ for all i .

   b) $f_n(x_0, \ldots, x_{n-1}, y_0, \ldots, y_{n-1}) = 1$ iff $\sum_{0\leq i\leq n-1} x_i 2^i > \sum_{0\leq i\leq n-1} y_i 2^i$.

   c) $f_n(x_1, \ldots, x_n) = 1$ iff $x_1 + \cdots + x_n \geq 2$.

9. Which functions $f \in B_2$ build a complete basis of one function ?

10. Which of the following bases are complete even if the constants are not given for free ?

   a) $\{\wedge, \neg\}$,   b) $\{\vee, \neg\}$,   c) $\{\oplus, \wedge\}$.

11. sel $\in B_3$ is defined by $sel(x,y,z) = y$, if $x = 0$, and $sel(x,y,z) = z$, if $x = 1$. Is $\{$ sel $\}$ a complete basis ?

12. Each function computed by an $\{\wedge, \vee\}$ - circuit is monotone.

13. Let Ω, Ω' be complete bases. Define constants c and d such that each Ω' - circuit S' can be simulated by an Ω - circuit S such that $C(S) \leq c\,C(S')$ and $D(S) \leq d\,D(S')$.

14. Compute $l(\{f\})$ (see § 4) for each nonconstant $f \in B_2$.

15. Construct a sequence of graphs G_n such that the algorithm of Johnson et al. constructs graphs G_n' whose depth $d(G_n')$ grows faster than $c\,d(G_n)$ for any constant c if $s = 2$.

16. Specify for the following functions "easy" functions with the same asymptotic behavior.
    a) $n^2 / (n - \log^3 n)$
    b) $\sum\limits_{1 \leq i \leq n} \log i$
    c) $\sum\limits_{1 \leq i \leq n} i^{-1}$
    d) $\sum\limits_{1 \leq i \leq n} i\,2^{-i}$.

17. $\log n = o(n^\varepsilon)$ for all $\varepsilon > 0$.

18. $n^{\log n}$ does not grow polynomially and also not exponentially.

19. If f grows polynomially, there exists a constant k such that $f(n) \leq n^k + k$ for all n.

2. THE MINIMIZATION OF BOOLEAN FUNCTIONS

2.1 Basic definitions

How can we design good circuits ? If we consider specific functions like addition or multiplication we take advantage of our knowledge about the structure of the function (see Ch.3). Here we treat the design of circuits for rather structureless functions. Unfortunately, this situation is not unrealistic, in particular for the hardware construction of computers. The inputs of such a Boolean function $f \in B_{n,m}$ may be the outputs of another Boolean function $g \in B_{k,n}$. The properties of f are described by a table $x \to f(x)$. Since the image of g may be a proper subset of $\{0,1\}^n$, f is not always defined for all $a \in \{0,1\}^n$. Such Boolean functions are called partially defined.

DEFINITION 1.1 : A partially defined Boolean function is a function $f : \{0,1\}^n \to \{0,1, ? \}$. B_n^* is the set of all partially defined Boolean functions on n variables.

A circuit computes $f \in B_n^*$ at gate G iff $f(x) = res_G(x)$ for all $x \in f^{-1}(\{0,1\})$.

Since inputs outside of $f^{-1}(\{0,1\})$ are not possible (or just not expected ?!), it does not matter which output a circuit produces for inputs $a \in f^{-1}(?)$. Since $B_n \subseteq B_n^*$, all our considerations are valid also for completely defined Boolean functions. We assume that f is given by a table of length $N = 2^n$. We are looking for efficient procedures for the construction of good circuits. The running time of these algorithms has to be measured in terms of their input size, namely N, the length of the table, and not n, the length of the inputs of f.

The knowledge of circuits, especially of efficient circuits for an arbitrary function is far away from the knowledge that is required to design always efficient circuits. Therefore one has restricted oneself to a subclass of circuits. The term "minimization of a Boolean function" stands for the design of an optimal circuit in the class of Σ_2-circuits (for generalizations of the concept of Σ_2-circuits see Ch.11). Inputs of Σ_2- circuits are all literals $x_1, \bar{x}_1, \ldots, x_n, \bar{x}_n$. In the first step we may compute arbitrary conjunctions (products) of literals. In the second step we compute the disjunction (sum) of all terms computed in the first step. We obtain a sum-of-products for f which also is called polynomial for f. The DNF of f is an example of a polynomial for f. Here we look for minimal polynomials, i.e. polynomials of minimal cost.

From the practical point of view polynomials have the advantage that there are only two logical levels needed, the level of disjunctions is following the level of conjunctions.

DEFINITION 1.2 :

i)   A monom m is a product (conjunction) of some literals. The cost of m is equal to the number of literals of m.

ii) A polynomial p is a sum (disjunction) of monoms. The cost of p is equal to the sum of the costs of all m which are summed up by p.

iii) A polynomial p computes $f \in B_n^*$ if $p(x) = f(x)$ for $x \in f^{-1}(\{0,1\})$. p is a minimal polynomial for f, if p computes f and no polynomial computing f has smaller cost than p.

Sometimes the cost of a polynomial p is defined as the number of monoms summed up by p. By both cost measures the cost of the circuit belonging to p is approximately reflected. On the one hand we need at least one gate for the computation of a monom, and on the other hand l gates are sufficient to compute a monom of length l and to add it to the other monoms. Since different monoms may share the same submonom we may save gates by computing these submonoms only once. The following considerations apply to both cost measures.

Let $p = m_1 v \cdots v m_k$ be a polynomial for f . $m_i(a) = 1$ implies $p(a) = 1$ and $f(a) \in \{1,?\}$. If $m_i^{-1}(1) \subseteq f^{-1}(?)$, we could cancel m_i and would obtain a cheaper polynomial for f .

DEFINITION 1.3 : A monom m is an implicant of f if $m^{-1}(1) \subseteq f^{-1}(\{1,?\})$ and $m^{-1}(1) \not\subseteq f^{-1}(?)$. $I(f)$ is the set of all implicants of f .

We have already seen that minimal polynomials consist of implicants only. Obviously the sum of all implicants computes f . If m and m' are implicants, but m is a proper submonom of m', $m v m' = m$ by the law of simplification, and we may cancel m' .

DEFINITION 1.4 : An implicant $m \in I(f)$ is called prime implicant if no proper submonom of m is an implicant of f . $PI(f)$ is the set of all prime implicants of f .

To sum up we have proved

THEOREM 1.1 : Minimal polynomials for f consist only of prime implicants.

All algorithms for the minimization of Boolean functions start with the computation of all prime implicants. Afterwards $PI(f)$ is used to construct a minimal polynomial. It is not known whether one may compute efficiently minimal polynomials without computing implicitly $PI(f)$.

2.2 The computation of all prime implicants and reductions of the table of prime implicants

The set of prime implicants PI(f) may be computed quite efficiently by the so-called Quine and McCluskey algorithm (McCluskey (56), Quine (52) and (55)). It is sufficient to present the algorithm for completely defined Boolean functions $f \in B_n$. The easy generalization to partially defined Boolean functions is left to the reader. Since f is given by its table $x \to f(x)$ implicants of length n can be found directly. For each $a \in f^{-1}(1)$ the corresponding minterm m_a is an implicant. It is sufficient to know how all implicants of length $i - 1$ can be computed if one knows all implicants of length i .

LEMMA 2.1 : Let m be a monom not containing x_j or $\bar{x}_j$. m is an implicant of f iff mx_j and $m\bar{x}_j$ are implicants of f .

Proof : If $m \in I(f)$, we can conclude $mx_j(a) = 1 \Rightarrow m(a) = 1 \Rightarrow f(a) = 1$, hence $mx_j \in I(f)$. Similarly $m\bar{x}_j \in I(f)$. If mx_j , $m\bar{x}_j \in I(f)$, we can conclude $m(a) = 1 \Rightarrow mx_j(a) = 1$ or $m\bar{x}_j(a) = 1 \Rightarrow f(a) = 1$, hence $m \in I(f)$.

□

ALGORITHM 2.1 (Quine and McCluskey) :

Input : The table (a,f(a)) of some $f \in B_n$.

Output : The nonempty sets Q_k and P_k of all implicants and prime implicants resp. of f with length k . In particular PI(f) is the union of all P_k .

Q_n is the set of all minterms m_a such that $f(a) = 1$, $i = n$.

While $Q_i \neq \phi$

  i   := i - 1 ;

  Q_i := { m | $\exists$ j : $x_j, \bar{x}_j$ are not in m but mx_j , $m\bar{x}_j \in Q_{i+1}$ };

$$P_{i+1} := \{ m \in Q_{i+1} \mid \forall\ m' \in Q_i : m' \text{ is not a proper submonom of } m \}.$$

By Lemma 2.1 the sets Q_k are computed correctly. Also the sets of prime implicants P_k are computed correctly. If an implicant of length k has no proper shortening of length $k-1$ which is an implicant, then it has no proper shortening which is an implicant and therefore it is a prime implicant. In order to obtain an efficient implementation of Algorithm 2.1 we should make sure that Q_i does not contain any monom twice. During the construction of Q_i it is not necessary to test for all pairs (m',m'') of monoms in Q_{i+1} whether $m' = mx_j$ and $m'' = m\bar{x}_j$ for some j. It is sufficient to consider pairs (m',m'') where the number of negated variables in m'' is by 1 larger than the corresponding number in m'. Let $Q_{i+1,l}$ be the set of $m \in Q_{i+1}$ with l negated variables. For $m' \in Q_{i+1,l}$ and all negated variables $\bar{x}_j$ in m' it is sufficient to test whether the monom m'_j where we have replaced $\bar{x}_j$ in m' by x_j is in $Q_{i+1,l-1}$. Finally we should mark all $m \in Q_{i+1}$ which have shortenings in Q_i. Then P_{i+1} is the set of unmarked monoms $m \in Q_{i+1}$.

We are content with a rough estimation of the running time of the Quine and McCluskey algorithm. The number of different monoms is 3^n. For each j either x_j is in m or $\bar{x}_j$ is in m or both are not in m. Each monom is compared with at most n other monoms. By binary search according to the lexicographical order $O(n)$ comparisons are sufficient to test whether m is already contained in the appropriate $Q_{i,l}$. This search has to be carried out not more than two times for each of the at most $n\,3^n$ tests. So the running time of the algorithm is bounded by $O(n^2\,3^n)$. The input length is $N = 2^n$. Using the abbreviation log for $\log_2$ we have estimated the running time by $O(N^{\log 3} \log N)$. Mileto and Putzolu (64) and (65) investigated the average running time of the algorithm for randomly chosen Boolean functions.

The relevant data on f is now represented by the table of prime implicants.

DEFINITION 2.1 : The table of prime implicants (PI - table) for f is a matrix whose rows correspond to the prime implicants $m_1, \ldots, m_k$ of f and whose columns correspond to the inputs $y_1, \ldots, y_s \in f^{-1}(1)$. The matrix entry at place (i,j) equals $m_i(y_j)$.

Due to the properties of prime implicants the disjunction of all prime implicants equals f and for a disjunction of some prime implicants g we know that $g \leq f$. We are looking for a cheap set of prime implicants whose disjunction equals f. It is sufficient and necessary to choose for each $y_j \in f^{-1}(1)$ some m_i such that $m_i(y_j) = 1$. A choice of prime implicants is a choice of rows in the PI - table. If and only if the submatrix consisting of the chosen rows contains no column without any 1 the disjunction of the chosen prime implicants equals f.

We can simplify our problem by two easy reduction rules. Let r_i be the row corresponding to the prime implicant m_i and let c_j be the column corresponding to $y_j \in f^{-1}(1)$.

LEMMA 2.2 :

i)   If the only 1-entry of c_j is contained in r_i, we have to choose m_i and may cancel r_i and all c_k such that $m_i(y_k) = 1$.

ii) If $c_j \leq c_{j'}$ for some $j \neq j'$, we may cancel $c_{j'}$.

Proof : i) Obviously m_i is the only prime implicant such that $m_i(y_j) = 1$. Therefore we have to choose m_i. If $m_i(y_k) = 1$, we have done the job for the input y_k.
ii) We still have to choose a prime implicant m_i such that $m_i(y_j) = 1$. Since $c_j \leq c_{j'}$ implies $m_i(y_{j'}) = 1$, we ensure that we choose a prime implicant for input $y_{j'}$.

□

We perform the reductions until no further reductions are possible. The result of this procedure is called a reduced PI - table.

EXAMPLE 2.1 : We save the first step and define $f \in B_4$ by Q_4, the set of implicants of length 4 .

Q_4: $Q_{4,4} = \phi$, $Q_{4,3} = \{ \bar{a}\bar{b}c\bar{d}, \bar{a}b\bar{c}\bar{d} \}$, $Q_{4,2} = \{ \bar{a}bcd, \bar{a}b\bar{c}d, ab\bar{c}\bar{d} \}$,
$\quad Q_{4,1} = \{ \bar{a}bcd, a\bar{b}cd, abc\bar{d} \}$, $Q_{4,0} = \{ abcd \}$.

Q_3: $Q_{3,3} = \phi$, $Q_{3,2} = \{ \bar{a}\bar{b}c, \bar{a}b\bar{c}, \bar{b}c\bar{d} \}$,
$\quad Q_{3,1} = \{ \bar{a}bd, \bar{a}cd, a\bar{b}c, ac\bar{d}, \bar{b}cd \}$, $Q_{3,0} = \{ abc, acd, bcd \}$.

$P_4 = \phi$.

Q_2: $Q_{2,2} = \phi$, $Q_{2,1} = \{ \bar{b}c \}$, $Q_{2,0} = \{ cd, ac \}$.

$P_3 = \{ \bar{a}b\bar{c}, \bar{a}bd \}$.

$Q_1 = \phi$.

$P_2 = Q_2$.

$\quad$ PI(f) $= \{ \bar{a}b\bar{c}, \bar{a}bd, \bar{b}c, cd, ac \}$.

The PI - table of f

	0010	0011	0100	0101	0111	1010	1011	1110	1111
$\bar{a}b\bar{c}$	0	0	1	1	0	0	0	0	0
$\bar{a}bd$	0	0	0	1	1	0	0	0	0
$\bar{b}c$	1	1	0	0	0	1	1	0	0
cd	0	1	0	0	1	0	1	0	1
ac	0	0	0	0	0	1	1	1	1

c_1, c_3 and c_8 have a single one . Therefore a minimal polynomial has to contain $\bar{a}b\bar{c}, \bar{b}c$ and ac . We may cancel r_1, r_3 and r_5 and all columns up to c_5 . We could have cancelled c_6 since $c_8 \leq c_6$ or c_7 since $c_9 \leq c_7$. We obtain the following reduced table.

5

	0111
$\bar{a}$ b d	1
c d	1

For a minimal polynomial we choose the cheaper prime implicant $c\,d$. Here the minimal polynomial is uniquely determined and equals $\bar{a}\,b\,\bar{c} \vee \bar{b}\,c \vee a\,c \vee c\,d$. Using three logical levels we obtain a more efficient circuit by the representation $\bar{a}\,b\,\bar{c} \vee c(\bar{b} \vee a \vee d)$.

In our example the construction of a minimal polynomial from the reduced PI - table was trivial. In general, this is a hard problem as we shall see in § 5 .

2.3 The minimization method of Karnaugh

For larger n , at least for $n \geq 7$, computers should be used for the minimization of Boolean functions. The method of Karnaugh (53) is advantageous if one tries to perform the minimization for $n \leq 6$ with one's own hand. The main idea is a better representation of our information.

The set of inputs $\{0,1\}^n$ is an n-dimensional cube. A monom m of length k corresponds to an (n-k) - dimensional subcube where the k variables of m are fixed in the right way. f is a coloring of $\{0,1\}^n$ by the colors 0 and 1 . m is an implicant iff the corresponding subcube is 1-colored. It is even a prime implicant iff no larger subcube, i.e. shorter monom, is 1-colored. A vector $a \in \{0,1\}^n$ has n neighbors which differ from a in exactly one position. The recognition of neighborhoods is exceptionally simple in the Karnaugh diagrams.

EXAMPLE 3.1 : The Karnaugh diagram for the function of Example 2.1

a b c d	00	01	11	10
00	0	1	0	0
01	0	1	0	0
11	1	1	1	1
10	1	0	1	1

We find f(a,b,c,d) in column ab and row cd . Where are the neighbors of (a,b,c,d) ? It is easy to check that the neighbors can be reached by one step in one of the four directions. The left neighbor of an element in the first column is the last element in the same row, and so on. These diagrams are clearly arranged for n = 4 . For n < 4 , we even obtain smaller diagrams. For n = 5 , we use two of the diagrams above, one for e = 0 and one for e = 1 . Then the fifth neighbor may be found at the same position of the other diagram. For n = 6 , we already have to work with 4 of these diagrams. For n ≥ 7 the situation becomes unintelligible and Karnaugh diagrams should not be used.

In our example each one in the diagram corresponds to an implicant of length 4 . Ones which are neighbors correspond to implicants of length 3 . The ones in the first column correspond to $\bar{a}\bar{b}c$ and the first two ones in the second column correspond to $\bar{a}b\bar{c}$. The 1-colored subcube for $\bar{a}\bar{b}c$ can be enlarged to the 1-colored subcube of the ones in the first and last column corresponding to the implicant $\bar{b}c$. Since the 1-colored subcube for $\bar{a}b\bar{c}$ cannot be enlarged, $\bar{a}b\bar{c}$ is a prime implicant. We easily detect prime implicants in Karnaugh diagrams. Furthermore, we see that the one in the first row is contained only in one maximal 1-colored subcube, namely for $\bar{a}b\bar{c}$, which therefore has to be contained in a minimal polynomial. Altogether we follow the same procedure as described in § 2 but we have a more adequat representation of the information. Veitch (52) suggested a similar procedure.

2.4 The minimization of monotone functions

Quine (53) has shown that the computation of the always unique minimal polynomial for a monotone Boolean function is easy.

THEOREM 4.1 : Each prime implicant of a monotone function $f \in M_n$ only contains positive literals.

Proof : Let $m = m'\bar{x}_j \in I(f)$. It is sufficient to prove that the shortening $m' \in I(f)$. If $m'(a) = 1$ either $a_j = 0$ implying $m'\bar{x}_j(a) = 1$ and $f(a) = 1$ or $a_j = 1$. In the last case let b be defined by $b_j = 0$ and $b_i = a_i$ for $i \neq j$. Then $m'\bar{x}_j(b) = 1$ implying $f(b) = 1$. Since $b \leq a$ and f is monotone, also $f(a) = 1$. In either case $m'(a) = 1$ implies $f(a) = 1$. Hence $m' \in I(f)$.

$\square$

THEOREM 4.2 : For monotone functions f the unique minimal polynomial consists of all prime implicants.

Proof : By Lemma 2.2 it is sufficient to construct for each $m \in PI(f)$ some input $a \in f^{-1}(1)$ such that $m(a) = 1$ and $m'(a) = 0$ for all $m' \in PI(f)$, $m' \neq m$. By Theorem 4.1 we may assume w.l.o.g. that $m(x) = x_1 \cdots x_k$. Let $a_i = 1$ iff $i \leq k$. Obviously $m(a) = 1$. If $m'(a) = 1$, $m' \neq m$ and $m' \in PI(f)$, m' can contain by Theorem 4.1

and by definition of a only variables x_i where $i \le k$. Therefore m'
is a proper submonom of m and m is no prime implicant. Contradiction.

$\square$

The minimal polynomial for $f \in M_n$ is also called monotone disjunctive normal form (MDNF).

THEOREM 4.3 : The set of functions computable by monotone circuits, i.e. $\{\wedge, \vee\}$ - circuits, is equal to the set of monotone functions.

Proof : By Theorem 4.1 each monotone function may be computed
by a monotone circuit. By induction on the number of gates of a
monotone circuit we prove that monotone circuits compute only
monotone functions. The inputs $0, 1, x_1, \ldots, x_n$ are monotone. For
the induction step it is sufficient to prove that $f \wedge g$ and $f \vee g$ are
monotone if f and g are monotone. Let $a \le b$. Then

$$(f \wedge g)(a) = \min \{f(a), g(a)\} \le \min \{f(b), g(b)\} = (f \wedge g)(b) \qquad (4.1)$$

and

$$(f \vee g)(a) = \max \{f(a), g(a)\} \le \max \{f(b), g(b)\} = (f \vee g)(b). \qquad (4.2)$$

$\square$

Monotone circuits will be investigated in detail in Ch.6 . The
monotone basis $\{\wedge, \vee\}$ is denoted by Ω_m and the corresponding
complexity measures are denoted by C_m and D_m.

2.5 The complexity of minimizing

So far we have described efficient algorithms for the computation of PI(f) and the reduced PI-table. No efficient algorithm for the second part, the computation of a minimal polynomial from the reduced PI-table, is known. We argue that with high probability no such algorithm exists. For this purpose we use the concept of NP-completeness (see Garey and Johnson (79)). For all those who are not familiar with the NP-theory we give the following short explanation. Many (more than 1000) problems are known to be NP-complete. It can be proved that one of the following statements is correct. Either all NP-complete problems have polynomial algorithms or no NP-complete problem may be solved by a polynomial algorithm. The conjecture of most of the experts is that the second statement holds. One of the well-known NP-complete problems is the set cover problem which we prove to be equivalent to our minimization problem.

DEFINITION 5.1 : An instance of the set cover problem is given by different sets $S_1, \ldots, S_m \subseteq \{1,...,n\}$ such that the union of all S_i is $\{1,...,n\}$, and some number $k \leq m$. The problem is to decide whether the union of k of the sets S_i equals $\{1,...,n\}$.

The problem of determining the minimum k such that k subsets are sufficient to cover $\{1,...,n\}$ is not easier. The connection with our minimization problem is easy to see. The inputs $a \in f^{-1}(1)$ correspond to the elements $1,...,n$ and the prime implicants correspond to the sets S_i . In particular, $j \in S_i$ iff $m_i(y_j) = 1$. We may still hope that minimization problems only lead to easy instances of the set cover problem. This hope has been destroyed by Paul (75).

DEFINITION 5.2 : A 0-1-matrix is called reduced if each row contains at least one 1-entry, each column contains at least two 1-entries and if no columns c and c' have the property $c \le c'$.

THEOREM 5.1 : For each reduced matrix M there exists a Boolean function f , whose reduced PI-table equals M . Furthermore f can be chosen such that all prime implicants of the reduced PI-table have the same length.

Proof : Let n be the number of rows of M and let S be the set of columns of M . It will turn out that the following function $f \in B_{n+2}$ satisfies the assertion of the theorem.
For $a \in \{0,1\}^n$ we denote $a_1 \oplus \cdots \oplus a_n$, the parity of a , by $|a|$. The vector of zeros only is denoted by $\underline{0}$.

$$f(a,0,0) = 1 \quad \text{iff } a \ne \underline{0}. \tag{5.1}$$

$$f(a,1,1) = 0 \quad \text{for all } a \in \{0,1\}^n . \tag{5.2}$$

$$f(a,1,0) = 1 \quad \text{iff } a \ne \underline{0}, \ a \notin S \text{ and } |a| = 0 . \tag{5.3}$$

$$f(a,0,1) = 1 \quad \text{iff } a \ne \underline{0}, \ a \notin S \text{ and } |a| = 1 . \tag{5.4}$$

We claim that $PI(f)$ consists of the following three subsets where m_a again is the minterm for a .

$$PI(f) = \{ m_a \, \bar{x}_{n+1} \mid a \ne \underline{0}, \ a \notin S, \ |a| = 1 \} \tag{5.5}$$

$$\cup \ \{ m_a \, \bar{x}_{n+2} \mid a \ne \underline{0}, \ a \notin S, \ |a| = 0 \}$$

$$\cup \ \{ x_i \, \bar{x}_{n+1} \, \bar{x}_{n+2} \mid 1 \le i \le n \} .$$

At first it is easy to see that all monoms in (5.5) are implicants and no monom is a shortening of another one. Therefore it is sufficient to prove that all other implicants of f are lengthenings of the monoms in (5.5).

Let $t \in I(f)$. Because of (5.2) t contains either $\bar{x}_{n+1}$ or $\bar{x}_{n+2}$ or both of them. Because of (5.1) t contains some x_i if it contains

$\bar{x}_{n+1}$ and $\bar{x}_{n+2}$. If t contains $\bar{x}_{n+1}$ but not $\bar{x}_{n+2}$, then t contains a full minterm m_a . Otherwise t does not contain x_i and $\bar{x}_i$ for some i and we find vectors a and a' differing only at position i such that $t(a,0,1) = t(a',0,1) = 1$ implying $f(a,0,1) = f(a',0,1) = 1$. Because of (5.4) $|a| = |a'| = 1$ which is impossible if a and a' differ only at one position. Altogether t contains $\bar{x}_{n+1}$ and m_a for some $a \in \{0,1\}^n$. Again (5.4) implies that $a \neq \underline{0}$, $a \notin S$ and $|a| = 1$. Similar arguments hold if t contains $\bar{x}_{n+2}$ but not $\bar{x}_{n+1}$. Altogether we have proved (5.5).

We consider the PI - table of f . The column for $(a,0,1) \in f^{-1}(1)$ has a single one in the row $m_a \bar{x}_{n+1}$. The PI - table may be reduced by eliminating the row $m_a \bar{x}_{n+1}$ and the columns $(a,0,1)$ and $(a,0,0)$. Similar arguments hold for rows $m_a \bar{x}_{n+2}$ and inputs $(a,1,0) \in f^{-1}(1)$. We obtain the following partially reduced PI - table M' . M' has rows for $x_i \bar{x}_{n+1} \bar{x}_{n+2}$ $(1 \leq i \leq n)$ and columns for $(a,0,0)$ and some $a \in S$. The columns $(a,0,1)$ and $(a,1,0)$ have all been eliminated. Column $(a,0,0)$ has been eliminated either during the elimination of row $m_a \bar{x}_{n+1}$ iff $a \notin S$ and $|a| = 1$ or during the elimination of row $m_a \bar{x}_{n+2}$ iff $a \notin S$ and $|a| = 0$. Furthermore $x_i \bar{x}_{n+1} \bar{x}_{n+2} (a,0,0) = a_i$. Therefore the partially reduced PI - table M' is equal to the given matrix M . Since M is reduced, M' is reduced too. All prime implicants have length 3 .

$\square$

2.6 Discussion

As we have shown the minimization of a Boolean function is (probably) a hard problem. Furthermore, a minimal polynomial for f does not lead to an optimal circuit for f . We only obtain an optimal circuit in the rather restricted class of two-level-circuits. The following example of Lupanov (65 a) shows that a very simple function may have an expensive minimal polynomial.

PROPOSITION 6.1 : Let $f(x) = x_1 \oplus \cdots \oplus x_n$ be the parity function.
Then $C(f) \leq n-1$ but the minimal polynomial consists of 2^{n-1} prime
implicants of length n each.

— size or complexity of a circuit = # gates

Proof : By definition $C(f) \leq n-1$. $PI(f)$ is the set of minterms m_a
such that $a_1 \oplus \cdots \oplus a_n = 1$. Since $|m_a^{-1}(1)| = 1$, all prime implicants
are necessary for the minimal polynomial.

$\square$

In Ch.11 we show that even k-level-circuits computing the parity function require an exponential number of gates. Of course parity
is an extreme example. Korshunov (81 b) and Kuznetsov (83 b)
have shown that for almost all $f \in B_n$ the number of prime impli-
cants in a minimal polynomial is at least $(1 - \varepsilon_n) \, 2^n/(\log n \, \log\log n)$
where $\varepsilon_n \to 0$ and at most $1.6 \, 2^n/(\log n \, \log\log n)$. In Ch.4 we construct efficiently a circuit with at most $2^n/n + o(2^n/n)$ gates for each
$f \in B_n$.

Finally we mention that it is possible to develop a dual theory by
exchanging the roles of $\wedge$ and $\vee$ and of 0 and 1 . Instead of
monoms we obtain Boolean sums and instead of (prime) implicants
(prime) clauses. For monotone functions the monotone conjunctive
normal form (MCNF) is the counterpart of the MDNF .

EXERCISES

1. Compute a minimal polynomial for
    $f(a,b,c,d) = \bar{a}\bar{b}\bar{c}d \vee \bar{a}\bar{b}cd \vee \bar{a}b\bar{c}d \vee \bar{a}b\bar{c}d \vee ab\bar{c}d \vee abc\bar{d} \vee abcd$.

2. How often do we obtain $m \in Q_i$ while constructing Q_i according
    to the Quine and McCluskey algorithm ?

3. Describe the set of prime implicants of $f \in B_n$ where f computes 1 iff $x_1 + \cdots + x_n \not\equiv 0 \mod k$.

4. Define a function $f \in B_n$ with $\Omega(3^n/n)$ prime implicants.

5. $D(f) \leq n + \log n$ for all $f \in B_n$.

6. Define a function $f \in B_n$ which has not a unique minimal polynomial.

7. Design polynomial $\{\wedge, \vee, \neg\}$ - circuits for the parity function such that the number of logical levels grows as slowly as possible.

8. Prove the dual counterpart of Proposition 6.1 for the parity function.

9. Let $f, g \in M_n$. $f \leq g \iff \forall\ p \in PI(f)\ \exists\ q \in PI(g) : p \leq q$.

10. Compute all prime implicants and prime clauses of T_k^n, the k-th threshold function, computing 1 iff the number of ones in the input is at least k.

For the following problems (Oberschelp (84)) we need some definitions. Let $S = \{0,...,s-1\}$ and let $i \oplus j \equiv i + j \mod s$. An interval $[a,b]$ contains a, $a \oplus 1$,..., b. A (generalized) rectangle is a Cartesian product of intervals. For a rectangle $D \subseteq S^n$ and some $c \in S - \{0\}$ the corresponding monom m is defined by $m(x) = c$ if $x \in D$ and $m(x) = 0$ otherwise. $m \in I(f)$ if $m \leq f$. $m \in PI(f)$ if no implicant $m' \in I(f)$ corresponds to D' and c' such that $D \subseteq D'$, $D \neq D'$ and $c = c'$ or $D = D'$ and $c < c'$. The partial derivative of f at a with respect to x_i is defined by

$$\partial f / \partial x_i(a) = \min\{f(a_1, \ldots, a_{i-1}, a_i \oplus 1, a_{i+1}, \ldots, a_n), f(a_1, \ldots, a_n)\}.$$

11. For $s = 2$ the above definitions of monoms and (prime) implicants are equal to the definitions in § 1 .

12. The order of partial derivatives is arbitrary.

13. $\partial f / \partial^j x_i = \partial f / \partial^{j'} x_i$ if $j, j' \geq s - 1$.

14. Describe the set of functions $f : S^n \to S$ such that $\partial f / \partial^{i(1)} x_1 \cdots \partial^{i(n)} x_n(a) = b$.

15. $g : S^n \to S$ has a local maximum at a if $g(b_i) < g(a)$ for all $b_i = (a_1, \ldots, a_{i-1}, a_i \oplus 1, a_{i+1}, \ldots, a_n)$.
If $g = \partial f / \partial^{i(1)} x_1 \cdots \partial^{i(n)} x_n$ has a local maximum at a , the monom h corresponding to $D = [a_1, a_1 \oplus i(1)] \times \ldots \times [a_n, a_n \oplus i(n)]$ and $c = g(a)$ is a prime implicant of f .

16. By the consideration of all local maxima we do not detect all prime implicants. Describe an algorithm for the computation of all prime implicants. Consider at first the case $s = 2$.

3. THE DESIGN OF EFFICIENT CIRCUITS FOR SOME FUNDAMENTAL FUNCTIONS

In this chapter we design for some fundamental functions circuits of small size and small depth. The design methods we use are important, since they are quite general. It may be astonishing that we already need clever and subtle methods for the design of efficient addition, multiplication and division circuits. The basic methods learnt in school are not efficient enough. In order to estimate the value of our circuits we mention that for all functions $f \in B_{n,m}$ considered in this chapter $n-1$ gates and depth $\lceil \log n \rceil$ are necessary (see Ch. 5). Here and in the rest of the book we use the so-called upper and lower Gaussian brackets.

$$\lceil x \rceil = \min \{ z \in \mathbb{Z} \mid z \geq x \} \quad \text{and} \quad \lfloor x \rfloor = \max \{ z \in \mathbb{Z} \mid z \leq x \} .$$

The binary number $a = (a_{n-1}, \ldots, a_0) \in \{0,1\}^n$ has the value $|a| = a_0 2^0 + \cdots + a_{n-1} 2^{n-1}$.

3.1 Addition and subtraction

DEFINITION 1.1 : The addition function $f_n^{add} \in B_{2n,n+1}$ has two n - bit numbers x and y as inputs and computes the $(n+1)$-bit representation s of $|x| + |y|$.

In this section f_n means f_n^{add} . How efficient is the addition method we learnt in school ? We use a halfadder to compute $s_0 = x_0 \oplus y_0$ and the carry bit $c_0 = x_0 \wedge y_0$. Afterwards we use $n-1$ fulladders for the computation of s_i and c_i from x_i, y_i and c_{i-1} . Finally $s_n = c_{n-1}$. Already in Ch.1 we have defined a fulladder of size 5 and depth 3 by

$$s_j = x_j \oplus y_j \oplus c_{j-1} \quad \text{and} \tag{1.1}$$

$$c_j = x_j \, y_j \vee (x_j \oplus y_j) \, c_{j-1} \, . \tag{1.2}$$

Altogether we obtain a circuit of size $5n - 3$ and depth $2n - 1$. Here we compute in parallel all $x_j \, y_j$ and $x_j \oplus y_j$. Afterwards s_j and c_j can be computed in depth 2 if c_{j-1} is computed.

THEOREM 1.1 : The school method of addition leads to a circuit of size $5n - 3$ and depth $2n - 1$.

This circuit is of minimal size (see Ch. 5). But its depth is far too large. This is not astonishing, since the method has been designed for sequentially working people. We try to reduce the depth. The problem is the computation of the carry bits. Later we compute all carry bits in advance. Now we compute the sum under the condition that the carry bits have certain values. Afterwards we select the right output. This procedure due to Sklansky (60 a) and (60 b) is called Conditional Sum Adder.

For the sake of simplicity we assume that $n = 2^k$. It should always be easy for the reader to generalize the algorithms to arbitrary n .

The numbers x and y have $n = 2^k$ bits and can be divided into 2^{n-l} blocks each of length 2^l . The i-th block of x of length $L = 2^l$, namely $(x_{iL-1}, \ldots, x_{(i-1)L})$, is denoted by $X_{i,l}$. Our problem is the addition of $X_{1,k}$ (the number x) and $Y_{1,k}$ where the carry bit at position 0 is 0 .

The subproblem $P_{i,l,c}$ where $0 \le l \le k$, $1 \le i \le 2^{k-l}$ and $c \in \{0,1\}$ is the problem of adding X_{il} , namely $(x_{iL-1}, \ldots, x_{(i-1)L})$, Y_{il} , namely $(y_{iL-1}, \ldots, y_{(i-1)L})$, and c . Altogether we have to solve $P_{1,k,0}$.

Since we are looking for a circuit of small depth, we solve the problems $P_{i,l,c}$ for fixed l in parallel. For $l = 0$ and $c = 0$ we have to compute the sum bits $x_j \oplus y_j$ and the carry bits $x_j \wedge y_j$. For $l = 0$ and $c = 1$ we have to compute the sum bits $x_j \oplus \bar{y}_j$ and the carry bits $x_j \vee y_j$. Altogether step 0 , the solution of all $P_{i,0,c}$, can be realized with 4n gates in depth 1 .

In step l $(1 \leq l \leq k)$ we solve all problems $P_{i,l,c}$ where we may use the results of all problems $P_{i,l-1,c}$. Let us consider $P_{i,l,c}$ in more detail. We have to add the summands $(x_{iL-1}, \ldots, x_{(i-1)L})$, $(y_{iL-1}, \ldots, y_{(i-1)L})$ and c . In order to use the solutions of smaller problems, we describe the summands in another way where $L' = 2^{l-1}$.

Summands for $P_{i,l,c}$:

$$(x_{2iL'-1}, \cdots, x_{(2i-1)L'}, x_{(2i-1)L'-1}, \cdots, x_{(2i-2)L'}) , \tag{1.3}$$

$$(y_{2iL'-1}, \cdots, y_{(2i-1)L'}, y_{(2i-1)L'-1}, \cdots, y_{(2i-2)L'}) \text{ and } c .$$

By (1.3) the second half of the solution of $P_{i,l,c}$ is the solution of $P_{2i-1,l-1,c}$ without the foremost carry c' . The first half of the solution of $P_{i,l,c}$ is the solution of $P_{2i,l-1,c'}$. Since c is given we may directly use the solution of $P_{2i-1,l-1,c}$. But c' is not known in advance. c' is an output of $P_{2i-1,l-1,c}$. Let z_j^0 ($(2i-1)L' \leq j \leq 2iL'$) and z_j^1 be the output bits of $P_{2i,l-1,0}$ and $P_{2i,l-1,1}$ resp. Using c' we may select the right output bit (z_j^0 if c' = 0 or z_j^1 if c' = 1) by

$$z_j = (c' \wedge z_j^1) \vee (\overline{c'} \wedge z_j^0) \tag{1.4}$$

in depth 2 using 3 gates. Altogether step l can be realized in depth 2 using for each of the $2^{k-l} \cdot 2$ problems $3(2^{l-1}+1)$ gates. The circuit size of step l is $3(2^k + 2^{k-l+1})$.

The depth of the whole circuit is $1 + 2k = 2 \log n + 1$ and the size is

$$4n + \sum_{1 \leq l \leq k} 3(2^k + 2^{k-l+1}) = 4n + 3k 2^k + 3(2^{k+1} - 2)$$

$$= 3n \log n + 10n - 6 . \tag{1.5}$$

THEOREM 1.2 : The Conditional Sum Adder may be realized (if $n = 2^k$) in depth $2 \log n + 1$ and size $3 n \log n + 10 n - 6$.

According to our remark at the beginning of this chapter the depth of this circuit is only double the size of the lower bound. But the size of the circuit is not linear. The Carry Look Ahead Adder due to Ofman (63) simultaneously has size $O(n)$ and depth $O(\log n)$. Constant factors for depth have stronger consequences than constant factors for size. Therefore the adder of Brent (70) of size $O(n \log n)$ and depth $\log n + O(\log^{1/2} n)$ is interesting. Krapchenko (70) came up with an adder of linear size and depth $\log n + O(\log^{1/2} n)$.

THEOREM 1.3 : Krapchenko's adder for n-bit numbers has size $3n + 6 \cdot 2^m$ and depth $m + 7 (2m)^{1/2} + 16$ where $m = \lceil \log n \rceil$.

For $n = 2^k$ the size of Krapchenko's adder is only by the factor of 1.8 larger than the minimal size for an adder. The additive term $7 (2m)^{1/2} + 16$ for the depth seems to be quite large, in particular for small n . In fact the additive term is smaller but our estimations are not exact. The following proof is long and technically involved, although the ideas are easy.

Proof of Theorem 1.3 : Krapchenko's adder S consists of five parts $S_1, \ldots, S_5$. In S_1 $u_j = x_j y_j$ and $v_j = x_j \oplus y_j$ are computed by n half-adders. The crucial part is the computation of the carry bits c_j in S_2, S_3 and S_4 . Afterwards, it is easy to compute in S_5 the outputs $s_0 = v_0 , s_j = v_j \oplus c_{j-1}$ for $1 \le j \le n-1$ and $s_n = c_{n-1}$. Therefore

$$C(S_1) = 2n \qquad D(S_1) = 1 \qquad \text{and} \qquad (1.6)$$

$$C(S_5) = n-1 \qquad D(S_5) = 1 . \qquad (1.7)$$

By applying (1.2) for $j+1$ times we can compute c_j from the u - and v - parameters.

$$
\begin{aligned}
c_j &= u_j \vee v_j c_{j-1} = u_j \vee u_{j-1} v_j \vee v_{j-1} v_j c_{j-2} = \cdots = \\
&= \bigvee_{0 \le i \le j} u_i v_{i+1} \cdots v_j .
\end{aligned}
\qquad (1.8)
$$

This can be interpreted in the following way. Carry $c_j = 1$ iff for some $i \le j$ at position i we have two ones ($u_i = 1$) and at the positions $i+1,...,j$ exactly a zero and a one ($v_{i+1} = \cdots = v_j = 1$). More generally, we define for $b \geq a$

$$G_{b,a} = g_{b-a+1}(u_b, v_b, \cdots, u_{a+1}, v_{a+1}, u_a) =$$

$$= \bigvee_{a \leq i \leq b} u_i v_{i+1} \cdots v_b \qquad (1.9)$$

$$V_{b,a} = v_a \cdots v_b . \qquad (1.10)$$

In particular $c_j = G_{j,0}$. In Fig. 1.1 we give a triangle representation for $G_{d,a}$ where one has to combine the rows by disjunctions. Let $a < b < d$. Since

$$G_{d,a} = G_{d,b+1} \vee G_{b,a} V_{d,b+1} \quad \text{and} \qquad (1.11)$$

$$V_{d,a} = V_{b,a} V_{d,b+1} . \qquad (1.12)$$

According to Fig. 1.1 G-functions are called triangles and V-functions are called rectangles.

In S_2 we compute some not too large triangles and rectangles. For some parameter τ to be chosen later we partition $\{0,...,n-1\}$ to blocks of size $2, 4, ..., 2^\tau$ and compute the corresponding triangles and rectangles. These results are used in S_3 for the computation of all carry bits c_j where $j = k\,2^\tau - 1$ for some k . In S_4 we fill the gaps and compute all c_j .

We have already computed triangles of size 1 , namely u_j , and rectangles of size 1 , namely v_j . By (1.11) and (1.12) we may compute rectangles and triangles of size 2^l from the rectangles and triangles of size 2^{l-1} with 1 and 2 gates resp. in depth 2 . The number of blocks of size 2^l may be estimated by 2^{m-l} . Altogether

$$C(S_2) \le 3 \cdot 2^m (1 - 2^{-\tau}) \quad \text{and} \quad D(S_2) = 2\tau . \tag{1.13}$$

S_4 is rather simple too. In S_3 we have computed all $c_{k\,2^\tau - 1}$ The other carry bits are computed in τ steps where we compute all $c_{k\,2^{\tau-l} - 1}$ in step l . For even k these carry bits have already been computed. For odd $k = 2j+1$ by $(1.8) - (1.12)$

$$c_{(2j+1)\,2^{\tau-l}-1} = \tag{1.14}$$

$$G_{(2j+1)\,2^{\tau-l}-1,\,(2j)\,2^{\tau-l}} \vee V_{(2j+1)\,2^{\tau-l}-1,\,(2j)\,2^{\tau-l}}\, c_{(2j)\,2^{\tau-l}-1}$$

The terms on the right-hand side are computed in S_2, S_3 or in earlier steps of S_4 . The depth of step l is 2 while the size is 2 for each new carry. j may take values in $\{0 , \ldots, 2^{m-\tau+l-1} - 1\}$. Thus

$$C(S_4) \le 2 \cdot 2^m (1 - 2^{-\tau}) \quad \text{and} \quad D(S_4) = 2\tau . \tag{1.15}$$

In S_3 we use the triangles u_j' and rectangles v_j' of size 2^τ as inputs $(0 \le j \le 2^{m-\tau} - 1)$ and compute all $G_{j,0}' = g_{j+1}(u_j', v_j', \ldots, u_0')$. By (1.11) and (1.12) we can conclude that $G_{j,0}'$ is the carry bit at position $(j+1)\,2^\tau - 1$. We have to solve the problem of computing all carry bits but the input size has been reduced from n to $2^{m-\tau}$.

At first we explain our ideas by an implementation of small depth and large size. Afterwards we bound depth and size simultaneously. Considering depth only to consider one output only is sufficient, say $G_{2^m-1,0} = g_{2^m}(u_{2^m-1}, v_{2^m-1}, \ldots, u_0)$. Again by (1.11) and (1.12)

$$G_{2^m-1,0} = \tag{1.16}$$

$$\bigvee_{0 \le i \le 2^{m-r}-1} G_{2^m-i2^r-1,\, 2^m-(i+1)2^r} \bigvee_{2^m-1,\, 2^m-i2^r} \cdot$$

All triangles on the right side have length 2^r, the rectangles can be computed in depth m, all conjunctions between triangles and rectangles can be done in parallel and by divide-and-conquer, the outer disjunction can be performed in depth $m-r$.

$$D(g_{2m}) \le m-r+1 + \max\{ D(g_{2^r}), m\} , \tag{1.17}$$

since all triangles and rectangles can be computed in parallel. For the sake of simplicity let us assume that $m = h(l) = \binom{l}{2}$. Then we choose $r = h(l-1)$. By induction we can prove that

$$D(g_{2h(l)}) \le h(l+1) . \tag{1.18}$$

For $l=1$, $m=0$ and g_1 has depth $0 \le h(2) = 1$. For the induction step $l-1 \to l$ we apply (1.17). By induction hypothesis the depth of g_{2^r} is bounded by $h(l) = m$. Thus the depth of g_{2m} is bounded by $2m - r + 1$ or $2\binom{l}{2} - \binom{l-1}{2} + 1 = \binom{l+1}{2} = h(l+1)$. Furthermore $\binom{l+1}{2} = \binom{l}{2} + l = m + O(m^{1/2})$ and for $n \le 2^m$ the depth of g_n is bounded by $\log n + O(\log^{1/2} n)$.

In order to guarantee also linear size we have reduced the number of inputs by the use of S_2 and S_4 and we use a more complicated implementation of all g - functions. Here we have $2^{m'}$ inputs where $m' = m - \tau$. We choose the smallest t such that $m' \le \binom{t}{2} = h(t)$. Since $\binom{t-1}{2} < m'$, it is easy to prove that

$$t < (2m')^{1/2} + 2 . \tag{1.19}$$

For $1 \le l \le t$ and $0 \le j \le 2^{m'}-1$ let $d(l,j)$ be the largest multiple of $2^{h(l)}$ not larger than j. Then

$$j - 2^{h(l)} + 1 \le d(l,j) \le j , \quad \text{in particular } d(t,j) = 0 . \tag{1.20}$$

For $2 \le l \le t$ and $0 \le j \le 2^{m'}-1$ let

$$e(l,j) = (d(l-1,j) - d(l,j)) / 2^{h(l-1)}. \tag{1.21}$$

By (1.20) we obtain for $l < t$

$$e(l,j) \le (j - d(l,j))/2^{h(l-1)} < 2^{h(l)-h(l-1)} = 2^{l-1} \quad \text{and} \tag{1.22}$$

$$e(t,j) = d(t-1,j)/2^{h(t-1)} \le j / 2^{h(t-1)} < 2^{m'-h(t-1)} \le 2^{l-1}. \tag{1.23}$$

We now compute all triangles G' and rectangles V' based on the inputs u_j' and v_j'. The rectangles are computed in $t-1$ steps $(1 \le l \le t-1)$. In step l we compute for $1 \le k \le e(l+1,j)$ and $0 \le j \le 2^{m'}-1$

$$V'_{j,d(l,j)-k\,2^{h(l)}} = \tag{1.24}$$

$$V'_{j,d(l,j)} \wedge \bigwedge_{1 \le r \le k} V'_{d(l,j)-(r-1)2^{h(l)}-1,\, d(l,j)-r\,2^{h(l)}}.$$

The correctness of (1.24) is obvious. It is necessary to prove that the rectangles on the right side are computed before step l. For $k = e(l,j)$, we get $d(l,j) = d(l-1,j) - k\,2^{h(l-1)}$ by (1.21). Therefore $V'_{j,d(l,j)}$ has been computed before. For the other rectangles let $j' = d(l,j) - (r-1)\,2^{h(l)} - 1$. By definition of $d(l,j)$ we can find some k such that $d(l,j) = k\,2^{h(l)}$, thus $j' = (k-r)\,2^{h(l)} + 2^{h(l)} - 1$. Furthermore $d(l,j) - r\,2^{h(l)} = (k-r)\,2^{h(l)} = d(l,j')$ by definition of d. So also the other rectangles are of the form $V'_{j',d(l,j')}$ and are computed before step l.

The triangles are computed in $t-1$ steps $(2 \le l \le t)$. In step l we compute for $0 \le j \le 2^{m'}-1$

$$G'_{j,d(l,j)} = G'_{j,d(l-1,j)} \vee$$

$$\bigvee_{1 \le r \le e(l,j)} V'_{j,d(l-1,j)-(r-1)2^{h(l-1)}} \wedge \tag{1.25}$$

$$G'_{d(l-1,j)-(r-1)2^{h(l-1)},\, d(l-1,j)-r\,2^{h(l-1)}}.$$

(1.25) is correct by our standard arguments. The rectangles are computed before step l as has been shown above. The triangles on the right have been computed at step $l-1$. Finally $G'_{j,d(t,j)} = G'_{j,0}$ is the carry bit at position $(j+1)\,2^{\tau} - 1$.

We estimate the depth and size of S_3 . In (1.24) we compute the conjunction of at most $e(l+1,j)$ rectangles. By (1.22) and (1.23) this can be done in depth l . In (1.25) we perform the conjunctions in depth 1 in parallel. Afterwards we compute the disjunction of at most $e(l,j) + 1$ terms. By (1.22) the depth of step l is bounded by l and by (1.23) the depth of step t is bounded by $m' - h(t-1) + 1$. Altogether by (1.19)

$$D(S_3) \leq 1 + ... + t - 1 + m' - h(t-1) + 1 = m' + t \tag{1.26}$$

$$< m' + (2m')^{1/2} + 2 .$$

The size of S_3 is estimated in the same way. For the computation of all rectangles the following number of gates is sufficient.

$$\sum_{1 \leq l \leq t-1} \sum_{0 \leq j \leq 2^{m'}-1} \sum_{1 \leq k \leq e(l+1,j)} k \leq \sum_{1 \leq l \leq t-1} \sum_{0 \leq j \leq 2^{m'}-1} 2^l(2^l-1)/2 \tag{1.27}$$

$$= 2^{m'}(2(4^{t-1}-1)/3 - 2^{t-1}) .$$

The number of gates for the triangles is estimated by

$$\sum_{2 \leq l \leq t} \sum_{0 \leq j \leq 2^{m'}-1} 2\,e(l,j) \leq 2^{m'}(2^{t+1} - 2t - 1) . \tag{1.28}$$

By (1.27) and (1.28)

$$C(S_3) \leq 2^{m'}\, 2^{2t-1} . \tag{1.29}$$

We summarize our complexity estimations.

$$D(S) \leq m' + (2m')^{1/2} + 4\tau + 4 = m + (2m')^{1/2} + 3\tau + 4 \tag{1.30}$$

and

$$C(S) \leq 3n + 5 \cdot 2^m(1 - 2^{-\tau}) + 2^{m'}\, 2^{2t-1} \tag{1.31}$$

where $m = \lceil \log n \rceil$, $m' = m - \tau$ and $t < (2m')^{1/2} + 2$. For

$$\tau = \lceil 2\,(2m)^{1/2} \rceil + 3 \tag{1.32}$$

$m' + 2t - 1 \leq m$ and the bounds of the theorem are proved.

□

Since addition is the most fundamental operation, we present another adder which simultaneously has linear size and logarithmic depth (Ladner and Fischer (80)). The structure of this adder is easier than Krapchenko's adder. At first we solve the prefix problem, the efficient computation of all prefixes $p_i = x_1 \circ \cdots \circ x_i$ for an associative operation $\circ$. Later we explain how the prefix problem may be used for the design of an efficient adder. Ladner and Fischer present a family of algorithms $A_k(n)$ for inputs of length n . For $n = 1$ nothing has to be done. Let $n > 1$.

$A_0(n)$: In parallel we apply $A_1(\lceil n/2 \rceil)$ to $x_1, \ldots, x_{\lceil n/2 \rceil}$ and $A_0(\lfloor n/2 \rfloor)$ to $x_{\lceil n/2 \rceil+1}, \ldots, x_n$. Afterwards p_i is computed for $i \leq \lceil n/2 \rceil$. All $p_i = (x_1 \circ \cdots \circ x_{\lceil n/2 \rceil}) \circ (x_{\lceil n/2 \rceil+1} \circ \cdots \circ x_i)$ for $i > \lceil n/2 \rceil$ may be computed in one step each in parallel.

$A_k(n)$ $(k \geq 1)$: In parallel we compute the $\lfloor n/2 \rfloor$ pairs $x_1 \circ x_2$, $x_3 \circ x_4, \ldots$. Afterwards we apply $A_{k-1}(\lceil n/2 \rceil)$ to these pairs and, if n is odd, x_n . We compute all p_{2i}, p_1 and p_n . The missing $\lfloor n/2 \rfloor - 1$ prefixes $p_{2i+1} = p_{2i} \circ x_{2i+1}$ can be computed in parallel.

By $C(k,n)$ and $D(k,n)$ we denote the size and depth resp. of $A_k(n)$. Furthermore $D^*(k,n)$ is the depth of p_n using $A_k(n)$. Considering the description of the algorithms we conclude

$$C(k,1) = D(k,1) = 0 , \tag{1.33}$$

$$C(0,n) = C(1,\lceil n/2 \rceil) + C(0,\lfloor n/2 \rfloor) + \lfloor n/2 \rfloor , \tag{1.34}$$

$$D(0,n) = \max \{ D(1,\lceil n/2 \rceil), D^*(1,\lceil n/2 \rceil) + 1 , D(0,\lfloor n/2 \rfloor) + 1 \} , \tag{1.35}$$

$$C(k,n) = C(k-1,\lceil n/2 \rceil) + 2\lfloor n/2 \rfloor - 1 , \tag{1.36}$$

$$D(k,n) \leq D(k-1,\lceil n/2 \rceil) + 2 , \tag{1.37}$$

$$D^*(k,n) \leq D(k-1,\lceil n/2 \rceil) + 1 . \tag{1.38}$$

We have used the fact that $A_k(n)$ computes p_n before the last step. The solution of (1.33) - (1.38) easily follows from induction.

THEOREM 1.4 : The prefix problem is solved by $A_k(n)$. For $0 \leq k \leq \lceil \log n \rceil$

$\quad C(k,n) \leq 2n(1 + 2^{-k})$ $\qquad$ and $\qquad\qquad\qquad\qquad$ (1.39)

$\quad D(k,n) \leq k + \lceil \log n \rceil .$ $\qquad\qquad\qquad\qquad\qquad\qquad$ (1.40)

How can we use the prefix problem for the addition of binary numbers ? We use the subcircuits S_1 and S_5 of Krapchenko's adder with size $2n$ and $n-1$ resp. and depth 1 each. S_1 computes a coding of the inputs bits.

$\quad u_j = x_j y_j \quad , \quad v_j = x_j \oplus y_j .$ $\qquad\qquad\qquad\qquad\qquad$ (1.41)

After having computed the carry bits we compute the result by

$\quad s_0 = v_0 \ , \ s_j = v_j \oplus c_{j-1} \text{ for } 1 \leq j \leq n-1 \ , \ s_n = c_{n-1} .$ $\quad$ (1.42)

We know that $c_j = u_j \vee v_j c_{j-1}$. Since (u_j, v_j) may take the values $(0,0)$, $(0,1)$ and $(1,0)$ we consider the functions $A(0,0)$, $A(0,1)$ and $A(1,0)$ where

$\quad A(u,v)(c) = u \vee v c \qquad \text{for } c \in \{0,1\} .$ $\qquad\qquad\qquad$ (1.43)

By definition we may compute the carry bits by

$\quad c_i = A(u_i,v_i) \circ \cdots \circ A(u_0,v_0)(0) .$ $\qquad\qquad\qquad\qquad$ (1.44)

This looks like the prefix problem.
We have to prove that $G = (\{ A(0,0),A(0,1),A(1,0)\} , \circ)$ is a monoid . Since the functions are defined on $\{0,1\}$ it is easy to check by case inspection that

$\quad A(0,0) \circ A(u,v) = A(0,0) ,$ $\qquad\qquad\qquad\qquad\qquad\qquad$ (1.45)

$\quad A(0,1) \circ A(u,v) = A(u,v) , \text{ and}$ $\qquad\qquad\qquad\qquad\quad$ (1.46)

$\quad A(1,0) \circ A(u,v) = A(1,0) .$ $\qquad\qquad\qquad\qquad\qquad\qquad$ (1.47)

The operation $\circ$ on sets of functions is always associative. Therefore the conditions for the application of the prefix algorithms are fulfilled. We only have to design a circuit for the operation $\circ$. Let $A(u,v) = A(u_2,v_2) \circ A(u_1,v_1) .$ Again by (1.45) - (1.47) it is easy to check that

$$(u,v) = (u_2 \vee u_1 v_2 , v_1 v_2) .$$
$$(1.48)$$

Here we find again the characteristic computation of triangles and rectangles as in Krapchenko's adder. By (1.48) a subcircuit for the operation $\circ$ has size 3 and depth 2 . By the prefix algorithm $A_k(n)$ we may compute all $(G_i, V_i) \in \{(0,0),(0,1),(1,0)\}$ such that $A(G_i, V_i)$ is equal to $A(u_i, v_i) \circ \cdots \circ A(u_0, v_0)$ with a circuit of size $3\,C(k,n)$ and depth $2\,D(k,n)$. By (1.43) and (1.44) $c_i = A(G_i, V_i)(0) = G_i$. We may save n gates, since we may eliminate the gates for the computation of V_i. V_i is not necessary for the computation of c_i , and the prefix algorithm uses V_i only for the computation of other V_j (see (1.48)).

Summarizing, the depth of the resulting circuit is $2\,D(k,n) + 2$ and its size is $3\,C(k,n) + 2n - 1$. By Theorem 1.4 we have proved

THEOREM 1.5 : For $0 \leq k \leq \lceil \log n \rceil$ there exist adders based on prefix algorithms whose size is $(8 + 6 \cdot 2^{-k})\, n$ and whose depth is $2\lceil \log n \rceil + 2k + 2$.

Even the most fundamental operation, the addition, is as we have seen a fascinating problem.

We do not consider the subtraction of binary numbers in detail. The complexity of subtraction is nearly the same as the complexity of addition. If we use the first bit of a number as a sign (0 = negative number , 1 = positive number), we have to distinguish between the different cases. More appropriate is the use of the well-known 1 - complement or 2 - complement of binary numbers. These representations of binary numbers are easy to compute. Afterwards we may use the same algorithms for addition and subtraction (see e.g. Spaniol (76)).

3.2 Multiplication

DEFINITION 2.1 : The multiplication function $f_n^{mult} \in B_{2n,2n}$ has two n-bit numbers x and y as inputs and computes the 2n-bit representation p of $|x| \cdot |y|$.

We learnt in school how to multiply x and y . For each i we multiply y_i by x , the result is $z_i = (z_{i,n-1}, \ldots, z_{i,0})$ where $z_{i,j} = y_i x_j$. By a shift which is gratis in circuits we compute $|z_i| \, 2^i$. Finally we add all $|z_i| \, 2^i$ in order to compute the product of x and y . The computation of all $z_{i,j}$ can be done by n^2 gates in depth 1 . By divide-and-conquer we can add the n numbers in $\lceil \log n \rceil$ addition steps. With the efficient adders of § 1 we obtain the following result.

LEMMA 2.1 : The school method for the multiplication implemented with efficient addition circuits leads to a circuit of size $O(n^2)$ and depth $O(\log^2 n)$.

The depth can be reduced by an easy trick due to Ofman (63) and Wallace (64). Since the addition of n - bit numbers requires depth $\Omega(\log n)$, they used Carry Save Adder (CSA gates). CSA gates have three n - bit numbers a,b,c as inputs and produce two (n+1)- bit numbers u and v as outputs such that $|a| + |b| + |c| = |u| + |v|$.

LEMMA 2.2 : CSA gates may be realized in size 5 n and depth 3 .

Proof : We use n fulladders. By the i-th fulladder we add a_i, b_i and c_i and produce the sum bit u_i and the carry bit v_{i+1} $(0 \leq i \leq n-1)$. Moreover $u_n = v_0 = 0$. Finally

$$|a| + |b| + |c| = \sum_{0 \leq i \leq n-1} (a_i + b_i + c_i) \, 2^i = \sum_{0 \leq i \leq n-1} (u_i + 2 \, v_{i+1}) \, 2^i \qquad (2.1)$$

$$= \sum_{0 \le i \le n} u_i \, 2^i + \sum_{0 \le i \le n} v_i \, 2^i = |u| + |v| \, .$$

$\square$

We improve the school method for multiplication by the application of this ingenious but nevertheless simple idea. The numbers z_i again are computed with n^2 gates in depth 1 . The following CSA gates work on numbers whose length is bounded by $2n$, thus all CSA gates have linear size and depth 3 . The number of summands is reduced by 1 by each CSA gate. Therefore $n-2$ CSA gates are sufficient to reduce the number of summands from n to 2 . Finally we use Krapchenko's adder to add these two summands. The resulting circuit has quadratic size. In order to reduce the depth we always use the largest possible number of CSA gates in parallel. If we still have $3k + i$ summands where $i \in \{0,1,2\}$ we may reduce the number of summands to $2k + i$ by k parallel CSA gates. Let $n_0 = n$ and let n_j be the number of summands after the j-th step. Obviously $n_1 \le \frac{2}{3}n + \frac{2}{3}$ and by induction

$$n_j \le (\frac{2}{3})^j n + \left[\frac{2}{3} + (\frac{2}{3})^2 + \cdots + (\frac{2}{3})^j \right] \le (\frac{2}{3})^j \cdot n + 2 \, . \tag{2.2}$$

For $j = \lfloor \log_{3/2} n \rfloor$, we conclude $n_j \le 3$. So $\lfloor \log_{3/2} n \rfloor + 1$ steps are sufficient to reduce the number of summands to 2 .

THEOREM 2.1 : The school method for multiplication implemented with CSA gates and a Krapchenko adder leads to a circuit of size $O(n^2)$ and depth $O(\log n)$.

This multiplication circuit is asymptotically optimal with respect to depth. It is hard to imagine that $o(n^2)$ gates are sufficient for multiplication. Let us try a divide-and-conquer algorithm. Let $n = 2^k$ and let $x = (x',x'')$ and $y = (y',y'')$ be divided into two parts of length $n/2$. Then

$$|p| = |x||y| = (2^{n/2}|x'| + |x''|)(2^{n/2}|y'| + |y''|)$$
$$= 2^n|x'||y'| + 2^{n/2}(|x'||y''| + |x''||y'|) + |x''||y''|.$$

(2.3)

In (2.3) we multiply four times numbers of length $n/2$. The multiplications by 2^n or $2^{n/2}$ are shifts which are gratis in circuits. Moreover we perform three additions which have linear size. For the size of the resulting circuit $C^*(n)$ we obtain the recursion

$$C^*(n) \leq 4 C^*(n/2) + c^* n \quad \text{and} \quad C^*(1) = 1$$

(2.4)

for some constant c^*. By Exercise 1 $C^*(n) = \Theta(n^2)$ and nothing has been gained. Karatsuba and Ofman (63) reduced the number of multiplications of $n/2$ bit-numbers from 4 to 3.
We compute $|p_1| = |x'||y'|$, $|p_2| = |x''||y''|$ and $|p_3| = (|x'| + |x''|)(|y'| + |y''|)$. Now the term $|x'||y''| + |x''||y'|$ can be obtained as $|p_3| - (|p_1| + |p_2|)$. We note that p_3 is a product of two numbers of length $n/2 + 1$. It is easy to see that $C(n) \leq C(n-1) + O(n)$ for the size $C(n)$ of multiplication circuits. Besides the three multiplications the circuit has by earlier results size $O(n)$ and depth $O(\log n)$. Altogether, since the multiplications can be done in parallel,

$$C(n) \leq 3 C(n/2) + O(n) \quad , \quad D(n) \leq D(n/2) + O(\log n) \quad ,$$
$$C(1) = D(1) = 1.$$

(2.5)

Obviously $D(n) = O(\log^2 n)$ and, by Exercise 1, $C(n) = O(n^{\log 3})$.

THEOREM 2.2 : Circuits for multiplication may have size $O(n^{\log 3})$ and depth $O(\log^2 n)$. $\log 3 \approx 1.585$.

For sequential computations the school method of addition is optimal whereas the school method of multiplication is not. Only for rather long numbers the multiplication method of Karatsuba and Ofman is better than the school method. The reader is asked to investigate exactly the following multiplication method $M(k)$. If $n \leq k$, use the school method and, if $n > k$, start with the method of Karatsuba and Ofman but solve subproblems for numbers with at most k bits by the school method. The optimal k is $k_{opt} = 17$. Since $2^{20} \approx 10^6$, we have improved the school method for numbers of reasonable size.

The depth of the Karatsuba and Ofman circuit can also be reduced to $O(\log n)$. Such a reduction was easy for the school method by the use of CSA gates. Here we have to consider additions, subtractions and multiplications by powers of 2. In the following we present a redundant representation of numbers where these operations can be performed efficiently. We know that $|p| < 2^{2n}$ and therefore we can compute $|p|$ exactly if we perform our calculations mod m, i.e. in $\mathbb{Z}_m$, for some $m \geq 2^{2n}$. The following representation of numbers has been investigated by Mehlhorn and Preparata (83).

DEFINITION 2.2 : A radix - 4 representation of $x \in \mathbb{Z}_m$, where $\mathbb{Z}_m$ is a Fermat ring, i.e. $m = 2^p + 1$ and p even, is a vector $(x_{L-1}, \ldots, x_0)$ such that $L = p/2 + 1$, $-3 \leq x_i \leq 3$ and $x = \sum\limits_{0 \leq i \leq L-1} x_i \, 4^i$.

Radix - 4 representations and computations in Fermat rings will also play an important role in a further multiplication method that we discuss later. The binary representation $(x'_p, \ldots, x'_0)$ of x can be understood as a radix - 4 representation by taking $x_i = x'_{2i} + 2x'_{2i+1}$. Obviously it is easy to change the sign in constant depth and linear size. Therefore we do not have to consider subtractions but only additions.

Let $(x_{L-1}, \ldots, x_0)$ and $(y_{L-1}, \ldots, y_0)$ be radix - 4 representations of x and y which we like to add. We start our computation similar to a CSA gate. We compute v_i and c_i such that $x_i + y_i = v_i + 4c_i$. Since $-6 \leq x_i + y_i \leq 6$, it is possible to choose $v_i \in \{-2, -1, 0, 1, 2\}$ and $c_i \in \{-1, 0, 1\}$. The exact definition of v_i and c_i is given in Tab. 2.1.

The trick is to represent 3 not as $0 \cdot 4 + 3 \cdot 1$, but as $1 \cdot 4 + (-1) \cdot 1$. By this trick, $-3 \leq s_i^* = v_i + c_{i-1} \leq 3$. If $c_{L-1} = 0$, we have computed by $(s_{L-1}^*, \ldots, s_0^*)$ a radix - 4 representation of $x + y$. Otherwise we have to add s^*, whose radix - 4 representation is

$x_i + y_i$	-6	-5	-4	-3	-2	-1	0	1	2	3	4	5	6
v_i	-2	-1	0	1	-2	-1	0	1	2	-1	0	1	2
c_i	-1	-1	-1	-1	0	0	0	0	0	1	1	1	1

Tab. 2.1

$(s_{L-1}^*, \ldots, s_0^*)$, and $c_{L-1} 4^L$. By definition,

$$4^L = 4 \cdot 2^P = 4m - 4 \equiv -4 \mod m \tag{2.6}$$

and $(0,\ldots,0,-c_{L-1},0)$ is a radix-4 representation of $c_{L-1} 4^L \mod m$. Either $-3 \le s_1^* - c_{L-1} \le 3$ or $c_{L-1} = -1$ and $s_1^* = 3$ or $c_{L-1} = 1$ and $s_1^* = -3$. In the first case we obtain a radix-4 representation of $x + y$ by $(s_{L-1}', \ldots, s_0')$ where $s_1' = s_1^* - c_{L-1}$ and $s_i' = s_i^*$ for all other i. In the other cases we have to work harder. In our description of the algorithm we use if-tests which are not possible in circuits. In circuits we have to perform the computations for both situations and at the end to select the right result (such a selection has been described in detail in § 1 for the Conditional Sum Adder). If $|s_1^* - c_{L-1}| = 4$, we add $(s_{L-1}^*, \ldots, s_0^*)$ and $(0,\ldots,0,-c_{L-1},0)$ by the same procedure as we started to add $(x_{L-1}, \ldots, x_0)$ and $(y_{L-1}, \ldots, y_0)$. We claim that the procedure stops. Since $|s_1^* - c_{L-1}| = 4$, we get $v_1^* = 0$ and $|c_0^*| \le 1$. Therefore we obtain the vector $(s_{L-1}^{**}, \ldots, s_0^{**})$ where $|s_1^{**}| = |v_1^* + c_0^*| \le 1$. Since $|c_{L-1}^*| \le 1$, it is not possible that $|s_1^{**} - c_{L-1}^*| = 4$. Hence $(s_{L-1}^{**}, \ldots, s_2^{**}, s_1^{**} - c_{L-1}^*, s_0^{**})$ is a radix-4 representation of $x + y$.

We also have to consider the computation of a radix - 4 representation for $x \, 2^s \mod m$. A multiplication by a power of 2 consists of a multiplication by a power of 4 and, if necessary, a multiplication by 2, i.e. an addition. That is why we consider only the computation of $x \, 4^r \mod m$. Since $4^L \equiv -4 \mod m$, as already shown,

$$x \, 4^r \equiv \sum_{r \leq h \leq L-1} x_{h-r} \, 4^h + \sum_{0 \leq h \leq r-1} x_{L-r+h} \, 4^h (-4) \mod m \qquad (2.7)$$

for $0 \leq r \leq L-1$. Therefore it is sufficient to add the radix-4 representations $(x_{L-1-r}, \ldots, x_0, 0, \ldots, 0)$ and $(0, \ldots, 0, -x_{L-1}, \ldots, -x_{L-r}, 0)$.

Finally we consider the transformation of a radix - 4 representation $(x_{L-1}, \ldots, x_0)$ of some number x into its binary representation. Let $x_i^+ = \max \{x_i, 0\}$ and $x_i^- = \min \{x_i, 0\}$. Let $(x_{i,1}^+, x_{i,0}^+)$ and $(x_{i,1}^-, x_{i,0}^-)$ be the binary representation of x_i^+ and $-x_i^-$ resp. We obtain the binary representation of x by an ordinary subtraction of x^+ and x^- which have the binary representations $(x_{L-1,1}^+, x_{L-1,0}^+, \ldots, x_{0,1}^+, x_{0,0}^+)$ and $(x_{L-1,1}^-, \ldots, x_{0,0}^-)$. We summarize our results.

THEOREM 2.3 : The binary representation of x is also a radix - 4 representation of x. Numbers in radix - 4 representation can be added, subtracted and can be multiplied by a power of 2 with circuits of linear size and constant depth. Furthermore, they can be transformed into binary representation in linear size and logarithmic depth.

Since the recursion depth of the Karatsuba - Ofman algorithm is $\log n$, we obtain the following improvement of Theorem 2.2.

THEOREM 2.4 : The Karatsuba and Ofman algorithm for multiplication can be implemented such that the resulting circuit has size $O(n^{\log 3})$ and depth $O(\log n)$.

In the rest of this section we present a circuit for multiplication due to Schönhage and Strassen (71). The circuit simultaneously has size $O(n \log n \log\log n)$ and depth $O(\log n)$. No multiplication circuit of smaller size is known. The problem whether multiplication circuits of linear size exist or whether multiplication is harder than addition with respect to circuit size is still open. Unfortunately the multiplication circuit beats the other circuits only for very long numbers. These long numbers are interesting for special applications, e.g. public key cryptosystems. The algorithm is recursive, so we should solve small subproblems with other methods.

To ensure that the subproblems are of the same type as the initial problem, we make the following assumptions. $n = 2^k$, $0 \leq |x|, |y| \leq 2^n$, and we are only interested in $|p| \mod (2^n + 1)$. We obtain the correct result if we start with $n/2$ - bit numbers. In the following we do not distinguish between $|x|$ and x. Also we assume that $x, y \leq 2^n - 1$. The cases $x = 2^n$ or $y = 2^n$ are easy and are treated in parallel. At the end the correct result is selected. Since $2^n \equiv -1 \mod (2^n + 1)$, $2^n y \equiv 2^n + 1 - y \mod (2^n + 1)$ and we only have to subtract y from $2^n + 1$. If $x, y \leq 2^n - 1$, their binary representations have length n.

After these preliminary remarks we discuss the ideas of the multiplication method of Schönhage and Strassen. While it is obvious that for the multiplication of polynomials we have to multiply numbers, it is interesting to see that the multiplication of numbers can be done by the multiplication of polynomials. We partition x and y into b blocks of l bits each, i.e. $x = (x_{b-1}, \ldots, x_0)$ and $y = (y_{b-1}, \ldots, y_0)$, where $x_i, y_i \in \{0,1\}^l$. The parameters are chosen as

$$b = 2^{\lfloor k/2 \rfloor} \quad \text{and} \quad l = n/b = 2^{\lceil k/2 \rceil}. \tag{2.8}$$

Let $f(z) = \sum_{0 \leq i \leq b-1} x_i z^i$ and $g(z) = \sum_{0 \leq i \leq b-1} y_i z^i$ be polynomials. By definition $x = f(2^l)$ and $y = g(2^l)$, thus $p = xy = h(2^l)$ where $h = fg$. Therefore we can multiply x and y by multiplying the polynomials f and g and evaluating h at 2^l. How can we compute the coefficients v_k of h? By the law of distributivity v_k is the sum of all $x_i y_j$ where $i + j = k$.

DEFINITION 2.3 : The convolution $v = (v_{2b-2}, \ldots, v_0)$ of $x = (x_{b-1}, \ldots, x_0)$ and $y = (y_{b-1}, \ldots, y_0)$ is given by

$$v_k = \sum_{i+j=k} x_i \cdot y_j . \tag{2.9}$$

If we compute all v_k by (2.9) we have to perform b^2 multiplications of l-bit numbers. Since $bl = n$, this is no improvement to previous methods. The following trick is convenient. By the fundamental theorem of algebra a polynomial f of degree $d-1$ is uniquely determined by the value of f at d different inputs. For the sake of simplicity we treat h as a polynomial of degree $2b-1$. Altogether we may multiply the polynomials f and g by evaluating f and g at $2b$ different inputs $a_1, \ldots, a_{2b}$, by computing $h(a_i) = f(a_i) \, g(a_i)$ and by computing the coefficients of h from $h(a_1), \ldots, h(a_{2b})$.

Later we shall see that the computation of $f(a_1), \ldots, f(a_{2b})$ can be done very efficiently if we choose the right values for $a_1, \ldots, a_{2b}$. In the second step we have to perform $2b$ multiplications. The method can only be efficient if the numbers to be multiplied are much shorter than x and y. Schönhage and Strassen observed that the length of the numbers can be reduced by Chinese Remaindering (explained later in this section) and that the number of multiplications can be reduced to b by replacing the convolution by its negative envelope.

DEFINITION 2.4 : The negative envelope $w = (w_{b-1}, \ldots, w_0)$ of the convolution v of x and y is given by

$$w_i = \sum_{0 \le j \le i} x_j \cdot y_{i-j} - \sum_{i < j \le b-1} x_j \cdot y_{b+i-j} . \tag{2.10}$$

If we define $v_{2b-1} = 0$, we obtain the following connection between the convolution and its negative envelope, $w_i = v_i - v_{b+i}$. Now we are able to present the main steps of the multiplication algorithm.

ALGORITHM 2.1 : We use the notation introduced above.

Step 1 : Compute $w_i' = w_i \bmod (2^{2l} + 1)$ for $0 \le i \le b-1$.
(This will be done by the recursive procedure we have discussed.)

Step 2 : Compute $w_i'' = w_i \bmod b$ for $0 \le i \le b-1$.
(This will be done directly.)

Step 3 : Compute w_i from w_i' and w_i'' for $0 \le i \le b-1$.
(This will be done by Chinese Remaindering.)

Step 4 : Compute p , the product of x and y , from $(w_{b-1}, \ldots, w_0)$.
(This will be done by standard methods.)

We still have to work hard to implement the four steps of the algorithm efficiently. At first we discuss the efficiency of the algorithm. In Step 1 we perform recursively b multiplications of numbers of length $2l$. These multiplications are done in parallel. All other work will be done by a circuit of size $O(bl \log b) = O(n \log n)$ and depth $O(\log n)$. So we obtain a circuit of size $C(n)$ and depth $D(n)$, where

$$C(n) \le b\, C(2l) + O(n \log n) \quad \text{and} \tag{2.11}$$

$$D(n) \le D(2l) + O(\log n) . \tag{2.12}$$

Since $l \le (2n)^{1/2}$, it is easy to show that $D(n) = O(\log n)$. For $C'(n) = C(n)/n$ we obtain by (2.11)

$$C'(n) \le 2\, C'(4\, n^{1/2}) + O(\log n) . \tag{2.13}$$

Now it is not difficult (though a little bit tedious) to prove $C'(n) = O(\log n \log \log n)$ and $C(n) = O(n \log n \log \log n)$.

For the implementation we do the easier steps first. Why is it sufficient to compute the negative envelope of the convolution ?

LEMMA 2.3 : $\quad p \equiv \sum_{0 \le i \le b-1} w_i\, 2^{il} \bmod (2^n + 1) .$

Proof : We have already seen that

$$p = h(2^l) = \sum_{0 \le i \le 2b-1} v_i \cdot 2^{il} , \qquad (2.14)$$

where $v_{2b-1} = 0$. Since $w_i = v_i - v_{b+i}$, it is sufficient to prove that $v_{b+i} \cdot 2^{(b+i)l}$ equals $-v_{b+i} \cdot 2^{il}$ mod $(2^n + 1)$. This is obvious since $2^{bl} = 2^n \equiv -1$ mod $(2^n + 1)$.

$\square$

By (2.10) we can estimate w_i by

$$-(b-1-i) \cdot 2^{2l} < w_i < (i+1) \cdot 2^{2l} . \qquad (2.15)$$

Therefore w_i mod $(b(2^{2l} + 1))$ is sufficient for the unique identification of w_i . The length of a radix-4 representation of w_i mod $(b(2^{2l} + 1))$ is $O(l \log b)$. We have to add b numbers, therefore the depth is bounded by $O(\log n)$. We estimate the length of the numbers. In particular, we do not add $w_0\, 2^{0l}$ and $w_{b-1}\, 2^{(b-1)l}$ at the beginning, but always "neighboring" numbers. After the j-th addition step we have computed sums of 2^j "neighboring" numbers. Due to the structure of the numbers $w_i\, 2^{il}$ the length of these $O(b\, 2^{-j})$ sums is $O(l \log b + 2^j\, l)$. The number of gates of the j-th addition step is bounded by $O(2^{-j}\, n \log n + n)$. Summing up for $j \in \{0,\dots,\lceil \log n \rceil\}$, the size is bounded by $O(n \log n)$. We now have computed the sum p^* of all $w_i\, 2^{il}$. It is necessary to compute $p \equiv p^*$ mod $(2^n + 1)$. Since $w_i < b\,(2^{2l} + 1)$, $p^* \le 2^{3n}$. We partition the binary representation of p^* to three blocks of length n each, i.e. $p^* = p_2\, 2^{2n} + p_1\, 2^n + p_0$. Since $2^n \equiv -1$ mod $(2^n + 1)$, $p \equiv p_2 - p_1 + p_0$ mod $(2^n + 1)$. We compute $p' = p_2 - p_1 + p_0$. Obviously $-2^n < p' \le 2^{n+1}$. We compute p' , $p' + 2^n + 1$ and $p' - (2^n + 1)$ and select the number in $\{0,\dots,2^n\}$ as p . Altogether we have implemented Step 4 efficiently.

For the implementation of Step 3 we make use of the Chinese Remainder Theorem which we prove in its general form. In § 3 we apply the theorem in its general form.

THEOREM 2.5 (**Chinese Remainder Theorem**) : Let $m_1, \ldots, m_k$ be relatively prime and $m = m_1 \cdot \ldots \cdot m_k$. For given $a_1, \ldots, a_k$ there is a unique $a \in \{0, \ldots, m-1\}$ such that $a \equiv a_i \mod m_i$ for all i. This a is given by

$$a \equiv \sum_{1 \le i \le k} a_i \cdot r_i \cdot s_i \mod m$$
(2.16)

where $r_i = m / m_i$ and $s_i \equiv (m / m_i)^{-1} \mod m_i$.

Proof : It is an easy fact from elementary number theory that s_i is well defined, since m_i and m / m_i are relatively prime. Since m_j is a factor of m / m_i if $i \ne j$, $r_i \equiv 0 \mod m_j$. By definition $r_i s_i \equiv 1 \mod m_i$. So $a \equiv a_i \mod m_i$. The uniqueness of the solution is easy to prove too. If a and b are solutions, $a - b \equiv 0 \mod m_i$. Because of the relative primality of all m_i even $a - b \equiv 0 \mod m$. Since $a, b \in \{0, \ldots, m-1\}$, we conclude $a = b$.

$\square$

Here we like to compute $w_i \mod (b(2^{2l} + 1))$ from $w_i' \equiv w_i \mod (2^{2l} + 1)$ and $w_i'' \equiv w_i \mod b$. Since b is a power of 2, b and $2^{2l} + 1$ are relatively prime. We claim

$$w_i = w_i' + (2^{2l} + 1) [(w_i'' - w_i') \mod b].$$
(2.17)

By the Chinese Remainder Theorem it is sufficient to investigate $w_i \mod b$ and $w_i \mod (2^{2l} + 1)$. The second number equals w_i'. Since $b \le 2^{2l}$, $2^{2l} \equiv 0 \mod b$. Therefore the right-hand side of (2.17) mod b is equal to w_i''. By (2.17) all w_i can be computed in size $O(n \log n)$ and depth $O(\log n)$. Also Step 3 is implemented efficiently.

The computation of all $w_i'' \equiv w_i \mod b$ is rather easy since b is rather small. Since b is a power of 2 we know $x_i' \equiv x_i \mod b$ and $y_i' \equiv y_i \mod b$. We hide all computations in a multiplication of long but not too long numbers. Let $f'(z) = \sum_{0 \le i \le b-1} x_i' z^i$ and $g'(z) =$

$\sum\limits_{0 \leq i \leq b-1} y'_i z^i$. For $m = 3 \log b$ let $x'' = f'(2^m)$ and $y'' = g'(2^m) \cdot x''$ is the sequence x'_{b-1} , $2 \log b$ zeros , x'_{b-2} ,...., $2 \log b$ zeros , x'_0 , similarly for y'' . By Theorem 2.4 we may compute $x'' \cdot y'' = f'g'(2^m)$ by a circuit of size $O((b \log b)^{\log 3})$ $= o(n \log n)$ and depth $O(\log(b \log b)) = O(\log n)$. By definition of the convolution vector v' of x' and y' we know that $f'g'(2^m) = \sum\limits_{0 \leq k \leq 2b-1} v'_k 2^{mk}$. Since $x'_i, y'_i \in \{0,...,b-1\}$, $0 \leq v'_k < b^3 = 2^m$. Thus $f'g'(2^m)$ contains all v'_k as substrings. Now it is easy to compute efficiently all $w''_i \equiv (v'_i - v'_{b+i}) \mod b$.

The most difficult part is the computation of all $w'_i \equiv w_i \mod (2^{2l} + 1)$ in Step 1 . Here we use the recursive procedure discussed at the beginning. The ideas for the computation of the negative envelope of convolution are discussed here in the general situation that vectors $a = (a_0, \ldots, a_{n-1})$ and $b = (b_0, \ldots, b_{n-1})$ are given. a_i and b_i are elements of a commutative ring with a one . The negative envelope $w = (w_0, \ldots, w_{n-1})$ is defined similarly to (2.10) . We like to evaluate the polynomials f and g whose vectors of coefficients are a and b , resp., at 2n (for the convolution) or n (for the negative envelope) different inputs. The naive procedure has $\Theta(n^2)$ arithmetic operations. By choosing the inputs carefully we get by with only $O(n \log n)$ arithmetic operations.

This so-called Fast Fourier Transform has already been described by Runge and König (24) and has been rediscovered for computer science by Cooley and Tukey (65). As inputs we choose $r^0, r^1, \ldots, r^{n-1}$ where r is an n-th root of identity.

DEFINITION 2.5 : r is an n-th root of identity in a commutative ring R with one if $r \neq 1$, $r^n = 1$ and $\sum\limits_{0 \leq j \leq n-1} r^{jk} = 0$ for $1 \leq k \leq n-1$.

First of all we prove the existence of roots of identity in some Fermat rings.

LEMMA 2.4 : Let n and $r \neq 1$ be powers of 2 and $m = r^{n/2} + 1$. Then r is an n-th root of identity in $\mathbb{Z}_m$ and n^{-1} and r^{-1} are defined in $\mathbb{Z}_m$.

Proof : The existence of n^{-1} and r^{-1} again follows from elementary number theory, since n and r are relatively prime to m. By definition $r \neq 1$. Since $r^{n/2} \equiv -1 \mod m$, $r^n \equiv 1 \mod m$. For the last condition we prove by induction on $p = \log n$

$$\sum_{0 \le j \le n-1} r^{jk} = \prod_{0 \le i \le p-1} (1 + r^{2^i k}). \tag{2.18}$$

This claim is obvious for $p = 1$. The induction step follows from the following elementary calculation

$$\sum_{0 \le j \le n-1} r^{jk} = (1 + r^k) \sum_{0 \le j \le (n/2)-1} (r^2)^{jk} \tag{2.19}$$

$$= (1 + r^k) \prod_{0 \le i \le p-2} (1 + (r^2)^{2^i k}) = \prod_{0 \le i \le p-1} (1 + r^{2^i k}).$$

Now it is sufficient to prove that one of the factors $1 + r^{2^i k} \equiv 0 \mod m$. Let $k = 2^s k'$ and k' odd. Then $0 \le s < p$. Furthermore, if $i = p - 1 - s$, $2^i k = 2^{p-1-s} 2^s k' = k' \, n/2$. Since $r^{n/2} \equiv -1 \mod m$, $1 + r^{2^i k} \equiv (1 + (-1)^{k'}) \equiv 0 \mod m$. $\square$

Later we apply the Fast Fourier Transform for $m = 2^{2l} + 1$ and $n = b$. Since $l = b$ or $l = 2b$, the existence of a b-th and a $2b$-th root of identity is guaranteed and so is the existence of b^{-1}, $(2b)^{-1}$ and r^{-1}.

DEFINITION 2.6 : Let $a = (a_0, \ldots, a_{n-1}) \in R^n$ and let r be an n-th root of identity in R. Let f be the polynomial of degree n whose coefficients are $a_0, \ldots, a_{n-1}$. The Discrete Fourier Transform $DFT_n(a)$ is given by $f(r^0), \ldots, f(r^{n-1})$.
In particular $f_j := f(r^j) = \sum_{0 \le i \le n-1} a_i r^{ij}$.

DFT_n can be written as matrix vector product of the matrix A , whose elements are r^{ij} , and the column vector a .

THEOREM 2.6 : The Discrete Fourier Transform $DFT_n(a)$ can be computed by an arithmetic circuit ($\{+,-,*\}$ - circuit) of size $O(n \log n)$ and depth $O(\log n)$.

Proof : This efficient algorithm again is based on divide - and - conquer and on the properties of roots of identity.

$$f_j = \sum_{0 \leq i \leq n-1} a_i \, r^{ij} =$$

$$= \sum_{0 \leq i \leq (n/2)-1} a_{2i} \, (r^{2j})^i + r^j \sum_{0 \leq i \leq (n/2)-1} a_{2i+1} \, (r^{2j})^i \, . \qquad (2.20)$$

Instead of evaluating f at $r^0, r^1, \cdots, r^{n-1}$ we may evaluate the polynomials given by $(a_0, a_2, \ldots, a_{n-2})$ and $(a_1, a_3, \ldots, a_{n-1})$ at $r^0, r^2, \ldots, r^{2n-2}$. Since $r^n = 1$, it is even sufficient to evaluate both polynomials of degree $(n/2)-1$ at $r^0, r^2, \ldots, r^{n-2}$. Since it is easy to prove that r^2 is an $(n/2)$-th root of identity, we may compute $DFT_{n/2}(a_0, a_2, \ldots, a_{n-2})$ and $DFT_{n/2}(a_1, a_3, \ldots, a_{n-1})$ by the same procedure. To start with we compute $r^0, r^1, \ldots, r^{n-1}$. Afterwards we may compute f_j with two further operations. The preprocessing, the computation of all r^i , can be done in linear size and logarithmic depth. The problem is not harder than the prefix problem (see § 1). For the complexity of the other computations we obtain the following recurring relations

$$C(n) \leq 2\,C(n/2) + 2n \quad \text{and} \quad D(n) \leq D(n/2) + 2 \, . \qquad (2.21)$$

Here we took advantage of the fact that the two subproblems and afterwards the computation of all f_j can be done in parallel. By (2.21) the claim of the theorem follows.

□

Now we know how to evaluate polynomials efficiently at certain inputs. We have already discussed that we also like to compute efficiently the coefficients of a polynomial given by its values at these well-chosen inputs. $DFT_n(a) = A\,a$ is a matrix vector product. If A^{-1} exists, $DFT_n^{-1}(b) = A^{-1}\,b$ is the inverse Discrete Fourier Transform. If $b = DFT_n(a)$, also $a = DFT_n^{-1}(b)$.

LEMMA 2.5 : If n^{-1} and r^{-1} exist, then A^{-1} exists also, and its elements are $n^{-1}\,r^{-ij}$.

Proof : We prove that the product of $A = (\,r^{ij}\,)$ and $B = (\,n^{-1}\,r^{-ij}\,)$ is the identity matrix.

The elements of AB are given by $n^{-1} \displaystyle\sum_{0\le k\le n-1} r^{ik}\,r^{-jk}$. If $i = j$, this equals 1. For $i > j$ (the case $i < j$ is analogous)

$$\sum_{0\le k\le n-1} r^{ik}\,r^{-jk} = \sum_{0\le k\le n-1} r^{(i-j)k} = 0 \tag{2.22}$$

by the last property of roots of identity.

$\square$

Since r^{-1} also is an n-th root of identity (it is easy to check the three properties) we obtain the following corollary.

COROLLARY 2.1 : The inverse Discrete Fourier Transform $DFT_n^{-1}(a)$ can be computed by an arithmetic circuit of size $O(n \log n)$ and depth $O(\log n)$.

Now we combine our observations and compute the negative envelope of convolution.

THEOREM 2.7 : Let R be a commutative ring with a one, $a = (a_0, \ldots, a_{n-1}, 0, \ldots, 0)$, $b = (b_0, \ldots, b_{n-1}, 0, \ldots, 0) \in R^{2n}$, r be an n-th root of identity such that r^{-1} and n^{-1} exist.

i) $DFT_{2n}^{-1}\,(DFT_{2n}(a) * DFT_{2n}(b))$, where $*$ is the componentwise multiplication, is the convolution of a and b.

ii) Let s be a $(2n)$-th root of identity and $r = s^2$.

Let $a^* = (a_0, sa_1, \cdots, s^{n-1}a_{n-1})$, $b^* = (b_0, sb_1, \cdots, s^{n-1}b_{n-1})$ and

$w^* = (w_0, s w_1, \cdots, s^{n-1} w_{n-1})$ where $w = (w_0, \ldots, w_{n-1})$ is the negative envelope of $a = (a_0, \ldots, a_{n-1})$ and $b = (b_0, \ldots, b_{n-1})$.
Then $w^* = DFT_n^{-1} (DFT_n(a^*) * DFT_n(b^*))$.

Proof : Part i) is a formal description of the algorithm for the computation of the convolution already discussed. At first both polynomials are evaluated at the same $2n$ inputs. Then the product polynomial is evaluated at these inputs, and finally the coefficients of the product polynomial are computed.

For Part ii) let $(f_0, \ldots, f_{n-1}) = DFT_n(a^*)$, $(g_0, \ldots, g_{n-1}) = DFT_n(b^*)$ and $(h_0, \ldots, h_{n-1})$ be the vector claimed to be equal to w^*. Then by definition

$$h_m = n^{-1} \sum_{0 \le i \le n-1} f_i \, g_i \, r^{-im} \qquad (2.23)$$

$$= n^{-1} \sum_{0 \le i \le n-1} \sum_{0 \le j \le n-1} \sum_{0 \le k \le n-1} s^j x_j \, s^k y_k \, r^{(j+k-m)i}$$

$$= \sum_{0 \le j \le n-1} \sum_{0 \le k \le n-1} s^{j+k} x_j y_k \cdot \left[n^{-1} \sum_{0 \le i \le n-1} r^{(j+k-m)i} \right] .$$

If $j + k = m$ or $j + k = m + n$ the inner sum is 1, since $r^n = 1$. Otherwise the inner sum is 0. Therefore

$$h_m = s^m \left(\sum_{j+k=m} x_j y_k + s^n \sum_{j+k=n+m} x_j y_k \right) \qquad (2.24)$$

$$= s^m (v_m - v_{n+m}) = s^m w_m .$$

Here we used the fact that $s^n = r^{n/2} = -1$.

$\square$

We apply Theorem 2.7.b for the computation of all $w_i' \equiv w_i \bmod (2^{2l} + 1)$. We work in the Fermat ring $\mathbb{Z}_m$ where $m = 2^{2l} + 1$. The roots of identity and the multiplicative inverses we need are well-defined. In our application n is replaced by b, a power of 2. Also the $(2b)$–th root of identity s and the b-th root of identity $r = s^2$ can be chosen by Lemma 2.4 as power of 2 . Since $r^b = s^{2b} = 1$, also $r^{-1} = r^{b-1}$, $s^{-1} = s^{2b-1}$ and $b^{-1} = 2^{-\lfloor k/2 \rfloor} = r^b \, 2^{-\lfloor k/2 \rfloor}$ can be chosen as power of 2 . Using radix - 4 representations all additions and all multiplications by a power of 2 have size $O(l)$ and constant depth. By Theorem 2.6 , Corollary 2.1 and Theorem 2.7 we have to perform $O(b \log b)$ of these operations and b multiplications of numbers of $2l$ bits. These b multiplications can be done in parallel. The depth of the other operations is $O(\log b) = O(\log n)$. Since $O(bl \log b) = O(n \log n)$, the algorithm of Schönhage and Strassen fulfils the complexity estimations of (2.11) and (2.12) . We have proved the following result.

THEOREM 2.8 : The algorithm of Schönhage and Strassen leads to a circuit for multiplication of size $O(n \log n \log\log n)$ and depth $O(\log n)$.

3.3 Division

Since $y/z = y\,(1/z)$, we consider only the computation of the inverse z^{-1} . In general the binary expansion of z^{-1} is not finite, e.g. for $z = 3$. So we are satisfied with the computation of the n most significant bits of z^{-1} . W.l.o.g. $1/2 \le z < 1$.

DEFINITION 3.1 : The division function $f_n^{div} \in B_{n-1,n}$ has $(z_{n-1} = 1, z_{n-2}, \cdots, z_0)$ as input.
For $z = 1/2\, z_{n-1} + (1/2)^2 z_{n-2} + \cdots + (1/2)^n z_0$ the n most significant bits of z^{-1} build the output of f_n^{div} .

The school method of division produces the output bits one after another. The divisor always is $(z_{n-1}, \ldots, z_0)$, the "actual" dividend changes. At first the dividend is $(1,0,...,0)$. During one step we subtract the divisor from the dividend if the divisor is not larger than the dividend. If the divisor is not larger the next output bit is 1, otherwise 0. We obtain the new dividend by multiplying (in the first case) the result of the subtraction or (in the second case) the old dividend by 2. By our previous results we are able to estimate the efficiency of the school method.

THEOREM 3.1 : The school method of division leads to a circuit of size $O(n^2)$ and depth $O(n \log n)$.

The depth of such a circuit cannot be accepted. Anderson, Earle, Goldschmidt and Powers (67) presented a circuit of depth $O(\log^2 n)$. At the beginning of § 2 we have reduced the multiplication of two numbers to the addition of n numbers. Here we reduce division to repeated multiplication. Let $x = 1 - z$. Then $0 < x \leq 1/2$ and by the binomial formula we obtain the following basic relation where $x(j)$ stands for x^{2^j}.

$$\frac{1}{z} = \frac{1}{1-x} = \frac{1}{1-x} \cdot \frac{1+x(0)}{1+x(0)} \cdot \frac{1+x(1)}{1+x(1)} \cdots \frac{1+x(k-1)}{1+x(k-1)} =$$

$$= \frac{P_k(x)}{1-x(k)} . \tag{3.1}$$

Since $x \leq 1/2$, the denominator is approximately 1. We compute approximations for all $x(j)$, afterwards an approximation $P_k^*(x)$ for $P_k(x)$. Since $1 < z^{-1} \leq 2$, we may take the n most significant bits of $P_k^*(x)$ as output bits if

$$|P_k^*(x) - z^{-1}| \leq 2^{-n+1} . \tag{3.2}$$

We compute $x^*(j)$ by computing the first s bits of $(x^*(j-1))^2$ following the binary point. Similarly we compute $P_j^*(x)$ by computing the first s bits of $P_{j-1}^*(x) \cdot (1 + x^*(j-1))$ following the binary point. How large do we have to choose s and k such that $P_k^*(x)$ fulfils (3.2) ?

Let $\delta = 2^{-s}$. In each step we are rounding off the result by at most δ. Since the old errors are squared, the errors are growing slowly.

LEMMA 3.1 : $x(j) - 2\delta \leq x^*(j) \leq x(j)$.

Proof : The second inequality is obvious since we are only rounding off the results. The first inequality is proved by induction.
For $j = 0$ the assertion is obvious. Since $x \leq 1/2$, $x(j) \leq 1/4$ for $j \geq 1$ and $4\delta x(j) \leq \delta$. By induction hypothesis

$$x^*(j+1) \geq x^*(j)^2 - \delta \geq (x(j) - 2\delta)^2 - \delta \geq x(j)^2 - 4\delta x(j) - \delta$$
$$\geq x(j+1) - 2\delta \; .$$

$$(3.3)$$

$\square$

LEMMA 3.2 : $P_j(x) - \varepsilon_j(x) \leq P_j^*(x) \leq P_j(x)$
where $\varepsilon_j(x) = (3j - 2)\,\delta\,(1 - x(j-1))/(1 - x)$.

Proof : Again the second inequality is obvious. Since $\varepsilon_1(x) = \delta$ and $P_1(x) = 1 + x$, the first inequality holds for $j = 1$. Since we are rounding off the results by at most δ , we can conclude by induction hypothesis and Lemma 3.1 that

$$P_j^*(x) \geq P_{j-1}^*(x)\,(1 + x^*(j-1)) - \delta$$

$$(3.4)$$

$$\geq (P_{j-1}(x) - \varepsilon_{j-1}(x))\,(1 + x(j-1) - 2\delta) - \delta$$

$$\geq P_{j-1}(x)\,(1 + x(j-1)) - \varepsilon_{j-1}(x)\,(1 + x(j-1)) - 2\delta P_{j-1}(x) - \delta \; .$$

The first term is equal to $P_j(x)$. Since $x(j-1) < x(j-2)$,

$$\varepsilon_{j-1}(x)(1 + x(j-1)) < (3j - 5)\,\delta\,(1 - x(j-2))\,(1 + x(j-2))/(1 - x)$$
$$= (3j - 5)\,\delta\,(1 - x(j-1))/(1 - x) \; .$$

$$(3.5)$$

Furthermore by definition $2\delta P_{j-1}(x) = 2\delta(1 - x(j-1))/(1 - x)$ and

$\delta < \delta(1 - x(j-1))/(1-x)$. By these estimations, (3.4) and (3.5)

$$P_j^*(x) > P_j(x) - (3j-2)(1-x(j-1))/(1-x) = P_j(x) - \varepsilon_j(x) . \qquad (3.6)$$

□

We combine our estimations. By the triangle inequality

$$|z^{-1} - P_k^*(x)| \leq |z^{-1} - P_k(x)| + |P_k(x) - P_k^*(x)| . \qquad (3.7)$$

By (3.1)

$$|z^{-1} - P_k(x)| = |z^{-1} - (1-x(k))z^{-1}| \qquad (3.8)$$

$$= x(k)/(1-x) \leq 2 \cdot 2^{-2^k} .$$

By Lemma 3.2

$$|P_k(x) - P_k^*(x)| \leq \varepsilon_k(x) \leq (3k-2) \cdot 2 \cdot 2^{-s} . \qquad (3.9)$$

(3.8) and (3.9) can be estimated by 2^{-n} if we choose

$$k = \lceil \log n \rceil + 1 \quad \text{and} \quad s = n + 3 + \lceil \log k \rceil . \qquad (3.10)$$

By this choice $|z^{-1} - P_k^*(x)| \leq 2^{-n+1}$ and we may output the n most significant bits of $P_k^*(x)$. Altogether we perform one subtraction and 2k - 2 multiplications of (s+1)-bit numbers which have to be performed sequentially.

THEOREM 3.2 : The algorithm of Anderson et al. leads to a circuit for division which has depth $O(\log^2 n)$ and size $O(n^2 \log n)$ (if we use convential multiplication circuits) or size $O(n \log^2 n \log \log n)$ (if we use Schönhage and Strassen multiplication circuits).

For several years one believed, that depth $O(\log^2 n)$ is necessary for division circuits. Reif (83) was the first to beat this bound. Generalizing the ideas of Schönhage and Strassen (see § 2) to the multiplication of n numbers he designed a division circuit of polynomial size and depth $O(\log n \log \log n)$. Afterwards Beame, Cook and Hoover (84) applied methods of McKenzie and Cook (84) and proved that the depth of division is $\Theta(\log n)$.

One-output circuits of depth d have at most $2^d - 1$ gates. Therefore circuits of depth $O(\log n)$ always have polynomial size. Since the new division circuit beats the older ones only for rather large n, we do not estimate accurately the depth of the new circuit. Because of the approximation algorithm introduced at the beginning of this section, it is sufficient to prove that n n-bit numbers may be multiplied in depth $O(\log n)$. Then we can compute all $x^*(j)$ in parallel in depth $O(\log n)$ and afterwards we multiply all $1 + x^*(j)$ in depth $O(\log n)$.

For the basic results of number theory that we apply the reader is referred to any textbook on number theory, e.g. Ayoub (63). For our algorithm it is crucial that problems for small numbers may be solved efficiently by table-look-up . Let T be a table (a_1, b_1) ,...., (a_N, b_N) where N and the length of each a_i are bounded by a polynomial in n. If all a_i are different, we may compute for $x \in \{a_1, \ldots, a_N\}$ in depth $O(\log n)$ that b_i which has the same index as $x = a_i$. Obviously we can test in depth $O(\log n)$ whether $x = a_j$. Let $c_j = 1$ iff $x = a_j$. All c_j can be computed in parallel. Afterwards all y_m where y_m is the m-th output bit, can be computed in parallel as disjunction of all $c_j \wedge b_{jm}$ $(1 \le j \le N)$. Here b_{jm} is the m-th bit of b_j. Altogether the circuit has depth $O(\log n)$. In general, tables of functions f have exponential length and table-look-up is not very efficient.

By table-look-up circuits we multiply the input numbers modulo small prime numbers. By the Chinese Remainder Theorem these products are sufficient to compute the product exactly. The size of the product is bounded by $M = (2^n - 1)^n$. Therefore it is sufficient to compute the product mod m for some $m > M$. We describe the main steps of our algorithm before we discuss their efficient implementation.

ALGORITHM 3.1 :

Input : $x_1, \ldots, x_n$, n n-bit numbers.

Output : x , the product of all x_i , as binary number.

Step 1 : Choose the smallest r such that p , the product of the r smallest primes $p_1, \ldots, p_r$, is larger than M .

Step 2 : Compute $y_{ij} \equiv x_i \bmod p_j$ for all $1 \le i \le n$ and $1 \le j \le r$.

Step 3 : Compute $x^j \equiv \prod_{1 \le i \le n} y_{ij} \equiv \prod_{1 \le i \le n} x_i \bmod p_j$ for $1 \le j \le r$.

Step 4 : Use the Chinese Remainder Theorem to compute x (or x mod p , which is the same) from all x^j .

The computations in Step 1 depend only on the input length which is fixed for circuits. All p_i and p can be computed in advance and are inputs of the circuit. Since $p_i \ge 2$, $r \le n^2$. Better estimations of r can be computed by the prime number theorem . Likewise by the prime number theorem $p_{max} = \max \{p_1, \ldots, p_r\}$ is bounded by a polynomial q(n) .

The computation of all y_{ij} in Step 2 can be done in parallel. All $a_{jk} \equiv 2^k \bmod p_j$ are independent of the input and can be computed in advance, i.e. all a_{jk} are inputs of the circuit. Let x_{ik} be the k-th bit of x_i . Then

$$x_i = \sum_{0 \le k \le n-1} x_{ik} 2^k \equiv \sum_{0 \le k \le n-1} x_{ik} a_{jk} \bmod p_j . \qquad (3.11)$$

Since $x_{ik} \in \{0,1\}$, all $x_{ik} a_{jk}$ can be computed in depth 1. As we already know (see § 2), the sum s_{ij} of all $x_{ik} a_{jk}$ can be computed in depth $O(\log n)$. Since $0 \le s_{ij} < np_j$, we may compute a table of all $s_{ij} - l p_j$ for $0 \le l < n$ in depth $O(\log n)$. By table-look-up we choose that $s_{ij} - l p_j$ which lies in $\{0, \ldots, p_j - 1\}$ and is therefore equal to y_{ij} .

In Step 3 we take advantage of some properties of prime numbers. $G_j = \{1, \ldots, p_j - 1\}$ is a cyclic group with respect to multiplication mod p_j . This implies the existence of a generator $g \in G_j$ such that for all $k \in G_j$ there exists a unique index $ind(k) \in \{0, \ldots, p_j - 2\}$ with respect to g and G_j such that

$$k \equiv g^{\text{ind}(k)} \bmod p_j .\tag{3.12}$$

At first we test in parallel whether some $y_{ij} = 0$ $(1 \le i \le n)$. In this case $x^j = 0$. Otherwise we compute x^j in the following way. The table $(k, \text{ind } k)$ for $1 \le k \le p_j - 1$ (with respect to g and G_j) does not depend on the input and is computed in advance. By table-look-up we compute in parallel in depth $O(\log n)$ all $\text{ind}(y_{ij})$. Afterwards we compute in parallel in depth $O(\log n)$ all $I(j)$, where $I(j)$ is the sum of all $\text{ind}(y_{ij})$. Since $0 \le I(j) < n(p_j - 1)$, we can compute in parallel in depth $O(\log n)$ all $I^*(j) \equiv I(j) \bmod (p_j - 1)$. These computations are done similarly to the computation of y_{ij} from s_{ij} in Step 2. It is an easy fact from elementary number theory that $g^{p'-1} \equiv 1 \bmod p'$ for prime numbers p'. Therefore

$$x^j \equiv \prod_{1 \le i \le n} y_{ij} \equiv \prod_{1 \le i \le n} g^{\text{ind}(y_{ij})} \equiv g^{I(j)} \equiv g^{I^*(j)} \bmod p_j .\tag{3.13}$$

Finally we can compute x^j from $I^*(j)$ by table-look-up. Instead of multiplying all y_{ij}, it is sufficient to add all $\text{ind}(y_{ij})$, and we know already that the sum of n numbers can be computed efficiently.

By the Chinese Remainder Theorem 2.5

$$x \equiv \sum_{1 \le j \le n} x^j\, r_j \bmod p \tag{3.14}$$

where $r_j = u_j v_j$, $u_j = p / p_j$ and $v_j \equiv (p / p_j)^{-1} \bmod p_j$. The numbers r_j do not depend on the input and can be computed in advance. We multiply in parallel all x^j and r_j. Since $0 \le x^j < p_j$ and $0 \le r_j < p$, these multiplications have depth $O(\log n)$ as has the addition of all $x^j r_j$. Obviously, $0 \le x^* < p n p_{\max}$ for the sum x^* of all $x^j r_j$, and x can be computed from x^* in depth $O(\log n)$ similarly to the computation of y_{ij} from s_{ij} in Step 2.

Altogether we obtain an efficient implementation of Algorithm 3.1 .

THEOREM 3.3 : The algorithm of Beame, Cook and Hoover leads to a division circuit of depth $O(\log n)$ and polynomial size.

It is still an open problem whether one can design a division circuit whose depth is bounded by c log n for a small constant c and whose size is acceptable.

The methods for the design of the division circuit may also be applied to the approximation of power series. The computation of the n most significant bits of e.g. e^x or ln x is possible in depth O(log n) (Alt (84)).

3.4 Symmetric functions

The class of symmetric functions contains many fundamental functions like sorting and all types of counting functions.

DEFINITION 4.1 : $S_{n,m}$ is the class of all symmetric functions $f \in B_{n,m}$, that is all functions f such that for all permutations $\pi \in \Sigma_n$
$$f(x_1, \ldots, x_n) = f(x_{\pi(1)}, \ldots, x_{\pi(n)}) .$$

Each vector $a \in \{0,1\}^n$ with exactly i ones is a permutation of any other vector with exactly i ones. That is why f is symmetric iff f only depends on the number of ones in the input. For symmetric functions we may shorten the table (a , f(a)) for f to the (value) vector $v(f) = (v_0, \ldots, v_n)$ such that $f(x) = v_i$ if $x_1 + \cdots + x_n = i$. We introduce some fundamental symmetric functions.

DEFINITION 4.2 :

i) $E_k^n(x) = 1$ iff $x_1 + \cdots + x_n = k$ (exactly - k - function).

ii) $T_k^n(x) = 1$ iff $x_1 + \cdots + x_n \geq k$ (threshold - k - function).

iii) $S^n(x) = (T_1^n(x), \cdots, T_n^n(x))$ (sorting function).

iv) $C_{k,m}^n(x) = 1$ iff $x_1 + \cdots + x_n \equiv k \mod m$ (counting function).

If the input length (and upper index) n is uniquely determined by the context, then we can omit n . The term sorting function for S^n is justified, since for inputs x with exactly k ones $T_1(x) = ... = T_k(x)$ = 1 but $T_{k+1}(x) = ... = T_n(x) = 0$. The output is the sorted sequence of the inputs. The functions $E_0, ..., E_n$ build a kind of basis for all symmetric functions, since for all $f \in S_n$

$$f(x) = \bigvee_{0 \le k \le n} E_k(x) \wedge v_k .$$

(4.1)

$v_0, ..., v_n$ are constants independent from the input, thus

$$C(f) \le C(E_0, ..., E_n) + n \quad \text{and}$$

(4.2)

$$D(f) \le D(E_0, ..., E_n) + \lceil \log (n+1) \rceil .$$

(4.3)

Furthermore $T_k = E_k \vee \cdots \vee E_n$. Because of the algorithms for the prefix problem (see § 1) we can compute S^n from $E_1, ..., E_n$ by a circuit of linear size and logarithmic depth.

Due to these observations it is essential to design an efficient circuit for the computation of $E_0, ..., E_n$. At first we compute with $n-2$ CSA gates and one Krapchenko adder the binary representation $a = (a_{k-1}, ..., a_0)$ of $x_1 + \cdots + x_n$. Here $k = \lceil \log (n+1) \rceil$. The depth of this circuit is $O(\log n)$. The length of the summands is 1 .

At step j of the adder-tree the inputs of the CSA gates are of length j , hence the CSA gates have size $O(j)$. The number of CSA gates at step j may be estimated by $\frac{1}{3} (\frac{2}{3})^{j-1} n$. Since the sum of all $(\frac{2}{3})^{j-1} j$ is a constant, the size of the adder-tree is $O(n)$.

$E_i(x) = 1$ iff the number $|a|$ represented by a is equal to i . Therefore $E_i(x)$ is a minterm on $a_{k-1}, ..., a_0$. We compute $E_0, ..., E_n$ by the computation of all minterms on $a_{k-1}, ..., a_0$.

LEMMA 4.1 : All minterms on $x_1, ..., x_n$ can be computed by a circuit of size $2^n + O(n 2^{n/2})$ and depth $O(\log n)$.

Proof : $O(n 2^{n/2})$ gates are sufficient to compute in parallel all

$2^{\lceil n/2 \rceil}$ minterms on $x_1, \ldots, x_{\lceil n/2 \rceil}$ and all $2^{\lfloor n/2 \rfloor}$ minterms on $x_{\lceil n/2 \rceil + 1}, \ldots, x_n$. Afterwards each of the 2^n minterms on $x_1, \ldots, x_n$ can be computed with one gate. □

By this lemma $E_0, \ldots, E_n$ can be computed from a in linear size and logarithmic depth since $k = \lceil \log(n+1) \rceil$. Altogether we obtain an efficient circuit for all symmetric functions.

THEOREM 4.1 : Each symmetric function $f \in S_n$ with one output as well as the sorting function may be computed by a circuit of size $O(n)$ and depth $O(\log n)$.

The proof of Theorem 4.1 is due to Muller and Preparata (75) though the result has been proved implicitly already by Lupanov (62a). By Theorem 4.1 we have designed efficient circuits for several fundamental functions.

3.5 Storage access

DEFINITION 5.1 : The storage access function $SA_n \in B_{n+k}$ where $n = 2^k$ is defined on a k-bit number $a = (a_{k-1}, \ldots, a_0)$ and n variables $x = (x_0, \ldots, x_{n-1})$. $SA_n(a,x) = x_{|a|}$.

We consider a storage of n memory cells containing the 1-bit informations $x_0, \ldots, x_{n-1}$. The vector a contains the number of the memory cell whose contents is interesting for us. $SA_n(a,x)$ computes the contents of this memory cell. Bit a_{k-1} decides whether we should search in the first or in the second half of the memory. Therefore

$$SA_n(a_{k-1}, \ldots, a_0, x_0, \ldots, x_{n-1}) = \tag{5.1}$$

$$= (a_{k-1} \wedge SA_{n/2}(a_{k-2}, \ldots, a_0, x_{n/2}, \ldots, x_{n-1})) \vee$$

$$\vee (\bar{a}_{k-1} \wedge SA_{n/2}(a_{k-2}, \ldots, a_0, x_0, \ldots, x_{(n/2)-1})).$$

Since $SA_1(x_0) = x_0$, (5.1) leads to a circuit for SA_n of size $C(n)$ and depth $D(n)$ where

$$C(n) = 2C(n/2) + 3 \quad, \quad D(n) = D(n/2) + 2,$$
$$C(1) = D(1) = 0. \tag{5.2}$$

The solution of this recurring relation is $C(n) = 3n - 3$ and $D(n) = 2\log n$.

LEMMA 5.1 : The storage access function SA_n can be computed by a circuit of size $3n$ - 3 and depth $2\log n$.

In Ch. 5 we prove a lower bound of $2n - 2$ for the circuit size of SA_n . Klein and Paterson (80) proved that this lower bound is nearly optimal.

Let $M_i(a)$ be the minterm of length k computing 1 iff $|a| = i$. Obviously

$$SA_n(a,x) = \bigvee_{0 \le i \le n-1} M_i(a) \wedge x_i. \tag{5.3}$$

In order to beat the $(3n - 3)$-bound of Lemma 5.1 we partition a into two halves $b = (a_{k-1}, \ldots, a_{\lceil k/2 \rceil})$ and $c = (a_{\lceil k/2 \rceil - 1}, \ldots, a_0)$. Then $|a| = |b| 2^{\lceil k/2 \rceil} + |c|$. For $r = 2^{\lceil k/2 \rceil}$ and $s = 2^{\lceil k/2 \rceil}$ we conclude from (5.3) by the law of distributivity that

$$SA_n(a,x) = \bigvee_{0 \le i \le r-1} \bigvee_{0 \le j \le s-1} M_i(b) \wedge M_j(c) \wedge x_{is+j} \tag{5.4}$$

$$= \bigvee_{0 \le i \le r-1} M_i(b) \wedge \left[\bigvee_{0 \le j \le s-1} M_j(c) \wedge x_{is+j} \right].$$

By Lemma 4.1 we can compute all $M_i(b)$ and all $M_j(c)$ by a circuit of size $r+s+o(r+s) = O(n^{1/2})$ and depth $\lceil \log (k/2) \rceil = \lceil \log\log n \rceil - 1$. For the computation of all $\bigvee M_j(c) \wedge x_{is+j}$ n $\wedge$-gates and $n-r$ $\vee$-gates are sufficient, the depth of this part of the circuit is $\lfloor k/2 \rfloor + 1$. Afterwards $SA_n(a,x)$ can be computed by r $\wedge$-gates and $r-1$ $\vee$-gates in depth $\lceil k/2 \rceil + 1$. This way we have proved

THEOREM 5.1 : The storage access function SA_n can be computed by circuits of size $2n + O(n^{1/2})$ and depth $\log n + \lceil \log\log n \rceil + 1$.

3.6 Matrix product

For the sake of simplicity we consider here only square matrices of n rows and n columns. As it is well known the matrix product of two matrices of integers or reals is defined by

$$z_{ij} = \sum_{1 \le k \le n} x_{ik} y_{kj} . \tag{6.1}$$

We investigate arithmetic circuits ($\{+,-,*\}$ - circuits, straight line programs) for the computation of $Z = (z_{ij})$. Arithmetic circuits lead to Boolean circuits if we replace each arithmetic operation by a Boolean circuit of suitable input size for this operation. Furthermore we are interested in the Boolean matrix product which is useful in graph theory (see Exercises). Here we consider matrices $X = (x_{ij})$ and $Y = (y_{ij})$ of ones and zeros only. The Boolean matrix product $Z = (z_{ij})$ is defined by

$$z_{ij} = \bigvee_{1 \le k \le n} x_{ik} \wedge y_{kj} . \tag{6.2}$$

Obviously the Boolean (arithmetic) matrix product can be computed with n^3 conjunctions (multiplications) and $n^3 - n^2$ disjunctions (additions) in depth $\lceil \log n \rceil + 1$. Strassen (69) proved in his pioneering paper that this school method is not optimal for the arithmetic matrix product. His arithmetic circuit has size $O(n^{\log 7})$ and depth $O(\log n)$. Arlazarov, Dinic, Kronrod and Faradzev (70) designed an arithmetic circuit of size $O(n^3/\log n)$ that only works for 0-1 - matrices but is better than the school method also for very small n . For 9 years no one improved Strassen's algorithm. Then a violent development started. Its end was the arithmetic circuit of Coppersmith and Winograd (82) whose size is $O(n^c)$ for some $c < 2.496$. Pan (84) gives a survey on this development. Now Strassen (86) improved the exponent to some $c < 2.479$. We describe here only Strassen's classical algorithm and point out how the computation of the Boolean matrix product may be improved by this algorithm too.

Strassen's algorithm depends on divide-and-conquer. Again we assume $n = 2^k$. We partition X,Y and Z into four matrices of $n/2$ rows and $n/2$ columns each.

$$
X = \begin{bmatrix} X_{11} & X_{12} \\ X_{21} & X_{22} \end{bmatrix} \; , \quad Y = \begin{bmatrix} Y_{11} & Y_{12} \\ Y_{21} & Y_{22} \end{bmatrix} \; , \quad Z = \begin{bmatrix} Z_{11} & Z_{12} \\ Z_{21} & Z_{22} \end{bmatrix} .
$$

It is easy to see that the submatrices Z_{ij} may be computed similarly to the product of 2×2 - matrices, e.g. $Z_{12} = X_{11}Y_{12} + X_{12}Y_{22}$. Here additions and multiplications are operations on $(n/2) \times (n/2)$ - matrices. By the school method we perform 8 matrix multiplications and 4 matrix additions. The addition of two $n \times n$ - matrices obviously can be performed with n^2 additions in depth 1 while multiplications seem to be harder.

By our experience with divide-and-conquer algorithms we should try to get by with less than 8 multiplications. It was a long way from this knowledge to the following algorithm. Though it is difficult to discover such an algorithm, it is easy to check its correctness. We describe the 7 multiplications of the algorithm, but before these multiplications we have to perform 10 additions and subtractions to compute the factors.

$$m_1 = (X_{12} - X_{22}) \cdot (Y_{21} + Y_{22}) \quad , \quad m_2 = (X_{11} + X_{22}) \cdot (Y_{11} + Y_{12}) \ ,$$

$$m_3 = (X_{11} - X_{21}) \cdot (Y_{11} + Y_{12}) \quad , \quad m_4 = (X_{11} + X_{12}) \cdot Y_{22} \ ,$$

$$m_5 = X_{11} \cdot (Y_{12} - Y_{22}) \qquad\qquad , \quad m_6 = X_{22} \cdot (Y_{21} - Y_{11}) \ , \tag{6.3}$$

$$m_7 = (X_{21} + X_{22}) \cdot Y_{11} \ .$$

Now it is easy to verify that

$$Z = \begin{bmatrix} m_1 + m_2 - m_4 + m_6 & m_4 + m_5 \\ m_6 + m_7 & m_2 - m_3 + m_5 - m_7 \end{bmatrix} . \tag{6.4}$$

Let $C(n)$ and $D(n)$ be the size and depth resp. of Strassen's arithmetic circuit. Then

$$C(n) = 7 C(n/2) + 18 (n/2)^2 \quad , \quad D(n) = D(n/2) + 3 \ ,$$

$$C(1) = D(1) = 1 \tag{6.5}$$

implying

THEOREM 6.1 : Strassen's algorithm leads to an arithmetic circuit for matrix multiplication of size $7 n^{\log 7} - 6 n^2$ and depth $3 \log n + 1$. ($\log 7 \approx 2.81$).

We emphasize that Strassen's algorithm as well as Karatsuba and Ofman's multiplication algorithm is based on additions, multiplications **and** subtractions. If only additions and multiplications (of positive numbers) are admissible operations, then the school method cannot be improved (see Ch. 6). The profitable use of subtractions for a problem where subtractions seem to be superfluous should be taken as a warning. One should be very careful with stating that certain operations are obviously not efficient for certain problems.

Fischer and Meyer (71) applied Strassen's algorithm to Boolean matrix multiplication. Similar results for the other matrix multiplication methods have been obtained by Lotti and Romani (80) and Adleman, Booth, Preparata and Ruzzo (78).

The inputs of the Boolean matrix product are numbers $x_{ij}, y_{ij} \in \{0,1\}$. Let z_{ij} be the Boolean matrix product and z_{ij}^* the conventional matrix product. Obviously

$$0 \leq z_{ij}^* \leq n \quad , \quad z_{ij}^* \text{ is an integer, and}$$

$$z_{ij}^* = 0 \quad \Leftrightarrow \quad z_{ij} = 0 \,. \tag{6.6}$$

Strassen's algorithm consists of additions, substractions and multiplications. Therefore, by (6.6), we can compute z_{ij}^* correctly if we perform all computations in $\mathbb{Z}_m$ for some $m > n$. In particular, the length of the numbers is $O(\log n)$. Finally all z_{ij}, by (6.6) the disjunction of all bits of z_{ij}^*, can be computed in parallel in depth $O(\log \log n)$. Since all multiplications of Strassen's agorithm can be done in parallel, we may estimate the complexity of the new algorithm for the Boolean matrix product by our results of § 1 and § 2.

Theorem 6.2 : The Boolean matrix product can be computed in size $O(n^{\log 7} \log n \log\log n \log\log\log n)$ and depth $O(\log n)$.

3.7 Determinant

In Ch. 9 we consider the simulation of programs by circuits in general. Here we investigate as a second example the computation of the determinant (the first one was the Boolean matrix product). The well known algorithm based on Gaussian elimination whose time complexity is $O(n^3)$ can be simulated by a circuit of size $O(n^3)$. Gaussian elimination is a typical sequential algorithm, so we need additional tricks to reduce the depth.

DEFINITION 7.1 : The determinant of a Boolean $n \times n$ - matrix X with respect to the field $\mathbb{Z}_2$ is $\det_n(X) = \underset{\pi \in \Sigma_n}{\oplus} x_{1,\pi(1)} \cdot \,\cdots\, \cdot x_{n,\pi(n)}$.

ALGORITHM 7.1 (Gaussian elimination) (see e.g. MacLane and Birkhoff (67)) :

1. $\det(x_{11}) = x_{11}$.

2. If the first column of X consists of zeros only, $\det_n(X) = 0$.

3. The componentwise addition (in $\mathbb{Z}_2$) of one row of X to another does not change the determinant of the matrix. If the first column of X contains a one , e.g. $x_{m,1} = 1$, we add the m-th row to all other rows starting with a one . We obtain a matrix X' with a single one in the first column and $\det_n(X) = \det_n(X')$.

4. By expansion according to the first column of X' we eliminate the first column and the m-th row and obtain an $(n-1) \times (n-1)$ - matrix X'' where $\det_{n-1}(X'') = \det_n(X)$.

THEOREM 7.1 : $\det_n$ may be computed by a circuit of size $3n^3 + n^2 - 4n$.

Proof : We simulate the Gaussian elimination algorithm. Let $X = X^n, X^{n-1}, \ldots, X^1$ be the matrices constructed by the algorithm. Since X^i has i columns and i rows, we can test with $i-1$ gates whether the first column of X^i contains zeros only ($g_i = 0$) or at least a one ($g_i = 1$) . $\det_n(X) = g_1 \cdot \,\cdots\, \cdot g_n$ can be computed with $n-1$ gates.

We only have to describe how to compute X^{k-1} from $X^k = (y_{ij})$. We may assume that $g_k = 1$, otherwise $\det_n(X) = 0$ will be computed correctly independent from $g_{k-1}, \ldots, g_1$. $u_m = \bar{y}_{11} \wedge \,\cdots\, \wedge \bar{y}_{m-1,1} \wedge y_{m1}$ $= 1$ iff the m-th row of X^k is the first one starting with a one . All $u_1, \ldots, u_k$ can be computed by $2k-3$ gates (if $k \geq 2$) . We use these pointers for selecting $v = (v_1, \ldots, v_k)$, the first row of X^k starting with a one . Obviously v_j , the disjunction of all $u_r y_{rj}$, can be computed by $2k-1$ gates. v is added (componentwise in $\mathbb{Z}_2$) to all rows of X^k starting with a one . Since we eliminate afterwards the first column we do not compute this column. We compute

$$z_{ij} = \bar{y}_{i1} \wedge y_{ij} \vee (y_{i1} \wedge (v_r \oplus y_{ij})) \quad (1 \leq i \leq k , 2 \leq j \leq k) \quad (7.1)$$

by altogether $4k(k-1)$ gates. Finally we have to eliminate the m-th row where $u_m = 1$. Let $t_1 = u_1$ and $t_j = t_{j-1} \vee u_j$. $t_1, \ldots, t_{k-1}$ can be computed by $k-2$ gates. Then $t_1 = \cdots = t_{m-1} = 0$ while $t_m = \cdots = t_{k-1} = 1$. Therefore the elements y_{ij}^* of X^{k-1} can be computed by

$$y_{ij}^* = \bar{t}_i z_{ij} \vee t_i z_{i+1,j} \quad (7.2)$$

by $3(k-1)^2$ gates. Altogether the number of gates for the computation of g_k and X^{k-1} from X^k equals

$$(k-1) + (2k-3) + k(2k-1) + 4k(k-1) + (k-2) + 3(k-1)^2$$
$$= 9k^2 - 7k - 3 , \quad (7.3)$$

and the number of gates in the whole circuit equals

$$n-1 + \sum_{2 \leq k \leq n} (9k^2 - 7k - 3) = 3n^3 + n^2 - 4n . \quad (7.4)$$

□

EXERCISES

1. Prove that the recursion relation $R(n) = a R(n/b) + cn$, $R(1) = c$ for $n = b^k$, $b > 1$, $a,c > 0$ has the solution $R(n) = \Theta(n)$, if $a < b$, $R(n) = \Theta(n \log n)$, if $a = b$, $R(n) = \Theta(n^{\log_b a})$, if $a > b$.

2. The Carry-Look-Ahead Adder partitions the input bits into $g(n)$ groups of nearly the same size. If we know the carry bit for some group we add the bits of this group using the school method and we compute directly by (1.8) the carry bit for the next group. Estimate size and depth of this adder.

3. The Carry-Look-Ahead Adder of second order adds the bits of a group by a Carry-Look-Ahead Adder (of first order). Estimate size and depth of this adder.

4. Estimate size and depth of the Conditional-Sum Adder, if the numbers are partitioned into
    a) 3   b) k   parts of nearly the same size.

5. Design efficient circuits for the transformation of an integer given by its sign and the binary representation of its absolute value into its 2-complement representation and vice versa.

6. Design efficient circuits for subtraction.

7. The adder tree of $n-2$ CSA gates has at least depth $\log_{3/2}(n/2)$.

8. Investigate the mixed multiplication algorithm $M(k)$.

9. Two complex numbers can be multiplied with only three multiplications of reals and some additions and subtractions.

10. Let X and Y be independent random variables that take the value $k \in \{0,...,n-1\}$ with probability p_k and q_k resp. Compute the distribution of $X+Y$, the so-called convolution of X and Y .

11. $\mathbb{R}$ has only for $n=2$ an n-th root of identity.

12. $e^{i2\pi/n}$ is an n-th root of identity in $\mathbb{C}$.

13. Design an efficient circuit for the computation of $x\,2^{-k}$, where x is given by a radix-4 representation.

14. Solve the recurring relations (2.11) and (2.12).

15. Design a circuit for division based on Newton's approximation method.

16. Multiply $(0,1,0)$, $(1,0,1)$ and $(1,1,1)$ by the method of Beame, Cook and Hoover.

17. For $f \in S_n$ (4.1) consists either for f or for $\bar{f}$ of at most $(n+1)/2$ summands.

18. Design a circuit for $f \in S_n$ whose size is bounded by $11.5\,n + o(n)$.

19. Prove a good upper bound on $C(f)$ for $f \in S_{n,m}$.

20. Estimate the size of the circuit for $(E_0, \ldots, E_n)$ in § 4 as exact as possible.

21. Let $G(x) = (\{1,\ldots,n\}, E(x))$ be a graph defined by the variables x_{ij} $(1 \le i < j \le n)$, i.e. $\{i,j\} \in E(x)$ iff $x_{ij} = 1$. X^k, the k-th Boolean power of matrix $X = (x_{ij})$ (where $x_{ij} = x_{ji}$ and $x_{ii} = 1$) contains a one at position (i,j) iff $G(x)$ contains a path from i to j of length bounded by k .

22. Design an efficient circuit for the decision whether the graph $G(x)$ is connected.

23. Implement Strassen's algorithm for arbitrary n and compute the number of arithmetic operations.

24. Compute the number of arithmetic operations of the following algorithm $A(l)$ for matrix multiplication. Let $n = 2^k$. If $k > l$ the algorithm applies Strassen's method. Problems and subproblems

of size $m \leq 2^l$ are solved by the school method. (See Mehlhorn (77) for a discussion of $A(l)$.)

25. Design for $f \in B_{n,n}$ where $f_i(x)$ is the conjunction of all x_j $(i \neq j)$ a circuit of size not larger than $3n - 6$.

26. $f(x_1, \ldots, x_n, y_1, \ldots, y_n) = \displaystyle\bigvee_{1 \leq i,j \leq n, |i-j| \leq m} x_i\, y_j$ has linear circuit size for all m.

27. $f(x_1, \ldots, x_n) = x_1 \vee (x_2 \wedge (x_3 \vee (\cdots)))$ has logarithmic depth.

28. Design efficient circuits for $f,g \in S_n$ where

$f(x) = 1$ iff $x_1 + \cdots + x_n \bmod 4 \in \{1,3\}$

$g(x) = 1$ iff $x_1 + \cdots + x_n \bmod 5 \in \{1,3\}$.

4. ASYMPTOTIC RESULTS AND UNIVERSAL CIRCUITS

4.1 The Shannon effect

For many fundamental functions we have designed efficient circuits. Is it possible to compute each function by an efficient circuit ? In this chapter we prove that almost all functions are hard functions, optimal circuits for almost all functions have exponential size and linear depth. This can be proved quite easily using Shannon's counting argument (Shannon (49)). The number of circuits with small circuit size or small depth grows much slower than the number of different Boolean functions implying that almost all functions are hard. This means that a random Boolean function is hard with very large probability. We obtain a random Boolean function by 2^n independent coin tosses with an unbiased coin, for each input a the output $f(a)$ is determined by one of the coin tosses. By this experiment we can expect a Boolean function that has no recognizable structure. This lack of structure implies that the function is hard. The converse is not correct. We shall see later that certain functions whose structure is easy to describe are (probably) hard. Hence, the structure of our fundamental functions is only a necessary condition for the existence of efficient circuits.

In this chapter we investigate the complexity of almost all functions, or equivalently, the expected complexity of a random function. It turns out that almost all functions have nearly the same complexity as the hardest function. This effect is called Shannon effect by Lupanov (70).

DEFINITION 1.1 : The notion "almost all functions f of a class $F_n \subseteq B_n$ have property P " stands for the assertion that

$$|\{ f \in F_n \mid f \text{ has } P \}| / |F_n| \to 1 \quad \text{as} \quad n \to \infty . \tag{1.1}$$

DEFINITION 1.2 : For a complexity measure CM and a class of functions F_n we denote by $CM(F_n)$ the complexity of the hardest functions in F_n, i.e. $\max \{ CM(f) \mid f \in F_n \}$.

DEFINITION 1.3 : The Shannon effect is valid for a class of functions F_n and a complexity measure CM if $CM(f) \geq CM(F_n) - o(CM(F_n))$ for almost all $f \in F_n$.

We prove that the Shannon effect is valid for several classes of Boolean functions and complexity measures. With Shannon's counting argument we prove that almost all functions are hard, i.e. their complexity is at least $a_n - o(a_n)$ for some large a_n. Then we design circuits (or formulas) for all functions whose complexity is bounded by a_n.

For almost all functions we obtain nearly optimal circuits. These circuits may be used for $f \in B_n$ if we have no idea of designing a better circuit for f. In Ch. 3 we have seen that we can design much more efficient circuits for many fundamental functions.

4.2 Circuits over complete bases

In order to apply Shannon's counting argument we estimate the number of B_2 - circuits of size b.

LEMMA 2.1 : At most $S(b,n) = (b+n+1)^{2b}\, 16^b\, b/\, b!$ functions $f \in B_n$ can be computed by B_2 - circuits of size b.

Proof : We estimate the number of B_2 - circuits of size b. For each gate there are $|B_2| = 16$ possibilities to choose its type and $b+n+1$ possibilities to choose each of its two predecessors, namely the other

$b - 1$ gates, n variables and 2 constants. Each B_2-circuit computes at most b different functions at its gates. Finally we take into account that each circuit is counted b! times, namely for b! different numberings of its gates. Altogether we obtain the claimed bound.

□

If $b = b(n) = C(B_n)$, $|B_n|$ functions in B_n can be computed by a B_2-circuit of size b. By Lemma 2.1 we can conclude $S(b,n) \geq |B_n|$. We use this inequality for an estimation of b. When considering $S(b,n)$ and $|B_n|$ as functions of n we see that $S(b,n)$ is exponential while $|B_n|$ is even double exponential. Since $S(b,n)$ as a function of b is also only exponential, $b = b(n)$ grows exponentially. We now estimate b more exactly. By Stirling's Formula $b! \geq c\, b^{b+1/2} e^{-b}$ for some constant $c > 0$ and thus

$$\log S(b,n) \geq \log |B_n| \quad \Rightarrow \tag{2.1}$$

$$2b \log(b+n+1) + 4b + \log b - (b+1/2)\log b + b \log e - \log c \geq 2^n.$$

For n sufficiently large, $b \geq n+1$ and therefore

$$b \log b + (6 + \log e)b + (1/2)\log b - \log c \geq 2^n. \tag{2.2}$$

If $b \leq 2^n\, n^{-1}$, we could conclude

$$2^n\, n^{-1}(n - \log n + 6 + \log e) + (1/2)(n - \log n) - \log c \geq 2^n \tag{2.3}$$

which for large n is false. Therefore

$$C(B_n) \geq 2^n\, n^{-1} \quad \text{for sufficiently large n}. \tag{2.4}$$

We can prove even more. If we consider a subclass B_n^* of B_n such that

$$\log |B_n^*| \geq 2^n - 2^n\, n^{-1} \log\log n =: a(n)$$

we can prove in the same way that $C(B_n^*) \geq 2^n n^{-1}$ for sufficiently large n. In particular, we may choose B_n^* as the class of those $2^{a(n)}$ functions in B_n of the smallest circuit size.

THEOREM 2.1 : For sufficiently large n at least $|B_n| (1 - 2^{-r(n)})$ of the $|B_n|$ functions in B_n , where $r(n) = 2^n n^{-1} \log\log n$, have circuit size at least $2^n n^{-1}$. In particular, almost all $f \in B_n$ have circuit size at least $2^n n^{-1}$.

We now show that $2^n n^{-1} + o(2^n n^{-1})$ gates are sufficient for the computation of an arbitrary $f \in B_n$. At first we present two less efficient circuits. The first one is called decoding circuit. Let $f_0 \in B_{n-1}$ and $f_1 \in B_{n-1}$ be the subfunctions of $f \in B_n$ for $x_n = 0$ and $x_n = 1$ resp. Obviously

$$f = (\bar{x}_n \wedge f_0) \vee (x_n \wedge f_1) \tag{2.5}$$

implying

$$C(B_n) \leq 2 C(B_{n-1}) + 3 \quad , \quad C(B_2) = 1 \quad \text{and} \tag{2.6}$$

$$C(B_n) \leq 2^n - 3 \quad . \tag{2.7}$$

We note that decoding circuits are even formulas. Decoding circuits can be improved in the following simple way. In a decoding circuit we compute all 2^{n-3} subfunctions in B_3 in disjoint subcircuits. It is much more efficient to compute all 2^8 functions in B_3 in advance. Let $C^*(B_k)$ be the circuit complexity for the computation of all functions in B_k . By (2.5)

$$C^*(B_k) \leq C^*(B_{k-1}) + 3 |B_k| \quad \text{and} \tag{2.8}$$

$$C^*(B_2) \leq 16 \quad , \text{hence}$$

$$C^*(B_k) \leq 3 \cdot 2^{2^k} + 6 \cdot 2^{2^{k-1}} \tag{2.9}$$

For the computation of f we compute at first all functions in B_k . The decoding circuit for f can stop after $n - k$ steps, since all necessary subfunctions are already computed. Similarly to (2.7) $3 \cdot 2^{n-k} - 3$ gates are sufficient to compute f if the functions in B_k are given. Hence

$$C(B_n) \leq 3(2^{n-k} + 2^{2^k}) + 6 \cdot 2^{2^{k-1}} \qquad \text{for arbitrary } k . \qquad (2.10)$$

For $k = \lceil \log n \rceil - 1$

$$C(B_n) \leq 12 \cdot 2^n n^{-1} + o(2^n n^{-1}) . \qquad (2.11)$$

These simple ideas already lead to circuits whose size is for almost all Boolean functions only by a factor of 12 larger than the size of an optimal circuit.

In order to eliminate the factor 12, we have to work harder. Lupanov (58) introduced the so-called (k,s) - Lupanov representation of Boolean functions. We represent the values of f by a table of 2^k rows for the different values of $(x_1, \ldots, x_k)$ and 2^{n-k} columns for the different values of $(x_{k+1}, \ldots, x_n)$. The rows are partitioned to $p = \lceil 2^k s^{-1} \rceil \leq 2^k s^{-1} + 1$ blocks $A_1, \ldots, A_p$ such that $A_1, \ldots, A_{p-1}$ contain s rows and A_p contains $s' \leq s$ rows. We try to find simpler functions than f and to reduce f to several of these simpler functions. Let $f_i(x) = f(x)$ if $(x_1, \ldots, x_k) \in A_i$ and $f_i(x) = 0$ otherwise. Obviously $f = f_1 \vee \cdots \vee f_p$.

Let $B_{i,w}$ be the set of columns whose intersection with A_i is equal to $w \in \{0,1\}^s$ (for $i = p$, $w \in \{0,1\}^{s'}$) and let $f_{i,w}(x) = f_i(x)$ if $(x_{k+1}, \ldots, x_n) \in B_{i,w}$ and $f_{i,w}(x) = 0$ otherwise. Obviously f is the disjunction of all $f_{i,w}$. Now consider the $2^k \times 2^{n-k}$ table of $f_{i,w}$. All rows outside of A_i consist of zeros only, the rows of A_i have only two different types of columns, columns w and columns of zeros only. We represent $f_{i,w}$ as the conjunction of $f_{i,w}^1$ and $f_{i,w}^2$ where $f_{i,w}^1(x) = 1$ iff for some j $w_j = 1$ and $(x_1, \ldots, x_k)$ is the j-th row of A_i, and $f_{i,w}^2(x) = 1$ iff $(x_{k+1}, \ldots, x_n) \in B_{i,w}$. Altogether we obtain Lupanov's (k,s)-representation

$$f(x_1, \ldots, x_n) = \bigvee_{1 \leq i \leq p} \bigvee_w f_{i,w}^1(x_1, \ldots, x_k) \wedge f_{i,w}^2(x_{k+1}, \ldots, x_n) . \qquad (2.12)$$

We may compute f now in the following way.

Step 1 : By Lemma 4.1, Ch.3, we compute with $O(2^k + 2^{n-k})$ gates all minterms on $\{x_1, \ldots, x_k\}$ and on $\{x_{k+1}, \ldots, x_n\}$.

Step 2 : We compute all $f_{i,w}^1$ by their DNF, the minterms are already computed. Since the blocks A_i are disjoint, each minterm is used at most once for fixed w . Altogether $2^s 2^k$ gates are sufficient.

Step 3 : We compute all $f_{i,w}^2$ by their DNF, the minterms are already computed. Since the blocks $B_{i,w}$ are disjoint for fixed i , each minterm is used once for fixed i . Altogether $p\, 2^{n-k}$ gates are sufficient.

Step 4 : By (2.12) $2 p\, 2^s$ gates are sufficient to compute f if all $f_{i,w}^1$ and $f_{i,w}^2$ are given.

The number of gates of our circuit can be estimated, since $p \leq 2^k s^{-1} + 1$, by

$$O(2^k + 2^{n-k}) + 2^{s+k} + 2^n s^{-1} + 2^{n-k} + 2^{k+s+1} s^{-1} + 2^{s+1} . \qquad (2.13)$$

We choose $k = \lceil 3 \log n \rceil$ and $s = n - \lceil 5 \log n \rceil$.

THEOREM 2.2 : $C(f) \leq 2^n n^{-1} + o(2^n n^{-1})$ for all $f \in B_n$.

By Theorem 2.1 and Theorem 2.2 we have proved that the Shannon effect is valid for B_n and B_2-circuit size.

Lupanov's circuits are nearly optimal and for almost all Boolean functions much better than minimal polynomials, i.e. optimal circuits of 2 logical levels. Lupanov's circuits have only 4 logical levels.

4.3 Formulas over complete bases

We proceed as in § 2 .

LEMMA 3.1 : At most $F(b,n) = (n+2)^{b+1} \, 16^b \, 4^b$ functions $f \in B_n$ can be computed by B_2 - formulas of size b .

Proof : We estimate the number of B_2-formulas of size b . W.l.o.g. the last gate is the only one without successor and the output is computed at the last gate. As already discussed in Ch.2 B_2-formulas are binary trees if we copy the variables and constants. There exist less than 4^b binary trees with b inner nodes. For each gate starting at the root of the tree we have for each of the two predecessors at most the two possibilities of choosing an inner node or a leaf. Each gate is labelled by one of the 16 functions of B_2 . Finally each of the $b+1$ leaves is labelled by one of the n variables or the 2 constants. Altogether we obtain the claimed bound.

□

If $b = b(n) = L(B_n)$, $\log F(b,n) \geq \log |B_n|$ implying

$$(b+1) \log (n+2) + 6b \; \geq \; 2^n . \tag{3.1}$$

(3.1) is not fulfilled for $b = 2^n \log^{-1} n \, (1 - (\log\log n)^{-1})$ and sufficiently large n . The same estimation holds for classes $B_n^* \subseteq B_n$ where $\log |B_n^*| = 2^n (1 - \log^{-1} n)$.

THEOREM 3.1 : For sufficiently large n at least $|B_n| \, (1 - 2^{-s(n)})$ of the $|B_n|$ functions in B_n , where $s(n) = 2^n \log^{-1} n$, are of formula size at least $2^n \log^{-1} n \, (1 - (\log\log n)^{-1})$. In particular, almost all $f \in B_n$ are of formula size at least $2^n \log^{-1} n \, (1 - (\log\log n)^{-1})$.

We already proved in § 2 an upper bound of $2^n - 3$ on $L(B_n)$. By

Lupanov's (k,s)-representation we shall obtain for each $f \in B_n$ a B_2-formula with 6 logical levels and $(2 + o(1)) 2^n \log^{-1} n$ gates. Since in formulas all gates have fan-out 1 we have to compute the functions $f_{i,w}^1$ and $f_{i,w}^2$ in another way as in § 1 . As only a few inputs are mapped to 1 by $f_{i,w}^1$ or $f_{i,w}^2$, we consider functions $f \in B_n$ where $|f^{-1}(1)| = r$ is small.

DEFINITION 3.1 : $L(r,n) = \max \{ L(f) \mid f \in B_n , |f^{-1}(1)| = r \}$.

The obvious upper bound on $L(r,n)$ is $rn - 1$, consider the DNF . This upper bound has been improved by Finikov (57) for small r.

LEMMA 3.2 : $L(r,n) \leq 2n - 1 + r 2^{r-1}$.

Proof : We describe a function $f \in B_n$ where $|f^{-1}(1)| = r$ by an $r \times n$-matrix consisting of the r inputs in $f^{-1}(1)$. For small r , in particular $r < \log n$, several columns of the matrix are the same. We make the most of this fact.

We do not increase the formula size of f by interchanging the roles of x_j and $\bar{x}_j$. With such interchanges we obtain a matrix whose first row consists of zeros only. Now the number l of different columns in the matrix is bounded by 2^{r-1} . Let $c_1, \ldots, c_l$ be the different columns and $A(i)$ be the set of numbers j such that the j-th column equals c_i . Let $a(i)$ be the minimal element of $A(i)$.

By definition, $f(x) = 1$ iff x equals one of the rows of the matrix. This can now be tested efficiently. f_1 tests whether for each i all variables x_j ($j \in A(i)$) have the same value, and afterwards f_2 tests whether x and some row agree at the positions $a(i)$ $(1 \leq i \leq l)$. f_2 is the disjunction of r monoms of length l , hence $L(f_2) \leq rl - 1$, and

$$f_1(x) = \bigwedge_{1 \leq i \leq l} \left(\bigwedge_{p \in A(i)} x_p \vee \bigwedge_{p \in A(i)} \bar{x}_p \right) \tag{3.2}$$

implying $L(f_1) \le 2n-1$. Since $f = f_1 \wedge f_2$ and $l \le 2^{r-1}$, we have proved the lemma.

□

LEMMA 3.3 : $L(r,n) \le (2 + o(1)) \, n \, r \log^{-1} n$ if $r \ge \log^2 n$.

Proof : For $r' = \lceil \log(n \log^{-2} n) \rceil$ we represent f as a disjunction of $\lceil r/r' \rceil$ functions f_i , where $|f_i^{-1}(1)| \le r'$. We apply Lemma 3.2 to all f_i . Therefore, if $r \ge \log^2 n$,

$$L(r,n) \le \lceil r/r' \rceil - 1 + \lceil r/r' \rceil (2n-1 + r'2^{r'-1}) \tag{3.3}$$

$$= (2 + o(1)) \, n \, r \log^{-1} n .$$

□

Lupanov (62 b) applied this result to the construction of efficient formulas.

THEOREM 3.2 : The formula size of all $f \in B_n$ is bounded by $(2 + o(1)) \, 2^n \log^{-1} n$.

Proof : We use Lupanov's (k,s)-representation. Again by (2.12) $2p2^s$ gates are sufficient if all $f_{i,w}^1$ and $f_{i,w}^2$ are computed. By definition, each $f_{i,w}^1$ can be computed as disjunction of at most s minterms of length k . All $f_{i,w}^1$ can be computed by disjoint formulas with altogether $p2^s ks$ gates.

Let $q_i(r)$ be the number of vectors w which appear exactly r times as a column in block A_i . The sum of all $q_i(r)$ equals the number of different vectors w and is therefore bounded by 2^s . The sum of all $r q_i(r)$ equals 2^{n-k} , which is the number of columns. If w appears r times as a column in A_i , $|(f_{i,w}^2)^{-1}(1)| = r$. $f_{i,w}^2$ is defined on $m = n-k$ variables. If $r < \log^2 m$, we compute $f_{i,w}^2$ by its DNF, otherwise we apply Lemma 3.3 . Altogether for each block A_i

$$\sum_{w} L(f_{i,w}^2) \le \sum_{r} L(r,m) \, q_i(r) \tag{3.4}$$

$$\le \sum_{r < \log^2 m} (rm-1) \, q_i(r) + \sum_{r \ge \log^2 m} (2 + o(1)) \, r \, m \log^{-1} m \, q_i(r)$$

$$\le m \log^2 m \sum_{r} q_i(r) + (2 + o(1)) \, m \log^{-1} m \sum_{r} r \, q_i(r)$$

$$\le 2^s \, m \log^2 m + (2 + o(1)) \, 2^m \, m \log^{-1} m .$$

Altogether we obtain a formula for f of at most

$$2p \, 2^s + p \, 2^s ks + p \, 2^s m \log^2 m + (2 + o(1)) \, p \, 2^m m \log^{-1} m \tag{3.5}$$

gates. We prove the theorem by choosing $k = \lceil 2 \log n \rceil$ and $s = n - \lceil 3 \log n \rceil$, implying $m = n - \lceil 2 \log n \rceil$ and , since $p \le 2^k s^{-1} + 1$, $p = O(n)$ as well as $p \, 2^m \le 2^n s^{-1} + 2^m$. $\square$

4.4 The depth over complete bases

Here the lower bound for almost all Boolean functions can be derived easily from the results on formula size by the following fundamental lemma. A partial converse is proved in Ch.7 .

LEMMA 4.1 : $D(f) \ge \lceil \log (L(f) + 1) \rceil$ for all Boolean functions.

Proof : Using the results of § 4 , Ch.1 , we can consider a Boolean formula of depth $D(f)$ for f . A formula is a binary tree. Binary trees of depth d have at most $2^d - 1$ inner gates. Therefore our formula for f has size l bounded by $2^{D(f)} - 1$. Hence $L(f) \le l \le 2^{D(f)} - 1$ and the lemma follows. $\square$

We combine Theorem 3.1 with Lemma 4.1 .

THEOREM 4.1 : The depth of almost all $f \in B_n$ is at least $n - \log\log n - o(1)$.

THEOREM 4.2 : The depth of each $f \in B_n$ is not larger than $n + \lceil \log n \rceil - 1$.

Proof : W.l.o.g. we assume that $|f^{-1}(1)| \leq 2^{n-1}$ and use the DNF. Otherwise we could use the CNF. All minterms can be computed in parallel in depth $\lceil \log n \rceil$. As the number of minterms is bounded by 2^{n-1} , we can sum up the minterms in depth $n - 1$. $\square$

By Theorem 4.1 and Theorem 4.2 the Shannon effect is valid for B_n and the depth of B_2-circuits. The trivial upper bound of Theorem 4.2 has been improved several times. We describe the history of these improvements.

DEFINITION 4.1 : Let $\log^{(1)} x = \log x$ and $\log^{(k)} x = \log\log^{(k-1)} x$. For $x \leq 1$, $\log^* x = 0$ and , for $x > 1$, $\log^* x$ is the minimal k such that $\log^{(k)} x \leq 1$.

$\log^* x$ is an increasing function tending to ∞ as $x \to \infty$. But $\log^* x$ is growing rather slowly. So $\log^* x \leq 5$ for all $x \leq 2^{65536}$.
Let $a(n)$ be the following number sequence : $a(0) = 8$, $a(i) = 2^{a(i-1)} + a(i-1)$. Now we are able to describe the improved bounds on $D(B_n)$.

Spira (71 b): $n + \log^* n$.
Muller and Preparata (71): $n + i$ for $n \leq a(i)$.
McColl and Paterson (77): $n + 1$.
Gaskov (78): $n - \log\log n + 2 + o(1)$.

The bound of Gaskov is optimal at least up to small additive terms (see Theorem 4.1). McColl and Paterson even use a circuit scheme, i.e. a fixed underlying graph. For different functions only the types of the gates are changed. By easy counting arguments one can prove that the depth of a circuit scheme cannot be smaller than $n-1$.

Because already the simple construction of Theorem 4.2 is not too bad, we only discuss some ideas of the construction of McColl and Paterson. For each partition of the set of variables X to an m-element set Z and an $(n-m)$-element set Y we can generalize (2.5) to

$$f(y,z) = \bigvee_{c \in \{0,1\}^m} m_c(z) \wedge f(y,c) = \bigwedge_{c \in \{0,1\}^m} (s_c(z) \vee f(y,c)). \tag{4.1}$$

McColl and Paterson "smuggled" the computation of $m_c(z)$ or $s_c(z)$ into the computation of $f(y,c)$. This leads to a saving of depth if we are content with the computation of an approximation of f. These approximations can be chosen such that f can be computed efficiently from its approximations.

4.5 Monotone functions

The importance of the class of monotone functions will be discussed in Ch.6. We know already that the minimal polynomial of a monotone function is the unique MDNF. We have considered in Ch.3 the following monotone functions: threshold functions, sorting function, and Boolean matrix product. Further examples can be found in Ch.6.

In order to apply Shannon's counting argument to the estimation of $C(M_n)$ and $C_m(M_n)$ we have to estimate $|M_n|$. This problem has been formulated (in another context) already by Dedekind. Contributions to this problem can be traced back to Alekseev (73), Gilbert (54), Hansel (66), Kleitman (69) and (73), Kleitman and Markowsky (75), and Korshunov (77) and (81 a). We cite the results of Korshunov who obtained his exact bounds by a description of the structure of almost all $f \in M_n$.

DEFINITION 5.1 : Let M_n^t contain all $f \in M_n$ such that

$$x_1 + \cdots + x_n < t-1 \quad \Rightarrow \quad f(x) = 0 , \tag{5.1}$$

$$x_1 + \cdots + x_n > t+1 \quad \Rightarrow \quad f(x) = 1 , \tag{5.2}$$

$$|\{ x \mid x_1 + \cdots + x_n = t-1 \text{ and } f(x) = 1 \}| \leq 2^{\lfloor n/2 \rfloor} , \text{ and} \tag{5.3}$$

$$|\{ x \mid x_1 + \cdots + x_n = t+1 \text{ and } f(x) = 0 \}| \leq 2^{\lfloor n/2 \rfloor} . \tag{5.4}$$

THEOREM 5.1 : Let $k = \lfloor n/2 \rfloor$ and $E(n) = \binom{n}{k}$. Almost all $f \in M_n$ are in M_n^k , if n is even, and in $M_n^k \cup M_n^{k+1}$, if n is odd. Furthermore, let $a_n \sim b_n$ iff $a_n / b_n \to 1$ as $n \to \infty$. Then

$$|M_n| \sim 2^{E(n)} \exp\left[\binom{n}{n/2 - 1} (2^{-n/2} + n^2 2^{-n-5} - n 2^{-n-4}) \right] , \tag{5.5}$$

if n is even, and

$$|M_n| \sim 2 \cdot 2^{E(n)} \exp\left[\binom{n}{(n-3)/2} (2^{-(n+3)/2} - n^2 2^{-n-6} - n 2^{-n-3}) \right.$$
$$\left. + \binom{n}{(n-1)/2} (2^{-(n+1)/2} + n^2 2^{-n-4}) \right] ,$$

if n is odd.

By these results almost all monotone Boolean functions have only prime implicants and prime clauses whose length is about $n/2$. For our purposes (see also § 2 and § 3) a good estimation of $\log |M_n|$ is sufficient. Such a result is much easier to prove.

PROPOSITION 5.1 : The number of monotone functions $f \in M_n$ is larger than $2^{E(n)}$ where $E(n) = \binom{n}{\lfloor n/2 \rfloor}$ is larger than $c 2^n n^{-1/2}$ for some constant $c > 0$.

Proof : The estimation of $E(n)$ follows from Stirling's formula. $E(n)$ is the number of different monotone monoms of length $\lfloor n/2 \rfloor$. For each subset T of this set of monoms we define f_T as the disjunction of all $m \in T$. Since no monom of length $\lfloor n/2 \rfloor$ is a shortening of another, $Pl(f_T) = T$ and $f_T \neq f_{T'}$ if $T \neq T'$. We have defined $2^{E(n)}$ different functions $f_T \in M_n$.

□

Now we can apply the results in § 2 and § 3 on the number of circuits or formulas of size b . If we consider monotone circuits or formulas, we may replace the factor 16^b by 2^b , since $|\Omega_m| = 2$. By Shannon's counting argument we obtain from elementary calculations the following results.

THEOREM 5.2 : For some constants $c_1, c_2 > 0$ almost all $f \in M_n$ have (monotone) circuit size bounded below by $c_1 2^n n^{-3/2}$, (monotone) formula size bounded below by $c_2 2^n n^{-1/2} \log^{-1} n$, and (monotone) depth bounded below by $n - (1/2)\log n - \log\log n + \log c_2$.

What is known about upper bounds ? One can show for the (monotone) circuit size upper bounds of the same size as the lower bounds of Theorem 5.2 . Lupanov (62 a) and (65 b), who proved asymptotically optimal bounds on the circuit and formula size of almost all Boolean functions, could design for monotone functions only circuits of size larger than $2^n n^{-3/2}$. Pippenger (76) and (78) described for all monotone functions B_2-circuits of size $O(2^n n^{-3/2})$. The old $O(2^n n^{-3/2} \log^2 n)$ bound of Reznik (62) on $C_m(M_n)$ has been improved at first by Pippenger (76) to $O(2^n n^{-3/2} \log n)$, and finally Red'kin (79) proved that all monotone functions can be computed by monotone circuits of size $O(2^n n^{-3/2})$. This implies that for almost all monotone functions $f \in M_n$ $C(f)$ and $C_m(f)$ are of the same size. In Ch.6 we learn that for certain $f \in M_n$ $C(f)$ may be much smaller than $C_m(f)$.

Since the $O(2^n n^{-3/2})$ bounds are rather complicated, we only prove the $O(2^n n^{-3/2} \log n)$ bound of Pippenger for monotone circuits. More important than the actual size of the bound it is to learn why no monotone function belongs to the hardest functions in B_n . The following circuit design takes advantage of structural particularities of monotone functions.

The fundamental equality (2.5) for decoding circuits, namely $f = (\bar{x}_n \wedge f_0) \vee (x_n \wedge f_1)$, contains a negation. For monotone functions, $f_0 \leq f_1$, and, considering the cases $x_n = 0$ and $x_n = 1$, we can prove the following monotone decompositions of $f \in M_n$.

$$f = f_0 \vee (x_n \wedge f_1) = (x_n \vee f_0) \wedge f_1 \; . \tag{5.6}$$

Applying the first part of (5.6) n-m times, we obtain

$$f(x_1, \ldots, x_n) = \tag{5.7}$$

$$\bigvee_{i(m+1),\ldots,i(n) \in \{0,1\}} \left(\bigwedge_{i(j)=1} x_{i(j)} \wedge f(x_1, \ldots, x_m, i(m+1), \ldots, i(n)) \right) .$$

Later on we discuss how we compute the 2^{n-m} subfunctions of f on $x_1, \ldots, x_m$ efficiently in common. Furthermore we need all monotone monoms on $x_{m+1}, \ldots, x_n$. These monoms can be computed with $2^{n-m} - (n-m) - 1$ $\wedge$-gates, since the empty monom and the $n-m$ monoms of length 1 are given and each monom of length l can be computed with one $\wedge$-gate from a monom of length $l-1$ and a variable. After having computed the subfunctions of f in (5.7) , less than $3 \cdot 2^{n-m}$ gates are sufficient for the computation of f .

According to the law of simplification $xy \vee y = y$, it is not possible that both p and some proper shortening or lengthening of p are prime implicants of f . If $p_1, \ldots, p_r$ is a chain of monoms, i.e. p_{i+1} is the lengthening of p_i by one variable, then at most one monom of the chain is a prime implicant of f . We show how we may partition the set of monoms into the smallest possible number of chains. These chains are grouped into b blocks. Then we compute all subfunctions of f in the following three steps.

Step 1 : Compute all monoms on $x_1, \ldots, x_m$. This can be done with less than 2^m gates.

Step 2 : Compute for each block all monotone functions having only prime implicants of that block, or equivalently, having at most one prime implicant of each chain of the block.

Step 3 : Each subfunction f' of f on $x_1, \ldots, x_m$ can be computed as the disjunction of $f'_1, \ldots, f'_b$ where f'_i is the disjunction of all prime implicants of f' belonging to the i-th block. Thus Step 3 can be implemented with $(b-1)2^{n-m}$ $\vee$-gates.

As Step 2 will be implemented by $\vee$-gates only, the whole circuit will contain only 4 logical levels.

Since there exist $E(m) = \binom{m}{\lfloor m/2 \rfloor}$ monoms of length $\lfloor m/2 \rfloor$, which have to belong to different chains, $E(m)$ chains are necessary. By solving the marriage problem we prove that $E(m)$ chains suffice.

LEMMA 5.1 : Let $G = (A \cup B, E \subseteq A \times B)$ be a bipartite graph. For $A' \subseteq A$ let $\Gamma(A')$ be the set of vertices $b \in B$ such that $(a,b) \in E$ for some $a \in A'$. G contains $|A|$ vertex disjoint edges iff $|\Gamma A'| \geq |A'|$ for all $A' \subseteq A$.

Sketch of proof : Obviously the condition is necessary. For the sufficiency part of the proof $e = |E| \geq |A|$, since $|\Gamma A| \geq |A|$.

Case 1 : $e = |A|$. Since $|\Gamma A| \geq |A|$, all edges are vertex disjoint.

Case 2 : $\exists \ A' : \phi \neq A' \neq A$ and $|\Gamma A'| = |A'|$. Let $B' = \Gamma A'$, $A'' = A - A'$ and $B'' = B - B'$. The condition of the lemma is fulfilled for the smaller subgraphs on $A' \cup B'$ and $A'' \cup B''$. By induction hypothesis we obtain $|A'|$ and $|A''|$ vertex disjoint edges resp. on these subgraphs, altogether $|A|$ vertex disjoint edges.

Case 3 : $\forall \ A' \neq \phi : |\Gamma A'| > |A'|$. By eliminating an arbitrary edge we obtain a smaller graph fulfilling the condition of the lemma.

Case 4 : $\forall \ A' \neq \phi$, $A' \neq A$: $|\Gamma A'| > |A'|$, $|\Gamma A| = |A|$ and $|E| > |A|$. The degree of some $b \in B$ is at least 2. By eliminating some edge (a,b) we obtain a smaller graph fulfilling the condition of the lemma. $\qquad \square$

Now we build $E(m)$ chains containing all monoms on $x_1, \ldots, x_m$. We start on level $\lfloor m/2 \rfloor$ where each chain contains one monom of length $\lfloor m/2 \rfloor$. We show how the $\binom{m}{k+1}$ monoms of length $k+1$ can be added to the $\binom{m}{k}$ chains containing one monom of length $k \geq \lfloor m/2 \rfloor$. The addition of the short monoms can be performed in the same way.

Let A and B contain the monoms of length $k+1$ and k resp. $a \in A$ and $b \in B$ are connected by an edge iff a is a lengthening of b. If we find a set S of $|A|$ vertex disjoint edges, we can add each monom $a \in A$ to that chain ending in b where $(a,b) \in S$. We only have to check the condition of Lemma 5.1 . Let $A' \subseteq A$ be a set of l monoms. Each monom of length $k+1$ has $k+1$ shortenings in B, therefore $(k+1)l$ edges are leaving A' and go to $\Gamma A'$. Each monom of length k has $m-k$ lengthenings in A, therefore at most $(m-k)r$, where $r = |\Gamma A'|$, edges are gathered by $\Gamma A'$. Since all edges leaving A' are gathered by $\Gamma A'$,

$$(k + 1)l \leq (m - k)r \tag{5.8}$$

implying $l \leq r$, since $k+1 \geq m-k$. Since the condition of Lemma 5.1 is fulfilled, our construction is possible. The set of all monoms can be partitioned to $E(m)$ chains $C_1, \ldots, C_{E(m)}$.

If $C_1, \ldots, C_i$ build a block B, exactly

$$S(B) = \prod_{1 \leq j \leq i} (|C_j| + 1) \tag{5.9}$$

monotone functions have at most one prime implicant of each chain C_j $(1 \leq j \leq i)$ and no other prime implicant. These functions can be computed by a circuit of size $S(B)$, if the monoms on $x_1, \ldots, x_m$ are given. This is easy to see, since any function with l prime implicants can be computed with one v-gate from a function with $l-1$ prime implicants and a monom. If we join the chains to b blocks $B_1, \ldots, B_b$, Step 2 and 3 of our circuit can be implemented with $\Sigma S(B_i)$ and $(b-1) 2^{n-m}$ gates resp.

b has to be chosen such that Step 2 and 3 can both be implemented efficiently. The "size" $S(B)$ of the blocks should be bounded by some parameter 2^s. Since each chain C_j contains at most $m+1$ monoms, each chain increases the size of a block at most by the factor of $m+2$. So we build the blocks by adding as many chains as possible without skipping the size bound 2^s. Then at most one block has a size less than $2^s/(m+2)$. We estimate the number of blocks b. The sum of all $|C_j|$ is 2^m, since each monom is in exactly one chain. Let $H(C_j) = \log(|C_j|+1)$. Then for all blocks B with at most one exception by (5.9)

$$\sum_{C \in B} H(C) = \log S(B) \geq s - \log(m+2).\qquad (5.10)$$

Because of the concativity of $\log$

$$\sum_{1 \leq j \leq E(m)} H(C_j) = E(m) \sum_{1 \leq j \leq E(m)} E(m)^{-1} \log(|C_j|+1) \qquad (5.11)$$

$$\leq E(m) \log\left(\sum_{1 \leq j \leq E(m)} E(m)^{-1} (|C_j|+1) \right)$$

$$= E(m) \log\left(2^m E(m)^{-1} + 1 \right).$$

Combining (5.10) and (5.11) we can estimate b by

$$b \leq 1 + E(m)(\log(2^m E(m)^{-1} + 1))(s - \log(m+2))^{-1}.\qquad (5.12)$$

The size of the whole circuit can be estimated by

$$3 \cdot 2^{n-m} + 2^m + b \cdot 2^s + (b-1)2^{n-m},\qquad (5.13)$$

since, by definition, $S(B) \leq 2^s$ for all blocks B. We may choose m and s and can estimate b by (5.12). Let

$$m = \lfloor n/3 \rfloor \quad \text{and} \quad s = (2/3)n - \log n,\qquad (5.14)$$

then, by Stirling's formula, $E(m) = \Theta(2^{n/3} n^{-1/2})$, and s is linear in n, hence by (5.12)

$$b = O(2^{n/3} n^{-3/2} \log n).\qquad (5.15)$$

Inserting (5.14) and (5.15) into (5.13) we have proved the following upper bound on $C_m(M_n)$.

THEOREM 5.3 : Each monotone function $f \in M_n$ can be computed by a monotone circuit of size $O(2^n n^{-3/2} \log n)$.

McColl (78 b) proved the following upper bound on $D_m(M_n)$. The proof is rather simple, but contains the idea of smuggling computation steps into other computations.

THEOREM 5.4 : Each monotone function $f \in M_n$ can be computed by a monotone circuit of depth n.

Proof : We define for $f \in M_n$ functions $g_1, h_1, \ldots, g_{n-1}, h_{n-1}$ such that $D_m(g_i), D_m(h_i) \leq i$ and $f = g_1 \vee \cdots \vee g_{n-1}$ as well as $f = h_1 \wedge \cdots \wedge h_{n-1}$. This obviously implies the theorem. We prove the assertion by induction on n. For $n = 2$ the claim is obvious. For the induction step we use the representations of f in (5.6) , namely $f_0 \vee (x_n \wedge f_1)$ and $(x_n \vee f_0) \wedge f_1$. Since $f_0, f_1 \in M_{n-1}$, by induction hypothesis

$$f_0 = g_1 \vee \cdots \vee g_{n-2} \quad \text{where} \quad D_m(g_i) \leq i \qquad \text{and} \qquad (5.16)$$

$$f_1 = h_1 \wedge \cdots \wedge h_{n-2} \quad \text{where} \quad D_m(h_i) \leq i . \qquad (5.17)$$

g_1 has depth 1 . If g_1^* has depth 2 , $g_1^* \vee g_2 \vee \cdots \vee g_{n-2}$ also can be computed in depth $n-1$. Thus there is some place in the computation of f_0 where we may smuggle in x_n. $g_1^* = x_n \vee g_1$ has depth 2 , so $x_n \vee f_0$ has depth $n-1$. $f = (x_n \vee f_0) \wedge f_1$ has depth n where $f_1 = h_1 \wedge \cdots \wedge h_{n-2}$ and $h_{n-1} = x_n \vee f_0$ such that $D_m(h_i) \leq i$. By dual arguments we obtain the other representation of f. $\quad\Box$

We have seen that the Shannon effect is valid for M_n and monotone depth. Henno (79) generalized McColl's design to functions in m−valued logic. By a further improvement of Henno's design Wegener (82 b) proved the Shannon effect also for the monotone functions in m-valued logic and (monotone) depth.

4.6 The weak Shannon effect

The proof of the Shannon effect for various classes of functions and complexity measures is a main subject in Russian language literature. There also weak Shannon effects are studied intensively. The Shannon effect is valid for F_n and CM iff almost all functions $f \in F_n$ have nearly the same complexity $k(n)$ and $k(n) = CM(F_n)$ is the complexity of the hardest function in F_n. The weak Shannon effect concentrates on the first aspect.

DEFINITION 6.1 : The weak Shannon effect is valid for the class of functions F_n and the complexity measure CM if $CM(f) \geq k(n) - o(k(n))$ and $CM(f) \leq k(n) + o(k(n))$ for almost all $f \in F_n$ and some number sequence $k(n)$.

The validity of the weak Shannon effect for M_n and circuit size and monotone circuit size has been proved by Ugolnikov (76) and Nurmeev (81) resp. It is not known whether the Shannon effect is valid too. The complexity $k(n)$ of almost all functions is not even known for the (monotone) circuit size. How can the weak Shannon effect be proved without knowing $k(n)$? Often Nigmatullin's (73) variational principle is used. If the weak Shannon effect is not valid there exist some number sequence $k(n)$, some constant $c > 0$, and some subclasses $G_n, H_n \subseteq F_n$ such that for infinitely many n

$$|G_n|, |H_n| = \Omega(|F_n|) \quad , \tag{6.1}$$

$$CM(f) \leq k(n) \quad , \text{ if } f \in G_n , \text{ and} \tag{6.2}$$

$$CM(f) \geq (1+c)\,k(n) \quad , \text{ if } f \in H_n . \tag{6.3}$$

Since G_n and H_n are large subclasses, there are functions $g_n \in G_n$ and $h_n \in H_n$ which do not differ too much. Furthermore this implies that h_n cannot be much harder than g_n in contradiction to (6.2) and (6.3).

Nurmeev's proof is based on Korshunov's description of the structure of almost all $f \in M_n$ (see § 5). However, the proof is technically involved.

4.7 Boolean sums and quadratic functions

In contrast with the large classes of Boolean functions, B_n and M_n, we consider here the smaller classes of k-homogeneous functions.

DEFINITION 7.1 : A Boolean function $f \in M_n$ is called k-homogeneous if all prime implicants of f are of length k. H_n^k and $H_{n,m}^k$ are the classes of k-homogeneous functions. 1-homogeneous functions are called Boolean sums, 2-homogeneous functions are called quadratic.

Important examples are the threshold functions, the Boolean matrix product and the clique functions (see Ch.6).

Since there are $\binom{n}{k}$ monoms of length k and since a k-homogeneous function is a non empty disjunction of such monoms,

$$|H_n^k| = 2^{b(n,k)} - 1 \quad \text{where} \quad b(n,k) = \binom{n}{k}. \tag{7.1}$$

(For constant k, $\binom{n}{k} = \Theta(n^k)$). With Shannon's counting argument the following lower bounds can be proved.

THEOREM 7.1 : For constant k, the (monotone) circuit size as well as the (monotone) formula size of almost all $f \in H_n^k$ is $\Omega(n^k \log^{-1} n)$.

We shall see that these bounds are asymptotically optimal for $k \geq 2$. The case $k = 1$ is treated as an exercise. At first we prove that it is sufficient to investigate the case $k = 2$.

LEMMA 7.1 : i) $C(H_n^k) \leq C_m(H_n^k)$.

ii) $C_m(H_n^k) \leq C_m(H_{n,n}^{k-1}) + 2n - 1$.

iii) $C_m(H_{n,n}^k) \leq n\, C_m(H_n^k)$.

Proof : i) and iii) are obvious by definition. For ii) let $f \in H_n^k$ and let g_i' be the disjunction of all prime implicants of f containing x_i . We factor out x_i , hence $g_i' = x_i \wedge g_i$ for some $g_i \in H_n^{k-1}$. The assertion follows, since

$$f(x) = \bigvee_{1 \leq i \leq n} x_i \wedge g_i(x) .$$

$$(7.2)$$

$\square$

By Lemma 7.1 an $O(n^2 \log^{-1} n)$ -bound for $H_{n,n}^1$ implies the same bound for H_n^2 and $O(n^k \log^{-1} n)$-bounds for $H_{n,n}^{k-1}$ and H_n^k. Savage (74) presented the following design of monotone circuits for $f \in H_{n,n}^1$. The variables are partitioned to $b = \lceil n/\lfloor \log n \rfloor \rceil$ blocks of at most $\lfloor \log n \rfloor$ variables each. All Boolean sums on each block can be computed with less than $2^{\lfloor \log n \rfloor} \leq n$ $\vee$-gates similarly to the computation of monoms in § 5 . Now each $f_i \in H_n^1$ can be computed with $b - 1$ $\vee$-gates from its subfunctions on the blocks. Since we have n outputs and b blocks, we can compute f with $(2b - 1)n$ $\vee$-gates. We combine this result with Lemma 7.1 .

THEOREM 7.2 : Each k-homogeneous function $f \in H_n^k$ can be computed by a (monotone) circuit of size $(2 + o(1))\, n^k \log^{-1} n$, if $k \geq 2$.

We note that we have designed asymptotically optimal monotone circuits for almost all $f \in H_{n,n}^1$ which consist of $\vee$-gates only. In Ch.6 we get to know some $f \in H_{n,n}^1$ such that optimal monotone circuits for f have to contain $\wedge$-gates disproving the conjecture that Boolean sums may be computed optimally using $\vee$-gates only.

Similar results for formulas are much harder to achieve. Using the MDNF of f each prime implicant requires its own $\wedge$-gate. We can compute efficiently many prime implicants by the law of distributivity. With $m+r-1$ gates we can compute mr monoms of length 2 by $(x_1 \vee \cdots \vee x_m) \wedge (x_{m+1} \vee \cdots \vee x_{m+r})$. The ratio of profit, number of monoms, and costs, number of gates, is best, if $m = r$ and m is large. It is only useful to compute monoms of length 2 which are prime implicants of f .

For $f \in H_n^2$ we consider the following graph $G(f)$ on $\{1,...,n\}$. $G(f)$ contains the edge $\{i,j\}$ iff $x_i x_j \in PI(f)$. A complete bipartite graph on disjoint m-vertex sets A and B contained in $G(f)$ is called $K_{m,m}$. Such a $K_{m,m}$ corresponds to m^2 prime implicants which can be computed with $2m-1$ gates. Since the result has to be connected with other terms, we define the cost of a $K_{m,m}$ as $2m$. If we can cover $G(f)$ by $a(m)$ copies of $K_{m,m}$ $(1 \leq m \leq n/2)$, then f can be computed by a monotone formula of size

$$\sum_{1 \leq m \leq n/2} 2\,a(m)\,m - 1 \ . \tag{7.3}$$

This suggests the following greedy algorithm. Starting with $G(f)$ search the largest complete bipartite subgraph, $K_{m,m}$, compute its edges with $2m-1$ gates, eliminate the edges of this copy of $K_{m,m}$ in $G(f)$ and continue in the same way. At the end compute the disjunction of all intermediate results. It is highly probable that the so constructed monotone formula for f will not have size larger than $O(n^2 \log^{-1} n)$. But this is difficult to prove.

Bublitz (86) investigated an algorithm that leads to monotone formulas which might be not as good as the formulas of the greedy algorithm above. For some carefully selected decreasing sequence $m(1),...,m(k)=1$ he searches always for the largest $K_{m,m}$ where m equals some $m(i)$. By this approach it is easier to estimate the efficiency of the algorithm.

THEOREM 7.3 : $L(H_n^k) \leq L_m(H_n^k) \leq 22\,n^k \log^{-1} n$, if $k \geq 2$.

Proof : By (7.2) we have to prove the claim for $k=2$ only. For $n \leq 54$ we use the MDNF of f whose size is bounded by $2\binom{n}{2} = n^2 - n$ and smaller than $22 n^2 \log^{-1} n$.

For $n \geq 55$ let $k = \log^* n$ (see Def. 4.1) and

$$m(i) = \lfloor (\log n) / (4 \log^{(k-i)} n) \rfloor \quad \text{for } 1 \leq i \leq k-2 \text{ and } m(k-1) = 1. \quad (7.4)$$

We use the approach discussed above. Let $e(i)$ be the number of edges of $G(f)$ after the elimination of all $K_{m(i),m(i)}$. Obviously $e(0) = |PI(f)| \leq \binom{n}{2}$ and by results of graph theory (see Bollobás (78))

$$e(i) \leq n^2 (m(i)/n)^{1/m(i)} \quad \text{for } 1 \leq i \leq k-2 \text{ and } e(k-1) = 0. \quad (7.5)$$

By elementary but tedious computations one can prove for $n \geq 55$ that

$$e(i) \leq n^2 / (4^i \log^{(k-i-1)} n) \quad \text{for } 0 \leq i \leq k-2. \quad (7.6)$$

After the elimination of all $K_{m(i-1),m(i-1)}$ the graph has at most $e(i-1)$ edges, each $K_{m(i),m(i)}$ has $m(i)^2$ edges, therefore the algorithm selects at most $e(i-1)/m(i)^2$ copies of $K_{m(i),m(i)}$. The cost of these subgraphs altogether is bounded by $2 e(i-1)/m(i)$. According to (7.4) and (7.6) this can be estimated by $16 n^2 / (4^{i-1} \log n)$. Summing up these terms we obtain the upper bound of $22 n^2 \log^{-1} n$.

$\square$

We emphasize the power of Shannon's counting argument which leads to asymptotically optimal results for large classes like B_n and M_n as well as for small classes like H_n^k. For almost all functions in these classes we know nearly optimal circuits.

4.8 Universal circuits

Each circuit computes a definite Boolean function. We now discuss the concept of programmable circuits, which are also called universal circuits. What does it mean to program a circuit ? How do we "read in" such a program ? The only inputs of a Boolean circuit are Boolean variables. Programmable circuits have input variables $x_1, \ldots, x_n$, the true input variables, and $y_1, \ldots, y_m$, the program variables or control bits. For each of the 2^m input vectors for y, the 2^m admissible programs, some Boolean function $f_y \in B_n$ is computed by the circuit.

DEFINITION 8.1 : A programmable circuit S is called (n,c,d)-universal if it contains n true input variables and c distinguished gates such that for each circuit S' of size $c' \leq c$ and depth $d' \leq d$ there is some admissible program such that the i-th distinguished gate of S computes the same function as the i-th gate of S' $(1 \leq i \leq c')$.

Efficient universal circuits offer the possibility of applying the same circuit to several purposes. We design two types of universal circuits. The first one is optimal with respect to size but the depth is rather large (whether it is possible to reduce depth is discussed in § 2 of Ch.7) whereas the other one is optimal with respect to depth and also is of reasonable size. Since depth and time of parallel computers are related, we refer to some papers on the construction of universal parallel computers, namely Galil and Paul (83) and Meyer auf der Heide (86).

We begin with lower bounds. Each (n,c,d)-universal circuit obviously has depth $\Omega(d)$. What about its size ?

THEOREM 8.1 : Each (n,c,∞)-universal circuit has size $\Omega(c \log c)$ if $c = O(2^n n^{-1})$.

The condition $c = O(2^n n^{-1})$ is not really to be seen as a restriction, since each $f \in B_n$ has circuit size $O(2^n n^{-1})$ (see § 2).

Proof of Theorem 8.1 : We prove the theorem by counting arguments. If the universal circuit has m control bits, it can compute at most $2^m c$ different functions. For small r, each Boolean function $f \in B_r$ has circuit size bounded by c. Due to the results of § 2 r can be chosen as $\log c + \log\log c - k$ for some appropriate constant k . In particular

$$2^m c \geq |B_r| \quad \Rightarrow \quad m + \log c \geq 2^r = \Omega(c \log c) . \tag{8.1}$$

Since $m = \Omega(c \log c)$ and since we have to consider control bits of positive fan-out only, the size of the circuit is $\Omega(c \log c)$.

□

For the construction of universal circuits we design universal gates and universal graphs. A universal gate has two true inputs x_1 and x_2 , four control bits y_1, y_2, y_3 , and y_4 and computes

$$y_1 x_1 x_2 \vee y_2 x_1 \bar{x}_2 \vee y_3 \bar{x}_1 x_2 \vee y_4 \bar{x}_1 \bar{x}_2 . \tag{8.2}$$

For each $f \in B_2$ there are control bits such that the universal gate realizes $f(x_1, x_2)$ by its DNF.

The construction of universal graphs is much more difficult. Valiant (76 b) designed universal circuits of size $O(c \log c)$ if $c \geq n$. By the results of § 4, Ch. 1, we have to consider only circuits of fan-out 2. We have to simulate the gates $G'_1, \ldots, G'_{c'}$ of each circuit S' at the distinguished gates $G_1, \ldots, G_{c'}$ of the universal circuit S . The distinguished gates of S will be universal gates, i.e. that the type of G'_i can be simulated. Since G'_j may be a direct successor of G'_i in S', if $j > i$, we have to be able to transfer the result of G_i to any other gate G_j where $j > i$. We design the universal circuit in such a way that, if G'_j is direct successor of G'_i in S' , we have a path from G_i to G_j in S such that on all edges of this graph the result of G'_i is computed. Since the successors of G'_i are different for different S', we use universal switches consisting of two true inputs x_1 and x_2, one control bit y , and two output bits computing

$$z_1 = y x_1 \vee \bar{y} x_2 \quad \text{and} \quad z_2 = \bar{y} x_1 \vee y x_2 . \tag{8.3}$$

In either case both inputs are saved, but by setting the control bit y we control in which direction the inputs are transferred to. If $y = 1$, $z_1 = x_1$ and $z_2 = x_2$, and, if $y = 0$, $z_1 = x_2$ and $z_2 = x_1$.

We are looking for an $(n+c)$-universal circuit, i.e. a directed acyclic graph G of fan-out and fan-in 2 with the following properties. There are $n+c$ distinguished nodes for n true input variables and for the simulation of c gates. Furthermore, for each circuit S' with n inputs and c gates of fan-out and fan-in 2 we may map each edge (v',w') in S' to a path from the corresponding node v to w in S such that all these paths are edge disjoint. Replacing the c distinguished nodes for the gates in S by universal gates and all not distinguished nodes by universal switches, we may simulate all circuits S'. By the following lemma we reduce the problem to the simulation of graphs of fan-out and fan-in 1.

LEMMA 8.1 : Let $G = (V,E)$ be a directed acyclic graph of fan-out and fan-in 2. Then E may be partitioned to E_1 and E_2, such that $G_i = (V,E_i)$ has fan-out and fan-in 1 for $i = 1$ and $i = 2$.

Proof : Let $V = \{a_1, \ldots, a_n\}$, $V' = \{b_1, \ldots, b_n\}$, $V'' = \{c_1, \ldots, c_n\}$ and let $G^* = (V' \cup V'', E^*)$ be the bipartite graph containing the edge (b_i, c_j) if $(a_i, a_j) \in E$. We may add some edges such that all nodes of G^* have degree 2. Then the assumptions of Lemma 5.1 are fulfilled implying the existence of n vertex disjoint edges. If E_1 contains these edges and E_2 the other edges (and if we destroy the new edges), we obtain a partition of E as required.

□

Now it is sufficient to design an $(n+c)$ - universal circuit G^* for the simulation of graphs S' with fan-out and fan-in 1, such that in G^* the fan-out and fan-in of the distinguished nodes is 1. Then we take two copies of G^* and identify the distinguished nodes. This new graph has fan-out and fan-in 2 and may simulate all circuit graphs S' with fan-out and fan-in 2 and c gates. We partition the edge set of S' by Lemma 8.1 and simulate the edges of E_1 and E_2 in the first and second copy of G^* resp. This leads to the design of a size optimal universal circuit.

THEOREM 8.2 : If $c \geq n$, (n,c,∞) - universal circuits of size $O(c \log c)$ may be designed.

Proof : According to our preliminary remarks we only have to construct graphs $U(m)$ of size $O(m \log m)$, fan-out and fan-in 2 for all nodes, fan-out and fan-in 1 for m distinguished nodes, such that all directed acyclic graphs of size m and fan-out and fan-in 1 can be simulated. For $m = 1$ a single node and for $m = 2$ two connected nodes are appropriate. For $m \geq 4$ and $m = 2k+2$, we use a recursive construction whose skeleton is given in Fig. 8.1 . The edges are directed from left to right. For $m' = m-1$ we eliminate p_m . The skeleton of $U(m)$ has to be completed by two copies of $U(k)$ on $\{q_1, \ldots, q_k\}$ and on $\{r_1, \ldots, r_k\}$. Since the q- and r-nodes have fan-out and fan-in 1 in the skeleton of $U(m)$ as well as in $U(k)$ (by induction hypothesis), these nodes have fan-out and fan-in 2 in $U(m)$. Obviously the distinguished nodes $p_1, \ldots, p_m$ have fan-out and fan-in 1 in $U(m)$.

How can we simulate directed acyclic graphs G of size m and fan-out and fan-in 1 ? We understand the pairs (p_{2i-1}, p_{2i}) of nodes as supernodes. The fan-out and fan-in of the supernodes is 2 . By Lemma 8.1 we partition the set of edges of G to E_1 and E_2 . Edges (p_{2i-1}, p_{2i}) in G are simulated directly. The edges leaving a supernode, w.l.o.g. (p_1, p_2) , can be simulated in the following way. If the edge leaving p_1 is in E_1 and the edge leaving p_2 is in E_2 (the other case is similar), we shall use edge disjoint paths from p_1 to q_1 and

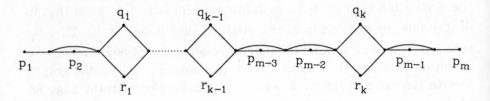

Fig. 8.1   The skeleton of $U(m)$

from p_2 to r_1 . If the edges leaving p_1 and p_2 end in the super-nodes $p_{2i-1,2i}$ and $p_{2j-1,2j}$ resp. we shall take a path from q_1 to q_{i-1} and from r_1 to r_{j-1} resp. in the appropriate $U(k)$. All these paths can be chosen edge disjoint by induction hypothesis. Finally the paths from q_{i-1} and r_{i-1} to p_{2i-1} and p_{2i} can be chosen edge disjoint. Thus the simulation is always successful.

Let $C(m)$ be the size of $U(m)$. Then, by construction

$$C(m) \leq 2C(\lceil m/2 \rceil - 1) + (5/2)m \; , \; C(1) = 1 \; , \; C(2) = 2 \; . \qquad (8.4)$$

This implies $C(m) = O(m \log m)$. In our application $m = n + c$. Since $n \leq c$, $U(n+c) = O(c \log c)$.

□

Cook and Hoover (85) designed a depth optimal universal circuit.

THEOREM 8.3 : If $c \geq n$ and $c \geq d \geq \log c$, (n,c,d) -universal circuits of size $O(c^3 d \log^{-1} c)$ and depth $O(d)$ may be designed.

The assumption $c \geq d \geq \log c$ is not really a restriction, since it is easy to see that $C(S) \geq D(S) \geq \log C(S)$ for all circuits S . Perhaps it is possible to design universal circuits of depth $O(d)$ and of smaller size. Until now we have some trade-off. If we use universal circuits of optimal depth the circuit size increases significantly. If we use the given circuits of size c and depth d , we have to pay the cost for the production of different types of circuits.

Proof of Theorem 8.3 : We want to simulate all circuits S' of size $c' \leq c$ and depth $d' \leq d$. What do we know about the depth of the i-th gate G_i' of S' ? Not much. G_i' may be a gate in depth 1 where some path of length d-1 starts. It may also be a gate in depth i . There-fore, in order to simulate all circuits S' in depth $O(d)$, we cannot wait until all possible predecessors of the i-th gate are simulated.

For some parameter h chosen later, we simulate the circuits in Step 0 ,...., Step $\lceil d/h \rceil$. Step 0 consists of the inputs of the circuit. In each further step we simulate all gates. Let $z_{i,m}$ be the simulation of the i-th gate in Step m . If the depth of the i-th gate in S' is at most mh , $z_{i,m}$ will simulate this gate correctly. Finally, each gate is simulated correctly after Step $\lceil d/h \rceil$.

We may choose $z_{i,0} = 0$. For the computation of $z_{i,m}$ we use the input variables and the simulations $z_{1,m-1}, \ldots, z_{c,m-1}$. In order to apply only correct simulations, if $z_{i,m}$ has to be correct, we look for the predecessors of the i-th gate in distance h . If a path starting from the i-th gate backwards ends after $l < h$ steps at some input, this input will be chosen 2^{h-l} times as predecessor in distance h . For each of the 2^h predecessors in distance h we have $n+c$ possibilities: $x_1, \ldots, x_n , z_{1,m-1}, \ldots, z_{c,m-1}$. We use a binary tree of depth $k = \lceil \log(n+c) \rceil$ with $n+c$ leaves for the $n+c$ possibilities. The nodes are universal selectors $yx_1 \vee \bar{y}x_2$ where y is a control bit. With these universal selector trees we may select the right predecessors in distance h . If we have to simulate the i-th gate correctly, its depth is at most mh , and the depth of its predecessors in distance h is at most $(m-1)h$, these gates are correctly simulated in the previous step.

Obviously each circuit of depth h can be simulated by a complete binary tree of depth h whose nodes are universal gates. Since we have chosen the predecessors correctly, we can compute $z_{i,m}$ by such a universal computation tree. Altogether we have designed an (n,c,d)-universal circuit.

What is the depth and size of it ? We have $\lceil d/h \rceil$ steps. Each step consists of parallel universal selector trees of depth $2\lceil \log(n+c) \rceil$ and parallel universal computation trees of depth 4h . Therefore the depth of the universal circuit is

$$\lceil d/h \rceil \, (2\lceil \log(n+c) \rceil + 4h) . \tag{8.5}$$

The depth is O(d) if $h = \Omega(\log c)$. We note that it is possible to bound the depth by approximately 6d . In each step each of the c gates is simulated by one universal computation tree of size $O(2^h)$ and 2^h universal selector trees of size $O(n+c) = O(c)$. Altogether the size may be estimated by

$$O(d\, h^{-1}\, c^2\, 2^h)\,.\tag{8.6}$$

For $h = \lceil \log c\rceil$ the size is $O(c^3\, d\, \log^{-1} c)\,.$

$\square$

If $h = \varepsilon \log c$ for some $\varepsilon > 0$, the depth still is $O(d)$ though the constant factor increases by approximately ε^{-1} but the size decreases to $O(c^{2+\varepsilon}\, d\, \log^{-1} c)\,.$

The concept of universal or programmable circuits leads to quite efficient circuit schemes.

EXERCISES

1. The Shannon effect is valid for B_n and $C_{\{\wedge,\vee,\neg\}}$.

2. Estimate $C(B_{n,m})$ for fixed m and discuss the result.

3. Prove Theorem 5.2.

4. Let $h(n) = |\Omega(n)|$. Apply Shannon's counting argument to $C_{\Omega(n)}(B_n)$. For which $h(n)$ the bounds are
    a) non exponential   b) polynomial ?

5. If $f(x) = x_{i(1)} \vee \cdots \vee x_{i(k)}$ for different $i(j)$, then $C(f) = C_m(f) = L(f) = L_m(f) = k-1$.

6. The weak Shannon effect but not the Shannon effect is valid for H_n^1 and C.

7. Define a class of Boolean functions such that Shannon's counting argument leads to much too small bounds.

8. Let $P_n^k \subseteq B_n$ be the class of functions f which may be computed by a polynomial whose monoms have not more than k literals. Estimate $C(P_n^k)$.

9. $f \in H_n^2$ can be computed with $n-1$ $\wedge$-gates.

10. Which is the smallest n such that each $f \in H_n^2$ can be computed with $n-2$ $\wedge$-gates ? (Bloniarz (79)).

11. $L_m(T_2^n) = O(n \log n)$.

12. Apply the algorithms of § 7 to T_2^n and estimate the size of the constructed formulas.

13. Estimate the depth of the universal graph $U(m)$ in § 8.

5. LOWER BOUNDS ON CIRCUIT COMPLEXITY

5.1 Discussion on methods

For almost all Boolean functions we know nearly optimal circuits (see Ch. 4). But almost all functions have circuit complexity $2^n n^{-1} + o(2^n n^{-1})$. Usually we are in another situation. The function for which we should design an efficient circuit is described by some of its properties, and it is quite easy to design a circuit of size $o(2^n n^{-1})$. For many fundamental functions (see Ch. 3) we can design circuits whose size is a polynomial of small degree. For other important functions, among them several NP-complete functions, the best known circuits have exponential size but size $2^{o(n)}$. In this situation we have to ask whether we can improve the best known circuits, and in the positive case, whether we can bound the possible improvements. For (explicitly defined) functions f we like to prove lower bounds on $C(f)$.

This is the hardest problem in the theory of Boolean functions. The results known are poor. Why is it more difficult to prove lower bounds than to prove upper bounds ? For an upper bound on $C(f)$ it is sufficient to design an efficient circuit, to prove that it computes f, and to estimate its size. We are concerned only with one circuit for f. For a lower bound on $C(f)$ it is necessary to prove that all circuits computing f have a certain circuit size. It is difficult to describe properties of all efficient circuits for f. Although e.g. subtractions and negations resp. seem to be useless for matrix multiplication, they are not useless at all. Optimal circuits cannot be designed without negations (see Ch. 3 and Ch. 6).

We used the notion "explicitly defined Boolean function" in order to exclude tricks like diagonalization. If we consider the lexicographical order on the tables of all $f_n \in B_n$ and if we define $f_n^* \in B_n$ as the lexicographically first function where $C(f_n^*) \geq 2^n n^{-1}$, we obtain by definition a sequence of hard functions. Everybody will admit that the sequence f_n^* is not "explicitly defined". We discuss this notion in § 6.

The Boolean functions we actually consider are explicitly defined. In particular, if the union of all $f_n^{-1}(1)$ is in NP , the sequence f_n is explicitly defined. Therefore, a reader who is not familiar with complexity theory should not have any problem. All functions known to him are explicitly defined, and he should not try tricks like the diagonalization trick for the definition of f_n^* above.

We need the notion "explicitly defined" to explain the poorness of the known results. Until now nobody was able to prove for some explicitly defined Boolean function $f_n \in B_n$ a lower bound on $C(f_n)$ larger than $3n$. Large lower bounds for non explicitly defined Boolean functions are easily achievable, but are of no use regarding our problem. Thus it is necessary to concentrate on the investigation of explicitly defined functions.

The situation is better for more restricted computation models. In Ch. 6, 8, 11, 12, and 14 we prove in several restricted models larger lower bounds for explicitly defined Boolean functions.

Since a long time it has been tried to prove lower bounds on circuit complexity (Yablonskii (57)). A simple but general lower bound has been derived by Lamagna and Savage (73).

DEFINITION 1.1 : $f \in B_n$ is called non degenerated if f depends essentially on all its variables, i.e. if the subfunctions of f for $x_i = 0$ and $x_i = 1$ are different.

THEOREM 1.1 : $C(f) \geq n - 1$ for any non degenerated $f \in B_n$.

Proof : We count the number of edges in an optimal circuit for f . If x_i has fan-out 0 , the output f of the circuit cannot depend essentially on x_i . If another gate than the output gate has fan-out 0 , this gate could be eliminated. Therefore the number of edges is at least

$n + c - 1$ where $c = C(f)$. Each gate has fan-in 2 implying that the number of edges equals $2c$. Hence $2c \geq n + c - 1$ and $c \geq n - 1$. □

This simple linear bound is optimal for some functions like $x_1 \oplus \cdots \oplus x_n$. Usually one does not consider degenerated one-output functions, since one can eliminate unnecessary variables. The situation is different for functions with many outputs. The Boolean matrix product consists of degenerated functions. The i-th output bit s_i of the addition function depends essentially on $x_i, y_i, \ldots, x_0, y_0$, only s_{n-1} and s_n are non degenerated. Applications and generalizations of the simple linear bound are treated in the exercises. Harper, Hsieh and Savage (75) and Hsieh (74) improved the lower bound for many functions to $(7/6)n - 1$.

The proof of Theorem 1.1 is based only on the graph structure of the circuit. The hope to prove nonlinear lower bounds by graph theoretical arguments only (described e.g. by Valiant (76 a)) has been destroyed. Though it is astonishing, graphs like superconcentrators may have linear size (Bassalygo (82), Gabber and Galil (79), Margulis (75), Pippenger (77 a)). Nevertheless graph theoretical arguments build a powerful tool for all types of lower bound proofs.

The (up to now) most successful method for general circuits is the elimination method. One replaces some variables in such a way by constants that one obtains a subfunction of the same type (in order to continue by induction) and that one may eliminate several unnecessary gates. A gate G becomes unnecessary if it computes a constant or a variable. If G is not an output gate, it becomes already unnecessary if one input is replaced by a constant. If the other input is g, the output of G is 0, 1, g or $\bar{g}$. $0,1$ and g are computed elsewhere. If G computes $\bar{g}$, we use g and change the type of the successors of G in the appropriate way. The disadvantage of this approach is that we analyze only the top of the circuit. The effect of the replacement of variables by constants on gates far off the inputs is hard to understand. This leads to the prediction that nonlinear lower bounds will not be proved by the elimination method. We discuss some applications of this method in § 2 - § 5 .

The most promising approach for the proof of nonlinear lower bounds is to analyze the value of each single gate for the computation of the considered function. Such an approach has already been suggested by Schnorr (76 b), but has been applied successfully only for monotone circuits (see Ch. 6).

In order to gather knowledge on the structure of optimal circuits one might try to characterize the class of all optimal circuits for some function. This problem is already hard. Even simple functions may have a large number of structurally different optimal circuits (see Sattler (81) and Blum and Seysen (84)).

5.2 2n - bounds by the elimination method

The first bound of size $2n - O(1)$ has been proved by Kloss and Malyshev (65). We discuss some other applications of the elimination method.

DEFINITION 2.1 : A Boolean function $f \in B_n$ belongs to the class $Q_{2,3}^n$ if for all different $i,j \in \{1,...,n\}$ we obtain at least three different subfunctions by replacing x_i and x_j by constants and if we obtain a subfunction in $Q_{2,3}^{n-1}$ (if $n \geq 4$) by replacing x_i by an appropriate constant c_i .

$Q_{2,3}^n$ is defined in such a way that a lower bound can be proved easily (Schnorr (74)).

THEOREM 2.1 : $C(f) \geq 2n - 3$ if $f \in Q_{2,3}^n$.

Proof : Each function $f \in Q_{2,3}^n$ is non degenerated. If f would not depend essentially on x_i, f could have at most two subfunctions with respect to x_i and x_j. Let G be the first gate in an optimal circuit S for f. Because of the optimality of S the predecessors of G are different variables x_i and x_j. If x_i and x_j both have fan-out 1, f depends on x_i and x_j only via G, which may compute only 0 or 1. Hence f can have at most two subfunctions with respect to x_i and x_j. W.l.o.g. we may assume that the fan-out of x_i is at least 2. If $n=3$, at least 4 edges are leaving the variables, and we may prove the existence of 3 gates by the method of Theorem 1.1. If $n \geq 4$, we replace x_i by c_i. At least the two successors of x_i can be eliminated. Furthermore we obtain a circuit for a function in $Q_{2,3}^{n-1}$ containing by induction hypothesis at least $2n-5$ gates. Therefore the original circuit contains at least $2n-3$ gates.

$\square$

COROLLARY 2.1 : The circuit size of the counting functions $C_{k,3}^n$ is at least $2n-3$ if $n \geq 3$.

Proof : By Def. 4.2, Ch. 3, $C_{k,3}^n(x) = 1$ iff $x_1 + \cdots + x_n \equiv k \mod 3$. The restrictions of $C_{k,3}^n$ with respect to x_i and x_j are the different functions $C_{k,3}^{n-2}$, $C_{k-1,3}^{n-2}$, and $C_{k-2,3}^{n-2}$. If $n \geq 4$, $C_{k,3}^{n-1}$, the subfunction of $C_{k,3}^n$ for $x_i=0$, is in $Q_{2,3}^{n-1}$.

$\square$

The following lower bound for the storage access function SA_n has been proved by Paul (77). We repeat that $SA_n(a,x) = x_{|a|}$.

THEOREM 2.2 : $C(SA_n) \geq 2n-2$.

Proof : Replacing some address variable a_i by a constant has the effect that the function becomes independent from half of the x-variables. Therefore we replace only x-variables, but this does not lead to storage access functions. In order to apply induction, we investigate a larger class of functions.

Let $F_s \subseteq B_{n+k}$ be the class of functions f such that

$$f(a_{k-1}, \ldots, a_0, x_0, \ldots, x_{n-1}) = x_{|a|} \quad \text{if} \quad |a| \in S \tag{2.1}$$

for some s-element set $S \subseteq \{0,\ldots,n-1\}$. Since $SA_n \in F_n$, it is sufficient to prove a $2s-2$ lower bound for functions in F_s . The assertion is trivial for $s = 1$. For $s \geq 2$ we prove that we obtain a circuit for a function in F_{s-1} after having eliminated 2 gates.

Case 1 : $\exists \ i \in S : x_i$ has fan-out at least 2 . Replace x_i by a constant. This eliminates at least the successors of x_i . S is replaced by $S - \{i\}$.

Case 2 : $\exists \ i \in S : x_i$ has fan-out 1 and the successor gate G is of type-$\wedge$ (see § 2, Ch.1). Then G computes $(x_i^b \wedge g^c)^d$ for some function g and some constants $b,c,d \in \{0,1\}$. If we replace x_i by $\overline{b}$, the output of G is replaced by the constant 0^d . Since the circuit computes a function in F_{s-1} , G cannot be the output gate. G and its successors, at least 2 gates, can be eliminated.

Case 3 : $\exists \ i \in S : x_i$ has fan-out 1 and the successor gate G is of type $-\oplus$ (see § 2, Ch.1). Then G computes $x_i \oplus g \oplus b$ for some function g and some constant $b \in \{0,1\}$. Again G is not the output gate. Let $j \in S - \{i\}$ and $|a| = j$. The circuit has to compute x_j independently from the value of x_i . A change of the value of x_i leads to a change of the result at G . Since for $|a| = j \in S - \{i\}$ the value of x_i does not have any influence on the output, we obtain a function in F_{s-1} , if we replace x_i by an arbitrary function. In particular, we choose the function g . Then G computes the constant b , and G and its successors, at least 2 gates, can be eliminated.

$\square$

In Ch. 3 we have proved an upper bound of $2n + O(n^{1/2})$ on $C(SA_n)$. An example where upper and lower bound exactly agree is the addition function. The $5n-3$ upper bound (Theorem 1.1, Ch.3, the school method for addition) has been proved to be optimal by Red'kin (81).

5.3 Lower bounds for some particular bases

The proof of Theorem 2.2 makes clear that type-$\oplus$ gates are more difficult to deal with than type-$\wedge$ gates. By replacing one input of a type-$\oplus$ gate by a constant it is impossible to replace its output by a constant. Therefore it is not astonishing that lower bounds for the basis $U_2 = B_2 - \{\oplus, \equiv\}$ are easier to prove. Schnorr (74) proved that parity requires in U_2-circuits three times as many gates as in B_2-circuits.

THEOREM 3.1 : For $n \geq 2$ and $c \in \{0,1\}$ the B_2-circuit complexity of the parity function $x_1 \oplus \cdots \oplus x_n \oplus c$ is $n-1$ while its U_2-circuit complexity equals $3(n-1)$.

Proof : The assertion on B_2-circuits follows from the definition and Theorem 1.1 . The upper bound for U_2-circuits follows, since $x \oplus y$ is equal to $(x \wedge \bar{y}) \vee (\bar{x} \wedge y)$. For the lower bound we prove the existence of some x_i whose replacement by a suitable constant eliminates 3 gates. This implies the assertion for $n = 2$ directly and for $n \geq 3$ by induction.

Let G be the first gate of an optimal circuit for parity. The inputs are different variables x_i and x_j. The fan-out of x_i is at least 2 . Otherwise, since G is of type-$\wedge$, we could replace x_j by a constant such that G is replaced by a constant. This would imply that the output became independent from x_i in contradiction to the definition of parity. We replace x_i by such a constant that G becomes replaced by a constant. Since parity is not replaced by a constant, G has positive fan-out. We may eliminate G and the successors of G and G', where G' is another successor of x_i . Either these are at least 3 gates, or G' is the only successor of G . Then G' as successor of G and x_i is replaced by a constant, and we can eliminate also the successors of G' . In either case we eliminate at least 3 gates. $\qquad \square$

As a further example we compute the complexity of the equality test $f_n^= \in B_{2n}$ defined by

$$f_n^=(x_1, \ldots, x_n, y_1, \ldots, y_n) = 1 \quad \text{iff} \quad (x_1, \ldots, x_n) = (y_1, \ldots, y_n). \quad (3.1)$$

THEOREM 3.2 : $C(f_n^=) = 2n - 1$ and $C_{U_2}(f_n^=) = 4n - 1$.

Proof : The upper bounds follow, since

$$f_n^=(x,y) = (x_1 \equiv y_1) \wedge \cdots \wedge (x_n \equiv y_n) \quad \text{and} \quad (3.2)$$

$$(x_i \equiv y_i) = (x_i \wedge y_i) \vee (\bar{x}_i \wedge \bar{y}_i). \quad (3.3)$$

The lower bound on $C(f_n^=)$ follows from Theorem 1.1 . The basis of the induction for the lower bound on the U_2 – complexity is contained in Theorem 3.1 .

Now it is sufficient to prove the existence of some pair (x_i, y_i) of variables and some constant c such that we may eliminate 4 gates if we replace x_i and y_i by c . Similarly to the proof of Theorem 3.1 we find some variable z , whose replacement by a suitable constant c eliminates 3 gates. Afterwards the function is not independent from the partner z' of z . Replacing z' also by c eliminates at least one further gate.

$\square$

Red'kin (73) proved that the $\{\wedge, \vee, \neg\}$ - complexity of $f_n^=$ is $5n - 1$. Furthermore parity has complexity $4(n-1)$ in $\{\wedge, \vee, \neg\}$-circuits and complexity $7(n-1)$ in $\{\wedge, \neg\}$- or $\{\vee, \neg\}$-circuits. Soprunenko (65) investigated the basis $\{NAND\}$. The complexity of $x_1 \wedge \cdots \wedge x_n$ is $2(n-1)$ whereas the complexity of $x_1 \vee \cdots \vee x_n$ is $3(n-1)$.

5.4 2.5 n - bounds for symmetric functions

The $2n$ lower bounds for B_2-circuits in § 2 were quite easy to prove. No easy proof of a larger lower bound is known. So Paul's (77) $2.5n$ bound for a generalized storage access function (of no practical relevance) was a qualitative improvement. Stockmeyer (77) applied the ideas of Paul to several fundamental symmetric functions. Here the value vector $v(f) = (v_0, \ldots, v_n)$ of a symmetric function $f \in S_n$ is written as a word $v_0 \cdots v_n$. By W we denote the words in $\{0,1\}^4$ having three different subwords of length 2. W has 8 elements, namely 0100, 0010, 0011, 0110, 1001, 1100, 1011, and 1101. Stockmeyer proved that symmetric functions where some $w \in W$ is near the middle of $v(f)$ are not very easy.

THEOREM 4.1 : If the value vector $v(f)$ of $f \in S_n$ can be written as $w'ww''$ where $w \in W$ and the length of w' as well as of w'' is at least k, f has circuit complexity at least $2n + k - 3$.

At first we apply this bound to threshold and counting functions.

COROLLARY 4.1 : $C(T_k^n) \geq 2n + \min\{k-2, n-k-1\} - 3$ if $2 \leq k \leq n-1$. In particular, $C(T_{\lceil n/2 \rceil}^n) \geq 2.5n - 5$.

Proof : $v(T_k^n) = 0^{k-2}(0011)1^{n-k-1}$ where 0^m is a word of m zeros. If $k = \lceil n/2 \rceil$, $k-2$ as well as $n-k-1$ is at least $0.5n - 2$. $\square$

COROLLARY 4.2 : $C(C_{k,m}^n) \geq 2.5n - 0.5m - 4$ if $0 \leq k < m < n$ and $m \geq 3$.

Proof : Exercise. $\square$

Proof of Theorem 4.1 : Let S_n^k be the subclass of symmetric functions $f \in S_n$ whose value vector has the form $w'ww''$ for some $w \in W$

and words w' and w" of a length of at least k . Let C(n,k) be the complexity of the easiest function in S_n^k . Then we have to prove that

$$C(n,k) \geq 2n + k - 3 .$$ (4.1)

Subfunctions of symmetric functions f are easy to describe. If $v(f) = v_0 \cdots v_n$, the subfunction of f where we replace some x_i by 0 or 1, has value vector $v_0 \cdots v_{n-1}$ or $v_1 \cdots v_n$ resp.

We prove (4.1) by induction on k . For k = 0 we prove $S_n^0 \subseteq Q_{2,3}^n$ and apply Theorem 2.1 . Since $f \in S_n^0$, $v(f)$ contains some subword $v_m v_{m+1} v_{m+2} v_{m+3} \in W$. Let f_{00} , f_{01} , and f_{11} be the subfunctions of f where we have replaced x_i and x_j both by zeros, by different values, and both by ones resp. We consider only the positions m and m + 1 of the value vectors of f_{00} , f_{01} , and f_{11} . These subwords are $v_m v_{m+1}$, $v_{m+1} v_{m+2}$ and $v_{m+2} v_{m+3}$ and by definition of W f_{00} , f_{01} and f_{11} are different. If $n \geq 4$, we may replace x_i by a constant such that $v_m \cdots v_{m+3}$ is a subword of the value vector of the produced subfunction f' . Hence $f' \in S_{n-1}^0$.

For $k \geq 1$ we prove

$$C(n,k) \geq \min \{ C(n-1,k-1) + 3 , C(n-2,k-1) + 5 \}$$ (4.2)

by the elimination method. (4.1) can be derived from (4.2) by induction. For the proof of (4.2) it is sufficient to prove that we either may eliminate 3 gates by replacing some x_i by a constant (the subfunction of f obviously is in S_{n-1}^{k-1}), or we may eliminate 5 gates by replacing some x_i and x_j by different constants (in this case the subfunction of f is in S_{n-2}^{k-1}).

We investigate an optimal circuit for $f \in S_n^k$. Furthermore we choose among all optimal circuits one where the number of edges leaving the variables is as small as possible. At the moment we may forget this condition, it will be useful in the last case of the proof. We do not replace more than 2 variables by constants. Since $k \geq 1$, $n \geq 5$ and we cannot obtain constant subfunctions. Therefore gates being replaced by constants have at least one successor which also can be eliminated.

If some variable x_i has fan-out at least 3 or fan-out 2 and some type-$\wedge$ gate as a direct successor, we may eliminate 3 gates by replacing x_i by an appropriate constant.

In all other cases we consider the first gate A of the circuit and its different inputs x_i and x_j. Since $f \in S_n^k \subseteq S_n^0 \subseteq Q_{2,3}^n$, we may conclude as in the proof of Theorem 2.1 that w.l.o.g. x_j has fan-out 2. Let C_1 be the second successor of x_j and B_1 the second successor of x_i if such a successor exists. In the following we assume the existence of B_1, otherwise the proof is easier.

By our preliminary remarks all gates A, B_1 and C_1 are type-$\oplus$ gates. Because of the optimality of the circuit $B_1 \neq C_1$. We build the maximal chain of gates $C_1, \ldots, C_q$ such that C_r is of type-$\oplus$ and is the only successor of C_{r-1}. Hence either C_q is the output gate or it is of type-$\wedge$ or it has at least two successors. Let E_r be that predecessor of C_r different from C_{r-1}. Similarly we build the chain $B_1, \ldots, B_p$. The part of the circuit we consider is described in Fig. 4.1. The label of a gate describes only the type of the gate. We rebuild this circuit such that the C - chain has length 1. It is impossible that $B_l = C_m$. Otherwise $x_i = x_j = 0$ and $x_i = x_j = 1$ would lead to the same subfunction contradicting $f \in Q_{2,3}^n$. If B_1 exists, the

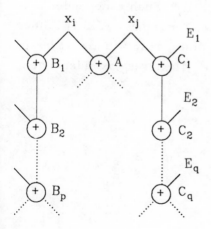

Fig. 4.1

circuit is symmetric with respect to x_i and x_j . W.l.o.g. we assume that no path leads from B_p to C_q . This implies $B_p \neq E_m$. Furthermore $B_l \neq E_m$ for $l < p$, since otherwise $B_{l+1} = C_m$. Indeed no path can lead from B_l to E_m . Such a path would pass through B_p and could be extended to C_q . Altogether the C - chain receives no information from the B - chain.

Let e_m be the function computed at E_m . At C_q we compute $x_j \oplus e_1 \oplus \cdots \oplus e_q \oplus a$ for some $a \in \{0,1\}$. The intermediate results at $C_1, \ldots, C_{q-1}$ are necessary only for the computation of the result at C_q , since all C_i $(i < q)$ have fan-out 1 . Without increasing the number of gates or the number of edges leaving the variables we rebuild the circuit by computing at some gate E the function $e_1 \oplus \cdots \oplus e_q \oplus a$ and at gate C the function $x_j \oplus res_E$. The new situation is shown in Fig. 4.2 .

Either C is the output gate or C has fan-out at least 2 or C has exactly one successor which is of type-$\wedge$. No path leads from B_1 to E . Because of the optimality of the circuit $A \neq E$.

It is essential that we do not decide which of the variables x_i and x_j is replaced by 0 and which is replaced by 1 . In place of that we replace for some appropriate $e \in \{0,1\}$ x_i by $res_E \oplus \bar{e}$. How can this be done if res_E depends on x_i and/or x_j ? Such a dependence is possible only via A where $res_A = x_i \oplus x_j \oplus c$ for some $c \in \{0,1\}$. Since x_i and x_j will be replaced by different values, res_A will always be replaced by $\bar{c}$. At first we replace A by $\bar{c}$. Then res_E is independent

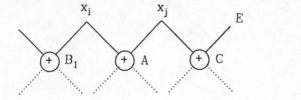

Fig. 4.2

from x_i and x_j, and we can perform the intended replacements of x_i and x_j. We obtain a subfunction $f' \in S_{n-2}^{k-1}$ of f. It is sufficient to show that we can eliminate A, C and 3 further gates. Let G be the set of direct successors of A or C. Since $A \neq E$, $A, C \notin G$. All gates in G can be eliminated, since at least one input is constant.

Case 1: $|G| \geq 3$. We eliminate at least 3 further gates.

Case 2: $|G| = 2$. Let G be a direct successor of A and $H \neq G$ be a direct successor of C. Since $|G| = 2$, the fan-out of C is bounded by 2. We distinguish three subcases as shown in Fig. 4.3.

Case 2.1: C has fan-out 2. Since res_A and res_C are constant, also res_G is constant. If $D \neq H$, we eliminate G, H and D. If $D = H$, res_D is constant, and we eliminate G, H, and the successors of H.

Case 2.2: C has fan-out 1. By construction the only successor H of C is of type-$\wedge$. We choose the constant e (see above) in such a way that H is replaced by a constant. Therefore H has a successor D.

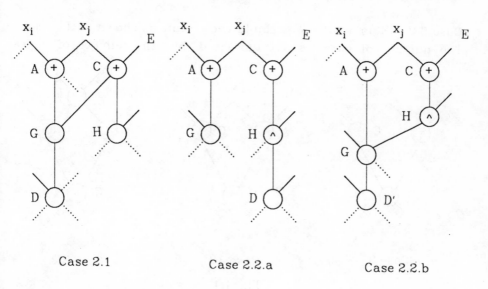

Case 2.1   Case 2.2.a   Case 2.2.b

Fig. 4.3

If $D \neq G$, we eliminate G , H , and D (Case 2.2.a). If $D = G$, res_G is constant, and we eliminate G , H , and the successors of G (Case 2.2.b).

Case 3 : $|G| = 1$. The only successor of A and C is gate G of type-$\wedge$ (see Fig. 4.4).

Case 3.1 : E is a variable, say x_m . We show that Case 3.1 is impossible. Because of the optimality of the circuit $m \notin \{i,j\}$. For suitable constants $a, b, c \in \{0,1\}$

$$\mathrm{res}_G = (x_i \oplus x_j \oplus a) \wedge (x_j \oplus x_m \oplus b) \oplus c \qquad (4.3)$$

$$= x_j (x_i \oplus x_m \oplus 1 \oplus a \oplus b) \oplus x_i x_m \oplus a x_m \oplus b x_i \oplus a b \oplus c .$$

If we replace x_i by 0 and x_m by $1 \oplus a \oplus b$, res_G and therefore the whole circuit becomes independent from x_j . But the subfunction f' of f we have to compute is not constant. Since f' is symmetric, it depends essentially on x_j . Contradiction.

Case 3.2 : E is a gate. We rebuild the circuit as shown in Fig. 4.4 . The number of gates is not increased, but the number of edges

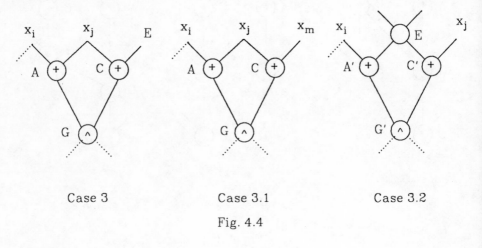

Case 3   Case 3.1   Case 3.2

Fig. 4.4

leaving variables is decreased by 1. If $\text{res}_G = \text{res}_{G'}$, this is a contradiction to our specific choice of the optimal circuit at the beginning of the proof. For suitable constants $c_0, c_1, c_2 \in \{0,1\}$

$$\text{res}_G = (x_i \oplus x_j \oplus c_0) \wedge (x_j \oplus \text{res}_E \oplus c_1) \oplus c_2 . \tag{4.4}$$

Similarly

$$\text{res}_{G'} = (x_i \oplus \text{res}_E \oplus d_0) \wedge (x_j \oplus \text{res}_E \oplus d_1) \oplus d_2 \tag{4.5}$$

where we may choose $d_0, d_1, d_2 \in \{0,1\}$ in an arbitrary way. If we define $d_0 = 1 \oplus c_0 \oplus c_1$, $d_1 = c_1$ and $d_2 = c_2$, then $\text{res}_G = \text{res}_{G'}$. Also Case 3.2 is impossible. We have proved (4.2).

$\square$

5.5 A 3n - bound

The methods of Paul (77) have been further developed by Schnorr (80) whose proof of a $3n$-bound is not complete. Blum (84) stepped into the breach. He modified the function considered by Schnorr. Then he could apply many of Schnorr's ideas in such a way that the problems in Schnorr's proof discovered by the author do not occur. In contrast to the functions considered up to now this function is of no practical relevance.

DEFINITION 5.1 : Let $n = 2^k$, $a = (a_{k-1}, \ldots, a_0)$, $b = (b_{k-1}, \ldots, b_0)$, $c = (c_{k-1}, \ldots, c_0)$, $x = (x_0, \ldots, x_{n-1})$ and p, q, r be Boolean variables. $f \in B_{n+3k+3}$ is defined by

$$f(a,b,c,p,q,r,x) = q \wedge [(x_{|a|} \wedge x_{|b|}) \vee (p \wedge x_{|b|} \wedge x_{|c|}^r)] \vee \overline{q} \wedge (x_{|a|} \oplus x_{|b|}) . \tag{5.1}$$

For $p = 0$ we obtain the function considered by Paul (77). The object of this section is the proof of the following theorem.

Theorem 5.1 : $C(f) \geq 3n - 3$.

Since f is based on the storage access function, we consider the class F_s of all functions $g \in B_{n+3k+3}$ which agree with f if $|a|, |b|, |c| \in S$ for some s -element set S . Since $f \in F_n$, it is sufficient to prove a $3s - 3$ lower bound for all $g \in F_s$. This is done by induction on s . For $s = 1$ the lower bound is trivial.
The following cases can be dealt with the methods of § 4 .

- $\exists \ i \in S :$ x_i has fan-out at least 3 .

- $\exists \ i \in S :$ x_i has fan-out 2 and some direct successor is a gate of type- $\wedge$.

- $\exists \ i \in S :$ all direct successors of x_i are gates of type- $\oplus$.

In all these cases we may replace x_i by some constant or some function $res_E \oplus e$ (for a gate E and a constant e) such that we can eliminate 3 gates and obtain a circuit for a function in F_{s-1} . The case, that each x_i has exactly one successor G_i of type- $\wedge$, cannot be excluded here as it could in § 4 . If some G_i had at least two successors, we again could eliminate 3 gates by replacing x_i by an appropriate constant. Therefore we assume that Q_i is the unique successor of the type- $\wedge$ gate G_i for $i \in S$. By G and Q we denote the sets of all G_i and Q_i .

In this last case the elimination method was not successful. By a precise analysis of the structure of optimal circuits we prove the existence of $3s - 3$ gates.

LEMMA 5.1 : G contains s gates.

Proof : Otherwise $G_i = G_j$ for some $i \neq j$. Replacing x_i by an appropriate constant the output of the circuit becomes independent from x_j in contradiction to the definition of F_s . $\square$

We introduce some notation for the analysis of optimal circuits.

DEFINITION 5.2 : A path from gate A to gate B is denoted by [A,B] . R is the output gate where the result is computed. A path [A,B] is called free if no inner node of the path is contained in G . A gate A is called split if its fan-out is at least 2 . A split B is called free if there are free paths [B,R] via at least two direct successors of B . A gate C is a collector of free paths $[G_i,R]$ and $[G_j,R]$ $(i \neq j)$ if C lies on both paths, and if the paths enter C via different edges.

LEMMA 5.2 : If $i \in S$, then there exists a free path $[G_i,R]$.

Proof : Otherwise we could replace all x_j $(j \in S - \{i\})$ in such a way by constants that res_R becomes independent from x_i in contradiction to the definition of F_s . $\square$

LEMMA 5.3 : Let C be a collector of free paths $[G_i,R]$ and $[G_j,R]$. Then at least one of the statements (*) or (**) holds :
(*) There exists a free split $B \neq C$ on $[G_i,C]$ or $[G_j,C]$.
(**) C is of type-⊕ , and there exists a free path $[G_i,G_j]$ or $[G_j,G_i]$.

Proof : We assume that (*) and (**) are both false.
Case 1 : C is of type-⊕ . We replace all variables but x_i and x_j by constants. $|a|=i$, $|b|=j$, $|c| \in S$, $p=0$, $q=1$, r and x_m $(m \notin S)$ arbitrary , x_k $(k \in S - \{i,j\})$ such that G_k computes a constant. By definition f is replaced by $x_i \wedge x_j$. Since (*) and (**) both are false, all information on x_i and x_j is transmitted via the unique free paths $[G_i,C]$ and $[G_j,C]$. One input of C is x_i^u , the other x_j^v , hence its output is $x_i \oplus x_j \oplus w$ for some $u,v,w \in \{0,1\}$. The output of C is the same for $x_i = x_j = 0$ or $x_i = x_j = 1$. The same must hold for R where $x_i \wedge x_j$ is computed. Contradiction.

Case 2 : C is of type-∧ . We replace the variables in the same way as in Case 1 with the only exception that $q=0$. Hence f is replaced by

$x_i \oplus x_j$. If the result of G_i depends essentially on x_j , we shall replace x_j by an appropriate constant such that the result at G_i and therefore the output at R become independent from x_i . This contradicts the fact that $x_i \oplus x_j$ is computed at R . Therefore the result at gate C is $(x_i^u \wedge x_j^v)^w$ for some $u, v, w \in \{0,1\}$ and all information on x_i and x_j is transmitted via C . This is the same contradiction as before, since we may replace x_j by $\bar{v}$ in order to make R independent of x_i .
$\qquad\qquad\qquad\qquad\qquad\qquad\qquad\qquad\qquad\qquad\qquad\qquad$ □

Now it is quite easy to prove that $G \cup Q$ contains exactly $2s$ gates.

Lemma 5.4 : $G \cup Q$ contains $2s$ gates.

Proof : By Lemma 5.1 , G contains s gates. If $Q_i = Q_j$ for some $i \neq j$, Q_i would be the collector of all free paths $[G_i, R]$ and $[G_j, R]$. Since statement (*) cannot hold, statement (**) of Lemma 5.3 holds. A free path $[G_i, G_j]$ passes Q_i and can be extended via G_j to $Q_j = Q_i$. The circuit would not be cycle free.

It remains to prove that $G_j \neq Q_i$. If $i = j$, this follows by definition. If $i \neq j$ and $G_j = Q_i$, all information concerning x_i is transmitted via G_j . By an appropriate replacement of x_j by a constant the circuit would become independent from x_i in contradiction to the definition of F_s .
$\qquad\qquad\qquad\qquad\qquad\qquad\qquad\qquad\qquad\qquad\qquad\qquad$ □

LEMMA 5.5 : The circuit contains at least $s - 2$ free splits.

Before we prove this essential lemma we deduce from it by a wire counting argument the theorem.

Proof of Theorem 5.1 : At least $2(s-2)$ free edges (wires) are leaving free splits by Lemma 5.5 . At least 2 of the s gates of Q do not belong to the considered $s - 2$ free splits. By Lemma 5.2 at least one free edge is leaving each Q_i . We consider the graph consisting of those $2s - 2$ free edges we have found and those free paths leading these free edges to R . By definition we do not consider any gate in G. The gates in Q are gathering at most s of these edges, since the other s input edges are entering from gates in G. In order to gather the other $s - 2$ free edges to the output R further $s - 3$ gates are necessary. □

Proof of Lemma 5.5 : We choose $j \in S$ such that G_j is the last G - gate in the numbering of the gates. In the following we refer always to the numbering of gates. Let C be the first collector of free paths $[G_k,R]$ and $[G_l,R]$ where $k,l \in S - \{j\}$ and $k \neq l$. By Lemma 5.3 we either find a free split $D \neq C$ on $[G_k,C]$ or $[G_l,C]$ or we find a free path $[G_k,G_l]$ or vice versa. By Lemma 5.2 there is a split on $[G_k,G_l]$. If we find a free split on these paths we shall choose the first free split, otherwise the first split. If the chosen split is on $[G_k,C]$ or $[G_k,G_l]$ we exclude x_k from further consideration, otherwise we exclude x_l . At the end of this procedure we have chosen $s - 2$ different splits.

We prove that we indeed have chosen $s - 2$ free splits. Otherwise for some first collector C of free paths $[G_k,R]$ and $[G_l,R]$ ($k,l \in S - \{j\}$, $k \neq l$) we cannot find any free split on $[G_k,C]$ or $[G_l,C]$. By Lemma 5.3 C is of type-$\oplus$ and w.l.o.g. the free path $[G_k,G_l]$ has no free split. We prove for all $m \in S - \{k,l\}$ (including $m = j$) the existence of a free path $[G_m,G_k]$ or $[G_m,G_l]$ in contradiction to the choice of j . We assume that this claim is false. We replace all variables but x_k, x_l, x_m and r by constants. $|a| = k$, $|b| = l$, $|c| = m$, $q = 1$, $p = 1$, x_i ($i \notin S$) arbitrary and x_i ($i \in S - \{k,l,m\}$) such that G_i is replaced by a constant. By definition R is replaced by $x_k x_l \vee x_l x_m^r$.

Case 1 : The result of G_l does not depend essentially on x_k. We replace x_m such that G_m is replaced by a constant and r such that $x_m^r = 0$. Then R is replaced by $x_k x_l$. We deduce a contradiction in the same way as in Case 1 of the proof of Lemma 5.3 .

Case 2 : The result of G_l depends essentially on x_k . Then for some $d \in \{0,1\}$ the result of G_l still depends on x_k if we replace r by d . If no free path $[G_m, G_k]$ or $[G_m, G_l]$ exists, then the function computed at G_l can be represented as $(x_k^u \wedge x_l^v)^w$ for some $u, v, w \in \{0,1\}$. If $x_k = \bar{u}$, G_l is replaced by a constant and the circuit becomes independent from x_l . But the function computed at R , namely $\bar{u} x_l \vee x_l x_m^d$, depends essentially on x_l for arbitrary u and d . Contradiction.

$\square$

The lower bound of Theorem 5.1 based on $N = n + 3k + 3$, the number of variables, is of size $3N - o(N)$.

The proofs of § 4 and § 5 are so burdensome that one is convinced that this is not the right way to obtain much larger lower bounds. But the reader should not lose his courage and try out his own ideas for the proof of lower bounds.

5.6 Complexity theory and lower bounds on circuit complexity

In § 1 we have shown that it is easy to define a sequence of provably hard functions by the simple trick of diagonalization. In this section we discuss more generally whether and how concepts (like diagonalization) and results of complexity theory may lead to lower bounds on circuit complexity. Furthermore we discuss the notion "explicitly defined". For the rest of this section we assume that the reader is familiar with fundamental concepts of complexity theory. But if the reader should not have this knowledge, this section should still give him a better understanding of the problems we are faced with.

The sequence of functions f_n^* defined by diagonalization in § 1 can be computed by a Turing machine whose working tape is $2^{O(n)}$-

bounded. For an input $x = (x_1, \ldots, x_n) \in \{0,1\}^n$ we may write the table of a function $f \in B_n$ on the working tape and can compute the lexicographical successor of f. We start with the lexicographically first function, the constant 0. For each function f we produce one after another each circuit of size $\lceil 2^n n^{-1} \rceil - 1$ and compare its output with f. If we find a circuit for f we produce the next Boolean function. Otherwise the considered function f is equal to f_n^*, and by table-look-up we compute the output $f_n^*(x)$. Therefore Turing machines with large resources are powerful enough to construct hard Boolean functions. Nevertheless explicitly defined Boolean functions are defined via Turing machines.

DEFINITION 6.1 : Let $s : \mathbb{N} \to \mathbb{N}$. The sequence $f_n \in B_n$ of Boolean functions is s-explicitly defined if the language $L = \bigcup_n f_n^{-1}(1)$ can be decided by a Turing machine whose working tape is bounded by $O(s(n))$.

Because of our above considerations we should not use exponential s. Furthermore, Scarpellini (85) has defined by diagonalization n^{k+1}-explicitly Boolean functions $f_n \in B_n$ of circuit size $\Omega(n^k \log^{-1} n)$. But many fundamental functions (those considered in Ch. 3 e.g.) can be computed on working tapes of polylog length $(O(\log^k n))$, and many NP-complete functions can be computed at least on linear working tapes. Therefore Definition 6.1 is interesting for functions s growing at most linear.

Diagonalization is not the only trick to define non explicitly hard functions (see e.g. Ehrenfeucht (72) and Stockmeyer (74)). We shall prove for a whole class of Boolean functions exponential lower bounds. These functions are not defined by diagonalization. Nevertheless they are not s-explicitly defined for any polynomial s.

DEFINITION 6.2 : A language $L \subseteq \{0,1\}^*$ is called EXP-TAPE-HARD if each language $L' \subseteq \{0,1\}^*$, which can be decided for some polynomial p by a Turing machine of working tape $2^{p(n)}$, is polynomially reducible to L (L' $\leq_p$ L) . L' $\leq_p$ L if there exists a Turing machine M whose time complexity is bounded by a polynomial and whose output $res_M(w)$ for input w is in L iff w $\in$ L' .

Meyer and Stockmeyer (72) proved that the following language L is EXP-TAPE-HARD . L consists of all binary codings of two regular expressions for the same language where the coding allows the abbreviation α^2 for the concatenation of α and α .

THEOREM 6.1 : Let L be EXP-TAPE-HARD . Let $g_n \in B_n$ be defined by $g_n^{-1}(1) = L \cap \{0,1\}^n$. Then for some d , $\varepsilon > 0$ and infinitely many n

$$C(g_n) \geq d\, 2^{n^{\varepsilon}} . \tag{6.1}$$

Proof : Let $f_n^* \in B_n$ be the sequence of Boolean functions defined by diagonalization in § 1 . Then $C(f_n^*) \geq 2^n n^{-1}$. Let L' be the union of all $f_n^{*-1}(1)$. Since L' can be decided by a $2^{O(n)}$ tape bounded Turing machine, L' $\leq_p$ L . Let M be a Turing machine for this reduction.

We design a circuit for f_n^* consisting of subcircuits for $g_1, \ldots, g_n$ and beyond that only a polynomial number of gates. Since $C(f_n^*)$ is large, some of the circuits for g-functions cannot be efficient. We apply a result which we shall prove in § 2 , Ch. 9 . If the Turing machine M^* is t(n) time bounded and decides L^* , the circuit complexity of h_n , defined by $h_n^{-1}(1) = L^* \cap \{0,1\}^n$ is bounded by $O(t(n) \log t(n))$.

Since the reduction machine M is p(n) time bounded for some polynomial p , also the length of its output is bounded by p(n) if the input w has length n . We extend the outputs, if necessary, by blanks B such that the output (for each input of length n) has length p(n) . These outputs can be encoded by $(a_1, b_1, \ldots, a_{p(n)}, b_{p(n)})$ $\in \{0,1\}^{2p(n)}$ where (a_i, b_i) is an encoding of the i-th output letter. By the result cited above all a_i and b_i can be computed by a circuit of size $O(p(n) \log p(n))$.

Now we apply in parallel the circuits $S_1, \ldots, S_{p(n)}$. S_i tests whether exactly $(a_1, b_1), \ldots, (a_i, b_i)$ are encodings of zeros and ones. It computes $x = (x_1, \ldots, x_i) \in \{0,1\}^i$ where $x_j = 1$ iff (a_j, b_j) is an encoding of 1 . Then S_i applies an optimal circuit for g_i to compute $g_i(x)$. Finally S_i computes y_i such that $y_i = 1$ iff $g_i(x) = 1$ and $res_M(w)$ has length i . Hence

$$f_n^*(w) = 1 \iff w \in L' \iff res_M(w) \in L \tag{6.2}$$

$$\iff y_1 \vee \cdots \vee y_{p(n)} = 1 \ .$$

The so constructed circuit for f_n^* contains one copy of an optimal circuit for g_i $(1 \le i \le p(n))$ and beyond that $q(n)$ gates for a polynomial q . Therefore

$$2^n n^{-1} \le C(f_n^*) \le q(n) + \sum_{1 \le i \le p(n)} C(g_i) \ . \tag{6.3}$$

We define $i(n) \in \{1, \ldots, p(n)\}$ such that $g_{i(n)}$ is one of the hardest functions among $g_1, \ldots, g_{p(n)}$. By (6.3)

$$C(g_{i(n)}) \ge (2^n n^{-1} - q(n)) / p(n) \ . \tag{6.4}$$

As the results of § 2 , Ch. 4 , show, $C(g_{i(n)})$ is bounded by $O(2^{i(n)} i(n)^{-1})$. Therefore the sequence $i(n)$ has infinitely many different values. Furthermore $i(n) \le p(n) \le c n^k$ for appropriate constants c and k implying $n \ge (i(n)/c)^{1/k}$ and

$$C(g_{i(n)}) \ge d \, 2^{(i(n))^\varepsilon} \quad \text{for some } d; \varepsilon > 0 \ . \tag{6.5}$$

$\square$

Many arguments used in this chapter have not been published. Some of them were developed during discussions with several colleagues, others, I got to know by hearsay. Some of the colleagues who have contributed to these arguments are M. Fürer, A. Meyer, W. Paul,

142

B. Scarpellini, and L. Valiant.

EXERCISES

1. Apply the simple linear bound (Theorem 1.1) to the functions considered in Ch. 3 .

2. Generalize the simple linear bound to Ω-circuits where $\Omega \subseteq B_r$.

3. If $f_1, \ldots, f_m$ are different functions

   $$C(f_1, \ldots, f_m) \geq m - 1 + \min \{C(f_1), \ldots, C(f_m)\} .$$

4. Let $g(x,y) = (\ldots(f(x) \, \Delta y_1)\ldots\Delta y_m)$ for some $\Delta \in B_2$ and some non constant f . For which Δ the equality $C(g) = C(f) + m$ holds ?

5. Let S be an optimal circuit for f with respect to circuit size. Let g and h be the input functions of the output gate. Then $\max \{C(g), C(h)\} \geq \lceil C(f) / 2 \rceil - 1$.

6. Let S be an optimal circuit for f with respect to depth. Let g and h be the input functions of the output gate. Then $\max \{D(g), D(h)\} = D(f) - 1$.

7. The fulladder for the addition of 3 bits has 5 gates. Prove that
   a) 4   b) 5   gates are necessary.

8. Let $f_n \in B_{n,2}$ be defined by $f_n(x) = (x_1 \wedge \cdots \wedge x_n, x_1 \oplus \cdots \oplus x_n)$. Then $C(f_n) = 2n - 2$.

9. Design optimal circuits for the function f_n of Exercise 8 which have (if $n \geq 3$) gates of fan-out larger than 1 .

10. Estimate the circuit complexity of f_n where $f_n(x) = 1$ iff $x_1 + \cdots + x_n$ is even (0 is not even).

11. Let $f_n(x) = (x_1 \oplus \cdots \oplus x_{n-1}) \vee (x_2 \wedge \cdots \wedge x_n)$. Then $C(f_n) = 2n - 3$.

12. Let $f_n(x) = x_1 \cdots x_n \vee \bar{x}_1 \cdots \bar{x}_n$. By the elimination method one can prove only a lower bound of size $n + \Omega(1)$. Try to prove larger lower bounds.

13. Prove lower bounds for the functions defined in the Exercises 26, 27, and 28 in Ch. 3.

14. $f_n^{\geq} \in B_{2n}$ is defined by $f_n^{\geq}(x,y) = 1$ iff $|x| \geq |y|$. The B_2-complexity of $f_n^{\geq}$ is at least $2n - 1$, its U_2-complexity is at least $4n - 3$.

15. Let G_n be the class of those functions $g \in B_n$ such that for some disjoint partition of $\{1,...,n\}$ to $\{i(1),...,i(m)\}$, $\{j(1),...,j(l)\}$ and $\{k(1),...,k(l)\}$

$$g(x) = \bigoplus_{1 \leq r \leq m} x_{i(r)} \oplus \bigoplus_{1 \leq r \leq l} x_{j(r)} x_{k(r)}.$$

Estimate the circuit complexity of functions $g \in G_{n,2}$ (Sattler (81)).

16. Almost all $f \in S_n$ have circuit complexity bounded below by $2.5n - o(n)$.

17. Count the number of $f \in S_n$ whose value vector does not contain any word in W as a subword. Design efficient circuits for these functions.

18. Prove Corollary 4.2.

19. Apply Theorem 4.1 to E_k^n (see Def. 4.2, Ch. 3).

20. Complete the proof of Theorem 5.1 .

21. Let $f_n(a,b,c,r,x) = x_{|a|}^r \wedge (x_{|b|} \oplus x_{|c|})$ (compare Def. 5.1). Modify the proof of Theorem 5.1 and prove that $C(f_n) \geq 3n - 3$.

22. Define a short 0-1-encoding of circuits. Describe how a Turing machine with short working tape can simulate encoded circuits.

6. MONOTONE CIRCUITS

6.1 Introduction

The most important incomplete basis is the monotone basis $\Omega_m = \{\wedge, \vee\}$. We know already that a Boolean function is computable over Ω_m iff it is monotone. Although monotone circuits cannot be more efficient than circuits over complete bases, the investigation of monotone circuits is a fundamental subject.

One main problem is the testing of the correctness of circuits. Monotone circuits can be tested much easier than circuits over complete bases (see e.g. Lee (78)). Furthermore, the monotone disjunctive normal form is a natural and monotone computation of a monotone function.

If we replace in a monotone disjunctive normal form for f conjunctions by multiplications and disjunctions by additions, we obtain a monotone polynomial $p(f)$. Lower bounds on the monotone circuit complexity of f imply lower bounds of the same size on the monotone arithmetic complexity of $p(f)$ (see Exercises). Monotone computations of monotone polynomials have absolute numerical stability (see e.g. Miller (75)).

Can negations be useful for the computation of monotone functions ? The best circuits for sorting and Boolean matrix product both include negations (see Ch. 3). How large is $C_m(f) / C(f)$ for these and other monotone functions ? The quotient is $\Theta(\log n)$ for sorting, $\omega(n^{1/4})$ for the Boolean matrix product, and $\Omega(n^{1/2} / (\log^2 n \log\log n))$ for the Boolean convolution (n is the number of variables). For the logical permanent (deciding whether a graph includes a perfect matching) the quotient even is superpolynomial ($n^{\Omega(\log n)}$). The question whether negation may be exponentially powerful is still not answered.

Lower bounds on $C_m(f) / C(f)$ require lower bounds on $C_m(f)$. We present several methods for the proof of polynomial lower bounds and Razborov's bound for exponential lower bounds.

Since the logical permanent (see above) has polynomial circuit complexity one might suppose that lower bounds on $C_m(f)$ cannot have any implications on $C(f)$. But for the fundamental class of slice functions f we can prove that $C_m(f) - C(f)$ is bounded by $O(n \log^2 n)$. Therefore lower bounds of size $\omega(n \log^2 n)$ on $C_m(f)$ imply lower bounds of the same size on $C(f)$. Since we know NP – complete slice functions, the $NP \neq P$ – conjecture might be proved by lower bounds on the monotone circuit complexity. From the theory of slice functions we can learn a lot about the structure of circuits, and we obtain a new model for the proof of lower bounds on the circuit complexity of explicitly defined Boolean functions.

The theory of slice functions is presented in § 13 - § 15 . In § 2 we design efficient monotone circuits for threshold functions and sorting. In § 3 - § 12 we discuss lower bound methods. The lower bounds we obtain may be generalized to many other functions by reduction methods (see also Ch. 10, § 3).

DEFINITION 1.1 : $f(x_1, \ldots, x_n)$ is called a projection of $g(y_1, \ldots, y_m)$ if $f(x_1, \ldots, x_n) = g(\sigma(y_1), \ldots, \sigma(y_m))$ for some mapping σ : $\{y_1, \ldots, y_m\} \to \{0, 1, x_1, \bar{x}_1, \ldots, x_n, \bar{x}_n\}$. The projection is monotone if $\sigma(y_j)$ $(1 \leq j \leq m)$ is not a negated variable.

PROPOSITION 1.1 : $C(f) \leq C(g)$ if f is a projection of g . $C_m(f) \leq C_m(g)$ if f is a monotone projection of g .

Skyum and Valiant (85) and Valiant (79) studied monotone projections intensively. For a sequence of functions $g_n \in B_n$ and some Boolean functions f the (monotone) P-complexity of f with respect to (g_n) is the smallest m such that f is a (monotone) projection of g_m . In this model negation can be exponentially powerful (Skyum (83)) as it can be in arithmetic computations (Valiant (80)).

At the end of this introduction we discuss some properties of monotone circuits. Why is it much more difficult to investigate $\{\wedge, \vee, \neg\}$-circuits than to investigate monotone circuits ? If $f \in B_n$ is given by $PI(f)$ it is a hard problem to compute $PI(\neg f)$. If $f, g \in M_n$ are given by $PI(f)$ and $PI(g)$ it is easy to compute $PI(f \vee g)$ and $PI(f \wedge g)$. By definition

$$f \vee g = \bigvee_{t \in PI(f)} t \vee \bigvee_{t' \in PI(g)} t' = \bigvee_{t \in PI(f) \cup PI(g)} t \ . \tag{1.1}$$

We have proved in Theorem 4.2 ,Ch. 2, that each monotone polynomial for a monotone function includes all prime implicants. Hence

$$PI(f \vee g) \subseteq PI(f) \cup PI(g) \ . \tag{1.2}$$

A monom $t \in PI(f) \cup PI(g)$ is not a prime implicant of $f \vee g$ iff some proper shortening of t is an element of $PI(f) \cup PI(g)$. Hence we obtain the following characterization of $PI(f \vee g)$.

$$PI(f \vee g) = \{t \in PI(f) \cup PI(g) \mid \nexists \ t' \in PI(f) \cup PI(g) : t \lneq t' \} \ . \tag{1.3}$$

No new prime implicant is computed at an $\vee$-gate. Similarly we conclude that

$$f \wedge g = (\bigvee_{t \in PI(f)} t) \wedge (\bigvee_{t' \in PI(g)} t') \tag{1.4}$$

$$= \bigvee_{t \in PI(f), t' \in PI(g)} t \, t'$$

and

$$PI(f \wedge g) = \{t t' \mid t \in PI(f), t' \in PI(g) , \tag{1.5}$$

$$\nexists \ u \in PI(f), u' \in PI(g) : t t' \lneq u u' \} \ .$$

We compute $PI(f \wedge g)$ by listing all $t t'$ where $t \in PI(f)$ and $t' \in PI(g)$ and by erasing afterwards all monoms for which we find a proper shortening in the list. A prime implicant t of f is also a prime implicant of $f \wedge g$ iff some (not necessarily proper) shortening t' of t is a prime implicant of g .

6.2 Design of circuits for sorting and threshold functions

The only symmetric and monotone functions are the threshold functions. The sorting function consists of all nontrivial threshold functions. The efficient computation of threshold functions by monotone circuits is fundamental for the theory of slice functions. The linear sorting circuit of Ch. 3 is not monotone. In that circuit the inputs x_i are summed up which cannot be done in monotone circuits. Most of the well-known sorting algorithms (see e.g. Aho, Hopcroft and Ullman (74)) use if−tests. These algorithms cannot be simulated by monotone circuits. But comparisons (x,y) → $(\min(x,y),\max(x,y))$ can be realized easily by two gates (x,y) → $(x \wedge y, x \vee y)$. We use these comparisons as basic gates. The variables $x_1, \ldots, x_n$ are given in an array A. The meaning of the basic step (i,j) $(1 \le i < j \le n)$ is the following. We compare $A(i)$ and $A(j)$ and store the minimum at array place i and the maximum at array place j. Algorithms of this type are called sorting networks.

It is easy to simulate the well-known bubble sort. In step k $(0 \le k \le n-2)$ we carry out the basic steps $(1,2)$, $(2,3)$, $\ldots$, $(n-k-1,n-k)$. Afterwards the $k+1$ largest inputs are in increasing order at the array places $n-k, \ldots, n$. The large inputs climb up the array like bubbles. Altogether $\binom{n}{2}$ comparisons and $n(n-1)$ monotone gates are sufficient for the computation of the sorting function. If we want to compute T_k^n we may stop the sorting algorithm after step $k-2$. T_k^n is the disjunction of the elements at the array places $1,\ldots,n+1-k$. Hence

$$C_m(T_k^n) \le 2((n-1) + \cdots + (n-k+1)) + (n-k) \qquad (2.1)$$

$$= 2(k-1)n - k^2 .$$

This result is interesting for small k. For large k we apply the duality principle for monotone functions. The dual function f_d of f is $\neg f(\bar{x}_1, \ldots, \bar{x}_n)$. By the rules of de Morgan we obtain a monotone circuit for f_d by replacing in a monotone circuit for f $\wedge$-gates by $\vee$-

gates and vice versa. Obviously $C_m(f) = C_m(f_d)$. The dual function of T_k^n is $\neg T_k^n(\bar{x}_1, \ldots, \bar{x}_n)$. $(T_k^n)_d$ computes 1 iff at most $k-1$ of the negated variables are 1 iff at least $n-k+1$ of the variables are 1. Hence $(T_k^n)_d = T_{n-k+1}^n$. We summarize our results.

PROPOSITION 2.1 : i) $C_m(T_k^n) = C_m(T_{n-k+1}^n)$.

ii) $C_m(S^n) \leq n(n-1)$.

iii) $C_m(T_k^n) \leq (2k-1)n - k^2$.

The reader is asked to look for improvements of these simple upper bounds. We present a sorting network (Batcher (68)) whose size is $O(n \log^2 n)$ and whose depth is $O(\log^2 n)$. This sorting network is based on the "sorting by merging" principle. W.l.o.g. $n = 2^k$.

ALGORITHM 2.1.a :

Input : Boolean variables $x_1, \ldots, x_n$.

Output : $S^n(x_1, \ldots, x_n) = (T_n^n(x_1, \ldots, x_n), \ldots, T_1^n(x_1, \ldots, x_n))$.

Step 1. If $n = 1$ nothing has to be done.

Step 2. If $n = 2^k > 1$ call this algorithm for $x_1, \ldots, x_{n/2}$ and for $x_{n/2+1}, \ldots, x_n$. This can be done in parallel.

Step 3. Use a merging algorithm to merge the two output sequences of Step 2 .

Batcher designed an efficient monotone merging circuit. Merging is much easier in non monotone circuits where we can simulate if-tests. Batcher's merging algorithm is recursive. Let $a_1 \leq \cdots \leq a_m$ and $b_1 \leq \cdots \leq b_m$ be the sorted input sequences. a_i may be smaller than b_1 , but a_i also may be larger than b_m . Altogether $m+1$ rank numbers are possible for a_i . We merge the subsequences of elements with odd indices and also the subsequences of elements with even indices (odd-even-merge). After having done this we still have to merge

150

two sorted lists. But only two rank numbers are possible for each element.

ALGORITHM 2.1.b :

Input : $a_1, \ldots, a_m$ and $b_1, \ldots, b_m$, two sorted lists of Boolean variables.

Output : $z_1, \ldots, z_n$ $(n = 2m)$, the sorted list of all a_i and b_j .

Step 1. If $m = 1$ one comparison is sufficient.

Step 2. If $m > 1$ call this algorithm for the sequences of all a_i (i odd) and all b_j (j odd) , and also call this algorithm for the sequences of all a_i (i even) and all b_j (j even). This can be done in parallel. Let $v_1, \ldots, v_m$ and $w_1, \ldots, w_m$ be the output sequences.

Step 3. Compute by $m-1$ (parallel) comparisons $z_1 = v_1$, $z_n = w_m$, $z_{2i} = \min(v_{i+1}, w_i)$ and $z_{2i+1} = \max(v_{i+1}, w_i)$ for $1 \le i \le m-1$.

We prove the correctness of Algorithm 2.1 . This is obvious for part a . Let k and l be the number of zeros in $(a_1, \ldots, a_m)$ and $(b_1, \ldots, b_m)$ resp. $\lceil k/2 \rceil$ of the 0-elements of the a-sequence have an odd index, and $\lfloor k/2 \rfloor$ have an even index. Hence the v-sequence contains $p = \lceil k/2 \rceil + \lceil l/2 \rceil$ zeros, and the w-sequence contains $q = \lfloor k/2 \rfloor + \lfloor l/2 \rfloor$ zeros. Obviously $0 \le p-q \le 2$. For the three possible values of $p-q$ we represent the v- and the w-sequence in such a way that w_i, which we compare with v_{i+1} in step 3, stands below v_{i+1} .

$$p$$
$$0\,0 \ldots 0\,1\,1 \ldots 1$$
$$0 \ldots 0\,0\,1 \ldots 1\,1$$
$$p-q = 0$$

$$p$$
$$0\,0 \ldots 0\,0\,1 \ldots 1$$
$$0 \ldots 0\,0\,1 \ldots 1\,1$$
$$p-q = 1$$

$$p$$
$$0\,0 \ldots 0\,0\,1 \ldots 1$$
$$0 \ldots 0\,1\,1 \ldots 1\,1$$
$$p-q = 2$$

Now it is obvious that $z_1, \ldots, z_n$ is the sorted sequence of the inputs.

What is the complexity of Batcher's algorithm ? Let $M(m)$ and $DM(m)$ be the number of comparisons and the depth of the merging algorithm for m a power of 2.

$$M(m) = 2\,M(m/2) + m - 1 \quad \text{and} \quad M(1) = 1 \text{ , hence} \qquad (2.2)$$

$$M(m) = m\log m + 1 \text{ .} \qquad (2.3)$$

$$DM(m) = DM(m/2) + 1 \qquad \text{and} \quad DM(1) = 1 \text{ , hence} \qquad (2.4)$$

$$DM(m) = \log m + 1 \text{ .} \qquad (2.5)$$

Let $S(n)$ and $DS(n)$ be the number of comparisons and the depth of Batcher's sorting algorithm for $n = 2^k$.

$$S(n) = 2\,S(n/2) + M(n/2) \quad \text{and} \quad S(1) = 0 \text{ , hence} \qquad (2.6)$$

$$S(n) = n\,(\log n)(\log n - 1)/4 + n - 1 \text{ ,} \qquad (2.7)$$

$$DS(n) = DS(n/2) + DM(n/2) \quad \text{and} \quad DS(1) = 0 \text{ , hence} \qquad (2.8)$$

$$DS(n) = (\log n)(\log n + 1)/2 \text{ .} \qquad (2.9)$$

DEFINITION 2.1 : The merging function M^n is the partial Boolean function which is equal to the sorting function if $x_1 \leq \cdots \leq x_{\lfloor n/2 \rfloor}$ and $x_{\lfloor n/2 \rfloor + 1} \leq \cdots \leq x_n$.

THEOREM 2.1 : If $n = 2^k$

$$C_m(S^n) \leq n\,(\log n)(\log n - 1)/2 + 2n - 2 \text{ ,} \qquad (2.10)$$

$$D_m(S^n) \leq (\log n)(\log n + 1)/2 \text{ ,} \qquad (2.11)$$

$$C_m(M^n) \leq n\log n - n + 2 \quad \text{and} \qquad (2.12)$$

$$D_m(M^n) \leq \log n \text{ .} \qquad (2.13)$$

Batcher's algorithm is appropriate for practical purposes. Not only $x_1, \ldots, x_n$ is sorted but also all blocks of length 2^i ($1 \leq i \leq k$)

namely $x_{j+1}, \ldots, x_{j'}$ where $j = r2^i$ $(0 \le r < 2^{k-i})$ and $j' = j + 2^i$ are sorted. In § 4 we prove that Batcher's merging algorithm is asymptotically optimal. The upper bound for sorting has been improved by Ajtai, Komlós and Szemerédi (83).

THEOREM 2.2 : One can design a sorting network of size $O(n \log n)$ and depth $O(\log n)$.

We do not present this AKS sorting network as it is rather complicated. Theorem 2.2 is a powerful theoretical result. But the AKS sorting network beats Batcher's sorting network only for very large n , in particular, only for n larger than in real life applications (see e.g. Paterson (83)). The AKS sorting network sorts the input sequence but no subsequence. It is an open problem whether Batcher's algorithm can be improved significantly for small n .

For the majority function we do not know of any monotone circuit of size $o(n \log n)$. The monotone complexity of the majority function is still unknown. For constant k we improve Proposition 2.1 . We design a monotone circuit of size $kn + o(n)$. This result has been announced by Adleman and has been proved by Dunne (84). The conjecture that $kn - o(n)$ monotone gates are necessary is also open.

THEOREM 2.3 : $C_m(T_k^n) \le kn + o(n)$ for constant k .

Proof : T_k^n is the disjunction of all monotone monoms of length k . If $B_1, \ldots, B_r$ form a partition of $X = \{x_1, \ldots, x_n\}$ the function $T_k^r(T_1(B_1), \ldots, T_1(B_r))$ has only prime implicants of length k . The number of prime implicants is large if all B_i are of almost the same size. Certainly, we do not obtain all prime implicants of length k . Therefore we use several partitions of X .

For the sake of simplicity we concentrate on those n where $n = p^k$ for some natural number p . Let $p(k) = p^k$ and $r = p(k-1)$. We prove that k partitions $B_1^q, \ldots, B_{p(k-1)}^q$ $(1 \le q \le k)$ are sufficient, namely that

$$T_k^{p(k)}(X) = \bigvee_{1 \leq q \leq k} T_k^{p(k-1)}(T_1^p(B_1^q), \ldots, T_1^p(B_{p(k-1)}^q)) .$$ (2.14)

In order to obtain all monoms of length k, we have to ensure for all different $j(1)$, ..., $j(k)$ the existence of some q such that $x_{j(1)}, \ldots, x_{j(k)}$ are elements of different sets of the q-th partition. Such a construction will be explained later. At first we estimate the size of the circuit. For the computation of T_k^p at the end we apply the circuit of Proposition 2.1 . Besides the computation of $T_k^{p(k-1)}$ we only need $k-1+k(n-p(k-1)) \leq kn$ gates. Since $p = n^{1/k}$

$$C_m(T_k^{p(k)}) \leq kn + k C_m(T_k^{p(k-1)})$$ (2.15)

$$\leq kn(1+(k/p)+(k/p)^2+\cdots) + k^{k-1}(2kp) = kn + o(n) .$$

A number $r \in \{1, \ldots, p^k\}$ or $r \in \{1, \ldots, p^{k-1}\}$ is represented by a vector $r = (r_1, \ldots, r_k) \in \{0, \ldots, p-1\}^k$ or $r = (r_1, \ldots, r_{k-1}) \in \{0, \ldots, p-1\}^{k-1}$. For $1 \leq r \leq p^{k-1}$ the set B_r^q includes the p variables x_i where $i = (r_1, \ldots, r_{q-1}, j, r_q, \ldots, r_{k-1})$ for some $0 \leq j \leq p-1$. It is obvious that the sets B_r^q $(1 \leq r \leq p^{k-1})$ build a partition of X . We claim that we find for different $j(1), \ldots, j(k) \in \{1, \ldots, p^k\}$ some q such that $x_{j(1)}, \ldots, x_{j(k)}$ are in different sets of the q-th partition.

If x_i and x_j are in the same set B_r^q , i and j agree at all but the q-th position. If $i \neq j$ and $q \neq q'$, it is impossible that $x_i, x_j \in B_r^q \cap B_{r'}^{q'}$. This proves the claim for $k=2$. For $k>2$ either $q=k$ is appropriate or two indices, w.l.o.g. $j(k-1)$ and $j(k)$, agree on all but the last position. We obtain $j'(l)$ by cancelling the last position of $j(l)$. Then $j'(k-1) = j'(k)$ and among $j'(1), \ldots, j'(k)$ are at most $k-1$ different vectors. We obtain $B_r'^q$ $(1 \leq q \leq k-1)$ by cancelling the last position of all elements in B_r^q . By induction hypothesis we find some $q \in \{1, \ldots, k-1\}$ such that for $l \neq m$ either $j'(l) = j'(m)$ or $x_{j'(l)}$ and $x_{j'(m)}$ are not in the same set $B_r'^q$. This q is appropriate. If $j'(l) = j'(m)$, $j(l)$ and $j(m)$ differ at the last position, hence $x_{j(l)}$ and $x_{j(m)}$ are for $l \neq m$ not in the same set B_r^q .

□

6.3 Lower bounds for threshold functions

We consider T_1^n, T_2^n, T_3^n and the majority function $T_{\lceil n/2 \rceil}^n$. By $C_m^\vee(f)$ and $C_m^\wedge(f)$ we denote the minimal number of $\vee$-gates and $\wedge$-gates resp. in a monotone circuit for f. In monotone circuits we cannot apply the deMorgan rules, and we cannot replace $\wedge$-gates by $\vee$-gates or vice versa. Alon and Boppana (85) proved that many $\vee$-gates are only useful if there also are several $\wedge$-gates available.

PROPOSITION 3.1 : Let $f \in M_n$. Then for $k = \max \{ C_m^\wedge(f), 1 \}$

$$C_m^\wedge(f) + C_m^\vee(f) \le C_m(f) \le kn + \binom{k-1}{2} - 1 .$$

(3.1)

Proof : The first inequality is obvious as is the second inequality for $C_m^\wedge(f) = 0$. For $C_m^\wedge(f) > 0$ let us consider a monotone circuit for f with k $\wedge$-gates, and let $f_1, \ldots, f_{k-1}$ be the outputs of the first $k-1$ $\wedge$-gates and let $f_k = f$. It is sufficient to prove that f_i can be computed out of the "inputs" $x_1, \ldots, x_n, f_1, \ldots, f_{i-1}$ with $n+i-2$ additional gates. $f_i = s_1 \vee (s_2 \wedge s_3)$ where s_j is the disjunction of some of the "inputs". If input t is in s_1, then it can be cancelled in s_2 and s_3. Hence we can choose s_1, s_2 and s_3 in such a way that each input is contained in at most one s_j. By this representation we can compute f_i with at most $n+i-2$ additional gates. $\qquad \square$

THEOREM 3.1 : i) $C_m^\wedge(T_1^n) = 0$, $C_m^\vee(T_1^n) = C_m(T_1^n) = n-1$.

ii) $C_m^\wedge(T_2^n) = \lceil \log n \rceil$, $C_m^\vee(T_2^n) = 2n-4$.

iii) $C_m(T_2^n) > 2n - 4 + \lceil \log n \rceil$.

Proof : Part i) is obvious. The first claim of Part ii) is left as an exercise. We omit the proof of Part iii) (Bloniarz (79)). Later we get to know another example where $C_m^\wedge(f) + C_m^\vee(f) < C_m(f)$.

We only prove that $C_m^v(T_2^n) = 2n - 4$. In a sorting network the following $2n - 3$ comparisons are sufficient $(1,2)$,..., $(n-1,n)$, $(1,2)$,..., $(n-2,n-1)$. We may save one v-gate, since we do not have to compute T_1^n , the maximum of the comparison $(n-1,n)$. This proves the upper bound.

The lower bound is proved by the elimination method and induction on n . The claim is obvious for $n = 2$. For $n > 2$ we consider a monotone circuit for T_2^n with the minimal number of v-gates. It is sufficient to find some i such that the replacement $x_i = 0$ eliminates at least 2 v-gates.

Let G be the first gate of the circuit. Its predecessors are different variables x_i and x_j . The outdegree of x_i is at least 2 (see Ch. 5). Each path from x_i to the output gate contains an v-gate. Otherwise $x_i = 0$ would replace T_2^n by 0 . The first v-gates on these paths may be eliminated. The only case to be considered, is that one where only one such v-gate H exists. Let I and J be the predecessors of H . If there are paths from x_i to I and from x_i to J we replace the outputs of I , J and H by 0 for $x_i = 0$. Similarly to the above arguments each path from H to the output gate contains an v-gate, and the first v-gate can also be eliminated. Otherwise there is no path from x_i to (w.l.o.g.) I . All paths from x_i to the output pass through J . In particular, there is some path from x_j via G to J consisting of $\wedge$-gates only. If $x_j = 0$, res_j is replaced by 0 , and the output becomes independent from x_i in contradiction to the fact that T_2^n is replaced by T_2^{n-1} for $x_j = 0$.

$\square$

We only cite the largest lower bounds known on $C_m(T_3^n)$ and $C_m(T_{\lceil n/2 \rceil}^n)$ (Dunne (84)).

THEOREM 3.2 : $C_m(T_3^n) \geq 2.5n - 5.5n$.

THEOREM 3.3 : $C_m(T_{\lceil n/2 \rceil}^n) \geq 3.5n - O(1)$.

We prove a weaker result containing most of the ideas of the proof of Theorem 3.3 . Theorem 3.4 combined with Theorem 3.2 leads to a $3.25\,n - 11$ lower bound on $C_m(T_{\lceil n/2\rceil})$.

THEOREM 3.4 : $C_m(T^n_{\lceil n/2\rceil}) \geq C_m(T^l_3) + 4(n-l) - 1$ for some $l \leq \lfloor n/2 \rfloor + 3$, if $n \geq 5$.

Proof : If $n = 5$ or $n = 6$ we may choose $l = n$. If $n > 6$ we apply the elimination method. We prove that we can eliminate at least 4 or 8 gates by replacing 1 or 2 variables resp. by constants. This replacement is performed until we obtain a subfunction T^l_3 , T^l_{l-2} , T^{l-1}_2 or T^{l-1}_{l-2} . In the last two cases we replace in the last step only one variable. Then we eliminate at least 3 gates. Altogether we eliminate at least $4(n-l) - 1$ gates and obtain a circuit for T^l_3 or T^l_{l-2} . By the duality principle $C_m(T^l_3) = C_m(T^l_{l-2})$. It is easy to see that $l \leq \lfloor n/2 \rfloor + 3$.

We investigate a monotone circuit for T^r_k where $3 < k < r - 2$.

Case 1 : $\exists\, x_i$: outdegree$(x_i) \geq 3$ or outdegree$(x_i) = 2$ and one of the direct successors of x_i has outdegree bounded below by 2 .

We replace x_i by a constant in such a way that a direct successor of the highest outdegree is replaced by a constant. At least 4 gates can be eliminated.

Case 2 : $\exists\, x_i$: outdegree$(x_i) = 2$ and the direct successors of x_i are of the same type, w.l.o.g. of type-$\wedge$.

We can eliminate at least 4 gates if x_i is replaced by 0 .

In all other cases we consider some gate G where a longest path of the circuit starts. The inputs of G are different variables x_i and x_j of outdegree 2 . W.l.o.g. G is of type-$\vee$. The other direct successors of x_i and x_j , namely G_1 and G_2 , are of type-$\wedge$. The gates G , G_1 and G_2 have outdegree 1 . The situation is shown in Fig. 3.1 .

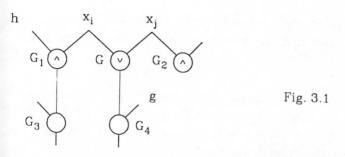

Fig. 3.1

If G_3 is of type-$\wedge$, we can eliminate at least 4 gates if $x_i = 0$. Therefore we assume that G_3 is of type-$\vee$ and, with similar arguments,
that G_4 is of type-$\wedge$. In particular $G_3 \neq G_4$. Since the longest path
of the circuit starts at G, either $g = x_k$ or $g = x_k \wedge x_l$ or $g = x_k \vee x_l$.
If $g = x_k$, outdegree $(x_k) \geq 2$. Otherwise the circuit is independent
from x_k if $x_i = x_j = 0$. If $x_k = 0$ we can eliminate at least 4 gates:
G, G_4, the direct successors of G_4 and the other direct successor of
x_k. If $g = x_k \wedge x_l$ or $g = x_k \vee x_l$ we go through the same discussion
about G', the gate where g is computed. The only situation we still
have to discuss is described in Fig. 3.2.

If $x_i = x_j = 0$, we can eliminate G, G_1, G_2 and G_5 and hence also G'.
Since G_1, G_2 and G_5 are replaced by 0, we can even eliminate 3 additional gates. If only one variable is to be replaced, we choose

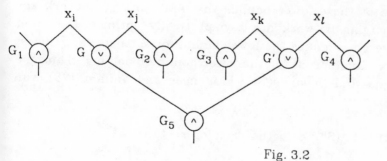

Fig. 3.2

$x_i = 0$. At least 3 gates can be eliminated. We should mention that $G_1 \ne G_2$. Otherwise the output would be independent from x_i if $x_j = x_k = x_l = 0$. □

Before Razborov's superpolynomial lower bounds were discovered (see § 10 - § 12) the following bound based on Theorem 3.1 and the duality principle was the largest one for explicitly defined monotone functions of one output (Tiekenheinrich (84)).

THEOREM 3.5 : $C_m(f) \ge 4n - 12$ for $f \in M_n$ defined by

$$f(x_1, \ldots, x_n) = T_{n-2}^{n-1}(x_1, \ldots, x_{n-1}) \vee (x_n \wedge T_2^{n-1}(x_1, \ldots, x_{n-1})) \quad (3.2)$$

Proof : $C_m^\vee(f) \ge 2(n-1) - 4 = 2n - 6$, since T_2^{n-1} is a subfunction of f (for $x_n = 1$) . $C_m^\wedge(f) \ge 2n - 6$, since T_{n-2}^{n-1} is a subfunction of f (for $x_n = 0$) and $C_m^\wedge(T_{n-2}^{n-1}) = C_m^\vee(T_2^{n-1})$ by the duality principle. □

6.4 Lower bounds for sorting and merging

We prove $\Omega(n \log n)$ lower bounds for sorting as well as for merging. Because of these lower bounds the AKS sorting network and Batcher's merging network are asymptotically optimal. The lower bound for merging implies the lower bound for sorting. Nevertheless we present a simple proof for the lower bound on sorting (Lamagna (75), Lamagna and Savage (74), Pippenger and Valiant (76), van Voorhis (72)).

THEOREM 4.1 : $C_m(S^n) \ge \log(n!) \ge n \log n - O(n)$.

Proof : $\log(n!) = n \log n - O(n)$ by Stirling's formula. We apply the elimination method. We prove the existence of some input x_i such that $\lceil \log n \rceil$ gates can be eliminated if $x_i = 0$. Afterwards the circuit computes S^{n-1}. Hence

$$C_m(S^n) \geq \lceil \log n \rceil + C_m(S^{n-1}) \geq \sum_{1 \leq i \leq n} \lceil \log i \rceil \geq \log(n!) . \qquad (4.1)$$

If $x_i = 0$, T_n^n is replaced by the constant 0. In a monotone circuit we compute the constant 0 at some gate G only if at some input of G the constant 0 is computed. By backtracking we find a path P_i from x_i to the output T_n^n such that all gates compute 0 if $x_i = 0$. Since the indegree of all gates is 2, at least one path P_i $(1 \leq i \leq n)$ is of length not smaller than $\lceil \log n \rceil$. We replace the corresponding input x_i by 0.

□

The lower bound for the merging function has been proved by Lamagna (79).

THEOREM 4.2 : $C_m(M^n) \geq (1/2)n \log n - O(n)$.

Proof : Let $n = 2k$. We only consider inputs where $x_k \leq \cdots \leq x_1$ and $y_k \leq \cdots \leq y_1$. Then the outputs are $T_1^n, \ldots, T_n^n$. $T_i^n, \ldots, T_{i+k}^n$ depend essentially on x_i. If $x_1 = \cdots = x_{i-1} = 1$, $x_{i+1} = \cdots = x_k = 0$, $y_1 = \cdots = y_j = 1$ and $y_{j+1} = \cdots = y_k = 0$, then T_{i+j}^n is equal to x_i. In this situation only the functions $0, 1$ and x_i are computed in the circuit. x_i can be computed at gate G only if at least one input equals x_i. Therefore there is some path from input x_i to output T_{i+j}^n such that at each gate on this path x_i is computed.

Let $d(i,j)$ be the length of a shortest path from x_i to T_j^n if $i \leq j \leq i+k$ and $d(i,j) = 0$ else. Let $e(j) = j$, if $j \leq k$, and $e(j) = n - j + 1$, if $j > k$. Then at least $e(j)$ x-variables are connected with output T_j^n. Hence, for fixed j, the sum of all $d(i,j)$ is the external path length of some binary tree with at least $e(j)$ leaves. The following lower bound on the external path length is well-known (or can be proved as an easy exercise).

$$\sum_{1 \le i \le k} d(i,j) \ge e(j) \lceil \log e(j) \rceil - 2^{\lceil \log e(j) \rceil} + e(j) =: t(j) . \tag{4.2}$$

Let $y_1 = \cdots = y_l = 1$ and $y_{l+1} = \cdots = y_k = 0$. Then $T_{l+1}^n, \ldots, T_{l+k}^n$ are not constant. If $x_1 = \cdots = x_k = 0$ they all compute 0 . We increase at first x_1 , then $x_2, \ldots$, then x_k from 0 to 1 . The output T_{l+i}^n switches from 0 to 1 after we have switched x_i . We find some path $p(i)$ from x_i to T_{l+i}^n such that the results at all gates switch at that moment from 0 to 1 . Because of monotonicity these paths $p(1), \ldots, p(k)$ are disjoint. Hence we have proved the existence of

$$\sum_{1 \le i \le k} d(i, i+l) \tag{4.3}$$

gates. The largest of these lower bounds is at least as large as the average lower bound.

$$C_m(M^n) \ge \frac{1}{k+1} \sum_{0 \le l \le k} \sum_{1 \le i \le k} d(i, i+l) \tag{4.4}$$

$$= \frac{1}{k+1} \sum_{1 \le j \le n} \sum_{1 \le i \le k} d(i,j) \ge \frac{1}{k+1} \sum_{1 \le j \le n} t(j)$$

$$= \frac{1}{2} n \log n - O(n)$$

by (4.2) and the definition of $e(j)$. $\qquad\qquad\square$

6.5 Replacement rules

A replacement rule for monotone circuits is a theorem of the following type: "If some monotone circuit for f computes at some gate G a function g with certain properties and if we replace gate G by a circuit for the monotone function h (depending perhaps on g), then the new circuit also computes f ." If h is a constant or a variable, the given circuit is not optimal. In particular, we obtain results on the structure of optimal monotone circuits. Later we apply replacement rules also in situations where h is a more complicated function. Nechiporuk (71) and Paterson (75) used already replacement rules. Mehlhorn and Galil (76) presented the replacement rules in the generalized form we discuss here.

It is easy to verify the correctness of the replacement rules, but it is difficult and more important to get a feeling why such replacement rules work. Let g be computed in a monotone circuit for f. If $t \in PI(g)$ but $tt' \notin PI(f)$ for all monoms t' (including the empty monom), t is of no use for the computation of f. At $\wedge$-gates t can only be lengthened. At $\vee$-gates either t is saved or t is eliminated by the law of simplification. Because of the conditions on t we have to eliminate t and all its lengthenings. Hence it is reasonable to conjecture that g can be replaced by h where $PI(h) = PI(g) - \{t\}$. If all prime implicants of f have a length of at most k and if all prime implicants of g have a length of at least $k+1$, we can apply the same replacement rule several times and can replace g by the constant 0.

THEOREM 5.1 : Let $f,g \in M_n$ and $t \in PI(g)$ where $tt' \notin PI(f)$ for all monoms t' (including the empty monom). Let h be defined by $PI(h) = PI(g) - \{t\}$. If g is computed in some monotone circuit for f and if we replace g by h the new circuit also computes f.

Proof : Let S be the given circuit for f and let S' be the new circuit computing f'. By definition $h \leq g$. Hence by monotonicity $f' \leq f$. If $f' \neq f$ we choose some input a where $f'(a) = 0$ and $f(a) = 1$. Since we have changed S only at one gate, $h(a) = 0$ and $g(a) = 1$. Since $g = h \vee t$, $t(a) = 1$. Let t^* be a prime implicant of f where $t^*(a) = 1$. We prove that t is a submonom of t^* in contradiction to the definition of t.

Let x_i be a variable in t. $a_i = 1$ since $t(a) = 1$. Let $b_i = 0$ and $b_j = a_j$ if $j \neq i$. Obviously $b \leq a$ and $t(b) = 0$. Hence $f'(b) = 0$, $h(b) = 0$ and $g(b) = 0$. For input b the circuits S and S' compute the same output since they compute the same value at that gate where they differ. Hence $f(b) = f'(b) = 0$. In particular $t^*(b) = 0$. Since b and a differ only at position i , x_i is a variable in t^* and t is a submonom of t^* . $\qquad\square$

THEOREM 5.2 : Let $g \in M_n$ be a function which is computed in some monotone circuit S for $f \in M_n$. Let t, t_1 and t_2 be monoms such that

$$tt_1 , tt_2 \in I(g) \qquad \text{and} \qquad (5.1)$$

$$\forall\ t^* \text{ monom} : t^*tt_1 , t^*tt_2 \in I(f)\ \Rightarrow\ t^*t \in I(f) . \qquad (5.2)$$

If we replace g by $h = g \vee t$ the new circuit S' also computes f .

We motivate the replacement rule by the following considerations. We assume that tt_1 and tt_2 are even prime implicants of g . Following the discussion for the first replacement rule only (not necessarily proper) lengthenings of tt_1 and tt_2 are useful for the computation of f . Since both monoms are prime implicants of the same function, " S treats tt_1 the same way as tt_2 ". By (5.2) for all common useful lengthenings of tt_1 and tt_2 already the appropriate lengthening of t is useful. In $h = g \vee t$ we replace tt_1 and tt_2 by t .

Proof of Theorem 5.2 : Let f' be the function computed by S' . $f' \geq f$ by monotonicity since $h \geq g$. If $f' \neq f$ we choose some input a where $f'(a) = 1$ and $f(a) = 0$. In particular $h(a) = 1$, $g(a) = 0$ and $t(a) = 1$. We choose $t' \in PI(f')$ where $t'(a) = 1$. If $tt' \in I(f)$, we could conclude that $f(a) = 1$ in contradiction to the construction of a . By (5.2) it is sufficient to prove $t't t_j \in I(f)$ for $j = 1$ and $j = 2$. Let b be an input where $t't t_j(b) = 1$. Then $f'(b) = 1$ (since $t' \in PI(f')$), $g(b) = 1$ (since $tt_j \in I(g)$) and $h(b) = 1$ (since $h \geq g$). For input b the circuits S and S' compute the same output since they compute the same value at that gate where they differ. Hence $f(b) = f'(b) = 1$. Altogether $t't t_j \in I(f)$ since $t't t_j(b) = 1$ implies $f(b) = 1$. $\qquad\square$

6.6 Boolean sums

A Boolean sum f with one output is the disjunction of some, e.g. s, variables. Obviously $C_m(f) = C_{\{\lor\}}(f) = s - 1$. The class of Boolean sums $f \in M_{n,n}$ with n outputs has been investigated very thoroughly, since on the one hand the complexity of each single output is well-known, but on the other hand it is difficult to determine the complexity of n – output functions. At first we prove lower bounds on $C_{\{\lor\}}(f)$, and then we prove that $\land$-gates are only of little help for Boolean sums.

DEFINITION 6.1 : A Boolean sum $f \in M_{n,n}$ is called (h,k) - disjoint, if each sample of $h + 1$ outputs has at most k common summands.

The following results are based on Mehlhorn (79) who generalized the results of Nechiporuk (71) and Wegener (80). Independently Pippenger (77) investigated $(2,2)$ - disjoint Boolean sums.

LEMMA 6.1 : Let $f = (f_1, \ldots, f_n) \in M_{n,n}$ and let f_i be a Boolean sum of s_i variables. Then

$$\sum_{1 \le i \le n} (\lceil s_i k^{-1} \rceil - 1) h^{-1} \le C_{\{\lor\}}(f) \le \sum_{1 \le i \le n} (s_i - 1) . \tag{6.1}$$

Proof : The upper bound is obvious. For the lower bound we consider an optimal $\{\lor\}$-circuit for f . The only functions computed in $\{\lor\}$-circuits are Boolean sums, since constants may be eliminated. At least $s_i - 1$ gates are necessary for the computation of f_i and at least $\lceil s_i k^{-1} \rceil - 1$ of the functions computed at these gates are Boolean sums of more than k summands. We only count these gates. By Definition 6.1 such a gate is useful for at most h outputs. Hence the lower bound follows.

□

One might conjecture that $\wedge$-gates are powerless for Boolean sums. This has been disproved by Tarjan (78).

THEOREM 6.1 : Let $f \in M_{11,14}$ be defined by

$$f_1 = p \vee y , \qquad f_2 = q \vee z , \qquad f_3 = r \vee y , \qquad f_4 = s \vee z ,$$

$$f_5 = x_1 \vee y , \qquad f_6 = x_1 \vee x_2 \vee y , \qquad f_7 = x_1 \vee x_2 \vee x_3 \vee y ,$$

$$f_8 = x_1 \vee z , \qquad f_9 = x_1 \vee x_2 \vee z , \qquad f_{10} = x_1 \vee x_2 \vee x_3 \vee z ,$$

$$f_{11} = p \vee u \vee x_1 \vee x_2 \vee x_3 \vee y , \qquad f_{12} = q \vee u \vee x_1 \vee x_2 \vee x_3 \vee z ,$$

$$f_{13} = r \vee w \vee x_1 \vee x_2 \vee x_3 \vee y , \qquad f_{14} = s \vee w \vee x_1 \vee x_2 \vee x_3 \vee z .$$

Then $C_m(f) \le 17 < 18 = C_{\{\vee\}}(f)$.

Proof : At first we compute $f_1, \ldots, f_{10}$ with 10 gates. Let

$$g = f_7 \wedge f_{10} = x_1 \vee x_2 \vee x_3 \vee yz . \tag{6.2}$$

Then

$$f_{11} = f_1 \vee (g \vee u) , \quad f_{12} = f_2 \vee (g \vee u) , \tag{6.3}$$

$$f_{13} = f_3 \vee (g \vee w) , \quad f_{14} = f_4 \vee (g \vee w) .$$

One $\wedge$-gate and 6 $\vee$-gates are sufficient for the computation of $f_{11}, \ldots, f_{14}$ if $f_1, \ldots, f_{10}$ and the variables are given. Hence $C_m(f) \le 17$. Obviously $C_{\{\vee\}}(f) \le 18$. For the lower bound it is sufficient to prove that 8 $\vee$-gates are necessary for the computation of $f_{11}, \ldots, f_{14}$ if $f_1, \ldots, f_{10}$ and the variables are given and if $\wedge$-gates are not available. This proof is left as an exercise. $\square$

This function is (see Exercises) a further example where

$$C_m^\wedge(f) + C_m^\vee(f) = 0 + 16 < 17 \le C_m(f) . \tag{6.4}$$

Now we estimate the power of $\wedge$-gates for Boolean sums.

THEOREM 6.2 : Let $f \in M_{n,n}$ be an (h,k) - disjoint Boolean sum where f_i is a Boolean sum of s_i variables. Let $h' = \max\{1, h-1\}$. Then

$$(h\,h')^{-1} \sum_{1\leq i\leq n} (\lceil s_i\,k^{-1}\rceil - 1) \leq C_m(f) \leq C_{\{v\}}(f) \leq \sum_{1\leq i\leq n} (s_i - 1) . \qquad (6.5)$$

Proof : We only have to prove the lower bound. We represent $g \in M_n$ as $g_1 \vee g_2$ where g_1 consists of the prime implicants of g of length 1. All prime implicants of the outputs f_i are of length 1. By our first replacement rule (Theorem 5.1) we can replace g by g_1. If g_1 is a constant or a variable we save the gate for the computation of g. If g_1 is a Boolean sum of two variables we replace the gate for the computation of g by a gate for the computation of g_1. If g_1 is a sum of more than two variables it might be expensive to compute g_1. For such a situation Wegener (80) introduced the assumption that some functions besides the variables are given for nothing. Here this is the class of all Boolean sums of at most k variables. The set of functions given for nothing is to be chosen carefully. If the set is too large, it may be easy to compute f. It the set is too small, we cannot apply the replacement rules in sufficiently many situations. Let C_m^* and $C_{\{v\}}^*$ denote the complexity measures C_m and $C_{\{v\}}$ if the Boolean sums of at most k variables are given for nothing. By the same arguments as before we prove the bounds of (6.1) also for $C_{\{v\}}^*(f)$.

Let us consider an optimal monotone $*$-circuit for f. Let a and b be the number of $\vee$- and $\wedge$-gates resp. in this circuit. We prove that we can replace each $\wedge$-gate by at most h new $\vee$-gates. After such a replacement we can even eliminate some other gate. At the end of this procedure we obtain a $*$-circuit over the basis $\{v\}$ for f. Hence

$$C_{\{v\}}^*(f) \leq a + (h-1)b \leq h'(a+b) = h'\,C_m^*(f) \leq h'\,C_m(f) . \qquad (6.6)$$

Applying Lemma 6.1 in its generalized form, we obtain the lower bound (6.5).

We always replace the last $\wedge$-gate G where g is computed and s and t are input functions. Again we represent $g = g_1 \vee g_2$. If the number of prime implicants of g_1 is at most k we replace g by g_1

which is given as input of the *-circuit. In this case we are done.

In the other case let w.l.o.g. $f_1, \ldots, f_l$ be the outputs which are successors of G. Since the prime implicants of g_1 have length 1, and since no $\wedge$-gate is a successor of G, the outputs $f_1, \ldots, f_l$ have the prime implicants of g_1 in common. These are more than k variables. $l \leq h$, since f is (h,k)-disjoint. We replace gate G by the constant 0. Then f_j $(1 \leq j \leq l)$ is replaced by h_j. We claim that

$$f_j = s \vee h_j \quad \text{or} \quad f_j = t \vee h_j \quad \text{for} \quad j \in \{1, \ldots, l\}. \tag{6.7}$$

By (6.7) we can replace G by at most $l \leq h$ $\vee$-gates. Since G is replaced by 0 we can eliminate also the direct successors of G. If G has no direct successor, $h_j = 0$ and we need no new gate. Altogether it is sufficient to prove (6.7).

$f_j \leq s \vee h_j$ and $f_j \leq t \vee h_j$, since $f_j = g \vee h_j$ and $g = s \wedge t$. If (6.7) does not hold, we can choose inputs a and b where $f_j(a) = f_j(b) = 0$ but $(s \vee h_j)(a) = (t \vee h_j)(b) = 1$. Let input c be defined by $c_i = a_i \vee b_i$. $(s \vee h_j)(c) = (t \vee h_j)(c) = 1$, since $c \geq a$ and $c \geq b$. Furthermore

$$f_j(c) = (g \vee h_j)(c) = [(s \wedge t) \vee h_j](c) = 1. \tag{6.8}$$

Hence $x_i \in PI(f_j)$ and $c_i = 1$ for some i. By definition of c either $a_i = 1$ or $b_i = 1$ in contradiction to the fact that $f_j(a) = f_j(b) = 0$. For this last argument it is essential that f_j is a Boolean sum. $\quad\square$

COROLLARY 6.1 : Optimal monotone circuits for $(1,1)$ - disjoint Boolean sums consist of $\vee$-gates only.

The explicit construction of (h,k)-disjoint Boolean sums which maximize $s_1 + \cdots + s_n$ is equivalent to the explicit solution of Zarankiewicz's problem. A Boolean sum $f \in M_{n,n}$ can be represented by a bipartite graph $G(f)$ on the vertices $x_1, \ldots, x_n$ and $f_1, \ldots, f_n$. $G(f)$ contains the edge (f_i, x_j) iff $x_j \in PI(f_i)$. f is (h,k)-disjoint iff $G(f)$ does not contain any complete bipartite graph $K_{h+1,k+1}$. Such a $K_{h+1,k+1}$ consists of $h+1$ vertices of the first and $k+1$ vertices of the second class such that all edges between these vertices exist. Let $z(n,j)$ be the maximal number of edges in a bipartite graph G where G does not contain any $K_{j,j}$ and G consists of $2n$ vertices. It is known (see Bollobás (78)) that

$$\lfloor (1 - (\frac{1}{j!})^2) \, n^{2-2/(j+1)} \rfloor \, \le \, z(n,j) \, < \, (j-1)^{1/j} \, n^{2-1/j} + \frac{t-1}{2} n \,. \qquad (6.9)$$

In general it is not known how to construct such graphs. Constructive solutions are only known for $j=2$ (Kovari, Sós and Turán (54)) and $j=3$ (Brown (66)).

COROLLARY 6.2 : We can define explicitly $(1,1)$ - disjoint and $(2,2)$ - disjoint Boolean sums whose monotone complexity is $\Theta(n^{3/2})$ and $\Theta(n^{5/3})$ resp.

We present only the construction of the most complex $(1,1)$ - disjoint Boolean sums. Let $n = p^2$ for some prime number p . The construction is based on the fact that straight lines in $\mathbb{Z}_p$ intersect in at most one point (projective geometry). For later applications we present the Boolean sum or the corresponding bipartite graph by an $n \times n$ - matrix M with elements in $\{0,1\}$. $M(i,j) = 1$ iff $x_j \in PI(f_i)$ for $0 \le i,j < n$. Let $i = a+bp$ and $j = c+dp$ for $0 \le a,b,c,d < p$. Then $M(i,j) = 1$ iff $c \equiv a+bd \bmod p$. This definition is illustrated by the submatrix $M_{b,d}$ of all elements with constant b and d . Then

$$M_{b,d} = \begin{bmatrix} \overset{q}{\begin{array}{c} \end{array}} \\ 0\,0\,\cdots\,0\,1\,0\,0\,\cdots\,0 \\ 0\,0\,\cdots\,0\,0\,1\,0\,\cdots\,0 \\ \hline 0\,0\,\cdots\,0\,0\,0\,0\,\cdots\,1 \\ 1\,0\,\cdots\,0\,0\,0\,0\,\cdots\,0 \\ \hline 0\,0\,\cdots\,1\,0\,0\,0\,\cdots\,0 \end{bmatrix} \quad q \equiv b\,d \bmod p \,. \qquad (6.10)$$

The corresponding Boolean sums are $(1,1)$-disjoint. Otherwise we could find some $i_k = a_k + b_k p$ and $j_l = c_l + d_l p$ $(1 \le k,l \le 2)$ such that $i_1 \neq i_2$, $j_1 \neq j_2$ and $M(i_k, j_l) = 1$.
By definition

$$c_l \equiv a_k + b_k\, d_l \bmod p \quad \text{for} \quad 1 \le k, l \le 2 \quad \text{and} \tag{6.11}$$

$$b_1(d_1 - d_2) \equiv c_1 - c_2 \equiv b_2(d_1 - d_2) \bmod p . \tag{6.12}$$

Since p is prime either $b_1 = b_2$ or $d_1 = d_2$. Either both rows or both columns belong to the same submatrices. But by (6.10) these submatrices do not have two ones in the same row or in the same column. The Boolean sums are $(1,1)$ - disjoint and each f_i is the sum of p variables. By Theorem 6.2 $C_m(i)$ is equal to $n(p-1) = n^{3/2} - n$.

6.7 Boolean convolution

We repeat the definition of the Boolean convolution.

$$f_k(x_0, \ldots, x_{n-1}, y_0, \ldots, y_{n-1}) = \bigvee_{i+j=k} x_i\, y_j \quad (0 \le k \le 2n-2) . \tag{7.1}$$

By (7.1) $2n^2 - 2n - 1$ gates suffice. One conjectures that this number of gates is also necessary in monotone circuits. Negations are powerful for the Boolean convolution. By the results of Ch. 3 we compute the Boolean convolution if we multiply the binary numbers

$$x' = \sum_{0 \le i < n} x_i\, 2^{ki} \quad \text{and} \quad y' = \sum_{0 \le i < n} y_i\, 2^{ki}$$

where $k = \lceil \log n \rceil + 1$, i.e. we separate x_i and x_{i+1} by $\lceil \log n \rceil$ zeros. x' and y' are binary numbers of length $\Theta(n \log n)$ and can be multiplied by the method of Schönhage and Strassen with $O(n \log^2 n \log\log n)$ gates.

For the monotone complexity of the Boolean convolution several lower bounds have been proved, namely lower bounds of size $n \log n$ (Pippenger and Valiant (76)), $n^{4/3}$ (Blum (85)), and $n^{3/2}$ (Weiß (83)), see also Wegener (84 b) when comparing the methods. Weiß applies the elimination method in conjunction with information flow arguments. We investigate a larger class of functions since the subfunctions of the Boolean convolution are not convolution functions.

DEFINITION 7.1 : A monotone function $f : X \cup Y \rightarrow \{0,1\}^m$ is bilinear if each prime implicant of f consists of one x-variable and one y-variable. f is even semi - disjoint if $PI(f_i) \cap PI(f_j) = \phi$ for $i \neq j$ and each variable is contained in at most one prime implicant of each output.

Obviously the Boolean convolution is a semi - disjoint bilinear form.

THEOREM 7.1 : Let f be a semi-disjoint bilinear form and let r_i be the number of outputs depending essentially on x_i . Then

$$C_m(f) \geq \sum_{1 \leq i \leq n} r_i^{1/2} .$$

$$(7.2)$$

COROLLARY 7.1 : The monotone complexity of the Boolean convolution is at least $n^{3/2}$ while its circuit complexity is $O(n \log^2 n \log \log n)$.

Proof of Theorem 7.1 : If we replace x_1 by 0 we obtain a subfunction of f which is a semi-disjoint bilinear form with unchanged parameters $r_2, \ldots, r_n$. Therefore it is sufficient to prove that we can eliminate at least $r_1^{1/2}$ gates if $x_1 = 0$. Let s_1 be the number of outputs depending essentially on x_1 and consisting of only one prime implicant. If $x_1 = 0$ we can eliminate those s_1 $\wedge$-gates where such outputs are computed. In the following we eliminate at least $(r_1 - s_1)^{1/2}$ v-gates, altogether at least $r_1^{1/2}$ gates.

We consider only outputs f_k that depend essentially on x_1 and have more than one prime implicant. Let $G_0, \ldots, G_m$ be a path from x_1 to f_k . This path includes at least one v-gate G_l where $x_i y_j$ for some $i \neq 1$ and some j is an implicant of the computed function g_l . Otherwise each prime implicant of g_l would include either x_1 or two x-variables or two y-variables. For $x_1 = 0$ g_l could be replaced by Theorem 5.1 by 0 and this would also hold for f_k in contradiction to the assumptions.

Let G^* be the set of all first v-gates on the paths from x_1 to the considered outputs f_k where some $x_i y_j$ for $i \neq 1$ is implicant. By our above-mentioned arguments one input of each gate in G^* can be replaced by 0 if $x_1 = 0$. Therefore all gates in G^* can be eliminated if $x_1 = 0$. The gates in G^* form a bottleneck. We prove that this bottleneck cannot be too tight.

Let $G^* = \{G_1, \ldots, G_p\}$. We choose $i(1),\ldots,i(p) \neq 1$ and $j(1),\ldots,j(p)$ such that $x_{i(l)} y_{j(l)} \in I(g_l)$ where g_l is computed at G_l. If $x_{i(l)} = y_{j(l)} = 1$ for $1 \leq l \leq p$ all gates in G^* compute the constant 1. The output f_k does not depend on x_1 any longer. Let s be chosen such that $x_1 y_s \in PI(f_k)$. Since variables are only replaced by ones, either f_k is replaced by 1 or f_k is replaced by a function f_k' where $y_s \in PI(f_k')$. The second possibility would imply that $x_{i(l)} y_s \in PI(f_k)$ for some l. This contradicts the definition of semi-disjoint bilinear forms since $i(l) \neq 1$. Hence f_k is replaced by 1 and $x_{i(l)} y_{j(m)} \in PI(f_k)$ for some $1 \leq l,m \leq p$. This conclusion holds for all $r_1 - s_1$ outputs considered.

Due to the definition of semi-disjoint bilinear forms the prime implicants are different for different outputs. Only p^2 different prime implicants can be constructed from the chosen p x-variables and p y-variables. Hence $p^2 \geq r_1 - s_1$ and $|G^*| = p \geq (r_1 - s_1)^{1/2}$ □

6.8 Boolean matrix product

The Boolean (I,J,K) - matrix product f_{IJK} of an $I \times K$-matrix and a $K \times J$-matrix is defined by

$$z_{ij} = \bigvee_{1 \le k \le K} x_{ik} y_{kj} \quad (1 \le i \le I, 1 \le j \le J).$$

(8.1)

THEOREM 8.1 : $C_m^{\vee}(f_{IJK}) = IJ(K-1)$, $C_m^{\wedge}(f_{IJK}) = IJK$ and $C_m(f_{IJK}) = 2IJK - IJ$.

The upper bounds follow from definition. Pratt (75 a) proved the necessity of $IJK/2$ $\wedge$-gates, before Paterson (75) and Mehlhorn and Galil (76) proved independently the exact bounds. The proof of the lower bound for $\vee$-gates can be simplified by using the methods of Weiß (83) (see § 7). Before we prove Theorem 8.1 we investigate the Boolean matrix product f_n of two $n \times n$ - matrices. By Theorem 8.1 $C_m(f_n) = 2n^3 - n^2$ and by the results of Ch. 3 $C(f_n) = O(n^c)$ for some constant $c < 5/2$. Since f_n is defined on $2n^2$ variables and has n^2 outputs we should express the bounds in dependence of $N = n^2$.

COROLLARY 8.1 : The monotone complexity of the Boolean matrix product $f_n \in M_{2N,N}$ is $2N^{3/2} - N$ while its circuit complexity is $O(N^c)$ for some $c < 5/4$.

Proof of Theorem 8.1 , $\vee$-gates : It is obvious that the Boolean matrix product is a semi-disjoint bilinear form. But the lower bound of Theorem 7.1 is not sharp enough for our purposes. We prove that we can always eliminate at least J $\vee$-gates if we replace x_{ik} $(1 \le i \le I, 1 \le k \le K-1)$ by 0 . There are J outputs z_{ij} $(1 \le j \le J)$ that depend essentially on x_{ik} and have at least two prime implicants. We prove that the bottleneck G^* of Theorem 7.1 has at least J gates.

Let $G^* = \{G_1, \ldots, G_p\}$ be the bottleneck for x_{ik} . Then we find sets X^* and Y^* of p x-variables and p y-variables resp. such that the replacement of these variables by ones forces all z_{ij} $(1 \le j \le J)$ to compute 1 . Hence Y^* contains some $y_{k(j),j}$ $(1 \le j \le J)$ and $|G^*| = p \ge J$.

□

For the lower bound on the number of $\land$-gates we apply the second replacement rule of Theorem 5.2 .

DEFINITION 8.1 : The variables x_{ik} ($1 \leq i \leq I$) and y_{kj} ($1 \leq j \leq J$) are called variables of type k .

LEMMA 8.1 : Let g be computed in a monotone circuit for the Boolean matrix product. If two different variables of type k are prime implicants of g , g can be replaced by the constant 1 .

Proof : Let $t_1, t_2 \in PI(g)$ be variables of type k . If $t = 1$, tt_1 , $tt_2 \in PI(g)$. In order to apply Theorem 5.2 we only have to establish (5.2). Let t^* be a monom and z_{ij} be an output where $t^* tt_1, t^* tt_2 \in I(z_{ij})$. Hence for some k' and k'' $t^* tt_1$ is a lengthening of $x_{ik'} y_{k'j}$ and $t^* tt_2$ is a lengthening of $x_{ik''} y_{k''j}$. If already $t^* t$ is a lengthening of one of these monoms, $t^* t \in I(z_{ij})$, and we have proved (5.2) . Otherwise $k' = k = k''$, since t_1 and t_2 are variables of type k . $t^* tt_1$ and $t^* tt_2$ are lengthenings of $x_{ik} y_{kj}$ but $t^* t$ is not. Since $t_1 \neq t_2$, $t_1 = x_{ik}$ and $t_2 = y_{kj}$ or vice versa. To make $x_{ik} y_{kj}$ a part of $t^* tt_1$ and $t^* tt_2$, x_{ik} and y_{kj} have to be members of $t^* t$ and $t^* t \in I(z_{ij})$. $\square$

Proof of Theorem 8.1 , $\land$**-gates** : We replace all x_{i1} ($1 \leq i \leq I$) by 1 and all y_{1j} ($1 \leq j \leq J$) by 0 . Then the circuit computes an $(I, J, K-1)$ - matrix product and we can proceed by induction. It is sufficient to prove that we can eliminate at least IJ $\land$-gates by the replacement considered.

Let G_{ij} be the first gate where we compute a function g_{ij} such that $x_{i1} y_{1j} \in PI(g_{ij})$. By definition of z_{ij}, G_{ij} is well defined, and because of the considerations of § 1 G_{ij} is an $\land$-gate (at $\lor$-gates no new prime implicant is created). Let g_1 and g_2 be the inputs of G_{ij} . By definition of G_{ij} and (1.5) w.l.o.g. $t_1 = x_{i1} \in PI(g_1)$ and $t_2 = y_{1j} \in$

$PI(g_2)$. If $x_{i1} = 1$, g_1 is replaced by 1 and G_{ij} can be eliminated. It is sufficient to prove that $G_{ij} \neq G_{i'j'}$ if $(i,j) \neq (i',j')$. Otherwise each variable $x_{i1}, x_{i'1}, y_{1j}$ and $y_{1j'}$ of type 1 is a prime implicant of g_1 or g_2. Since $i \neq i'$ or $j \neq j'$, either g_1 or g_2 has two different variables of type 1 as prime implicant. This input can be replaced by 1 (see Lemma 8.1). W.l.o.g. we assume that such replacements are done in advance.

$\square$

6.9 A generalized Boolean matrix product

Several new methods for the proof of lower bounds on the complexity of monotone circuits have been developed during the investigation of the following generalized Boolean matrix product (Wegener (79 a) and (82 a)). Let Y be the Boolean matrix product of matrix X_1 and the transposed of matrix X_2 . $y_{ij} = 1$ iff the i-th row of X_1 and the j-th row of X_2 "have a common 1" . This consideration of the Boolean matrix product can be generalized to a "direct" matrix product of m $M \times N$ - matrices $X_1, \ldots, X_m$. For each choice of one row of each matrix the corresponding output computes 1 iff the chosen rows have a common 1 .

DEFINITION 9.1 : The generalized Boolean matrix product f_{MN}^m is a monotone function on mMN variables with M^m outputs $(m, M \geq 2)$. The variables form m $M \times N$ - matrices. x_{hl}^i is the element of the i-th matrix at position (h, l). x_{hl}^i is a variable of type l.
For $1 \leq h_1, \ldots, h_m \leq M$ let

$$y_{h_1, \ldots, h_m} = \bigvee_{1 \leq l \leq N} x_{h_1 l}^1 x_{h_2 l}^2 \cdots x_{h_m l}^m . \tag{9.1}$$

$(h_1, \ldots, h_m, l) = x_{h_1 l}^1 \cdots x_{h_m l}^m$ is a prime implicant of type l .

THEOREM 9.1 : $C_m(f_{MN}^m) \leq NM^m(2+(M-1)^{-1}) \leq 3NM^m$.

Proof : NM^i ∧-gates are sufficient to compute all $(h_1, \ldots, h_i, l)$ if all $(1, \ldots, h_{i-1}, l)$ are already computed. Hence the number of ∧-gates may be estimated by

$$N \sum_{2 \leq i \leq m} M^i \leq N(M^{m+1}-1)(M-1)^{-1} \leq NM^m(1+(M-1)^{-1}) . \qquad (9.2)$$

Afterwards each output can be computed with $N-1$ ∨-gates. □

It is possible to save a small amount of the ∧-gates. For the simple Boolean matrix product we proved in § 8 that one ∧-gate is necessary for each prime implicant, and that K-1 ∨-gates are necessary for outputs with K prime implicants. If we could generalize these ideas to f_{MN}^m , we would obtain the following lower bounds: NM^m on the number of ∧-gates and $(N-1)M^m$ on the number of ∨-gates. It was proved (Wegener (79 a)) that the number of ∨-gates can be reduced (for m constant and M large) approximately to $NM^m(m-1)^{-1}$ (see Exercises). No good lower bound on the number of ∨-gates is known. We can prove the necessity of $(1/2)NM^m$ ∧-gates. At first we carry out an analysis of the structure of optimal monotone circuits for f_{MN}^m . Again we apply replacement rules. Notation: $x_{0l}^i = 1$.

LEMMA 9.1 : Let g be computed in a monotone circuit for f_{MN}^m . Let $(i_1, \ldots, i_m, l)$, $(j_1, \ldots, j_m, l) \in PI(g)$ for some $l \in \{1, \ldots, N\}$ and $i_k, j_k \in \{0,1,\ldots,M\}$. Let $A = \{k \mid i_k = j_k\}$, and let t be the conjunction of all $x_{i_k l}^k$ where $k \in A$. Then g can be replaced by $h = g \vee t$.

Proof : Let $t_1 = \bigwedge_{k \notin A} x_{i_k l}^k$ and $t_2 = \bigwedge_{k \notin A} x_{j_k l}^k$. By definition of A , t_1 and t_2 have no common variable. According to Theorem 5.2 it is sufficient to prove (5.1) and (5.2) . (5.1) is fulfilled by assumption. If

(5.2) was not fulfilled, we would choose a monom t^* and an output $(h_1, \ldots, h_m) = y_{h_1, \ldots, h_m}$ such that t^*tt_1 and t^*tt_2 are implicants of $(h_1, \ldots, h_m)$ but t^*t is not. Then t^*tt_1 includes some $(h_1, \ldots, h_m, l')$ but t^*t does not include $(h_1, \ldots, h_m, l')$. Hence $l = l'$. The same holds for t^*tt_2. That means $(h_1, \ldots, h_m, l)$ is a submonom of t^*tt_1 and t^*tt_2 but not of t^*t. The variable that is not included in t^*t is a common variable of t_1 and t_2 in contradiction to the definition of t_1 and t_2. $\qquad\Box$

We interpret this lemma. A monom is "useful" for some f_{MN}^m if it is a (not necessarily proper) shortening of a prime implicant of f_{MN}^m. If g includes several useful monoms of type l, we can replace g by $g \vee t$ where t is the common part of all useful monoms of type l, i.e. t is the monom consisting of all variables which are members of all useful monoms of type l. The replacement of g by $g \vee t$ should not cause any costs. Therefore we do not count $\vee$-gates and assume that all monoms of less than m variables are given as inputs. The length of a useful monom is bounded by m and the common part of different useful monoms includes less than m variables.

Circuits in this model (only $\wedge$-gates are counted, monoms of length less than m are given as inputs) are called $*$-circuits, the appropriate complexity measure is C_m^*. A $*$-circuit S for f_{MN}^m can now be transformed into a "standard" $*$-circuit for f_{MN}^m of the same complexity. We manipulate the gates of S according to their natural numbering. Let g be computed at some gate. Let $t_l = 0$, if g includes at most one useful monom of type l, and let t_l be the common part of all useful monoms of type l which are prime implicants of g, otherwise. We can replace g by $g \vee t_1 \vee \cdots \vee t_N$ without any costs. We obtain a $*$-circuit S' for f_{MN}^m. In S' all inputs and outputs of $\wedge$-gates have at most one useful monom of type l as prime implicant. This standard form of $*$-circuits makes the following considerations much more easier. The assumption that certain functions besides the variables and constants are given as inputs has been applied for the first time in circuit theory to the generalized matrix product (Wegener (79 a)).

In that paper a $(2/m)NM^m$ lower bound has been proved using the elimination method and the pigeon hole principle. Wegener (82 a) improved that bound and proved a $(1/2)NM^m$ lower bound which is only by a small constant factor smaller than the known upper bounds. More important than the new bound was the application of a new method for proving lower bounds. The method is based on the definition of a suitable value function to estimate the value of each gate for the computation of the outputs.

THEOREM 9.2 : $C_m(f_{MN}^m) \geq C_m^{\wedge}(f_{MN}^m) \geq C_m^*(f_{MN}^m) > (1/2)NM^m$ if $m \geq 2$.

For $m=2$ or $m=3$ the $(2/m)NM^m$ - bound is better than the bound of Theorem 9.2 .

COROLLARY 9.1 : For $n \geq 4$ let $m(n) = \lfloor \log n \rfloor$, $M(n) = 2$, $N(n) = \lfloor n/(2\log n) \rfloor$ and $h_n = f_{M(n)N(n)}^{m(n)}$. h_n is defined on at most n variables and has at most n outputs. The monotone circuit complexity of h_n is of size $n^2/\log n$.

Proof of Theorem 9.2 : We only have to prove the last inequality. Let S be an optimal $*$-circuit for f_{MN}^m . We assume that S is in standard form, i.e. the inputs and outputs of $\wedge$-gates have at most one prime implicant which is a useful monom of type l . We try to estimate the value of each $\wedge$-gate G for the computation of each prime implicant $(h_1, \ldots, h_m, l)$. A function $v_G : PI(f_{MN}^m) \to [0,1]$ is called value function if

$$v(G) := \sum_{1 \leq h_1, \ldots, h_m \leq M} \sum_{1 \leq l \leq N} v_G(h_1, \ldots, h_m, l) \leq 1 . \qquad (9.3)$$

At each gate we can distribute at most the value 1 among the prime implicants. This ensures that for an optimal $*$-circuit S

$$v(S) := \sum_{G \wedge\text{-gate in S}} v(G) \leq C^{\wedge}_m(S) = C^*_m(f^m_{MN}) \tag{9.4}$$

is a lower bound on $C^*_m(f^m_{MN})$. Finally we prove the necessity of giving value $1/2$ to each prime implicant, i.e. we prove for all $(h_1, \ldots, h_m, l)$ that

$$v(h_1, \ldots, h_m, l) := \sum_{G \wedge\text{-gate in S}} v_G(h_1, \ldots, h_m, l) > 1/2 . \tag{9.5}$$

Combining (9.3) - (9.5) we have proved that

$$C^*_m(f^m_{MN}) \geq \sum_{1 \leq h_1, \ldots, h_m \leq M} \sum_{1 \leq l \leq N} v(h_1, \ldots, h_m, l) \tag{9.6}$$

$$> (1/2) \, N \, M^m .$$

At first we define a value function. Then we discuss why we think that such a value function works. Let G be an $\wedge$-gate in an optimal $*$-circuit for f^m_{MN}. Let g' and g'' be the inputs of G and $g = \text{res}_G$. We define v_G as the sum of v'_G and v''_G. Let $i_1, \ldots, i_{q'} \in \{1, \ldots, N\}$ be the types such that some $t_j \in PI(f^m_{MN})$ of type i_j is prime implicant of g but not of g'. Then

$$v'_G(t_j) = 1/(2q') \quad \text{for } 1 \leq j \leq q' \qquad \text{and} \tag{9.7}$$

$$v'_G(t) = 0 \qquad \text{for all other } t \in PI(f^m_{MN}) .$$

Obviously

$$v'(G) := \sum_{1 \leq h_1, \ldots, h_m \leq M} \sum_{1 \leq l \leq N} v'_G(h_1, \ldots, h_m, l) \leq 1/2 . \tag{9.8}$$

v''_G is defined in the same way but with respect to g'' instead of g'. Then (9.3) is fulfilled. It remains to prove (9.5).

We discuss some arguments what makes the value function v a good choice. v is relatively simple, the image of v_G has at most 4 elements. $v_G(t)$ is equal to

- $\dfrac{1}{2q'} + \dfrac{1}{2q''}$ if $t \in PI(g)$, $t \notin PI(g') \cup PI(g'')$, these prime implicants are created at G ,

- $\dfrac{1}{2q'}$ if $t \in PI(g) \cap PI(g'')$, $t \notin PI(g')$,

- $\dfrac{1}{2q''}$ if $t \in PI(g) \cap PI(g')$, $t \notin PI(g'')$, these prime implicants are
preserved at G ,

- 0 if $t \notin PI(g)$ or $t \in PI(g) \cap PI(g') \cap PI(g'')$.

The prime implicants created at G get the highest score at G . This
is in accordance with our intuition. This score is quite small if q'
and q'' are quite large. What reasons are there for hoping that each
of these prime implicants t scores enough, i.e. $v(t) > 1/2$? If q'
and q'' are both large, then g has many prime implicants with variables of different types. These "dirty" monoms cannot be lengthened
to prime implicants of f_{MN}^m . The only possibility to eliminate these
dirty monoms is that t scores sufficiently often.

Proof of (9.5) : We consider the prime implicant $t = (h_1, \ldots, h_m, l)$
and the corresponding output $y_t := y_{h_1, \ldots, h_m}$. Let S be an optimal
$*$-circuit for f_{MN}^m in standard form, and let $S(t)$ be the subcircuit
consisting of the following inputs and gates. A gate G of S belongs
to $S(t)$ if some path in S leads from G to the output y_t and if t is
a prime implicant of all functions computed on this path (including
G). Furthermore the inputs of the gates we just discussed belong to
$S(t)$. $S(t)$ is a connected subcircuit with output y_t . For each input
g of $S(t)$, $t \notin PI(g)$, but t is a prime implicant of all functions computed within the circuit.

If both direct predecessors of some gate G are inputs of $S(t)$, G
is an $\wedge$-gate. Otherwise $t \notin PI(res_G)$. If an input of $S(t)$ has an $\wedge$-
gate as direct successor, some proper shortening of t is a prime implicant of that input.

Let $s_1, \ldots, s_D$ be the inputs of $S(t)$ leading directly into an $\wedge$-gate. Let $G(i)$ be an $\wedge$-gate with input s_i and let $v_{G(i)}^* = v_{G(i)}'$ if s_i is the first input of $G(i)$ and $v_{G(i)}^* = v_{G(i)}''$ otherwise. In either case $v_{G(i)}^*(t) > 0$. Instead of (9.5) we prove the stronger result

$$b_1 + \cdots + b_D > 1/2 \tag{9.9}$$

for $b_i = v_{G(i)}^*(t)$. W.l.o.g. $b_1 \geq \cdots \geq b_D$. We choose some $w_i \in PI(s_i)$ such that some proper lengthening w_i^* of w_i is prime implicant of $\mathrm{res}_{G(i)}$, $v_{G(i)}^*(w_i^*) > 0$, and the type of w_i^* differs from the types of $w_1^*, \ldots, w_{i-1}^*$. We can always choose $w_1^* = t$. If the choice of w_i according to our rules is impossible, $v_{G(i)}^*$ is positive for at most $i-1$ prime implicants.
Hence $b_i \geq (2(i-1))^{-1}$ and, since $b_1 \geq \cdots \geq b_D$,

$$b_1 + \cdots + b_D \geq i\,b_i > 1/2 . \tag{9.10}$$

In the following we assume that $w_1, \ldots, w_D$ are chosen according to our rules. By construction $w_i \in PI(s_i)$ and

$$w_1 \cdots w_D \leq s_1 \cdots s_D . \tag{9.11}$$

We claim that

$$s_1 \cdots s_D \leq y_t . \tag{9.12}$$

Let a be an input where $s_i(a) = 1$ for $1 \leq i \leq D$. $S(t)$ is a circuit where all inputs leading into $\wedge$-gates are equal to 1 . Furthermore no $\vee$-gate of $S(t)$ has two inputs of $S(t)$ as direct predecessors. Now it is easy to prove by induction that for input a all gates of $S(t)$ compute 1 , in particular $y_t(a) = 1$. Because of (9.11) and (9.12)

$$w_1 \cdots w_D \leq y_t . \tag{9.13}$$

We consider that input a where all variables of $w_1 \cdots w_D$ are set to 1 and all other variables are set to 0 . By (9.13) $y_t(a) = 1$. All variables of w_i are of type l_i and $l_1, \ldots, l_D$ are different. Since w_i is a proper shortening of w_i^* and $v_{G(i)}^*(w_i^*) > 0$, w_i includes at most $m-1$ variables. Hence a is an input where for each type at most $m-1$ variables are set to 1 . By definition of f_{MN}^m $y_t(a) = 0$. Because of this contradiction it is impossible to choose $w_1, \ldots, w_D$ according to our rules.

$\square$

6.10 Razborov's method

In § 3 - § 9 we heard about several methods for the proof of lower bounds on the monotone complexity of Boolean functions. For functions with one output we proved only linear bounds, and for functions with n outputs the largest bound is of size $\Theta(n^2 \log^{-1} n)$ (see § 9). Razborov (85 a) and (85 b) developed a method for the proof of exponential lower bounds. The method itself can be described in a rather simple way (like the elimination method or the method of value functions). The ingenious part is the successful application to important functions.

In monotone circuits we work in the lattice $(M_n, \wedge, \vee)$. Instead of $f \in M_n$ we consider now $f^{-1}(1)$. Let M_n^* be the set of all $f^{-1}(1)$ where $f \in M_n$, i.e. the set of all up-sets. Then we work in the lattice $(M_n^*, \cap, \cup)$. Razborov investigates computations in sublattices of $M^* = M_n^*$. We state formally the concepts before we discuss the method.

DEFINITION 10.1 : $(L, \cap, \cup)$ is called a legitimate lattice if the following conditions are fulfilled.

i) $L \subseteq M^*$, $x_1^{-1}(1), \ldots, x_n^{-1}(1)$, ϕ , $\{0,1\}^n \in L$.

ii) For $M, N \in L$ the meet (the lattice theoretic intersection) $M \sqcap N \in$ L is well defined and $M \sqcap N \subseteq M \cap N$.

iii) For $M, N \in L$ the join (the lattice theoretic union) $M \sqcup N \in L$ is well defined and $M \sqcup N \supseteq M \cup N$.

The deviation of the operations $\sqcap$ and $\sqcup$ from $\cap$ and $\cup$ is measured by $\delta_\sqcap(M, N) = (M \cap N) - (M \sqcap N)$ and $\delta_\sqcup(M, N) = (M \sqcup N) - (M \cup N)$.

DEFINITION 10.2 : The complexity of $f \in M_n$ (or $f^{-1}(1) \in M^*$) with respect to a legitimate lattice L is defined by

$$C_L(f) = \min \{ t \mid \exists \, M, M_1, N_1, \ldots, M_t, N_t \in L : \qquad (10.1)$$

$$M \subseteq f^{-1}(1) \cup \bigcup_{1 \leq i \leq t} \delta_\sqcup(M_i, N_i) \text{ and}$$

$$f^{-1}(1) \subseteq M \cup \bigcup_{1 \leq i \leq t} \delta_\sqcap(M_i, N_i) \}.$$

THEOREM 10.1 : $C_L(f)$ is a lower bound on $C_m(f)$ for $f \in M_n$ and each legitimate lattice L.

Proof : Let S be an optimal monotone circuit for f. Let f_i and g_i $(1 \leq i \leq t = C_m(f))$ be the inputs of the i-th gate of S. S^* results from S by the replacements $x_i \rightarrow x_i^{-1}(1)$, $0 \rightarrow \phi$, $1 \rightarrow \{0,1\}^n$, $\wedge \rightarrow \sqcap$, $\vee \rightarrow \sqcup$. S^* is a computation in L. Let M_i and N_i be the inputs of the i-th gate of S^*, and let M be the output of S^*. We prove by induction on t that these sets fulfil the conditions described in (10.1). The basis of the induction $(t = 0)$ is obvious. For the induction step we distinguish whether the t-th gate is an $\vee$-gate ((10.2) and (10.3)) or an $\wedge$-gate ((10.4) and (10.5)). By definition and induction hypothesis

$$M = M_t \sqcup N_t = M_t \cup N_t \cup \delta_\sqcup(M_t, N_t) \qquad (10.2)$$

$$\subseteq f_t^{-1}(1) \cup g_t^{-1}(1) \cup \bigcup_{1 \leq i \leq t} \delta_\sqcup(M_i, N_i) = f^{-1}(1) \cup \bigcup_{1 \leq i \leq t} \delta_\sqcup(M_i, N_i),$$

$$f^{-1}(1) = f_t^{-1}(1) \cup g_t^{-1}(1) \subseteq M_t \cup N_t \cup \bigcup_{1 \le i \le t-1} \delta_\cap(M_i, N_i) \qquad (10.3)$$

$$\subseteq M_t \cup N_t \cup \bigcup_{1 \le i \le t} \delta_\cap(M_i, N_i) \subseteq M \cup \bigcup_{1 \le i \le t} \delta_\cap(M_i, N_i) ,$$

$$M = M_t \cap N_t \subseteq M_t \cap N_t \subseteq (f_t^{-1}(1) \cap g_t^{-1}(1)) \cup \bigcup_{1 \le i \le t-1} \delta_\cup(M_i, N_i) \qquad (10.4)$$

$$\subseteq f^{-1}(1) \cup \bigcup_{1 \le i \le t} \delta_\cup(M_i, N_i) \quad \text{and}$$

$$f^{-1}(1) = f_t^{-1}(1) \cap g_t^{-1}(1) \subseteq (M_t \cap N_t) \cup \bigcup_{1 \le i \le t-1} \delta_\cap(M_i, N_i) \qquad (10.5)$$

$$= M_t \cap N_t \cup \bigcup_{1 \le i \le t} \delta_\cap(M_i, N_i) = M \cup \bigcup_{1 \le i \le t} \delta_\cap(M_i, N_i) .$$

$$\square$$

A more careful analysis of (10.3) and (10.4) shows that we even proved

$$M \subseteq f^{-1}(1) \cup \bigcup_{i \,|\, i\text{-th gate is an } \wedge\text{-gate}} \delta_\cup(M_i, N_i) \quad \text{and} \qquad (10.6)$$

$$f^{-1}(1) \subseteq M \cup \bigcup_{i \,|\, i\text{-th gate is an } \vee\text{-gate}} \delta_\cap(M_i, N_i) . \qquad (10.7)$$

We try to better understand computations in L . Exactly the functions f where $f^{-1}(1) \in L$ have C_L-complexity 0 . Again we have to choose an appropriate class of functions which are given as inputs. If $f^{-1}(1) \notin L$, then $f^{-1}(1)$ cannot be computed in an L−circuit. (10.1) describes sufficiently good approximations M of $f^{-1}(1)$. We do not demand that the approximating sets M, M_i and N_i can be computed in an L−circuit of size t .

How should we choose a lattice L where it can be proved that $C_L(f)$ is large ? If L is too "dense", we can choose M in such a way that $f^{-1}(1) - M$ and $M - f^{-1}(1)$ are small sets. Then these sets can be covered with a small number of δ-sets. If L is too "coarse-grained", i.e. has only few elements, δ-sets are large and again $f^{-1}(1) - M$ and

$M - f^{-1}(1)$ can be covered by a small number of δ-sets. In the extreme case L consists only of $x_i^{-1}(1)$ for $1 \le i \le n$, ϕ and $\{0,1\}^n$ and $M' \cap N' = \phi$ and $M' \cup N' = \{0,1\}^n$ for $M', N' \in L$. Then $C_L(f) \le 1$, since we can choose $M = \{0,1\}^n$ and $M_1 = N_1 = \phi$.

The lattice we choose should depend on the function f whose monotone complexity we like to estimate. L should not contain a good approximation of f and δ-sets should be small. Razborov used lattices where $\delta_\sqcap$-sets include only a small number of minimal elements of $f^{-1}(1)$ (prime implicants) and $\delta_\sqcup$-sets include only a small number of maximal elements of $f^{-1}(0)$ (prime clauses). Furthermore L includes only sets M where $f^{-1}(1) - M$ or $M - f^{-1}(1)$ is large. In particular, we prove a lower bound min on the minimal number of prime implicants and prime clauses in $(f^{-1}(1) - M) \cup (M - f^{-1}(1))$ for $M \in L$. Then we prove an upper bound max on the number of prime implicants in $\delta_\sqcap$-sets and of prime clauses in $\delta_\sqcup$-sets. Then $C_L(f) \ge$ min/max. By max we estimate the maximal value of one computation step with respect to L. The value necessary for the computation of f in an L-circuit is at least min. Hence Razborov generalized the concepts that certain functions besides the variables and constants are given as inputs and that one should try to estimate the value of computation steps. His estimations are much more rough than those in § 9. This might be the key to the success of Razborov's method.

These general considerations are useful for understanding Razborov's method. Nevertheless it is difficult to choose a good lattice. So far, only one type of lattice has been applied successfully. Razborov proved $n^{\Omega(\log n)}$-bounds. Alon and Boppana (85) improved these bounds to exponential bounds by a better analysis of Razborov's lattice.

6.11 An exponential lower bound for clique functions

DEFINITION 11.1 : The clique function $cl_{n,m} \in M_N$ where $N = \binom{n}{2}$ is defined on the variables $x_{i,j}$ $(1 \leq i < j \leq n)$. $cl_{n,m}(x) = 1$ iff $G(x) = (V = \{1,...,n\}$, $E(x) = \{(i,j) \mid x_{i,j} = 1\})$ includes an m-clique, i.e. m vertices which are all directly connected by an edge.

The clique function is NP-complete if $m = n/2$. Hence we suppose that circuits for $cl_{n,n/2}$ cannot have polynomial size. For monotone circuits we can prove an exponential lower bound. At first we define a legitimate lattice $L = L(n,r,l)$ where the parameters $l \geq 2$ and $r \geq 2$ are fixed later.

DEFINITION 11.2 : Let $W, W_1, \ldots, W_r$ be (not necessarily different) sets and A a class of sets.

i) $W_1, \ldots, W_r$ imply W $(W_1, \ldots, W_r \vdash W)$ if $|W| \leq l$, $|W_i| \leq l$ for $1 \leq i \leq r$ and $W_i \cap W_j \subseteq W$ for all $i \neq j$.

ii) A implies W $(A \vdash W)$ if $W_1, \ldots, W_r \vdash W$ for some $W_1, \ldots, W_r \in A$.

iii) A is closed if $(A \vdash W)$ implies $(W \in A)$.

iv) A^* is the intersection of all closed $B \supseteq A$.

LEMMA 11.1 : i) A^* is closed.

ii) $A \subseteq A^*$.

iii) $(A^*)^* = A^*$.

iv) $A \subseteq B$ $\Rightarrow$ $A^* \subseteq B^*$.

Proof : ii) and iv) follow by definition, and iii) follows from i) . For the proof of i) we assume that $A^* \vdash W$. If B is closed and $B \supseteq A$, by definition $B \supseteq A^*$ and hence $B \vdash W$. Since B is closed, $W \in B$ for all closed $B \supseteq A$. This implies $W \in A^*$, and A^* is closed. $\square$

DEFINITION 11.3 : Let $V = \{1,...,n\}$ and $V(l) = \{\, W \subseteq V \mid |W| \leq l \,\}$. For $A \subseteq V(l)$ let $[A]$ be the set of graphs on V containing a clique on some $W \in A$. $(L, \sqcap, \sqcup)$ is defined by

$$L = L(n,r,l) = \{ [A] \mid A \subseteq V(l) \text{ is closed } \} \cup \{ \phi \} , \qquad (11.1)$$

$$[A] \sqcap [B] = [A \cap B] \quad \text{and} \qquad (11.2)$$

$$[A] \sqcup [B] = [(A \cup B)^*] . \qquad (11.3)$$

LEMMA 11.2 : $(L, \sqcap, \sqcup)$ is a legitimate lattice.

Proof : The properties we have to establish are described in Definition 10.1 .

i) $L \subseteq M_N^*$, since we identify graphs and vectors in $\{0,1\}^N$ (see Definition 11.1) . $\phi \in L$ by definition. $[V(l)] = \{0,1\}^N \in L$, since $V(l)$ is closed. Let F_{ij} be the class of all $W \in V(l)$ including i and j . F_{ij} is closed. Hence $[F_{ij}] = x_{ij}^{-1}(1) \in L$.

ii) Let $A,B \subseteq V(l)$ be closed. Similar to the proof of Lemma 11.1 it follows that $A \cap B \subseteq V(l)$ is closed. Hence $[A \cap B] \in L$. If $G \in [A] \sqcap [B] = [A \cap B]$, G contains a clique on some $W \in A \cap B$. Hence $G \in [A] \cap [B]$.

iii) By Lemma 11.1 $(A \cup B)^* \subseteq V(l)$ is closed and $[(A \cup B)^*] \in L$. If $G \in [A] \sqcup [B]$, G contains a clique on some $W \in A \cup B \subseteq (A \cup B)^*$. Hence $G \in [A] \sqcup [B]$.

□

Before we estimate the L-complexity of clique functions, we investigate the structure of closed systems A . If $B \in A$, also all $B' \supseteq B$ where $|B'| \leq l$ are elements of A . Obviously $B, ..., B \vdash B'$. This observation allows us to describe closed systems by their minimal sets, namely sets $B \in A$ where no proper subset of B is included in A . A consists of its minimal sets, and all sets of at most l elements including a minimal set. Later we shall establish relations between prime implicants in δ −sets and minimal sets in closed systems.

Therefore it is important to prove that closed systems have not too many minimal sets.

LEMMA 11.3 : In each closed system A the number of minimal sets with at most k elements is bounded by $(r-1)^k$.

Proof : A system F of sets of at most k elements has the property $P(r,k)$ if there are no sets $W, W_1, \ldots, W_r \in F$ and $U \subsetneq W$ such that $W_i \cap W_j \subseteq U$ for all $i \neq j$. The system of all minimal sets of A with at most k elements has property $P(r,k)$. Otherwise, by definition of the notion closed, U would be a set in A and W would not be minimal. We prove by induction on r that systems F with property $P(r,k)$ contain at most $(r-1)^k$ sets.

If F would contain different sets W_1 and W_2 for $r = 2$, we could choose $U = W_1 \cap W_2$. Since W_1 and W_2 are both minimal sets, U is a proper subset of W_1 and W_2 and for $W = W_1$ we have proved that F does not fulfil property $P(2,k)$.

For the induction step let F be a system with property $P(r,k)$. We fix $D \in F$. For $C \subseteq D$ let

$$F_C = \{ W - C \mid W \in F, W \cap D = C \} . \tag{11.4}$$

F_C has property $P(r-1, k-|C|)$. Otherwise we choose $W', W_1', \ldots, W_{r-1}' \in F_C$, $U' \subsetneq W'$ such that $W_i' \cap W_j' \subseteq U'$ for $i \neq j$. Let $W = W' \cup C \in F$, $U = U' \cup C \subsetneq W$, $W_i = W_i' \cup C \in F$ for $1 \leq i \leq r-1$ and $W_r = D \in F$. Since $C \subseteq D$, $W_i \cap W_j \subseteq U$ for $i \neq j$ in contradiction to the assumption that F has property $P(r,k)$. By induction hypothesis $|F_C| \leq (r-2)^{k-|C|}$. Since D is fixed, the condition $W \cap D = C$ is fulfilled for only one set C . If $W \cap D = C = W' \cap D$ but $W \neq W'$, also $W - C \neq W' - C$. Finally we make use of the fact that $|D| \leq k$, since $D \in F$.

$$|F| = \sum_{C \subseteq D} |F_C| \leq \sum_{0 \leq i \leq |D|} \binom{|D|}{i} (r-2)^{k-i} \tag{11.5}$$

$$\leq \sum_{0 \leq i \leq k} \binom{k}{i} (r-2)^{k-i} = (r-1)^k .$$

□

We provide some auxiliary means for the estimation of the size of δ_u-sets. These sets can be described as $\lceil C^* \rceil - \lceil C \rceil$ for some appropriate system C. How can C^* be constructed out of C ?

Let $C' = \{ W \notin C \mid C \vdash W \}$. By definition $C^* = C$ iff $C' = \phi$. If $C' \neq \phi$ we improve C by choosing some minimal set $W \in C'$ and adding W and all sets $W' \supseteq W$ where $|W'| \leq l$ to C. We obtain a system B where $C \subsetneq B \subset C^*$ and $B^* = C^*$. We continue with B in the same way. The number of such improvement steps is bounded by $|V(l)| \leq n^l$, since the improving set $W \in V(l)$. This upper bound may be improved to $l! \, (r+1)^l$ but this is not essential for our purposes.

(m-1)-partite graphs correspond to inputs in $cl_{n,m}^{-1}(0)$. Such a graph G can be described by a coloring $h : V \to \{1,...,m-1\}$ of the vertices. The vertices i and j are connected by an edge in $G(h)$ iff $h(i) \neq h(j)$. Later we have difficulties to choose the right (m-1)-partite graph. Therefore we investigate randomly chosen (m-1)-partite graphs or random colorings of graphs. For a coloring h the graph $G(h)$ contains a clique on the vertex set $W \subseteq V$ iff the vertices of W have different colors, i.e. W is colored. The uniform distribution on all g^n colorings of V with g colors yields a random coloring of V.

LEMMA 11.4 : Let $g \geq l$, $A \subseteq V(l)$, $W, W_1, \ldots, W_r \in A$, $W_1, \ldots, W_r \vdash W$. Let E (or E_i) be the event that W (or W_i) is colored. Let CE_i be the complementary event of E_i. Then

$$\Pr(E \cap CE_1 \cap \cdots \cap CE_r) \leq \left[1 - \frac{g(g-1) \cdots (g-l+1)}{g^l} \right]^r . \tag{11.6}$$

Proof : Since $W_i \cap W_j \subseteq W$, the events $CE_1, \ldots, CE_r$ are independent if W is colored, i.e. if E happens. This follows since the sets $W_i - W$

are disjoint. Hence

$$Pr(E \cap CE_1 \cap \cdots \cap CE_r) \leq Pr(CE_1 \cap \cdots \cap CE_r \mid E) \qquad (11.7)$$

$$= \prod_{1 \leq i \leq r} Pr(CE_i \mid E) = \prod_{1 \leq i \leq r} (1 - Pr(E_i \mid E)).$$

By (11.7) it suffices to prove that $Pr(E_i \mid E)$ is at least $g \cdots (g - l + 1) / g^l$. Let $p(i) = |W_i \cap W|$ and $q(i) = |W_i - W|$. Then $p(i) + q(i) = |W_i| \leq l$. The event E implies for the set W_i that $W_i \cap W$ is colored with $p(i)$ different colors. The probability that then the $q(i)$ elements of $W - W_i$ get other and different colors is

$$\prod_{0 \leq j < q(i)} \frac{g - p(i) - j}{g} \geq \prod_{0 \leq j < l} \frac{g - j}{g} = \frac{g \cdots (g - l + 1)}{g^l}. \qquad (11.8)$$

□

LEMMA 11.5 : Let $C \subseteq V(l)$, $g \geq l$ and h be a random coloring of V. Then

$$Pr(G(h) \in \lceil C^* \rceil - \lceil C \rceil) \leq n^l \left[1 - \frac{g \cdots (g - l + 1)}{g^l} \right]^r. \qquad (11.9)$$

Proof : We already described a construction of C^* out of C in at most n^l steps. Let $C_0 = C$, $C_1, \ldots, C_p = C^*$ be the steps of this construction $(0 \leq p \leq n^l)$. It is sufficient to prove that

$$Pr(G(h) \in \lceil C_i \rceil - \lceil C_{i-1} \rceil) \leq \left[1 - \frac{g \cdots (g - l + 1)}{g^l} \right]^r. \qquad (11.10)$$

Let W_i be the chosen set for the construction of C_i out of C_{i-1}. $G(h)$ contains a clique on D iff D is colored. $G(h)$ is not in $\lceil C_{i-1} \rceil$ iff all sets in C_{i-1} are not colored. $G(h)$ is in $\lceil C_i \rceil$ iff some set in C_i is colored. By construction W_i has to be colored. Furthermore by construction $C_{i-1} \vdash W_i$, i.e. $B_1, \ldots, B_r \vdash W_i$ for sets $B_j \in C_{i-1}$. Altogether the event $G(h) \in \lceil C_i \rceil - \lceil C_{i-1} \rceil$ implies that $B_1, \ldots, B_r$ are not colored but W_i is colored. The probability of this event has been estimated in Lemma 11.4 .

□

Lemma 11.5 is a useful bound for the probability that a random $(m-1)$-partite graph is in some δ_u-set. Now we are prepared to prove the lower bound.

THEOREM 11.1 : Let $4 \le m \le (1/4)(n/\log n)^{2/3}$, $l = \lceil m^{1/2} \rceil$ and $r = \lceil 4\, m^{1/2} \log n \rceil$. Then

$$C_m(cl_{n,m}) \ge C_{L(n,r,l)}(cl_{n,m}) \tag{11.11}$$

$$\ge \frac{1}{8} \left[\frac{n}{m(r-1)} \right]^{\lceil (l+1)/2 \rceil} \ge \frac{1}{8} \left[\frac{n}{4\, m^{3/2} \log n} \right]^{(m^{1/2}+1)/2}$$

In particular for $m = \lfloor (1/4)(n/\log n)^{2/3} \rfloor$

$$C_m(cl_{n,m}) = \exp\left(\Omega((n/\log n)^{1/3})\right). \tag{11.12}$$

Proof : The first inequality of (11.11) follows from Theorem 10.1 . The last inequalities of (11.11) and (11.12) follow from easy calculations. The lower bound on $C_L(cl_{n,m})$ is still to be proved.

Let $t = C_L(cl_{n,m})$ and let $M, M_1, N_1, \ldots, M_t, N_t$ be sets fulfilling the conditions of (10.1), the definition of C_L. By definition we can choose closed systems $A, A_1, B_1, \cdots, A_t, B_t$ in $V(l)$ where $M = \lceil A \rceil$, $M_i = \lceil A_i \rceil$ and $N_i = \lceil B_i \rceil$.

Case 1 : M is not the set of all graphs.

We consider those $\binom{n}{m}$ graphs which contain exactly the edges of an m-clique, i.e. the graphs corresponding to prime implicants. Each of these graphs is by (10.1) contained in M or some $\delta_n(M_i, N_i)$. We prove that M can include at most half of these graphs, and that each δ_n-set can include at most $4\,(m(r-1)/n)^{\lceil (l+1)/2 \rceil} \binom{n}{m}$ of these graphs. In order to cover all m-cliques, it is necessary that

$$4 \left[\frac{m(r-1)}{n} \right]^{\lceil (l+1)/2 \rceil} \binom{n}{m} t + \frac{1}{2} \binom{n}{m} \ge \binom{n}{m}. \tag{11.13}$$

(11.13) implies (11.11) .

At first we estimate the quantity of m-cliques that can be included in M . Each set $W \in A$ has at least two elements, since each graph contains each clique on one vertex and M is not the set of all graphs. Let B be a set of m elements where the clique on B belongs to M . Then we find some minimal set $D \in A$ where $D \subseteq B$. By Lemma 11.3 A has at most $(r-1)^k$ minimal sets D with k elements. D can be responsible only for $\binom{n-k}{m-k}$ m-cliques, because this is the number of m-element sets $B \supseteq D$. Hence the number of m-cliques in M is bounded by

$$\sum_{2 \le k \le l} (r-1)^k \binom{n-k}{m-k} . \tag{11.14}$$

By elementary calculations $\binom{n}{m} / \binom{n-k}{m-k} \ge (n/m)^k$ and $m(r-1)/n \le 1/2$. Hence

$$\sum_{2 \le k \le l} (r-1)^k \binom{n-k}{m-k} \le \sum_{2 \le k \le l} (r-1)^k \binom{n}{m} (m/n)^k \tag{11.15}$$

$$\le \binom{n}{m} \sum_{2 \le k \le l} (1/2)^k \le (1/2) \binom{n}{m} .$$

By similar methods we investigate $\delta_n(M_i, N_i)$. By definition

$$\delta_n(M_i, N_i) = (M_i \cap N_i) - (M_i \cap N_i) = \lceil A_i \rceil \cap \lceil B_i \rceil - \lceil A_i \cap B_i \rceil . \tag{11.16}$$

If the m-clique on Z belongs to $\delta_n(M_i, N_i)$ we can find some minimal set $U \subseteq Z$ in A_i and some minimal set $W \subseteq Z$ in B_i , but no subset of Z belongs to $A_i \cap B_i$. Since A_i and B_i are closed, $U \cup W \subseteq Z$ will be in $A_i \cap B_i$ if $|U \cup W| \le l$. Hence $|U \cup W| > l$, and one of the sets U or W includes at least $\lceil (l+1)/2 \rceil$ elements. If the m-clique on Z belongs to $\delta_n(M_i, N_i)$, a minimal set of A_i or of B_i with at least $\lceil (l+1)/2 \rceil$ elements is included in Z . In the same way as before we can estimate the number of m-cliques in $\delta_n(M_i, N_i)$ by

$$\sum_{\lceil(l+1)/2\rceil \leq k \leq l} 2\,(r-1)^k \binom{n-k}{m-k} \leq 2\binom{n}{m}\left(\frac{m(r-1)}{n}\right)^{\lceil(l+1)/2\rceil} \sum_{0 \leq i < \infty}\left(\frac{1}{2}\right)^i$$

$$= 4\binom{n}{m}\left(\frac{m(r-1)}{n}\right)^{\lceil(l+1)/2\rceil} \tag{11.17}$$

Case 2 : M is the set of all graphs.

We consider the class of complete $(m-1)$ – partite graphs, this class includes only graphs in $cl_{n,m}^{-1}(0)$. By (10.1) each of these graphs is contained in some $\delta_\sqcup(M_i,N_i)$. For $C_i = A_i \cup B_i$

$$\delta_\sqcup(M_i,N_i) = (M_i \sqcup N_i) - (M_i \cup N_i) \tag{11.18}$$

$$= \lceil(A_i \cup B_i)^*\rceil - \lceil A_i \cup B_i\rceil = \lceil C_i^*\rceil - \lceil C_i\rceil .$$

Let h be a random $(m\text{-}1)$ - coloring of V , then G(h) is a complete $(m\text{-}1)$ - partite graph. By Lemma 11.5 , the definitions of l and r and an elementary calculation

$$\Pr(G(h) \in \lceil C_i^*\rceil - \lceil C_i\rceil) \leq n^l\left[1-(m-1)\cdots(m-l)/(m-1)^l\right]^r \tag{11.19}$$

$$\leq n^{\sqrt{m}}\,n^{-2\sqrt{m}} = n^{-\sqrt{m}} \qquad \text{and}$$

$$\Pr(\exists\ 1 \leq i \leq t : G(h) \in \lceil C_i^*\rceil - \lceil C_i\rceil) \leq t\,n^{-\sqrt{m}} . \tag{11.20}$$

Since all complete $(m\text{-}1)$ - partite graphs are in the union of all $\delta_\sqcup$ - sets, the left-hand probability of (11.20) is equal to 1 . Hence $t \geq n^{\sqrt{m}}$. The claim follows since for $m \geq 4$

$$n^{\sqrt{m}} \geq \frac{1}{8}\left(\frac{n}{m(r-1)}\right)^{\lceil(l+1)/2\rceil} \tag{11.21}$$

$\square$

6.12 Other applications of Razborov's method

By similar methods Alon and Boppana (85) proved also the following bounds.

DEFINITION 12.1 : $cl_{n,p,q}$ is the class of all monotone functions $f \in M_N$ (where $N = \binom{n}{2}$) such that $f(x) = 0$ if $G(x)$ (see Def. 11.1) contains no p-clique and $f(x) = 1$ if $G(x)$ contains a q-clique.

THEOREM 12.1 : Let $f \in cl_{n,p,q}$, $4 \leq p \leq q$ and $p^* q \leq n / (8 \log n)$ for $p^* = p^{1/2}$. Then

$$C_m(f) \geq \frac{1}{8} \left(\frac{n}{4 p^* q \log n} \right)^{(p^*+1)/2} \geq \frac{1}{8} 2^{(p^*+1)/2} . \qquad (12.1)$$

In particular, for $p = \lfloor \log^4 n \rfloor$ and $q = \lfloor n / (8 \log^3 n) \rfloor$

$$C_m(f) = n^{\Omega(\log n)} . \qquad (12.2)$$

Hence it is even difficult to approximate clique functions.

THEOREM 12.2 : $C_m(cl_{n,m}) = \Omega(n^m / \log^m n)$ for constant m.

Theorem 12.2 improves an $\Omega(n^m / \log^{2m} n)$ − bound of Razborov. This bound is not far away from the obvious $O(n^m)$ - upper bound. We show that negations are powerful for the computation of clique functions.

THEOREM 12.3 : Let BM_n be the Boolean matrix product of $n \times n$-matrices. For constant m and $t = \binom{n}{\lceil m/3 \rceil}$

$$C(cl_{n,m}) = O(C(BM_t)) = o(n^{(5/2)\lceil m/3 \rceil}) . \qquad (12.3)$$

Proof : The second equality holds, since $t \leq n^{\lceil m/3 \rceil}$ and

$C(BM_t) = o(t^{5/2})$ (Coppersmith and Winograd (82), see Ch.3 , § 6). For the first assertion we assume that 6 is a divisor of m . Otherwise we could add up to 5 vertices to the graph which are all connected to all other vertices.

How can we reduce the clique function to matrix multiplication ? The rows and columns of the $t \times t$-matrix correspond to the vertex sets $A \subseteq V$ of size $m/3$. The matrix entry $y_{A,B}$ should be equal to 1 iff A and B are disjoint and the graph $G(x)$ implied by the input vector x contains the clique on $A \cup B$. Obviously $G(x)$ includes an m-clique iff for some sets A, B and C $y_{A,B} = y_{A,C} = y_{B,C} = 1$. We compute the Boolean matrix product $Z = Y^2$. By definition $z_{A,B} = 1$ iff for some C $y_{A,C} = y_{C,B} = 1$. Hence we can compute

$$cl_{n,m}(x) = \bigvee_{A,B} z_{A,B} y_{A,B} \tag{12.4}$$

with $O(t^2)$ gates. Since BM_t has t^2 different outputs, $C(BM_t) \geq t^2$, and it is sufficient to prove that all $y_{A,B}$ can be computed with $O(t^2)$ gates. Let $y_A = 1$ iff $G(x)$ includes the clique on A . All y_A $(|A| = m/3)$ can be computed with $O(t)$ gates, since m is constant. $y_{A,B} = 0$ if A and B are not disjoint. If A and B are disjoint, we partition A to A' and A'' and B to B' and B'' where the partition sets are of size $m/6$. Obviously

$$y_{A,B} = y_{A' \cup B'} \wedge y_{A' \cup B''} \wedge y_{A'' \cup B'} \wedge y_{A'' \cup B''} \wedge y_A \wedge y_B , \tag{12.5}$$

and all $y_{A,B}$ can be computed with $O(t^2)$ gates.

□

We know now that $C(f) = o(C_m(f))$ for sorting, Boolean convolution, Boolean matrix product, and certain clique functions. The lower bounds known on $C_m(f) / C(f)$ are polynomial. Can this quotient be superpolynomial or even exponential ? To answer this question we consider perfect matchings.

DEFINITION 12.2 : PM_n is defined on n^2 variables x_{ij} $(1 \leq i, j \leq n)$.

$$PM_n(x) = \bigvee_{\pi \in \Sigma_n} x_{1,\pi(1)} \wedge \cdots \wedge x_{n,\pi(n)}. \tag{12.6}$$

PM_n is called logical permanent (if $\vee$ is replaced by $\oplus$ we obtain the determinant). $PM_n(x) = 1$ iff the bipartite graph $G(x)$ on $V \cup W = \{v_1, w_1, \ldots, v_n, w_n\}$ with edge set $E(x) = \{ (v_i, w_j) \mid x_{ij} = 1 \}$ includes a perfect matching, i.e. n vertex disjoint edges.

Hopcroft and Karp (73) designed a polynomial algorithm for the decision whether or not a bipartite graph includes a perfect matching. Therefore (see Ch. 9) we can design circuits of polynomial size for PM_n. Razborov (85 a) proved that the monotone complexity is superpolynomial.

THEOREM 12.4 : $C_m(PM_n) = n^{\Omega(\log n)}$ but $C(PM_n) = n^{O(1)}$. In particular, $C_m(PM_n) / C(PM_n)$ is superpolynomial.

It is still an open problem whether $C_m(f) / C(f)$ can be exponential. Finally we present the largest lower bound known on the monotone complexity of explicitly defined Boolean functions. We should notice that $cl_{n,m}$ is defined on $\Theta(n^2)$ variables. The following bound has been proved by Alon and Boppana (85) with Razborov's method, the first exponential bound for this function is due to Andreev (85) .

DEFINITION 12.3 : $Poly_{q,s}$ is defined on $n = q^2$ variables x_{ij} ($1 \le i,j \le q$) where q is prime. Let $G(x)$ be the bipartite graph specified by x (see Def. 12.2).
$Poly_{q,s}(x) = 1$ iff a polynomial p over the field $\mathbb{Z}_q$ exists such that $degree(p) \le s - 1$ and $G(x)$ includes all edges $(v_i, w_{p(i)})$.

THEOREM 12.5 : $C_m(Poly_{q,s}) = exp(\Omega(n^{1/4} \log^{1/2} n))$
for $s = (1/2) (q/ \log q)^{1/2}$.

Superpolynomial and exponential lower bounds on the monotone circuit complexity of other Boolean functions can be proved via monotone projections (see § 1) or other monotone reductions (see Ch. 10, § 3).

6.13 Negation is powerless for slice functions

Because of Theorem 12.4 one might conjecture that lower bounds on $C_m(f)$ have no implications on $C(f)$. In the following we present a fundamental class of functions where negation is almost powerless, we prove that $C_m(f) = O(C(f) + n\log^2 n)$ for slice functions. Lower bounds on $C_m(f)$ of size $\omega(n\log^2 n)$ imply lower bounds of the same size on $C(f)$.

Our problem is the simulation of circuits by monotone circuits. At first we switch to the complete basis $\{\wedge, \vee, \neg\}$, the number of gates only needs to be increased by a constant factor (see Ch. 1, § 3). Then we double all $\wedge$-gates and $\vee$-gates, one output of a pair is negated, the other one not. After that we can apply the deMorgan rules without increasing the number of gates. Finally we obtain a so-called standard circuit where only variables are negated. The most difficult problem is the replacement of $\bar{x}_i$ by a monotone function. Such a replacement depends on the output of the circuit, since $\bar{x}_i$ is not monotone. The concept of pseudo complements is due to Berkowitz (82).

DEFINITION 13.1 : Let $f \in M_{n,m}$. A function $h_i \in M_n$ is a pseudo complement for x_i with respect to f if in each standard circuit for f $\bar{x}_i$ can be replaced by h_i .

DEFINITION 13.2 : $f \in B_n$ is called $k-$slice if $f(x) = 0$ for inputs x with less than k ones and $f(x) = 1$ for inputs x with more than k ones.
$f = (f_1, \ldots, f_m) \in B_{n,m}$ is called k-slice if all $f_i \in B_n$ are k-slices.

Slice functions are monotone. The interesting inputs for a k-slice are those with exactly k ones, the elements of the k-th slice of $\{0,1\}^n$.

THEOREM 13.1 : Let $X = \{x_1, \ldots, x_n\}$ and $X_i = X - \{x_i\}$. $T_k^{n-1}(X_i)$ is a pseudo complement for x_i with respect to k-slices f.

Proof : Let f' be that function computed by a standard circuit for f after we have replaced $\bar{x}_i$ by $T_k^{n-1}(X_i)$. We claim that $f' = f$. If input a includes less than k ones, $f(a) = 0$ and $T_k^{n-1}(X_i)(a) = 0 \le \bar{a}_i$. $f'(a) = 0$, since standard circuits are monotone below the inputs. If input a includes more than k ones, $f(a) = 1$, $T_k^{n-1}(X_i)(a) = 1 \ge \bar{a}_i$ and $f'(a) = 1$ by monotonicity. If input a includes exactly k ones

$$\bar{a}_i = 1 \quad \Leftrightarrow \quad a_i = 0 \quad \Leftrightarrow \quad T_k^{n-1}(X_i)(a) = 1 . \tag{13.1}$$

$f(a) = f'(a)$, since we do not have changed the circuit for these inputs. Altogether $f' = f$. □

The following generalization of Dunne (84) is left as an exercise.

PROPOSITION 13.1 : $h_i \in M_n$ is a pseudo complement for x_i with respect to $f \in M_{n,m}$ iff

$$\forall \ 1 \le j \le m : \ f_{j|x_i=0} \le h_i \le f_{j|x_i=1} . \tag{13.2}$$

All $f \in M_n$ have pseudo complements, but these pseudo complements may be hard to compute. Slice functions have pseudo complements which are easy to compute. Moreover, slice functions set up a basis of all monotone functions (Wegener (85 a) and (86 b)).

DEFINITION 13.3 : The k-th slice f^k of $f \in B_n$ is defined by

$$f^k = (f \wedge E_k^n) \vee T_{k+1}^n = (f \wedge T_k^n) \vee T_{k+1}^n . \tag{13.3}$$

THEOREM 13.2 : i) $C(f) \leq C(f^0, \ldots, f^n) + O(n)$.

ii) $C(f^0, \ldots, f^n) \leq C(f) + O(n)$.

iii) $C_m(f^0, \ldots, f^n) \leq C_m(f) + O(n \log n)$ if f monotone.

iv) $C_m(f^k) \leq C_m(f) + O(n)$ if f monotone and k constant.

Proof : ii) , iii) , and iv) follow from (13.3) and the known upper bounds on the complexity of threshold functions. i) follows from

$$f = \bigvee_{0 \leq k \leq n} (f^k \wedge E_k^n) .$$

$$(13.4)$$

$\square$

Since $C(f) = \Theta(C(f^0, \ldots, f^n))$, if $C(f) = \Omega(n)$, we can investigate $(f^0, \ldots, f^n)$ instead of f . $(f^0, \ldots, f^n)$ is called monotone representation of f , since f^k is monotone. Even for non monotone $f \in B_n$ we can compare $C(f^0, \ldots, f^n)$ with $C_m(f^0, \ldots, f^n)$. Theorem 13.1 has the following corollary.

COROLLARY 13.1 : i) $C_m(f^k) \leq O(C(f^k)) + C_m(k)$ where $C_m(k) = C_m(T_k^{n-1}(X_i) \mid 1 \leq i \leq n)$.

ii) $C_m(f^0, \ldots, f^n) \leq \sum_{0 \leq k \leq n} O(C(f^k)) + C_m(0, \ldots, n)$ where $C_m(0, \ldots, n) = C_m(T_k^{n-1}(X_i) \mid 1 \leq i \leq n , 0 \leq k \leq n)$.

Lower bounds on the **monotone** complexity of the k-th slice f^k of some explicitly defined $f \in B_n$ of size $\omega(C_m(k))$ imply a lower bound of the same size on the circuit complexity of f . This fact offers a strong motivation for the investigation of monotone circuits and slice functions. We point out that we can use efficient circuits (over the basis B_2) for $f \in M_n$ for the design of efficient monotone circuits for $(f^0, \ldots, f^n)$ but not for the design of efficient monotone circuits for f. (13.4) has no monotone analogue.

What is the monotone complexity of the pseudo complements for slice functions ? The sets X_i are more or less alike. One might believe that it is sufficient to sort X and to remove x_i afterwards. But this last step is impossible in monotone circuits. The best monotone circuits for all $T_k^{n-1}(X_i)$ $(1 \le i \le n)$ have been designed by Paterson (pers. comm.), Valiant (86), and Wegener (85 a).

THEOREM 13.3 : $C_m(k) = O(n \min \{k, n-k, \log^2 n\})$.

Proof : The following circuit is suitable for small k . Obviously

$$T_k^{n-1}(X_i) = \bigvee_{0 \le p \le k} T_p^{i-1}(x_1, \dots, x_{i-1}) \wedge T_{k-p}^{n-i}(x_{i+1}, \dots, x_n) \text{ and} \qquad (13.5)$$

$$T_p^i(x_1, \dots, x_i) = T_p^{i-1}(x_1, \dots, x_{i-1}) \vee (T_{p-1}^{i-1}(x_1, \dots, x_{i-1}) \wedge x_i) . \qquad (13.6)$$

Because of (13.6) all $T_p^i(x_1, \dots, x_i)$ $(1 \le i \le n, 1 \le p \le k)$ can be computed with at most $2nk$ gates, the same holds for all $T_{k-p}^{n-i}(x_{i+1}, \dots, x_n)$ $(0 \le i \le n-1, 0 \le p \le k-1)$. Because of (13.5) $2nk$ further gates suffice for the computation of all $T_k^{n-1}(X_i)$. Hence $C_m(k) \le 6nk$ and by the duality principle also $C_m(k) \le 6n(n-k)$.

For k not too small and not too large the following attack is promising. W.l.o.g. $n = 2^m$. For each $r \in \{0, \dots, m\}$ we partition X to 2^{m-r} blocks of successive variables of 2^r variables. Let X_{ir} be the 2^r-block that includes x_i .

We use a Batcher sorting network to sort X with $O(n \log^2 n)$ gates. As mentioned in §2 we sort simultaneously all X_{ir} . $X_i = X - \{x_i\}$ is the disjoint union of $Z_{i,m-1}, \dots, Z_{i,0}$ where Z_{ir} is some 2^r-block. We can sort X_i and compute $T_k^{n-1}(X_i)$ by merging $Z_{i,m-1}, \dots, Z_{i,0}$. If we merge the small blocks at first, the intermediate results are of interest only for $T_k^{n-1}(X_i)$. If we merge $Z_{i,m-1}$ and $Z_{i,m-2}$, the result is of interest for all those 2^{m-2} sets X_j where $x_j \notin Z_{i,m-1} \cup Z_{i,m-2}$. Using this approach we merge always a large set and a smaller one. Now we make the most of the fact that we only compute $T_k^{n-1}(X_i)$ and that we do not sort X_i .

By Y_{ir} we denote the union of $Z_{i,m-1}, \dots, Z_{i,r}$, in particular $Y_{i0} = X_i$. Since $Y_{ir} = X - X_{ir}$, only 2^{m-r} sets Y_{ir} are different. We are interested in the element of rank k in Y_{i0} (the k-th largest element of Y_{i0}). If we know the elements of rank $k-1$ and k in Y_{i1}, we can merge them with the 1-block Z_{i0}, and the middle element is equal to $T_k^{n-1}(X_i)$. In general it suffices to know the elements of rank $k-2^{r+1}+1, \ldots, k$ in $Y_{i,r+1}$. Since Y_{ir} is the disjoint union of $Y_{i,r+1}$ and Z_{ir}, the elements of rank $k-2^r+1, \ldots, k$ of Y_{ir} are the 2^r middle elements in the output of a merging network if we merge the elements of rank $k-2^{r+1}+1, \ldots, k$ in $Y_{i,r+1}$ with the elements in $Z_{i,r}$. All other elements in $Y_{i,r+1}$ cannot be elements of rank $k-2^r+1, \ldots, k$ in Y_{ir}.

Thus we start with the sorted sets $Y_{i,m-1} = Z_{i,m-1}, \ldots, Z_{i0}$. For $r = m-2, \ldots, 0$ we compute the elements of rank $k-2^r+1, \ldots, k$ in Y_{ir} by merging the elements of rank $k-2^{r+1}+1, \ldots, k$ in $Y_{i,r+1}$ and the elements in Z_{ir}. The middle 2^r elements are the elements we are looking for. Using the Batcher merging network $O((r+1) \, 2^{r+1})$ gates suffice. For fixed r we need 2^{m-r} of these merging networks, hence $O((r+1) \, 2^m) = O((r+1) \, n)$ gates. For all r together $O(n \, m^2) = O(n \log^2 n)$ gates suffice.

$\square$

For practical purposes it is important to notice that the circuits in the proof of Theorem 13.3 are not only asymptotically efficient but also efficient for small n.

We do not know of a nonlinear lower bound on the monotone complexity of some explicitly defined slice function $f \in M_n$. Razborov's method cannot be applied directly to slice functions. Till today this is only a hypothesis many experts believe in, among them Razborov (pers. comm.). One should try to formalize this hypothesis and to prove the formal statement.

In § 14 we discuss central slices, i.e. $n/2$-slices, and argue why they are more important than k-slices for constant k. For central slices we have to prove $\omega(n \log^2 n)$ bounds on the monotone complexity in order to obtain results for circuits over complete bases.

Smaller lower bounds can work only for functions which have more efficient pseudo complements. Such classes of functions were introduced by Wegener (86 b).

DEFINITION 13.4 : $F_n^k \subseteq M_n$ is the class of all k -slices f for which the set of variables can be partitioned in such a way into k disjoint sets $X^1, \ldots, X^k$ that each prime implicant of f of length k includes exactly one variable of each class. (The disjunction of the prime implicants of length k is a multilinear form.)

The j-th variable of X^i is denoted by x_j^i $(1 \le i \le k, 1 \le j \le n(i) = |X^i|)$. Let h_i be the disjunction of all variables in X^i and let g_i be the conjunction of all h_j $(j \ne i)$. Obviously $n - k$ gates suffice for the computation of all h_i. Then $3k - 6$ gates suffice, if $k \ge 2$, for the computation of all g_i (Exercise 25, Ch. 3, generalized to monotone circuits). If we estimate the number of gates by $3k - 3$, the estimation holds also for $k = 1$. Let

$$y_j^i = x_j^i \wedge g_i \quad \text{and} \quad z_j^i = \bigvee_{m \ne j} y_m^i. \tag{13.7}$$

All y_j^i can be computed with n gates, afterwards all z_j^i for fixed i can be computed with at most $3n(i) - 3$ gates. Altogether we can compute all y_j^i and z_j^i with at most $5n - k - 3$ gates. y_j^i and z_j^i are almost pseudo inputs and pseudo complements for x_j^i with respect to functions in F_n^k.

THEOREM 13.4 : All y_j^i and z_j^i can be computed with $O(n)$ gates. If we replace in a standard circuit for $f \in F_n^k$ x_j^i by y_j^i and $\bar{x}_j^i$ by z_j^i, then f is replaced by some function f^* where $f = f^* \vee T_{k+1}^n$. Hence

$$C_m(f) = O(C(f)) + O(n) + C_m(T_{k+1}^n). \tag{13.8}$$

Proof : We only have to prove that $f = f^* \vee T_{k+1}^n$. If input a includes either less than k ones or exactly k ones but not from k different classes, $f(a) = 0$ and $T_{k+1}^n(a) = 0$. Since $y_j^i(a) = 0 \le x_j^i(a)$ and

$z_j^i(a) = 0 \le \bar{x}_j^i(a)$, $f^*(a) = 0$ by monotonicity. If input a includes exactly k ones from different classes, $T_{k+1}^n(a) = 0$. The set of prime implicants of y_j^i is the set of all monoms including exactly one variable of each class among them x_j^i. $PI(z_j^i)$ is the set of all monoms including exactly one variable of each class but not x_j^i. Hence $x_j^i(a) = y_j^i(a)$, $\bar{x}_j^i(a) = z_j^i(a)$ and $f(a) = f^*(a)$. If a includes more than k ones, $T_{k+1}^n(a) = 1$ and $f(a) = 1$, since f is a k-slice. In this case the correcting term T_{k+1}^n is necessary.

$\square$

DEFINITION 13.5 : $G_n^k \subseteq M_n$ is the class of all $g = g^* \vee T_2^*$ for which the set of variables can be partitioned in such a way into k disjoint sets $X^1, \ldots, X^k$ that each prime implicant of g^* includes exactly one variable of each class. $T_2^*(X)$ is the disjunction of all $T_2^{n(i)}(X^i)$.

THEOREM 13.5 : If we replace in a standard circuit for $g \in G_n^k$ x_j^i by y_j^i and $\bar{x}_j^i$ by z_j^i , then g is replaced by some function g' where $g = g' \vee T_2^*$. Hence

$$C_m(g) = O(C(g)) + O(n) . \qquad (13.9)$$

Proof : The proof is similar to that of Theorem 13.4 . $C_m(T_2^*) = O(n)$, since $C_m(T_2^{n(i)}) = O(n(i))$. $\square$

COROLLARY 13.2 : i) $C(f) = \Theta(C_m(f))$ for $f \in F_n^k$ if $C_m(f) = \omega(n \min\{k, n-k, \log n\})$.

ii) $C(g) = \Theta(C_m(g))$ for $g \in G_n^k$.

According to Corollary 13.2 already lower bounds of size $n \log n$ or $n \log^* n$ on the monotone complexity of certain functions imply similar bounds for circuits over complete bases.

Dunne (84) applied the concept of slice functions and proved for the most complex $(n-k)$ - homogeneous functions $f \in H_n^{n-k}$ (see Ch. 4, § 7) that $C(f) = \Theta(C_m(f))$. More precisely, $C_m(f) = O(C(f)) + O(n^{k-1})$ for $f \in H_n^{n-k}$ and constant k .

The monotone complexity of the set of all pseudo complements has been determined by Wegener (86 b).

THEOREM 13.6 : $C_m(0,...,n) = \Theta(n^2)$.

Proof : The lower bound is obvious, since we consider $n(n-1)$ different outputs $T_p^{n-1}(X_i)$ $(1 \le p \le n-1 , 1 \le i \le n)$.

For the upper bound we analyze Batcher's merging network for merging sorted lists of different size $k = 2^i$ and $l = 2^j$, w.l.o.g. $k \ge l$. We only modify Step 1 of Algorithm 2.1.b . If $l = 1$, k comparisons suffice. Hence $M(k,l)$, the number of comparisons, fulfils the following recursion equation.

$$M(k,l) = 2M(k/2,l/2) + (k+l)/2 - 1 \quad \text{and} \quad M(k,1) = k . \quad (13.10)$$

Since the depth of recursion is only $\log l$,

$$M(k,l) = (k+l)(\log l)/2 + k - l + 1 . \quad (13.11)$$

W.l.o.g. $n = 2^m$. We apply a Batcher sorting network and sort X and all $n 2^{-r}$ blocks of 2^r successive variables. For this step $O(n \log^2 n)$ gates suffice. As in the proof of Theorem 13.3 X_i is the disjoint union of $Z_{i,m-1}, \ldots, Z_{i,0}$ where Z_{ir} is some 2^r-block. Again Y_{ir} is the union of $Z_{i,m-1}, \ldots, Z_{ir}$, hence $Y_{i0} = X_i$. We sort Y_{ir} by merging $Y_{i,r+1}$ and Z_{ir} . The size of $Y_{i,r+1}$ is bounded by n , hence $M(n,2^r) \le nr + n$ comparisons suffice. For fixed r $(0 \le r \le m-2)$ we need 2^{m-r} of these merging networks, hence

$$2^{m-r}(nr + n) = n^2(r + 1) 2^{-r} \quad (13.12)$$

comparisons. Summing up for all r we can esimate the number of gates by $6 n^2$. $\square$

This result implies that for all functions $f \in B_n$ which cannot be computed very efficiently, it is almost sufficient to investigate the monotone complexity of the monotone representation $(f^0, \ldots, f^n)$ of f . More precisely, $C(f) = \Omega(C_m(f^0, \ldots, f^n) / n)$ and $C(f) = \Theta(C(f^0, \ldots, f^n))$.

6.14 Hard slices of NP-complete functions

According to Theorem 13.2 there is for each $f \in B_n$ some k such that $C(f^k) = \Omega(C(f) / n)$. Difficult functions have difficult slices, but they also may have easy slices, e.g. for $k = 0$ or $k = n$. We like to know which slice is hard, and we ask for relations between the complexity of f^k and f^{k+1} .

As examples for probably hard functions we consider NP-complete functions, in particular the clique function $cl_{n,m}$ for $m = n/2$ (see Def. 11.1). $cl_{n,m}$ has $\binom{n}{m}$ prime implicants, one for each vertex set A of size m . All prime implicants t_A are of length $\binom{m}{2}$, t_A is testing whether all edges on A exist. The $\binom{m}{2}$ - slice of $cl_{n,m}$ has the same prime implicants and additional prime implicants of length $\binom{m}{2}$ + 1 . This slice looks similar to $cl_{n,m}$, but this slice is easy to compute (Wegener (85 a)).

DEFINITION 14.1 : If $f \in M_n$ has only prime implicants of length k , f^k is called the canonical slice of f .

THEOREM 14.1 : The circuit complexity of the canonical slice of $cl_{n,m} \in M_N$ where $N = \binom{n}{2}$ is $O(N)$, its monotone complexity $O(N \log N)$, for constant m only $O(N)$.

Proof : The canonical slice is the M - slice for $M = (\frac{m}{2})$.

$$cl_{n,m}^M = (cl_{n,m} \wedge E_M^N) \vee T_{M+1}^N = (cl_{n,m} \wedge T_M^N) \vee T_{M+1}^N . \tag{14.1}$$

In (14.1) we can replace $cl_{n,m}$ by any function g which equals $cl_{n,m}$ on graphs with exactly M edges. T_M^N and T_{M+1}^N have circuit complexity $O(N)$.

A graph with exactly M edges includes an m-clique iff the M edges set up an m-clique. This happens iff at least m vertices have degree at least $m-1$. This condition can be expressed by threshold functions. Let $X_i = \{ x_{1i}, \ldots, x_{i-1,i}, x_{i,i+1}, \ldots, x_{in}\}$. X_i includes the variables describing the edges adjacent to vertex i . In (14.1) we can replace $cl_{n,m}$ by T_m^n ($T_{m-1}^{n-1}(X_1)$,...., $T_{m-1}^{n-1}(X_n))$. All these $n+1$ threshold functions have circuit complexity $O(n)$, altogether $O(n^2)$ $= O(N)$. The results for monotone circuits follow in the same way. $\square$

DEFINITION 14.2 : $f^* = f^{\lceil n/2 \rceil}$ is the central slice of $f \in B_n$.

THEOREM 14.2 : For n even and $l \geq (\frac{n/2}{2})$

$$C_m(cl_{n,n/2}^l) \leq C_m(cl_{5n,5n/2}^*) . \tag{14.2}$$

If $l < (\frac{n/2}{2})$, $cl_{n,n/2}^l = T_{l+1}^N$ for $N = (\frac{n}{2})$.

This theorem due to Dunne (84) implies that the central slice of $cl_{n,n/2}$ has polynomial (monotone) circuits iff $cl_{n,n/2}$ has polynomial circuits. Furthermore $cl_{n,n/2}^*$ is an NP-complete predicate, since the reduction in the following proof can be computed in polynomial time.

Proof of Theorem 14.2 : It is sufficient to prove that $cl_{n,n/2}^l$ is a subfunction of $cl_{5n,5n/2}^*$. We denote the vertices by $v_1, \ldots, v_n, w_1, \ldots, w_{4n}$ and replace all variables corresponding to edges which are adjacent to some w-node by an appropriate constant. The vertices $w_1, \ldots, w_{2n}$ form a $2n$-clique, and these vertices are connected to all v-vertices. The variables for the edges (w_i, w_{2n+i}) $(1 \leq i \leq 2n)$ are replaced by 0.

Altogether $\binom{4n}{2} + 4n^2$ variables should be replaced by constants. Until now we have decided that $\binom{2n}{2} + 2n^2$ edges exist and that $2n$ edges do not exist. We still have to decide about

$$\binom{4n}{2} + 4n^2 - \binom{2n}{2} - 2n^2 - 2n = 8n^2 - 3n \qquad (14.3)$$

edges. Let $r = \lceil \binom{5n}{2}/2 \rceil - l - (\binom{2n}{2} + 2n^2)$. Then $0 \leq r \leq 8n^2 - 3n$. We decide that exactly r of the $8n^2 - 3n$ variable edges exist. Altogether the graph contains now $\lceil \binom{5n}{2}/2 \rceil - l$ edges.

It remains to be proved that the graph on V includes an $n/2$-clique or more than l edges iff the graph on $V \cup W$ includes an $5n/2$-clique or more than $\lceil \binom{5n}{2}/2 \rceil$ edges. Each $n/2$-clique on V can be extended to a $5n/2$-clique on $V \cup W$ by adding $w_1, \ldots, w_{2n}$. If the graph on W included a $(2n+1)$-clique, this clique would include for some i the vertices w_i and w_{2n+i}. This is impossible, since w_i and w_{2n+i} are not connected. Hence a $5n/2$-clique on $V \cup W$ implies an $n/2$-clique on V. The assertion on the number of edges is obvious, since the graph includes $\lceil \binom{5n}{2}/2 \rceil - l$ edges adjacent to some w-vertex. $\qquad \square$

Results similar to those in Theorem 14.1 and 14.2 can also be proved for other NP-complete predicates (see Exercises). In order to obtain more results on the complexity of the slices of some function, we compare the complexity of the k-slice with the complexity of the $(k+1)$-slice of some function f. Dunne (84) proved that f^{k+1} is not much harder than f^k, whereas Wegener (86 b) proved that f^{k+1} may be much easier than f^k.

Theorem 14.3 : Let $f \in M_n$ have prime implicants of length k only.

Then $C_m(f^{k+l}) = O(n\, C_m(f^{k+l-1}))$ for $l \geq 1$.

Proof : The key to the proof is the realization of f^{k+l} by

$$f^{k+l}(x) = \bigvee_{1 \leq i \leq n} f^{k+l-1}(h_i(x)) \wedge T^n_{k+l}(x) \vee T^n_{k+l+1}(x) \tag{14.4}$$

for $h_i(x) = y$ where $y_i = 0$ and $y_j = x_i x_j$ for $i \neq j$. (14.4) implies the theorem, since $C_m(f^{k+l-1}) = \Omega(n)$, $C_m(T^n_{k+l}, T^n_{k+l+1}) = O(n^2)$ and $C_m(h_1, \ldots, h_n) = O(n^2)$.

(14.4) is obvious for inputs with less or more than $k+l$ ones. Let a be an input with exactly $k+l$ ones. W.l.o.g. $a_i = 1$ iff $i \leq k+l$. If $i > k+l$, $h_i(a) = (0, \ldots, 0)$ and $f^{k+l-1}(h_i(a)) = 0$. If $i \leq k+l$, $h_i(a)$ differs from a only at position i, in particular $h_i(a)$ includes $k+l-1$ ones.

If $f^{k+l-1}(h_i(a)) = 1$, $p(h_i(a)) = 1$ for some $p \in PI(f)$. Since $h_i(a) \leq a$, $p(a) = 1$ and $f^{k+l}(a) = 1$.

If $f^{k+l}(a) = 1$, $p(a) = 1$ for some $p \in PI(f)$. By our assumption p has length k. By definition of a the variables of p have indices $j \leq k+l$. Since $l \geq 1$, $p(h_i(a)) = 1$ for some i such that x_i is not in p. Hence $f^{k+l-1}(h_i(a)) = 1$.

□

Theorem 14.4 : Let $c(k,n) = \binom{n-1}{k-1} \left(\log \binom{n-1}{k-1}\right)^{-1}$. There are functions $f \in M_n$ with prime implicants of length k only, such that $C_m(f^k) = \Omega(c(k,n))$ and $C_m(f^l) = O(n \log n)$ for $l > k$.

Proof : Let $F_{k,n}$ be the set of all functions f such that all prime implicants have length k and each monom of length k not including x_1 is a prime implicant of f. Then $f \in F_{k,n}$ is defined by a subset of all monoms of length k including x_1. Hence $\log |F_{k,n}| = \binom{n-1}{k-1}$. By Shannon's counting argument $C_m(f^k) = \Omega(c(k,n))$ for almost all $f \in F_{k,n}$.

It suffices to prove that $f^l = T_l^n$ for $f \in F_{k,n}$ and $l > k$. By definition $f^l = (f \wedge T_l^n) \vee T_{l+1}^n$. Obviously $f^l \le T_l^n$. Let $T_l^n(a) = 1$. Then a includes l ones. Since $l > k$, input b, defined by $b_1 = 0$ and $b_i = a_i$ for $i \neq 1$, includes at least k ones, and, by definition of $F_{k,n}$, $f(b) = 1$.

$\square$

6.15 Set circuits - a new model for proving lower bounds

We are not able to prove non linear lower bounds on the circuit complexity of explicitly defined Boolean functions. For monotone circuits we know several methods for the proof of lower bounds, and for slice functions f lower bounds on $C_m(f)$ imply lower bounds on $C(f)$. Hence we should apply our lower bound methods to slice functions. The reader should convince himself that our bounds (at least in their pure form) do not work for slice functions. In this section we discuss some particularities of monotone circuits for slice functions f and present some problems whose solution implies lower bounds on $C_m(f)$ and therefore also on $C(f)$ (Wegener (85 a) and (86 b)).

Let $PI_k(g)$ be the set of prime implicants of g whose length is k. Let M_n^k be the set of $f \in M_n$ where $PI_l(f) = \phi$ for $l < k$. M_n^k includes all k-slices.

LEMMA 15.1 : Let S be a monotone circuit for $f \in M_n^k$. If we replace the inputs x_i by $y_i = x_i \wedge T_k^n$, then the new circuit S' also computes f.

The proof of this and the following lemmas is left to the reader. For the computation of the pseudo inputs $n + C_m(T_k^n)$ gates suffice. All functions computed in S' are in M_n^k. In the following sense slice functions are the easiest functions in M_n^k.

LEMMA 15.2 : Let $f, f' \in M_n^k$ and $PI_k(f) = PI_k(f')$. If f is a k-slice , $f = f' \vee T_{k+1}^n$ and $C_m(f) \leq C_m(f') + C_m(T_{k+1}^n) + 1$.

Hence we consider prime implicants of length k only. If we do not compute any shorter prime implicants, prime implicants of length k will not be eliminated by the law of simplification.

LEMMA 15.3 : Let $f, g \in M_n^k$. Then

$$PI_k(f \vee g) = PI_k(f) \cup PI_k(g) \quad \text{and} \tag{15.1}$$

$$PI_k(f \wedge g) = PI_k(f) \cap PI_k(g) . \tag{15.2}$$

These lemmas motivate the so-called set circuits.

DEFINITION 15.1 : The inputs of a set circuit are for some k the sets $Y_i = PI(x_i \wedge T_n^k)$ and the operations are binary unions and intersections. The set complexity of $f \in M_n^k$, denoted by $SC(f)$, is the least number of gates in a set circuit for $PI_k(f)$.

THEOREM 15.1 : Let f be a k-slice. Then

i) $C_m(f) \leq SC(f) + C_m(T_k^n, T_{k+1}^n) + n + 1$.

ii) $SC(f) \leq C_m(f) \leq O(C(f)) + O(n \min\{k, n-k, \log^2 n\})$.

Proof : We only combine the assertions of Lemma 15.1, 15.2, 15.3, Theorem 13.1, Corollary 13.1, and Theorem 13.3 . $\qquad \square$

Set circuits form the principal item of monotone circuits and circuits for slice functions. So we obtain a set theoretical or combinatorial representation of circuits.

For the classes of functions F_n^k and G_n^k (see Definition 13.4 and 13.5) we can use the pseudo inputs y_j^i and in set circuits the sets $Y_j^i = PI(y_j^i)$, the prime implicants in Y_j^i all have exactly one variable of each class X^i. This holds for all gates of a set circuit with inputs Y_j^i. This leads to both a geometrical and combinatorial representation of set circuits.

The set of monoms with exactly one variable of each class X^i ($1 \le i \le k$) can be represented as the set theoretical product $Q = \underset{1 \le i \le n}{\times} \{1,...,n(i)\}$ where $(r(1),...,r(k)) \in Q$ corresponds to the monom $x_{r(1)}^1 \cdots x_{r(k)}^k$. Q is a k-dimensional, discrete cuboid. Input Y_j^i corresponds to the $(k-1)$-dimensional subcuboid of all $(r(1),...,r(k))$ where $r(i) = j$. The set of prime implicants of $f \in F_n^k$ or $g \in G_n^k$ corresponding to vertices in Q forms a subset $Q(f)$ or $Q(g)$ of Q, called pattern of f or g. Set circuits for f or g correspond to computations of $Q(f)$ or $Q(g)$ by unions and intersections out of the $(k-1)$-dimensional subcuboids of Q.

For $n = 2k$ and $n(1) = \cdots = n(k) = 2$ we work on the k-dimensional cube $\{0,1\}^k$ (or $\{1,2\}^k$). There is a one-to-one relation between subsets Q' of $\{0,1\}^k$ and functions in F_n^k or G_n^k. If we could prove for some explicitly defined set $Q' \subseteq \{0,1\}^k$ that $\omega(n)$ binary unions and intersections are necessary for the computation of Q' out of all $(k-1)$-dimensional subcubes of $\{0,1\}^k$, then we would have proved a lower bound of the same size on the circuit complexity of the corresponding $g \in G_n^k$.

In order to illustrate our geometrical approach as well as for later purposes, we prove that the canonical slice of the Boolean convolution has linear complexity.

THEOREM 15.2 : The monotone complexity of the canonical slice of the Boolean convolution is linear.

Proof : The canonical slice is the 2-slice, the Boolean convolution is a function in $F_{2n,2n-1}^2$. Hence the cuboid considered is the square $\{1,...,n\}^2$. The i-th row corresponds to the set of monoms $A_i = \{x_i y_1, ..., x_i y_n\}$ and the j-th column corresponds to $B_j = \{x_1 y_j, ..., x_n y_j\}$. These sets are inputs of the set circuit. We have to compute the Boolean convolution , i.e. the diagonal sets $T_k = \{x_i y_j \mid i+j = k\}$. It is sufficient to design a set circuit of linear size for $T_2, \ldots, T_{2n}$.

W.l.o.g. $n = m^2$. We partition the square to m^2 subsquares of side length m each (see Fig. 15.1).

1. $D_l = A_{(l-1)m+1} \cup \cdots \cup A_{(l-1)m+m}$ $(1 \leq l \leq m)$ $(m^2 - m$ gates$)$.

2. $E_l = B_{(l-1)m+1} \cup \cdots \cup B_{(l-1)m+m}$ $(1 \leq l \leq m)$ $(m^2 - m$ gates$)$.

3. $F_{ij} = D_i \cap E_j$ $(1 \leq i,j \leq m)$ $(m^2$ gates$)$.

   F_{ij} are the subsquares of side length m .

4. $G_{ij} = \underset{i+j=l}{\cup} F_{ij}$ $(2 \leq l \leq 2m)$ $(m^2 - 2m + 1$ gates$)$.

   G_l is the l-th diagonal consisting of subsquares.

5. $H_l = A_l \cup A_{m+l} \cup \cdots \cup A_{(m-1)m+l}$ $(1 \leq l \leq m)$ $(m^2 - m$ gates$)$.

6. $I_l = B_l \cup B_{m+l} \cup \cdots \cup B_{(m-1)m+l}$ $(1 \leq l \leq m)$ $(m^2 - m$ gates$)$.

7. $J_{ij} = H_i \cap I_j$ $(1 \leq i,j \leq m)$ $(m^2$ gates$)$.

   J_{ij} includes of each subsquare the element at position (i,j) .

8. $K_l = \underset{i+j=l}{\cup} J_{ij}$ $(2 \leq l \leq 2m)$ $(m^2 - 2m + 1$ gates$)$.

   K_l consists of all l-th diagonals of subsquares.

T_k cuts at most two adjacent diagonals of subsquares, say $G_{h(k)}$ and perhaps $G_{h(k)+1}$ (see Fig. 15.1). The intersection of T_k and $G_{h(k)}$ consists of all $d'(k)$-th diagonals of the subsquares in $G_{h(k)}$. Let $d''(k)$ be the corresponding parameter for the intersection of $G_{h(k)+1}$ and T_k . Hence

9. $T_k = (G_{h(k)} \cap K_{d'(k)}) \cup (G_{h(k)+1} \cap K_{d''(k)})$ if $k-1$ is not a multiple of m and $m+2 \leq k \leq m^2 - m$, and

   $T_k = G_{h(k)} \cap K_{d'(k)}$ otherwise.

   Here $2 \leq k \leq 2n$ and $6n - 8m + 3$ gates suffice.

Altogether the set circuit consists of $14n - 16m + 5$ gates.

□

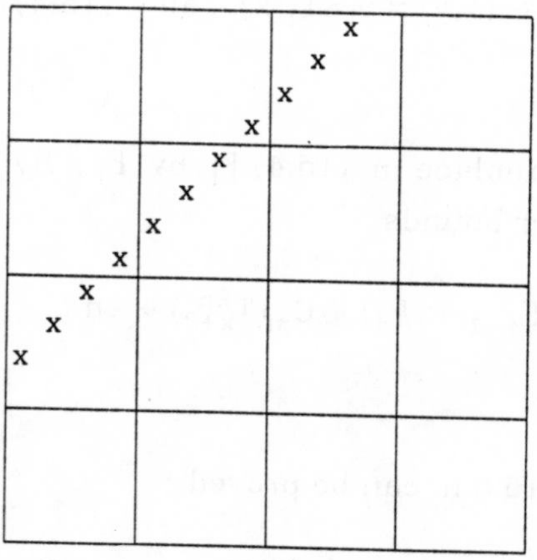

$$n = 16 \,,\, m = 4 \,,\, k = 12 \,,\, h(k) = 3 \,,$$
$$d_1(k) = 8 \,,\, d_2(k) = 4 \,,$$
$$T_{12} = (G_3 \cap K_8) \cup (G_4 \cap K_4)$$

Fig. 15.1

At the end of this section we discuss relations between functions of n outputs and their corresponding one output function. These considerations result in another combinatorial problem whose solution would probably imply lower bounds for slice functions.

Let $x = (x_1, \ldots, x_n)$ and $y = (y_1, \ldots, y_n)$. For $f_1, \ldots, f_n \in M_n$ we define $g, g_1, \ldots, g_n \in M_n$ by

$$g_i(x,y) = y_i \wedge f_i(x) \quad \text{and} \quad g(x,y) = \bigvee_{1 \leq i \leq n} g_i(x,y) \,. \tag{15.3}$$

LEMMA 15.4 : i) $C_m(g_1, \ldots, g_n) = C_m(f_1, \ldots, f_n) + n$.

ii) $C_m(g) \leq C_m(g_1, \ldots, g_n) + n - 1$.

Proof : The upper bounds follow from the definition and the lower bound can be proved by the elimination method.

□

For many functions, in particular those functions we have investigated in § 4 - § 9 , we suppose that equality holds in Lemma 15.4 ii). Let us consider k-slices $F_1, \ldots, F_n \in M_n$. Then $F_i = F_i' \vee T_{k+1}^n$ where $PI(F_i') = PI_k(F_i)$. Since $y_i \wedge F_i$ is in general no slice, we define the $(k+1)$-slices $G, G_1, \ldots, G_n$ by

$$G_i(x,y) = G_i'(x,y) \vee T_{k+2}^{2n}(x,y) \text{ where } G_i'(x,y) = y_i \wedge F_i'(x) \text{ , and} \quad (15.4)$$

$$G(x,y) = \bigvee_{1 \leq i \leq n} G_i(x,y) . \quad (15.5)$$

Since $y_i \wedge T_{k+1}^n(x) \leq T_{k+2}^{2n}(x,y)$, we can replace in (15.4) F_i' by F_i . By definition we obtain the following upper bounds.

LEMMA 15.5 : i) $C_m(G_1, \ldots, G_n) \leq C_m(F_1, \ldots, F_n) + C_m(T_{k+2}^{2n}) + 2n$.

ii) $C_m(G) \leq C_m(G_1, \ldots, G_n) + n - 1$.

Even a partial converse of Lemma 15.5 ii can be proved.

LEMMA 15.6 : $C_\Omega(G_1, \ldots, G_n) \leq C_\Omega(G) + C_\Omega(T_{k+2}^{2n}) + 2n$ for $\Omega \in \{B_2, \Omega_m\}$.

Proof : The assertion follows from the following representation of G_i .

$$G(x,y) \wedge y_i \vee T_{k+2}^{2n}(x,y) \quad (15.6)$$

$$= \bigvee_{1 \leq j \leq n} (y_j \wedge F_j'(x) \vee T_{k+2}^{2n}(x,y)) \wedge y_i \vee T_{k+2}^{2n}(x,y)$$

$$= (F_i'(x) \wedge y_i) \vee (\bigvee_{j \neq i} F_j'(x) \wedge y_j \wedge y_i) \vee (T_{k+2}^{2n}(x,y) \wedge y_i) \vee T_{k+2}^{2n}(x,y)$$

$$= (F_i'(x) \wedge y_i) \vee T_{k+2}^{2n}(x,y) = G_i(x,y) . \qquad \square$$

What about a partial converse of Lemma 15.5 i ? In opposition to Lemma 15.4 i we cannot apply the elimination method. If we set $y_1 = \cdots = y_n = 1$ and if $k \leq n-2$, $T_{k+2}^{2n}(x,y) = 1$ and $G_i(x,y) = 1$. We even suppose that $C_m(F_1, \ldots, F_n)$ can be much larger than $C_m(G_1, \ldots, G_n)$. To underpin this supposition, let $F_1, \ldots, F_n \in F_n^k$, i.e. our geometrical view works for $F_1, \ldots, F_n$. Then $G_1, \ldots, G_n \in F_n^{k+1}$, the (k+1)-st dimension concerns the y-variables. The patterns $F_1, \ldots, F_n$ are defined on the same k-dimensional cuboid Q . G_i has to be constructed on a (k+1)-dimensional cuboid Q' . More precisely, the pattern of G_i equals the pattern of F_i and has to be constructed on that k-dimensional subcuboid Q_i of Q' where the last dimension is fixed to i . $G_1, \ldots, G_n$ can be constructed "in parallel" on the disjoint subcuboids Q_i of Q' , but $F_1, \ldots, F_n$ have to be constructed on the same cuboid Q . Obviously Q and Q_i are isomorphic. We illustrate these considerations in an example.

Let $f_1, \ldots, f_n$ be the Nechiporuk Boolean sums (see § 6) . Then $C_m(f_1, \ldots, f_n) = \Theta(n^{3/2})$. Let $F_1, \ldots, F_n$ be the canonical slices, i.e. the 1 −slices, of $f_1, \ldots, f_n$, and let $G, G_1, \ldots, G_n$ be defined by (15.4) and (15.5) . We consider the pattern of G , which is a subset of the square $\{1, \ldots, n\}^2$. The pattern of G consists of the subpatterns $M_{b,d}$ of (6.10) , so G is composed of small diagonals.
Similarly to Theorem 15.2 we can prove

LEMMA 15.7 : $C_m(G) = O(n)$.

By Lemma 15.6 also $C_m(G_1, \ldots, G_n) = O(n)$. Lemma 15.6 can now be made clear. G is a pattern in the square $\{1, \ldots, n\}^2$, G_i the sub-pattern in the i-th row. Let us consider again the algorithm for the proof of Theorem 15.2 . We compute "in parallel" different useful patterns in different rows. This approach cannot be used for the computation of $F_1, \ldots, F_n$. In that case we work on the cuboid $\{1, \ldots, n\}^1$, i.e. the set $\{1, \ldots, n\}$, and we cannot work "in parallel". We suppose that $SC(f_1, \ldots, f_n)$, $C_m(F_1, \ldots, F_n)$ and therefore also $C(F_1, \ldots, F_n)$ are nonlinear. We reformulate in a pure set theoretical setting the problem of computing $SC(f_1, \ldots, f_n)$. Nonlinear lower bounds for this problem imply lower bounds of the same size on the circuit complexity of the explicitly defined Boolean sums $f_1, \ldots, f_n$.

Inputs :　　$\{1\}, \ldots, \{n\}$.

Operations :　$\cap$, $\cup$ (binary) .

Outputs :　　$H_1, \ldots, H_n$ where $H_i = \{ j \mid x_j \in PI(f_i) \}$.

Problem :　　$SC(H_1, \ldots, H_n) = ? (= \sum_{1 \le i \le n} (|H_i| - 1) ?)$.

EXERCISES :

1. Let $f \in M_n$ be in MDNF . If we replace $\wedge$ by $*$ and $\vee$ by $+$, we obtain the polynomial $p(f)$. Then $C_m(f) \leq C_{\{+, *\}}(p(f))$, but equality does not hold in general.

2. If a sorting network sorts all $0-1$-sequences, it also sorts all sequences of real numbers.

3. $C_m^{\wedge}(T_2^n) = \lceil \log n \rceil$.

4. $C_m^{\wedge}(f) = 2n$ for $f(x_1, \ldots, x_{3n}) = \bigvee_{1 \leq i \leq n} T_2^3(x_{3i-2}, x_{3i-1}, x_{3i})$.

5. $C_m^{\wedge}(S^n) = C_m^{\vee}(S^n) = \Omega(n \log n)$.

6. Each monotone circuit for S^n includes a permutation network, i.e. for $\pi \in \Sigma^n$ there are disjoint paths from x_i to the output $T_{\pi(i)}^n$.

7. The minimal external path length of binary trees with n leaves is $n \lceil \log n \rceil - 2^{\lceil \log n \rceil} + n$.

8. Let f be a semi-disjoint bilinear form.
Then $C_m(f) \geq \min \{|X|, |Y|\}^{-1} (t(1) + \cdots + t(m))$ where $t(j)$ is defined in (4.2) .

9. Formulate the replacement rules dual to Theorem 5.1 and 5.2 and discuss applications.

10. The replacement rules of Theorem 5.1 and 5.2 are powerless for slice functions.

11. Let g be computed in a monotone circuit for the Boolean convolution. Let $t, t' \in PI_1(g)$. Can g be replaced by the constant 1 ?

12. Let g be computed in a monotone circuit for f.
    a) g can be replaced by $0 \iff \forall \, t \in PI(g) \, \forall \, t'$ monom $t \, t' \notin PI(f)$.
    b) g can be replaced by $1 \iff (gh \leq f \implies h \leq f)$.

13. Let f be the Boolean sum of Theorem 6.1 . Then $C_m(f) = 17$ and $C_{\{v\}}(f) = 18$.

14. Which is the largest lower bound that can be proved using (6.9) and Theorem 6.2 ?

15. Apply the methods of the proof of Theorem 7.1 to $(1,1)$-disjoint Boolean sums.

16. For a semi-disjoint bilinear form f let $G(f)$ be the bipartite graph including the edge (r,s) iff $x_r y_s \in PI(f_k)$ for some k . Let $V(r,s)$ be the connected component including the edge (r,s) . f is called a disjoint bilinear form iff $V(r,s)$ and $PI(f_k)$ have at most one edge (or prime implicant) in common.
    a) The Boolean matrix product is a disjoint bilinear form.
    b) The Boolean convolution is not a disjoint bilinear form.

17. If $f \in M_{n,n}$ is a disjoint bilinear form, $|PI(f)| = O(n^{3/2})$.

18. If $f \in M_{n,m}$ is a disjoint bilinear form, $C_m^\wedge(f) = \sum_{1 \leq k \leq m} |PI(f_k)|$.

19. The monograph Savage (76) contains a proof that $C_m^\vee(f) = \sum_{1 \leq k \leq m} (|PI(f_k)| - 1)$ for disjoint bilinear forms.
    a) The proof is incorrect. Find the error.

b) Barth (80) presented the following counterexample. g is defined on x_i, y_i $(0 \le i < 2n^2)$. The output g_k ($k = (k_0, \ldots, k_3) \in \{0,\ldots,n\text{-}1\}^4$) has the prime implicants $x_{a(k)} y_{b(k)}$ and $x_{c(k)} y_{d(k)}$ where $a(k) = k_3 n + k_0$, $b(k) = k_2 n + k_1$, $c(k) = n^2 + k_1 n + k_0$, $d(k) = n^2 + k_3 n + k_2$. Hint: Consider the MCNF of g .

20. Optimal monotone circuits for the Boolean matrix product are unique up to associativity and commutativity.

21. Maximize $N M^m$ for $mMN \le n$ and $M^m \le n$.

22. Apply the elimination method to the generalized matrix product f_{MN}^m .

23. Let $P(n)$ be the circuit complexity of the Boolean matrix product. Prove upper bounds on $C(f_{MN}^m)$ depending on n and $P(n)$.

24. Investigate the MCNF of f_{MN}^m . How many $\vee$-gates are sufficient for the computation of f_{MN}^m ?

25. Design $*-$circuits for f_{MN}^m with $N M^m$ $\wedge$-gates where $v(h_1, \ldots, h_m, l) = \dfrac{i+1}{2i}$ for all prime implicants (i fixed, m large).
a) For almost all gates $v(G) = \dfrac{1}{2}$.
b) For almost half of the gates $v(G) = 0$, for the other gates $v(G) = 1$.

26. $B \subseteq PI(f)$ is called isolated if $r = s$ or $r = t$ for $r \in PI(f)$. Compute the size of the largest isolated set for
a) the Boolean convolution   b) the clique function.

27. Schnorr (76 c) conjectured by analogy with his results on arithmetic circuits that $C_m^\vee(f) \ge |B|$ for isolated sets B . Wegener (79

b) presented the following counterexample. Let $y_{hh'h''}$ be the outputs of f_{M2}^3 and let g be defined on $M^3 + 6M^2$ variables by

$$g(x_{jl}^i, z_{hh'h''}) = \bigvee_{1 \le h,h',h'' \le M} y_{hh'h''} z_{hh'h''} \cdot$$

$PI(g)$ is isolated but $C_m^v(g) \le M^3 + 6M^2 + 3M - 1$ (use the MCNF for f_{M2}^3).

28. $C_m(f) = \Theta(2^n n^{-3/2})$ for almost all slices $f \in M_n$.

29. If $C(f) = \Omega(2^n n^{-1})$, f has $\Omega(n^{1/2})$ slices of complexity $\Omega(2^n n^{-2})$.

30. Prove Proposition 13.1.

31. The canonical slice of the Boolean matrix product has complexity $O(n^2)$.

32. Design efficient circuits for the canonical slices of the following functions:
a) Perfect matching PM_n (see Definition 12.2).
b) UHC_n (and DHC_n). $UHC_n(x) = 1$ iff the undirected graph $G(x)$ on n vertices specified by the variables x includes a Hamiltonian circuit, i.e. a circuit of length n. DHC is the same function for directed graphs.

33. $C_m(DHC_n^l) \le C_m(DHC_{7n}^*)$ if $n \le l \le n(n-1)$.

34. Prove Lemma 15.1, 15.2, 15.3, and 15.7.

7. RELATIONS BETWEEN CIRCUIT SIZE, FORMULA SIZE AND DEPTH

We investigate the relations between the complexity measures circuit size C , formula size L and depth D . A more intensive study of formulas (in Ch. 8) is motivated by the result that $D(f) = \Theta(\log L(f))$. For practical purposes circuits of small size and depth are preferred. It is an open problem, whether functions of small circuit size and small depth always have circuits of small size and depth. Trade-offs can be proved only for formula size and depth.

7.1 Formula size vs. depth

The relations between formula size and depth have been investigated also for arithmetic computations (Brent, Kuck and Murayama (73), Muller and Preparata (76), and Preparata and Muller (76)). The results are similar to those for Boolean formulas, $D(f) = \Theta(\log L(f))$, hence formula size is also a complexity measure for parallel time.

DEFINITION 1.1 : The selection function $sel \in B_3$ is defined by

$$sel(x,y,z) = \bar{x}y \vee xz .$$ (1.1)

For a basis Ω

$$k(\Omega) = \frac{D_\Omega(sel) + 1}{\log 3 - 1} .$$ (1.2)

The variable x decides which of the variables y or z we select. If sel is computable over Ω , $k(\Omega)$ is small. In particular, $k(B_2) = 3/(\log 3 - 1) \approx 5.13$. Obviously sel is not monotone. Let $sel'(x,y,z) = y \vee xz$. Then $sel' = sel$ for all inputs where $y \leq z$. Since $D_m(sel') = 2$, we define $k(\Omega_m) = 3/(\log 3 - 1)$. The following theorem has been proved for complete bases by Spira (71 a) and for the monotone basis by Wegener (83). Krapchenko (81) improved the constant factor of the upper bound for several bases.

THEOREM 1.1 : Let $f \in B_n$ and $\Omega \subseteq B_2$ complete, or $f \in M_n$ and $\Omega = \Omega_m$. Then

$$\log(L_\Omega(f) + 1) \leq D_\Omega(f) \leq k(\Omega) \log(L_\Omega(f) + 1).$$ (1.3)

Proof : The first inequality is rather easy. Let S be a depth optimal circuit and let $d = D_\Omega(f)$. We find a formula F for f of depth d (see Ch. 1). F is a binary tree of depth d, hence the number of gates (inner nodes) of F is bounded by $2^d - 1$. Hence $L_\Omega(f) \leq 2^d - 1$.

The second inequality is proved by induction on $l = L_\Omega(f)$. The assertion is obvious for $l \leq 2$, since $k(\Omega) > 2$. Let $l \geq 3$ and let F be an optimal formula for f. If the depth of F is too large, we shall re-build F such that the depth decreases. During this procedure the size can increase exponentially. F is a binary tree. Let F_1 and F_2 be the right and left subtree of F computing f_1 and f_2 resp. The size of F_1 or F_2 is denoted by l_1 or l_2 resp. W.l.o.g. $l_1 \leq l_2$. Then

$$l_1 + l_2 = l - 1 \ , \ 0 \leq l_1 \leq (l-1)/2 \ , \ 1 \leq (l-1)/2 \leq l_2 \leq l - 1.$$ (1.4)

We apply the induction hypothesis to F_1, since this subtree is small enough. For F_2 we have to work harder. Let F_0 be the smallest subtree of F_2 with at least $\lceil l_2 / 3 \rceil$ gates. Both the right and the left subtree of F_0 have at most $\lceil l_2 / 3 \rceil - 1$ gates. Hence we can estimate l_0, the size of F_0, by

$$1 \leq \lceil l_2 / 3 \rceil \leq l_0 \leq 2(\lceil l_2 / 3 \rceil - 1) + 1 \leq (2l_2 + 1)/3.$$ (1.5)

F_0 is a subtree of F_2 of medium size. Let f_0 be the function computed by F_0, and let $f_{2,i}$ for $i \in \{0,1\}$ be the function computed by F_2 if we replace the subformula F_0 by the constant i. By definition

$$f_2 = \mathrm{sel}(f_0, f_{2,0}, f_{2,1}).$$ (1.6)

If F_2 is a monotone formula, $f_{2,0} \leq f_{2,1}$ and

$$f_2 = \text{sel}'(f_0, f_{2,0}, f_{2,1}) \,. \tag{1.7}$$

We compute $f_0, f_{2,0}$ and $f_{2,1}$ in parallel and f_2 by (1.6) or (1.7) . In the following we identify sel and sel' . Then

$$D_\Omega(f_2) \leq D_\Omega(\text{sel}) + \max\{D_\Omega(f_0), D_\Omega(f_{2,0}), D_\Omega(f_{2,1})\} \text{ and} \tag{1.8}$$

$$D_\Omega(f) \leq 1 + \max\{D_\Omega(f_1), D_\Omega(f_2)\} \,. \tag{1.9}$$

We apply the induction hypothesis to $f_0, f_1, f_{2,0}$ and $f_{2,1}$. Because of (1.4), (1.5) and the definition of $f_{2,0}$ and $f_{2,1}$

$$L_\Omega(f_0) \leq (2l_2+1)/3 \leq (2l-1)/3 \text{ and} \tag{1.10}$$

$$L_\Omega(f_{2,i}) \leq l_2 - l_0 \leq 2l_2/3 \leq (2l-1)/3 \,. \tag{1.11}$$

Hence

$$D_\Omega(f_2) \leq D_\Omega(\text{sel}) + k(\Omega) \log((2l-1)/3+1) \,. \tag{1.12}$$

Since $L_\Omega(f_1) = l_1 \leq (l-1)/2$, we obtain by induction hypothesis for $D_\Omega(f_1)$ a smaller upper bound than for $D_\Omega(f_2)$ in (1.12) . Hence by definition of $k(\Omega)$

$$D_\Omega(f) \leq 1 + D_\Omega(\text{sel}) + k(\Omega) \log(2/3) + k(\Omega) \log(l+1) \tag{1.13}$$

$$= k(\Omega) \log(l+1) \,.$$

$\square$

The lower bound is optimal, since $D(f) = \lceil \log n \rceil$ and $L(f) = n - 1$ for $f(x) = x_1 \wedge \cdots \wedge x_n$. We know that $D_\Omega(f) \leq c\, D_{\Omega'}(f)$ for complete bases Ω and Ω' and some constant $c = c(\Omega, \Omega')$. In connection with Theorem 1.1 we obtain

COROLLARY 1.1 : Let $\Omega, \Omega' \in B_2$ be complete bases. Then

$$L_\Omega(f) \leq (L_{\Omega'}(f)+1)^{c\,k(\Omega')} - 1 \text{ for some constant } c \,. \tag{1.14}$$

For complete bases Ω and Ω' the complexity measures L_Ω and $L_{\Omega'}$ are polynomially connected. Pratt (75 b) investigated more precisely the effect of a change of basis for complete bases $\Omega \subseteq B_2$. The exponent $ck(\Omega')$ in (1.14) can be replaced by $\log_3 10 \approx 2.096$. This result is almost optimal, since $L(x_1 \oplus \cdots \oplus x_n) = n-1$ and $L_{\{\wedge,\vee,\neg\}}(x_1 \oplus \cdots \oplus x_n) = \Theta(n^2)$ (see Ch. 8).

7.2 Circuit size vs. formula size and depth

We know hardly anything about the dependence of circuit size on depth. The best result is due to Paterson and Valiant (76).

THEOREM 2.1 : $\log(C(f)+1) \leq D(f) = O(C(f)\log^{-1}C(f))$.

The first inequality is obvious, since $C(f) \leq L(f)$, and optimal, since $C(x_1 \wedge \cdots \wedge x_n) = n-1$. The upper bound is not much better than the trivial bound $D(f) \leq C(f)$. The largest known lower bound on the formula size (over a complete basis) of an explicitly defined function is of size n^2 (see Ch. 8). According to Theorem 1.1 we do not know any $\omega(\log n)$ bound on the depth of explicitly defined functions. In particular, we cannot prove $D(f) = \omega(\log C(f))$ for some function f.

Proof of Theorem 2.1 : The idea of the proof can be described rather easily. Its realization is technically involved. We partition a size optimal circuit for f into two parts of nearly the same size such that no path leads from the second part to the first one. If this partition cuts many edges, the circuit has large width, and it is sufficient to reduce the depth of both parts. If this partition cuts only a small number of m edges, the output f depends on the first part only via the functions $g_1, \ldots, g_m$ computed on these edges. Let $f_c(x)$ be the output if $(g_1(x), \ldots, g_m(x)) = c \in \{0,1\}^m$. Then

$$f(x) = \bigvee_{c \in \{0,1\}^m} g_1(x)^{c(1)} \wedge \cdots \wedge g_m(x)^{c(m)} \wedge f_c(x) \qquad (2.1)$$

is the "disjunctive normal form of f with respect to the inputs

$g_1, \ldots, g_m$ " . We compute $g_1, \ldots, g_m$ and all f_c in parallel with small depth and compute f by (2.1) . Since in this case m is small, we hope to obtain a circuit of small depth.

We measure the size of a circuit S by the number $E(S)$ of its edges starting in gates. Obviously $E(S) \le 2C(S)$ and $E(f) \le 2C(f)$ for the proper complexity measure E . Let

$$D(z) = \max \{ D(f) \mid E(f) \le z \} \tag{2.2}$$

be the maximum depth of a function f whose size is bounded by z . We look for an upper bound on D . Let

$$A(d) = \max \{ z \mid D(z) \le d \} . \tag{2.3}$$

Hence, by definition,

$$D(A(d)) \le d , \tag{2.4}$$

and A is almost the inverse of D . D is an increasing function, which can only increase slowly. Let $D(f) = D(z)$ and let S be a circuit for f where $E(S) \le z$. If we replace the first gate of S by a new variable, we obtain a circuit S' for f' where $E(S') \le z-1$. Hence

$$D(z-1) \le D(z) = D(f) \le D(f') + 1 \le D(z-1) + 1 . \tag{2.5}$$

After these definitions we explain in detail our ideas discussed above. We choose some function f where $E(f) = A(r) + 1$ and $D(f) > r$. Let S be a circuit for f where $z := E(S) = E(f)$ and let $G_1, \ldots, G_c$ be the gates of S . As indicated, we partition S into two parts $X = \{G_1, \ldots, G_i\}$ and $Y = \{G_{i+1}, \ldots, G_c\}$. What is a good choice for i ? Let $M \subseteq X$ be the set of gates having a direct successor in Y . Let $m = |M|$ and let x and y be the number of edges between gates in X and Y resp. Then

$$x + y + m \le z , \tag{2.6}$$

since at least m edges connect a gate in X with a gate in Y . We investigate $2x + m - z$ in dependence of i . If $i = c$, then $x = z$, $m = 0$, and $2x + m - z = z$. If $i = 0$, then $x = m = 0$ and $2x + m - z = -z$. If we decrease i by 1 , one gate G switches from X to Y , x decreases at most by 2 (the edges for the inputs of G) , m decreases at most by 1 (the gate G) . Hence $2x + m - z$ decreases at most by 5 , and we can choose some i such that

$$|2x + m - z| \leq 2 . \tag{2.7}$$

We claim that

$$2w + m \leq z + 2 \quad \text{for} \quad w = \max\{x,y\} . \tag{2.8}$$

(2.8) follows from (2.7) if $w = x$. By (2.6) and (2.7)

$$x + y + m \leq z \leq 2x + m + 2 \quad , \text{hence} \quad y \leq x + 2 . \tag{2.9}$$

If $w = y$, $2w + m \leq y + (x+2) + m \leq z+2$, and (2.8) holds.

On the one hand we can compute the functions computed at gates $G \in M$ in depth $D(x)$ and then f in depth $D(y)$. Hence

$$D(f) \leq D(x) + D(y) \leq 2 D(w) \quad \text{and} \tag{2.10}$$

$$D(w) \geq D(f) / 2 > \lfloor r/2 \rfloor .$$

On the other hand we can apply the representation of f in (2.1) . All g_i can be computed in parallel in depth $D(x)$, their conjunction can be computed in depth $\lceil \log m \rceil$. Parallel to this we can compute all f_c in parallel in depth $D(y)$. Afterwards f can be computed in depth $1 + m$. Hence by (2.8)

$$D(f) \leq \max\{ D(x) + \lceil \log m \rceil , D(y) \} + 1 + m \tag{2.11}$$

$$\leq D(w) + \lceil \log m \rceil + 1 + m \leq D(w) - 2w + z + 3 + \lceil \log m \rceil .$$

The rest of the proof is a tedious computation. By (2.10) and the definition of A

$$A(\lfloor r/2 \rfloor) < w . \tag{2.12}$$

The function $w \to D(w) - 2w$ is strictly decreasing, since by (2.5)

$$D(w) - 2w \leq D(w-1) + 1 - 2w < D(w-1) - 2(w-1) . \tag{2.13}$$

We use (2.11) and estimate w by (2.12) and m by z (see (2.9)). Hence by the definition of f , (2.11), (2.4) and (2.5)

$$r < D(f) \leq D(A(\lfloor r/2 \rfloor) + 1) - 2(A(\lfloor r/2 \rfloor) + 1) + z + 3 + \lceil \log z \rceil \tag{2.14}$$

$$\leq \lfloor r/2 \rfloor + 1 - 2A(\lfloor r/2 \rfloor) + z + 1 + \lceil \log z \rceil .$$

By definition $z = A(r) + 1$. Hence by (2.14)

$2A(\lfloor r/2 \rfloor) + \lceil r/2 \rceil - 2 < z + \lceil \log z \rceil = A(r) + 1 + \lceil \log(A(r)+1) \rceil$. (2.15)

For a constant $k \geq 1$ we define

$$H(r) = (r/2) \log r + 2 \log r - kr. \qquad (2.16)$$

By elementary transformations it can be shown that for sufficiently large R, all $k \geq 1$ and $r > R$

$$2 H(\lfloor r/2 \rfloor) + \lceil r/2 \rceil - 2 > H(r) + 1 + \lceil \log(H(r)+1) \rceil. \qquad (2.17)$$

We claim that $A(r) \geq H(r)$ for some appropriate k and all r. Parameter k is chosen such that $A(r) \geq H(r)$ for $r \leq R$. If $r > R$ by (2.15), the induction hypothesis and (2.17)

$$A(r) + 1 + \lceil \log(A(r)+1) \rceil > 2 A(\lfloor r/2 \rfloor) + \lceil r/2 \rceil - 2 \qquad (2.18)$$

$$\geq 2 H(\lfloor r/2 \rfloor) + \lceil r/2 \rceil - 2 > H(r) + 1 + \lceil \log(H(r)+1) \rceil,$$

hence $A(r) \geq H(r)$.

We summarize our results.

$$2 C(f) \geq E(f) > A(r) \geq H(r) \geq (r/2) \log r - kr \quad \text{and} \qquad (2.19)$$

$$D(f) = D(z) \leq D(z-1) + 1 = D(A(r)) + 1 \leq r + 1. \qquad (2.20)$$

For sufficiently large r the function $(r/2) \log r - kr$ is increasing. Hence for some appropriate constant $k' > 0$

$$C(f) \geq (1/4)(D(f)-1) \log(D(f)-1) - (k/2)(D(f)-1) \qquad (2.21)$$

$$\geq k' D(f) \log D(f).$$

This implies $D(f) = O(C(f) \log^{-1} C(f))$.

□

We add some remarks on the relations between circuit size and formula size. Obviously $C(f) \leq L(f)$, and this bound is optimal for $x_1 \wedge \cdots \wedge x_n$. By Theorem 1.1 and 2.1 we conclude that

$$\log L(f) = O(C(f) \log^{-1} C(f)). \qquad (2.22)$$

The largest differences known between $L(f)$ and $C(f)$ are proved in Ch. 8. For a storage access function f for indirect addresses $C(f) = \Theta(n)$ but $L(f) = \Omega(n^2 \log^{-1} n)$ and for the parity function g and $\Omega = \{\wedge, \vee, \neg\}$ $C_\Omega(g) = \Theta(n)$ but $L_\Omega(f) = \Theta(n^2)$.

7.3 Joint minimization of depth and circuit size, trade-offs

A circuit is efficient if size **and** depth are small. For the existence of efficient circuits for f it is not sufficient that $C(f)$ and $D(f)$ are small. It might be possible that all circuits of small depth have large size and vice versa. In Ch. 3 we have designed circuits of small depth and size, the only exception is division. We do not know whether there is a division circuit of size $O(n \log^2 n \log \log n)$ and depth $O(\log n)$. For the joint minimization of depth and circuit size we define a new complexity measure PCD (P = product).

DEFINITION 3.1 : For $f \in B_n$ and a basis Ω

$$PCD_\Omega(f) = \min \{ C(S) D(S) \mid S \text{ is an } \Omega-\text{circuit for } f \} \quad \text{and} \quad (3.1)$$

$$PLD_\Omega(f) = \min \{ L(S) D(S) \mid S \text{ is an } \Omega-\text{formula for } f \} . \quad (3.2)$$

Obviously $C_\Omega(f) D_\Omega(f) \le PCD_\Omega(f)$. For many functions we have proved that $C(f) D(f) = \Theta(PCD(f))$, e.g. for addition both are of size $n \log n$. Are there functions where $PCD(f)$ is asymptotically larger than $C(f) D(f)$? What is the smallest upper bound on $PCD(f) / C(f) D(f)$? All these problems are unsolved. We know that $C(f) D(f) = \Omega(n \log n)$ for all $f \in B_n$ depending essentially on n variables. But we cannot prove for any explicitly defined function $f \in B_n$ that all circuits of logarithmic depth have nonlinear size. In § 4 we present a function f where $L(f) D(f) = o(PLD(f))$. This result is called a trade-off result. In general, trade-offs are results of the following type. We have two types of resources c_1 and c_2 for some problem P which we like to minimize simultaneously. But for each solution S where $c_1(S)$ is small $c_2(S)$ is not small and vice versa. Results of this type have been proved for several problems. We refer to Carlson and Savage (83) for the problem of optimal representations of trees and graphs and to Paterson and Hewitt (80) for the investigation of pebble games which are models for time − place trade-offs for sequential computations. For VLSI chips (see also Ch. 12, § 2) one tries to minimize the area A of the chip and simultaneously the cycle length T. It has turned out that AT^2 is a suitable joint complexity measure. By information flow arguments one can prove for many problems, among them the multiplication of binary numbers, that $AT^2 = \Omega(n^2)$. Since for multiplication $A = \Omega(n)$ and $T = \Omega(\log n)$ chips where $AT^2 = O(n^2)$ may exist only for $\Omega(\log n) = T = O(n^{1/2})$. Mehlhorn and Preparata (83) designed for this range of T VLSI chips optimal with respect to AT^2. The user himself can decide whether A or T is more important to him. We are far away from similar results for circuit size and depth.

7.4 A trade-off result

Since no trade-off between circuit size and depth is known, we present a trade-off between formula size and depth. Although $D_\Omega(f) = \Theta(\log L_\Omega(f))$ for all $f \in B_n$, this result does not imply that $PLD_\Omega(f) = \Theta(L_\Omega(f) D_\Omega(f))$. On the contrary we present an example f where $L_\Omega(f) D_\Omega(f) = o(PLD_\Omega(f))$ for $\Omega = \Omega_m$ and $\Omega = \{\wedge, \vee, \neg\}$. Furthermore we get to know methods for such trade-offs.

DEFINITION 4.1 : The carry function $f_n \in B_{2n}$ is defined by

$$f_n(x_1, \ldots, x_n, y_1, \ldots, y_n) = \bigvee_{1 \leq i \leq n} x_i y_i \cdots y_n. \tag{4.1}$$

This function is important for the addition of binary numbers a and b. Let $x_i = a_i \wedge b_i$ and $y_i = a_i \oplus b_i$. Then $f_n(x,y)$ is the foremost carry (see Ch. 3, (1.8)). Hence by the results of Ch. 3, § 1 $C_\Omega(f_n) = \Theta(n)$, $D_\Omega(f_n) = \Theta(\log n)$ and $PCD_\Omega(f_n) = \Theta(n \log n)$ for $\Omega \in \{B_2, \{\wedge, \vee, \neg\}, \Omega_m\}$, and there is no trade-off. But here we investigate formula size and depth.

THEOREM 4.1 : i) There is a monotone formula for f_n of size $O(n)$ and depth $O(n)$.

ii) There is a monotone formula for f_n of size $O(n \log n)$ and depth $O(\log n)$.

iii) $PLD_\Omega(f_n) = O(n \log^2 n)$ for $\Omega \in \{\Omega_m, \{\wedge, \vee, \neg\}, B_2\}$.

iv) $L_\Omega(f_n) = \Theta(n)$ for $\Omega \in \{\Omega_m, \{\wedge, \vee, \neg\}, B_2\}$.

v) $D_\Omega(f_n) = \Theta(\log n)$ for $\Omega \in \{\Omega_m, \{\wedge, \vee, \neg\}, B_2\}$.

Proof : iii) , iv) and v) follow from i) and ii) . i) follows from the Horner scheme

$$f_n(x,y) = y_n \wedge (x_n \vee (y_{n-1} \wedge \cdots (y_1 \wedge x_1) \cdots)) . \tag{4.2}$$

The second assertion can be proved by a recursive approach. Here and in the rest of this chapter we do not count the gates of a formula but the leaves of the proper binary tree which is by 1 larger than the real formula size. W.l.o.g. $n = 2^k$. We divide $x = (x', x'')$ and $y = (y', y'')$ in two parts of the same length. Then

$$f_n(x,y) = (f_{n/2}(x',y') \wedge y_{n/2+1} \wedge \cdots \wedge y_n) \vee f_{n/2}(x'',y'') . \tag{4.3}$$

For this formula F_n

$$L(F_n) = 2 L(F_{n/2}) + n/2 \quad , \quad L(F_1) = 2 \quad , \quad \text{hence} \tag{4.4}$$

$$L(F_n) = (1/2) n \log n + 2n \, ,$$

$$D(F_n) = \max \{ D(F_{n/2}), \log (n/2) \} + 2 \quad , \quad D(F_1) = 1 \, , \tag{4.5}$$

hence

$$D(F_n) = 2 \log n + 1 . \qquad \qquad \square$$

The following trade-offs have been proved by Commentz-Walter (79) for the monotone basis and by Commentz-Walter and Sattler (80) for the basis $\{\wedge, \vee, \neg\}$.

THEOREM 4.2 : $PLD_m(f_n) \geq \dfrac{1}{128} n \log^2 n$.

228

THEOREM 4.3 : $\text{PLD}_{\{\wedge,\vee,\neg\}}(f_n) \geq \frac{1}{8} n \log n \log\log n (\log\log\log\log n)^{-1}$.

Actually these are only asymptotic results. Obviously, for both bases $\Omega = \Omega_m$ and $\Omega = \{\wedge,\vee,\neg\}$, $L_\Omega(f_n) \geq 2n$ and $D_\Omega(f_n) \geq \log(2n)$, hence $\text{PLD}_\Omega(f_n) \geq 2n \log(2n)$. The lower bound of Theorem 4.2 is not better than this simple bound if $n \leq 2^{256}$, and the bound of Theorem 4.3 does not beat the simple bound if $n \leq 2^{2^{38}}$.

Before we discuss the essential ideas of the proof of Theorem 4.2 we anticipate some technical lemmas. The proof of Theorem 4.3 is based on the same ideas but is technically even more involved and therefore omitted.

LEMMA 4.1 : If we replace for $j \notin J \subseteq \{1,...,n\}$ x_j by 0 and y_j by 1 we obtain the subfunction f_m , where $m = |J|$, on the set of variables $\{x_j, y_j \mid j \in J\}$.

Proof : Obvious. □

LEMMA 4.2 : If we replace x_1 and y_n by 1 we obtain $f_{n-1}^d(y_1, \ldots, y_{n-1}, x_2, \ldots, x_n)$ where f_{n-1}^d is the dual function of f_{n-1} .

Proof : We apply the rules of deMorgan and the law of distributivity.

$$f_{n-1}^d(y_1, \ldots, y_{n-1}, x_2, \ldots, x_n) = \neg f_{n-1}(\bar{y}_1, \ldots, \bar{y}_{n-1}, \bar{x}_2, \ldots, \bar{x}_n) \quad (4.6)$$

$$= \neg \bigvee_{1\leq i\leq n-1} \bar{y}_i \bar{x}_{i+1} \cdots \bar{x}_n = \neg(\neg \bigwedge_{1\leq i\leq n-1} (y_i \vee x_{i+1} \cdots \vee x_n))$$

$$= x_n \vee x_{n-1} y_{n-1} \vee x_{n-2} y_{n-2} y_{n-1} \vee \cdots \vee x_2 y_2 \cdots y_{n-1} \vee y_1 \cdots y_{n-1}$$

$$= f_n(1, x_2, \ldots, x_n, y_1, \ldots, y_{n-1}, 1) .$$ □

LEMMA 4.3 : $\binom{d-1+s-1}{d-1} + \binom{d-1+s}{d-1} \leq \binom{d+s}{d}$ if $s \geq 1$.

Proof : Elementary. □

LEMMA 4.4 : Let $m(p) = \max \{ \binom{d+s}{d} \mid ds \le p \}$. Then $\log m(p) \le 2 p^{1/2}$.

Proof : By Stirling's formula we can approximate $n!$ by $(2\pi)^{1/2} n^{n+1/2} e^{-n}$, more precisely, the quotient of $n!$ and its approximation is in the interval $[1 , e^{1/(11n)}]$. Hence

$$\log \binom{d+s}{d} \le \frac{1}{11(d+s)} \log e - \frac{1}{2} \log(2\pi) + \frac{1}{2} \log(\frac{d+s}{ds}) \qquad (4.7)$$

$$+ (d+s) \log(d+s) - d \log d - s \log s$$

$$\le d \log(d+s) - d \log d + s \log(d+s) - s \log s$$

$$= (d+s) (-\frac{d}{d+s} \log \frac{d}{d+s} - \frac{s}{d+s} \log \frac{s}{d+s})$$

$$= (d+s) H(\frac{d}{d+s}, \frac{s}{d+s})$$

where

$$H(x, 1-x) = -x \log x - (1-x) \log(1-x) \qquad (4.8)$$

is the entropy function. W.l.o.g. $d \le s$. Since

$$H(x, 1-x) \le -2x \log x \qquad \text{for } x \le 1/2 , \qquad (4.9)$$

$$\log \binom{d+s}{d} \le 2d \log(\frac{d+s}{d}) = 2d \log(1 + \frac{s}{d}) . \qquad (4.10)$$

We only investigate numbers d and s where $ds \le p$ and $d \le s$, hence $d^2 \le p$ and $\alpha := p/d^2 \ge 1$. Furthermore $d = (p/\alpha)^{1/2}$ and $s/d = sd/d^2 \le p/d^2 = \alpha$. Hence

$$\log m(p) \le \max \{ 2 (\frac{p}{\alpha})^{1/2} \log(1+\alpha) \mid \alpha \ge 1 \} . \qquad (4.11)$$

Let $g(\alpha) = \alpha^{-1/2} \log(1+\alpha)$. Then $g(1) = 1$ and g is decreasing for $\alpha \ge 1$. Hence the maximum in (4.11) is $2 p^{1/2}$.

$\square$

Now we begin with the proof of Theorem 4.2 . Instead of designing a formula for f_n of minimal complexity with respect to PLD_m we choose another way. For given d and s we look for the maximal $n =: t(d,s)$ such that there is a monotone formula F_n for f_n where $D(F_n) \le d$ and $L(F_n)/n \le s$. Upper bounds on $t(d,s)$ imply lower bounds on $PLD_m(f_n)$. The main result is the following lemma.

LEMMA 4.5 : $\forall$ $d > 0$, $s > 1$: $\log t(d,s) \le 8 \, (d \, s)^{1/2}$.

We prove at first, how this lemma implies the theorem.

Proof of Theorem 4.2 : Let F_n be an optimal formula for f_n with respect to PLD_m . Let $d = D(F_n)$ and s be chosen such that $s - 1 < L(F_n)/n \le s$. Obviously $s \ge 2$. By definition $n \le t(d,s)$ and by Lemma 4.5

$$PLD_m(f_n) = L(F_n)\, D(F_n) \ge n(s-1)d \ge \frac{1}{2} n s d \qquad (4.12)$$

$$\ge \frac{1}{128} n \log^2 t(d,s) \ge \frac{1}{128} n \log^2 n .$$

$\square$

It is easier to work with $t(d,s)$ than with PLD_m . The main reason is that depth and formula size are both bounded independently. s is a bound for the average number of leaves of the formula labelled by x_i or y_i . It would be more convenient to have bounds on the number of x_i- and y_j-leaves (for fixed i and j) and not only on the average number. Let $t'(d,s)$ be the maximal n such that there is a monotone formula F_n for f_n such that $D(F_n) \le d$ and for $i,j \in \{1,...,n\}$ the number of x_i- and y_j-leaves is bounded by s . Obviously $t'(d,s) \le t(d,s)$. We prove an upper bound on $t(d,s)$ depending on $t'(d,s)$, and afterwards we estimate the more manageable measure $t'(d,s)$.

LEMMA 4.6 : $t(d,s) \le 3 \, t'(d,6 \, s)$.

Proof : Let F_n be a monotone formula for f_n where $n = t(d,s)$, $D(F_n) \leq d$ and $L(F_n) \leq sn$. Let I be the set of all i such that the number of x_i-leaves in F_n is bounded by $3s$. Since $L(F_n) \leq sn$, $|I| \geq (2/3)n$. Let J be the corresponding set for the y-variables. Then $|J| \geq (2/3)n$ and $|H| \geq (1/3)n$ for $H = I \cap J$. For $i \notin H$ we replace x_i by 0 and y_i by 1 . By Lemma 4.1 we obtain a formula F' for $f_{|H|}$ where $D(F') \leq d$, and each variable is the label of at most $3s$ leaves. Hence

$$t(d,s) = n \leq 3|H| \leq 3\,t'(d,6\,s) . \tag{4.13}$$

$\square$

LEMMA 4.7 : $t'(d,s) \leq \binom{d+s}{d} - 1$.

This lemma is the main step of the proof. Again we first show that this lemma implies the theorem.

Proof of Lemma 4.5 : By Lemma 4.7 $t'(d,s)$ is bounded by $m(ds)$ for the function m of Lemma 4.4 . Hence

$$\log t(d,s) \leq \log t'(d,6\,s) + \log 3 \leq 2\,(6\,ds)^{1/2} + \log 3 \tag{4.14}$$

$$\leq 8\,(ds)^{1/2} . \qquad\qquad\qquad \square$$

For the proof of Lemma 4.7 we investigate the last gate of monotone formulas for f_n . If this gate is an $\wedge$-gate we apply Lemma 4.2 and investigate the corresponding dual formula whose last gate is an $\vee$-gate. If $f_n = g_1 \vee g_2$, we find by the following lemma large subfunctions of f_n in g_1 and g_2 .

LEMMA 4.8 : If $f_n = g_1 \vee g_2$, there is a partition of $\{1,...,n\}$ to I and J such that we may replace the variables x_i and y_i for $i \notin I$ $(i \notin J)$ by constants in order to obtain the subfunction $f_{|I|}$ $(f_{|J|})$. Furthermore g_1 or g_2 depends essentially on all y-variables.

Proof : Since $x_1 y_1 \cdots y_n \in PI(f_n) \subseteq PI(g_1) \cup PI(g_2)$, $x_1 y_1 \cdots y_n$ is a prime implicant of g_j for $j = 1$ or $j = 2$, in particular g_j depends essentially on all y-variables.

$p_i = x_i y_i \cdots y_n$ $(1 \leq i \leq n)$ are the prime implicants of f_n . Let I be the set of all i where $p_i \in PI(g_1)$ and $J = \{1,...,n\} - I$. Then $p_j \in PI(g_2)$ for $j \in J$. We set $x_k = 0$ and $y_k = 1$ for $k \notin I$. Each prime implicant of g_1 equals some p_i $(i \in I)$ or is a lengthening of some p_k $(k \notin I)$. These p_k are replaced by 0 , since $x_k = 0$. In p_i $(i \in I)$ the y-variables y_k $(k \notin I)$ are replaced by 1 . Altogether g_1 is replaced by $f_{|I|}$. The same arguments work for g_2 . $\qquad\qquad\Box$

Finally we finish the proof of Theorem 4.2 by the proof of Lemma 4.7 .

Proof of Lemma 4.7 : Induction on d . The assertion is trivial if $d = 0$ or $s \leq 1$, since $t'(d,s) = 0$. Let $d > 0$ and $s > 1$ and let us assume that the assertion holds for all $d' < d$. Let F be a monotone formula for f_n where $n = t'(d,s)$, $D(F) \leq d$, and for all $i,j \in \{1,...,n\}$ the number of x_i- and y_j-leaves is bounded by s .

Case 1 : The last gate of F is an $\vee$-gate.

Let g_1 and g_2 be the inputs of the last gate, hence $f_n = g_1 \vee g_2$. By Lemma 4.8 we assume w.l.o.g. that g_1 depends essentially on all y-variables. Let I and J form the partition of $\{1,...,n\}$ whose existence also has been proved in Lemma 4.8 . The depth of the formulas for g_1 and g_2 is bounded by $d - 1$. For all $i,j \in \{1,...,n\}$ the number of x_i- and y_j-leaves in the formula for g_2 is bounded by $s - 1$, since the formula for g_1 includes at least one y_j-leaf. Hence $|I| + |J| = n$, $|I| \leq t'(d-1,s)$ and $|J| \leq t'(d-1,s-1)$ and by Lemma 4.3 and the induction hypothesis

$$t'(d,s) = n \leq |I| + |J| + 1 \leq t'(d-1,s) + t'(d-1,s-1) + 1 \qquad (4.15)$$

$$\leq \binom{d-1+s}{d-1} - 1 + \binom{d-1+s-1}{d-1} - 1 + 1 \leq \binom{d+s}{d} - 1 .$$

Case 2 : The last gate of F is an $\wedge$-gate.

Let $x_1 = 1$ and $y_n = 1$. Then f_n is replaced by f_{n-1}^d. If we replace $\wedge$-gates by $\vee$-gates and vice versa, we obtain a monotone formula for f_{n-1} whose last gate is an $\vee$-gate. Similarly to Case 1 we can prove that $|I| \leq t'(d-1,s)$ and $|J| \leq t'(d-1,s-1)$ for some partition I and J of $\{1,...,n-1\}$. Here $|I| + |J| = n-1$. (4.15) works also in this situation. □

As already acknowledged we do not know much about trade-offs between formula size or circuit size and depth.

EXERCISES

1. Generalize Spira's theorem to complete bases $\Omega \subseteq B_r$.

2. Compute $C_\Omega(\text{sel})$ and $D_\Omega(\text{sel})$ for different bases $\Omega \subseteq B_2$, in particular $\Omega = \{ \text{NAND} \}$ and $\Omega = \{\oplus,\wedge\}$.

3. Let F be a formula of size l and let F' be the equivalent formula constructed in the proof of Spira's theorem. Estimate the size of F'.

4. Which functions are candidates for the relation $D(f) = \omega(\log C(f))$?

5. Let $n = 2^m$ and let f be the Boolean matrix product of $n \times n$ - matrices. What is the minimal size of a monotone circuit for f whose depth is bounded by $m+1$?

6. Generalize the result of Exercise 5 to B_2-circuits.

7. Let $f = (f_0, \ldots, f_{2n-2})$ be the Boolean convolution and $n = 2^m$. Let $g_i = f_i \vee f_{i+n}$ for $0 \le i \le n-2$ and $g_{n-1} = f_{n-1}$. Solve the problems of Exercise 5 and 6 for $g_0, \ldots, g_{n-1}$.

8. FORMULA SIZE

The depth of a circuit corresponds to the parallel computation time. Since $D(f) = \Theta(\log L(f))$ (Theorem of Spira, see Ch. 7, § 1), the study of the formula size of Boolean functions is well motivated.

The formula size of f is equal to the minimal number of gates in a formula for f. The number of gates or inner nodes of a binary tree is by 1 less than the number of leaves of the tree. Often it is easier to deal with the number of leaves, e.g. the number of leaves of a binary tree is equal to the sum of the number of leaves in the left subtree and the number of leaves in the right subtree. Hence we denote the formula size of f by $L^*(f)$ and we define $L(f) = L^*(f) + 1$. It causes no problems to call L also formula size.

Because of their central role, we investigate threshold functions in § 1 - § 3 and symmetric functions in § 4. In § 5 - § 8 we present and apply some methods for the proof of lower bounds on the formula size of explicitly defined functions.

8.1 Threshold - 2

We know that the (monotone) circuit complexity of T_k^n is linear for fixed k (see Ch. 6, § 2). The monotone formula size is superlinear, it is of size $n \log n$.

THEOREM 1.1 : $L_m(T_2^n) = O(n \log n)$. If $n = 2^k$, $L_m(T_2^n) \le n \log n$.

Proof : W.l.o.g. $n = 2^k$. Otherwise we add some 0-inputs. Let $x = (x', x'')$ where x' and x'' consist of $n/2$ variables each. Obviously

$$T_2^n(x) = (T_1^{n/2}(x') \wedge T_1^{n/2}(x'')) \vee T_2^{n/2}(x') \vee T_2^{n/2}(x'') . \tag{1.1}$$

Since $L_m(T_1^n) = n$, we conclude that

$$L_m(T_2^n) \leq n + 2L_m(T_2^{n/2}) \quad \text{and} \quad L_m(T_2^2) = 2 . \tag{1.2}$$

Hence $L_m(T_2^n) \leq n \log n$.

$\square$

This simple approach is optimal if $n = 2^k$. We prove this claim for the monotone basis (Hansel (64)). For the complete basis $\{\wedge, \vee, \neg\}$ we refer to Krichevskii (64). We investigate the structure of monotone formulas for T_2^n and prove the existence of an optimal monotone single-level formula.

DEFINITION 1.1 : A monotone formula or circuit is a single-level formula or circuit if no directed path combines $\wedge$-gates.

It is reasonable to conjecture that all quadratic functions (all prime implicants are monotone and have length 2) have optimal single-level formulas and circuits. This claim is open for circuits and has been disproved for formulas (see Exercises).

LEMMA 1.1 : There is an optimal monotone formula for T_2^n which is a single-level formula.

Proof : Let F be an optimal monotone formula for T_2^n . We reconstruct F until we obtain a single-level formula F' for T_2^n of the same size as F . If F is not a single-level formula, let G be the first $\wedge$-gate of F which has some $\wedge$-gate as (not necessarily direct) predecessor. Let $g = \text{res}_G$ and let g_1 and g_2 be the inputs of G . Then g_1 and g_2 are computed by single-level formulas. Hence $g_1 = t_1 \vee u_1 \vee \cdots \vee u_p$ where t_1 is a Boolean sum and all u_j are computed at $\wedge$-gates H_j . Let u_{j1} and u_{j2} be the inputs of H_j . Then $u_j = u_{j1} \wedge u_{j2}$ and u_{j1} and u_{j2} are Boolean sums. If u_{j1} and u_{j2} contain the same variable x_i , the subformula for u_j is not optimal. We may replace x_i in u_{j1} and in u_{j2} by 0 . Then u_j is replaced by u_j' where $u_j = u_j' \vee x_i$. Instead of two x_i-leaves one x_i-leaf suffices. Hence u_{j1} and u_{j2} have no common variable and all prime implicants have length 2 . Similarly

$g_2 = t_2 \vee w_1 \vee \cdots \vee w_q$.

We rearrange the $\vee$-gates in the formulas for g_1 and g_2 , such that t_1, t_2, $u = u_1 \vee \cdots \vee u_p$, and $w = w_1 \vee \cdots \vee w_q$ are computed. Then $g_1 = t_1 \vee u$, $g_2 = t_2 \vee w$ and

$$g = g_1 g_2 = t_1 t_2 \vee t_1 w \vee t_2 u \vee u w . \tag{1.3}$$

We replace the subformula for g by a subformula for

$$g' = t_1 t_2 \vee u \vee w \tag{1.4}$$

of the same size. Let f be the function computed by the new formula. $T_2^n \leq f'$, since $g \leq g'$. Let us assume, that $T_2^n(a) = 0$ but $f'(a) = 1$ for some input a . Then $g(a) = 0$ and $g'(a) = 1$. This is only possible if $u(a) = 1$ or $w(a) = 1$. But u and w have only prime implicants of length 2 , hence $T_2^n(a) = 1$ in contradiction to the assumption. The new formula is an optimal monotone formula for T_2^n . We continue in the same way until we obtain a single-level formula.

$\square$

THEOREM 1.2 : $L_m(T_2^n) \geq n \log n$.

Proof : We investigate an optimal monotone formula F for T_2^n . W.l.o.g. (see Lemma 1.1) we assume that F is a single-level formula. Let $G_1, \ldots, G_p$ be the $\wedge$-gates where $u_i = u_{i1} \wedge u_{i2}$ $(1 \leq i \leq p)$ are computed. u_{i1} and u_{i2} are disjoint Boolean sums. For $(j(1), \ldots, j(p)) \in \{1,2\}^p$ we replace all variables in $u_{1,j(1)}, \ldots, u_{p,j(p)}$ by 0 . Since the output of F is 0 we have replaced at least $n-1$ variables by 0 . If x_i is not replaced by 0 , $(j(1), \ldots, j(p))$ is an element of M_i . If all variables are replaced by 0 , $(j(1), \ldots, j(p))$ is an element of M_0 . Hence $M_0, M_1, \ldots, M_n$ build a partition of $\{1,2\}^p$.

Let $(j(1), \ldots, j(p)) \in M_m$ and $m \geq 1$. If x_m is a summand of $u_{i,1}$ (or $u_{i,2}$) , then $j(i) = 2$ (or $j(i) = 1$) . If x_m is neither a summand of $u_{i,1}$ nor of $u_{i,2}$, $j(i)$ may be 1 or 2 . Let $p(m)$ be the number of indices i such that u_i does not depend on x_m . Then $|M_m| = 2^{p(m)}$ and $p - p(m)$ is the number of x_m-leaves. Hence

$$L_m(T_2^n) = \sum_{1 \le m \le n} (p - p(m)) = np - \sum_{1 \le m \le n} \log |M_m| \qquad (1.5)$$

$$= np - n \log \left(\prod_{1 \le m \le n} |M_m|^{1/n} \right).$$

We apply the well-known inequality between the arithmetic and the geometric mean :

$$(1/n) \sum_{1 \le i \le n} a_i \ge \left(\prod_{1 \le i \le n} a_i \right)^{1/n}. \qquad (1.6)$$

Since the sets $M_1, \ldots, M_n$ are disjoint, $|M_1| + \cdots + |M_n| \le 2^p$. Hence

$$L_m(T_2^n) \ge np - n \log \left((1/n) \sum_{1 \le m \le n} |M_m| \right) \qquad (1.7)$$

$$\ge np - n \log(1/n) - n \log 2^p = n \log n.$$

$\square$

COROLLARY 1.1 : $L_m(T_k^n) = \Omega(n \log n)$ if $1 < k < n$.

Proof : For $k \le \lceil n/2 \rceil$ we use the fact that T_2^{n-k+2} is a subfunction of T_k^n. For $k > \lceil n/2 \rceil$ we apply the duality principle, which implies $L_m(T_k^n) = L_m(T_{n+1-k}^n)$.

$\square$

In § 2 we prove that this bound is asymptotically optimal if k or $n-k$ is constant. For $k = n/2$ we prove better lower bounds in § 8 (for the basis $\{\wedge, \vee, \neg\}$).

8.2 Design of efficient formulas for threshold - k

It is quite easy to design an optimal monotone formula for T_2^n but it is much harder to design optimal formulas for T_k^n, if $k > 2$ is constant. The reader is asked to design a formula of size $o(n \log^2 n)$ for T_3^n. The methods of § 1 lead to the recursive approach

$$T_k^n(x) = \bigvee_{0 \leq p \leq k} T_p^{n/2}(x') \wedge T_{k-p}^{n/2}(x'') .$$

$$(2.1)$$

These formulas for T_k^n have size $O(n (\log n)^{k-1})$ (Korobkov (56) and Exercises). Khasin (69) constructed formulas of size $O(n (\log n)^{k-1} / (\log \log n)^{k-2})$, Kleiman and Pippenger (78) improved the upper bound to $O((\frac{k}{2})^{\log^* n} n \log n)$ and Friedman (84) designed asymptotically optimal formulas of size $O(n \log n)$. All these bounds are proved constructively, i.e. there is an algorithm which constructs for given n formulas of the announced size for T_k^n and the running time of the algorithm is a polynomial $p(n)$.

Much earlier Khasin (70) proved that $L_m(T_k^n) = O(n \log n)$, but his proof is not constructive. We only discuss the main ideas of Khasin's paper. T_k^n is the disjunction of all monotone monoms of length k. It is easy to compute many of these prime implicants by a small formula. W.l.o.g. $n = mk$. Let $A(1), ..., A(k)$ be a partition of $\{1,...,n\}$ into k blocks of size m each. Then for each permutation $\pi \in \Sigma_n$

$$f_\pi(x) = \bigwedge_{1 \leq j \leq k} \bigvee_{i \in A(j)} x_\pi(i)$$

$$(2.2)$$

is a formula of size n and f_π is the disjunction of many, exactly m^k, prime implicants of length k each. We hope that T_k^n is the disjunction of a small number of functions f_π. Which permutations should be chosen ? Since Khasin could not solve this problem, he computed the mean number of missing prime implicants if one chooses randomly $O(\log n)$ permutations π. This number is $O(n \log n)$. So there is a good choice of $O(\log n)$ permutations π such that T_k^n is the disjunction of $O(\log n)$ formulas f_π of size n each and $O(n \log n)$ prime implicants of length k each. Hence the size of the formula for T_k^n is $O(n \log n)$.

We present the constructive solution due to Friedman (84). We obtain a formula of size $c\,n\log n$ for a quite large c. It is possible to reduce c by more complicated considerations. We again consider functions f as described in (2.2). If $A(1)$,...., $A(k)$ is an arbitrary partition of $\{1,....,n\}$, f has formula size n and $f \le T_k^n$. $x_{i(1)} \cdots x_{i(k)} \in PI(f)$ iff the variables $x_{i(1)}, \ldots, x_{i(k)}$ are in different sets of the partition. Hence we are looking for sets $A_{m,j}$ ($1 \le m \le k$, $1 \le j \le r$) with the following properties

- $A_{1,j}, \ldots, A_{k,j}$ are disjoint subsets of $\{1,....,n\}$ for each j,
- for different $i(1),....,i(k) \in \{1,....,n\}$ we find some j such that each $A_{m,j}$ contains exactly one of the elements $i(1),....,i(k)$.

Then

$$T_k^n = F_1 \vee \cdots \vee F_r \quad \text{where} \quad F_j = \bigwedge_{1 \le m \le k} \bigvee_{i \in A_{m,j}} x_i. \tag{2.3}$$

The first property ensures that all prime implicants have length k. The second property ensures that each monom of length k is a prime implicant of some F_j. A class of sets $A_{m,j}$ with these properties is called an (n,k)-scheme of size r. The size of the corresponding formula is $r\,n$.

We explain the new ideas for $k = 2$. W.l.o.g. $n = 2^r$. Let $pos_j(l)$ be the j-th bit of the binary representation of $l \in \{1, \ldots, 2^r\}$ where $1 \le j \le r$. The sets

$$A_{m,j} = \{l \mid pos_j(l) = m\} \quad \text{for } 0 \le m \le 1 \text{ and } 1 \le j \le r \tag{2.4}$$

build an $(n,2)$-scheme of size $r = \log n$. This simple construction is successful since for different $l,l' \in \{1,....,2^r\}$ we find a position j where $pos_j(l) \ne pos_j(l')$.

If $k = 3$, we could try to work with the ternary representation of numbers. In general we cannot find for different numbers $l,l',l'' \in \{1,....,n\}$ a position j such that $pos_j(l)$, $pos_j(l')$ and $pos_j(l'')$ (ternary representation) are different. For example : $1 \to (0,1)$,

$2 \to (0,2)$, $4 \to (1,1)$. Instead of that we work with b-ary numbers for some large but constant b. We look for a large set $S \subseteq \{1,...,b\}^r$ such that two vectors in S agree at less than $(1/3)m$ positions. Let l, $l', l'' \in S$ be different. We label all positions where at least two of these vectors agree. Altogether we label less than $3(1/3)m = m$ positions, since there are $3 = \binom{3}{2}$ different pairs of vectors. The vectors l, l', l'' differ at all positions which are not labelled. Let

$$A_{m,(j,t(1),t(2),t(3))} = \{ s \in S \mid pos_j(s) = t(m) \} \qquad (2.5)$$

for $1 \le m \le 3$, $1 \le j \le r$, $1 \le t(1) < t(2) < t(3) \le b$.

If we fix $T = (j,t(1),t(2),t(3))$, the sets $A_{1,T}, A_{2,T}$ and $A_{3,T}$ are disjoint. Let $s_1, s_2, s_3 \in S$ be different. Then there is some j , an unlabelled position, such that $pos_j(s_1)$, $pos_j(s_2)$ and $pos_j(s_3)$ are different. Let $t(1) < t(2) < t(3)$ be the ordered sequence of $pos_j(s_i)$ $(1 \le i \le 3)$. Then s_1, s_2, s_3 are in different sets $A_{1,T}, A_{2,T}$ and $A_{3,T}$ for $T = (j,t(1),t(2),t(3))$. Hence we have constructed a $(|S|,3)$-scheme of size $r\binom{b}{3}$. Since b is constant, r should be of size $O(\log|S|)$.

The same idea works for arbitrary k . For some constant b we look for a large set $S \subseteq \{1,...,b\}^r$ such that two vectors in S agree at less than $r/\binom{k}{2}$ positions. Let $s_1, \ldots, s_k$ be different elements of S. For each of the $\binom{k}{2}$ pairs of vectors there are less than $r/\binom{k}{2}$ positions where these vectors agree. Hence there is some position $j = j(s_1, \ldots, s_k)$ where all vectors differ. By

$$A_{m,(j,t(1),...,t(k))} = \{ s \in S \mid pos_j(s) = t(m) \} \qquad (2.6)$$

for $1 \le m \le k$, $1 \le j \le r$, $1 \le t(1) < ... < t(k) \le b$

we obtain a $(|S|,k)$ - scheme of size $r\binom{b}{k}$. If it is possible to choose S in such a way that $r = O(\log |S|)$ we are done. We then choose r large enough that $|S| \ge n$. Afterwards we identify $1,...,n$ with different elements of S . By (2.3) we obtain a formula for T^n_k of size $r\binom{b}{k} n = O(n \log n)$.

For the construction we apply a greedy algorithm.

LEMMA 2.1 : Let $l = \binom{k}{2}$, $b = 2^{2l}$, $c = 2l$ and $r=cr'$ for some r' . Then there is an algorithm which constructs some set $S \subseteq \{1,...,b\}^r$ of size $b^{r'}$ such that two vectors in S agree at less than $r / \binom{k}{2}$ positions. The running time of the algorithm is a polynomial $p(b^{r'})$.

Before we prove this lemma we show that it implies the main result of this section.

THEOREM 2.1 : For constant k monotone formulas for T_k^n of size $O(n \log n)$ can be constructed in polynomial time.

Proof : We apply the algorithm of Lemma 2.1 for the smallest r' such that $b^{r'} \geq n$ and obtain an (n,k)-scheme of size $r \binom{b}{k} n$. Since $r' = O(\log n)$, also $r = O(\log n)$ and the formula has size $O(n \log n)$. $\square$

Proof of Lemma 2.1 : We consider an r-dimensional array for the elements of $\{1,...,b\}^r$. If we choose some vector s as an element of S, all vectors which differ from s in at most $R = (1 - (1/l))r$ positions are forbidden as further vectors in S . The number of forbidden vectors is at most $\binom{r}{R} b^R$. We use the rough estimate $\binom{r}{R} < 2^r$. Hence the number of forbidden vectors is bounded by

$$b^{r \log_b 2 + R} \qquad \text{where} \qquad (2.7)$$

$$r \log_b 2 + R = r (\log_b 2 + 1 - (1/l)) = r (1 - (1/2l)) \qquad (2.8)$$

$$= r (1 - (1/c)) = r - r' .$$

Here we used the fact that $\log_b 2 = 1/(2l)$. The greedy algorithm works as follows. Choose $s_1 \in \{1,...,b\}^r$ arbitrary. Label all forbidden vectors. If $s_1, \ldots, s_{i-1}$ are chosen, choose $s_i \in \{1,...,b\}^r$ as an arbitrary non-forbidden vector and label all vectors forbidden by s_i. If

$i \leq b^{r'}$, the number of vectors forbidden by $s_1, \ldots, s_{i-1}$ is bounded by $(i-1)b^{r-r'} < b^r$ and s_i can be chosen. Hence the algorithm works. The running time is bounded by a polynomial $p(b^r)$ and hence by a polynomial $q(b^{r'})$.

□

8.3 Efficient formulas for all threshold functions

It is a hard struggle to design asymptotically optimal (monotone) formulas for T_k^n and constant k. The design of a polynomial formula is easy, since we can take the MDNF which consists of $\binom{n}{k}$ prime implicants. In general $\binom{n}{k}$ is not polynomially bounded. Since T_k^n is a subfunction of T_n^{2n}, we consider only the majority function T_m^n where $n = 2m$.

Since some time $\{\wedge, \vee, \neg\}$ - formulas of size $O(n^{3.37})$ are known. We are more interested in the monotone formula size of the threshold functions. Polynomial monotone formulas for all threshold functions imply (see Ch. 6, § 13 - § 15) that the monotone formula size of slice functions is only by polynomial factors larger than the formula size over the basis $\{\wedge, \vee, \neg\}$ and also over all complete bases (see Ch. 7, § 1). By Theorem 1.1 in Ch. 7 the monotone depth of slice functions is then of the same size as the depth of these functions.

The sorting network of Ajtai et al. (83) has depth $O(\log n)$. Hence the monotone formula size of all threshold functions is polynomially bounded. The degree of this polynomial is very large (see Ch. 6, § 2). We prove non constructively the existence of monotone formulas for the majority function of size $O(n^{5.3})$ (Valiant (84)).

We consider random formulas of different levels. For some p chosen later a random formula of level 0 equals x_j $(1 \leq j \leq n)$ with probability p and equals 0 with probability $1 - np$. A random formula F_i of level i equals

$$F_i = (G_1 \vee G_2) \wedge (G_3 \vee G_4) \tag{3.1}$$

where $G_1, \ldots, G_4$ are independently chosen random formulas of level $i-1$. The size of F_i is bounded by $4^i = 2^{2i}$. If the probability that $F_i = T_m^n$ is positive, then there is some monotone formula of size 2^{2i} for T_m^n. Why do we hope that F_i sometimes equals T_m^n? In $G_1 \vee G_2$ and $G_3 \vee G_4$ prime implicants are shortened but are lengthened again by the following conjunction. Furthermore the experiment is symmetric with respect to all variables.

It is sufficient to prove that for all $a \in \{0,1\}^n$

$$\text{Prob}\,(F_i(a) \neq T_m^n(a)) < 2^{-n-1}. \tag{3.2}$$

This implies

$$\text{Prob}\,(F_i \neq T_m^n) \leq \sum_{a \in \{0,1\}^n} \text{Prob}\,(F_i(a) \neq T_m^n(a)) \leq \tag{3.3}$$

$$\leq 2^n\, 2^{-n-1} = 1/2.$$

Hence

$$L_m(T_m^n) \leq 2^{2i}. \tag{3.4}$$

Let

$$f_i = \max\,\{\,\text{Prob}(F_i(a) = 1) \mid T_m^n(a) = 0\,\} \quad \text{and} \tag{3.5}$$

$$h_i = \max\,\{\,\text{Prob}(F_i(a) = 0) \mid T_m^n(a) = 1\,\}.$$

LEMMA 3.1 : $f_i = f_{i-1}^4 - 4f_{i-1}^3 + 4f_{i-1}^2$ and $h_i = -h_{i-1}^4 + 2h_{i-1}^2$.

Proof : Because of the monotonicity of F_i and its symmetry with respect to all variables F_i has its worst behavior on inputs with exactly $m-1$ or m ones. Let a be an input with $m-1$ ones. The event $G_j(a) = 1$ has probability f_{i-1} by definition. The event $(G_1 \vee G_2)(a) = 1$ has probability $1 - (1-f_{i-1})^2$ as has the event $(G_3 \vee G_4)(a) = 1$. Hence the event that $F_i(a) = 1$ has probability

$$(1 - (1 - f_{i-1})^2)^2 = f_i .$$

Let b be an input with m ones. The event $G_j(b) = 0$ has probability h_{i-1} by definition. The event $(G_1 \vee G_2)(b) = 0$ has probability h_{i-1}^2 as has the event $(G_3 \vee G_4)(b) = 0$. Hence the event that $F_i(b) = 0$ has probability $1 - (1 - h_{i-1}^2)^2 = h_i$.

□

What is the behavior of the sequence $f_0, f_1, \ldots$ for some given f_0 ? By elementary calculations

$$f_i = f_{i-1} \iff f_{i-1} \in \{0, \alpha, 1, (3 + \sqrt{5})/2\} \tag{3.6}$$

for $\alpha = (3 - \sqrt{5})/2$ and

$$h_i = h_{i-1} \iff h_{i-1} \in \{ -(1 + \sqrt{5})/2, 0, 1 - \alpha, 1 \} . \tag{3.7}$$

The only fix points in the interval $(0,1)$ are $f_{i-1} = \alpha$ and $h_{i-1} = 1 - \alpha$. Considering the representation of f_i and h_i in Lemma 3.1 we note that $f_i < f_{i-1}$ iff $f_{i-1} < \alpha$ and that $h_i < h_{i-1}$ iff $h_{i-1} < 1 - \alpha$. If $f_0 < \alpha$ and $h_0 < 1 - \alpha$, then f_i and h_i are decreasing sequences converging to 0 . To us it is important that $f_l, h_l < 2^{-n-1}$ for some $l = O(\log n)$ (see (3.2) - (3.4)).

It turned out that $p = 2\alpha / (2m - 1)$ is a good choice. Let a be an input with $m - 1$ ones. Then

$$f_0 = \mathrm{Prob}(F_0(a) = 1) = (m-1)p = \alpha - \alpha/(n-1) \tag{3.8}$$

$$= \alpha - \Omega(n^{-1}) .$$

Let b be an input with m ones. Then

$$h_0 = \mathrm{Prob}(F_0(a) = 0) = 1 - \mathrm{Prob}(F_0(b) = 1) = 1 - mp \tag{3.9}$$

$$= 1 - \alpha - \alpha/(n-1) = 1 - \alpha - \Omega(n^{-1}) .$$

We shall see that $\alpha - f_0$ and $1 - \alpha - h_0$ are large enough such that f_i and h_i decrease fast enough.

The function $f_i - f_{i-1}$ is continuous (in f_{i-1}). Hence $f_i - f_{i-1}$ is bounded below by a positive constant if $f_{i-1} \in [\varepsilon', \alpha - \varepsilon]$ for some fixed

$\varepsilon, \varepsilon' > 0$. If $f_i < \alpha - \varepsilon$, $f_j < \varepsilon'$ for some $j = i + O(1)$. But for which i it holds that $f_i < \alpha - \varepsilon$ if $f_0 = \alpha - \Omega(n^{-1})$? For which l $f_l < 2^{-n-1}$ if $f_j < \varepsilon'$?

By Lemma 3.1 $f_i < 4 f_{i-1}^2$ and $h_i < 4 h_{i-1}^2$ for $f_{i-1}, h_{i-1} \in (0,1]$. Let $\varepsilon' = 1/16$ and $f_j, h_j < \varepsilon'$. For $l > j$ and $k = 2^{l-j}$

$$f_l < 4 f_{l-1}^2 < 4^3 f_{l-2}^4 < \cdots < 4^{k-1} f_j^k < (1/4)^k = 2^{-2k} \qquad (3.10)$$

and also $h_l < 2^{-2k}$. If $l = j + \lceil \log n \rceil$, $k \geq n$ and

$$f_l, h_l < 2^{-2k} \leq 2^{-2n} \leq 2^{-n-1}. \qquad (3.11)$$

If $f_i < \alpha - \varepsilon$ and $h_i < 1 - \alpha - \varepsilon$, then $f_l, h_l < 2^{-n-1}$ for $l = i + \lceil \log n \rceil + O(1)$.

It is easy to check that for $\delta > 0$

$$f_{i-1} = \alpha - \delta \quad \Rightarrow \quad f_i = \alpha - 4\alpha\delta + O(\delta^2) \text{ and} \qquad (3.12)$$

$$h_{i-1} = 1 - \alpha - \delta \quad \Rightarrow \quad h_i = 1 - \alpha - 4\alpha\delta + O(\delta^2). \qquad (3.13)$$

Hence

$$\forall \gamma < 4\alpha \; \exists \varepsilon > 0 \; \forall 0 < \delta < \varepsilon : f_i = \alpha - \delta \quad \Rightarrow \quad f_i < \alpha - \gamma\delta \text{ and} \qquad (3.14)$$

$$h_{i-1} = 1 - \alpha - \delta \Rightarrow h_i < 1 - \alpha - \gamma\delta.$$

We know that $f_0 \leq \alpha - cn^{-1}$ for some $c > 0$. Hence by (3.14) $f_i \leq \alpha - \gamma^i cn^{-1}$ if $\gamma^{i-1} cn^{-1} < \varepsilon$. If we choose $i = (\log n)/(\log \gamma) + c'$ for some appropriate c', then $f_i < \alpha - \varepsilon$ and (by similar arguments) $h_i < 1 - \alpha - \varepsilon$. Altogether $\text{Prob}(F_l = T_m^n) \geq 1/2$ for all $\gamma < 4\alpha$, some appropriate c'' depending on γ and

$$l = (\log n)(1 + \log^{-1} \gamma) + c''. \qquad (3.15)$$

The size of F_l is bounded by

$$2^{2l} = O(n^\beta) \quad \text{where} \quad \beta = 2(1 + \log^{-1}\gamma), \; \gamma < 4\alpha = 2(3 - \sqrt{5}). \qquad (3.16)$$

Choosing $\gamma = 4\alpha - \eta$ for some small η we obtain a monotone formula for T_m^n of size $O(n^{5.271})$.

THEOREM 3.1 : The monotone formula size of each threshold function T_k^n is bounded by $O(n^{5.271})$.

The best lower bounds on the formula size of the majority function (over the monotone basis and over $\{\wedge,\vee,\neg\}$) are of size $\Omega(n^2)$. Hence the investigation of the (monotone) formula size of threshold functions is not yet complete.

8.4 The depth of symmetric functions

We are not able to prove $\omega(\log n)$ lower bounds on the depth of explicitly defined Boolean functions. For functions depending essentially on n variables a $\lceil \log n \rceil$ lower bound is obvious. Most of the lower bounds of size $c \log n$ for some $c > 1$ follow from $\Omega(n^c)$ bounds on the formula size. There are only few exceptions where lower bounds on the depth are proved directly. McColl (78 c) proved such bounds for symmetric functions and the complete bases $\{NAND\}$ and $\{NAND, \rightarrow\}$. Since the methods are similar, we concentrate us on the basis $\{NAND\}$. Further results for special functions are proved by McColl (76).

We know already (see Theorem 4.1, Ch. 3) that the depth of all symmetric functions is $\Theta(\log n)$. For the proof of lower bounds over the basis $\{NAND\}$ we make the most of the cognition that NAND - circuits of small depth compute only functions of short prime implicants.

LEMMA 4.1 : If f can be computed by a NAND -circuit of depth $2d + 1$, the length of each prime implicant of f is bounded by 2^d .

Proof : Induction on d . If $d = 0$, the depth is bounded by 1 . The only functions which are computable in depth 1 are x_i , $\bar{x}_i = NAND(x_i, x_i)$ and $\bar{x}_i \vee \bar{x}_j = NAND(x_i, x_j)$. All prime implicants have length $2^d = 1$. Let us now assume that the lemma holds for all functions of depth $d' \le 2d + 1$. Let f be a function of depth $2d + 2$ or

$2d+3$, and let S be a depth optimal circuit for f. At least one of the direct predecessors of the output gate is also a gate. Hence

$$f = NAND(NAND(h_1,h_2),NAND(h_3,h_4)) = (h_1 \wedge h_2) \vee (h_3 \wedge h_4) \quad (4.1)$$

or $f = NAND(NAND(h_1,h_2),x_i) = (h_1 \wedge h_2) \vee \bar{x}_i$

for functions $h_1, \ldots, h_4$ whose prime implicants have by induction hypothesis lengths bounded by 2^d. Thus the length of the prime implicants of f is bounded by 2^{d+1}.

$\square$

LEMMA 4.2 : Let t be an implicant of $f \in S_n$ of length s. Then the value vector $v(f)$ of f contains a substring of length $n-s+1$ consisting of ones only.

Proof : We replace s variables by constants in such a way that t and hence also f are replaced by 1. The substring of $v(f)$ for this subfunction has length $n-s+1$ and consists of ones only.

$\square$

THEOREM 4.1 : If $f \in S_n$ is not constant,

$$D_{\{NAND\}}(f) \geq 2 \log n - (2 \log 3 - 1). \quad (4.2)$$

Proof : Since $\neg f = NAND(f,f)$, f and $\neg f$ have almost the same depth. If the depth is small, the prime implicants of f and $\neg f$ are short and $v(f)$ and $v(\neg f)$ have long substrings consisting of ones only. Hence $v(f)$ has a long substring of ones only and a long substring of zeros only. The length of the shorter substring is bounded by $(n+1)/2$.

Case 1 : $2^k \leq n < 3 \cdot 2^{k-1}$.

We choose d so that $D_{\{NAND\}}(f) \in \{2d-1,2d\}$. Then $D_{\{NAND\}}(\neg f) \leq 2d+1$. By Lemma 4.1 the lengths of the prime implicants of f and $\neg f$ are bounded by 2^d. $v(f)$ contains a 0-sequence whose length is at least $n+1-2^d$ and a 1-sequence whose length is at least $n+1-2^d$. The length of $v(f)$ is $n+1$. Hence

$$n + 1 \geq 2(n+1-2^d) \quad \text{and} \quad 2^{d+1} \geq n+1 \geq 2^k + 1 . \tag{4.3}$$

Since d and k are natural numbers

$$D_{\{NAND\}}(f) \geq 2d - 1 \geq 2k - 1 = 2(k-1) + 1 \tag{4.4}$$

$$> 2\log(n/3) + 1 = 2\log n - (2\log 3 - 1) .$$

Case 2 : $3 \cdot 2^{k-1} \leq n < 2^{k+1}$.

We use similar arguments. Let $D_{\{NAND\}}(f) \in \{2d, 2d+1\}$, hence $D_{\{NAND\}}(\neg f) \leq 2d+2$. $v(f)$ contains a 1-sequence (0-sequence) whose length is at least $n+1-2^d$ ($n+1-2^{d+1}$) . Hence

$$n+1 \geq n+1-2^d +n+1-2^{d+1} \;\Rightarrow\; 3 \cdot 2^d \geq n+1 \geq 3 \cdot 2^{k-1} + 1 \tag{4.5}$$

$$\Rightarrow \; D_{\{NAND\}}(f) \geq 2d \geq 2k \geq 2(\log n - 1) \geq 2\log n - (2\log 3 - 1) .$$

□

8.5 The Hodes and Specker method

After intensive studies on the depth and formula size of symmetric functions and above all threshold functions we switch over to general methods for the proof of lower bounds on the formula size of Boolean functions. Many applications on the Hodes and Specker method are presented by Hodes (70). Hodes and Specker (68) stated only that their method yields nonlinear bounds. Vilfan (72) proved that the bounds actually are of size $n \log^* n$. Pudlák (84 a) combined the results of Hodes and Specker and the Ramsey theory (see e.g. Graham, Rothschild and Spencer (80)) and proved the following theorem.

THEOREM 5.1 : For each binary basis Ω there is some $\varepsilon_\Omega > 0$ such that the following statement holds for all $r \geq 3$ and all $f \in B_n$ whose formula size with respect to Ω is bounded above by $\varepsilon_\Omega \, n(\log\log n - r)$. There is a set of $n-r$ variables such that the subfunction $f' \in B_r$ of f where we have replaced these $n-r$ variables by zeros is symmetric, and its value vector $v(f') = (v_0, \ldots, v_r)$ has the following form: $v_1 = v_3 = v_5 = \cdots$ and $v_2 = v_4 = v_6 = \cdots$. Hence f' is uniquely defined by v_0, v_1 and v_2.

The proof is based on the fundamental principle of the Ramsey theory. Simple objects, here formulas of small size, are locally simple, i.e. have very simple symmetric functions on not too few variables as subfunctions. We leave out the proof here. A direct application of the Ramsey theory to lower bounds on the formula size has been worked out by Pudlák (83). Since the Ramsey numbers are increasing very fast, such lower bounds have to be of small size.

Here we explain only one simple application of this method, more applications are posed as exercises.

THEOREM 5.2 : $L(T_2^n) = \Omega(n \log\log n)$.

Proof : Let $r = 3$. If we replace $n-3$ variables by zeros, T_2^n is replaced by T_2^3. For the value vector of T_2^3 $v_1 \neq v_3$. $\qquad\square$

This is the largest known lower bound on $L(T_2^n)$.

8.6 The Fischer, Meyer and Paterson method

Also the method due to Fischer, Meyer and Paterson (82) is based on the fact that simple functions have very simple subfunctions. This method yields larger lower bounds than the Hodes and Specker method but for a smaller class of functions. The class of very simple functions is the class of affine functions $x_1 \oplus \cdots \oplus x_m \oplus c$ for $c \in \{0,1\}$. The size of an affine function is the number of variables on which it depends essentially. A subfunction f' of f is called a central restriction of f if $n_1 - n_0 \in \{0,1\}$ for the number of variables replaced by ones (n_1) and zeros (n_0).

THEOREM 6.1 : Let $a(f)$ be the maximal size of an affine subfunction of f when considering only central restrictions. Then for all Boolean functions $f \in B_n$ $(n \in \mathbb{N})$

$$L(f) \geq \varepsilon n (\log n - \log a(f)) \quad \text{for some constant } \varepsilon > 0 . \tag{6.1}$$

We also omit the tedious proof of this theorem. The following result states a rather general criterion for an application of this method. Afterwards we present a function for which the bound of Theorem 6.1 is tight.

THEOREM 6.2 : If $f(a) = c$ for all inputs with exactly k ones and $f(a) = \bar{c}$ for all inputs with exactly $k+2$ ones, then

$$L(f) \geq \varepsilon' n \log (\min \{k, n-k\}) \quad \text{for some constant } \varepsilon' > 0 . \tag{6.2}$$

Proof : W.l.o.g. $k \leq \lfloor n/2 \rfloor$. At first we prove the assertion for $k = \lfloor n/2 \rfloor$. It is sufficient to prove that $a(f) \leq 2$. Let us consider a central restriction $f' \in B_3$ of f. Then $\lceil (n-3)/2 \rceil$ variables have been replaced by ones and $\lfloor (n-3)/2 \rfloor$ variables have been replaced by zeros. Since $k - \lceil (n-3)/2 \rceil = 1$, $f'(1,0,0) = c$ but $f'(1,1,1) = \bar{c}$. Hence f' is not affine.

If $k < \lfloor n/2 \rfloor$, we consider an optimal formula F for f. Let b_i be the number of leaves of F labelled by x_i. Then we replace those $n - 2k$ variables by zeros which have the largest b-values. The formula size of the subfunction $f' \in B_{2k}$ is at least $\varepsilon'(2k) \log k$ as we have proved in the last paragraph. Hence there is some variable x_i such that at least $\varepsilon' \log k$ leaves of the subformula F' of F are labelled by x_i. By definition, $b_j \geq \varepsilon' \log k$ for all x_j which we have replaced by zeros. Hence

$$L(f) = L(F) \geq (n - 2k)\, \varepsilon' \log k + \varepsilon'(2k) \log k = \varepsilon' n \log k . \qquad (6.3)$$

□

THEOREM 6.3 : $L(C_{0,4}^n) = \Theta(n \log n)$ for the counting function $C_{0,4}^n$.

Proof : $C_{0,4}^n(a) = 1$ iff $a_1 + \cdots + a_n \equiv 0 \bmod 4$ (see Def. 4.1, Ch. 3). The lower bound follows from Theorem 6.2, since each substring of $v(C_{0,4}^n)$ of length 4 contains exactly one 1. Hence we may choose k such that $n/2 - 2 \leq k \leq n/2 + 2$.

For the upper bound we assume w.l.o.g. that $n = 2^m$. Let $D_1^n(x)$ and $D_0^n(x)$ be the last two bits of $x_1 + \cdots + x_n$. Then $C_{0,4}^n(x) = \mathrm{NOR}(D_1^n(x), D_0^n(x))$. Obviously $L(D_0^n(x)) = n$, since $D_0^n(x) = x_1 \oplus \cdots \oplus x_n$. Let $x = (x',x'')$ where x' and x'' contain $n/2$ variables each. Then

$$D_1^n(x) = D_1^{n/2}(x') \oplus D_1^{n/2}(x'') \oplus (D_0^{n/2}(x') \wedge D_0^{n/2}(x'')), \qquad (6.4)$$

$$L(D_1^n) \leq 2\, L(D_1^{n/2}) + n \quad \text{and} \quad L(D_1^2) = 2 . \qquad (6.5)$$

Hence $L(D_1^n) \leq n \log n$ and $L(C_{0,4}^n) \leq n(1 + \log n)$.

□

8.7 The Nechiporuk method

The lower bound due to Nechiporuk (66) is based on the observation that there cannot be a small formula for a function with many different subfunctions. There have to be different subformulas for different subfunctions.

DEFINITION 7.1 : Let $S \subseteq X$ be a set of variables. All subfunctions f' of f, defined on S, are called S-subfunctions.

THEOREM 7.1 : Let $f \in B_n$ depend essentially on all its variables, let $S_1, \ldots, S_k \subseteq X$ be disjoint sets of variables, and let s_i be the number of S_i-subfunctions of f. Then

$$L(f) \geq N(S_1, \ldots, S_k) := (1/4) \sum_{1 \leq i \leq k} \log s_i . \qquad (7.1)$$

Proof : Let F be an optimal formula for f and let a_i be the number of leaves labelled by variables $x_j \in S_i$. It is sufficient to prove that $a_i \geq (1/4) \log s_i$. Let T_i be that subtree of F consisting of all leaves labelled by some $x_j \in S_i$ and consisting of all paths from these leaves to the output of F . The indegree of the nodes of T_i is 0, 1 or 2 . Let W_i be the set of nodes of indegree 2 . Since it is obvious that $|W_i| = a_i - 1$, it is sufficient to prove that

$$|W_i| \geq (1/4) \log s_i - 1 . \qquad (7.2)$$

Let P_i be the set of paths in T_i starting from a leaf or a node in W_i, ending in a node in W_i or at the root of T_i and containing no node in W_i as inner node. There are at most $|W_i| + 1$ different end-points of paths in P_i . Because of the definition of P_i there are at most two P_i-paths ending in some gate G . These paths can be found by starting in G and going backwards until a node in W_i or a leaf is reached. Hence

$$|P_i| \leq 2(|W_i| + 1).$$ (7.3)

The different replacements of the variables $x_j \notin S_i$ lead to s_i different subformulas. We measure the local influence of different replacements. Let p be a path in P_i and let us fix a replacement of all variables $x_j \notin S_i$. If h is computed at the first gate of p, then the function computed on the last edge of p is 0, 1, h or $\bar{h}$, since no variable $x_k \in S_i$ has any influence on this path. Since T_i can be partitioned into the paths $p \in P_i$, the number of S_i-subfunctions is bounded by $4^{|P_i|}$. Hence

$$s_i \leq 4^{|P_i|}$$ (7.4)

and (7.2) follows from (7.3) and (7.4).

□

What is the largest possible size of the Nechiporuk bound $N(S_1, \ldots, S_k)$?

THEOREM 7.2 : If $f \in B_n$, the Nechiporuk bound $N(S_1, \ldots, S_k)$ is not larger than $2n \log^{-1} n$.

Proof : Let $t(i) = |S_i|$. There are $2^{n-t(i)}$ possibilities of replacing the variables $x_j \notin S_i$ by constants, and there are not more than $2^{2^{t(i)}}$ functions on S_i. Hence

$$\log s_i \leq \min \{ n - t(i), 2^{t(i)} \}.$$ (7.5)

W.l.o.g. $t(i) > \log n$ iff $i \leq q$. Since the sets S_i are disjoint, $q < n \log^{-1} n$ and

$$\sum_{1 \leq i \leq q} \log s_i \leq \sum_{1 \leq i \leq q} (n - t(i)) \leq n^2 \log^{-1} n.$$ (7.6)

Furthermore

$$\sum_{q < i \leq k} \log s_i \leq \sum_{q < i \leq k} 2^{t(i)}.$$ (7.7)

Since the function $x \to 2^x$ is convex, the right-hand side of (7.7) is maximal if as many $t(i)$ as possible are equal to $\log n$, the upper bound for these $t(i)$. Hence also (7.7) is bounded by $n^2 \log^{-1} n$.

□

Indeed it is possible to prove by Nechiporuk's method bounds of size $n^2 \log^{-1} n$. The Nechiporuk function is dealt with in the Exercises. We prove a bound of this size for a storage access function for indirect addressing (Paul (77)).

DEFINITION 7.2 : The storage access function (for indirect addressing) $ISA_n \in B_n$ where $n = 2p + k$ for some $p = 2^{2^l}$ and $k = \log p - \log\log p$ is defined on the variables $x = (x_1, \ldots, x_p)$, $y = (y_0, \ldots, y_{p-1})$ and $a = (a_0, \ldots, a_{k-1})$.
Let $d = (x_{|a|\log p + 1}, \ldots, x_{(|a|+1)\log p})$ where $|a|$ is the binary number represented by a. Then $ISA_n(x,y,a) = y_{|d|}$.

THEOREM 7.3 : $L(ISA_n) = \Omega(n^2 \log^{-1} n)$ and $C(ISA_n) \le 2n + o(n)$.

Proof : Let $S_i = \{x_{i\log p + 1}, \ldots, x_{(i+1)\log p}\}$ for $0 \le i \le p \log^{-1} p - 1$. For fixed i we replace the a-variables by constants so that $|a| = i$. Then y is the value table of the S_i-subfunction. All 2^p different value tables lead to different S_i-subfunctions. Hence $s_i \ge 2^p$ and by the Nechiporuk method

$$L(ISA_n) \ge (1/4) p^2 \log^{-1} p = \Omega(n^2 \log^{-1} n). \tag{7.8}$$

By Theorem 5.1 , Ch. 3, the circuit complexity of SA_n , the storage access function for direct addressing, is bounded by $2n + o(n)$. Hence each $x_{|a|\log p + j}$ $(1 \le j \le \log p)$ can be computed by $2p \log^{-1} p + o(p \log^{-1} p)$ gates. The whole vector d can be computed with $2p + o(p)$ gates. Afterwards ISA_n can be computed with $2p + o(p)$ gates. Altogether $4p + o(p) = 2n + o(n)$ gates are sufficient for the computation of ISA_n.

□

Nechiporuk's method has been applied to many functions. We refer to Harper and Savage (72) for the marriage problem and to Paterson (73) for the recognition of context free languages. We investigate the determinant (Kloss (66)) and the clique functions (Schürfeld (84)). The determinant $\det_n \in B_N$ where $N = n^2$ is defined by

$$\det_n(x_{11}, \ldots, x_{nn}) = \bigoplus_{\pi \in \Sigma_n} x_{1,\pi(1)} \cdots x_{n,\pi(n)} . \tag{7.9}$$

THEOREM 7.4 : $L(\det_n) \geq (1/8)(n^3 - n^2)$.

Proof : Let $S_i = \{x_{j,(i+j) \bmod n} \mid 1 \leq j \leq n\}$ contain the variables of some secondary diagonal. Since the determinant does not change if we interchange rows or columns, we conclude that $s_1 = \cdots = s_n$. We only consider S_n , the variables of the main diagonal, and prove the existence of $2^{(n^2-n)/2}$ S_n-subfunctions. Then the theorem follows by the Nechiporuk method.

Let $y_j = x_{jj}$. We replace the variables below the main diagonal by fixed constants in the following way.

$$g_c(y_1, \ldots, y_n) = \det_n \begin{bmatrix} y_1 & c_{12} & c_{13} & \cdots & c_{1,n-2} & c_{1,n-1} & c_{1n} \\ 1 & y_2 & c_{23} & \cdots & c_{2,n-2} & c_{2,n-1} & c_{2n} \\ 0 & 1 & y_3 & \cdots & c_{3,n-2} & c_{3,n-1} & c_{3n} \\ \cdots & \cdots & \cdots & \cdots & \cdots & \cdots & \cdots \\ 0 & 0 & 0 & \cdots & 1 & y_{n-1} & c_{n-1,n} \\ 0 & 0 & 0 & \cdots & 0 & 1 & y_n \end{bmatrix} . \tag{7.10}$$

Since there are $(n^2-n)/2$ matrix elements c_{ij} $(i < j)$ above the main diagonal, it is sufficient to prove that g_c and $g_{c'}$ are different functions for different c and c' .
For $n = 2$ $g_c(y_1, y_2) = y_1 y_2 \oplus c_{12}$ and the assertion is obvious. The case $n = 3$ is left as an exercise.

For $n > 3$ we apply matrix operations which do not change the determinant. We multiply the second row by y_1 and add the result to the first row. The new first row equals

$$(0 , y_1 y_2 \oplus c_{12} , y_1 c_{23} \oplus c_{13} , \cdots , y_1 c_{2n} \oplus c_{1n}) . \tag{7.11}$$

The first column has a one in the second row and zeros in all other rows. Hence we can erase the first column and the second row of the matrix. For $y_1 = 1$ we obtain an $(n-1) \times (n-1)$-matrix of type (7.10). By induction hypothesis we conclude that g_c and $g_{c'}$ differ if $c_{ij} \neq c_{ij}'$ for some $i \geq 3$ or $c_{1k} \oplus c_{2k} \neq c_{1k}' \oplus c_{2k}'$ for some $k \geq 3$.

By similar arguments for the last two columns (instead of the first two rows) we conclude that g_c and $g_{c'}$ differ if $c_{ij} \neq c_{ij}'$ for some $j \leq n-2$ or $c_{k,n-1} \oplus c_{kn} \neq c_{k,n-1}' \oplus c_{kn}'$ for some $k \leq n-2$. Altogether we have to consider only the situation where $c_{ij} = c_{ij}'$ for all $(i,j) \notin \{(1,n-1),(1,n),(2,n-1),(2,n)\}$ and $c_{1k} \oplus c_{2k} = c_{1k}' \oplus c_{2k}'$ for $k \in \{n-1,n\}$. Let $y_1 = 0$. Then we can erase the first column and the second row of the matrix. We obtain $(n-1) \times (n-1)$ - matrices M and M' which agree at all positions except perhaps the last two positions of the first row. Since $c \neq c'$ and $c_{1k} \oplus c_{2k} = c_{1k}' \oplus c_{2k}'$ for $k \in \{n-1,n\}$, $c_{1,n-1} \neq c_{1,n-1}'$ or $c_{1n} \neq c_{1n}'$ or both. By an expansion according to the first row we compute the determinants of M and M' . The summands for the first $n-3$ positions are equal for both matrices. The $(n-2)$-th summand is y_n if $c_{1,n-1} = 1$ ($c_{1,n-1}' = 1$ resp.) and 0 else, and the last summand is 1 if $c_{1n} = 1$ ($c_{1n}' = 1$ resp.) and 0 else. Hence $g_c(y) \oplus g_{c'}(y)$ is equal to y_n or 1 or $y_n \oplus 1$ according to the three cases above. This ensures that $g_c \neq g_{c'}$ if $c \neq c'$.

$\square$

The clique function $cl_{n,m} \in M_N$ where $N = \binom{n}{2}$ (see Def.11.1, Ch.6) checks whether the graph $G(x)$ contains an m-clique.

THEOREM 7.5 : $L(cl_{n,m}) \geq (1/48) (n-m)^3 - o((n-m)^3)$ if $m \geq 3$.

Proof : It is sufficient to prove the claim for $m = 3$, since $cl_{n-(m-3),3}$ is a subfunction of $cl_{n,m}$. We only have to replace all edges adjacent to the nodes $n - m + 4 , \ldots , n$ by ones.

Let $S_i = \{x_{i,i+1}, \ldots, x_{in}\}$ for $1 \le i \le n - 1$. In order to estimate the number of S_i-subfunctions, we replace all edges adjacent to the nodes $1, \ldots, i-1$ by zeros. These nodes are isolated and cannot belong to a 3-clique. We replace the variables x_{kl} ($i + 1 \le k < l \le n$) in such a way by constants, that the graph on the nodes $i + 1, \ldots, n$ does not contain a 3-clique. Different replacements lead to different S_i-subfunctions. If $a_{kl} = 1$ for one replacement and $a'_{kl} = 0$ for another replacement, let $x_{ik} = x_{il} = 1$ and $x_{ij} = 0$ for all other j . The first graph contains the 3-clique on $\{i, k, l\}$, but the second graph does not contain any 3-clique at all.

Hence the number of S_i-subfunctions is not smaller than the number of graphs on $n - i$ vertices without any 3-clique. We partition the set of vertices into two sets M_1 and M_2 of size $\lceil (n-i)/2 \rceil$ and $\lfloor (n-i)/2 \rfloor$ resp. No bipartite graph contains a 3-clique. Hence the number of S_i-subfunctions is at least $2^{\lceil (n-i)/2 \rceil \lfloor (n-i)/2 \rfloor}$. By the Nechiporuk method

$$L(cl_{n,3}) \ge (1/4) \sum_{1 \le i \le n-1} \lceil (n-i)/2 \rceil \lfloor (n-i)/2 \rfloor \tag{7.12}$$

$$= (1/16) \sum_{1 \le i \le n-1} (n-i)^2 - o(n^3) = (1/48) \, n^3 - o(n^3) \, . \qquad \square$$

8.8 The Krapchenko method

The lower bound methods of § 5 - § 7 work for all (binary) bases. Then the parity function $f(x) = x_1 \oplus \cdots \oplus x_n$ is a simple function. For an input $a \in f^{-1}(c)$ all neighbors, i.e. all inputs b which differ from a at exactly one position, are elements of $f^{-1}(\bar{c})$. For the functions $g(x) = x_i$ computed at the inputs each vector $a \in g^{-1}(c)$ has exactly one neighbor in $g^{-1}(\bar{c})$. Using only gates of type-$\wedge$, i.e. using the basis $U = B_2 - \{\oplus, \equiv\}$, the number of pairs of neighbors (a,b) , such that $h(a) \neq h(b)$ for the computed function h , is increasing only slowly. This observation is the principal item of the Krapchenko method. Hence this method works only for the basis U .

We assume that the leaves of a formula can be labelled by any literal $(x_i$ or $\bar{x}_i)$. Then we can apply the rules of deMorgan, and all inner nodes are labelled by $\wedge$ or $\vee$. We do not present the proof due to Krapchenko (71, 72 b) but a simpler proof due to Paterson (pers. comm.).

DEFINITION 8.1 : A formal complexity measure FC is a function $FC : B_n \rightarrow \mathbb{N}$ such that

i) $FC(x_i)$ = 1   for $1 \leq i \leq n$,
ii) $FC(f)$ = $FC(\neg f)$ for $f \in B_n$ and
iii) $FC(f \vee g) \leq FC(f) + FC(g)$ for $f,g \in B_n$.

By this definition and the rules of deMorgan also $FC(f \wedge g) \leq FC(f) + FC(g)$. L_U is a formal complexity measure. Moreover L_U is the largest formal complexity measure.

LEMMA 8.1 : $L_U(f) \geq FC(f)$ for any $f \in B_n$ and any formal complexity measure FC .

Proof : By induction on $l = L_U(f)$. If $l = 1$, $f = x_i$ or $f = \bar{x}_i$, and $FC(f) = 1$. Let $l = L_U(f) > 1$ and let F be an optimal U-formula for f . W.l.o.g. the last gate of F is an $\vee$-gate whose input functions are g and h . Hence $f = g \vee h$. The subformulas for g and h are optimal, too. By the induction hypothesis

$$L_U(f) = L_U(g) + L_U(h) \geq FC(g) + FC(h) \geq FC(f) . \qquad (8.1)$$

$\square$

We look for a formal complexity measure FC such that for many difficult functions f   FC(f) is large and can be estimated easily.

DEFINITION 8.2 : Let H(A,B) be the set of neighbors (a,b) $\in$ A$\times$B . Let

$$K_{AB} = |H(A,B)|^2 |A|^{-1} |B|^{-1} \quad \text{and} \tag{8.2}$$

$$K(f) = \max \{ K_{AB} \mid A \subseteq f^{-1}(1) , B \subseteq f^{-1}(0) \} . \tag{8.3}$$

THEOREM 8.1 : $L_U(f) \geq K(f)$ for all Boolean functions f .

Proof : It is sufficient to prove that the Krapchenko measure K is a formal complexity measure.

i) **Claim** : $K(x_i) = 1$.

" $\geq$ " : Let B be the set containing only the zero vector, and let A be the set containing only the i-th unit vector.

" $\leq$ " : Each vector in $x_i^{-1}(0)$ has only one neighbor in $x_i^{-1}(1)$ and vice versa.

ii) $K(f) = K(\neg f)$ by definition, since the definition of K(f) is symmetric with respect to $f^{-1}(0)$ and $f^{-1}(1)$.

iii) **Claim** : $K(f \vee g) \leq K(f) + K(g)$.
We choose $A \subseteq (f \vee g)^{-1}(1)$ and $B \subseteq (f \vee g)^{-1}(0)$ in such a way that $K(f \vee g) = K_{AB}$. Then $B \subseteq f^{-1}(0)$ and $B \subseteq g^{-1}(0)$. We partition A into disjoint sets $A_f \subseteq f^{-1}(1)$ and $A_g \subseteq g^{-1}(1)$. Then H(A,B) is the disjoint union of $H(A_f,B)$ and $H(A_g,B)$. Let $a_g = |A_g|$, $h_f = |H(A_f,B)|$ and so on. Then

$$K(f \vee g) = h^2 a^{-1} b^{-1} \quad \text{and} \tag{8.4}$$

$$K(f) + K(g) \geq h_f^2 a_f^{-1} b^{-1} + h_g^2 a_g^{-1} b^{-1} .$$

It is sufficient to prove that

$$h^2 a^{-1} b^{-1} \leq h_f^2 a_f^{-1} b^{-1} + h_g^2 a_g^{-1} b^{-1} . \tag{8.5}$$

We make use of the facts that $h = h_f + h_g$ and $a = a_f + a_g$. Hence

$$(8.5) \iff (h_f + h_g)^2 a_f a_g \leq h_f^2 a_g (a_f + a_g) + h_g^2 a_f (a_f + a_g) \tag{8.6}$$

$$\Leftrightarrow \quad 0 \leq h_f^2 a_g^2 - 2 h_f h_g a_f a_g + h_g^2 a_f^2 = (h_f a_g - h_g a_f)^2 .$$

$\square$

LEMMA 8.2 : $K(f) \leq n^2$ for all $f \in B_n$.

Proof : $|H(A,B)| \leq \min \{n|A|, n|B|\}$, since each vector has only n neighbors.

$\square$

THEOREM 8.2 : For the parity function $f_n(x) = x_1 \oplus \cdots \oplus x_n$ $L(f_n) = n$ and $L_U(f_n) \geq n^2$. If $n = 2^k$, $L_U(f_n) = n^2$.

Proof : Obviously $L(f_n) = n$. If $A = f_n^{-1}(1)$ and $B = f_n^{-1}(0)$, $|A| = |B| = 2^{n-1}$. Each neighbor of $a \in A$ lies in B and vice versa, i.e. $|H(A,B)| = n 2^{n-1}$. Hence $L_U(f_n) \geq n^2$ by Theorem 8.1 .

We still have to prove an upper bound on $L_U(f_n)$ for $n = 2^k$. Let $x = (x', x'')$ where x' and x'' have length $n/2$ each.

$$f_n(x) = (f_{n/2}(x') \wedge (\neg f_{n/2}(x''))) \vee ((\neg f_{n/2}(x')) \wedge f_{n/2}(x'')) . \qquad (8.7)$$

Hence

$$L_U(f_n) \leq 4 L_U(f_{n/2}) , \quad L_U(f_1) = 1 , \text{ and } L_U(f_n) \leq n^2 . \qquad (8.8)$$

$\square$

This difference between the bases B_2 and U has been proved by Krapchenko (72 a). The Krapchenko method yields good lower bounds for several symmetric functions (see Theorem 8.2 and Exercises). It is easy to prove that the Nechiporuk bound is linear for all symmetric functions. The Nechiporuk method is sometimes useful also for functions with short prime implicants ($cl_{n,3}$ in Theorem 7.5). For such functions no nonlinear lower bound can be proved by the Krapchenko bound (Schürfeld (84)).

THEOREM 8.3 : Let $l_{PI}(f)$ be the smallest number such that some polynomial for f contains only prime implicants of length $l \leq l_{PI}(f)$.

Let $l_{PC}(f)$ be defined in a similar way for prime clauses. Then $K(f) \leq l_{PI}(f) \, l_{PC}(f)$.

Proof : Let $A \subseteq f^{-1}(1)$ and $B \subseteq f^{-1}(0)$. For $a \in A$ we find some prime implicant t of f such that $t(a) = 1$ and the length of t is bounded by $l_{PI}(f)$. If $a' \in f^{-1}(0)$ is a neighbor of a , $t(a') = 0$. Hence a and a' differ in a position i where x_i or $\bar{x}_i$ is a literal of t .
This implies $|H(A,B)| \leq l_{PI}(f)|A|$. Similarly $|H(A,B)| \leq l_{PC}(f)|B|$. Altogether $K_{A,B} \leq l_{PI}(f) \, l_{PC}(f)$.

$\square$

As a further example we apply the Krapchenko method to the determinant.

THEOREM 8.4 : $L_U(\det_n) \geq (1/12) \, n^4$.

Proof : Let $A = \det_n^{-1}(1)$ and $B = \det_n^{-1}(0)$. $|A|$ is the number of regular $n \times n$ – matrices over the field $\mathbb{Z}_2 = (\{0,1\}, \oplus, \wedge)$. The first row of such a matrix has to be different from the zero vector, we have $2^n - 1$ possibilites for the choice of this row. If we have chosen $i - 1$ linearly independent vectors, these vectors are spanning a vector space of 2^{i-1} vectors. For the choice of the i-th row we have therefore $2^n - 2^{i-1}$ possibilities. Hence

$$|A| = \prod_{1 \leq i \leq n} (2^n - 2^{i-1}) = \alpha_n \, 2^{n^2} \text{ where } \alpha_n = \prod_{1 \leq i \leq n} (1 - 2^{-i}) . \quad (8.9)$$

Since $(1-a)(1-b) \geq 1-a-b$ for $a,b \geq 0$,

$$\alpha_n = (1/2) \prod_{2 \leq i \leq n} (1 - 2^{-i}) \geq (1/2)(1 - \sum_{2 \leq i \leq n} 2^{-i}) \geq (1/4) . \quad (8.10)$$

Furthermore $\alpha_n / (1 - \alpha_n) \geq 1/3$ and $\alpha_{n-1} \geq \alpha_n$.

Let M be a given $n \times n$-matrix and M' a neighbor of M . W.l.o.g. M and M' differ exactly at position $(1,1)$. We compute $\det_n M$ and $\det_n M'$ by an expansion of the first row. Then $\det_n M \neq \det_n M'$ iff the $(n-1) \times (n-1)$-matrix M^* consisting of the last $n-1$ rows and columns of M (or M') is regular. We have n^2 possibilities for the choice of the position where M and M' differ, $\alpha_{n-1} 2^{(n-1)^2}$ possibilities for the choice of M^* and $2^{2(n-1)}$ possibilities for the choice of the other members of the i-th row and the j-th column if M and M' differ at position (i,j). Hence

$$|H(A,B)| = n^2 2^{2(n-1)} \alpha_{n-1} 2^{(n-1)^2} = (1/2)\, \alpha_{n-1}\, n^2\, 2^{n^2}. \qquad (8.11)$$

Altogether

$$K(\det_n) \geq \frac{(1/4)\, \alpha_{n-1}^2\, n^4\, 2^{2n^2}}{\alpha_n\, 2^{n^2}\,(1-\alpha_n)\, 2^{n^2}} = \frac{1}{4}\, \frac{\alpha_{n-1}}{\alpha_n}\, \frac{\alpha_{n-1}}{1-\alpha_n}\, n^4 \geq \frac{1}{12}\, n^4. \qquad (8.12)$$

$\square$

EXERCISES

1. $L(f \vee g) = L(f) + L(g)$ if f and g depend essentially on disjoint sets of variables.

2. (Bublitz (86)) Let

    $f(x_1, \ldots, x_6) = x_1 x_4 \vee x_1 x_6 \vee x_2 x_4 \vee x_2 x_6 \vee x_3 x_6 \vee x_4 x_5 \vee x_4 x_6$.

    a) There is a single-level circuit of size 7 for f.
    b) $C_m(f) = 7$.
    c) $L_m^*(f) = 7$.
    d) All single-level formulas for f have at least 8 gates.

3. Let $L_m^\wedge(f)$ and $L_m^\vee(f)$ be the minimal number of $\wedge$-gates and $\vee$-gates resp. in monotone formulas for f.

    a) $L_m^\wedge(f) + L_m^\vee(f) \leq L_m^*(f)$.
    b) $L_m^*(T_2^4) = 7$.
    c) $L_m^\wedge(T_2^4) = 2$.

d) $L_m^\vee(T_2^4) = 4$.

4. Prove that the Korobkov formulas for T_k^n (see (2.1)) have size $O(n(\log n)^{k-1})$.

5. The Fibonacci numbers are defined by $a_0 = a_1 = 1$ and $a_n = a_{n-1} + a_{n-2}$. It is well-known that

$$a_n = (\Phi^{n+1} - (\Phi - \sqrt{5})^{n+1})/\sqrt{5} \quad \text{for} \quad \Phi = (1/2)(1 + \sqrt{5}) .$$

Let $\Omega = \{NAND, \rightarrow\}$ where $(x \rightarrow y) = \bar{x} \vee y$ and $D_\Omega(f) \le d$. Then f is a disjunction of monoms whose length is bounded by a_d .

6. We use the notation of Exercise 5 . If $f \in S_n$ is not constant, $D_\Omega(f) \ge \log_\Phi(\sqrt{5}\, n) - 3$.

7. Let $1 < k < n - 3$, $f \in B_n$, $f(a) = 0$ for inputs a with exactly k ones and $f(a) = 1$ for inputs a with exactly $k + 2$ ones. Then $L(f) = \Omega(n \log \log n)$.

8. Let $f, f' \in S_n$, $v(f) = (v_0, \dots, v_n)$ and $v(f') = (v_n, \dots, v_0)$. Estimate $L(f) - L(f')$.

9. There are 16 symmetric functions $f_n \in S_n$ with linear formula size. For all other $f_n \in S_n$ $L(f_n) = \Omega(n \log \log n)$.

10. Design efficient formulas for $C_{0,8}^n$ and for $C_{0,3}^n$.

11. Apply the Meyer, Fischer and Paterson method and the Hodes and Specker method to threshold functions.

12. How large is the fraction of $f \in S_n$ with $L(f) = o(n \log n)$?

13. Apply the Nechiporuk method to circuits over B_r .

14. The Nechiporuk method yields only linear bounds for symmetric functions.

15. (Nechiporuk (66)) Let m and n be powers of 2 , m = O(log n) , m and n large enough that there are different $y_{ij} \in \{0,1\}^m$, $1 \le i \le l = n/m$, $1 \le j \le m$, having at least two ones each. Let x_{ij} be variables, and let $g_{i,j,k}(x)$ be the disjunction of all x_{kl} such that y_{ij} has a 1 at position l . Let

$$f(x) = \bigoplus_{1 \le i \le l, 1 \le j \le m} x_{ij} \wedge (\bigoplus_{1 \le k \le l, k \ne i} g_{i,j,k}(x)) .$$

Then $L(f) = \Omega(n^2 \log^{-1} n)$.

16. (Schürfeld (84), just as 17. and 18.) Let $f \in M_N$. Let k be the maximal length of a prime implicant of f . Then f has at most $2|S_i|^{k-1}$ S_i-subfunctions. The Nechiporuk bound is not larger than $N^{2-(1/k)}$.

17. Let $f(x,y,z) = \bigvee_{1 \le i,j,k \le n} z_{ij} x_{ik} y_{kj}$ be the one-output function corresponding to the Boolean matrix product (see § 15, Ch. 6). Then $L(f) = \Theta(n^3)$.

18. We generalize the definition of f in Exercise 17 . Let $k \ge 3$ and let $X^1, \ldots, X^{k-1}, Z$ be (k-1)-dimensional $n \times \cdots \times n$ - matrices of Boolean variables. For $N = kn^{k-1}$ let $f \in M_N$ be the disjunction of all

$$z_{i(1) \cdots i(k-1)} x^1_{r(1) \cdots r(k-2)i(1)} \cdots x^{k-1}_{r(1) \cdots r(k-2)i(k-1)}$$

$(1 \le i(j), r(j) \le n)$. Then $L(f) = \Omega(N^{2-1/(k-1)})$.

19. Describe all $f \in B_n$ where $K(f) = n^2$ for the Krapchenko measure K.

20. Let $f \in B_n$. Let $f(a) = c$ for all inputs a with exactly k ones and $f(a) = \bar{c}$ for all inputs a with exactly $k + 1$ ones. Estimate $K(f)$.

21. $\lceil 2 \log n \rceil \leq D_U(x_1 \oplus \cdots \oplus x_n) \leq 2 \lceil \log n \rceil$.

9. CIRCUITS AND OTHER NON UNIFORM COMPUTATION MODELS VS. TURING MACHINES AND OTHER UNIFORM COMPUTATION MODELS

9.1 Introduction

Circuits represent a hardware model for the computation of Boolean functions. For a given sequence $f_n \in B_n$ we look for circuits S_n computing f_n with small size (cost of the circuit, computation time for sequential computations) and small depth (computation time for parallel computations). Moreover we prefer circuits where $n \rightarrow S_n$ can be computed by an efficient algorithm. It is easy to check that most of the circuits we have designed can be constructed efficiently. An exception is the monotone formula for the majority function (Ch. 8, § 3), and also the $O(\log n)$ - depth division circuit (Ch. 3, § 3) cannot be computed very efficiently. A circuit has to be designed only once and can be applied afterwards for many computations. So the time for the construction of a circuit is not so important as the computation time of the circuit.

How do circuits differ from software models ? A circuit works only for inputs of a definite length, whereas a reasonable program works for inputs of arbitrary length. A hardware problem is a Boolean function $f_n \in B_n$. Obviously each f_n is computable. A software problem is a language $L \subseteq \{0,1\}^*$, i.e. a subset of the set of all finite $0-1$-sequences. It is well-known that many languages are not computable. So we look for conditions implying that there is an efficient uniform algorithm for L if there is a sequence S_n of efficient non uniform circuits for f_n where $f_n^{-1}(1) = L \cap \{0,1\}^n$. And we ask whether we can design efficient circuits S_n for f_n if we know an efficient algorithm for L , the union of all $f_n^{-1}(1)$ $(n \in \mathbb{N})$.

Efficient simulations are known between the different uniform computation models (models for the software of computers). So we consider Turing machines as a representative of uniform computation models. In §2 and §3 we present efficient simulations of Turing machines by circuits. Since there are non computable (non recursive) languages, we cannot simulate in general sequences of circuits by Turing machines. In §4 we simulate efficiently circuits by non uniform Turing machines.

Are there languages $L \subseteq \{0,1\}^*$ for which we do not know any polynomial Turing program but for which we can design efficient circuits, more precisely, efficient circuits S_n for f_n defined by $f_n^{-1}(1) = L \cap \{0,1\}^n$? In §5 we characterize languages with polynomial circuits, and in §6 we simulate efficiently probabilistic Turing machines by circuits. Nevertheless it is not believed that NP - complete languages can have polynomial circuits. In §7 we discuss some consequences if certain NP - complete languages would have polynomial circuits.

We prefer efficient circuits S_n for $f_n \in B_n$, which can be constructed efficiently. In §8 we compare some definitions for such circuits called uniform circuits. We close this introduction with a short survey of some concepts of the complexity theory.

A (deterministic) Turing machine works on one on both sides unlimited working tape. Each register $i \in \mathbb{Z}$ of the tape contains a letter of a finite alphabet Σ. At the beginning the input $(x_1, \ldots, x_n)$ is contained in the registers $0, \ldots, n-1$, all other registers are empty (contain the letter B = blank). The central unit of the machine is at each point of time in one state $q \in Q$ where Q is finite. The state at the beginning of the computation is defined by q_0. The machine has a head which can read one register and which can move from register i to register $i-1$ or $i+1$. The head starts at register 0. The program is given by a transition function $\delta : Q \times \Sigma \rightarrow Q \times \Sigma \times \{R,L,N\}$. If the machine is in state q and reads a and if $\delta(q,a) = (q',a',d)$, then the machine replaces the contents of the considered register by a', the new state of the machine is q', and the head moves one step in direction d (R = right , L = left , N = no move). The computation stops in some definite state q^*. The result of the computation can be read

consecutively in the registers starting at register 0 until the first register contains the letter B. Turing machines may have more than
one tape. Then there is one head for each of the k tapes ($k \in \mathbb{N}$),
and the action of the machine depends on all letters which are read
by the k heads.

For input x let $t(x)$ be the number of steps until the machine
stops and let $s(x)$ be the number of different registers which are
scanned by the head of the machine. The computation time t and
the space s of the Turing machine are defined by

$$t(n) = \max \{ t(x) \mid |x| = n \} \tag{1.1}$$

where $|x|$ is the length of x and

$$s(n) = \max \{ s(x) \mid |x| = n \} . \tag{1.2}$$

For $S,T : \mathbb{N} \to \mathbb{N}$ we denote by DTIME(T) and DSPACE(S) the set of
languages which can be decided by deterministic Turing machines in
time $O(T(n))$ or space $O(S(n))$ resp. A machine decides L if it computes 1 if $x \in L$ and 0 if $x \notin L$.

DEFINITION 1.1 : P is the class of languages which can be decided by
deterministic Turing machines in polynomial time.

In order to classify languages according to their complexity, one
considers non deterministic Turing machines. Then $\delta(q,a)$ is a subset of $Q \times \Sigma \times \{R,L,N\}$. There is a number of admissible computation
steps. A non deterministic Turing machine accepts L if there is some
admissible computation on x with output 1 iff $x \in L$. For $x \in L$ the
computation time $t_{ndet}(x)$ is the length of a shortest accepting computation path. Moreover

$$t_{ndet}(n) = \max (\{ t_{ndet}(x) \mid |x| = n , x \in L \} \cup \{1\}) . \tag{1.3}$$

DEFINITION 1.2 : NP is the class of languages which can be decided
by non deterministic Turing machines in polynomial time.

The subclass of NP-complete languages contains the most difficult problems in NP in the following sense. Either $P = NP$ or no NP-complete language is in P (see Cook (71), Karp (72), Specker and Strassen (76) , and Garey and Johnson (79)). The majority of the experts believes that $NP \neq P$. Then all NP-complete languages (one knows of more than 1000 ones) have no polynomial algorithm. We mention only two NP-complete languages, the set of all n-vertex graphs (n arbitrary) with an $n/2$ - clique and the class of all sets of Boolean clauses (disjunctions of literals) which can be satisfied simultaneously (SAT = satisfiability problem).

In order to describe the complexity of a language L relative to another language A , one considers Turing machines with oracle A . These machines have an extra tape called oracle tape. If the machine reaches the oracle state, it can decide in one step whether the word y written on the oracle tape is an element of A . If one can design an efficient Turing machine with oracle A for L the following holds. An efficient algorithm for A implies an efficient algorithm for L , because we can use the algorithm for A as a subroutine replacing the oracle queries of the Turing machines with oracle A .

DEFINITION 1.3 : Let A be a language. $P(A)$ or $NP(A)$ is the class of languages which can be decided by a polynomial deterministic or non deterministic resp. Turing machine with oracle A . For a class C of languages $P(C)$ is the union of all $P(A)$ where $A \in C$, $NP(C)$ is defined similarly.

DEFINITION 1.4 : The following hierarchy of languages is called the Stockmeyer hierarchy (Stockmeyer (76)). $\Sigma_0 = \Pi_0 = \Delta_0 = P$. $\Sigma_n = NP(\Sigma_{n-1})$, in particular $\Sigma_1 = NP$. Π_n consists of all L whose complement is contained in Σ_n and $\Delta_n = P(\Sigma_{n-1})$.

Obviously $\Sigma_{n-1} \subseteq \Sigma_n$. It is an open problem whether this hierarchy is proper. If $\Sigma_n = \Sigma_{n+1}$, also $\Sigma_n = \Sigma_{n+k}$ for all $k \geq 0$. In order to prove $NP \neq P$, it is sufficient to prove that $\Sigma_n \neq P$ for some $n \geq 1$. Kannan (82) proved by diagonalization the existence of languages

$L_k \in \Sigma_3 \cap \Pi_3$ such that $|L_k \cap \{0,1\}^n|$ is polynomially bounded and L_k has no circuits of size $O(n^k)$. At the end of this survey we state a characterization of the classes Σ_n and Π_n (Stockmeyer (76)).

THEOREM 1.1 : $L \in \Sigma_n$ ($L \in \Pi_n$) iff the predicate " $x \in L$ " can be expressed by a quantified formula

$$(Q_1 x_1) \cdots (Q_n x_n) \ T(x, x_1, \ldots, x_n) \tag{1.4}$$

where $x_1, \ldots, x_n$ are vectors of variables of polynomial length, T is a predicate which can be decided in polynomial time and where $Q_1, \ldots, Q_n$ is an alternating sequence of quantifiers $\exists$ and $\forall$ and $Q_1 = \exists$ ($Q_1 = \forall$) .

The problem whether $\Sigma_n = \Sigma_{n+1}$ is the problem whether we can eliminate efficiently quantifiers.

9.2 The simulation of Turing machines by circuits: time and size

We like to simulate efficiently Turing machines by circuits. Let M be a deterministic Turing machine deciding $L \subseteq \{0,1\}^*$ in time $t(n)$. We look for circuits S_n for f_n defined by $f_n^{-1}(1) = L \cap \{0,1\}^n$ whose size is small with respect to $t(n)$. The easiest solution is a step-by-step simulation. The difficulty is the simulation of the head (if - tests). After t steps the position of the head $l(t)$ can take any value in $\{-t, \ldots, 0, \ldots, t\}$ depending on the input. For this reason we simulate Turing machines at first by special Turing machines with simple head moves. These Turing machines can be simulated easily by circuits.

DEFINITION 2.1 : A Turing machine is called oblivious if the sequence of head moves is the same for all inputs of the same length.

For oblivious Turing machines $pos(t,n)$, the position of the head on inputs of length n after $t \leq t(n)$ steps, is well defined. The t-th configuration of an oblivious Turing machine M on an input x of length n is described uniquely by its state $q(t,x)$ and the contents $b(t,x,j)$ of register j where $-t(n) \leq j \leq t(n)$. We use an arbitrary encoding of Q and Σ by $0-1$-sequences of length $\lceil \log |Q| \rceil$ and $\lceil \log |\Sigma| \rceil$ resp. The 0-th configuration is known, since $q(0,x) = q_0$, $b(0,x,j) = x_{j+1}$ if $0 \leq j \leq n-1$ and $b(0,x,j) = B$ otherwise. The output is $b(t(n),x,0)$. Let δ_1 and δ_2 be the first two projections of the transition function δ . Then

$$q(t+1,x) \quad = \quad \delta_1(q(t,x),b(t,x,pos(t,n))) , \qquad (2.1)$$

$$b(t+1,x,j) \quad = \quad b(t,x,j) \quad \text{if} \quad j \neq pos(t,n) , \text{ and} \qquad (2.2)$$

$$b(t+1,x,pos(t,n)) \quad = \quad \delta_2(q(t,x),b(t,x,pos(t,n))) . \qquad (2.3)$$

Since δ is a finite function, there is a circuit of size $O(1)$ for δ . Since $pos(t,n)$ is known in advance, we can simulate M by $t(n)$ copies of the circuit for δ .

THEOREM 2.1 : If L can be decided by an oblivious Turing machine in time $t(n)$, $f_n \in B_n$ defined by $f_n^{-1}(1) = L \cap \{0,1\}^n$ can be computed by a circuit of size $O(t(n))$.

This theorem holds also for oblivious Turing machines with k tapes. The problem is the simulation of Turing machines M by oblivious ones: At first we describe a simple simulation which will be improved later. The simulation works step-by-step. We use markers # (a new letter not contained in the alphabet of M) and the alphabet $(\Sigma \cup \{\#\})^2$. Then there is space for two letters in each register. After the simulation of the t-th step of M the registers $-t-1$ and $t+n$ of M' contain the mark $(\#,\#)$. The first letter in register $j \in \{-t,...,t+n-1\}$ equals the contents of this register after the t-th step of M . The second letter is equal to # for that register read by the head of M , all other second letters equal B . The head of M' is at the left mark $(\#,\#)$.

In $O(n)$ steps the " 0-th step " can be simulated. For the simulation of the t-th step M' has to know the state q of M . The left mark is shifted by one position to the left, then the head of M' turns to the right until it finds the marked register $(a,\#)$. M' evaluates in its central unit $\delta(q,a) = (q',a',d)$, it bears in mind q' instead of q , replaces the contents of the register by (a',B) , if $d = R$, and by $(a',\#)$, if $d = L$ or $d = N$. If $d = R$, the next register to the right with contents (b,B) is marked by $(b,\#)$ in the next step. One goes right to the right mark $(\#,\#)$ which is shifted one position to the right. The head turns back to the left. If $d = L$, $(a',\#)$ is replaced by (a',B) , and the register to the left containing (a'',B) is marked by $(a'',\#)$. The simulation stops when the left mark $(\#,\#)$ is reached. M' is oblivious, and the t-th computation step is simulated in $O(t+n)$ steps. Altogether $t'(n) = O(t(n)^2)$ for the running time of M' . A more efficient simulation is due to Fischer and Pippenger ((73) and (79)) (see also Schnorr (76 a)).

THEOREM 2.2 : A deterministic Turing machine M with time complexity $t(n)$ can be simulated by an oblivious Turing machine M' with time complexity $O(t(n) \log t(n))$.

Proof : Again we use a step-by-step simulation. We shift the information of the tape in such a way that each step is "simulated in register 0 ". A move of the head to the right (left) is simulated by a shift of the information to the left (right). This idea again leads to an $O((t(n)^2)$ algorithm. To improve the running time we divide the information into blocks such that a few small blocks have to be shifted often, but large blocks have to be shifted rarely.

We like to shift a block of length $l = 2^m$ in time $O(l)$ l positions to the right or left. This can be done by an oblivious Turing machine with 3 tapes. One extra tape is used for adding always 1 until the sum equals l which is stored on a second track of the tape. The second extra tape is used to copy the information.

On the working tape we use 3 tracks, namely the alphabet $(\Sigma \cup \{\#\})^3$ for a new letter $\#$. If a register with contents $a \in \Sigma$ is scanned for the first time, this contents is identified with $(a, \#, \#)$. Each track $j \in \{1,2,3\}$ is divided into blocks B_i^j ($i \in \mathbb{Z}$) where B_0^j contains position 0 of track j and B_i^j for $i \neq 0$ contains the $2^{|i|-1}$ positions $2^{i-1}, \ldots, 2^i - 1$ if $i > 0$ or $-(2^{|i|} - 1), \ldots, -2^{|i|-1}$ if $i < 0$ of track j . A block is called empty when it contains only $\#$'s and is called full when it contains no $\#$. The segment S_i consists of the blocks B_i^1, B_i^2 and B_i^3 . A segment is called clean if the number of full blocks is 1 or 2 . At the beginning all blocks are either full or empty, and all segments are clean. Clean segments contain some information and provide space for further informations. They serve as a buffer.

The program $\text{sim}(k)$ simulates 2^k steps of M . We demand that the following statements hold after each simulation step.

(1) Each block is either full or empty.

(2) The contents of the tape of M after t computation steps can be read after t simulation steps by reading the full blocks B_i^j according to the lexicographical order on the pairs (i, j) .

(3) The head of M' scans register 0 , segment S_0 . In the first track of this register is the information that M reads at that time.

(4) During the simulation of 2^m steps the head only visits the segments $S_{-(m+1)}, \ldots, S_{m+1}$. At the end of the simulation $S_{-m}, \ldots, S_m$ are clean, and the number of full blocks of $S_{-(m+1)}$ (or S_{m+1}) is at most by 1 larger or smaller than at the beginning.

At the beginning of the simulation (1) - (4) are fulfilled. $\text{sim}(0)$ is a simple program which easily can be performed obliviously. M' knows the state q of the simulated machine M and reads in the first track of S_0 the same information a as M does. Let $\delta(q,a) = (q',a',d)$. M' bears q' in mind instead of q . It replaces in the first track a by a' . If $d = L$, the letter in the last full block of S_{-1} is transmitted to the first block of S_0 , all informations in S_0 are transmitted from B_0^j to B_0^{j+1} ($j \leq 2$). If now B_0^3 is full, its information is transmitted to B_1^1 , the information of B_1^1 is transmitted to

B_1^{j+1} ($j \le 2$) . If $d = R$, the contents of B_0^1 is transmitted to the last empty block of S_{-1} , the information of B_0^j ($j \ge 2$) is transmitted to B_0^{j-1} . If B_0^1 is empty now, the information of B_1^1 is transmitted to B_0^1 , the information of B_1^j ($j \ge 2$) is transmitted to B_1^{j-1} . At the end the head is at position 0 . All these transmissions are possible, since S_{-1}, S_0 and S_1 are clean at the beginning. Hence S_0 is clean at the end of sim(0) . Altogether sim(0) is an oblivious program of constant time complexity fulfilling (1) - (4) .

sim(k) is defined for $k > 0$ recursively by

$$\text{sim(k)} : \text{sim(k}-1) ; \text{clean(k)} ; \text{sim(k}-1) ; \text{clean(k)} . \qquad (2.4)$$

The program clean(k) should clean up S_{-k} and S_k . We have seen that after the application of sim(0) S_{-1} and S_1 can be unclean. Let us investigate sim(k) as a non recursive procedure. sim(k) consists of 2^k simulation steps sim(0) where the t-th step is followed by clean(1),..., clean(l) for $l = \max \{ m \mid 2^{m-1}$ divides $t \}$. By counting the number of simulation steps, it is easy to see which clean-procedures have to be performed.

We explain how clean(k) cleans up S_k (a similar program cleans S_{-k}). The head turns to the right until it scans the first register of S_k . This can be done easily by counting the number of steps on an extra tape. We distinguish three cases. In order to have the program oblivious, the head simulates all three cases, but the actions are performed only for the right case. If S_k is clean, there is nothing to be done. If all blocks of S_k are empty, the first block of S_{k+1} is broken into two pieces and transmitted to the first two blocks of S_k . The contents of B_{k+1}^j ($j \ge 2$) is transmitted to B_{k+1}^{j-1}. If all blocks of S_k are full, the last two blocks are concatenated and transmitted to the first block of S_{k+1} . The contents of B_{k+1}^j ($j \le 2$) is transmitted to B_{k+1}^{j+1} .

We prove by induction on k that sim(k) fulfils (1) - (4) . This has been proved already for $k = 0$. We investigate sim(k) for $k > 0$. By induction hypothesis sim(k-1) fulfils (1) - (4) . By (4) $S_{-(k+1)}$ and S_{k+1} are clean, since they are not visited during sim(k-1) . Hence clean(k) works. Afterwards $S_{-k}, \ldots, S_k$ are clean, and by induction hypothesis sim(k-1) works correctly. Afterwards clean(k) is called for the second time. This call for clean(k) would cause problems only if S_k is empty and S_k was empty before the first call of clean(k) or S_k is full in both situations. In the first case S_{k+1} may be empty now, in the second case S_{k+1} may be full now. But such situations do not occur. If S_k was empty before the first call of clean(k) , we have filled it up with two full blocks. Because of (4) the number of full blocks is decreased by the second call of sim(k-1) at most by 1 , and S_k cannot be empty again. If S_k was full before the first call of clean(k) , we have cleared out two blocks. Because of (4) the number of full blocks is increased by the second call of sim(k-1) at most by 1 , and S_k cannot be full again. Hence clean(k) works. Altogether sim(k) works and fulfils (1) - (4) .

By our considerations $\text{sim}(\lceil \log t(n) \rceil)$ is an oblivious Turing machine M' simulating M . The running time is $O(t(n))$ for all calls of sim(0) and $O(2^k)$ for each call of clean(k) . Since clean(k) is called only once for 2^k simulation steps, the whole time spent for clean(k) is $O(t(n))$. If $k > \lceil \log t(n) \rceil$, $\text{sim}(\lceil \log t(n) \rceil)$ does not call clean(k) at all. Hence the running time of M' is $t'(n) = O(t(n) \log t(n))$. □

If we want to simulate the Turing machine M by circuits, we can assume that s(n) is known to the circuit designer. We use markers ## in the registers $-s(n)$ and s(n) which do not change M since M never reaches these registers. The simulating oblivious Turing machine can omit all calls of clean(k) for $k > \lceil \log s(n) \rceil$. Information from $S_{-(k+1)}$ or S_{k+1} will never be used in register 0 . Then the running time of the oblivious Turing machine is only $O(t(n) \log s(n))$. From these considerations, Theorem 2.1 and Theorem 2.2 we obtain the main result of this chapter.

THEOREM 2.3 : If L can be decided by a deterministic Turing

machine in time $t(n)$ and space $s(n)$, $f_n \in B_n$ defined by $f_n^{-1}(1) = L \cap \{0,1\}^n$ can be computed by a circuit of size $O(t(n) \log s(n))$.

9.3 The simulation of Turing machines by circuits: space and depth

The circuit we have constructed in § 2 has large depth $O(t(n) \log s(n))$, since we have simulated the sequential computation of the given Turing machine step-by-step. Here we design circuits of small depth with respect to the space complexity of the Turing machine.

If $f_n \in B_n$ depends essentially on all n variables, the space complexity of each Turing machine for the union of all $f_n^{-1}(1)$ fulfils $s(n) \geq n$. The Turing machine has to read all inputs, but the space is not used for work. Therefore we assume that the input is given on a read - only input tape. The space complexity $s(x)$ for input x is the number of different registers that the Turing machine scans on the working tape, if x is the input. Now it is possible that Turing machines need only sublinear space $s(n) = o(n)$.

For example the language of all sequences consisting of ones only can now be decided with 1 register (for the output) on the working tape. The corresponding Boolean functions $f_n(x) = x_1 \wedge \cdots \wedge x_n$ have circuit depth $\lceil \log n \rceil$. All functions depending essentially on n variables have depth $\Omega(\log n)$. Hence it is not astonishing that the depth of our circuit depends on

$$l(n) = \max \{s(n), \lceil \log n \rceil\} \tag{3.1}$$

and not only on $s(n)$. Before we formulate the main result of this section (Borodin (77)), we prove a simple connection between the time complexity and the space complexity of Turing machines. If a Turing machine runs too long on a short working tape, it reaches some configuration for the second time. This computation cycle is repeated infinitely often, and the machine never stops. Let the registers of the working tape be numbered by $1,...,s(n)$ when the input x has length n. Then a configuration is a vector

$$(q,i,a_1, \cdots ,a_{s(n)},j) \tag{3.2}$$

where $q \in Q$ is the current state, $i \in \{1,...,n\}$ is the position of the head on the input tape, $j \in \{1,...,s(n)\}$ is the position of the head on the working tape, and $a_k \in \Sigma$ is the contents of register k. Hence $k(n)$, the number of different configurations, fulfils

$$\log k(n) \leq \log|Q| + \log n + s(n) \log|\Sigma| + \log s(n). \tag{3.3}$$

If $t(n) > k(n)$, the Turing machine runs for some input in a cycle and does not stop at all on this input. Hence by (3.3)

$$\log t(n) \leq \log k(n) = O(l(n)). \tag{3.4}$$

THEOREM 3.1 : If L can be decided by a deterministic Turing machine in time $t(n)$ and space $s(n)$, then

$$D(f_n) = O(l(n)\log t(n)) = O(l(n)^2) \text{ for } f_n^{-1}(1) = L \cap \{0,1\}^n. \tag{3.5}$$

Proof : We assume that the Turing machine does not stop in q^*, but that it remains in q^* and does not change the contents of the registers of the working tape. Then the computation on x can be described by the sequence of configurations $k_0(x) ,..., k_{t(n)}(x)$ and $x \in L$ iff register 1 of the working tape contains a 1 in $k_{t(n)}(x)$.

For each configuration $k(x)$ the direct successor $k'(x)$ is unique. $k'(x)$ does not depend on the whole input vector but only on that bit x_i which is read by the Turing machine in configuration $k(x)$. Let $A = A(x)$ be the $k(n) \times k(n)$-matrix where $a_{k,k'} = 1$ (k,k' configurations) iff k' is the direct successor of k on input x. Since $a_{k,k'}$ depends only on one bit of x, A can be computed in depth 1. Let $A^i = (a^i_{k,k'})$ be the i-th power of A with respect to Boolean matrix multiplications. Since

$$a^i_{k,k'} = \bigvee_{k''} a^{i-1}_{k,k''} \wedge a_{k'',k'}, \tag{3.6}$$

$a^i_{k,k'} = 1$ iff on input x and starting in configuration k we reach configuration k' after t steps. We compute by $\lceil \log t(n) \rceil$ Boolean matrix multiplications A^T for $T = 2^{\lceil \log t(n) \rceil}$. The depth of each matrix multiplication is $\lceil \log k(n) \rceil + 1$. Finally

$$f_n(x) = \underset{k \in K_a}{\vee} a^T_{k_0,k} \tag{3.7}$$

for the starting configuration k_0 and the set of accepting configurations K_a. Altogether $f_n(x)$ can be computed in depth $1 + \lceil \log t(n) \rceil \, (\lceil \log k(n) \rceil + 1) + \lceil \log k(n) \rceil$. The theorem follows from (3.4).

$\square$

9.4 The simulation of circuits by Turing machines with oracles

Each Boolean function $f_n \in B_n$ can be computed by a Turing machine in n steps without working tape. The machine bears in mind the whole input x and accepts iff $x \in f_n^{-1}(1)$. But the number of states of the machine is of size 2^n and grows with n. We like to design a Turing machine which decides L, the union of all $f_n^{-1}(1)$ where $f_n \in B_n$. But L can be non recursive even if $C(f_n)$ is bounded by a polynomial. A simulation of circuits by Turing machines is possible if we provide the Turing machine with some extra information depending on the length of the input but not on the input itself (Pippenger (77 b),(79), Cook (80)).

DEFINITION 4.1 : A non uniform Turing machine M is a Turing machine provided with an extra read-only tape (oracle tape) containing for inputs x of length n an oracle a_n. The computation time $t(x)$ is defined in the usual way, the space $s(x)$ is the sum of the number of different registers on the working tape scanned on input x and $\lceil \log |a_n| \rceil$.

The summand $\lceil \log |a_n| \rceil$ for the space complexity is necessary for the generalization of the results of § 3 . We have to add $m \in \{1, \ldots, |a_n|\}$, the position of the head on the oracle tape, to a configuration vector $k = (q, i, a_1, \ldots, a_{s(n)}, j)$ (see (3.2)). If the space complexity is defined as done in Definition 4.1 , the estimation (3.4) holds also for non uniform Turing machines. Hence the results of § 2 and § 3 hold also for non uniform Turing machines.

THEOREM 4.1 : If $c_n = C(f_n) = \Omega(n)$, L , the union of all $f_n^{-1}(1)$, can be decided by a non uniform Turing machine where $t(n) = O(c_n^2)$ and $s(n) = O(c_n)$.

Proof : The oracle a_n is an encoding of an optimal circuit S_n for $f_n \in B_n$. We number the inputs and gates of S_n by $1, \ldots, n + c_n$. A gate is encoded by its number, its type and the numbers of its direct predecessors. The encoding of a gate has length $O(\log c_n)$, the encoding a_n of S_n has length $O(c_n \log c_n)$, hence $\log |a_n| = O(\log c_n)$.

The Turing machine can now simulate the circuit given in the oracle step-by-step. After the simulation of $i - 1$ gates, the results of these gates are written on the working tape. The i-th gate is simulated by looking for the inputs of the gate (on the input tape or on the working tape), by applying the appropriate $\omega \in B_2$ to these inputs and by writing the result on the working tape. It is easy to see that each gate can be simulated in time $O(c_n)$ and we obviously need c_n registers on one working tape for the results of the gates and $O(\log c_n)$ registers on another working tape for counting. □

THEOREM 4.2 : If $d_n = D(f_n) = \Omega(\log n)$, L , the union of all $f_n^{-1}(1)$, can be decided by a non uniform Turing machine where $t(n) = O(n\, 2^{d_n})$ and $s(n) = O(d_n)$.

Proof : The oracle a_n is an encoding of a depth optimal formula F_n for f_n . Formulas can be simulated with very little working tape, since the result of each gate is used only once. We number the gates of a formula of depth d_n in postorder. The postorder of a binary tree T with left subtree T_l and right subtree T_r is defined by

$$\text{postorder}(T) = \text{postorder}(T_l)\,\text{postorder}(T_r)\,\text{root}(T)\,. \tag{4.1}$$

A gate is encoded by its type and numbers $i_l, i_r \in \{0,...,n\}$. If $i_l = 0$, the left direct predecessor is another gate and, if $i_l = j \in \{1,...,n\}$, the left direct predecessor is the variable x_j. In the same way i_r is an encoding of the right predecessor. Each gate is encoded by $O(\log n)$ bits. Since formulas of depth d contain at most $2^d - 1$ gates, $\log|a_n| = O(d_n)$.

The Turing machine simulates the formula given in the oracle step-by-step. If we consider the definition of the postorder, we conclude that gate G has to be simulated immediately after we have simulated the left and the right subtree of the tree rooted at G. If we erase all results that we have already used, only the results of the roots of the two subtrees are not erased. Hence the inputs of G can be found in the following way. The value of variables is looked up on the input tape, the result of the $j \in \{0,1,2\}$ inputs which are other gates are the last j bits on the working tape. These j bits are read and erased, and the result of G is added at the right end of the working tape.

Since each gate can be simulated in time $O(n)$ the claim on the computation time of the Turing machine follows. It is easy to prove by induction on the depth of the formula that we never store more than d_n results on that working tape where we store the results of the gates. We use $O(\log n)$ registers on a further working tape for counting. Hence the space complexity $s(n)$ of the Turing machine is bounded by $O(d_n)$. $\qquad\square$

DEFINITION 4.2 : Let $T\,,\,S : \mathbb{N} \to \mathbb{N}$.

i) SIZE(T) or DEPTH(S) is the class of sequences $f_n \in B_n$ which can be computed by circuits of size $O(T(n))$ or depth $O(S(n))$ resp.

ii) NUTIME(T) or NUSPACE(S) is the class of languages $L \subseteq \{0,1\}^*$ which can be decided by non uniform Turing machines in time $O(T(n))$ or space $O(S(n))$ resp.

In § 2 and Theorem 4.1 we compared the size of circuits with the time of Turing machines. In § 3 and Theorem 4.2 we have found a tight relation between the depth of circuits and the space of Turing machines. We collect these results in the following theorem, again identifying languages and sequences of Boolean functions.

THEOREM 4.3 : i) $SIZE(T^{O(1)}) = NUTIME(T^{O(1)})$ if $T(n) = \Omega(n)$.

ii) $DEPTH(S^{O(1)}) = NUSPACE(S^{O(1)})$ if $S(n) = \Omega(\log n)$.

Savage (72) considered another type of non uniform Turing machines. These Turing machines compute only a single Boolean function $f_n \in B_n$. The complexity $C(n)$ of the Turing machine is measured by $\|p\| \, t(n) \log s(n)$ where $\|p\|$ is the number of bits in the Turing machine program. Such a Turing machine can be simulated by a circuit of size $O(C(n))$, the proof makes use of the ideas in the proof of Theorem 2.3 .

9.5 A characterization of languages with polynomial circuits

Based on the knowledge gained in § 2 - § 4 we prove a general characterization of languages with polynomial circuits (Karp and Lipton (80)). This characterization is used later for a simulation of probabilistic Turing machines by circuits.

DEFINITION 5.1 : Let F be a class of functions $h : \mathbb{N} \to \Sigma^*$. Poly is the class of all h where $|h(n)|$ is bounded by a polynomial. Let C be a class of languages $L \subseteq \{0,1\}^*$ and let $<.,.> : (\{0,1\}^*)^2 \to \{0,1\}^*$ be an injective encoding where $|<x,y>| = O(|x|+|y|)$ and (x,y) can be computed in time $O(|x|+|y|)$ from $<x,y>$. Then

$$C/F = \{L \subseteq \{0,1\}^* \mid \exists\ B \in C, h \in F : L = \{x \mid <x,h(|x|)> \in B\}\} \qquad (5.1)$$

is the class of languages L which are relative to some oracle function $h \in F$ in the class C.

For $P/Poly$ (see Def. 1.1 for the definition of P) the oracle word of polynomial length can be the encoding of a circuit of polynomial size. Hence the following theorem (Pippenger (79)) is not surprising.

THEOREM 5.1 : $L \in P/Poly$ iff f_n defined by $f_n^{-1}(1) = L \cap \{0,1\}^n$ has polynomial circuit size.

Proof : If $L \in P/Poly$, then

$$L = \{\ x \mid <x,h(|x|)> \in B\ \} \qquad (5.2)$$

for some $B \in P$ and $h \in Poly$. Hence there is some non uniform polynomially time bounded Turing machine with oracle $h(n)$ deciding whether $<x,h(|x|)> \in B$. This Turing machine M decides L by (5.2). By Theorem 2.3 M can be simulated by circuits of polynomial size.

If $C(f_n) \leq p(n)$ for some polynomial p, let $h(n)$ be the standard encoding of a circuit S_n for f_n of size $p(n)$. Let B be the set of all $<x,y>$ where y is an encoding of a circuit on $|x|$ inputs computing 1 on input x. It is an easy exercise to prove that $B \in P$. By definition $L = \{x \mid <x,h(|x|)> \in B\}$ and hence $L \in P/Poly$.

$\square$

It is interesting that also $NP/Poly$ can be described by properties of circuits.

DEFINITION 5.2 : The language $L \subseteq \{0,1\}^*$ has polynomial generating circuits S_n ($n \in \mathbb{N}$) if $k(n)$, the number of inputs of S_n, and $g(n)$, the number of gates of S_n, are bounded by a polynomial and if for some selected gates or inputs $G(0,n) , ..., G(n,n)$ of S_n

$$L \cap \{0,1\}^n = \{ (res_{G(1,n)}(a), \ldots , res_{G(n,n)}(a)) \mid a \in \{0,1\}^{k(n)}, \qquad (5.3)$$

$$res_{G(0,n)}(a) = 1 \} .$$

We explain this definition by the following considerations. Let L have polynomial circuits, i.e. there are circuits S_n of polynomial size for f_n where $f_n^{-1}(1) = L \cap \{0,1\}^n$. Then these circuits are also generating. We choose the inputs $x_1, \ldots, x_n$ as $G(1,n) , ..., G(n,n)$ and the output gate as $G(0,n)$. Then (5.3) is fulfilled by definition of f_n . This result is also a corollary of the following theorem (Schöning (84), Yap (83)), since $P/\text{Poly} \subseteq NP/\text{Poly}$.

THEOREM 5.2 : $L \in NP/\text{Poly}$ iff L has polynomial generating circuits.

Proof : If $L \in NP/\text{Poly}$, then
$$L = \{ x \mid <x,h(|x|)> \in B \} \qquad (5.4)$$
for some $B \in NP$ and $h \in \text{Poly}$. Since $NP = \Sigma_1$, there is by Theorem 1.1 some $L' \in P$ and some polynomial p such that
$$L = \{ x \mid \exists\, y \in \{0,1\}^{p(|x|)} : <x,h(|x|),y> \in L' \} . \qquad (5.5)$$
Since $L' \in P$, we find circuits S_n of polynomial size $q(n)$ working on $n + p(n)$ input variables (x,y) and the oracle $h(n)$ as constant input and computing 1 iff $<x,h(n),y> \in L'$. S_n are generating circuits for L' . We define $G(1,n) , ..., G(n,n)$ as the inputs $x_1, \ldots, x_n$ and $G(0,n)$ as the output gate of S_n .

If S_n is a sequence of polynomial generating circuits for L , we define $h(n)$ as the encoding of S_n , $G(0,n) , ..., G(n,n)$ and $k(n)$. Then $h \in \text{Poly}$. Let B be the set of all $<x,y>$ where for $n = |x|$ y is the encoding of a circuit on $k(n)$ inputs and of $n + 1$ gates $G(0,n) , ...,$ $G(n,n)$ and of $k(n)$ such that there is an input $a \in \{0,1\}^{k(n)}$ for which $res_{G(0,n)}(a) = 1$ and $res_{G(i,n)}(a) = x_i$ for $1 \le i \le n$. $B \in NP$, since a non deterministic Turing machine guesses a correctly. Moreover

$$L = \{ x \mid <x,h(|x|)> \in B \} \tag{5.6}$$

and hence $L \in NP / Poly$.

$\square$

It is an open problem whether $P / Poly \neq NP / Poly$.

9.6 Circuits and probabilistic Turing machines

DEFINITION 6.1 : For probabilistic Turing machines the set of states Q contains three selected states q_a, q_r and $q_?$. If one of these states is reached, the machine stops. If the stopping state is q_a , the input is accepted (output 1), if it is q_r , the input is rejected (output 0), if it is $q_?$, the machine does not decide about the input (no output). If $q \notin \{q_a, q_r, q_?\}$, $\delta(q,a) \in (Q \times \Sigma \times \{R,L,N\})^2$. Each of the two admissible computation steps is performed with probability $1/2$.

Probabilistic Turing machines can simulate deterministic computation steps. Then both triples in $\delta(q,a)$ are the same. The output $M(x)$ of a probabilistic Turing machine M on input x is a random variable. The running time $t(n)$ is the length of the longest computation path on inputs of length n .

DEFINITION 6.2 : Let $\chi_L(x) = 1$ iff $x \in L$.

i) PP (probabilistic polynomial) is the class of languages $L \subseteq \{0,1\}^*$, such that there is some ppTm (polynomially time bounded probabilistic Turing machine) M where for all x

$$Prob(M(x) = \chi_L(x)) > 1/2 \quad \text{(Monte Carlo algorithms)} . \tag{6.1}$$

ii) BPP (probabilistic polynomial with bounded error) is the class of languages $L \subseteq \{0,1\}^*$ such that there is some ppTm M and some $\varepsilon > 0$ where for all x

$$\text{Prob}(M(x) = \chi_L(x)) > 1/2 + \varepsilon . \tag{6.2}$$

iii) R (random) is the class of languages $L \subseteq \{0,1\}^*$ such that there is some ppTm M where

$$\text{Prob}(M(x) = 1) > 1/2 \quad \text{for } x \in L \qquad \text{and} \tag{6.3}$$

$$\text{Prob}(M(x) = 0) = 1 \quad \text{for } x \notin L .$$

iv) ZPP (probabilistic polynomial with zero error) is the class of languages $L \subseteq \{0,1\}^*$ such that there is some ppTm M where

$$\text{Prob}(M(x) = 0) = 0 \text{ and } \text{Prob}(M(x) = 1) > 1/2 \text{ for } x \in L \tag{6.4}$$

and

$$\text{Prob}(M(x) = 1) = 0 \text{ and } \text{Prob}(M(x) = 0) > 1/2 \text{ for } x \notin L$$

(Las Vegas algorithms).

We do not like to discuss the quality of different casinos, but we state that Las Vegas algorithms never tell lies, whereas Monte Carlo algorithms may compute wrong results on nearly half of the computation paths. It is easy to prove (see Exercises) that

$$P \subseteq ZPP \subseteq R \subseteq BPP \subseteq PP \quad \text{and} \quad R \subseteq NP . \tag{6.5}$$

The error probability of BPP algorithms can be decreased by independent repetitions of the algorithm.

LEMMA 6.1 : Let M be a ppTm for $L \in BPP$ fulfilling (6.2). Let M_t (t odd) be that probabilistic Turing machine which simulates M for t times independently and which accepts (rejects) x if more than $t/2$ simulations accept (reject) x and which otherwise does not decide about x . Then

$$\text{Prob}(M_t(x) = \chi_L(x)) > 1 - 2^{-m} \quad \text{if} \tag{6.6}$$

$$t \geq -\frac{2}{\log(1-4\varepsilon^2)}(m-1).$$

(6.7)

Proof : Let E be an event whose probability p is larger than $1/2 + \varepsilon$. Then

$$p^i(1-p)^i < (1/2+\varepsilon)^i(1/2-\varepsilon)^i = (1/4-\varepsilon^2)^i.$$

(6.8)

Let a_i for $i \leq t/2$ be the probability that E happens exactly i times in t independent repetitions of the experiment. Then

$$a_i = \binom{t}{i}p^i(1-p)^{t-i} < \binom{t}{i}(1/4-\varepsilon^2)^{t/2}.$$

(6.9)

Hence

$$\text{Prob}(M_t(x)=\chi_L(x)) > 1 - (1/4-\varepsilon^2)^{t/2}\sum_{0\leq i\leq\lfloor t/2\rfloor}\binom{t}{i}$$

(6.10)

$$= 1 - (1/4-\varepsilon^2)^{t/2}2^{t-1} = 1 - (1/2)(1-4\varepsilon^2)^{t/2}.$$

Choosing t according to (6.7), (6.6) follows from (6.10).

□

If the number of repetitions is bounded by a polynomial, M_t is polynomially time bounded. Adleman (78) proved that languages $L \in R$ have polynomial circuits. Bennett and Gill (84) could generalize this result.

THEOREM 6.1 : If $L \in BPP$, f_n defined by $f_n^{-1}(1) = L \cap \{0,1\}^n$ has polynomial circuit size.

Proof : We look for a computation path which is correct for all inputs of the same length. Such a computation path will be used as an oracle.

We apply Lemma 6.1. This ensures the existence of a ppTm M for L whose error probability is bounded by $2^{-2|x|}$. W.l.o.g. M stops for all inputs x of length n after exactly $p(n)$ computation steps where p is a polynomial. A computation path is described by a vector $a \in \{0,1\}^{p(n)}$. In step t the $(a_t + 1)$-th possible computation step is performed. There are $2^{n+p(n)}$ pairs (x,a) of inputs of length n and computation paths a of length $p(n)$. For fixed x the number of computation paths leading to wrong results is bounded by $2^{p(n)-2n}$. Hence the number of pairs (x,a) where a is a wrong computation path for input x is bounded by $2^{p(n)-n}$. Since $2^{p(n)} - 2^{p(n)-n} \geq 1$, there is at least one computation path $h(n) \in \{0,1\}^{p(n)}$ which is correct for all inputs of length n. By definition $h \in$ Poly. Let

$$B = \{ <x,y> \mid y \in \{0,1\}^{p(|x|)}, M(x) = 1 \text{ on computation path } y \}. \quad (6.11)$$

Then $B \in P$, since a deterministic Turing machine can simulate directly a probabilistic Turing machine on a given computation path. Hence

$$L = \{ x \mid <x,h(|x|)> \in B \} \in P / \text{Poly} \qquad (6.12)$$

and, by Theorem 5.1, f_n defined by $f_n^{-1}(1) = L \cap \{0,1\}^n$ has polynomial circuit size. $\qquad \square$

BPP and R contain languages which are not known to be contained in P.

9.7 May NP-complete problems have polynomial circuits ?

If $NP = P$, all NP-complete problems have polynomial circuits. But let us assume like most of the experts do that $NP \neq P$. Nevertheless there is the possibility that NP-complete languages have polynomial circuits. This would imply for problems in NP that non uniform circuits are much more powerful than uniform Turing machines. Again, hardly anyone expects such a result. We corroborate this expectation in this section. If, for example, SAT (see § 1) has polynomial circuits, then Stockmeyer's hierarchy collapses at an early stage. Again, the experts do not expect that. But beware of experts. The experts also believed that non uniform algebraic decision trees cannot solve NP-complete problems in polynomial time. However Meyer auf der Heide (84) proved that the knapsack problem can be solved by algebraic decision trees in polynomial time.

DEFINITION 7.1 : A language L is called polynomially self-reducible if it can be decided by a polynomially time bounded Turing machine with oracle L which asks its oracle for inputs of length n only for words of length $m < n$.

LEMMA 7.1 : SAT is polynomially self-reducible.

Proof : Let the input be a set of clauses where at least one clause includes x_1 or $\bar{x}_1$. Then we replace at first x_1 by 1 and ask the oracle whether the new set of clauses can be satisfied. Afterwards we repeat this procedure for $x_1 = 0$. We accept iff one of the oracle questions is answered positively.

□

For a language L we denote by $L_{\leq n}$ the union of all $L_m = L \cap \{0,1\}^m$ for $m \leq n$. Let $L(M)$ or $L(M,B)$ be the language decided by the Turing machine M or the Turing machine M with oracle B resp.

LEMMA 7.2 : Let A be polynomially self-reducible, and let M be a polynomially time bounded Turing machine according to Definition 7.1 . If $L(M,B)_{\leq n} = B_{\leq n}$, then $A_{\leq n} = B_{\leq n}$.

Proof : By induction on n . If $n = 0$, M is not allowed to ask the oracle. Hence it does the same for all oracles.

$$A_{\leq 0} = L(M,A)_{\leq 0} = L(M,B)_{\leq 0} = B_{\leq 0} .$$

(7.1)

If $L(M,B)_{\leq n+1} = B_{\leq n+1}$, also $L(M,B)_{\leq n} = B_{\leq n}$ and by the induction hypothesis $A_{\leq n} = B_{\leq n}$. Since M asks on inputs x , where $|x| \leq n+1$, the oracle only for words y , where $|y| \leq n$,

$$A_{\leq n+1} = L(M,A)_{\leq n+1} = L(M,A_{\leq n})_{\leq n+1} = L(M,B_{\leq n})_{\leq n+1} \tag{7.2}$$

$$= L(M,B)_{\leq n+1} = B_{\leq n+1} .$$

$\square$

This lemma serves as technical tool for the proof of the following theorem (Balcazár, Book and Schöning (84)). The complexity classes Σ_k and $\Sigma_k(A)$ are defined in § 1 .

THEOREM 7.1 : Let $A \in \Sigma_k/$ Poly be polynomially self-reducible. Then $\Sigma_2(A) \subseteq \Sigma_{k+2}$.

Before we prove this theorem, we use it to prove the announced result due to Karp and Lipton (80).

THEOREM 7.2 : If SAT has polynomial circuits, then $\Sigma_3 = \Sigma_2$ and the Stockmeyer hierarchy collapses at the third stage.

Proof : If SAT has polynomial circuits, then SAT $\in$ P/ Poly $= \Sigma_0/$ Poly (Theorem 5.1) . Hence $\Sigma_2(SAT) \subseteq \Sigma_2 \subseteq \Sigma_3$ (Theorem 7.1 and Lemma 7.1). Since SAT is NP-complete, $\Sigma_3 = NP(NP(NP)) = \Sigma_2(SAT)$. Hence $\Sigma_2 = \Sigma_3$.

$\square$

Proof of Theorem 7.1 : Let M be a Turing machine deciding A and fulfilling the properties of Definition 7.1 . Since $A \in \Sigma_k/$ Poly , there are some language $B \in \Sigma_k$ and some $h \in$ Poly such that

$$A_{\leq n} = \{ x \mid <x,h(n)> \in B \}_{\leq n} . \tag{7.3}$$

Also $B_w = \{ x \mid <x,w> \in B \} \in \Sigma_k$. Let $L' \in \Sigma_2(A)$. We have to prove $L' \in \Sigma_{k+2}$. By Theorem 1.1 there is a polynomially time bounded Turing machine M' with oracle A such that

$$L' = \{ x \mid (\exists y)_q (\forall z)_q : <x,y,z> \in L(M',A) \} . \tag{7.4}$$

Here q is a polynomial where $q(|x|)$ is a bound for $|y|$ and $|z|$. Since M' is working in polynomial time $r(|x|)$, also the length of each oracle word is bounded by $r(|x|)$. Let p' be the polynomial $p \circ r$. We want to prove that

$$L' = \{ x \mid (\exists w)_{p'} : ((\forall u)_r R(u,w) \wedge (\exists y)_q (\forall z)_q S(w,x,y,z)) \} \tag{7.5}$$

where $R(u,w)$ holds iff $(u \in B_w \Leftrightarrow u \in L(M,B_w))$ and

$S(w,x,y,z)$ holds iff $<x,y> \in L(M',B_w)$.

$R,S \in P(\Sigma_k)$ since $B_w \in \Sigma_k$. (7.5) implies

$$L' = \{ x \mid (\exists w)_{p'} (\exists y)_q (\forall u)_r (\forall z)_q : R(u,w) \wedge S(w,x,y,z) \} . \tag{7.6}$$

Hence $L' \in \Sigma_{k+2}$ by Theorem 1.1. We still have to prove (7.5).

We claim that the predicate "$(\forall u)_r R(u,w)$" is equivalent to $A_{\leq r(n)} = (B_w)_{\leq r(n)}$. Since $|u| \leq r(n)$, the given predicate is equivalent to $(B_w)_{\leq r(n)} = L(M,B_w)_{\leq r(n)}$. This implies $A_{\leq r(n)} = (B_w)_{\leq r(n)}$ by Lemma 7.2. The other part follows from the definition of M.

By (7.3) there is always some w where $|w| \leq p'(|x|)$ and "$(\forall u)_r R(u,w)$" holds. Only for such words we have to consider the second predicate. Then we can replace the oracle B_w by A. By (7.4) $x \in L'$ iff "$(\exists y)_q (\forall z)_q S(w,x,y,z)$" holds. This proves (7.5).

$\square$

Schöning (83) introduced two hierarchies between P and NP. Ko and Schöning (85) proved for the so-called "low-hierarchy" (see Exercises), that languages $A \in NP$ with polynomial circuits are already contained in the third level of this hierarchy.

9.8 Uniform circuits

We have simulated deterministic non uniform Turing machines and also probabilistic Turing machines efficiently by circuits. Circuits can be simulated efficiently only by non uniform Turing machines. Instead of considering the more powerful non uniform Turing machines, we ask for restricted circuits such that these so-called uniform circuits can be simulated efficiently by (uniform) Turing machines. We only give a brief introduction (without proofs) to this subject.

The standard encoding SC_n of a circuit S_n is the encoding of its gates by the type of the gate and the numbers of the direct predecessors (see § 4). If $n \to SC_n$ can be computed efficiently with respect to n, then the circuits S_n can be simulated efficiently (again see § 4). There are a lot of possibilities how we can define what "efficient computation of $n \to SC_n$" means.

DEFINITION 8.1 : A sequence of circuits S_n of size c_n and depth d_n is called U_B-uniform or U_{BC}-uniform , if $n \to SC_n$ can be computed by a Turing machine whose space is bounded by $O(d_n)$ or $O(\log c_n)$ resp.

Here B stands for Borodin (77) and C for Cook (79). Cook also introduced the classes NC and NC_k (NC = Nick's Class celebrating the paper of Pippenger (79)). These classes (with the modification of unbounded fan-in $\wedge$- and $\vee$-gates) are important also as complexity classes for parallel computers. Since Ruzzo (81) characterized the classes NC_k by alternating Turing machines (see Chandra, Kozen and Stockmeyer (81)), this type of Turing machines describes parallel computers.

DEFINITION 8.2 : $NC = U_{BC}$ - SIZE,DEPTH($n^{O(1)},\log^{O(1)}n$) is the class of languages L such that f_n defined by $f_n^{-1}(1) = L \cap \{0,1\}^n$ can be computed by U_{BC}-uniform circuits of polynomial size and polylog

depth (the depth is a polynomial with respect to $\log n$).
$NC_k = U_{BC} - SIZE, DEPTH(n^{O(1)}, \log^k n)$.

THEOREM 8.1 : If $k \geq 2$, $NC_k = A - SPACE, TIME(\log n, \log^k n)$ is the class of languages which can be decided by an alternating Turing machine of space $O(\log n)$ and time $O(\log^k n)$.

Further definitions of uniform circuits (Ruzzo (81)) refer to the complexity of the structure of the circuits (Goldschlager (78)). For a gate G and $p = (p_1, \ldots, p_m) \in \{L,R\}^*$ let $G(p)$ be the gate G_m where $G_0 = G$ and G_i is the p_i-predecessor ($L =$ left , $R =$ right) of G_{i-1} . $G(\varepsilon) = G$ for the empty word ε .

DEFINITION 8.3 : The direct connection language DCL of a sequence of circuits S_n is the set of all $<n,g,p,y>$ where g is the number of some input or gate G in S_n , $p \in \{\varepsilon, L, R\}$ and y is the type of G if $p = \varepsilon$ or y is the number of $G(p)$ if $p \neq \varepsilon$. The extended connection language ECL of S_n ($n \in \mathbb{N}$) is defined in the same way but $p \in \{L,R\}^*$ and $|p| \leq \log c_n$.

DEFINITION 8.4 : Let S_n be a sequence of circuits of size c_n and depth d_n .

i) S_n is called U_D-uniform if DCL can be decided by Turing machines in time $O(\log c_n)$.

ii) S_n is called U_E-uniform if ECL can be decided by Turing machines in time $O(\log c_n)$.

iii) S_n is called U_{E^*}-uniform if ECL can be decided by alternating Turing machines in time $O(d_n)$ and space $O(\log c_n)$.

THEOREM 8.2 : Let S_n be a sequence of circuits of size c_n and depth d_n .

i) S_n U_E-uniform $\Rightarrow$ S_n U_D-uniform $\Rightarrow$ S_n U_{BC}-uniform $\Rightarrow$ S_n U_B-uniform.

ii) S_n U_E-uniform $\Rightarrow$ S_n U_{E^*}-uniform $\Rightarrow$ S_n U_B-uniform.

iii) S_n U_{BC}-uniform $\Rightarrow$ S_n U_{E^*}-uniform if $d_n \geq \log^2 c_n$.

These properties are easy to prove. More results have been proved by Ruzzo (81). They are summarized in the following theorem.

THEOREM 8.3 : Let $X \in \{D, E, E^*\}$.

i) $NC = U_X$ - SIZE, DEPTH$(n^{O(1)}, \log^{O(1)} n)$.

ii) If $k \geq 2$, $NC_k = U_X$ - SIZE, DEPTH$(n^{O(1)}, \log^k n)$.

Hence the proposed definitions are rather robust. Only the notion of U_B-uniformity seems to be too weak. Most of the circuits we have designed are uniform, many fundamental functions are in NC_k for small k.

EXERCISES

1. An oblivious $t(n)$ time bounded Turing machine with k tapes can be simulated by circuits of size $O(t(n))$.

2. A $t(n)$ time bounded Turing machine with k tapes can be simulated by an $O(t(n)^2)$ time bounded Turing machine with one tape.

3. Specify an oblivious Turing machine for sim(0).

4. Estimate the size of the circuits designed in §3.

5. Prove (6.5).

6. Let ACP (almost correct polynomial) be the class of languages L such that L is almost decided by a polynomial Turing machine, i.e. the number of errors on inputs of length n is bounded by a polynomial $q(n)$. If $L \in ACP$, L has polynomial circuits.

7. Let APT (almost polynomial time) be the class of languages L which can be decided by a Turing machine whose running time is for some polynomial p for at least $2^n - p(n)$ inputs of length n bounded by $p(n)$. If $L \in APT$, L has polynomial circuits.

8. Let $L_k = \{ A \in NP \mid \Sigma_k(A) \subset \Sigma_k \}$ (low hierarchy) and $H_k = \{ A \in NP \mid \Sigma_{k+1} \subset \Sigma_k(A) \}$ (high hierarchy). Let PH be the union of all Σ_k. If $PH \neq \Sigma_k$, then $L_k \cap H_k = \phi$.

9. If $PH = \Sigma_k$, then $L_k = H_k = NP$.

10. Let S_n be a sequence of circuits of size c_n and let $s(n) = \Omega(\log c_n)$. Then the following statements are equivalent:
    a) $(n \to SC_n) \in DSPACE(s(n))$.
    b) $ECL \in DSPACE(s(n))$.
    c) $DCL \in DSPACE(s(n))$.

11. Prove Theorem 8.2. Hint: $DSPACE(t) \subseteq A\text{-}SPACE, TIME(t,t^2)$.

12. Which of the circuits designed in Ch. 3 and Ch. 6 are uniform? Which of the functions investigated in Ch. 3 and Ch. 6 are in NC or in NC_k?

10. HIERARCHIES, MASS PRODUCTION AND REDUCTIONS

10.1 Hierarchies

How large are the "gaps" in the complexity hierarchies for Boolean functions with respect to circuit size, formula size and depth ? A gap is a non-empty interval of integers none of which is the complexity of any Boolean function. Other hierarchies are investigated in Ch. 11 and Ch. 14 .

Let B_n^* denote the set of all Boolean functions depending essentially on n variables, n is fixed for the rest of this section. For any complexity measure M , let M(r) be the set of all $f \in B_n^*$ where $M(f) \leq r$. The gap problem is to find for each r the smallest increment $r' = m(r)$ such that M(r) is a proper subset of $M(r+r')$.

We are interested in $c_\Omega(j)$, $l_\Omega(j)$ and $d_\Omega(j)$ for binary bases Ω . Tiekenheinrich (83) generalized the depth results to arbitrary bases. Obviously $c_\Omega(j)$ is only interesting for those j where $C_\Omega(j+1) \neq \phi$ and $C_\Omega(j) \neq B_n^*$. For any complexity measure M , let $M(B_n^*)$ be the complexity of the hardest function in B_n^* with respect to M . It has been conjectured that

$$d_\Omega(j) = c_\Omega(j) = l_\Omega(j) = 1 \quad \text{for all } \Omega \text{ and all interesting j} . \quad (1.1)$$

It is easy to prove that $d_\Omega(j) \leq 2$ and $c_\Omega(j), l_\Omega(j) \leq j+1$ (McColl (78 a)). The best results are summarized in the following theorem (Wegener (81) and Paterson and Wegener (86)).

THEOREM 1.1 :

$$d_\Omega(j) = 1 \quad \text{for all } \Omega \subseteq B_2 \text{ and } \lceil \log n \rceil - 1 \leq j < D_\Omega(B_n^*) . \quad (1.2)$$

Let $\Omega \in \{B_2, U_2, \Omega_m\}$. Then

$$c_\Omega(j) = 1 \quad \text{if } n-2 \le j \le C_\Omega(B^*_{n-1}) \, , \tag{1.3}$$

$$c_\Omega(j) \le n \quad \text{if } C_\Omega(B^*_{n-1}) < j < C_\Omega(B^*_n) \quad \text{and} \tag{1.4}$$

$$l_\Omega(j) \le n \quad \text{if } n-2 \le j < L_\Omega(B^*_n) \, . \tag{1.5}$$

For any complete basis $\Omega \subseteq B_2$ there is a constant $k(\Omega)$ such that

$$c_\Omega(j) \le k(\Omega) \quad \text{if } n-2 \le j \le C_\Omega(B^*_{n-1}) \quad \text{and} \tag{1.6}$$

$$c_\Omega(j) \le k(\Omega)n \quad \text{if } C_\Omega(B^*_{n-1}) < j < C_\Omega(B^*_n) \, . \tag{1.7}$$

The proof of the general claim (1.2) is technically involved. (1.5)-(1.7) can be proved by the same methods as (1.3) and (1.4). Hence we shall present the proof of (1.2)-(1.4) for the bases B_2, U_2 and Ω_m. Before doing so we state some counterexamples.

(1.1) is false for some bases and small n, and we even know an example where $c_\Omega(j) > n$. We note that $B^*_2 = U^*_2 \cup \{\oplus, \equiv\}$.

$\Omega = U_2$: $C_\Omega(U_2) = 1$ but $C_\Omega(\oplus) = C_\Omega(\equiv) = 3$ (Theorem 3.1, Ch. 5). Therefore $c_\Omega(1) = 2$. Similarly $l_\Omega(1) = 2$.

$\Omega = \{\wedge, \vee, \neg\}$: $C_\Omega(U_2) = 2$ but $C_\Omega(\oplus) = C_\Omega(\equiv) = 4$ (Red'kin (73)). Therefore $c_\Omega(2) = 2$. Similarly $l_\Omega(2) = 2$.

$\Omega = \{\wedge, \neg\}$: $C_\Omega(U_2) = 4$ but $C_\Omega(\oplus) = C_\Omega(\equiv) = 7$ (Red'kin (73)). Therefore $c_\Omega(5) = 2$ and $c_\Omega(4) = 3 > 2 = n$. Similarly $l_\Omega(4) = 3$.

Proof of Theorem 1.1 : The idea of the proof is to take some function f in B^*_n of maximal complexity and construct a chain of functions from the constant function 0 up to f such that the circuit size cannot increase by much at any step in the chain. We then conclude that there can be no large gaps.

Let $f \in B^*_n$ be a function of maximal circuit size with respect to Ω. Let $f^{-1}(1) = \{a_1, \ldots, a_r\}$. For the case $\Omega = \Omega_m$ we shall assume that the a's are ordered in some way, so that for $s < t$, a_t does not contain more ones than a_s. Let $f_0 \equiv 0, f_1, \ldots, f_r = f$ where

$$f_k^{-1}(1) = \{a_1, \ldots, a_k\} \quad \text{for} \quad 0 \leq k \leq r. \tag{1.8}$$

Obviously $D_\Omega(f_1) = \lceil \log n \rceil$, $C_\Omega(f_1) = n - 1$ and $f_1 \in B_n^*$. For the case $\Omega = \Omega_m$ each f_k is monotone. If $f_k(a) = 1$ and $b \geq a$, also $f(b) = 1$ and $i \leq j$ for $a_i = b$ and $a_j = a$. Hence $f_k(b) = 1$.

For any $a_k = (e(1), \ldots, e(n))$ define the minterm

$$m_k(x) = x_1^{e(1)} \wedge \cdots \wedge x_n^{e(n)} \tag{1.9}$$

and the monom

$$t_k(x) = \bigwedge_{i \mid e(i) = 1} x_i. \tag{1.10}$$

Then for $0 < k \leq r$ we have $f_k = f_{k-1} \vee m_k$ while in the monotone case we have also $f_k = f_{k-1} \vee t_k$. This follows, since $m_k(x) = 1$ iff $x = a_k$ and $t_k(x) = 1$ iff $x \geq a_k$. In all cases we see that

$$D_\Omega(f_k) \leq \max \{D_\Omega(f_{k-1}), \lceil \log n \rceil\} + 1 \quad \text{and} \tag{1.11}$$

$$C_\Omega(f_k) \leq C_k(f_{k-1}) + n. \tag{1.12}$$

It is possible that $f_k \notin B_n^*$. If f_k depends essentially only on m variables, we assume w.l.o.g. that these variables are $x_1, \ldots, x_m$. In $f_k = f_{k-1} \vee m_k$ or $f_k = f_{k-1} \vee t_k$ we replace $x_{m+1}, \ldots, x_n$ by 0. Therefore (1.12) is improved to

$$C_\Omega(f_k) \leq C_\Omega(f_{k-1}) + m. \tag{1.13}$$

Let $p(x) = x_{m+1} \wedge \cdots \wedge x_n$. Then $f_k^* = f_k \vee p \in B_n^*$. Let m_k' and t_k' be the subfunctions of m_k and t_k resp. for $x_{m+1} = \cdots = x_n = 0$. Then the depth of $m_k' \vee p$ and $t_k' \vee p$ is bounded by $\lceil \log n \rceil + 1$, and the circuit size of these functions is bounded by $n - 1$. Obviously f_k is a subfunction of f_k^*. Hence

$$D_\Omega(f_k) \leq D_\Omega(f_k^*) \leq \max \{D_\Omega(f_{k-1}), \lceil \log n \rceil + 1\} + 1 \tag{1.14}$$

$$\leq \max \{ D_\Omega(f_{k-1}^*), \lceil \log n \rceil + 1 \} + 1 \qquad \text{and}$$

$$C_\Omega(f_k) \leq C_\Omega(f_k^*) \leq C_\Omega(f_{k-1}^*) + n \leq C_\Omega(f_{k-1}^*) + n . \tag{1.15}$$

$D_\Omega(f_1^*) = \lceil \log n \rceil$ and for any $\lceil \log n \rceil + 2 \leq j \leq D_\Omega(B_n^*)$ we find some $i(j)$ such that $D_\Omega(f_{i(j)}^*) = j$. It is an exercise to prove the existence of some $g \in B_n^*$ such that $D_\Omega(g) = \lceil \log n \rceil + 1$. We have proved (1.2) and by (1.15) also (1.4).

To prove our optimal result (1.3) for the lower range of circuit size we need to go up from f_{k-1} to f_k in smaller steps. We will explain this construction only for the complete bases, since for the monotone case it is similar. Let $V(h)$ be the set of variables on which h is depending essentially. We shall construct a sequence $h_0, \ldots, h_m \in B_n$ with the following properties.

$$C_\Omega(h_i) \leq C_\Omega(h_{i-1}) + 1 \tag{1.16}$$

$$C_\Omega(h_0) = 0 , \quad C_\Omega(h_m) = C_\Omega(B_{n-1}^*) + 1 \tag{1.17}$$

$$V(h_{i-1}) \subseteq V(h_i) . \tag{1.18}$$

Let $g_i \in B_n^*$ be the disjunction of h_i and all variables not in $V(h_i)$. Then $C_\Omega(g_0) = n - 1$, $C_\Omega(g_m) = C_\Omega(B_{n-1}^*) + 1$ and

$$C_\Omega(g_i) = C_\Omega(h_i) + n - |V(h_i)| \leq C_\Omega(h_{i-1}) + 1 + n - |V(h_{i-1})| \tag{1.19}$$

$$= C_\Omega(g_{i-1}) + 1 .$$

For any $n - 1 \leq j \leq C_\Omega(B_{n-1}^*) + 1$ we find some $i(j)$ such that $C_\Omega(g_{i(j)}) = j$. This proves (1.3).

We construct $h_0, \ldots, h_m$. Let $f \in B_{n-1}^*$ be of maximal circuit size. Let $f_r = f$ and $r = |f^{-1}(1)|$. We construct f_{k-1} as before by removing a (minimal) element of $f_k^{-1}(1)$, but now regarding f_k as a member of $B_{s(k)}^*$ where $s(k) = |V(f_k)|$. The effect of this is to ensure that

$V(f_{k-1}) \subseteq V(f_k)$. Then $f_k = f_{k-1} \vee m_k$ where m_k is a minterm on the variables in $V(f_k)$. The procedure stops after $r - r'$ steps with $f_{r'} \equiv 0$. We note that no function f_k depends essentially on x_n. This variable is used as a pointer in an interpolating sequence. Let $m_k(x)$ be the conjunction of all $x_i^{e(i)}$ $(1 \le i \le s(k))$. Let

$$f_{k-1,i} = f_{k-1} \vee (x_n \wedge x_1^{e(1)} \wedge \cdots \wedge x_i^{e(i)}) \quad \text{for } 0 \le i \le s(k). \qquad (1.20)$$

Then the sequence $h_0, \ldots, h_m$ is defined as the sequence

$$f_{r',0}, \cdots, f_{r',s(r'+1)}, \cdots, f_{r-1,0}, \cdots, f_{r-1,s(r)}, f_{r,0}.$$

(1.17) is fulfilled, since $f_{r',0} = x_n$, $f_{r,0} = f_r \vee x_n$, $f_r \in B_{n-1}^*$ and $C_\Omega(f_r) = C_\Omega(B_{n-1}^*)$.

We prove (1.16). In an optimal circuit for $f_{k-1,i}$ we replace x_n by $z = x_n \wedge x_{i+1}^{e(i+1)}$. The new circuit has $C_\Omega(f_{k-1,i}) + 1$ gates. We interpret z as a new "variable" and conclude that the new circuit computes

$$f_{k-1} \vee z \wedge x_1^{e(1)} \wedge \cdots \wedge x_i^{e(i)} = f_{k-1,i+1}. \qquad (1.21)$$

In an optimal circuit for $f_{k-1,s(k)}$ we replace x_n by 1. Then we compute f_k (see (1.20)). Since $f_{k,0} = f_k \vee x_n$, also $C_\Omega(f_{k,0}) \le C_\Omega(f_{k-1,s(k)})$.

We prove (1.18). Let $s = s(k)$. $V(f_{k-1,i})$ is a subset of $\{x_1, \ldots, x_s, x_n\}$. We regard $f_{k-1,i}$ as a member of B_{s+1}. $f_{k-1,i}$ depends essentially on x_n. Let a_k be that vector which has been removed from $f_k^{-1}(1)$ for the construction of $f_{k-1}^{-1}(1)$. Then $a_k \in \{0,1\}^s$ and $f_{k-1,i}(a_k,0) = 0$ but $f_{k-1,i}(a_k,1) = 1$. If $x_n = 0$, $f_{k-1,i} = f_{k-1}$ and $f_{k-1,i}$ depends essentially on all variables in $V(f_{k-1}) = \{x_1, \ldots, x_{s'}\}$ where $s' = s(k-1)$. Moreover $f_{k-1,i}$ depends essentially on $x_1, \ldots, x_i$. If $f_{k-1,i}$ was not depending essentially on x_j $(j \le i)$ we could use the procedure for the proof of (1.16) and would obtain a circuit for f_k not depending on x_j. This would be a contradiction to the fact that f_k depends essentially on $x_1, \ldots, x_s$. For $s'' = \max \{s',i\}$, $V(f_{k-1,i}) = \{x_1, \ldots, x_{s''}, x_n\}$. Therefore $V(f_{k-1,i}) \subseteq V(f_{k-1,i+1})$ and $V(f_{k-1,s}) = \{x_1, \ldots, x_s, x_n\} = V(f_{k,0})$. $\qquad \square$

The counterexamples show that Theorem 1.1 is at least almost optimal. The general proof of (1.2) (Wegener (81)) is based on the assumption that the constants 0 and 1 are inputs of the circuit. Strangely enough, this assumption is necessary at least for small n. Let Ω be the complete basis $\{1, \wedge, \oplus\}$ (Ring-Sum-Expansion) and let 1 be not an input of the circuit. $B_1^* = \{x_1, \bar{x}_1\}$, $D_\Omega(x_1) = 0$ but $D_\Omega(\bar{x}_1) = 2$. Therefore $d_\Omega(0) = 2$.

10.2 Mass Production

Test sequences for the purpose of medical research, experiments in physical sciences or inquiries in social sciences often require large sample size. It is impossible to analyze directly all data. In some preprocessing phase one performs a data reduction, i.e. the same function is applied to the data of each single test.

DEFINITION 2.1 : The direct product $f \times g \in B_{n+m, k+l}$ of $f \in B_{n,k}$ and $g \in B_{m,l}$ is defined by

$$(f \times g)(x, y) = (f(x), g(y)).$$

$$(2.1)$$

Similarly $f_1 \times \cdots \times f_r$ is defined and $r \times f$ is the direct product of r copies of f.

It is possible to compute $r \times f$ by r copies of an optimal circuit for f. We ask whether one can save gates for the mass production of f. Obviously this is not possible for simple functions like $x_1 \wedge \cdots \wedge x_n$. Moreover one might believe that it makes no sense to compute functions depending on variables of different copies of f. But we have already seen that the encoding of independent information in a common bit string is useful for certain applications, see e.g. the application of the Chinese Remainder Theorem in Ch. 3.

Let us consider medical tests. If x is the data of some person, $f(x) = 1$ iff this person is infected by some definite pathogenic agent. If $r \times f$ has large complexity and if it is known that only a small number of people may be infected, it is useful to compute at first whether at all any person is infected.

DEFINITION 2.2 : The direct disjunction $v(f \times g) \in B_{n+m}$ of $f \in B_n$ and $g \in B_m$ is defined by

$$v(f \times g)(x,y) = f(x) \vee g(y) . \qquad (2.2)$$

Similarly $v(f_1 \times \cdots \times f_r)$ and $v(r \times f)$ are defined.

If $v(r \times f)$ can be computed more efficiently than $r \times f$, we use the following strategy. We compute $v(r \times f)$. If the output is 0, no person is infected and we stop. Otherwise we compute $v(s \times f)$ for some $s < r$ and some subset of persons and so on. Some remarks on how to choose good strategies are included in the monograph of Ahlswede and Wegener (86) . Here we investigate the complexity of $r \times f$ and $v(r \times f)$. The following table shows in which situation savings are possible for mass production.

	C	C_m	L
$f \times f$	Yes	No	No
$v(f \times f)$	Yes	Open problem	No

Tab. 2.1

It is easy to prove the results on formula size.

THEOREM 2.1 : i) $L_\Omega(f \times g) = L_\Omega(f) + L_\Omega(g)$ for all f, g and Ω .

ii) $L_\Omega(v(f \times g)) = L_\Omega(f) + L_\Omega(g) + 1$ if $v \in \Omega$ and f and g are not constant.

Proof : i) Because of the fan-out restriction of formulas we need disjoint formulas for f and g.

ii) The upper bound is obvious since $\vee \in \Omega$. Let $a \in f^{-1}(0)$. By definition $\vee(f \times g)(a,y) = g(y)$. Therefore each formula for $\vee(f \times g)$ has at least $L_\Omega(g) + 1$ leaves labelled by y-variables. The existence of $L_\Omega(f) + 1$ x-leaves is proved in the same way. Altogether each formula for $\vee(f \times g)$ has at least $L_\Omega(f) + L_\Omega(g) + 2$ leaves. This implies the lower bound.

□

The result on monotone circuits has been proved by Galbiati and Fischer (81).

THEOREM 2.2 : $C_m(f \times g) = C_m(f) + C_m(g)$.

Proof : We assume that an optimal monotone circuit S for $f \times g$ contains less than $C_m(f) + C_m(g)$ gates. Then there are gates in S having x- and y-variables as (not necessarily direct) predecessors. Let H be the first of these gates computing $h(x,y)$ out of the inputs $h_1(x)$ and $h_2(y)$. W.l.o.g. H is an $\wedge$-gate, $\vee$-gates are handled in the dual way. Let f' and g' be the functions computed instead of f and g resp. if we replace H by the constant 0. By monotonicity $f' \leq f$ and $g' \leq g$. If $f' \neq f$, there are a and b where $f'(a,b) = 0$ and $f(a,b) = 1$. Also $f'(a,0) = 0$, since the circuit is monotone (here 0 is also the vector consisting of zeros only). $f(a,0) = 1$, since f does not depend on the y-variables. Therefore $f'(a,0) \neq f(a,0)$ implying $h(a,0) = 1$ and $h_2(0) = 1$. Again by monotonicity $h_2 \equiv 1$ in contradiction to the optimality of S. Similar arguments prove $g' = g$. Hence $f' = f$ and $g' = g$ in contradiction to the optimality of S. □

We have proved that optimal monotone circuits for $f \times g$ consist of disjoint optimal monotone circuits for f and g. It does not help to join x- and y-variables. Uhlig ((74) and (84)) proved that the situation is totally different for circuits over complete bases.

THEOREM 2.3 : $C(r \times f) \leq 2^n n^{-1} + o(2^n n^{-1})$ if $f \in B_n$ and $\log r = o(n \log^{-1} n)$.

For hard functions mass production leads to extreme savings of resources. If $C(f) = \Omega(2^n n^{-1})$ (as for almost all $f \in B_n$, see Ch. 4), $\varepsilon > 0$ and n sufficiently large, the complexity of $2^{o(n/\log n)}$ copies of f is at most by a factor $1 + \varepsilon$ larger than the complexity of f. For all practical purposes this result is not of large value, since most of the interesting functions have circuit complexity bounded by $O(2^{\alpha n})$ for some $\alpha < 1$.

Theorem 2.3 holds also for $\vee(r \times f)$ which can be computed from $r \times f$ by $r - 1$ additional gates. The use of mass production for $\vee(r \times f)$ has also been proved by Paul (76). His methods differ from those of Uhlig. Paul considered Turing machines for the computation of $\vee(r \times f)$ and applied the efficient simulation of Turing machines by circuits (see Ch. 9, § 2). These results disprove the conjecture that Ashenhurst decompositions (Ashenhurst (57)) lead to optimal circuits.

DEFINITION 2.3 : An Ashenhurst decomposition of $f \in B_n$ is given by

$$f(x) = g(x_{\pi(1)}, \ldots, x_{\pi(m)}, h(x_{\pi(m+1)}, \ldots, x_{\pi(n)})) \tag{2.3}$$

for some $m \in \{1, \ldots, n-2\}$, $g \in B_{m+1}$ and permutation π.

The general proof of Theorem 2.3 is technically involved. Therefore we consider only the case $r = 2$. This is sufficient for the "Yes"-entries in Tab. 2.1.

Proof of Theorem 2.3 for $r = 2$: We design a circuit for $(f(x), f(y))$. For some k specified later let $x' = (x_1, \ldots, x_k)$ and $x'' = (x_{k+1}, \ldots, x_n)$. Similarly y' and y''. For $0 \leq l < 2^k$ let f_l be the subfunction of f where we replace the first k inputs of f by the binary representation (of length k) of l. By i and j we denote the numbers whose binary representations are x' and y' resp. Then we have to compute $f_i(x'')$ and $f_j(y'')$. Let $g_0 = f_0$, $g_l = f_{l-1} \oplus f_l$ for

$1 \leq l \leq 2^k - 1$ and $g_l = f_{l-1}$ for $l = L := 2^k$. Then

$$f_l = g_0 \oplus \cdots \oplus g_l = g_{l+1} \oplus \cdots \oplus g_L. \tag{2.4}$$

Let us assume for the moment that $i \leq j$. Then it is sufficient to compute $g_0(x''), \ldots, g_i(x'')$ and $g_{j+1}(y''), \ldots, g_L(y'')$.

We compute $z^l = x''$ if $0 \leq l \leq i$ and $z^l = y''$ if $i + 1 \leq l \leq L$. $O(k)$ gates are sufficient for each l to compute $\tau^l = 1$ iff $l \leq i$. Afterwards $O(1)$ gates are sufficient to select each of the $n - k$ bits of z^l. Altogether we need $O(n 2^k)$ gates for the computation of all z^l. For all l we compute $g_l(z^l)$. Since g_l depends only on $n - k$ variables, we need altogether (see Ch. 4, § 2) only

$$(2^k + 1)(2^{n-k}(n-k)^{-1} + o(2^{n-k}(n-k)^{-1})) \tag{2.5}$$

gates. Afterwards we compute $a^l = g_l(z^l)$ if $l \leq i$ and $a^l = 0$ else and also $b^l = g_l(z^l)$ if $l \geq j + 1$ and $b^l = 0$ else. This again can be done by $O(n 2^k)$ gates. Now $f(x) = f_i(x'')$ is the $\oplus$-sum of all a^l and $f(y) = f_j(y'')$ is the $\oplus$-sum of all b^l.

The total number of gates is $O(n 2^k)$ plus the number in (2.5). If $k = \omega(1)$ and $k = o(n)$ the number of gates is bounded by $2^n n^{-1} + o(2^n n^{-1})$.

In general we do not know whether $i \leq j$. $O(n)$ gates are sufficient to compute $\tau = 0$ iff $i \leq j$. We interchange x and y iff $\tau = 1$ ($O(n)$ gates). Then we use the circuit described above and compute $(f(x), f(y))$ if $\tau = 0$ and $(f(y), f(x))$ if $\tau = 1$. By $O(1)$ additional gates we compute $(f(x), f(y))$ in all cases.

□

The fundamental idea is the encoding of x'' and y'' by the z-vectors in such a way that only $2^k + 1$ and not 2^{k+1} functions on $n - k$ variables have to be computed. The idea is the same for larger r but the encoding is more difficult. For monotone functions we improve Theorem 2.3 using the asymptotic results of Ch. 4, § 5, and the fact that subfunctions of monotone functions are monotone and the methods of Uhlig.

COROLLARY 2.1 : $C(r \times f) = O(2^n n^{-3/2})$ if $f \in M_n$ and $\log r = o(n \log^{-1} n)$.

10.3 Reductions

Reducibility is a key concept in the complexity theory. Polynomial-time reducibility is central to the concept of NP-completeness (see Garey and Johnson (79)). Reducibility can be used to show that the complexities of different problems are related. This can be possible even though we do not know the complexity of some problem. Reducibility permits one to establish lower and upper bounds on the complexity of problem A relative to problem B or vice versa. If A is reducible to B , this means that A is not much harder than B . Lower bounds on the complexity of A translate to similar lower bounds on the complexity of B . An efficient algorithm for B translates to a similarly efficient algorithm for A . This requires that the necessary resources for the reducibility function are negligible compared to the complexity of A and B .

The monograph of Garey and Johnson (79) is an excellent guide to reducibility concepts based on Turing machine complexity. Because of the efficient simulations of Turing machines by circuits (Ch. 9, § 2-3) all these results can be translated to results on circuit complexity.

We discuss three reducibility concepts that were defined with view on the complexity of Boolean functions. The three concepts are NC_1-reducibility, projection reducibility and constant depth reducibility.

NC_1-reducibility is defined via circuits with oracles (Cook (83), Wilson (83)). We remember that NC_k is the class of all sequences $f_n \in B_n$ having U_{BC}-uniform circuits S_n of polynomial size and $O(\log^k n)$ depth (see Ch. 9, § 8).

DEFINITION 3.1 : For $g_n \in B_{n,m(n)}$ a circuit with oracle $g = (g_n)$ consists of B_2-gates and oracle gates computing some g_n . The size of a g_n-oracle gate is $n + m(n)$ and its depth is $\lceil \log n \rceil$.

DEFINITION 3.2 : The sequence $f = (f_n)$ is NC_1-reducible to $g = (g_n)$ if f_n can be computed by U_{BC}-uniform circuits S_n with oracle g and logarithmic depth.
Notation : $f \leq_1 g$.

NC_1-reducibility is reflexive ($f \leq_1 f$) and transitive ($f \leq_1 g \leq_1 h$ $\Rightarrow f \leq_1 h$) . The proof of these properties is left as an exercise. It is intuitively evident that f is not harder than g if $f \leq_1 g$. This intuition is made precise in the following theorem.

THEOREM 3.1 : $f \in NC_k$ if $f \leq_1 g$ and $g \in NC_k$.

Proof : Since $f \leq_1 g$, there are U_{BC}-uniform circuits S_n with oracle g and $O(\log n)$ depth computing f_n . The size of S_n is polynomially bounded as for all circuits of logarithmic depth. Since $g \in NC_k$, there are U_{BC}-uniform circuits T_n of polynomial size and $O(\log^k n)$ depth computing g_n . Let U_n be those circuits where we have replaced g_r-gates in S_n by copies of T_r . The circuits U_n are U_{BC}-uniform. They have polynomial size, since we have replaced polynomially many gates by circuits of polynomial size.

We estimate the length of a path p in U_n . Let p' be the corresponding path in S_n . Gates of depth 1 on p' have not been lengthened. Gates of depth $\lceil \log r \rceil$ on p' have been replaced by paths of length $O(\log^k r)$. Hence the length of p is bounded by $O(\log n)$ plus the sum of some $O(\log^k r_i)$ such that the sum of all $O(\log r_i)$ is bounded by $O(\log n)$. Since the function $x \to x^k$ is convex, the length of p is bounded by $O(\log^k n)$. This establishes the bound on the depth of U_n . $\square$

We often have used (see Ch. 3) implicitly the notion of NC_1-reducibility, although we have not discussed the uniformity of the circuits. In order to practise the use of this reducibility concept, we present some NC_1-reducibility results on arithmetic functions (Alt (84), Beame, Cook and Hoover (84)). Let MUL (more precisely MUL_n) be the multiplication of two n-bit integers, SQU the squaring of an n-bit integer, POW the powering of an n-bit number, i.e. the computation of $x, x^2, \ldots, x^n$ and DIV the computation of the n most significant bits of x^{-1}.

THEOREM 3.2 : $MUL =_1 SQU \leq_1 POW =_1 DIV$.

Proof : $MUL =_1 SQU$, since both problems are in NC_1. For this claim we use the circuits designed in Ch. 3. Nevertheless we state explicit reductions. $SQU \leq_1 MUL$, since $SQU(x) = MUL(x,x)$. $MUL \leq_1 SQU$, since

$$x y = (1/2) ((x+y)^2 - x^2 - y^2) \tag{3.1}$$

and there are U_{BC}-uniform circuits of logarithmic depth for addition, subtraction, and division by 2.

$SQU \leq_1 POW$, since SQU is a subproblem of POW.

$SQU \leq_1 DIV$ by transitivity and $POW \leq_1 DIV$. An explicit reduction is given by

$$x^2 = \cfrac{1}{\cfrac{1}{x} - \cfrac{1}{x+1}} - x. \tag{3.2}$$

$DIV \leq_1 POW$, since the most significant bits of x^{-1} can be computed by some approximation

$$x^{-1} \approx 1 + (1-x) + (1-x)^2 + \cdots + (1-x)^k \tag{3.3}$$

(see Ch. 3, § 3).

$POW \leq_1 DIV$. Let

$$y := 2^{2n^3} \frac{1}{1 - 2^{-2n^2}x} = 2^{2n^3} \sum_{0 \le i < \infty} 2^{-i2n^2} x^i \qquad (3.4)$$

$$= \sum_{0 \le i < \infty} 2^{2n^2(n-i)} x^i .$$

x^n has at most n^2 significant bits. After computing enough (but polynomially many) bits of y we can read off $x, x^2, \ldots, x^n$ in the binary representation of y.

□

We have proved $SQU \le_1 MUL$ by the relation $SQU(x) = MUL(x,x)$. The oracle circuit for SQU consists of a single oracle gate. Such reductions are called projections (see Ch. 6, § 1) by Skyum and Valiant (85).

DEFINITION 3.3 : The sequence $f = (f_n)$ is projection reducible to $g = (g_n)$ if

$$f_n(x_1, \ldots, x_n) = g_{p(n)}(\sigma_n(y_1), \ldots, \sigma_n(y_{p(n)})) \qquad (3.5)$$

for some polynomially bounded $p(n)$ and some $\sigma_n : \{y_1, \ldots, y_{p(n)}\} \to \{x_1, \bar{x}_1, \ldots, x_n, \bar{x}_n, 0, 1\}$.
Notation : $f \le_{proj} g$.

Projection reducibility is reflexive and transitive. There is a whole theory on projection reducibility which we only touch slightly. We summarize some results of Chandra, Stockmeyer and Vishkin (84).

DEFINITION 3.4 : Input UG (DG) means that the input is the adjacency matrix of an m-vertex undirected (directed) graph.
EUL CYC : Input: UG . Output 1 ⟺ G contains a cycle traversing every edge exactly once.
UCYC : Input: UG . Output 1 ⟺ G contains a cycle.
CON : Input: UG . Output 1 ⟺ G is connected.

STR CON : Input: DG . Output 1 $\Leftrightarrow$ G is strongly connected.

UST CON : Input: UG . Output 1 $\Leftrightarrow$ G contains a path $v_1 \to v_m$.

DST CON : Input: DG . Output 1 $\Leftrightarrow$ G contains a directed path $v_1 \to v_m$.

NET FLOW : Input: m-bit unary numbers $c(i,j)$ for $1 \le i,j \le m$ and an m^2-bit unary number f . The m-bit unary representation of k is $0^{m-k}1^k$. Output 1 $\Leftrightarrow$ The network with capacity $c(i,j)$ on edge (i,j) allows an integral flow of size at least f from v_1 to v_m . A flow is a function $\varphi : E \to \mathbb{N}_0$ where $\varphi(i,j) \le c(i,j)$, $\varphi(i,1) = 0$, $\varphi(m,j) = 0$ and $\sum_i \varphi(i,j) = \sum_k \varphi(j,k)$ for $j \ne 1$ and $j \ne m$.

BIP MATCH : Input: the adjacency matrix of a bipartite graph G on $2m$ vertices and an m-bit unary number k . Output 1 $\Leftrightarrow$ G contains a matching of size k , i.e. k vertex-disjoint edges.

BIP PERF MATCH : BIP MATCH for $k = m$.

CIRC VAL : Input: The (standard) encoding of a circuit S and the specification of an input a . Output 1 $\Leftrightarrow$ S computes 1 on a .

THEOREM 3.3 : EUL CYC $=_{proj}$ UCYC $=_{proj}$ CON $=_{proj}$ UST CON $\le_{proj}$ STR CON $=_{proj}$ DST CON $\le_{proj}$ NET FLOW $=_{proj}$ BIP MATCH $=_{proj}$ BIP PERF MATCH $\le_{proj}$ CIRC VAL .

Proof : We only prove some of the assertions in order to present some methods.

CON $\le_{proj}$ EUL CYC : Given an undirected graph G , we describe an undirected graph G' such that G is connected iff G' has an Eulerian cycle. Let $V = \{v_1, \ldots, v_m\}$ be the vertex set of G . Then G' has $3m + \binom{m}{2}$ vertices denoted by v_i, y_i, z_i $(1 \le i \le m)$ and u_{ij} $(1 \le i < j \le m)$. We declare that the edges $\{v_i, y_i\}$, $\{v_i, z_i\}$ and $\{y_i, z_i\}$ exist, i.e. the appropriate variables are replaced by the constant 1 . The edges $\{v_i, u_{ij}\}$, $\{v_j, u_{ij}\}$ and $\{v_i, v_j\}$ exist in G' iff $\{v_i, v_j\}$ exists in G , i.e. these variables are replaced by x_{ij} . All other edges do not exist, these variables are set to 0 .

We use the well-known fact that a graph contains an Eulerian cycle iff it is connected except for isolated vertices and the degree of all vertices is even. By construction the degree of all vertices in G' is always even. If G is connected, u_{ij} is either isolated or connected to v_i, so are z_i and y_i. Since all v-vertices are connected also in G', all non-isolated vertices in G' are connected. If G' is connected except for isolated vertices, v_i and v_j have to be connected by a path p without cycles in G'. If p uses the edges $\{v_k, u_{k\ell}\}$ and $\{u_{k\ell}, v_\ell\}$ (the only possibility of reaching $u_{k\ell}$) we may use instead of these two edges the edge $\{v_k, v_\ell\}$ and obtain a path from v_i to v_j in G.

DST CON $\leq_{proj}$ NET FLOW : Let $c(i,j) = 1$ if $(v_i, v_j) \in E$ and $c(i,j) = 0$ else. Let $f = 1$. There is a flow of size 1 or larger from v_1 to v_m iff there is a directed path from v_1 to v_m in the given graph G.

BIP PERF MATCH $\leq_{proj}$ BIP MATCH : This is obvious, since BIP PERF MATCH is BIP MATCH for $k = m$.

BIP MATCH $\leq_{proj}$ NET FLOW : Let G be the given bipartite graph on $u_1, \ldots, u_m$ and $v_1, \ldots, v_m$. For the flow problem we add two vertices s and t and look for a flow from s to t. The capacities are 1 for (s, u_i) and (v_i, t) for $1 \leq i \leq m$ and all edges (u_i, v_j) in G. All other capacities are 0. Obviously there is a flow of size f from s to t iff G contains a matching of size f.

BIP PERF MATCH $\leq_{proj}$ CIRC VAL : There is a polynomial algorithm for BIP PERF MATCH due to Hopcroft and Karp (73) (see also Ch. 6, § 12). By the simulations of Ch. 9, § 2 there are also polynomial circuits S_n for this problem. We consider CIRC VAL for circuits of size $c(S_n)$ and n^2 inputs. The variables for the encoding of a circuit are replaced by the constants describing the encoding of S_n, and the variables for the inputs are replaced by the variables for the edges in the bipartite graph.

□

$f \leq_{proj} g$ iff f_n is a special case of some g_m where m is not too large with respect to n . This happens if f is really a special case of g (as for BIP PERF MATCH $\leq_{proj}$ BIP PERF) or if g is a general model (as CIRC VAL) and also for problems which at the first glance have nothing in common (as for CON $\leq_{proj}$ EUL CYC) . Much more complicated projection reductions than those presented are known. If $f \leq_{proj} g$, (f_n) is not much harder than (g_n) .

Often weaker reducibility concepts are sufficient for the conclusion that (f_n) is not much harder than (g_n) . Let us compare parity PAR where $PAR_n(x_1, \ldots, x_n) = x_1 \oplus \cdots \oplus x_n$ and majority MAJ where $MAJ_n(x) = T^n_{\lceil n/2 \rceil}(x)$. MAJ $\not\leq_{proj}$ PAR , since each subfunction of a parity function is a parity function or a negated parity function. Also PAR $\not\leq_{proj}$ MAJ. Projections of MAJ_m are functions of the following type, the output is 1 iff $\sum_{1 \leq i \leq m} \alpha_i x_i \geq k$ for some k and $\alpha_i \in \mathbb{Z}$. This is not equal to PAR_n . Nevertheless PAR is not much harder than MAJ by the following reduction :

$$PAR_n(x) = \bigvee_{k \text{ odd}} T^n_k(x) \wedge (\neg T^n_{k+1}(x)) . \tag{3.6}$$

All T^n_k are subfunctions of MAJ_{2n} .

This leads to another reducibility concept, the so-called constant depth reducibility. It refers to bounded-depth circuits which we investigate in detail in the next chapter. For these circuits all literals $x_i, \bar{x}_i$ $(1 \leq i \leq n)$ are inputs, and all gates are $\wedge$-gates and $\vee$-gates of unbounded fan-in. Polynomials refer to depth 2 circuits.

DEFINITION 3.5 : SIZE - DEPTH$(S(n), D(n))$ is the class of all sequences $f_n \in B_n$ which can be computed by unbounded fan-in circuits of size at most $S(n)$ and depth at most $D(n)$ simultaneously. SIZE - DEPTH(poly , const) is the union of all SIZE - DEPTH$(c n^k, d)$.

DEFINITION 3.6 : The sequence $f = (f_n)$ is constant depth reducible to $g = (g_n)$ if there is a polynomial $p(n)$ and a constant c such that each f_n is computed by an unbounded fan-in circuit of depth at most c and size $p(n)$ containing oracle gates for g_j or $\bar{g}_j$ with $j \leq p(n)$ - the size and the depth of the oracle gates is 1 - and on each path is at most one oracle gate.

Notation : $f \leq_{cd} g$.

THEOREM 3.4 : i) $\leq_{cd}$ is reflexive and transitive.

ii) $f \leq_{proj} g \Rightarrow f \leq_{cd} g$.

iii) $f \leq_{cd} g$, $g \in$ SIZE-DEPTH($S(n),D(n)$) , S and D monotone $\Rightarrow$ $f \in$ SIZE-DEPTH($p(n)S(p(n))$, $cD(p(n))$) for some polynomial p and constant c . In particular $g \in$ SIZE-DEPTH(poly,const) $\Rightarrow$ $f \in$ SIZE-DEPTH(poly,const) .

The easy proof of this theorem is left as an exercise. By Theorem 3.4 ii the results of Theorem 3.3 hold also for constant depth reducibility. For "simple" problems like PAR and MAJ nothing can be proved with projection reducibility, but a lot is known about constant depth reducibility. Some of the following results have been proved by Furst, Saxe and Sipser (84) but most of them are due to Chandra, Stockmeyer and Vishkin (84).

DEFINITION 3.7 :

PAR : Input: $x_1, \ldots, x_n$. Output $x_1 \oplus \cdots \oplus x_n$.

ZMc (zero mod 2^c) : Input: $x_1, \ldots, x_n$. Output $1 \iff x_1 + \cdots + x_n \equiv 0 \bmod 2^c$.

MUL : Multiplication of two m-bit numbers, $n = 2m$.

SOR : The sorting problem for m m-bit numbers, $n = m^2$.

MADD (multiple addition) : The addition of m m-bit numbers, $n = m^2$.

THR : Input: $x_1, \ldots, x_m$ and an m-bit unary number k . Output $T_k^m(x)$, $n = 2m$.

MAJ : Input: $x_1, \ldots, x_n$. Output $T_{\lceil n/2 \rceil}^n(x)$.

BCOUNT : Input: $x_1, \ldots, x_n$. Output: the binary representation of $x_1 + \cdots + x_n$.

UCOUNT : Input: $x_1, \ldots, x_n$. Output: the n-bit unary representation of $x_1 + \cdots + x_n$.

THEOREM 3.5 : PAR $=_{cd}$ ZMc $\leq_{cd}$ MUL $=_{cd}$ SOR $=_{cd}$ MADD $=_{cd}$ THR $=_{cd}$ MAJ $=_{cd}$ BCOUNT $=_{cd}$ UCOUNT $\leq_{cd}$ UST CON .

By Theorem 3.4 ii we can combine the results of Theorem 3.3 and Theorem 3.5 . The lower bound for parity (which we prove in Ch. 11) translates to lower bounds for all problems in Theorem 3.3 and Theorem 3.5 . Again reducibility is a powerful tool.

We do not prove that MUL ,..., UCOUNT $\leq_{cd}$ UST CON , only the weaker claim PAR, ZMc $\leq_{cd}$ UST CON . This claim is sufficient for the translation of the lower bound on parity to the other problems.

Proof of Theorem 3.5 :

PAR $\leq_{cd}$ ZMc : We use 2^{c-1} copies of each x_i and an oracle gate for $\neg$ ZMc on these $n\,2^{c-1}$ inputs.

ZMc $\leq_{cd}$ PAR : Obviously PAR $= \neg$ ZMc for $c = 1$. Because of transitivity it is sufficient to prove ZMc $\leq_{cd}$ ZM(c-1) if $c \geq 2$. Let $x_1, \ldots, x_n$ be the inputs and let us compute $y_{ij} = x_i x_j$ for $1 \leq i < j \leq n$. It is sufficient to prove that

$$ZMc(x_1, \ldots, x_n) = ZM(c-1)(x_1, \ldots, x_n) \wedge ZM(c-1)(y_{12}, \ldots, y_{n-1,n}). \quad (3.7)$$

Let s be the sum of all x_i and t the sum of all y_{ij} . Then

$$t = \sum_{1 \leq i < j \leq n} y_{ij} = (1/2) \sum_{i \neq j} x_i x_j \quad (3.8)$$

$$= (1/2) \left(\left(\sum_{1 \leq i \leq n} x_i \right)^2 - \sum_{1 \leq i \leq n} x_i^2 \right) = (1/2)(s^2 - s) .$$

If $s \equiv 0 \bmod 2^c$, $s \equiv (s/2) \equiv 0 \bmod 2^{c-1}$ and $t \equiv 0 \bmod 2^{c-1}$, since $t = (s/2)(s-1)$. This proves $\leq$ in (3.7). If $s \equiv t \equiv 0 \bmod 2^{c-1}$ but $s \not\equiv 0 \bmod 2^c$, $s = j2^{c-1}$ for some odd j . Since $c \geq 2$, also $s-1$ is odd. Hence $(s-1)j$ is odd. Moreover

$$t = (s/2)(s-1) = (s-1)j\,2^{c-2} \qquad (3.9)$$

in contradiction to $t \equiv 0 \bmod 2^{c-1}$. This proves $\geq$ in (3.7).

PAR $\leq_{cd}$ **UCOUNT** : Because of transitivity this implies that the first group (PAR , ZMc) is constant depth reducible to the second group (MUL ,...., UCOUNT) of problems.

UCOUNT(x) equals $(T_n^n(x), \ldots, T_1^n(x))$. We compute UCOUNT(x) and $\neg$ UCOUNT(x) . Then we compute PAR(x) by (3.6) .

For the proof that the second group of problems contains equivalent problems with respect to constant depth reducibility it is (by transitivity) sufficient to prove that MAJ $\leq_{cd}$ MUL $\leq_{cd}$ MADD $\leq_{cd}$ BCOUNT $\leq_{cd}$ SOR $\leq_{cd}$ UCOUNT $\leq_{cd}$ THR $\leq_{cd}$ MAJ .

MAJ $\leq_{cd}$ **MUL** : If we are able to compute the binary representation c_n of $x_1 + \cdots + x_n$, we are done. $MAJ(x) = 1$ iff $x_1 + \cdots + x_n \geq \lceil n/2 \rceil$. This comparison can be performed in depth 2 and polynomial size by the disjunctive normal form, since the length of c_n is $k = \lceil \log(n+1) \rceil$. For the computation of c_n we use a padding trick already used in Ch. 3, § 2 . Let a be the binary number of length nk with x_i at position $k(i-1)$ and zeros elsewhere. Then a is the sum of all $x_i 2^{k(i-1)}$. Let b be the binary number of length nk with ones at the positions $k(i-1)$ for $1 \leq i \leq n$ and zeros elsewhere. Then b is the sum of all $2^{k(i-1)}$. We compute (at an oracle gate) c , the product of a and b . Then c is the sum of all $c_i 2^{k(i-1)}$ with k-bit numbers c_i contained in c . It is easy to see that $c_n = x_1 + \cdots + x_n$.

MUL $\leq_{cd}$ **MADD** : Obvious by the school method for multiplication.

MADD $\leq_{cd}$ **BCOUNT** : Let $a_i = (a_{i,m-1}, \ldots, a_{i,0})$ for $1 \leq i \leq m$ be the m numbers we have to sum up. We use in parallel oracle gates to compute the $l = \lceil \log(m+1) \rceil$-bit numbers $b_j = a_{1,j} + \cdots + a_{m,j}$. Then $s = a_1 + \cdots + a_m$ is also the sum of all $b_j 2^j$. Since the length of all b's is l, we add $b_j 2^j$ and $b_{j+l} 2^{j+l}$ without any gate by concatenating the strings for b_j and b_{j+l}. In this way we obtain l numbers of length

$m+l$ each whose sum equals s .

Again we add the bits at the same position. But we have (by Definition 3.6) no more oracle gates. Since l is already small, the disjunctive normal form has polynomial size with respect to $n = m^2$. We continue in the same way until we obtain two numbers x and y whose sum is s . At step 0 we have $l(0) = m$ summands. If $l(i-1)$ is the number of summands at step $i-1$, $l(i) = \lceil \log (l(i-1)+1) \rceil$. The number of necessary steps is not bounded by a constant. Therefore we use this procedure only for two steps and compute $l(2) = O(\log\log m)$ summands whose sum is s . We estimate the number of bits in these summands on which x_i or y_i depends essentially. Each bit of the summands in step 3 depends on $l(2)$ bits of the summands in step 2 . If the number of necessary steps is k , x_i or y_i depends on $l(2)l(3) \cdots l(k-1)$ bits. Since $l(j) = O(\log l(j-1))$, $l(j)l(j+1)^2 = o(l(j)^2)$ and by induction $l(j) \cdots l(k-1) = o(l(j)^2)$. Therefore x_i and y_i depend on $o(l(2)^2) = o(\log m)$ bits of the summands computed in step 2 . So we compute x_i and y_i by their disjunctive normal forms from the summands in step 2 . Finally we add x and y by a circuit of polynomial size and constant depth. The existence of such a circuit is proved in Ch. 11, § 2 . The proof is easy by the methods of Ch. 3, § 1 .

BCOUNT $\leq_{cd}$ SOR : Let $s = (s_{k-1}, \ldots, s_0)$ where $k = \lceil \log (n+1) \rceil$ be the binary representation of $x_1 + \cdots + x_n$. By sorting $x_1, \ldots, x_n$ with an oracle gate we obtain the unary representation $y = (y_n, \ldots, y_1)$ of s . Let $y_0 = 1$, $y_{n+1} = 0$ and $z_i = y_i \wedge \bar{y}_{i+1}$ for $0 \leq i \leq n$. Then $z_i = 1$ iff $i = s$. Let $b_i = (b_{i,k-1}, \ldots, b_{i,0})$ be the binary representation of i . Then s_j is the disjunction of all $z_i \wedge b_{ij}$.

SOR $\leq_{cd}$ UCOUNT : It is proved in Ch. 11, § 2 (or easy to see) that there are polynomial comparator circuits of constant depth. The output is 1 iff $x < y$ (or for another circuit $x \leq y$) . Let $a_1, \ldots, a_m$ be the m-bit numbers that have to be sorted. We compute $c_{ij} = 1$ iff $a_i < a_j$ or $a_i = a_j$ and $i \leq j$. Then we compute in parallel by oracle gates d_j , the sum of all c_{ij} . d_j is the unary representation of the position of a_j in the sorted list of $a_1, \ldots, a_m$. By similar methods as in the last reduction " BCOUNT $\leq_{cd}$ SOR " we compute the sorted list of $a_1, \ldots, a_m$.

UCOUNT $\leq_{cd}$ **THR** : We compute in parallel by oracle gates $y_i = THR(x_1, \ldots, x_n, i)$. Then $UCOUNT(x_1, \ldots, x_n) = (y_n, \ldots, y_1)$.

THR $\leq_{cd}$ **MAJ** : The input consists of $x_1, \ldots, x_m$ and $k = (k_m, \ldots, k_1)$, a number in unary representation. We compute by an oracle gate $z = MAJ(x_1, \ldots, x_m, \bar{k}_1, \ldots, \bar{k}_m, 1)$.

$z = 1$ iff $x_1 + \cdots + x_m + \bar{k}_1 + \cdots + \bar{k}_m + 1 \geq m+1$. There are l ones in k if k represents l. Then $\bar{k}_1 + \cdots + \bar{k}_m = m-l$. Hence $z = 1$ iff $x_1 + \cdots + x_m \geq l$ iff $THR(x,k) = 1$.

In order to relate the complexity of PAR and ZMc to all problems considered in Theorem 3.3 we prove **PAR** $\leq_{cd}$ **UST CON** .

We compute the adjacency matrix A of an undirected graph G on the vertices $v_0, \ldots, v_{n+1}$. Let $x_1, \ldots, x_n$ be the inputs of PAR and let $x_0 = x_{n+1} = 1$. Let $a_{ii} = 0$ and let

$$a_{ij} = x_i \wedge \bar{x}_{i+1} \wedge \cdots \wedge \bar{x}_{j-1} \wedge x_j \quad \text{for } i < j. \tag{3.10}$$

G contains exactly one path from v_0 to v_{n+1}, this path passes through all v_i with $x_i = 1$. The length of this path is even iff $x_1 \oplus \cdots \oplus x_n = 1$. We square in polynomial size and constant depth the Boolean matrix A. The result is B, the adjacency matrix of the graph G' where v_i and v_j are connected by an edge iff they are connected in G by a path of length 2. I.e. v_0 and v_{n+1} are connected by a path iff $x_1 \oplus \cdots \oplus x_n = 1$. Therefore one oracle gate for UST CON is sufficient for the computation of $x_1 \oplus \cdots \oplus x_n$. $\square$

Often it is easier to prove lower bounds by reduction than to prove lower bounds directly. The number of reducibility results is large.

EXERCISES

1. Let N_n^* be the class of all $f \in M_n^*$ whose prime implicants all have length $\lceil n/2 \rceil$. Then there is for each $\lceil \log n \rceil \le j \le D(N_n^*)$ (or $D_m(N_n^*)$) a function $g_j \in N_n^*$ where $D(g_j) = j$ (or $D_m(g_j) = j$).

2. Prove (1.2) for the bases $\{\wedge, \oplus\}$ and $\{NAND\}$.

3. Prove $d_\Omega(j) \le 2$ for all binary bases and all interesting j.

4. Prove (1.5).

5. Prove (1.3) and (1.4) for further bases.

6. $c_\Omega(j) = 1$ for $n = 2$, $0 \le j < C_\Omega(B_2^*)$ and $\Omega = \{\wedge, \oplus\}$ or $\Omega = \{NAND\}$.

7. Almost all $f \in B_n$ have no Ashenhurst decomposition.

8. Assume that $C_m(\vee(f \times g)) \ge C_m(f) + C_m(g)$ for arbitrary Boolean functions f and g. Prove by this assumption asymptotically optimal bounds on the monotone circuit size of the Boolean matrix product and the generalized Boolean matrix product (see Ch. 6, § 9).

9. Prove Theorem 2.2 using the replacement rule of Theorem 5.1, Ch. 6, and its dual version.

10. (Fischer and Galbiati (81) just as Exercise 11). Let $f \in M_{n+1}$ depend on $x_1, \ldots, x_n, z$ and $g \in M_{m+1}$ depend on $y_1, \ldots, y_m, z$. Then $C_m(f, g) = C_m(f) + C_m(g)$. Hint: A gate G is called mixed, if G has not only x-variables but also y-variables as predecessors.

Let H be the first mixed gate of a monotone circuit for (f,g), w.l.o.g. an $\wedge$-gate. Let $h(x,y,z) = res_H$ and let $h_1(x,z)$ and $h_2(y,z)$ be the inputs of H.

a) H can be replaced by 0 if $h_1(0,1) = h_2(0,1) = 0$.

b) If $h_1(0,1) = 1$ and H is not superfluous, $h_1(0,0) = h_2(0,0) = 0$, $\quad z \wedge h_2(0,z) = h_1(x,z) \wedge h_2(0,z) \quad$ and $z \wedge h_2(y,z) = h_1(0,z) \wedge h_2(y,z)$.

c) Either H can be replaced by 0 or h_1 or h_2 can be replaced by z.

11. Let $h \in B_n$, $x = (x_1, \ldots, x_n)$, $y = (y_1, \ldots, y_n)$, $f(x,z_1,z_2) = z_1 \wedge (z_2 \vee h(x))$ and $g(y,z_1,z_2) = z_2 \wedge (z_1 \vee h(y))$. Then $C_m(f,g) \le C_m(h) + 3n + 4$.

Hint: Compute $h(u_1, \ldots, u_n)$ with $u_i = x_i z_1 \vee y_i z_2$.

12. $\le_1$ is reflexive and transitive.

13. $\le_{proj}$ is reflexive and transitive.

14. Prove Theorem 3.4.

15. Prove directly $PAR \le_{cd} MUL$.

16. Try to prove directly more of the assertions of Theorem 3.5.

11. BOUNDED - DEPTH CIRCUITS

11.1 Introduction

A polynomial p for the Boolean function f is a disjunction of monoms computing f (see Ch. 2). Polynomials are circuits of two logical levels. All literals $x_1, \bar{x}_1, \ldots, x_n, \bar{x}_n$ are inputs. The monoms are computed on the first level, an $\wedge$-level. On the second level, an $\vee$-level, these monoms are combined by a disjunction. In this chapter we investigate circuits of k logical levels.

DEFINITION 1.1 : A Σ_k-circuit (Π_k-circuit) is a circuit consisting of k logical levels. All inputs of gates on level l are outputs of gates on level $l-1$. On level 0 we have the inputs $x_1, \bar{x}_1, \ldots, x_n, \bar{x}_n$. $\wedge$- and $\vee$-gates of unbounded fan-in are available. The levels $k, k-2, k-4, \ldots$ consist of $\vee$-gates ($\wedge$-gates) and the other levels consist of $\wedge$-gates ($\vee$-gates).

This model is robust. Negations inside the circuit are powerless. We copy all gates and negate one of the copies of each gate. No additional gate is necessary for the application of the deMorgan rules (bottom-up). At the end of this procedure only inputs are negated. If an input of an $\wedge$-gate G is the output of an $\wedge$-gate G' , we replace the edge from G' to G by edges from all direct predecessors of G' to G . Also the synchronization of Σ_k- and Π_k-circuits is no essential restriction. An edge from a gate G on level l to a gate G' on level $l' > l+1$ may be simulated by $l'-(l+1)$ new gates on the levels $l+1, \ldots, l'-1$ computing res_G . The size of the circuit is at most multiplied by the number of logical levels which should be small.

Hardware designers prefer circuits with a small number of logical levels. Hence it is a fundamental problem to decide whether sequences of functions $f_n \in B_n$ are in SIZE - DEPTH(poly,const) (see

Def. 3.5, Ch. 10). In § 3 we prove that polynomial circuits for the parity function have depth $\Omega((\log n)/(\log \log n))$. Applying the reducibility results of Ch. 10, § 3, we conclude that many fundamental functions with polynomial circuit size are not in SIZE-DEPTH(poly,const). Therefore we should use circuits where the number of logical levels is increasing with the input length.

In § 2 we prove for some fundamental functions that they are in SIZE-DEPTH(poly,const) and design almost optimal circuits for the parity function. The announced lower bound for the parity function is proved in § 3 . In § 4 we describe which symmetric functions are contained in SIZE-DEPTH(poly,const) . In § 5 we discuss hierarchy problems.

We finish this introduction with two concluding remarks. Bounded-depth circuits also represent an elegant model for PLAs (programmable logic arrays). Furthermore results on bounded-depth circuits are related to results on parallel computers (see Ch. 13).

11.2 The design of bounded-depth circuits

Let $f_n \in B_n$. If the number of prime implicants (or prime clauses) of f_n is bounded by a polynomial, then the sequence f_n ($n \in \mathbb{N}$) has polynomial Σ_2-circuits (Π_2-circuits) . Hence this sequence is in SIZE-DEPTH(poly,const) . We mention two examples, the threshold functions T_k^n and the clique functions $cl_{n,k}$ (see Def. 11.1 , Ch. 6) for constant k . Furthermore all functions depending essentially on only $O(\log n)$ input bits are in SIZE-DEPTH(poly,const) . An example is the transformation of the binary representation $(x_1, \ldots, x_k)$ ($n = 2^k$) of some number $x \in \{0, \ldots, n-1\}$ into its unary representation $(y_1, \ldots, y_n)$.

Chandra, Stockmeyer and Vishkin (84) proved that the following fundamental functions are in SIZE-DEPTH(poly,const) .

DEFINITION 2.1 :

ADD : Addition of two m-bit numbers, $n = 2m$.

COM : The comparison problem for two m-bit numbers $x = (x_{m-1}, \ldots, x_0)$ and $y = (y_{m-1}, \ldots, y_0)$. Output $1 \Leftrightarrow |x| > |y|$. $n = 2m$.

MAX : The computation of the maximum of m m-bit numbers, $n = m^2$.

MER : The merging problem for two sorted lists of m m-bit numbers, $n = 2m^2$.

U → B : Input: an n-bit unary number k. Output: the binary representation of k.

THEOREM 2.1 : ADD , COM , MAX , MER and U → B are in SIZE-DEPTH(poly,const).

Proof : **ADD** : We implement the carry look-ahead method (see Ch. 3, § 1). We compute $u_j = x_j y_j$ and $v_j = x_j \oplus y_j$ $(0 \le j \le m-1)$ in depth 2. The carry bit c_j is the disjunction of all $u_i v_{i+1} \cdots v_j$ $(0 \le i \le j)$ (see Ch. 3, (1.8)). The sum bits s_j are computed by $s_0 = v_0$, $s_n = c_{n-1}$ and $s_j = v_j \oplus c_{j-1}$ $(1 \le j \le n-1)$. The size of the circuit is $O(n^2)$ (the number of wires is $O(n^3)$) and the depth is 4 if v_j and s_j are computed by Π_2-circuits for $a \oplus b$.

COM : $|x| > |y|$ if there is an i such that $y_i = 0$, $x_i = 1$ and $y_j = x_j$ for all $j > i$. This can be computed by

$$\bigvee_{0 \le i \le m-1} \left(x_i \wedge \bar{y}_i \wedge \bigwedge_{i < j \le m-1} [(x_j \wedge y_j) \vee (\bar{x}_j \wedge \bar{y}_j)] \right). \tag{2.1}$$

The circuit size is $O(m^2) = O(n^2)$ and the depth is 4.

MAX : Let $a_1, \ldots, a_m$ be m m-bit numbers. We compute in depth 4 with $O(m^4)$ gates $c_{ij} = 1$ iff $a_i \ge a_j$ $(1 \le i,j \le m)$. Let d_i be the conjunction of all c_{ij}. Then $d_i = 1$ iff a_i is the maximum. The j-th bit of the output is computed as the disjunction of all $a_{ij} d_i$. The size of the circuit is $O(m^4) = O(n^2)$, and the depth is 6.

MER : Let $a_1 \leq \cdots \leq a_m$ and $b_1 \leq \cdots \leq b_m$ be sorted lists. We compute $c_{ij} = 1$ iff $b_i < a_j$. For each j , $c_{mj} \cdots c_{1j}$ is the unary representation of the number of b's less than a_j . Let $c_j = 0^{m-j} c_{mj} \cdots c_{1j} 1^j$. Then c_j is the unary representation of a_j's position in the merged list. In parallel we compute $d_{ij} = 1$ iff $a_i \leq b_j$ and $d_j = 0^{m-j} d_{mj} \cdots d_{1j} 1^j$, the unary representation of b_j's position in the merged list. For $z = z_{2m} \cdots z_1$, $z_{2m+1} = 0$ and $0 \leq k \leq 2m$, $EQ_k(z) = z_k \wedge \bar{z}_{k+1}$ tests whether z is the unary representation of k . Finally the i-th bit of the k-th number in the merged list is

$$\bigvee_{1 \leq j \leq m} (EQ_k(c_j) \wedge a_{ji}) \vee \bigvee_{1 \leq j \leq m} (EQ_k(d_j) \wedge b_{ji}) . \tag{2.2}$$

The size of the circuit is $O(m^4) = O(n^2)$, and the depth is 6 .

U → B : Let $(x_n, \ldots, x_1)$ be the input, $x_0 = 1$ and $x_{n+1} = 0$. Let $d_i = x_i \bar{x}_{i+1}$. Then $d_i = 1$ iff x is the unary representation of i , $0 \leq i \leq n$. The j-th bit of the output is the disjunction of all d_i such that the j-th bit of i is 1 . The number of gates is $O(n)$, the number of wires is $O(n \log n)$, and the depth is 2 .

□

THEOREM 2.2 : If $k(n) = O(\log^r n)$ for some fixed r , $T_{k(n)}^n$ is in SIZE - DEPTH(poly,const) .

The proof of this theorem is postponed to Ch. 12, § 3 . The proof is not constructive. We shall design efficient probabilistic circuits for $T_{k(n)}^n$ and shall show how such circuits are simulated by deterministic circuits.

There are only few papers on lower bounds for functions in SIZE - DEPTH(poly,const) . We refer to Chandra, Fortune and Lipton (83) and (85) and Hromkovic (85). It is more important to decide which functions belong to SIZE - DEPTH(poly,const) , the class of efficiently computable functions.

In the next section we prove that the parity function PAR_n does not belong to this class. Here we design almost optimal circuits for

PAR_n . PAR_n consists of 2^{n-1} prime implicants and 2^{n-1} prime clauses, all of them are necessary in Σ_2- and Π_2-circuits resp. Hence the complexity of PAR_n in depth 2 circuits is $2^{n-1}+1$. In the following we allow negations which we eliminate afterwards as described in § 1 .

For k-level circuits we compute PAR_n in $k-1$ steps. W.l.o.g. $n = r^{k-1}$. In Step 1 we compute PAR_r on r^{k-2} blocks of r variables each. In Step 2 we compute PAR_r on r^{k-3} blocks of r outputs of Step 1 each. Hence we compute the parity of r^2 bits at each output of Step 2 . We continue in the same way. After Step i we have computed the parity of r^{k-1-i} blocks of r^i variables each, in particular, we compute PAR_n in Step $k-1$. We use an alternating sequence of Σ_2- and Π_2-circuits for Step $1, \ldots, k-1$. Then it is possible to combine the second level of the Σ_2-circuits (Π_2-circuits) on Step i and the first level of the Π_2-circuits (Σ_2-circuits) on Step $i+1$. Altogether we obtain Σ_k-circuits and Π_k-circuits for PAR_n . The number of subcircuits for PAR_r is $r^{k-2}+r^{k-3}+\cdots+1 \le r^{k-1} = n$, each of these subcircuits contains $2^{r-1}+1$ gates.

THEOREM 2.3 : i) PAR has Σ_k- and Π_k-circuits of size
$O(n\, 2^{n^{1/(k-1)}})$.

ii) PAR has $\Sigma_{k(n)}$- and $\Pi_{k(n)}$-circuits of size $O(n^2 \log^{-1} n)$ if $k(n) = \lceil (\log n)/\log\log n \rceil + 1$.

Proof : i) has already been proved for $n = r^{k-1}$. The general case is left as an exercise.

ii) In Step i we combine the outputs of Step $i-1$ to the least number of blocks whose size is bounded by $\lceil \log n \rceil + 1$. The number of blocks in Step i is bounded by $\max\{1, \lfloor n/\log^i n \rfloor\}$. $k(n)-1$ steps are sufficient in order to obtain one block, since $(\log n)^{k(n)-1} \ge n$. Altogether we require less than $2\lfloor n/\log n \rfloor$ Σ_2- and Π_2-parity circuits working on at most $\lceil \log n \rceil + 1$ inputs. $\qquad\square$

11.3 An exponential lower bound for the parity function

The number of papers on Σ_2- and Π_2-circuits is immense, but there are almost no results on Σ_k- and Π_k-circuits for $k \geq 3$ which were proved before 1980. Then exponential lower bounds on the monotone Σ_3-complexity have been proved by Tkachev (80), Kuznetsov (83 a), Valiant (83) (for clique functions) and Yao (83) (for the majority function). Yao proved exponential lower bounds even on the monotone Σ_4-complexity of some clique functions.

The decisive break-through was the paper of Furst, Saxe and Sipser (84). They proved that parity is not in SIZE-DEPTH(poly,const). Their non polynomial lower bound for Σ_k-circuits was improved by an $\exp(\Omega(\log^2 n))$ - lower bound of Ajtai (83). The first exponential lower bound for arbitrary constant depth was proved by Boppana (84), but only for the monotone Σ_k-complexity of the majority function. Another break-through was the proof of exponential lower bounds for depth k parity circuits. The original bound and methods due to Yao (85) have been improved by Hastad (86).

THEOREM 3.1 : For some constant n_0 and $n \geq n_0^k$ Σ_k- and Π_k-circuits for the parity function $x_1 \oplus \cdots \oplus x_n$ have more than $2^{c(k)n^{1/(k-1)}}$ gates, $c(k) = (1/10)^{k/(k-1)} \approx 1/10$.

COROLLARY 3.1 : PAR is not in SIZE-DEPTH(poly,const).

COROLLARY 3.2 : Polynomial size parity circuits must have depth of at least $\dfrac{\log n}{c + \log\log n}$ for some constant c.

The corollaries follow easily from Theorem 3.1. Because of our upper bounds in Theorem 2.3, these results are nearly optimal.

We give an outline of the proof of Theorem 3.1 . The proof is by induction on k . The induction basis k = 2 is easy. For the induction step we try to convert depth k circuits to not very large depth $k-1$ circuits. If the second level is an $\wedge$-level, each function on level 2 is computed by a Π_2-circuit. It is possible to replace these Π_2-circuits by Σ_2-circuits for the same functions. Then the second and the third level of the circuit are $\vee$-levels which we combine in order to obtain depth $k-1$ circuits. The problem is that the Σ_2-complexity of g may be exponential even if the Π_2-complexity is small, say polynomial.

In the following way the problem can be avoided. We replace several variables in such a way by constants that all functions on level 2 have small Σ_2-circuits and that the number of remaining variables is yet large enough. Nobody knows how to construct such a replacement. Again we use probabilistic methods. We hope that many replacements serve our purposes. In order to prove the existence of a good replacement, it is sufficient to prove that the probability of a good replacement is positive.

DEFINITION 3.1 : A restriction is a function $\rho : \{x_1, \ldots, x_n\} \to \{0, 1, *\}$. Then g_ρ is the projection of g where we replace x_i by $\rho(x_i)$ if $\rho(x_i) \in \{0, 1\}$. For a random restriction $\rho \in R_p$ ($0 \le p \le 1$) the random variables $\rho(x_i)$ ($1 \le i \le n$) are independent and $\rho(x_i) = 0$ with probability $(1-p)/2$, $\rho(x_i) = 1$ with probability $(1-p)/2$ and $\rho(x_i) = *$ with probability p . For $\rho \in R_p$, g_ρ is a random function.

The following main lemma tells us that if we apply a random restriction, we can with high probability convert Π_2-circuits to equivalent Σ_2-circuits of small size. We need the notion of the 1-fan-in of a circuit. This is the maximal fan-in of all gates on the first level. The proof of the first technical lemma is left to the reader.

LEMMA 3.1 : The equation

$$(1 + \frac{4p}{(1+p)\alpha})^t = (1 + \frac{2p}{(1+p)\alpha})^t + 1 \tag{3.1}$$

has a unique positive root. If $p = o(1)$, $\alpha \approx (2p)\ln^{-1}\varphi < 5pt$, where φ is the golden ratio, i.e. the root of $\varphi^2 = \varphi + 1$.

MAIN LEMMA 3.2 : Let S be a Π_2-circuit of 1-fan-in t computing $g \in B_n$ and let $\rho \in R_p$. The probability that g_ρ can be computed by a Σ_2-circuit of 1-fan-in s is at least $1 - \alpha^s$.

The Main Lemma is equivalent to its dual version. We prove a more general version of the Main Lemma . Let $l_{PI}(f)$ denote the maximal length of a prime implicant of f . We use the convention that a conditional probability is 0 if the probability of the condition in question is 0 .

LEMMA 3.3 : Let $g_1, \ldots, g_m$ be sums of at most t literals each. Let $g = g_1 \wedge \cdots \wedge g_m$ and $f \in B_n$. For $\rho \in R_p$ we have

$$Pr(l_{PI}(g_\rho) \geq s \mid f_\rho \equiv 1) \leq \alpha^s . \tag{3.2}$$

Lemma 3.3 implies the Main Lemma 3.2 by choosing $f \equiv 1$.

Proof of Lemma 3.3 : We prove this lemma by induction on m . If $m = 0$, the lemma is obvious since $g \equiv 1$.

Let $m > 0$. Since $Pr(A) \leq \max \{Pr(A|B), Pr(A|\bar{B})\}$, also

$$Pr(l_{PI}(g_\rho) \geq s \mid f_\rho \equiv 1) \leq \tag{3.3}$$

$$\max \{Pr(l_{PI}(g_\rho) \geq s \mid f_\rho \equiv 1, g_{1\rho} \equiv 1), Pr(l_{PI}(g_\rho) \geq s \mid f_\rho \equiv 1, g_{1\rho} \not\equiv 1)\} .$$

The estimation of the first term is easy by the induction hypothesis. We choose $f \wedge g_1$ instead of f and $g' = g_2 \wedge \cdots \wedge g_m$ instead of g . If the condition $(f \wedge g_1)_\rho \equiv 1$ holds, $g_\rho = g'_\rho$. Therefore the first term is bounded by α^s .

The estimation of the second term is more difficult. W.l.o.g. g_1 is the sum of all $x_i \in T$ and $|T| \leq t$. Otherwise we interchange the roles of some x_i and $\bar{x}_i$. Let ρ' or ρ'' be that part of ρ which concerns the variables in T or not in T resp. Notation: $\rho = \rho'\rho''$. The condition $g_{1\rho} \not\equiv 1$ is equivalent to the condition that $\rho'(x_i) \not\equiv 1$ for all $x_i \in T$. Hence each prime implicant of g_ρ contains - if $g_{1\rho} \not\equiv 1$ - some $x_i \in T$. For $Y \subseteq T$ let $PIY(g_\rho)$ be the set of prime implicants of g_ρ containing, for $x_i \in T$, x_i or $\bar{x}_i$ iff $x_i \in Y$. Let $l_{PIY}(g_\rho)$ be the length of a longest prime implicant in $PIY(g_\rho)$ and let $\rho'(Y) \equiv *$ be the event that $\rho'(x_i) = *$ for all $x_i \in Y$. Then

$$\Pr(l_{PI}(g_\rho) \geq s \mid f_\rho \equiv 1 , g_{1\rho'} \not\equiv 1) \tag{3.4}$$

$$\leq \sum_{Y \subseteq T, Y \neq \phi} \Pr(l_{PIY}(g_\rho) \geq s \mid f_\rho \equiv 1, g_{1\rho'} \not\equiv 1)$$

$$= \sum_{Y \subseteq T, Y \neq \phi} \Pr(\rho'(Y) \equiv * \mid f_\rho \equiv 1, g_{1\rho'} \not\equiv 1) \cdot$$

$$\cdot \Pr(l_{PIY}(g_\rho) \geq s \mid f_\rho \equiv 1, g_{1\rho'} \not\equiv 1, \rho'(Y) \equiv *),$$

since $\Pr(l_{PIY}(g_\rho) \geq s \mid \rho'(Y) \not\equiv *) = 0$. We claim that

$$\Pr(\rho'(Y) \equiv * \mid f_\rho \equiv 1 , g_{1\rho'}(Y) \not\equiv 1) \leq \left(\frac{2p}{1+p}\right)^{|Y|} \quad \text{and} \tag{3.5}$$

$$\Pr(l_{PIY}(g_\rho) \geq s \mid f_\rho \equiv 1, g_{1\rho'} \not\equiv 1, \rho'(Y) \equiv *) \leq (2^{|Y|} - 1) \, \alpha^{s-|Y|} \tag{3.6}$$

hold. By (3.4) - (3.6) it is easy to estimate the second term in (3.3). We add in (3.4) the term for $Y = \phi$ which is estimated in (3.5) and (3.6) by 0. Hence, by the definition of α

$$\Pr(l_{PI}(g_\rho) \geq s \mid f_\rho \equiv 1 , g_{1\rho'} \not\equiv 1) \tag{3.7}$$

$$\leq \sum_{Y \subseteq T} \left(\frac{2p}{1+p}\right)^{|Y|} (2^{|Y|} - 1) \, \alpha^{s-|Y|}$$

$$\leq \alpha^s \sum_{0 \leq i \leq |T|} \binom{|T|}{i} \left(\frac{2p}{1+p}\right)^i (2^i - 1) \, \alpha^{-i}$$

$$\le \alpha^s \sum_{0 \le i \le t} \binom{t}{i} \left[\left(\frac{4p}{(1+p)\alpha} \right)^i - \left(\frac{2p}{(1+p)\alpha} \right)^i \right]$$

$$= \alpha^s \left[\left(1 + \frac{4p}{(1+p)\alpha} \right)^t - \left(1 + \frac{2p}{(1+p)\alpha} \right)^t \right] = \alpha^s .$$

Proof of (3.5) : The condition $g_{1\rho'} \not\equiv 1$ is equivalent to the condition that $\rho(x_i) \in \{0, *\}$ for $x_i \in T$. Then $\rho(x_i)$ takes the values 0 and $*$ with probability $(1-p)/(1+p)$ and $2p/(1+p)$ resp. Since all $\rho(x_i)$ are independent

$$\Pr(\rho'(Y) \equiv * \mid g_{1\rho'} \not\equiv 1) = \left(\frac{2p}{1+p} \right)^{|Y|} . \tag{3.8}$$

The additional condition $f_\rho \equiv 1$ implies a tendency that more variables are replaced by constants. Therefore the event $\rho'(Y) \equiv *$ should have smaller probability. For a definite proof we use the equivalence of the inequalities $\Pr(A|B) \le \Pr(A)$ and $\Pr(B|A) \le \Pr(B)$. For the proof of (3.5) it is by (3.8) and this equivalence sufficient to prove

$$\Pr(f_\rho \equiv 1 \mid \rho'(Y) \equiv *, g_{1\rho'} \not\equiv 1) \le \Pr(f_\rho \equiv 1 \mid g_{1\rho'} \not\equiv 1) . \tag{3.9}$$

Two restrictions are called equivalent if they agree on all $x_i \notin Y$. It is sufficient to prove (3.9) for all equivalence classes. Each equivalence class contains exactly one restriction ρ where $\rho'(Y) \equiv *$. If $f_\rho \not\equiv 1$ or $g_{1\rho'} \equiv 1$ for this restriction, the left-hand side of (3.9) equals 0 for this equivalence class and (3.9) holds. Otherwise $f_{\bar\rho} \equiv 1$ for all $\bar\rho$ equivalent to ρ , since the additional replacement of variables does not influence a constant.

Proof of (3.6) : We like to exclude g_1 from our considerations. Then it is possible to apply the induction hypothesis. The condition "$g_{1\rho'} \not\equiv 1$ and $\rho'(Y) \equiv *$" is satisfied iff $\rho'(x_i) \in \{0, *\}$ for $x_i \in T$ and $\rho'(x_i) = *$ for $x_i \in Y$. Here two restrictions are called equivalent if they agree on all $x_i \in T$. It is sufficient to prove for a fixed equivalence class

$$\Pr(\ell_{\text{PIY}}(g_\rho) \ge s \mid f_\rho \equiv 1) \le (2^{|Y|} - 1) \, \alpha^{s-|Y|} . \tag{3.10}$$

Each prime implicant $t \in PIY(g_\rho)$ is of the form $t = t't''$ for some monom t' on all variables in Y and some monom t'' on some variables $x_i \notin T$. If we replace the variables in Y such that t' is replaced by 1, we obtain a subfunction $g_{\rho\sigma(t)}$ of g_ρ where $t'' \in PI(g_{\rho\sigma(t)})$. Since g_1 is the sum of all $x_i \in T$, t' contains at least one $x_i \in T$. Hence $l_{PIY}(g_\rho) \geq s$ only if there is some $\sigma : Y \rightarrow \{0,1\}$, $\sigma \not\equiv 0$, such that the length of a longest prime implicant of $g_{\rho\sigma}$ (a monom on the variables $x_i \notin T$) is at least $s - |Y|$, notation $l_{PI}^*(g_{\rho\sigma}) \geq s - |Y|$. We conclude

$$\Pr(l_{PIY}(g_\rho) \geq s \mid f_\rho \equiv 1) \leq \qquad (3.11)$$

$$\leq \sum_{\sigma : Y \rightarrow \{0,1\}, \sigma \not\equiv 0} \Pr(l_{PI}^*(g_{\rho\sigma}) \geq s - |Y| \mid f_\rho \equiv 1) .$$

The right-hand side of (3.11) consists of $2^{|Y|} - 1$ terms. It is sufficient to estimate each of these terms by $\alpha^{s - |Y|}$.

We fix some $\sigma : Y \rightarrow \{0,1\}$, $\sigma \not\equiv 0$. We have fixed $\rho'\sigma$ but $\rho'' \in R_\rho$ is still a random restriction on the variables $x_i \notin T$. In order to apply the induction hypothesis we want to consider functions on the variables $x_i \notin T$. Let f^* be the conjunction of all functions which we obtain from $f_{\rho'}$ by replacing the variables in $(\rho')^{-1}(*)$ by constants. Then f^* is defined on the variables $x_i \notin T$. $f_{\rho''}^* \equiv 1$ iff $f_\rho \equiv 1$. Similarly let g^* be the conjunction of all functions which we obtain from $g_{\rho'\sigma}$ by replacing the variables in $(\rho')^{-1}(*) \cap (T-Y)$ by constants. Then g^* is defined on the variables $x_i \notin T$. The prime implicants of g^* are exactly those prime implicants of $g_{\rho'\sigma}$ containing only variables $x_i \notin T$. Let g_j^* be defined in a similar way. Then $g^* = g_1^* \wedge \cdots \wedge g_m^*$. Since g_1 is the sum of all $x_i \in Y$, $g_1^* \equiv 1$. For all legitimate replacements $(g_j)_{\rho'\sigma}$ is replaced by a constant or by some definite function g_j'. Hence, if $j \geq 2$, g_j^* is a sum of at most t literals and g^* is the conjunction of $m-1$ of those g_j^*. Since we have also shown that f^* and

g^* are defined on the variables $x_i \notin T$ and that $\rho'' \in R_p$ is a random restriction, it is possible to apply the induction hypothesis. We conclude

$$Pr(l^*_{PI}(g_{\rho\sigma}) \geq s - |Y| \mid f_\rho \equiv 1) = \qquad (3.12)$$

$$= Pr(l_{PI}(g^*_{\rho''}) \geq s - |Y| \mid f^*_{\rho''} \equiv 1) \leq \alpha^{s-|Y|}.$$

$\square$

The Main Lemma has many applications. The most appropriate function is the parity function, as all prime implicants and prime clauses of the parity function have length n, and all subfunctions are parity functions or negated parity functions.

LEMMA 3.4 : For some constant n_0, $n \geq n_0^{k-1}$ and $k \geq 2$ the parity function on n variables cannot be computed by a Σ_k- or Π_k-circuit which for $s = t = (1/10)n^{1/(k-1)}$ simultaneously has 1-fan-in bounded by t and at most 2^s gates on the levels $2,...,k$.

Proof : Induction on k. The claim is obvious for $k = 2$ since Σ_2- and Π_2-circuits for the parity function have 1-fan-in n.

We assume that the assertion holds for $k-1$ but not for k. Let S_n be depth k circuits for $x_1 \oplus \cdots \oplus x_n$ such that the 1-fan-in is bounded by t, and the number of gates on the levels $2,...,k$ is bounded by 2^s. W.l.o.g. the second level is an $\wedge$-level. The gates of this level are outputs of Π_2-circuits with 1-fan-in t. We apply the Main Lemma for $p = n^{-1/(k-1)}$. The expected number of remaining variables is $m = np = n^{(k-2)/(k-1)}$. For large n, the probability that at least m variables are left is larger than $1/3$. For each Π_2-circuit the probability of the circuit being converted to an equivalent Σ_2-circuit of 1-fan-in s is at least $1 - \alpha^s$. For large n, $\alpha < 5pt = 1/2$. Hence the probability of less than m variables being left or some Π_2-circuit cannot be converted in the described way is bounded by $(2/3) + (2\alpha)^s$. Since $2\alpha < 1$, this probability is less than 1 for large n. Then there is a partial replacement of variables such that the circuit computes the parity of $m = n^{(k-2)/(k-1)}$ variables, and all Π_2-circuits can be converted to equivalent Σ_2-circuits of 1-fan-in $s = (1/10)n^{1/(k-1)} = (1/10)m^{1/(k-2)}$. Afterwards the second and the third level are v-levels, and by merging them the depth of the circuit will decrease to $k-1$. The number of gates on the levels $2,...,k-1$ has not increased and is bounded by 2^s. Since $n \ge n_0^{k-1}$, also $m \ge n_0^{k-2}$. It is easy to prove that all conclusions hold for $n \ge n_0^{k-1}$. The depth $k-2$ circuit for the parity of m variables contradicts the induction hypothesis. $\qquad\square$

Now it is easy to prove Theorem 3.1.

Proof of Theorem 3.1: If the theorem is false, there is a depth k circuit for the parity of $n \ge n_0^k$ variables with at most 2^s gates, $s = (1/10)^{k/(k-1)}n^{1/(k-1)}$. This circuit can be understood as a depth $k+1$ circuit of 1-fan-in 1. Let $p = 1/10$ and $\rho \in R_p$. If $p = 1/10$ and $t = 1$, then $\alpha = 2/11$. If n_0 is chosen in the right way, there is a restriction such that the circuit computes the parity on $m = n/10$ variables, and all (w.l.o.g.) Π_2-circuits on level 2 can be converted to equivalent Σ_2-circuits of 1-fan-in s. If $n_0 \ge 10$, $m = n/10 \ge n_0^{k-1}$. Furthermore $s = (1/10)m^{1/(k-1)}$. The new depth k circuit for the parity on m variables contradicts Lemma 3.4, since the number of gates on the levels $2,...,k$ is bounded by 2^s. $\qquad\square$

11.4 The complexity of symmetric functions

Upper and lower bounds on the depth k complexity of the parity function almost agree, the upper bound is based on a simple design.

For all symmetric and almost all Boolean functions we decide in this section whether they belong to SIZE-DEPTH(poly,const) (Brustmann and Wegener (86)). Our results are based on the lower bound techniques due to Hastad (86). Weaker results based on the lower bound technique due to Furst, Saxe and Sipser (84) have been obtained by Fagin, Klawe, Pippenger and Stockmeyer (85) and Denenberg, Gurevich and Shelah (83). It is fundamental to know a lower bound for the majority function.

THEOREM 4.1 : For some constant n_0 and all $n \geq n_0^k$ Σ_k- and Π_k- circuits for the majority function have more than $2^{c(k)} n^{1/(k-1)}$ gates , $c(k) = (1/10)^{k/(k-1)} \approx 1/10$.

Proof : This theorem has been proved by Hastad (86) in a way similar to his bound for the parity function. The analysis of the probabilities is harder, since we have to ensure that the restriction gives out the same number of ones and zeros.

We are satisfied with the proof of a weaker bound based on the reducibility of parity to majority. Let $C_k(MAJ_n)$ be the Σ_k- complexity of the majority function. By duality the Π_k-complexity is the same. With less than $n\,C_k(MAJ_n)$ gates we compute in Π_k- circuits $E_l^{\lceil n/2 \rceil} = T_l^{\lceil n/2 \rceil} \wedge (\neg\, T_{l+1}^{\lceil n/2 \rceil})$ for all odd $l \in \{1, \ldots, \lceil n/2 \rceil\}$. $PAR_{\lceil n/2 \rceil}$ is the disjunction of these $E_l^{\lceil n/2 \rceil}$. Hence

$$C_{k+1}(PAR_{\lceil n/2 \rceil}) \leq n\,C_k(MAJ_n) \tag{4.1}$$

and by Theorem 3.1

$$C_k(MAJ_n) \geq n^{-1}\, 2^{c(k+1)}(n/2)^{1/k} \quad \text{for } n \geq n_0^{k+1} . \tag{4.2}$$

$\square$

From now on we denote by $C_k(f)$ the depth k complexity of f . We require some results on the structure of symmetric functions.

DEFINITION 4.1 : Let $v(f) = (v_0, \ldots, v_n)$ be the value vector of a symmetric function $f \in S_n$. By $v_{max}(f)$ we denote the length of a longest constant substring of $v(f)$. For $f \in B_n$ let $l_{min}(f)$ be the length of a shortest prime implicant or prime clause.

LEMMA 4.1 : $l_{min}(f) = n + 1 - v_{max}(f)$ for $f \in S_n$.

Proof : A prime implicant t of length k with l variables and $k-l$ negated variables implies $v_l = \cdots = v_{n-k+l} = 1$ and therefore the existence of a constant substring of $v(f)$ of length $n+1-k$. Furthermore, we obtain a maximal constant substring. If $v_{l-1} = 1$ or $v_{n-k+l+1} = 1$, we could shorten t by a variable or negated variable resp. If $v_l = \cdots = v_{n-k+l} = 1$ is a maximal constant substring of $v(f)$, then the monom $x_1 \cdots x_l \bar{x}_{l+1} \cdots \bar{x}_k$ is a prime implicant of f of length k . Dual arguments hold for prime clauses and substrings of $v(f)$ consisting of zeros. $\qquad\Box$

THEOREM 4.2 : For $c(k) = (1/10)^{k/(k-1)}$ we denote by $H(n,k)$ Hastad's lower bound function $2^{c(k)n^{1/(k-1)}}$.

i) If $f_n \in S_n$ and $l = l_{min}(f_n) = O(\log^r n)$ for some constant r , then $f = (f_n) \in SIZE\text{-}DEPTH(poly,const)$.

ii) If $f_n \in S_n$ and $l = l_{min}(f_n) \leq (n+1)/2$, then for $l \geq n_0^{k+1}$
$$C_k(f_n) \geq H(l,k+1)/l .\qquad\qquad(4.3)$$

iii) If $f_n \in S_n$ and $l = l_{min}(f_n) > (n+1)/2$, then for $w = v_{max}(f_n)$ and $w \geq n_0^{k+1}$
$$C_k(f_n) \geq H(w,k+1)/w \geq H(n+1-l,k+1)/l .\qquad(4.4)$$

iv) If $f_n \in B_n$ (not necessarily symmetric) and $l_{min}(f_n) \geq n - O(\log^r n)$ for some constant r , then for constant k and large n
$$C_k(f_n) \geq H(n,k) .\qquad\qquad(4.5)$$

Proof : We identify the vector $(v_0, \ldots, v_n)$ with the string $v_0 \cdots v_n$. By duality we assume that there is always a maximal constant substring consisting of zeros. For $w = v_{max}(f_n)$, $v(f) = s\,0^w s'$. W.l.o.g. (otherwise we negate the variables) s is not longer than s' .

i) $v_i = 1$ only for some $i \leq l-1$ and some $i \geq n-l+1$. f_n is the disjunction of all $T_i^n \wedge (\neg T_{i+1}^n)$ where $v_i = 1$. By Theorem 2.2 and by duality all these functions are in SIZE-DEPTH(poly,const).

ii) By our assumptions $s' = 1t$, and the length of s' is at least $\lceil l/2 \rceil$. Since $w \geq l$, $v(f)$ contains the substring $0^l 1t$ where the length of t is at least $\lceil l/2 \rceil - 1$. For $\lceil l/2 \rceil \leq m \leq l$ let $g_m \in S_l$ be that symmetric function whose value vector is a substring of $0^l 1t$ starting with $0^m 1$. All these value vectors start with $\lceil l/2 \rceil$ zeros, and g_m computes 1 for inputs with exactly m ones. Hence the disjunction of all g_m is the majority function on l variables. Since all g_m are subfunctions of f_n

$$C_{k+1}(MAJ_l) \leq (\lfloor l/2 \rfloor + 1) C_k(f_n) + 1 . \tag{4.6}$$

The lower bound (4.3) follows from Theorem 4.1.

iii) By Lemma 4.1 $w \leq (n+1)/2$. Hence $v(f)$ contains a substring $0^w 1t$ where the length of t is at least $\lceil w/2 \rceil - 1$. The lower bound (4.4) follows from similar arguments as (4.3).

iv) It is sufficient to prove that we can copy Hastad's proof for these functions. The Main Lemma works for all $f_n \in B_n$. In the proof of Lemma 3.4 and Theorem 3.1 only a few properties of the parity functions are used, namely the facts that $l_{min}(PAR_n) = n > n/10$ and that each subfunction of a parity function is a function of the same type.

$l_{min}(f)$ is the minimum number of variables which have to be replaced by constants in order to obtain a constant subfunction. Hence $l_{min}(g) \geq l_{min}(f) - (n-m)$ if $g \in B_m$ is a subfunction of $f \in B_n$. In his lower bound proof for depth k circuits Hastad constructed subfunctions on $n^{(k-2)/(k-1)}, n^{(k-3)/(k-1)}, ..., n^{1/(k-1)}, (1/10)n^{1/(k-1)}$ variables. For these functions $g \in B_m$ we have $l_{min}(g) \geq m - O(\log^r n) = m - O(\log^r m)$. All these functions belong to the class of functions with large l_{min}-value. Since $l_{min}(g)$ is a lower bound on the 1-fan-in of depth 2 circuits for g, the lower bound (4.5) can be proved by Hastad's proof, if n is large enough so that $l_{min}(g) > m/10$.

□

COROLLARY 4.1 : Let $f = (f_n)$ where $f_n \in S_n$.
Then $f \in$ SIZE-DEPTH(poly,const) iff $l_{min}(f_n) = O(\log^r n)$ for some constant r .

Proof : The if-part is Theorem 4.2 i . The only if-part follows from the definition of Hastad's function and the lower bounds in Theorem 4.2 ii - iv . $\square$

COROLLARY 4.2 : $C_k(f) \geq H(n,k)$ for almost all $f \in B_n$.

Proof : Bublitz, Schürfeld, Voigt and Wegener (86) investigated properties of l_{min} and proved the following assertion (see Theorem 7.8, Ch. 13). $l_{min}(f) \in I_n$ for almost all $f \in B_n$ and intervals I_n where $n - \lfloor \log n \rfloor \in I_n$ and the length of I_n is smaller than 2 . Hence the corollary follows from Theorem 4.2 iv . $\square$

The bounds we have proved depend only on $l_{min}(f)$. Is it reasonable to conjecture that $C_k(f)$ depends for all $f \in B_n$ essentially only on $l_{min}(f)$? The answer is negative. Let $n = m^2$ and let the set of variables be partitioned to m blocks of size m each. Let h_n compute 1 iff at least one block contains ones only. Then $l_{min}(h_n) = m = n^{1/2}$ but h_n has linear depth 2 circuits.

For symmetric functions $l_{min}(f)$ describes rather precisely the size and the structure of the set of all prime implicants and prime clauses and therefore the complexity of f . If $l_{min}(f)$ is not too small, a random subfunction of f is with large probability not a simple function. The same holds for arbitrary Boolean functions only if $l_{min}(f)$ is very large. For h_n defined above, $l_{min}(h_n)$ is quite large. It is highly probable that a random subfunction of h_n is a constant.

11.5 Hierarchy results

We have proved that the parity function has large complexity with respect to depth k circuits. This lower bound implies many others by the reducibility results of Ch. 10, § 3 . What happens if unbounded fan-in parity gates are added to the set of admissible gates ? Then ZMc is easy to compute, since ZMc $\leq_{cd}$ PAR . Razborov (86) proved that the complexity of the majority function in depth k $\{\wedge, \vee, \oplus\}$ - circuits of unbounded fan-in is exponential. This holds also for all functions f with MAJ $\leq_{cd}$ f . It is an open problem to decide which functions are difficult in depth k circuits consisting of threshold gates of unbounded fan-in.

Razborov's new and striking result belongs to the class of hierarchy results, since we increase the power of the basis in order to be able to solve more problems with polynomial circuits. We turn our thoughts to another type of hierarchy results.

DEFINITION 5.1 : Let $\Sigma_k(P)$ and $\Pi_k(P)$ be the class of all sequences $f = (f_n)$ of functions $f_n \in B_n$ which can be computed by polynomial Σ_k-circuits and Π_k-circuits resp. $\Sigma_k^m(P)$ and $\Pi_k^m(P)$ are defined in a similar way with respect to monotone depth k circuits.

Obviously for all k

$$\Sigma_k(P) \subseteq \Sigma_{k+1}(P) \subseteq \text{SIZE} - \text{DEPTH}(\text{poly}, \text{const}) , \tag{5.1}$$

$$\Pi_k(P) \subseteq \Pi_{k+1}(P) \subseteq \text{SIZE} - \text{DEPTH}(\text{poly}, \text{const}) , \tag{5.2}$$

$$\Sigma_k(P) \subseteq \Pi_{k+1}(P) , \ \Pi_k(P) \subseteq \Sigma_{k+1}(P) \qquad \text{and} \tag{5.3}$$

$$\Sigma_k^m(P) \subseteq \Sigma_k(P) \cap \{f = (f_n) \mid f_n \in M_n\} . \tag{5.4}$$

The problem is whether these inclusions are proper. The answer is always positive. This has been proved by Okol'nischkova (82) for (5.4) and by Sipser (83) for (5.1) - (5.3) . Sipser's proof is non constructive. One is interested in explicitly defined functions which separate the complexity classes. This was first done by Klawe, Paul, Pippenger and Yannakakis (84) for monotone depth k circuits and then by Yao (85) in the general case.

DEFINITION 5.2 : Let $n = m^k$. Let us denote the variables by $x_{i(1),\ldots,i(k)}$ $(1 \le i(j) \le m)$. Let $Q = \exists$, if k is odd, and $Q = \forall$, if k is even. Then $F_{k,n}(x) = 1$ iff the predicate

$$\exists\, i(1) \;\; \forall\, i(2) \;\; \exists\, i(3) \;\cdots\; Q\, i(k) \;:\; x_{i(1),\ldots,i(k)} = 1 \tag{5.5}$$

is satisfied.

In the preceding section we discussed already $F_{2,n} = h_n$.

THEOREM 5.1 : Let $F_k = (F_{k,n})$. Then $F_k \in \Sigma_k^m(P)$, but all depth $k-1$ circuits for F_k have exponential size.

Again Hastad (86) proved similar results with simpler proofs. We do not present the proofs which are based on the lower bound method for the parity function.

Such hierarchy results have further implications. Furst, Saxe and Sipser (84) have shown tight relations to classical complexity problems. The results of this chapter imply that the complexity classes Σ_k and Σ_{k+1} (see Definition 1.4, Ch. 9) as well as the complexity classes Σ_k and PSPACE can be separated by oracles.

EXERCISES

1. If a Σ_k-formula is defined on n variables and consists of b gates, then the number of wires can be bounded by $b(n+b)$ and the number of leaves can be bounded by bn .

2. Let f be computed by a Σ_k-circuit of size c. Estimate the Σ_k-formula size of f.

3. (Chandra, Stockmeyer and Vishkin (84)). Let $f_n \in B_n$ be computed by circuits of c_n binary gates and depth d_n. For $\varepsilon > 0$, f_n can be computed in depth $O(d_n/(\varepsilon \log\log n))$ circuits with $O(2^{(\log n)^\varepsilon} c_n)$ gates of unbounded fan-in.

4. Prove upper bounds on the depth k complexity of the majority function. Hint: Exercise 3.

5. (Chandra, Fortune and Lipton (83)). There is a constant k such that all $x_1 \vee \cdots \vee x_i$ ($1 \le i \le n$) can be computed by a Σ_k-circuit with $O(n)$ wires.

6. Design good Σ_k-circuits for $F_{k,n}$.

7. Prove Theorem 2.3 i for all n.

8. Prove Lemma 3.1.

9. Define l_{max} and v_{min} in the dual way to l_{min} and v_{max}. Then $l_{max}(f) + v_{min}(f) = n+1$ for $f \in S_n$.

10. $C_k(f) \ge H(n,k)$ for almost all $f \in S_n$.

11. Let $p(f)$ be the number of prime implicants and prime clauses of f. Prove for $f \in S_n$ upper and lower bounds on $p(f)$ depending on $l_{min}(f)$.

12. SYNCHRONOUS, PLANAR AND PROBABILISTIC CIRCUITS

In this chapter we investigate some more circuit models. Circuits should be synchronized and it should be possible to embed the circuits on chips of small area. In the last section we discuss efficient simulations of probabilistic circuits by deterministic circuits.

12.1 Synchronous circuits

DEFINITION 1.1 : A synchronous circuit is a circuit with the additional property that all paths from the inputs to some gate G have the same length.

In Ch. 11 we have considered only synchronous bounded-depth circuits, since this restriction does not change essentially the model of bounded-depth circuits. Let C_s and D_s be the complexity measures for synchronous circuits with binary gates. We remember that PCD(f) is the product complexity (see Def. 3.1, Ch. 7), namely the minimal $C(S) D(S)$ for all circuits S computing f .

THEOREM 1.1 : i) $D_s(f) = D(f)$ for all $f \in B_n$.

ii) $C_s(f) \le PCD(f) \le C(f)^2$ for all $f \in B_n$.

Proof : i) and the second inequality of ii) are obvious. Let S be a circuit for f where $C(S) D(S) = PCD(f)$. For each gate G , let $d(G)$ be the length of the longest path to G . Let G_1 and G_2 be the direct predecessors of G , w.l.o.g. $d(G_1) \ge d(G_2)$. Then $d(G_1) = d(G) - 1$. We add a path of $d(G) - d(G_2) - 1$ identity gates to the edge from G_2 to G . The resulting circuit S′ is synchronous, for each G in S we have added at most $D(S) - 1$ gates. Hence $C_s(f) \le C(S') \le C(S) D(S)$. □

If we had proved $\omega(n \log n)$ lower bounds on the synchronous circuit size of explicitly defined Boolean functions, we would obtain for the first time similar bounds for the product complexity. The best we can prove are lower bounds of size $n \log n$.

THEOREM 1.2 : The synchronous circuit size of the addition of two n-bit numbers is $\Theta(n \log n)$.

Proof : The upper bound is left as an exercise. Let $s = (s_n, \ldots, s_0)$ be the sum of $a = (a_{n-1}, \ldots, a_0)$ and $b = (b_{n-1}, \ldots, b_0)$. s_i depends essentially on $a_i, b_i, \ldots, a_0, b_0$. Hence the depth of $s_n, \ldots, s_{\lceil n/2 \rceil}$ is at least $\lceil \log n \rceil$. The vector $(s_n, \ldots, s_{\lceil n/2 \rceil})$ can take all 2^m values in $\{0,1\}^m$ where $m = \lfloor n/2 \rfloor + 1$. Let $G_1, \ldots, G_r$ be those gates whose depth equals $d \leq \lceil \log n \rceil$. These gates build a bottleneck for the information flow from the inputs to the outputs $s_n, \ldots, s_{\lceil n/2 \rceil}$. If $r < m$, we could not distinguish between 2^m situations. Hence $r \geq m \geq n/2$, and the circuit contains at least $(1/2) n \log n$ gates. $\square$

This result implies that the size of each synchronous adder is considerably larger than the size of an optimal asynchronous adder. For functions f with one output no example in which $C(f) = o(C_s(f))$ is known. One might think that the carry function c_n , the disjunction of all $u_i v_{i+1} \cdots v_n$ $(0 \leq i \leq n)$, is a candidate for such a gap (see also Ch. 7, § 4) . But $C_s(c_n)$ is linear (Wippersteg (82)). Harper (77) and Harper and Savage (79) generalized the bottleneck argument of Theorem 1.2 to functions with one output. The gates on level $l \leq D(f)$ contain all necessary information on f and all subfunctions of f . Therefore the number of gates on level l cannot be small if f has many subfunctions.

DEFINITION 1.2 : For $f \in B_n$ let $N(f,A)$ be the number of subfunctions g of f on the set of variables $A \subseteq X = \{x_1, \ldots, x_n\}$. Let

$$N'(f,a) = {\binom{n}{a}}^{-1} \sum_{A \subset X, |A|=a} \log N(f,A) \qquad (1.1)$$

be the average of all $\log N(f,a)$ for $|A| = a$.

If $N'(f,a)$ is large, f has many subfunctions. If also $D(f)$ is large, the number of gates on many levels cannot be very small. Hence $C_s(f)$ cannot be very small either.

LEMMA 1.1 : Let $f \in B_n$ depend essentially on the b variables in B. If $r = 2ab(n-a-b+1)^{-1} < 1$, then

$$N'(f,a) \le {\binom{n}{a}}^{-1} \sum_{0 \le k \le b} {\binom{b}{k}}{\binom{n-b}{a-k}} 2^k \le (1-r)^{-1}. \qquad (1.2)$$

Proof : The number of sets $A \subseteq X$ of size a where $|A \cap B| = k$ equals ${\binom{b}{k}}{\binom{n-b}{a-k}}$. The subfunctions of f on these sets A depend essentially at most on the variables in $A \cap B$. Hence $\log N(f,A) \le 2^k$ implying the first inequality.

Let $s(k) = {\binom{b}{k}}{\binom{n-b}{a-k}} 2^k$. Then

$$q(k) := \frac{s(k+1)}{s(k)} = 2 \frac{b-k}{k+1} \frac{a-k}{n-a-b+1+k} \qquad (1.3)$$

$$\le 2 \frac{ab}{n-a-b+1} = q(0).$$

Since $q(0) = r < 1$, we estimate the sum by a geometric series.

$${\binom{n}{a}}^{-1} \sum_{0 \le k \le b} s(k) \le {\binom{n}{a}}^{-1} {\binom{n-b}{a}} \sum_{0 \le k \le b} r^k \le (1-r)^{-1}. \qquad (1.4)$$

$\square$

THEOREM 1.3 : If $f \in B_n$ and

$$D(f) \ge d := \lfloor \log(\delta(n-a+1)/(2a+\delta)) \rfloor \qquad (1.5)$$

for some $0 < \delta < 1$ and $a \in \{1,...,n\}$, then

$$C_s(f) \geq (1 - \delta)\, d\, N'(f,a)\,. \tag{1.6}$$

Proof : It is sufficient to prove that each synchronous circuit for f contains on level $l \in \{1,...,d\}$ at least $(1-\delta)\, N'(f,a)$ gates. Let $G_1, \ldots, G_m$ be the gates on level l and let $g_1, \ldots, g_m$ be the functions computed at these gates. Since $f(x)$ is determined by $g(x) = (g_1(x),...,g_m(x))$,

$$N(f,A) \leq N(g,A) \leq \prod_{1 \leq i \leq m} N(g_i,A) \tag{1.7}$$

and by taking the logarithm and computing the average

$$N'(f,a) \leq \sum_{1 \leq i \leq m} N'(g_i,a)\,. \tag{1.8}$$

Since $D(g_i) \leq l \leq d$, g_i depends essentially on at most $2^d \leq \delta(n-a+1)/(2a+\delta) =: b$ variables. For this choice of b , the parameter r defined in Lemma 1.1 equals δ . Hence $r < 1$ and by Lemma 1.1

$$N'(g_i,a) \leq (1 - \delta)^{-1}\,. \tag{1.9}$$

By (1.8) and (1.9)

$$N'(f,a) \leq m\,(1-\delta)^{-1} \tag{1.10}$$

and the number of gates on each level $l \in \{1,...,d\}$ is at least $(1-\delta)\, N'(f,a)$.

$\square$

Obviously the lower bound of Theorem 1.3 cannot be larger than $O(n \log n)$. Harper and Savage (79) proved by this theorem an $\Omega(n \log n)$ lower bound on the synchronous circuit size of the determinant (see Def. 7.1, Ch. 3).

12.2 Planar and VLSI - circuits

The theory of VLSI-circuits is too extensive to be presented in a short section. For the technological aspects we refer to the monograph of Mead and Conway (80) and for the aspects of the complexity theory to Ullman (84). We discuss only the fundamental model of VLSI-circuits (Brent and Kung (80), Thompson (79) and (80)), some lower bound techniques and some relations to planar circuits.

DEFINITION 2.1 : A graph is planar if it can be embedded in the plane in such a way that no edges cross each other. A circuit is planar if its underlying graph is planar. $C_p^*(f)$ is the planar circuit size of f if the inputs can be copied. $C_p(f)$ is the planar circuit size of $f \in B_{n,m}$ if the inputs and outputs of the circuit occur once on an outer circle in the order $x_1,..,x_n, f_m(x), \ldots, f_1(x)$.

We talk about planar $*$-circuits and planar circuits shortly. Formulas can be simulated directly by planar $*$-circuits. For planar circuits we need planar circuits for crossings.

LEMMA 2.1 : Let $f(y,z) = (z,y)$. Then $C_p(f) = 3$.

Proof :

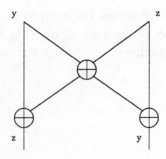

Fig. 2.1

THEOREM 2.1 : $C(f) \leq C_p^*(f) \leq C_p(f) \leq 6\, C(f)^2$ for all $f \in B_n$.

Proof : The first two inequalities follow from the definition. For the last inequality we consider an optimal circuit S for f . Let $c = C(f)$. We embed input x_i at $(i,0)$ and gate G_j at $(0,-j)$. An edge e from x_i or G_i to G_j is embedded by a continuous function $\alpha_e = (\alpha_{e,1}, \alpha_{e,2})$ where $\alpha_{e,k} : [0,1] \to \mathbb{R}$ for $k \in \{1,2\}$, $\alpha_e(0) = (i,0)$ or $\alpha_e(0) = (0,-i)$ resp. and $\alpha_e(1) = (0,-j)$. We define all embeddings such that $\alpha_{e,2}$ is decreasing. If the edges leading to $G_1, \ldots, G_{i-1}$ are embedded, then we embed the two edges leading to G_i in such a way that all previous edges are crossed once at most. Since the circuit contains $2c$ edges, the number of crossings is bounded by $\binom{2c}{2} = c(2c-1)$. We replace each crossing by the planar circuit of Lemma 2.1 . In addition to the c gates of S we obtain at most $3c(2c-1)$ new gates.

$\square$

The same ideas work for functions $f \in B_{n,m}$ with many outputs. If we ensure that the outputs are computed at the last gates, they can be embedded on an outer circle of the planar circuit. For this purpose it is sufficient to add at first $m-1$ new output gates.

The following claim is used implicitly in many papers.

CLAIM : If f is computed in a circuit with c gates and d crossings of edges, then $C_p(f) \le c + 3d$.

The Claim seems to be obvious. We only have to replace each crossing by the planar circuit of Lemma 2.1 . As was pointed out by McColl (pers. comm.) this is no proof of the Claim. It is not for sure that the produced circuit is cycle-free. Let us consider a circuit, like the sorting circuit in Ch. 3, § 4, whose width is linear at the top and at the bottom, but only logarithmic in the middle (see Fig. 2.2). Let G be the leftmost gate, and let G' be the rightmost gate at the bottom of the circuit. Let us assume that we like to compute at G'' , a new leftmost output, the conjunction of res_G and $res_{G'}$. We minimize the number of crossings, if we embed the edge from G' to G'' as described in Fig. 2.2 . The edges $e' = (v,w)$ and $e'' = (G',G'')$ lying on

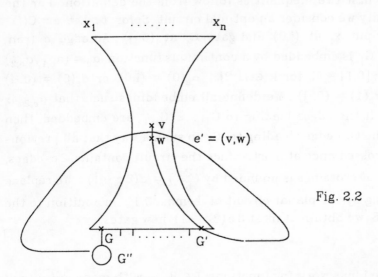

Fig. 2.2

the same path cross. If we replace this crossing by the planar circuit of Lemma 2.1 , we obtain a cycle starting at w leading via G' to the z -input of the "crossing-circuit", then leading to the y -output of the "crossing-circuit" and back to w .

This problem does not occur for our embedding in the proof of Theorem 2.1 . All edges are embedded top-down. If some edges e and e' lie on the same path, their embeddings do not cross.

Theorem 2.1 implies an upper bound of $O(2^{2n} n^{-2})$ on the planar circuit complexity of all $f \in B_n$. Savage (81) improved this simple bound.

THEOREM 2.2 : i) $C_p^*(f) \leq (2 + o(1)) \, 2^n \log^{-1} n$ for all $f \in B_n$.

ii) $C_p(f) \leq 5 \cdot 2^n$ for all $f \in B_n$.

Proof : i) follows from Theorem 3.2, Ch. 4, and the fact that $C_p^*(f) \leq L(f)$. For the proof of ii) we compute all minterms on $x_1, \ldots, x_n$. If all 2^{i-1} minterms on $x_1, \ldots, x_{i-1}$ are computed, we take a wire starting at x_i . This wire runs at the right hand side of the circuit to its bottom and crosses all 2^{i-1} wires for the monoms m on $x_1, \ldots, x_{i-1}$. Then we compute all mx_i and $m\bar{x}_i$. We have used 2^i gates for the computation of the minterms and $3 \cdot 2^{i-1}$ gates for the crossings, i.e. $5 \cdot 2^{i-1}$ gates in Step i . For all steps the number of gates is bounded by $5 \cdot 2^n$. f or $\neg f$ is the disjunction of at most 2^{n-1} minterms. If we do not compute unnecessary minterms in Step n , f or $\neg f$ can be computed with $5 \cdot 2^n$ gates. The Claim is proved, as $C_p(f) = C_p(\neg f)$. □

The upper bound on $C_p(f)$ has been improved by McColl and Paterson (84) to $(61/48) \, 2^n$. McColl (85 b) proved that for almost all $f \in B_n$ the planar circuit complexity is larger than $(1/8) \, 2^n - (1/4) \, n$. This implies that $C_p^*(f) = o(C_p(f))$ for almost all f $\in B_n$.

With information flow arguments and the Planar Separator Theorem due to Lipton and Tarjan ((79) and (80)), Savage (81) proved $\Omega(n^2)$-bounds on the planar circuit complexity of several n - output functions. Larger lower bounds imply (due to Theorem 2.1) nonlinear bounds on the circuit complexity of the same functions.

The investigation of planar circuits is motivated by the realization of circuits on chips. Today, chips consist of h levels, where h > 1 is a small constant. We introduce the fundamental VLSI - circuit model. For some constant $\lambda > 0$, gates occupy an area of λ^2 , and the minimum distance between two wires is λ . A VLSI - circuit of h levels on a rectangular chip of length $l \, \lambda$ and width $w \, \lambda$ consists of a three-dimensional array of cells of area λ^2. Each cell can contain a gate, a wire or a wire branching. Wires "cross" each other at different levels of the circuit. A crossing of wires occupies a constant amount of area. The area occupied by a wire depends on the embedding of the circuit.

VLSI - circuits are synchronized sequential machines. The output of gate G at the point of time t may be the input of gate G at the point of time t + 1 , i.e. the circuits are in general not cycle-free. For each input there is a definite input port, a cell at the border of the chip, where and a definite point of time when it is read. In particular, no input is copied. For each output there is a definite output port where and a definite point of time when it is produced.

The following complexity measures are of interest. $A = l \, w$, the area of the chip, T , the number of clock cycles from the first reading of an input to the production of the last output, and P , the period. VLSI - circuits may be pipelined, i.e. we may start the computation on the next input before the last computation is finished if this causes no problem. P is the minimum number of clock cycles between the starting of two independent computations. $D := n/P$ is called the data rate of the circuit.

We consider the addition of $a = (a_{n-1}, \ldots, a_0)$ and $b = (b_{n-1}, \ldots, b_0)$. At first we use only one synchronized fulladder of depth d . At the point of time $d \, t + 1$, a_t, b_t and the carry bit c_{t-1} are the inputs of the fulladder. Hence $A = \Theta(1)$, $T = d \, n$ and $P = T - d + 1$. If we connect n fulladders in series and input a_t, b_t and c_{t-1} to the $(t+1)$-st fulladder at the point of time $d \, t + 1$, then $A = \Theta(n)$, $T = d \, n$ and $P = 1$. It turned out that $A T^2$ is the appropriate complexity measure (see Ullman (84)).

Relations between (planar) circuits and VLSI - circuits have been studied by Savage ((81) and (82)). For each clock cycle a VSLI - circuit is a circuit with at most $h A$ gates. We simulate the T clock cycles by T copies of the circuit for one clock cycle. This implies the following theorem.

THEOREM 2.3 : If $f \in B_{n,m}$ is computed by a VLSI - circuit of area A in time T , then $C(f) \leq h A T$.

The T copies of the VLSI - circuits can be embedded in the plane in such a way that we obtain at most $O(A T \min(A,T)) = O(A T^2)$ crossings of wires.

What is the VLSI - complexity of almost all Boolean functions ? The planar circuit in the proof of Theorem 2.2 has some very long wires. Therefore a divide-and-conquer approach for the computation of all minterms is used. Using the H - pattern due to Mead and Rem (79), Kramer and van Leeuwen (82) designed VLSI - circuits for each $f \in B_n$ where $A = O(2^n)$, $T = O(n)$ and $P = O(1)$. This is optimal for almost all $f \in B_n$. The result on P is obviously optimal. The result on T cannot be improved, since $D(f)$ is a lower bound on the number of clock cycles of a VLSI - circuit. Finally there is only a finite number of types of cells. Hence the number of different circuits on a chip of area A is $O(c^A)$ for some constant c. In order to compute all $f \in B_n$, $A = \Omega(2^n)$ for almost all $f \in B_n$.

There is a large number of design methods for VLSI - circuits. So we make no attempt to present these methods. Most of the lower bounds are proved by information flow arguments. We present the method due to Vuillemin (83) leading to $\Omega(n^2)$-bounds on AT^2 for several fundamental functions.

DEFINITION 2.2 : Let Σ_n be the symmetric group of all permutations on $1,...,n$. A subgroup G of Σ_n is called transitive if for all $i,j \in \{1,...,n\}$ there is some $\pi \in G$ where $\pi(i) = j$.

DEFINITION 2.3 : $f \in B_{n+m,n}$ is called transitive of degree n if there is some transitive subgroup G of Σ_n such that for each $\pi \in G$ there is some $y^\pi = (y_1^\pi, \ldots, y_m^\pi)$ where

$$f(x_1, \ldots, x_n, y_1^\pi, \ldots, y_m^\pi) = (x_{\pi(1)}, \ldots, x_{\pi(n)}) . \tag{2.1}$$

If f is transitive of degree n, it must be possible to transport the i-th input bit $(1 \le i \le n)$ to the j-th output port. This data flow is possible in a short time only on a large area. Hence we hope to prove nontrivial lower bounds on AT^2 for functions f transitive of high degree. At first we present examples of transitive functions of high degree.

DEFINITION 2.4 : CYCSH : cyclic shifts. Input: $x_0, \ldots, x_{n-1}, y_1, \ldots, y_m$ where $m = \lceil \log n \rceil$. Let y be the binary number represented by $(y_1, \ldots, y_m)$. Output: $z_0, \ldots, z_{n-1}$ where $z_i = x_{(i+y) \bmod n}$.

MUL : Input: n-bit numbers x, y, M . Output: the n-bit number $z \equiv xy \bmod M$.

CYCCON : Cyclic convolution. Input: $2n$ k-bit numbers $x_0, y_0, \ldots, x_{n-1}, y_{n-1}$. Output: n k-bit numbers $z_0, \ldots, z_{n-1}$ where

$$z_l \equiv \sum_{i+j \,\equiv\, l \bmod n} x_i y_j \bmod M \quad \text{for} \quad M = 2^k - 1 . \tag{2.2}$$

MVP : matrix-vector-product. Input: n k-bit numbers $x_1, \ldots, x_n$ and an $n \times n$ - matrix $Y = (y_{ij})$ where $y_{ij} \in \{0,1\}$. Output: n k-bit numbers $z_1, \ldots, z_n$ where

$$z_l \equiv \sum_{1 \le i \le n} y_{li} x_i \bmod M \quad \text{for} \quad M = 2^k - 1 . \tag{2.3}$$

3-MATMUL : multiplication (mod M for $M = 2^k - 1$) of three $n \times n$ - matrices of k-bit numbers.

LEMMA 2.2 : CYCSH and MUL are transitive of degree n , CYCCON and MVP are transitive of degree nk , and 3-MATMUL is transitive of degree $n^2 k$.

Proof : CYCSH : Let G be the transitive group of all cyclic shifts π_j where $\pi_j(i) \equiv (i+j) \bmod n$. CYCSH computes this group by definition.

MUL : We fix $M = 2^n - 1$ and $y = 2^s$ for some $s \in \{0, \ldots, n-1\}$. Then $2^n \equiv 1 \bmod M$ and

$$z \equiv xy = \sum_{0 \le i \le n-1} x_i 2^{i+s} \tag{2.4}$$

$$\equiv \sum_{0 \le i \le n-s-1} x_i 2^{i+s} + \sum_{n-s \le i \le n-1} x_i 2^{i+s-n} \bmod M .$$

The binary representation of z is $(x_{n-s}, \ldots, x_{n-1}, x_0, \ldots, x_{n-s-1})$ and the cyclic shift π_{n-s} is computed. Hence MUL computes the transitive group of cyclic shifts.

CYCCON : Let G be the group of all permutations $\pi_{i,j}$ $(0 \leq i < n, 0 \leq j < k)$. For $\pi_{i,j}$ the cyclic shift π_i is applied to the vector $(x_0, \ldots, x_{n-1})$ and then the cyclic shift π_j is applied to each vector x_m $(0 \leq m \leq n-1)$. Obviously this group is transitive of degree nk. The permutation $\pi_{i,j}$ is computed if we set $y_i = 2^j$ and $y_m = 0$ for $m \neq i$. Then $z_l \equiv x_{l-i} y_i \bmod M$, if $l \geq i$, and $z_l \equiv x_{n+l-i} y_i \bmod M$, if $l < i$. In the same way as in the proof for MUL, it follows that z_l is equal to x_{l-i} or x_{n+l-i} shifted by j positions. Furthermore the x-vectors have been shifted by i positions.

MVP and **3-MATMUL** : These examples are left as exercises. $\qquad \square$

THEOREM 2.4 : If f is transitive of degree n, then $AT^2 = \Omega(n^2)$ for each VLSI - circuit computing f.

Proof : It is sufficient to prove $A = \Omega(D^2)$. Since $T \geq P = nD^{-1}$, it follows then that

$$AT^2 = \Omega(D^2(nD^{-1})^2) = \Omega(n^2). \tag{2.5}$$

The claim is trivial if $D = O(1)$. Otherwise let h be the number of levels, $l\lambda$ the length and $w\lambda$ the width of a VLSI - circuit for f. W.l.o.g. $w \geq l$. By a longitudinal cut we partition the chip into a right part R and a left part L. If this cut is shifted one cell, then the number of output ports in each part is increased or decreased by a constant summand. At most P outputs may leave the same output port. Since $P = nD^{-1}$ and $D = \omega(1)$, $P = o(n)$. Hence it is possible to cut the circuit in such a way that for R_{out} and L_{out}, the number of outputs leaving the circuit in the right part and left part resp.,

$$L_{out} \geq R_{out} = \Omega(n). \tag{2.6}$$

Since the cut is longitudinal, we have cut $c = O(l)$ wires. Since

$$A = lw \geq l^2 = \Omega(c^2), \tag{2.7}$$

it is sufficient to prove $c = \Omega(D)$.

Let G be the transitive group computed by f and let $\pi \in G$. If the control variables are fixed in such a way that we compute π, then x_i has to cross the cut if the input port for x_i is in another part of the circuit than the output port for the $\pi^{-1}(i)$-th output. In this case $k(i,\pi) := 1$, otherwise $k(i,\pi) := 0$.

Let G_{ij} be the set of all $\pi \in G$ where $\pi(i) = j$. It follows from elementary group theory (see e.g. Huppert (67)) that all G_{ij} are of the same size. Hence $\pi^{-1}(j) = i$ for $|G| n^{-1}$ permutations $\pi \in G$. It follows that

$$\sum_{\pi \in G} k(i,\pi) = |G| n^{-1} L_{out} , \qquad (2.8)$$

if the input port for x_i lies in R, and

$$\sum_{\pi \in G} k(i,\pi) = |G| n^{-1} R_{out} , \qquad (2.9)$$

if the input port for x_i lies in L. Therefore

$$\sum_{\pi \in G} \sum_{1 \le i \le n} k(i,\pi) \ge n |G| n^{-1} \min \{L_{out}, R_{out}\} = |G| R_{out} . \qquad (2.10)$$

In particular, there is some $\pi \in G$ such that for the computation of π at least R_{out} inputs have to cross the cut. Since only c wires connect the two parts of the circuit, P cannot be very small. If $P < R_{out} c^{-1}$, the data queue at the cut would be increasing. Hence, by (2.6),

$$n D^{-1} = P \ge R_{out} c^{-1} = \Omega(n c^{-1}) \qquad (2.11)$$

and $c = \Omega(D)$. $\qquad\qquad\qquad\qquad\qquad\qquad\qquad\qquad\qquad\qquad \square$

12.3 Probabilistic circuits

In Ch. 9, § 6, we have simulated probabilistic Turing machines efficiently by circuits. This approach leads e.g. to polynomial circuits for primality testing. Here we go the same way for probabilistic circuits.

DEFINITION 3.1 : The inputs of a probabilistic circuit S are the inputs $x_1, \ldots, x_n$ of a Boolean function and some further inputs $y_1, \ldots, y_m$ which take the values 0 and 1 independently with probability $1/2$. According to this probability distribution the output $S(x)$ of S on input x is a random variable.

DEFINITION 3.2: Let $A,B \subseteq \{0,1\}^n$ and $0 \le q < p \le 1$. The probabilistic circuit S separates A and B with respect to (p,q) if

$$\forall \ x \in A \ : \ \Pr(S(x)) = 1) \ge p \quad \text{and} \tag{3.1}$$

$$\forall \ x \in B \ : \ \Pr(S(x)) = 1) \le q. \tag{3.2}$$

Notation: (S,A,B,p,q).
S is an ε-computation of f , if $(S,f^{-1}(1),f^{-1}(0),(1/2)+\varepsilon,1/2)$ is satisfied.

The following considerations can be generalized to circuits with binary gates or formulas. But we concentrate our view upon bounded-depth circuits with gates of unbounded fan-in (see Ch. 11). We shall prove Theorem 2.2, Ch. 11, by designing probabilistic circuits for threshold functions.

At first, we present simple transformations and show how probabilistic circuits of very small error probability lead to deterministic circuits. Afterwards we investigate how we can reduce the error probability. On the one hand, we improve $\log^{-r} n$-computations to $\log^{-r+1} n$-computations, if $r \ge 2$, and on the other hand, we improve $\log^{-1} n$-computations to computations of very small error probability. All results are due to Ajtai and Ben-Or (84).

LEMMA 3.1 : Let (S,A,B,p,q) be satisfied for $A,B \subseteq \{0,1\}^n$ and $0 \le q < p \le 1$.

i) If $p \ge p' > q' \ge q$, (S,A,B,p',q') is satisfied.

ii) There is a probabilistic circuit S' such that $C(S') = C(S)$, $D(S') = D(S)$ and $(S',B,A,1-q,1-p)$ are satisfied.

iii) For each positive integer l there is a probabilistic circuit S_l such that $C(S_l) \le l \, C(S) + 1$, $D(S_l) \le D(S) + 1$ and (S_l,A,B,p^l,q^l)

are satisfied.

iv) If $q < 2^{-n}$ and $p > 1 - 2^{-n}$, there is a deterministic circuit S_d such that $C(S_d) \leq C(S)$, $D(S_d) \leq D(S)$ and $(S_d, A, B, 1, 0)$ are satisfied.

Proof : i) Obvious by definition.

ii) We negate the output of S and apply the deMorgan rules bottom-up.

iii) We use l copies of S with independent random inputs and combine the outputs by an $\wedge$-gate. $S_l(x) = 1$ iff all copies of S compute 1. The assertion follows since the copies of S have independent random inputs.

iv) Since $q < p$, A and B are disjoint. Let f be defined by $f^{-1}(1) = A$. For $x \in A \cup B$, the error probability, i.e. the probability that $S(x) \neq f(x)$, is smaller than 2^{-n}. Let $I(x)$ be the random variable where $I(x) = 1$ iff $S(x) \neq f(x)$ and $I(x) = 0$ otherwise. Then $E(I(x)) = \Pr(S(x) \neq f(x))$. Hence

$$E\left(\sum_{x \in A \cup B} I(x) \right) = \sum_{x \in A \cup B} E(I(x)) < 1 . \tag{3.3}$$

For fixed $y_1, \ldots, y_m$, I, the sum of all $I(x)$, is the number of errors on the inputs $x \in A \cup B$. I is always a nonnegative integer. By (3.3) $E(I) < 1$. Therefore there is a vector $(y_1^*, \ldots, y_m^*) \in \{0,1\}^m$ which leads to zero error. S_d is constructed by replacing the random inputs $y_1, \ldots, y_m$ by the constants $y_1^*, \ldots, y_m^*$. $\qquad \square$

No efficient algorithm for the computation of $y_1^*, \ldots, y_m^*$ is known. In general, the methods of this section lead only to non uniform circuits even if the given probabilistic circuits are uniform. The step in Lemma 3.1 iv is the only non uniform step.

LEMMA 3.2 : If $(S, A, B, (1 + \log^{-r} n)/2, 1/2)$ is satisfied for some $r \geq 2$, then there is a probabilistic circuit S' such that $C(S') =$

$O(n^2 (\log n) C(S))$, $D(S') \leq D(S) + 2$ and $(S',A,B,(1+\log^{-r+1} n)/2, 1/2)$ are satisfied.

Proof : W.l.o.g. $n = 2^k$. Then

$(S, A, B, (1 + \log^{-r} n)/2, 1/2)$ $\rightarrow$ L. 3.1 i & iii $\qquad$ (3.4)

$\qquad\qquad\qquad\qquad\qquad\qquad\qquad\qquad$ $l = 2 \log n$

$(S_1, A, B, n^{-2}(1 + 2\log^{-r+1} n), n^{-2})$ $\rightarrow$ L. 3.1 ii

$(S_2, B, A, 1 - n^{-2}, 1 - n^{-2}(1 + 2\log^{-r+1} n))$ $\rightarrow$ L. 3.1 i & iii

$\qquad\qquad\qquad\qquad\qquad\qquad\qquad\qquad$ $l = \lfloor (n^2 - 1) \ln 2 \rfloor$

$(S_3, B, A, 1/2, (1 - \log^{-r+1} n)/2)$ $\rightarrow$ L. 3.1 ii

$(S_4, A, B, (1 + \log^{-r+1} n)/2, 1/2)$.

Let $S' = S_4$. The assertions on $C(S')$ and $D(S')$ follow directly from Lemma 3.1 . The only crucial part is the computation of p^l and q^l if we apply L. 3.1 iii . This is easy for the first application of L. 3.1 iii , since

$$(1/2)^l = n^{-2} \qquad\qquad \text{and} \qquad\qquad (3.5)$$

$$(1 + \log^{-r} n)^{2 \log n} > 1 + (2 \log n)(\log^{-r} n) = 1 + 2 \log^{-r+1} n . \quad (3.6)$$

For the second application we assume that n is large. For small n we use the DNF for f defined by $f^{-1}(1) = B$. We set $\exp\{x\} = e^x$ and apply the well-known estimations

$$1 + x \leq e^x \qquad \text{and} \qquad \left(1 - \frac{x}{n}\right)^{n-1} \geq e^{-x} . \qquad (3.7)$$

Now $l = \lfloor (n^2 - 1) \ln 2 \rfloor \leq (n^2 - 1) \ln 2$ and $n^2 \ln 2 - l < 3 \ln 2$. Hence

$$(1 - n^{-2})^l \geq (1 - n^{-2})^{(n^2 - 1)\ln 2} \geq e^{-\ln 2} = 1/2 \qquad (3.8)$$

for the first term. For the second term

$$(1 - n^{-2}(1 + 2\log^{-r+1} n))^l \qquad\qquad\qquad\qquad (3.9)$$

$$< \exp\{-n^{-2}(n^2 - 3)(\ln 2)(1 + 2\log^{-r+1} n)\}$$

$$= (1/2)^{n^{-2}(n^2 - 3)} \exp\{-n^{-2}(n^2 - 3)(\ln 2) 2 \log^{-r+1} n\} .$$

We estimate the first factor by

$$(1/2)^{n^{-2}(n^2-3)} = (1/2) \, 8^{n^{-2}} = (1/2) \exp\{(\ln 8) \, n^{-2}\} \qquad (3.10)$$

$$= (1/2)(1 + O(n^{-2})).$$

For the second factor $2n^{-2}(n^2-3)(\ln 2) > 1.3$ for large n. If $x \geq 0$

$$\exp\{-x\} = \sum_{0 \leq i < \infty} \frac{(-x)^i}{i!} \leq 1 - x\left(1 - \frac{x}{2} - \frac{x^3}{4!} - \frac{x^5}{6!} - \cdots\right). \qquad (3.11)$$

Hence for large n

$$\exp\{-n^{-2}(n^2-3)(\ln 2) \, 2 \log^{-r+1} n\} < 1 - 1.2 \log^{-r+1} n. \qquad (3.12)$$

By (3.9), (3.10) and (3.12)

$$(1 - n^{-2}(1 + 2\log^{-r+1} n))^{\ell} < (1/2)(1 + O(n^{-2}))(1 - 1.2\log^{-r+1} n) \qquad (3.13)$$

$$< (1/2)(1 - \log^{-r+1} n) \quad \text{for large } n.$$

$$\square$$

LEMMA 3.3 : If $(S, A, B, (1 + \log^{-1} n)/2, 1/2)$ is satisfied, then there is a deterministic circuit S' such that $C(S') = O(n^6 (\log^2 n) C(S))$, $D(S') \leq D(S) + 4$ and $(S', A, B, 1, 0)$ are satisfied.

Proof : We leave the details to the reader and present only a sketch of the proof.

$(S, A, B, (1 + \log^{-1} n)/2, 1/2)$	$\rightarrow$	L. 3.1 i & iii	$\ell = 2 \log n$ (3.14)
$(S_1, A, B, 2n^{-2}, n^{-2})$	$\rightarrow$	L. 3.1 ii	
$(S_2, B, A, 1 - n^{-2}, 1 - 2n^{-2})$	$\rightarrow$	L. 3.1 i & iii	$\ell = 2n^2 \ln n$
$(S_3, B, A, n^{-2}, n^{-4})$	$\rightarrow$	L. 3.1 ii	
$(S_4, A, B, 1 - n^{-4}, 1 - n^{-2})$	$\rightarrow$	L. 3.1 i & iii	$\ell = n^3$
$(S_5, A, B, 1 - 2n^{-1}, e^{-n})$	$\rightarrow$	L. 3.1 ii	
$(S_6, B, A, 1 - e^{-n}, 2n^{-1})$	$\rightarrow$	L. 3.1 i & iii	$\ell = n$
$(S_7, B, A, 1 - 2ne^{-n}, (2n^{-1})^n)$	$\rightarrow$	L. 3.1 ii	

$(S_8, A, B, 1-(2n^{-1})^n, 2ne^{-n}) \quad \rightarrow \quad$ L. 3.1 iv

$(S', A, B, 1, 0)$ ◻

We combine Lemma 3.2 with Lemma 3.3 .

THEOREM 3.1 : If S_n is for some $r > 0$ a sequence of $\log^{-r} n$ - computations of $f_n \in B_n$, if $C(S_n)$ is bounded by a polynomial and if $D(S_n)$ is bounded by a constant, then $f = (f_n) \in$ SIZE - DEPTH(poly,const) .

We are now ready to prove Theorem 2.2 , Ch. 11 .

THEOREM 3.2 : If $k(n) = O(\log^r n)$ for some fixed r , then $f = (T^n_{k(n)}) \in$ SIZE - DEPTH(poly,const) .

Proof : W.l.o.g. $k = k(n) \leq \log^r n$ and $n = 2^l$. We design a probabilistic circuit S of size $n\lceil n/k\rceil + 1$ and depth 2 . We use $\lceil n/k\rceil$ blocks of random inputs, the block size is $l = \log n$. There exist n minterms $m^j_1, \ldots, m^j_n$ on the j-th block of random inputs. We compute $x_i \wedge m^j_i$ for all $1 \leq i \leq n$ and $1 \leq j \leq \lceil n/k\rceil$. The disjunction of all $x_i \wedge m^j_i$ for fixed j is a random x_r (according to the uniform distribution). We compute the disjunction of all $x_i \wedge m^j_i$, the disjunction of $\lceil n/k\rceil$ random x - inputs.

Let $p_k(s)$ be the probability that $S(x) = 1$ if the input contains s ones. Since $1 - \frac{s}{n}$ is the probability that a random x - input equals 0 , we conclude

$$p_k(s) = 1 - (1 - \frac{s}{n})^{\lceil n/k\rceil} \approx 1 - e^{-s/k} . \tag{3.15}$$

Obviously $s \rightarrow p_k(s)$ is increasing. Thus the circuit S satisfies $(S, (T^n_k)^{-1}(1), (T^n_k)^{-1}(0), p_k(k), p_k(k-1))$. For small k or n we use the DNF for T^n_k . Otherwise it is easy to prove that

$$p_k(k) \geq p_k(k-1)(1 + k^{-2}) \quad \text{and} \quad 0.5 \leq p_k(k-1) \leq 0.9 . \tag{3.16}$$

If $p_k(k-1) = 0.5$, we could apply directly Theorem 3.1 , since

$k^{-2} \geq \log^{-2r} n$. One possible way to deal with $p_k(k-1) > 0.5$ is described in Exercise 13.

□

We have seen that $\log^{-r} n$ - computations can be simulated efficiently by deterministic computations. What about $n^{-\varepsilon}$ - computations for some $\varepsilon > 0$? If they had been simulated efficiently, we would obtain by the construction in Theorem 3.2 and Theorem 3.1 circuits of polynomial size and constant depth for $T_{k(n)}^n$ and $k(n) = n^\varepsilon$. This would be a contradiction to Corollary 4.1 , Ch. 11 . Hence the simulation of Ajtai and Ben-Or is optimal if we allow a polynomial increase of the circuit size and a constant number of additional logical levels.

Although the majority function is not in SIZE - DEPTH(poly,const), it can be proved by the above methods that some approximation of the majority function is contained in this class (Stockmeyer (83), Ajtai and Ben-Or (84)).

THEOREM 3.3 : There is for constant r a sequence of circuits S_n of polynomial size and constant depth which compute functions $f_n \in B_n$ such that

$$f_n(x) = 1 \quad \text{if} \quad x_1 + \cdots + x_n \geq (n/2)(1 + \log^{-r} n) \quad \text{and} \quad (3.17)$$

$$f_n(x) = 0 \quad \text{if} \quad x_1 + \cdots + x_n < n/2 . \quad (3.18)$$

We have pointed out that the last step in our simulation of probabilistic circuits by deterministic circuits, the application of Lemma 3.1 iv , is non uniform. Hence it is possible that functions $f_n \in B_n$ can be computed by uniform probabilistic circuits of polynomial size and small error probability, but cannot be computed by uniform deterministic circuits of polynomial size. This leads to the definition of the complexity classes RNC and RNC_k (Cook (83), for the definition of NC and NC_k see Def. 8.2, Ch. 9). Here we consider circuits with binary gates.

DEFINITION 3.3 : RNC (RNC_k) is the class of languages L such that for f_n defined by $f_n^{-1}(1) = L \cap \{0,1\}^n$ there are U_{BC}-uniform probabilistic circuits of polynomial size and polylog depth (depth $O(\log^k n)$) satisfying

$$\Pr (S_n(x) = f_n(x) \mid x \in f_n^{-1}(a)) \geq 3/4 \quad \text{for} \quad a \in \{0,1\} . \tag{3.19}$$

We are content with this definition and the remark that many RNC_k algorithms are known.

EXERCISES

1. Prove the upper bound in Theorem 1.2 .

2. Each synchronous circuit for the addition of an n-bit number and a 1-bit number has size $\Omega(n \log n)$.

3. Estimate $C_s(f)$ for all $f \in B_n$ by synchronizing Lupanov's circuit (Ch. 4, § 2).

4. Each synchronous circuit for the computation of the pseudo complements of a k-slice (Ch. 6, § 13) contains at least $\lceil \log (n-1) \rceil \lceil \log (\binom{n}{k} + 2) \rceil$ gates.

5. The complete graph K_m is planar iff $m \leq 4$.

6. The complete bipartite graph $K_{3,3}$ is not planar.

7. (McColl (81)). The following functions are not computable in monotone, planar circuits.
   a) $f_1(x,y) = (y,x)$.

b) $f_2(x,y) = (xy,x)$.

c) $f_3(x,y) = (xy, x \lor y)$.

8. (McColl (85 a)). T_3^5 (and also T_k^n for $2 < k < n-1$) is not computable in a monotone, planar circuit.

9. (McColl (85 a)). T_2^n is computable in monotone, planar circuits.

10. Complete the proof of Lemma 2.2 for MVP and 3-MATMUL.

11. Prove results similar to Lemma 3.1 - 3.3 and Theorem 3.1 for probabilistic circuits with binary gates.

12. Let $0 \le q_i < p_i \le 1$ and let (S_i, A, B, p_i, q_i) be satisfied for $1 \le i \le m$. In $S^\lor$ and $S^\land$ we combine the outputs of all S_i by an $\lor$-gate and $\land$-gate resp. Compute $p_\lor, q_\lor, p_\land, q_\land$ such that $(S^\lor, A, B, p_\lor, q_\lor)$ and $(S^\land, A, B, p_\land, q_\land)$ are satisfied.

13. Let (S,A,B,p,q) be satisfied and $r \in \{0,\dots, 2^k - 1\}$. Then there is a circuit S' such that $C(S') \le C(S) + O(2^k)$, $D(S') \le D(S) + O(1)$ and $(S', A, B, (r+p)2^{-k}, (r+q)2^{-k})$ are satisfied.

14. Compare the construction of bounded-depth circuits for the threshold functions with the construction of monotone formulas for the majority function in Ch. 8, § 3 .

13. PRAMs AND WRAMs: PARALLEL RANDOM ACCESS MACHINES

13.1 Introduction

Circuits represent a hardware model of parallel computations but not a model of parallel computers. A parallel computer consists of many computers (so-called processors) which work together. Since several years vector computers are used, these are based on the SIMD concept (single-instruction-multiple-data-stream). At each single time step one can apply a definite type of operation (e.g. addition) to vectors and not only to numbers. This concept is appropriate for numerical applications (simulations in physics and geological explorations, meteorological computations for an improved weather-forecast, etc.), but for several combinatorial algorithms it is too restrictive.

Nowadays, one is designing MIMD computers (multiple-instruction-multiple-data-stream) that consist of up to 1024 processors. Each processor has its own program. The processors may work together by communicating with each other. If each pair of processors was connected by a communication channel, we would have $\binom{1024}{2} = 523\,776$ connections. Hence this approach is impractical. The communication graph (vertices are processors, edges are communication channels) should be a graph of small degree. There are communication graphs like for instance the cube-connected-cycle and the shuffle-exchange-network which have constant degree (for an arbitrary number of processors) and which allow fast communication between arbitrary processors.

It is difficult to design algorithms for these realistic parallel computers, since one always has to pay attention to the "distance" of processors which like to communicate. Hence one considers parallel computers of a simpler communication structure. Processors are not connected via communication channels, instead of that all processors have random access to a shared memory. Processor j obtains information from processor i by reading an information written by processor i . These parallel random access machines represent no realistic model, but on the one hand it is convenient to design algorithms in this model, and, on the other hand, efficient algorithms are known for the simulation of these algorithms on those realistic parallel computers discussed above (see e.g. Mehlhorn and Vishkin (84) or Alt, Hagerup, Mehlhorn and Preparata (86)). Hence we investigate only parallel random access machines, nowadays the standard model of parallel computers at least for the purposes of the complexity theory.

DEFINITION 1.1 : A parallel random access machine (PRAM) for n Boolean inputs consists of processors P_i $(1 \leq i \leq p(n))$, a read-only input tape of n cells $M_1, \ldots, M_n$ containing the inputs $x_1, \ldots, x_n$ and a shared memory of cells M_j $(n < j \leq n + c(n))$, all containing at first zeros. P_i starts in the state $q(i,0)$. At time step t , depending on its state $q(i,t)$, P_i reads the contents of some cell M_j of the shared memory, then, depending on $q(i,t)$ and the contents of M_j , it assumes a new state $q(i,t+1)$, and, depending on $q(i,t+1)$, it writes some information into some cell of the shared memory. The PRAM computes $f_n \in B_n$ in time $T(n)$ if the cell M_{n+1} of the shared memory contains on input $x = (x_1, \ldots, x_n)$ at time step $T(n)$ the output $f_n(x)$.

We distinguish between some models of PRAMs with different rules for solving read and write conflicts.

- An EREW PRAM (exclusive read, exclusive write) works correctly only if at any time step and for any cell at most one processor reads the contents of this cell and at most one processor writes into this cell.

- A CREW PRAM (concurrent read, exclusive write) or shortly PRAM allows that many processors read the contents of the same cell at the same time step, but it works correctly only if at any time step and for any cell at most one processor writes into this cell.

- A CRCW PRAM (concurrent read, concurrent write) or shortly WRAM solves write conflicts. If more than one processor tries to write at time step t into cell M_j , then the processor with the smallest number wins. This processor writes its information into M_j , all other competitors fail to write.

- A WRAM satisfies the common write rule (CO WRAM) if whenever several processors are trying to write into a single cell at the same time step, the values that they try to write are the same.

Our PRAM models are non uniform. Nevertheless, we shall design uniform algorithms. For efficient algorithms the computation time $T(n)$, the number of processors $p(n)$ and the communication width $c(n)$ should be simultaneously small. Moreover, the computation power of the single processors should be restricted realistically. For lower bounds we choose the model as general as possible.

In § 2 we compare the different models and obtain efficient algorithms via simulations. All functions with efficient circuits of bounded-depth can be computed efficiently by CO WRAMs . The reverse holds for WRAMs of restricted computation power. This result, which is proved in § 3 , enables us to generalize lower bounds proved in the previous chapters. In § 4 - § 6 we discuss lower bound methods. The lower bounds depend on combinatorial measures which we investigate in § 7 .

13.2 Upper bounds by simulations

THEOREM 2.1 : i) Each function $f_n \in B_n$ can be computed in time $\lceil \log n \rceil + 1$ by an EREW PRAM with n powerful processors and communication width n .

ii) Each $f_n \in B_n$ can be computed in time $\lceil \log n \rceil + 2$ by a PRAM with $n\,2^n$ realistic processors and communication width $n\,2^n$.

iii) Each $f_n \in B_n$ can be computed in time 2 by a CO WRAM with $n\,2^n$ realistic processors and communication width 2^n .

Proof : i) At time step 0 processor P_i reads the i-th input x_i , stores this value in its internal memory and writes it into Y_i , i.e. the i-th cell M_{n+i} of the shared memory. At time step t , processor P_i reads the contents of Y_j where $j = i + 2^{t-1}$. If $j > n$, P_i does nothing. If $j \leq n$, P_i concatenates the contents of its internal memory and the contents of Y_j . The result is stored in its internal memory and written into Y_i . It is easy to prove that P_i knows after time step t the vector $(x_i, \ldots, x_j)$ where $j = \min\{n, i + 2^t - 1\}$. After time step $\lceil \log n \rceil$, P_1 knows $(x_1, \ldots, x_n)$. P_1 evaluates $f(x_1, \ldots, x_n)$ and writes the result into the output cell Y_1 .

ii) We use the DNF of f . Each minterm can be evaluated in time $\lceil \log n \rceil + 1$ by n realistic processors and communication width n . A minterm is a conjunction of n literals $x_k^{a(k)}$. We use a binary tree as in the proof of i) , but the conjunction is a simple function. Instead of $(x_i, \ldots, x_j)$ we only store $x_i^{a(i)} \wedge \cdots \wedge x_j^{a(j)}$. All minterms can be evaluated in parallel by a PRAM . Before the last step there is for each $a \in f_n^{-1}(1)$ a processor $P(a)$ knowing $m_a(x)$. W.l.o.g. Y_1 contains 0 . $P(a)$ writes 1 into Y_1 iff $m_a(x) = 1$. There is no write conflict, since at most one minterm computes 1 .

iii) The disjunction of n literals can be computed by a CO WRAM consisting of n realistic processors in one time step and communication width 1 . Each processor reads one input and writes 1 into the output cell iff its literal equals 1 . We use the CNF of f and evaluate all maxterms in parallel. Moreover we write 1 into Y_1 . In the second step a processor $P(a)$ for $a \in f^{-1}(0)$ reads $s_a(x)$ and writes 0 into Y_1 iff $s_a(x) = 0$.

$\square$

These simple algorithms are not efficient algorithms, since either the number of processors grows exponentially or the processors are too powerful. We have seen that it is possible to simulate the DNF or CNF for f. This idea can be extended to circuits (van Leeuwen (83), Stockmeyer and Vishkin (84)).

THEOREM 2.2 : i) Let S be a circuit of binary gates computing $f_n \in B_n$ with s gates in depth d. Then there is a PRAM computing f_n in time $O(d)$ with $p = \lceil s/d \rceil$ realistic processors and communication width s.

ii) Let S be a circuit of unbounded fan-in gates computing $f_n \in B_n$ with s gates and e edges in depth d. Then there is a CO WRAM computing f_n in time $d+1$ with e realistic processors and communication width s.

Proof : i) The depth of a gate is the length of a longest path from an input to this gate. Let N_i be the number of gates of depth i in S. These gates are partitioned to p blocks of at most $\lceil N_i/p \rceil$ gates each. We simulate the circuit level by level. A processor may simulate a binary gate in two steps of time. Hence the i-th level is simulated in $2\lceil N_i/p \rceil$ steps by p processors. The result of each gate is written into a definite cell of the shared memory. The time for this simulation is estimated by

$$\sum_{1 \leq i \leq d} 2\lceil N_i/p \rceil \leq 2d + 2(N_1 + \cdots + N_d)/p \tag{2.1}$$

$$\leq 2d + 2s(d/s) = 4d.$$

ii) There is for each gate of the circuit a cell in the shared memory and for each edge of the circuit a processor. In time step 0 the contents of the cells representing $\wedge$-gates are replaced by ones. In time step i ($1 \leq i \leq d$) all gates on the i-th level are simulated. The processors for the edges leading to these gates read the inputs of the edges. If the level is an $\wedge$-level a processor writes 0 into the corresponding cell for the gate iff the processor has read 0. $\vee$-gates are simulated similarly. □

This theorem leads to efficient PRAM algorithms. We obtain for many fundamental functions $O(\log n)$ -time algorithms on PRAMs with a polynomial number of realistic processors and polynomial communication width (see Ch. 3). By the results of Ch. 10, § 3, and Ch. 11 we obtain for certain fundamental problems $O(1)$ -time algorithms on CO WRAMs with a polynomial number of realistic processors and polynomial communication width. In § 4 we prove $\Omega(\log n)$-bounds on the PRAM complexity of many fundamental functions even if the number of processors, the power of processors and the communication width are unlimited. These results imply that realistic CO WRAMs may be faster by a factor of $\Theta(\log n)$ than PRAMs of unlimited resources. This speed up is optimal because of the following results.

THEOREM 2.3 : A WRAM of p processors, communication width c and time complexity t may be simulated by an EREW PRAM with $(c+n)p$ processors, communication width $c+(c+n)p$ and time complexity $t(4 + 2\lceil \log p \rceil)$.

Proof : The simulation is step-by-step. The c cells of the shared memory are simulated directly by c cells. Furthermore each of the n input cells and the c cells of the shared memory is simulated once for each processor. We assume that we have simulated i computation steps. Then the information of each of the $c+n$ cells of the WRAM is copied and written into p definite cells. This can be done for each cell by p processors in time $\lceil \log p \rceil + 1$ without read conflicts. If the information is copied r times, r processors may read the information and may write it into r other cells and so on. Afterwards we simulate one computation step. Each processor can read the information in its own cells, i.e. without read conflict. Each processor simulates the internal computation and marks that of its cells representing the cell in which it tries to write. For each cell of the shared memory p processors are sufficient to compute in time

⌈log p⌉ + 1 the number of the processor who wins the write conflict according to the rules. This is simply the computation of the minimum of at most p numbers. Each processor is informed whether it has won the write conflict. Afterwards all winners write their information into the corresponding cells which causes no write conflict. The whole computation step has been simulated in $4 + 2\lceil \log p \rceil$ steps.

□

WRAMs can be simulated rather efficiently by simple EREW PRAMs. What is the difference between WRAMs and CO WRAMs ? This question has been answered by Kucera (82).

THEOREM 2.4 : A WRAM of p processors, communication width c and time complexity t may be simulated by a CO WRAM of $\binom{p}{2}$ processors, communication width $c + p$ and time complexity $4t$.

Proof : The simulation is step-by-step. We use processors P_j ($1 \leq j \leq p$) for the simulation and P_{ij} ($1 \leq i < j \leq p$) for some extra work. Since P_j and P_{ij} never work simultaneously $\binom{p}{2}$ processors are sufficient if $p \geq 3$. The case $p = 2$ is obvious. Each computation step is simulated in 4 steps. At first the processors P_j ($1 \leq j \leq n$) simulate the reading and the internal computations of the WRAM , and P_j writes into the j-th extra cell of the shared memory the number of that cell into which P_j likes to write. In the following two steps P_{ij} decides whether P_j loses a write conflict against P_i . P_{ij} writes a mark # into the j-th extra cell iff P_j has lost a write conflict against P_i . This causes no conflict for CO WRAMs . All processors writing at this time step write the same letter, namely the mark # . In the fourth step P_j reads whether it has lost a write conflict. Only if P_j has not lost a write conflict, P_j simulates the write phase of the WRAM . This causes no write conflict at all.

□

All these simulations lead to upper bounds on the time complexity of parallel computers. For several fundamental functions we obtain (nearly) optimal algorithms. For many other functions new ideas for the design of efficient parallel algorithms are needed. Because we did not present efficient algorithms for non fundamental functions, we shall not discuss efficient parallel algorithms for such functions.

13.3 Lower bounds by simulations

Stockmeyer and Vishkin (84) have proved that restricted WRAMs may be simulated efficiently by circuits of unbounded fan-in gates. We restrict the computation power of the single processors in such a way that each single step may be simulated by a polynomial circuit of constant depth. This is the only restriction we actually need.

Each processor p follows some program of $l(p)$ lines. Its current state $l \in \{1,\dots,l(p)\}$ describes the actual line of the program. The initial state is $l = 1$. The processor has a local random access memory. We give a list of legitimate operations.

- $M(r) = c$ (reading of constants). The constant c is written into the r-th cell of the local memory.

- $M(r) = M(i)$ (direct reading). The contents of the i-th cell of the local memory is written into the r-th cell of the local memory.

- $M(r) = M(i) \circ M(j)$ (computation step). Let x and y be the contents of the i-th and j-th cell of the local memory resp. Then $z = x \circ y$ is written into the r-th cell of the local memory. The function $\circ$ is one of a finite list of operations. We allow only operations which can be computed by polynomial circuits of constant depth and where the length $|z|$ of the output z is bounded by $\max \{|x| + 1, |y| + 1, n\}$. By the results of Ch. 11, § 2, the list may include addition, subtraction, comparison and also the multiplication of numbers of length $O(\log n)$.

- $M(r) = *M(i) \{l/c\}$ (indirect reading). Let I be the contents of the i-th cell of the local memory. The contents of the l-th cell of the local/common (or shared) memory is written into the r-th cell of the local memory.

- $*M(r) = M(i) \{l/c\}$ (indirect writing). The contents of the i-th cell of the local memory is written into the j-th cell of the local/common memory, j is the contents of the r-th cell of the local memory.

- GO TO l if $M(i) </= M(j)$ (if-tests). It is tested whether the contents of the i-th cell of the local memory is smaller than / equal to the contents of the j-th cell of the local memory. In the positive case we proceed to line l of the program. Otherwise we proceed (as usual) to the next line of the program.

- STOP (end of the program).

The so-restricted WRAMs are called RES WRAMs . The program size is the number of bits in the program.

THEOREM 3.1 : Let $f_n \in B_m$ where $m = n^2$. Let W_n be a sequence of RES WRAMs computing f_n , if the input is given in n blocks of n bits each, with $p(n)$ processors of program size $s(n)$, unlimited communication width and time complexity $t(n)$.
Then for some polynomial Q , there are circuits S_n computing f_n with $Q(n,p(n),s(n),t(n))$ unbounded fan-in gates in depth $O(t(n))$.

Proof : Although the communication width is unlimited, only a limited number of cells is available. The numbers of the input have length n and the length of the numbers in the programs is bounded by $s(n)$. RES WRAMs cannot produce large numbers in short time. The length of all numbers used by W_n is bounded by

$$L(n) = \max\{n, s(n)\} + t(n) . \tag{3.1}$$

We simulate W_n step-by-step. The difficulty is to find the information in the memories, since by numbers of length $L(n)$ one may address $2^{L(n)}$ different cells. These are $2^{L(n)}$ possible addresses. For each definite input each processor may change the contents of at most $t(n)$ cells. Therefore the circuits use an internal representation of the memories of W_n. Everything written at time step k gets the internal address k. If this information is deleted at a later time step, the information is marked as invalid. The index l refers to the local memory and index c to the common memory. For all $1 \le p \le p(n)$, $1 \le k \le t(n)$, $k \le t \le t(n)$ we shall define $a_l(p,k)$, $v_l(p,k)$ and $w_l(p,k,t)$. $a_l(p,k)$ is a number of length $L(n)$ and indicates the address of that cell of the local memory into which the p-th processor has written at time step k. $v_l(p,k)$ is also a number of length $L(n)$ and equals the number which the p-th processor has written at time step k. The bit $w_l(p,k,t)$ indicates whether at time step t the information the p-th processor has written into the local memory at time step k is still valid ($w_l(p,k,t) = 1$) or has been deleted ($w_l(p,k,t) = 0$). In the same way we define $a_c(p,k)$, $v_c(p,k)$ and $w_c(p,k,t)$. At the beginning all local cells contain zeros, only the first n cells of the common memory contain the input. Hence we define $a_c(i,0) = i$, $v_c(i,0) = x_i$ and $w_c(i,0,0) = 1$ for $1 \le i \le n$. Here we assume, like we do in the whole proof, that numbers are padded with zeros if they have not the necessary length. All other parameters are equal to 0 for $t = 0$.

Let $l(p)$ be the number of lines in the program of the p-th processor. Let $i(p,l)$, $j(p,l)$, $c(p,l)$ and $r(p,l)$ be the parameters in the l-th line of the p-th program. Here and in the following we assume that non existing parameters are replaced by zeros and that the empty disjunction is zero. Let $ic(p,l,t) = 1$ iff during the $(t+1)$-st computation step processor p is in line l of its program. Obviously $ic(p,l,0) = 1$ iff $l = 1$.

Let us assume that t computation steps of W_n have been simulated correctly. This is satisfied at the beginning for $t = 0$. We describe the simulation of the $(t+1)$-st computation step. Let $EQ(a,b) = 1$ iff $a = b$, let

$$a \wedge (b_1, \ldots, b_m) = (a \wedge b_1, \ldots, a \wedge b_m) \quad \text{and} \tag{3.2}$$

$$(a_1, \ldots, a_m) \vee (b_1, \ldots, b_m) = (a_1 \vee b_1, \ldots, a_m \vee b_m) \qquad (3.3)$$

for arbitrary m. We simulate each line of each program. Let $R(p,l,t)$ be the result produced by the p-th processor during the $(t+1)$-st computation step, if the processor is in line l of the program. The result is the information which will be written into some cell or the result of an if-test. Let $A(p,l,t)$ be the address of the cell into which $R(p,l,t)$ will be written. Let $I(p,l,t)$ be the contents of the $i(p,l)$-th cell of the local memory before the $(t+1)$-st computation step. Then

$$I(p,l,t) = \bigvee_{1 \le k \le t} [EQ(i(p,l), a_l(p,k)) \wedge w_l(p,k,t) \wedge v_l(p,k)]. \qquad (3.4)$$

The equality test ensures that we are looking for information at the correct address only, and the validity bit w_l ensures that we consider only valid information. If we consider a computation step or an if-test, we compute $J(p,l,t)$ in the same way. $R(p,l,t)$ equals $c(p,l)$ (reading of constants), or $I(p,l,t) \circ J(p,l,t)$ (computation step), or $I(p,l,t)$ (indirect writing), or 1 or 0 if $I(p,l,t) </= J(p,l,t)$ or $I(p,l,t) \ge / \ne J(p,l,t)$ resp. (if-test). For steps of indirect reading $R(p,l,t)$ equals the contents of the cell $I(P,l,t)$ of the local or common memory. Hence $R(p,l,t)$ can be computed by (3.4) if we replace $i(p,l)$ by $I(p,l,t)$. For the common memory we replace $a_l(p,k)$, $v_l(p,k)$, and $w_l(p,k,t)$ by $a_c(p',k)$, $v_c(p',k)$ and $w_c(p',k,t)$ resp. and compute the disjunction over all p', since each processor may have written into the common memory. In every case all $R(p,l,t)$ are computed in polynomial size and constant depth. Only for indirect writing, $A(p,l,t)$ is not a constant. Then $A(p,l,t)$ is computed in the same way as $R(p,l,t)$. Finally

$$R(p,t) = \bigvee_{1 \le l \le l(p)} ic(p,l,t) \wedge R(p,l,t) \quad \text{and} \qquad (3.5)$$

$$A(p,t) = \bigvee_{1 \le l \le l(p)} ic(p,l,t) \wedge A(p,l,t) \qquad (3.6)$$

are the actual results and addresses.

This information is used for an updating of our parameters. The instruction counter $ic(p,l,t+1)$ equals 1 iff $ic(p,l-1,t) = 1$ and line $l-1$ does not contain an if-test or $ic(p,l',t) = 1$, line l' contains an if-test and the result of this test leads us to line l. Hence all

$ic(p,l,t+1)$ are computed in polynomial size and constant depth.

Let $\lambda(p,t) = 1$ iff the p-th processor writes into its local memory during the $(t+1)$-st computation step. Let $\gamma(p,t) = 1$ iff the p-th processor tries to write into the common memory during the $(t+1)$-st computation step. $\lambda(p,t)$ as well as $\gamma(p,t)$ is the disjunction of some $ic(p,l,t)$. Now the local memories are updated. Let $a_l(p,t+1) = A(p,t)$, $v_l(p,t+1) = R(p,t)$ and $w_l(p,t+1,t+1) = \lambda(p,t)$. For $1 \leq k \leq t$, let $w_l(p,k,t+1) = 0$ iff $w_l(p,k,t) = 0$ or $\lambda(p,t) = 1$ and $a_l(p,k) = A(p,t)$. An information is not valid iff it was not valid before or the p-th processor writes into that cell of its local memory where this information has been stored.

For the updating of the common memory we have to decide write conflicts. Let $\gamma'(p,t) = 1$ iff the p-th processor actually writes some information into the common memory at the $(t+1)$-st computation step. Then

$$\gamma'(p,t) = \gamma(p,t) \wedge [\neg (\bigvee_{1 \leq q < p} \gamma(q,t) \wedge EQ(A(q,t),A(p,t)))] , \qquad (3.7)$$

since a processor loses a write conflict iff a processor with a smaller number tries to write into the same cell. Finally $a_c(p,t+1) = A(p,t)$, $v_c(p,t+1) = R(p,t)$ and $w_c(p,t+1,t+1) = \gamma'(p,t)$. For $1 \leq k \leq t$, $w_c(p,k,t+1) = 0$ iff $w_c(p,k,t) = 0$ or $\gamma'(p',t) = 1$ and $a_c(p',t) = A(p',t)$ for some p'. One computation step can be simulated in polynomial size and constant depth.

At the end of the simulation we compute the output in the same way as we have read the contents of cells.

$\square$

Combining this simulation and the lower bounds of Ch. 11 we obtain lower bounds on the complexity of RES WRAMs.

13.4 The complexity of PRAMs

We know (Theorem 2.1) that all Boolean functions $f \in B_n$ can be computed by an EREW PRAM in time $\lceil \log n \rceil + 1$. This upper bound is proved by doubling the information of each processor in each step. If a (very powerful) processor knows the whole input a, it can compute the output and write it into the output cell. Here we consider lower bounds. If a PRAM stops the computation with output 1, it has to be sure that $f(a) = 1$. Let t be a shortest prime implicant covering a, i.e. $t(a) = 1$. Let l be the length of t. If we have knowledge on less than l input bits, and if these bits agree with a, we do not know that the output equals 1.

DEFINITION 4.1 : Let $f \in B_n$. For $a \in f^{-1}(1)$ let $l(f,a)$ be the length of a shortest prime implicant $t \in PI(f)$ such that $t(a) = 1$. For $a \in f^{-1}(0)$ let $l(f,a)$ be the length of a shortest prime clause $s \in PC(f)$ such that $s(a) = 0$. Let

$$l_{max}(f) = \max \{l(f,a) \mid a \in \{0,1\}^n\} \qquad \text{and} \tag{4.1}$$

$$l_{min}(f) = \min \{l(f,a) \mid a \in \{0,1\}^n\} . \tag{4.2}$$

Obviously $l_{min}(f)$ is the length of a shortest prime implicant or prime clause and (4.2) agrees with Definition 4.1, Ch. 11. Since $l_{max}(f)$ and $l_{min}(f)$ will play an important role in the following sections, we interpret $l(f,a)$ also in another way. An implicant of length k corresponds to an $(n-k)$-dimensional subcube C of $\{0,1\}^n$ such that f computes 1 for all $a \in C$. A prime implicant t has the additional property that C cannot be extended, i.e. f is not constant on any cube C' where C is a proper subcube of C'. This implies the following characterization of $l(f,a)$.

LEMMA 4.1 : $l(f,a)$ is the maximum k such that f is not constant on any $(n-k+1)$-dimensional subcube of $\{0,1\}^n$ containing a.

$l(f,a)$ is called sensitive complexity of f at input a (Vishkin and Wigderson (85)). We believe that it is more adequate to interpret this measure using the fundamental notion of prime implicants and prime clauses.

We also remark that $l_{max}(f)$ may be small even when f has long prime implicants and prime clauses.

LEMMA 4.2 : Let $SA_n \in B_{n+k}$ where $n = 2^k$ be the storage access function. Then $l_{max}(SA_n) = l_{min}(SA_n) = k+1$ but SA_n has a prime implicant and a prime clause of length 2^k each.

Proof : The proof is left as an exercise. □

By our considerations above we have to know at least $l(f,a)$ bits, if the input is a , before we may know the output. One might believe that one can at most double his information in one computation step. This leads to the conjecture that the PRAM time complexity of f is not smaller than $\lceil \log l_{max}(f) \rceil$. For the disjunction OR_n of n variables, $l_{max}(OR_n) = n$. The conjecture is false, since OR_n can be computed by an EREW PRAM in less than $\lceil \log n \rceil$ steps (Cook, Dwork and Reischuk (86)).

THEOREM 4.1 : Let $a = ((1 + \sqrt{5})/2)^2 \approx 2.618$. OR_n can be computed by an EREW PRAM with n realistic processors and communication width n in time $\lceil \log_a n \rceil$.

Proof : It is essential that a processor may transfer information if it does not write. We consider the situation of two memory cells M and M' containing the Boolean variables x and y resp. and a processor P knowing the Boolean variable z . P reads the contents of M' , computes $r = y \vee z$ and writes 1 into M iff $r = 1$. Then M contains $x \vee y \vee z$, the disjunction of 3 variables. If $r = 1$, this value is written into M . If $r = 0$, $x \vee y \vee z = x$. M contains this information, since P does not write anything.

This idea can be generalized and parallelized. W.l.o.g. the input tape is not read-only, and we have no further memory cells. Let $OR(i,j)$ be the disjunction of $x_i, \ldots, x_{i+j-1}$. Let $P_t(i)$ be the knowledge of the i-th processor after t computation steps, and let $M_t(i)$ be the contents of the i-th memory cell after t computation steps. Then $P_0(i) = OR(i,G_0)$ for $G_0 = 0$ and $M_0(i) = OR(i,H_0)$ for $H_0 = 1$. Let $P_{t-1}(i) = OR(i,G_{t-1})$ and $M_{t-1}(i) = OR(i,H_{t-1})$.

During the t-th computation step the i-th processor reads the contents of the $(i+G_{t-1})$-th cell (if $i+G_{t-1} \leq n$) and computes

$$P_t(i) = P_{t-1}(i) \vee M_{t-1}(i+G_{t-1}) \tag{4.3}$$

$$= OR(i,G_{t-1}) \vee OR(i+G_{t-1},H_{t-1}) = OR(i,G_{t-1}+H_{t-1}) .$$

We have simplified the notation and have assumed that $x_j = 0$ if $j > n$. The i-th processor writes 1 into the $(i-H_{t-1})$-th cell (if $i-H_{t-1} \geq 1$) iff $P_t(i) = 1$. As in our example at the beginning of the proof

$$M_t(i) = M_{t-1}(i) \vee P_t(i+H_{t-1}) \tag{4.4}$$

$$= OR(i,H_{t-1}) \vee OR(i+H_{t-1},G_{t-1}+H_{t-1})$$

$$= OR(i, G_{t-1}+2H_{t-1}) .$$

Hence $G_t = G_{t-1} + H_{t-1}$ and $H_t = G_{t-1} + 2H_{t-1}$. We set $F_{2t} = G_t$ and $F_{2t+1} = H_t$. Then

$$F_0 = 0 , \quad F_1 = 1 , \quad F_{2t} = F_{2t-2} + F_{2t-1} , \quad F_{2t+1} = F_{2t-1} + F_{2t} . \tag{4.5}$$

This is the well-known recursion for the Fibonacci numbers

$$F_t = (\Phi^t - (\Phi - \sqrt{5})^t)/\sqrt{5} \quad \text{for} \quad \Phi = (\sqrt{5}+1)/2 . \tag{4.6}$$

Hence $M_t(1)$ is the disjunction of the first F_{2t+1} variables. We stop the computation if $F_{2t+1} \geq n$.

$\square$

By this result we have improved the obvious upper bound by a small constant factor. Cook, Dwork and Reischuk (86) have proved that this is nearly optimal. The PRAM complexity of OR_n is $\Theta(\log n)$. By Theorem 4.1 this result is not obvious.

THEOREM 4.2 : Let $b = (5 + \sqrt{21})/2 \approx 4.791$. The PRAM time complexity (number of processors, communication width and computation power of the processors are unlimited) of $f \in B_n$ is not smaller than $\log_b n$ if $l_{max}(f) = n$.

Proof : Let a^* be an input where $l(f,a^*) = n$. Then f is not constant on any 1-dimensional subcube of $\{0,1\}^n$ containing a^*. Hence $f(a^*(i)) \neq f(a^*)$ for the neighbors $a^*(i)$ of a^*, where $a^*(i)_j = a^*_j$ for $i \neq j$ and $a^*(i)_i = 1 - a^*_i$.

We introduce some notation. An index i influences a processor P at time step t on input a if the state of P at t on a differs from the state of P at t on $a(i)$. In a similar way we define the influence of an index on a memory cell. Let $K(P,t,a)$ and $L(M,t,a)$ be the set of indices influencing P and M resp. at t on a.

Obviously $K(P,0,a) = \phi$, $L(M_i,0,a) = \{i\}$ if $i \leq n$ and $L(M_i,0,a) = \phi$ if $i > n$. Let T be the computation time of a PRAM computing f and let M_1 be the output cell. Then $L(M_1,T,a^*) = \{1,...,n\}$, since $l(f,a^*) = n$. We shall estimate the information flow. If $L(M_1,t,a^*)$ grows only slowly with t, then T is large.

We anticipate the results of our estimations. We prove for

$$K_0 = 0 \ , \ L_0 = 1 \ , \ K_{t+1} = K_t + L_t \ , \ L_{t+1} = 3K_t + 4L_t , \qquad (4.7)$$

all processors P, memory cells M, inputs a and time steps t that

$$|K(P,t,a)| \leq K_t \quad \text{and} \quad |L(M,t,a)| \leq L_t . \qquad (4.8)$$

The recursion (4.7) has for $b' = (5 - \sqrt{21})/2$ the solution

$$K_t = (b^t - b'^t)/\sqrt{21} \quad \text{and} \qquad (4.9)$$

$$L_t = ((3 + \sqrt{21})b^t + (\sqrt{21} - 3)b'^t)/(2\sqrt{21}) \leq b^t . \qquad (4.10)$$

Hence

$$n = |L(M_1,T,a^*)| \leq L_T \leq b^T \quad \text{and} \quad T \geq \log_b n . \tag{4.11}$$

We prove (4.8) by induction on t . The assertion is obvious for $t = 0$. A processor P may store all available information and may read the contents of one memory cell M . Hence

$$K(P,t+1,a) \subseteq K(P,t,a) \cup L(M,t,a) \tag{4.12}$$

and by induction hypothesis

$$|K(P,t+1,a)| \leq K_t + L_t = K_{t+1} . \tag{4.13}$$

A memory cell M is influenced in a complicated way if no processor writes into M . If processor P writes into M at $t+1$ on a , then all information in M is deleted and M is influenced only by indices influencing P . Hence

$$L(M,t+1,a) \subseteq K(P,t+1,a) \quad \text{and} \tag{4.14}$$

$$|L(M,t+1,a)| \leq K_{t+1} = K_t + L_t \leq 3K_t + 4L_t = L_{t+1} . \tag{4.15}$$

If no processor writes into M at $t+1$ on a , then M may be influenced by those indices which have influenced M before. Furthermore, index i may influence M at $t+1$ on a if some processor P writes into M at $t+1$ on input $a(i)$. Hence

$$L(M,t+1,a) \subseteq L(M,t,a) \cup Y(M,t+1,a) \tag{4.16}$$

for the set $Y(M,t+1,a)$ of indices i such that some processor P writes into M at $t+1$ on $a(i)$ but not on a . It is sufficient to prove that

$$|Y(M,t+1,a)| \leq 3 K_{t+1} . \tag{4.17}$$

For a bound on the size of $Y(M,t+1,a)$ we investigate the situation where $1,2 \in Y(M,t+1,a)$. P' and P'' write into M at $t+1$ on $a(1)$ and $a(2)$ resp., and P' and P'' do not write into M at $t+1$ on a . This is possible only if $1 \in K(P',t+1,a(1))$ and $2 \in K(P'',t+1,a(2))$. The assumptions $1 \notin K(P'',t+1,a(2))$, $2 \notin K(P',t+1,a(1))$ and $P' \neq P''$ lead to a write conflict on the input $a' = a(1)(2) = a(2)(1)$. P' writes on $a(1)$ into M and is not influenced by index 2 . Hence P' writes on a' into M . The same holds for $P'' \neq P'$ in contradiction to the definition of PRAM programs.

We conclude that $P' = P''$ or $1 \in K(P'',t+1,a(2))$ or $2 \in K(P',t+1,a(1))$.

Now we investigate the general situation in which $Y(M,t+1,a) = \{u_1, \ldots, u_r\}$. Let z_i be the number of that processor which writes into M at $t+1$ on $a(u_i)$. We construct a bipartite graph G on the vertices $v_1, \ldots, v_r$ and $w_1, \ldots, w_r$. G contains the edge (v_i,w_j) iff $u_i \in K(P(z_j),t+1,a(u_j))$. Since $|K(P(z_j),t+1,a(u_j))| \leq K_{t+1}$, the degree of w_j is bounded by K_{t+1}. Hence

$$e \leq r K_{t+1} \tag{4.18}$$

for the number of edges e of G. Our preliminary investigations imply that for each pair (u_i,u_j) where $P(z_i) \neq P(z_j)$, G contains at least one of the edges (v_i,w_j) and (v_j,w_i). We estimate the number of these pairs. There are r possibilities for u_i. If $P(z_i) = P(z_j)$, then $u_j \in K(P(z_i),t+1,a)$. This is possible for at most K_{t+1} indices. Hence there are at least $r - K_{t+1}$ possibilities for u_j. We have counted each pair twice. Hence

$$e \geq r(r - K_{t+1})/2. \tag{4.19}$$

We combine (4.18) with (4.19) and obtain the following estimation for $r = |Y(M,t+1,a)|$.

$$r(r - K_{t+1})/2 \leq r K_{t+1} \quad \text{and} \quad r \leq 3 K_{t+1}. \tag{4.20}$$
$$\square$$

The following conjecture is a natural generalization of Theorem 4.2.

CONJECTURE : $T(f) = \Omega(\log l_{max}(f))$ for the PRAM time complexity $T(f)$ of Boolean functions f.

This conjecture is open. Only a (perhaps) weaker lower bound has been proved.

DEFINITION 4.2 : For $a \in \{0,1\}^n$, let $\Gamma(a)$ be the neighborhood of a consisting of those n vectors which differ from a at exactly one position. The critical complexity $c(f,a)$ of f at a is the number of neighbors $b \in \Gamma(a)$ where $f(a) \neq f(b)$. The critical complexity $c(f)$ of f is defined by

$$c(f) = \max \{ c(f,a) \mid a \in \{0,1\}^n \} . \qquad (4.21)$$

THEOREM 4.3 : $T(f) \geq \log_b c(f)$ for the PRAM time complexity of Boolean functions f and $b = (5 + \sqrt{21})/2$.

Proof : Let a^* be an input where $c(f,a^*) = c(f)$. W.l.o.g. $f(a^*) \neq f(a^*(i))$ for $1 \leq i \leq c(f)$. Let f' be that subfunction of f on $c(f)$ variables where we have replaced the variables x_j for $j > c(f)$ by a_j^*. Obviously $l(f',a^*) = c(f)$ is equal to the number of variables of f' . $T(f') \geq \log_b c(f)$ by Theorem 4.2 , and $T(f) \geq T(f')$, since f' is a subfunction of f .

$\square$

PROPOSITION 4.1 : $c(f) \leq l_{max}(f)$ for all $f \in B_n$.

Proof : It is sufficient to prove $c(f,a) \leq l(f,a)$ for all $a \in \{0,1\}^n$. Let $k = c(f,a)$. Then $f(b) \neq f(a)$ for k neighbors b of a , and f is not constant on any $(n-k+1)$-dimensional subcube of $\{0,1\}^n$ containing a .

$\square$

Because of Proposition 4.1 the conjecture is not weaker than Theorem 4.3 . The conjecture is a more natural assertion, since l_{max} is a more natural complexity measure than c . It is open, whether the conjecture is really stronger than Theorem 4.3 . What is the largest difference between $c(f)$ and l_{max} ?
Does there exist a sequence $f_n \in B_n$ such that $c(f_n) = o(l_{max}(f_n))$ or even $\log c(f_n) = o(\log l_{max}(f_n))$? Only in the second case the conjecture is stronger than Theorem 4.3 .

In § 7 we estimate the critical and the sensitive complexity of almost all functions and of the easiest functions. It will turn out that the bound of Theorem 4.3 is often tight.

13.5 The complexity of PRAMs and WRAMs with small communication width

It is reasonable to restrict the communication width of PRAMs and WRAMs (Vishkin and Wigderson (85)). We begin the discussion with an efficient algorithm.

THEOREM 5.1 : OR_n and PAR_n can be computed in time $O((n/m)^{1/2} + \log m)$ by an EREW PRAM with $O((nm)^{1/2})$ realistic processors and communication width m.

Proof : We consider only PAR_n, the algorithm for OR_n is similar. At first we consider the case $m = 1$. Let $\binom{k}{2} < n \le \binom{k+1}{2} = 1 + \cdots + k$. Then $k = O(n^{1/2})$. We compute the parity of $\binom{k+1}{2}$ variables by k processors in time $k + 1$. The set of inputs is partitioned to blocks $A_1, \ldots, A_k$ where $|A_i| = i$. The i-th processor computes in time i the parity of the variables in A_i. During the $(i+1)$-st computation step the i-th processor reads the contents of the common memory cell. If this is the parity of the variables in the blocks $A_1, \ldots, A_{i-1}$, the i-th processor computes the parity of the variables in the blocks $A_1, \ldots, A_i$ by a binary parity gate and writes the result into the common memory cell. By induction we conclude that the k-th processor writes the result into the common memory cell during the $(k+1)$-st computation step.

If $m > 1$, we partition the variables to m blocks of at most $\lceil n/m \rceil$ variables each. For each block $O((n/m)^{1/2})$ processors are sufficient to compute the parity in time $O((n/m)^{1/2})$ and communication width 1. Using $O((nm)^{1/2})$ processors and communication width m, these computations can be performed in parallel. Afterwards m processors compute in time $\lceil \log m \rceil + 1$ the parity of the m results and so the parity of all variables. W.l.o.g. $m \le n$, otherwise the result follows directly. □

COROLLARY 5.1 : Each $f \in B_n$ can be computed in time $O((n/m)^{1/2} + \log m)$ by an EREW PRAM with $O((nm)^{1/2})$ powerful processors and communication width m.

Proof : We use the approach of the proof of Theorem 5.1 and collect during each time step all available information as in the proof of Theorem 2.1 i . □

THEOREM 5.2 : If a WRAM computes $f_n \in B_n$ in time $T(f_n)$ with communication width m, then $T(f_n) \ge (l_{min}(f_n)/m)^{1/2}$.

The upper and lower bounds of Theorem 5.1 and 5.2 are of the same size if $l_{min}(f_n) = \Theta(n)$ and $m = O(n \log^{-2} n)$. In particular $l_{min}(PAR_n) = n$. In § 7 we prove that $l_{min}(f_n) = \Theta(n)$ for almost all $f_n \in B_n$, almost all $f_n \in M_n$, almost all $f_n \in S_n$ and several fundamental functions. Hence Theorem 5.2 is a powerful result. If $l_{min}(f_n)$ is small, the complexity of WRAMs of small communication width cannot be described correctly by $l_{min}(f_n)$. Obviously $l_{min}(OR_n) = 1$ and OR_n can be computed in time 1 with communication width 1 . Let

$$g_n(x_1, \ldots, x_n) = x_1 \lor (x_2 \oplus \cdots \oplus x_n) . \tag{5.1}$$

Then $l_{min}(g_n) = 1$, but by Theorem 5.2 and the fact that PAR_{n-1} is a subfunction of g_n the time complexity of g_n is not smaller than $((n-1)/m)^{1/2}$.

Proof of Theorem 5.2 : We add m processors with numbers larger than those of the given processors. The i-th additional processor always reads the contents of the i-th memory cell (not on the read-only input tape) and tries to write this information again into the same cell. Hence for each memory cell there is always a processor which writes into it.

Let $k = l_{min}(f)$. A processor which knows less than k inputs, does not know the output. The processors gather their information from reading inputs on the input tape or information in common memory cells. During t computation steps a processor may read directly at most t inputs. For efficient computations the amount of information flowing through the common memory cells needs to be large. We estimate this information flow. We construct (deterministic) restrictions such that for the so-constructed subfunctions the contents of all memory cells does not depend on the input.

At the beginning we consider all inputs, namely the cube $E_0 = \{0,1\}^n$. We construct cubes $E_{1,1}, \ldots, E_{1,m}, \ldots, E_{T,1}, \ldots, E_{T,m}$ ($T = T(f_n)$) such that each cube is a subcube of the one before. Let us construct $E_{t,l}$ and E' be the previous cube, namely $E_{t,l-1}$ if $l > 1$ or $E_{t-1,m}$ if $l = 1$. For $a \in E'$ let $p(a)$ be the number of the processor that writes into the l-th memory cell M_l at t on a. We choose $a_{t,l} \in E'$ such that $p(a_{t,l}) \leq p(a)$ for $a \in E'$. Let $i_1, \ldots, i_r$ be the indices of those inputs which the $p(a_{t,l})$-th processor has read during the first t computation steps directly on the input tape. Obviously $r \leq t$. Let $E_{t,l}$ be the set of all $a \in E'$ which agree with $a_{t,l}$ at the positions $i_1, \ldots, i_r$. $E_{t,l}$ is a subcube of E' whose dimension is by r smaller than the dimension of E'. Since $r \leq t$, the dimension of $E_{T,m}$ is at least

$$n - m \sum_{1 \leq t \leq T} t = n - m\,T(T+1)/2\,. \tag{5.2}$$

CLAIM: f_n is constant on $E_{T,m}$.

By this claim it is easy to prove the theorem. The largest subcube on which f_n is constant has dimension $n - l_{min}(f_n)$. Hence

$$l_{min}(f_n) \le m\,T(T+1)/2 \quad \text{and} \quad T \ge (l_{min}(f_n)/m)^{1/2}. \tag{5.3}$$

Proof of the Claim : The diction, that a processor writes the same in several situations, should also include the case that a processor never writes. We prove that the computation paths for the inputs $a \in E_{T,m}$ are essentially the same. The initial configuration does not depend on the input. Then we choose some input a' and a processor p' that writes on a' into the first common cell at $t = 1$ such that no processor $p < p'$ writes on some $a \in E_0$ into M_1 at $t = 1$. We restrict the input set to those inputs which agree with a' at that position which has been read by p'. Let $a \in E_{1,1}$. No processor $p < p'$ writes into M_1 on a at $t = 1$ (by construction). Processor p' cannot distinguish between a and a'. Hence p' writes on both inputs the same into M_1 and switches to the same state.

Let us consider $E_{t,l}$ and the previous cube E'. We assume that the contents of all M_i at the time steps $0,...,t-1$ and of M_i ($1 \le i \le l-1$) at time step t do not depend on $a \in E'$. Then we choose some input $a' \in E'$ and a processor p' writing on a' into M_l at time step t such that no processor $p < p'$ writes on some $a \in E'$ into M_l at t. We restrict the input set to those inputs which agree with a' at those positions which have been read by p' on the input tape. Let $a \in E_{t,l}$. No processor $p < p'$ writes into M_l on a at t (by construction). Processor p' does the same on a and a', since it has read the same information on the input tape and in the common memory. Hence p' writes the same on a and on a' into M_l and switches to the same state.

The contents of the output cell M_1 is for all $a \in E_{T,m}$ the same. Hence f is constant on $E_{T,m}$.

□

THEOREM 5.3 : If a PRAM computes $f_n \in B_n$ in time $T(f_n)$ with communication width m, then $T(f_n) \ge (l_{max}(f_n)/m)^{1/3}$.

This result improves the bound of Theorem 5.2 only for PRAMs and functions where $l_{max}(f_n)$ is much larger than $l_{min}(f_n)$. We present two examples. Obviously $l_{min}(OR_n) = 1$ but $l_{max}(OR_n) = n$. Obviously $l_{min}(cl_{n,3}) = 3$, and the reader may easily verify that $l_{max}(cl_{n,3}) = \binom{n-1}{2}$.

Proof of Theorem 5.3 : Let e be an input where $l(f,e) = l_{max}(f_n)$. Again we construct a sequence of cubes $E_0 = \{0,1\}^n, E_{1,1}, \ldots, E_{1,m}, \ldots, E_{T,1}, \ldots, E_{T,m}$ for $T = T(f_n)$. Each cube is a subcube of its predecessor. Since we only know that e is a difficult input, we ensure that $e \in E_{t,l}$. E.g. for OR_n , e consists of zeros only. If $e \notin E_{t,l}$, the subfunction of OR_n on $E_{t,l}$ is a simple function, namely a constant.

We discuss the construction of $E_{t,l}$ out of E' where $E' = E_{t,l-1}$ or $E' = E_{t-1,m}$ or $E' = E_0$.

Case 1 : There is no input $a \in E'$ such that a processor writes into M_l on a at time step t . Then $E_{t,l} = E'$.

Case 2 : The i-th processor writes into M_l on input e at t . Let $i_1, \ldots, i_r$ be the indices of those inputs which the i-th processor has read on e during the first t computation steps directly on the input tape. Then $r \leq t$. Let $E_{t,l}$ be the set of all $a \in E'$ which agree with e at the positions $i_1, \ldots, i_r$.

Case 3 : No processor writes into M_l on input e at t , but there are some input $a \in E'$ and some processor p such that p writes into M_l on a at t . Again $E_{t,l}$ is the set of all $a' \in E'$ which agree with e at some positions $i_1, \ldots, i_r$. Here we choose a minimal set of indices such that no processor writes into M_l on some input $b \in E_{t,l}$ at t .

CLAIM 1 : $e \in E_{T,m}$ and f is constant on $E_{T,m}$.

Proof : $e \in E_{t,l}$ for all t and l by our construction. The second part of the assertion is proved in the same way as the Claim in the proof of Theorem 5.2 . $\square$

CLAIM 2 : For the construction of $E_{t,l}$ we fix at most $t(t+1)/2$ additional variables.

The proof of this claim is postponed. It follows from the claim, that we altogether fix not more than

$$m \sum_{1 \le t \le T} t(t+1)/2 \le m T^3 \tag{5.4}$$

variables. By Claim 1 , f is constant on an $(n - mT^3)$-dimensional subcube of $\{0,1\}^n$ containing e . Hence

$$l_{max}(f_n) = l(f,e) \le m T^3 \quad \text{and} \quad T \ge (l_{max}(f_n)/m)^{1/3} . \tag{5.5}$$

It is sufficient to prove Claim 2 .

Proof of Claim 2 : We only have to consider Case 3 . Let $a(1)$,..., $a(k)$ be those inputs for which some processor writes into M_l at t . Let $i(j)$ be the number of the processor corresponding to $a(j)$. Let $E_{t,l}$ be the set of all $a \in E'$ which agree with e at all positions which have been read for some $j \in \{1,...,k\}$ by the $i(j)$-th processor on input $a(j)$ during the first t computation steps directly on the input tape. Obviously no processor writes into M_l on some input $b \in E_{t,l}$ at t . We have fixed at most kt variables. This estimate is too rough.

For a more profound analysis, we construct $E_{t,l}$ in a few more steps. We always consider one input only. Let $E_{t,l,0} = E'$. Let $E_{t,l,h}$ be the set of all $a \in E_{t,l,h-1}$ which agree with e at all positions which have been read by the $i(h)$-th processor on $a(h)$ during the first t computation steps. We assume w.l.o.g. that the inputs $a(i)$ are ordered in the following way. $a(1)$ is defined as before. If there is still some input $a \in E_{t,l,h-1}$ such that some processor writes into M_l at t, then $a(h) = a$. Otherwise the construction is finished, we set $E_{t,l} = E_{t,l,h-1}$. Now it is sufficient to prove that at most $\max\{0, t-h+1\}$ additional variables are fixed for the construction of $E_{t,l,h}$ out of $E_{t,l,h-1}$. Then the number of fixed variables can be estimated by $t + \cdots + 1 = t(t+1)/2$.

The new claim is proved by induction on h . The assertion is obvious for h = 1 , since a processor reads at most t inputs during t computation steps. For h > 1 , let R(h-1) and R(h) be the set of variables we fix for the construction of $E_{t,l,h-1}$ and $E_{t,l,h}$ resp. By the induction hypothesis, $|R(h-1)| \leq \max\{0, t-h+2\}$. Since a(h) was a candidate which could have been chosen as a(h-1) , also $|R'(h-1)| \leq \max\{0, t-h-2\}$ for the set of variables R'(h-1) which would have been fixed by variables if we chose a(h) as a(h-1) . Obviously R(h) = R'(h-1) - R(h-1) , so it is sufficient to prove that the intersection of R'(h-1) and R(h-1) is not empty. Then R(h) is a proper subset of R'(h-1) .

Let i(h-1) and i(h) be the numbers of those processors that write on a(h-1) and a(h) resp. at t into M_l .

Case 1 : $i(h-1) \neq i(h)$. If R'(h-1) and R(h-1) are disjoint, we define an input b in the following way.

$$
\begin{aligned}
b_j &= a(h-1)_j && \text{if} && j \in R(h-1) \\
b_j &= a(h)_j && \text{if} && j \in R'(h-1) \\
b_j &= e_j && \text{if} && j \notin (R(h-1) \cup R'(h-1)) .
\end{aligned}
$$

(5.6)

On input a(h-1) , the i(h-1)-st processor reads on the input tape during the first t computation steps only variables which either have been fixed for the construction of $E_{t,l,h-1}$ or have indices in R(h-1) . On input b , the i(h-1)-st processor reads the same information, as all fixed variables agree with e . Since the i(h-1)-st processor writes on a(h-1) into M_l at t , it writes also on b into M_l at t . In the same way we conclude that the i(h)-th processor writes on b into M_l at t . The assumption, that R'(h-1) and R(h-1) are disjoint, leads to a write conflict which cannot be solved by a PRAM .

Case 2 : i(h-1) = i(h) . The inputs a(h-1) and a(h) agree on all variables which have been fixed during the construction of $E_{t,l,h-2}$. Let t' be the first time step where the i(h)-th processor reads on the input tape on a(h-1) a variable which has not been fixed. During the computation steps 1,...,t'-1 the i(h)-th processor cannot distinguish between a(h-1) and a(h) . Hence it reads on both inputs at t' in the same input cell. The index of this cell is contained in $R(h-1)$ and in $R'(h-1)$.

□

Beame (published by Vishkin and Wigderson (85)) considered another complexity measure.

DEFINITION 5.1 : Let $m(f) = \min \{ |f^{-1}(0)| , |f^{-1}(1)| \}$ and let $M(f) = n - \log m(f)$.

THEOREM 5.4 : If a PRAM computes $f_n \in B_n$ in time $T(f_n)$ with communication width m , then $T(f_n) \geq (M(f_n)/m)^{1/2}$.

We omit the proof of this theorem. Obviously $M(PAR_n) = 1$ and we obtain a trivial bound. But $M(OR_n) = n$ and the lower bound $(n/m)^{1/3}$ of Theorem 5.3 is improved to $(n/m)^{1/2}$. This bound is optimal for OR_n if $m = O(n \log^{-2} n)$ (see Theorem 5.1). For a comparison of the lower bounds of Theorem 5.3 and 5.4 we remark that $M(f_n) \leq l_{max}(f_n)$ for all $f_n \in B_n$ and $M(f_n) = O(1)$ for almost all $f_n \in B_n$ (see Exercises).

13.6 The complexity of WRAMs with polynomial resources

In § 5 we have proved lower bounds on the time complexity of WRAMs with very small communication width. Other lower bounds under severe restrictions (either on the number of processors or on the computation power of the processors or on the input size (in the non Boolean case)) have been proved. Beame ((86 a) and (86 b)) proved the first optimal bounds for non-trivial Boolean functions and WRAMs with polynomial resources (number of processors or communication width). He proved an $\Omega((\log n)/\log\log n)$-bound for parity, but actually, the proof works as Hastad's proof (see Ch. 11) for all functions f where $l_{min}(f)$ is sufficiently large. The lower bound can be extended via the simulation of § 2 and the reducibility results of Ch. 10, § 3, to many fundamental functions and graph functions. The optimality of the lower bound follows from the simulation in § 2 and the upper bound of Ch. 11, § 2.

Beame's proof works with probabilistic methods. One of the crucial ideas is the description of a computation by processor and cell partitions.

DEFINITION 6.1 : For each WRAM , its i-th processor P_i , its j-th common memory cell M_j and any time step $t \in \{0,...,T\}$ we define the processor partition $P(i,t)$ and the cell partition $M(j,t)$. Two inputs x and y are equivalent with respect to $P(i,t)$ iff they lead to the same state of P_i at time step t . Two inputs x and y are equivalent with respect to $M(j,t)$ iff they lead to the same contents of M_j at time step t .

DEFINITION 6.2 : Let $A = (A_1, ... , A_m)$ be a partition of $\{0,1\}^n$. Let $f_i(x) = 1$ iff $x \in A_i$. Let (as in Ch. 11, § 3) $l_{PI}(f_i)$ denote the maximal length of a prime implicant of f_i . The degree $d(A)$ of A is the maximum of all $l_{PI}(f_i)$.

Since AND_n , the conjunction of n variables, can be computed by a WRAM in one step, the degree of a cell partition may increase violently during one step. But after having applied a random restriction ρ (see Def. 3.1, Ch. 11), with large probability the degree is not too large. The projection g_ρ of a parity function again is a parity function. Hence the degree of the output cell at the end of the computation, i.e. at time step T , is as large as the input size. We choose restrictions such that on the one hand the number of variables does not decrease too fast and, on the other hand, the degree of the partition does only increase slowly. Then the computation time T cannot be too small for the parity function.

Another fundamental notion is that of graded sets of Boolean functions.

DEFINITION 6.3 : A graded set of Boolean functions is a set F of Boolean functions on the same set of n variables together with a grade function $\gamma : F \to \mathbb{N} \cup \{\infty\}$ such that $\gamma(f) = \gamma(g)$ implies $f \wedge g \equiv 0$. F determines a partition $[F]$ of $\{0,1\}^n$. Two inputs x and y are equivalent with respect to $[F]$ iff either $f(x) = f(y) = 1$ for some $f \in F$ and $g(x) = g(y) = 0$ for all $g \in F$ where $\gamma(g) < \gamma(f)$ or $f(x) = f(y) = 0$ for all $f \in F$.

We often make use of the following fact. If ρ is a restriction shrinking the input set from $\{0,1\}^n$ to $\{0,1\}^n_\rho$, then $[F_\rho] = [F]_\rho$ where F_ρ is the class of all f_ρ for $f \in F$. In particular we are interested in the following graded set of Boolean functions.

DEFINITION 6.4 : Let $F(j,t)$ be the following graded set of Boolean functions for a given WRAM , a memory cell number j and a time step t . The function f describing an equivalence class with respect to $P(i,t)$ such that P_i tries to write on inputs of this equivalence class into the j-th memory cell at time step t is in $F(j,t)$ and has grade i. The function f describing an equivalence class with respect to $M(j,t-1)$ is in $F(j,t)$ and has grade ∞ .

LEMMA 6.1 : i) $F(j,t)$ is a graded set of Boolean functions.

ii) $[F(j,t)]$ is a refinement of $M(j,t)$.

Proof : i) follows directly from the definitions.

ii) We have to prove that x and y are equivalent with respect to $M(j,t)$ if they are equivalent with respect to $[F(j,t)]$.

Since $M(j,t-1)$ is a partition of $\{0,1\}^n$, it is impossible that $f(x) = 0$ for all $f \in [F(j,t)]$. Hence, if x and y are equivalent with respect to $[F(j,t)]$, then $f(x) = f(y) = 1$ for some $f \in F(j,t)$ and $g(x) = g(y) = 0$ for all $g \in F(j,t)$ where $\gamma(g) < \gamma(f)$. If $\gamma(f) = i < \infty$, the i-th processor is on x and y at t in the same state and tries to write the same information into the j-th memory cell. Since no processor with a number $l < i$ tries to write on x or y at t into M_j , the i-th processor wins the write conflict. On x and y the same information is written into the j-th cell at t . If $\gamma(f) = \infty$, no processor writes into the j-th cell at t for x or y . The contents of this cell remains unchanged. Since in this situation x and y are equivalent with respect to $M(j,t-1)$, the contents of the cell is the same for x and y . Hence x and y are equivalent with respect to $M(j,t)$.

$\square$

LEMMA 6.2 : If β satisfies $\left(\dfrac{4\,p}{\beta(1+p)} + 1 \right)^r = 2$, then

$$\beta = \frac{4\,p}{(1+p)(2^{1/r}-1)} < 6\,p\,r . \tag{6.1}$$

$\square$

Proof : The easy proof is left to the reader.

MAIN LEMMA 6.3 : i) Let F be a graded set of Boolean functions on $\{0,1\}^n$. Let $d([F]) \le r$ for some $r > 0$ and let $\rho \in R_p$ be a random restriction. Then

$$\Pr(d([F_\rho]) \ge s) \le \beta^s < (6\,p\,r)^s \tag{6.2}$$

for the constant β of Lemma 6.2 .

ii) The same assertion holds for arbitrary partitions A of $\{0,1\}^n$ instead of $[F]$.

This Main Lemma is proved by Beame (86 b) in a way similar to our proof of the Main Lemma 3.2 in Ch. 11 . Although the proof contains some new estimations we do not present it here.

THEOREM 6.1 : i) Let W be a WRAM computing the parity of n variables in time $T = T(n)$ with p(n) processors and communication width c(n) . Then for large n

$$p(n) + c(n) \geq \frac{1}{4} 2^{(1/24) n^{1/T}} , \qquad\qquad (6.3)$$

$$p(n) \qquad \geq \frac{1}{4} 2^{(1/96) n^{1/T}} \qquad , \text{ and} \qquad\qquad (6.4)$$

$$c(n) \qquad \geq \frac{1}{4} 2^{(1/12) (n/T!)^{1/T}} . \qquad\qquad (6.5)$$

ii) If $p(n)$ is bounded by a polynomial, then

$$T(n) \geq \frac{\log n}{O(1) + \log\log n} = \frac{\log n}{\log\log n} - O\left(\frac{\log n}{(\log\log n)^2} \right) . \qquad (6.6)$$

iii) If $c(n)$ is bounded by a polynomial, then

$$T(n) \geq \frac{\log n}{2 \log\log n} - O\left(\frac{\log n}{(\log\log n)^2} \right) . \qquad (6.7)$$

We again emphasize that these bounds hold for all functions f_n where $l_{\min}(f_n)$ is sufficiently large and for all functions $f_n \in B_n$ where $PAR \leq_{cd} f = (f_n)$. Part ii and Part iii of Theorem 6.1 are simple corollaries to (6.4) and (6.5) resp. The proofs of (6.3) - (6.5) follow the same pattern. We present the proof of (6.4) which seems to be the most important assertion.

Proof of (6.4) : We define restrictions $\rho(1), \ldots, \rho(T)$ such that $\rho(t)$ may be applied after $\rho(1), \ldots, \rho(t-1)$ have been applied. Let $\pi(t)$ be the composition of $\rho(1), \ldots, \rho(t)$. Let E_t be the subcube of $\{0,1\}^n$ on which $f_{\pi(t)}$ for $f \in B_n$ is defined. Let D_t be the dimension of E_t and let $s = \log 4 p(n)$.

We prove for $t \geq 1$ that we can choose $\pi(t)$ such that $D_t \geq (1/48) n (96 s)^{-(t-1)}$ and the degree of all partitions $P(i,t)_{\pi(t)}$ and $M(j,t)_{\pi(t)}$ is bounded by s . $P(i,t)_{\pi(t)}$ and $M(j,t)_{\pi(t)}$ are the partitions $P(i,t)$ and $M(j,t)$ restricted to $E_t = \{0,1\}^n_{\pi(t)}$.

First we show how this claim implies (6.4) . Let M_1 be the output cell. Then the degree of $M(1,T)_{\pi(T)}$ is equal to D_T . The claim implies that

$$s \geq d(M(1,T)_{\pi(T)}) = D_T \geq \frac{1}{48} n (96 s)^{-(T-1)}, \tag{6.8}$$

$$(96 s)^T \geq 2 n \geq n \quad \text{and} \quad s \geq (1/96) n^{1/T}. \tag{6.9}$$

Since $s = \log 4 p(n)$, (6.4) follows from (6.9).

We prove the claim by induction on t. At time step $t = 1$ the i-th processor reads one memory cell, and the state afterwards depends on a single input bit. Hence the degree of $P(i,1)$ is bounded by $1 \leq s$ and the degree of $P(i,1)_{\pi(1)}$ cannot be larger.

By Lemma 6.1 ii, $[F(j,1)]$ is a refinement of $M(j,1)$. By definition each $f \in F(j,1)$ is a function describing an equivalence class of some $P(i,1)$ or $M(j,0)$. All these functions depend on at most one variable. Let $\rho \in R_q$ for $q = 1/48$ be a random restriction. The Main Lemma implies for $r = 1$

$$\Pr(d([F(j,1)_\rho]) \geq s) \leq (6 q)^s = 8^{-s} = 2^{-2s-2} / p(n). \tag{6.10}$$

Each processor knows at most one variable. Hence there are at most two memory cells into which a definite processor may write at time step 1. For at most $2 p(n)$ memory cells M_j the degree of $[F(j,1)_\rho]$ may be larger than s. The probability that the degree of all $[F(j,1)_\rho]$ is less than s is at least $1 - 2^{-2s-1}$. Since $[F(j,1)_\rho]$ is a refinement of $M(j,1)_\rho$, the function f describing an equivalence class of $M(j,1)_\rho$ is the disjunction of some functions g_i describing equivalence classes of $[F(j,1)_\rho]$. If $l_{PI}(g_i) \leq s$, also $l_{PI}(f) \leq s$. Hence the degree of $M(j,1)_\rho$ is bounded by the degree of $[F(j,1)_\rho]$. The probability that $D_1 \geq n/48$, the expected number of remaining variables, is at least $1/3$. Hence we can choose a restriction $\rho(1)$ for which all conditions hold simultaneously.

For the induction step we assume that the claim holds for some $t \geq 1$. The state of the i-th processor at $t+1$ depends only on the state of this processor at t (the partition $P(i,t)$) and on the contents of that cell which the processor reads at t. For all inputs of an equivalence class of $P(i,t)$ this is the same cell. Hence each equivalence class of $P(i,t+1)$ is the intersection of some equivalence class of $P(i,t)$ and some equivalence class of some $M(j,t)$. If g'

describes the class of $P(i,t)$ and g'' describes the appropriate class of $M(j,t)$, then $g = g' \wedge g''$ describes the equivalence class of $P(i,t+1)$. Obviously $l_{PI}(g)$ is not larger than $l_{PI}(g') + l_{PI}(g'')$. Hence, by the induction hypothesis,

$$d(P(i,t+1)_{\pi(t)}) \leq d(P(i,t)_{\pi(t)}) + \max_j \{ M(j,t)_{\pi(t)} \} \leq 2s. \qquad (6.11)$$

We look for a restriction $\rho(t+1)$ which keeps the degrees of the processor and cell partitions small and keeps the number of variables large. Let $\rho \in R_q$ be a random restriction for some q chosen later. By (6.11) and the Main Lemma for $r = 2s$

$$\Pr(d(P(i,t+1)_{\pi(t),\rho}) \geq s) < (12\,q\,s)^s. \qquad (6.12)$$

Now we consider the j-th memory cell M_j. By Lemma 6.1 $[F(j,t+1)]$ is a refinement of $M(j,t+1)$, this holds also when we restrict the sets to E_t. By Definition 6.4 each equivalence class of some $[F(j,t+1)]_{\pi(t)}$ is an equivalence class of some $P(i,t+1)$ or an equivalence class of $M(j,t)$. By the induction hypothesis and (6.11)

$$d([F(j,t+1)]_{\pi(t)}) \leq 2s, \qquad (6.13)$$

and also the degree of $M(j,t+1)_{\pi(t)}$ is bounded by $2s$. If no processor writes into M_j at $t+1$, the degree is even bounded by s . In the same way as we have proved (6.12) we also conclude that

$$\Pr(d(M(j,t+1)_{\pi(t),\rho}) \geq s) < (12\,q\,s)^s. \qquad (6.14)$$

We hope that the degree of all processor and all cell partitions is simultaneously bounded by s for some restriction ρ . We have to consider $p(n)$ processors and infinitely many memory cells. But for those memory cells which no processor writes into at $t+1$ it is for sure by the induction hypothesis that the degree of $M(j,t+1)_{\pi(t),\rho}$ is bounded by s . By (6.11) the equivalence classes of $P(i,t+1)_{\pi(t)}$ are described by functions whose prime implicants have a length of at most $2s$. Such a prime implicant is satisfied for a fraction of 2^{-2s} of all inputs. Hence $P(i,t+1)_{\pi(t)}$ partitions the input set to at most 2^{2s} subsets. This implies that the i-th processor may write only into one of 2^{2s} different memory cells at $t+1$. Altogether for only $2^{2s}\,p(n)$ memory cells M_j it is not for sure that the degree of

$M(j,t+1)_{\pi(t),\rho}$ is bounded by s.

Let $q = 1/(96\,s)$. The probability that the degree of all processor and cell partitions (with respect to $\pi(t)$ and ρ) is not bounded by s is (since $s = 4\log p(n)$) at most

$$(2^{2s} + 1)\,p(n)\,(12\,q\,s)^s = (2^{2s} + 1)\,p(n)\,2^{-3s} \qquad (6.15)$$

$$= (1 + 2^{-2s})\,p(n)\,2^{-s}$$

$$= (1 + 2^{-2s})\,p(n)\,\frac{1}{4\,p(n)} = \frac{1}{4}(1 + 2^{-2s}).$$

The probability that D_{t+1} is less than its expected value $D_t / (96\,s) \geq (1/48)\,n\,(96\,s)^{-t}$ is bounded by $2/3$. Since

$$\frac{1}{4}(1 + 2^{-2s}) + \frac{2}{3} < 1, \qquad (6.16)$$

we can choose a restriction $\rho(t+1)$ such that all assertions are satisfied for time step $t+1$.

$\square$

Beame (86 b) generalized his methods (in a way similar to those of Hastad (86) for bounded-depth circuits, see Ch. 11, § 5) and defined explicitly functions for the following hierarchy results which we present without proofs.

THEOREM 6.2 : i) For any T such that

$$T = \frac{\log n}{3\log\log n} - \omega\left(\frac{\log n}{\log\log n^2}\right) \qquad (6.17)$$

there is a Boolean function $f \in B_n$ which can be computed by a WRAM with $p(n) = n^{O(1)}$ processors in time T but which cannot be computed by a WRAM with $p(n) = n^{O(1)}$ processors in time $T-1$.

The same holds if the number of processors $p(n)$ and the communication width $c(n)$ simultaneously are bounded by a polynomial.

ii) For any T such that

$$T = \frac{\log n}{5 \log\log n} - \omega \left(\frac{\log n}{\log\log n^2} \right) \tag{6.18}$$

there is a Boolean function $f \in B_n$ which can be computed by a WRAM with communication width $c(n) = n^{O(1)}$ in time T but which cannot be computed by a WRAM with communication width $c(n) = n^{O(1)}$ in time $T-1$.

Essentially the proof of Theorem 6.1 depends only on $l_{\min}(f_n)$. The only argument which depends on the parity function is the equality $d(M(1,T)_{\pi(T)}) = D_T$ in (6.8). The degree of $M(1,T)_{\pi(T)}$ equals the dimension of the restricted input set, since $l_{\min}(f_n) = n$ for the parity function f_n. In the general case the degree of $M(1,T)_{\pi(T)}$ is not smaller than $l_{PI}(g_n)$ where $g_n = (f_n)_{\pi(T)}$. $l_{PI}(g_n)$ is not smaller than $l_{\min}(f_n) - (n - D_T)$ (see the proof of Theorem 4.2 iv, Ch. 11). Hence

$$s \geq l_{\min}(f_n) - n + \frac{1}{48} n (96 s)^{-(T-1)} \tag{6.19}$$

for $s = \log 4 p(n)$. This implies

$$96^T s^{T-1} (s + n - l_{\min}(f_n)) \geq 2 n. \tag{6.20}$$

For almost all $f_n \in B_n$, $l_{\min}(f_n) \geq n - \lfloor \log n \rfloor - 1$ (see § 7). W.l.o.g. $p(n) \geq n$. Then $s \geq n - l_{\min}(f_n)$ and

$$2 n \leq 96^T s^{T-1} (s + n - l_{\min}(f_n)) \leq 2 \cdot 96^T s^T, \tag{6.21}$$

$$(96 s)^T \geq n \quad \text{and} \quad s \geq (1/96) n^{1/T}. \tag{6.22}$$

THEOREM 6.3 : The lower bounds of Theorem 6.1 hold for almost all $f_n \in B_n$.

Furthermore (6.20) holds for all $f_n \in B_n$. If $l_{\min}(f_n)$ is not too small, we obtain powerful lower bounds on the WRAM complexity of these functions.

13.7 Properties of complexity measures for PRAMs and WRAMs

All the powerful lower bounds for bounded-depth circuits, PRAMs or WRAMs depend essentially on one of the following three combinatorial complexity measures: $c(f)$, the critical complexity of f (Def. 4.2) , $l_{min}(f)$, the minimal sensitive complexity or the length of a shortest prime implicant or prime clause of f (Def. 4.1, Ch. 11 and Ch. 13) , and $l_{max}(f)$, the maximal sensitive complexity or the length of a longest necessary prime implicant or prime clause of f (Def. 4.1). We investigate these complexity measures in detail. If nothing else is stated explicitly the results are due to Bublitz, Schürfeld, Voigt and Wegener (86).

We begin with the relations between the single complexity measures.

THEOREM 7.1 : i) $l_{min}(f) \leq l_{max}(f)$ and $c(f) \leq l_{max}(f)$ for all $f \in B_n$.

ii) $l_{min}(OR_n) = 1$ but $c(OR_n) = l_{max}(OR_n) = n$ for the symmetric and monotone function $OR_n \in B_n$.

iii) There are functions $f_n \in B_n$ where $c(f_n) = \lfloor n/2 \rfloor + 2$ but $l_{max}(f_n) = n - 1$.

iv) For all $n = 6m$, there are functions $f_n \in B_n$ where $c(f_n) = (1/2)n$ but $l_{min}(f_n) = (5/6)n$.

v) $c(f) \geq l_{max}(f) 2^{l_{max}(f) - n}$ for all $f \in B_n$, in particular $c(f_n) = n$ iff $l_{max}(f_n) = n$ for $f_n \in B_n$.

Proof : i) The first part is obvious and the second part is Proposition 4.1 .

ii) is obvious.

iii) Let $f_n \in S_n$ be defined by its value vector $v(f_n) = (v_0, \ldots, v_n)$ where $v_i = 1$ iff $i \in \{\lfloor n/2 \rfloor, \lfloor n/2 \rfloor + 1\}$. The assertion holds for these functions. The proof is left to the reader (who should apply Theorem

7.3).

iv) Let $f \in B_4$ be defined by the following Karnaugh diagram.

f	0 0	0 1	1 1	1 0
0 0	0	1	1	1
0 1	0	0	0	1
1 1	1	1	0	1
1 0	0	1	0	0

By case inspection, $c(f) = 2$ and $l_{min}(f) = 3$. If $n = 4m$, let $f_n \in B_n$ be equal to the $\oplus$-sum of m copies of f on disjoint sets of variables. Then $c(f_n) = (1/2) n$ and $l_{min}(f_n) = (3/4) n$. Paterson (pers. comm.) defined some $f \in B_6$ where $c(f) = 3$ and $l_{min}(f) = 5$. This leads considering the above arguments to the claim of Part iv of the theorem.

v) We use a pigeon-hole argument. Let $k = l_{max}(f)$. Then we find an $(n-k)$-dimensional subcube S where f is constant such that f is not constant on any subcube S' which properly contains S. By definition

$$\sum_{a \in S} c(f,a) \le c(f) |S| = c(f) 2^{n-k} . \tag{7.1}$$

There are k dimensions to increase S, but in each dimension we find a neighbor b of some $a \in S$ where $f(a) \neq f(b)$. Hence

$$\sum_{a \in S} c(f,a) \ge k . \tag{7.2}$$

The assertion follows from (7.1) and (7.2).

□

It is an open problem to prove optimal bounds on $l_{min}(f_n) / c(f_n)$ or $l_{max}(f_n) / c(f_n)$. The importance of such bounds has already been discussed in § 4. We obtain optimal results for the classes M_n of monotone functions and S_n of symmetric functions (Wegener (85 b)).

THEOREM 7.2 : $c(f) = l_{max}(f)$ for all $f \in M_n$.

Proof : Because of Theorem 7.1 i it is sufficient to prove the $"\geq"$-part. Let t be a prime implicant of f of length k . Let $a \in \{0,1\}^n$ be defined such that $a_i = 1$ iff x_i is contained in t . Since $t(a) = 1$, also $f(a) = 1$. Monoms m , where $m(a) = 1$, are shortenings of t . Hence t is the unique prime implicant where $t(a) = 1$. If b is a neighbor of a such that $a_i = 1$ but $b_i = 0$ for some i , then $t(b) = 0$. By monotonicity $t'(b) = 0$ for all $t' \in PI(f)$ and $f(b) = 0$. Hence $c(f) \geq c(f,a) = k$. Dual arguments hold for prime clauses. $\square$

We remember that $v_{max}(f_n)$ and $v_{min}(f_n)$ denote for $f_n \in S_n$ the length of a longest and shortest maximal constant substring of $v(f_n)$ resp. (see Ch. 11, § 4 and Exercises).

THEOREM 7.3 : i) $l_{min}(f) = n + 1 - v_{max}(f)$ for $f \in S_n$.

ii) $l_{max}(f) = n + 1 - v_{min}(f)$ for $f \in S_n$.

iii) Let $v(f) = (v_0, \ldots, v_n)$ for $f \in S_n$ and let $v_{-1} = v_{n+1} = -1$. If $v_i \neq v_{i+1}$ and $v_i \neq v_{i-1}$ for some i , then $c(f) = n$. Otherwise

$$c(f) = \max \{k + 1, n - k \mid v_k \neq v_{k+1}, 0 \leq k \leq n-1\}. \tag{7.3}$$

iv) $l_{min}(f) \leq c(f) \leq l_{max}(f)$ for $f \in S_n$.

Proof : i) see Lemma 4.1 in Ch. 11 .

ii) see Exercise 9 in Ch. 11 .

iii) If $a \in \{0,1\}^n$ contains i ones, a has i neighbors with $i-1$ ones and $n-i$ neighbors with $i+1$ ones.

iv) is obvious by i and iii . $\square$

Later we prove that $c(f) \geq \lceil (n+1)/2 \rceil$ for all non constant $f \in S_n$. The example in the proof of Theorem 7.1 iii is that symmetric function where $l_{max}(f_n)/c(f_n)$ is maximum. Hence the quotient is bounded by 2.

By Theorem 7.3, $l_{min}(f)$, $c(f)$ and $l_{max}(f)$ can be computed for $f \in S_n$ from $v(f)$ in linear time $O(n)$. For further fundamental functions it is possible to compute the complexity with respect to these complexity measures. But in general this computation is NP-hard. Therefore it is helpful to know the complexity of an easiest function in some class. This yields a lower bound for all other functions in this class.

DEFINITION 7.1 : Let $F_n \subseteq B_n$ be a class of functions and let M be a complexity measure for the functions in F_n. Then $M(F_n)$ is the minimal $M(f)$ for all $f \in F_n$ depending essentially on all n variables.

Obviously $l_{min}(B_n) = l_{min}(M_n) = l_{min}(S_n) = 1$ and this assertion leads to useless lower bounds. The situation is different for the critical and the maximal sensitive complexity. The lower bounds of the following theorem have been proved by Simon (83) and the upper bounds by Wegener (85 b).

THEOREM 7.4 : If $n \geq 2$,

$$\frac{1}{2}\log n - \frac{1}{2}\log\log n + \frac{1}{2} \leq c(B_n) \leq l_{max}(B_n) \leq l_{max}(M_n) \qquad (7.4)$$

$$= c(M_n) \leq \frac{1}{2}\log n + \frac{1}{4}\log\log n + O(1).$$

Proof : It follows from Theorem 7.1 and Theorem 7.2 that $c(B_n) \leq l_{max}(B_n) \leq l_{max}(M_n) = c(M_n)$.

For the upper bound we define a monotone storage access function MSA_n on $n+k$ variables $x = (x_1, \ldots, x_k)$ and $y = (y_1, \ldots, y_n)$ where $n = \binom{k}{\lfloor k/2 \rfloor}$. Let A be the class of all subsets of $\{1,\ldots,k\}$ of size $\lfloor k/2 \rfloor$ and let $\alpha : A \rightarrow \{1,\ldots,n\}$ be one-to-one. Then

$$MSA_n(x,y) = T^k_{\lfloor k/2 \rfloor + 1}(x) \vee \bigvee_{A \in \mathcal{A}} \left(\bigwedge_{i \in A} x_i \wedge y_{\alpha(A)} \right).$$ (7.5)

Only address vectors with exactly $\lfloor k/2 \rfloor$ ones are valid for MSA_n. We claim that

$$c(MSA_n) = \lceil k/2 \rceil + 1.$$ (7.6)

Obviously the length of all prime implicants is $\lfloor k/2 \rfloor + 1$. For inputs in $MSA_n^{-1}(0)$ let l be the number of ones in x. If $l < \lfloor k/2 \rfloor - 1$, the input is 0-critical. If $l = \lfloor k/2 \rfloor - 1$, the input is at most $k - (\lfloor k/2 \rfloor - 1) = \lceil k/2 \rceil + 1$-critical, since we have to change some x_i from 0 to 1 in order to obtain an input in $MSA_n^{-1}(1)$. Some of these inputs are $\lceil k/2 \rceil + 1$ - critical, e.g. if all $y_j = 1$. If $l = \lfloor k/2 \rfloor$, we have to change one of the $k - \lfloor k/2 \rfloor = \lceil k/2 \rceil$ 0-entries in x or the appropriate y_j in order to find a neighbor in $MSA_n^{-1}(1)$. Since $l \leq \lfloor k/2 \rfloor$ for inputs in $MSA_n^{-1}(0)$, we have proved the claim.

For arbitrary n, we consider the smallest m such that MSA_m is defined on at least n variables. We define $f_n \in B_n$ as a subfunction of MSA_m where the appropriate number of y-variables is replaced by ones. Then f_n depends essentially on n variables and $c(f_n) \leq c(MSA_m)$. We obtain the upper bound in (7.4) by (7.6) and Stirling's formula.

The lower bound is proved by counting methods. At first we prove a simple combinatorial claim.

CLAIM : Let G be a subgraph of the cube $C_n = \{0,1\}^n$ where in C_n the vertices with Hamming distance 1 are connected by an edge. If the degree of each vertex in G is at least r, then G has at least 2^r vertices.

Proof of the Claim : By induction on n. Obviously $n \geq r$. If $n = r$, $G = C_n$ and G contains 2^n vertices. If $n > r$, we partition C_n to C^0_{n-1} and C^1_{n-1} by fixing the last dimension to 0 and 1 resp. If G is contained in C^0_{n-1} or in C^1_{n-1}, the claim follows from the induction hypothesis. Otherwise G is partitioned to $G_0 \subseteq C^0_{n-1}$ and $G_1 \subseteq C^1_{n-1}$. The degree of each vertex in G_0 or G_1 is at least $r-1$, since only one neighbor is in the other subcube. It follows from the induction hypothesis that G_0 and G_1 contain at least 2^{r-1} vertices each. Hence G contains at least 2^r vertices. □

For the proof of the lower bound let $f \in B_n$ depend essentially on n variables. We color the cube $C_n = \{0,1\}^n$ by coloring the vertex a by $f(a)$ and the edge (a,b) by 1 if $f(a) \neq f(b)$ and by 0 otherwise. Since $c(f,a) \leq c := c(f)$, each vertex is connected to at most c 1-edges. C_n contains at most $c\,2^{n-1}$ 1-edges.

We look for a lower estimate on the number of 1-edges. We fix $i \in \{1,...,n\}$. Let C_0 and C_1 be the $(n-1)$-dimensional subcubes where we have fixed the i-th dimension to 0 and 1 resp. We estimate the number of 1-edges between C_0 and C_1. Since f depends essentially on x_i there is a 1-edge between some $a \in C_0$ and $a(i) \in C_1$. Again $a(i)$ is the i-th neighbor of a. We consider the graph G of all vertices $(b,b(i))$ where $b \in C_0$. The vertices $(b,b(i))$ and $(b',b'(i))$ are connected by an edge iff b and b' are neighbors in C_0 and $f(b') = f(b) \neq f(b(i)) = f(b'(i))$. Let H be the set of vertices $(b,b(i))$ which can be reached in G from $(a,a(i))$. Since $f(b) \neq f(b(i))$ for $(b,b(i)) \in H$, at least $|H|$ 1-edges are connecting C_0 and C_1.

We claim that each $(b,b(i)) \in H$ has at least $n-2c+1$ neighbors in G. At most c 1-edges are leaving b, one of them leads to $b(i)$. At most c 1-edges are leaving $b(i)$, one of them leads to b. Hence there are at least $n-2c+1$ dimensions to which b and $b(i)$ are connected by 0-edges. These neighbors are in G. The graph of all b where $(b,b(i)) \in H$ is a subgraph of some $(n-1)$-dimensional cube where the degree of each vertex is at least $n-2c+1$. From the combinatorial claim it follows that this graph contains at least 2^{n-2c+1} vertices. Hence we have at least 2^{n-2c+1} 1-edges in the i-th dimension and altogether at least $n\,2^{n-2c+1}$ 1-edges. We combine this result with the upper bound $c\,2^{n-1}$ on the number of 1-edges. Thus

$$n\,2^{n-2c+1} \leq c\,2^{n-1} \quad \Rightarrow \quad 4n \leq c\,2^{2c} \tag{7.7}$$

$$\Rightarrow \quad c > \frac{1}{2} \log n - \frac{1}{2} \log \log n + \frac{1}{2} . \qquad \square$$

THEOREM 7.5 : i) If $f \in B_n$ depends essentially on n variables, then a PRAM computing f has time complexity $\Omega(\log \log n)$.

ii) MSA_n depends essentially on more than n variables and can be computed by a PRAM with $O(n \log n)$ processors and communication width $O(n \log n)$ in time $O(\log \log n)$.

Proof : i) follows from Theorem 7.4 and Theorem 4.3 . For the proof of ii we refer to Wegener (85 b). $\qquad \square$

This result indicates again how excellent the lower bound of Theorem 4.3 is.

THEOREM 7.6 : $c(S_n) = l_{max}(S_n) = \lceil (n+1)/2 \rceil$.

Proof : Obviously $c(S_n) \le l_{max}(S_n)$. For $f_n = T^n_{\lceil (n+1)/2 \rceil}$, $l_{max}(f_n) = \lceil (n+1)/2 \rceil$, since T^n_k has only prime implicants of length k and prime clauses of length $n+1-k$. Hence $l_{max}(S_n) \le \lceil (n+1)/2 \rceil$. If $f \in S_n$ is not constant, $v_i \ne v_{i+1}$ for some i . By Theorem 7.3 iii

$$c(f) \ge \max \{ i+1 , n-i \} \ge \lceil (n+1)/2 \rceil \qquad (7.8)$$

and $c(S_n) \ge \lceil (n+1)/2 \rceil$. $\qquad \square$

The lower bound of Theorem 7.4 is optimal, but it implies only a lower bound of $\Theta(\log n)$ on the critical and maximal sensitive complexity of Boolean functions. That is why one looked for fundamental classes of functions for which one can prove better results. One example is the class of symmetric functions (see Theorem 7.6), and another one is the class of graph properties.

DEFINITION 7.2 : A Boolean function f on $N = \binom{n}{2}$ variables x_{ij} $(1 \le i < j \le n)$ is a graph property if for all permutations $\pi \in \Sigma_n$

$$f(x_{1,2}, \ldots, x_{n-1,n}) = f(x_{\pi(1),\pi(2)}, \ldots, x_{\pi(n-1),\pi(n)}) \tag{7.9}$$

is satisfied. We denote the set of all (monotone) graph properties by G_N and MG_N resp.

Obviously all graph problems are described by graph properties. A graph problem does not depend on the numbering of the vertices.

THEOREM 7.7 : i) $\lfloor n/4 \rfloor < c(G_N) \le l_{max}(G_N) \le n-1$.

ii) $c(MG_N) = l_{max}(MG_N) = n-1$.

Part i has been proved by Turán (84), his conjecture that $c(G_N) = n-1$ is still open. Only the weaker assertion that $c(MG_N) = n-1$ has been proved by Wegener (85 b). We present only the proof of Part ii of the Theorem which includes the upper bound of Part i . The proof of the lower bound of Part ii is more typical than the proof of the lower bound of Part i and supports our philosophy that the complexity of functions is described by the length and structure of the prime implicants and prime clauses.

Proof of Theorem 7.7 ii : For the upper bound we investigate the graph property "no vertex is isolated" (Turán (84)). The proper function $f \in G_N$ is obviously monotone. Its monotone conjunctive normal form is

$$f(x) = \bigwedge_{1 \le i \le n} (\bigvee_{1 \le j < i} x_{ji} \vee \bigvee_{i < j \le n} x_{ij}) , \tag{7.10}$$

each prime clause has length $n-1$. The i-th clause computes 0 iff the i-th vertex is isolated. The prime implicants correspond to minimum graphs without isolated vertices. These are spanning forests where each tree contains at least 2 vertices. The number of edges in spanning forests, and therefore also the length of prime implicants, is bounded by $n-1$. Hence $l_{max}(MG_N) \le n-1$.

Since $MG_N \subseteq M_N$, $l_{max}(MG_N) = c(MG_N)$ by Theorem 7.2 . It is sufficient to prove that $l_{max}(MG_N) \ge n-1$. All prime implicants and prime clauses of monotone functions are necessary. Therefore it is sufficient to prove for $f \in MG_N$ the existence of a prime implicant or prime clause whose length is at least $n-1$. This is equivalent to the existence of a minimum satisfying graph with at least $n-1$ edges or a maximum non satisfying graph with at least $n-1$ missing edges. A graph G is called satisfying for $f \in G_N$ iff G satisfies the graph property described by f.

We assume that all minimum satisfying graphs have at most $n-2$ edges, otherwise we are done. We construct a maximum non satisfying graph with at least $n-1$ missing edges.

Let l be the maximal number of isolated vertices in a minimum satisfying graph. For a graph G let $m(G)$ be the minimal degree of a non isolated vertex. Let m be the minimal $m(G)$ for all minimum satisfying graphs with l isolated vertices. We claim that

$$m \leq \lfloor (2n-4) / (n-l) \rfloor . \qquad (7.11)$$

For the proof of this claim we investigate a graph G^* defining m. G^* has, by our assumption, at most $n-2$ edges. The sum of the degrees of all vertices is at most $2n-4$. The degree of each of the $n-l$ non isolated vertices is at least m. Hence the sum of the degrees of all vertices is at least $m(n-l)$. This implies $m(n-l) \leq 2n-4$ and (7.11).

We construct a maximum non satisfying graph G. Let G' consist of a complete graph K_{n-l-1} on the vertices $v_1, \ldots, v_{n-l-1}$ and $l+1$ isolated vertices $v_{n-l}, \ldots, v_n$. It follows from the definition of l that G' is non satisfying. We add as many edges as possible, until we obtain a maximum non satisfying graph G. For $i \geq n-l$, vertex v_i is connected to at most $m-1$ vertices v_k where $k < n-l$. Otherwise we could embed G^* into G and by monotonicity G would be satisfying. For this purpose we identify the vertices v_j $(j \neq i, j \geq n-l)$ with the l isolated vertices of G^*. We identify v_i with a vertex v^* of degree m in G^* and m neighbors of v_i with the m neighbors of v^*.

We prove that at least $n-1$ edges are missing in G. The number of missing edges between the vertex sets $v_1, \ldots, v_{n-l-1}$ and $v_{n-l}, \ldots, v_n$ is at least $(n-l-1-(m-1))(l+1)$. We are done if

$$(n - l - m)(l + 1) \geq n - 1 .\tag{7.12}$$

If $l = 0$, $m = 1$ by (7.11) and (7.12) is satisfied. Otherwise it is by (7.11) sufficient to prove that

$$(n - l - (2n - 4)/(n - l))(l + 1) \geq n - 1 .\tag{7.13}$$

If $l \geq 1$, this is equivalent to

$$l^2 - 2ln + l + n^2 - 3n + 3 \geq (n - 4)/l .\tag{7.14}$$

For $l \geq 1$ it is sufficient to have

$$l^2 - 2ln + l + n^2 - 3n + 3 \geq n - 4 \qquad \text{or}\tag{7.15}$$

$$l \leq n - (1/2) - (3n - 27/4)^{1/2} .\tag{7.16}$$

In particular, the assertion is proved for $n \leq 3$. To capture the cases where (7.16) is not satisfied we distinguish between two cases.

Case 1 : G^* is not the complete graph on $n - l$ vertices, K_{n-l}, together with l isolated vertices.

In this case $m \leq n - l - 2$ and $n - l - m \geq 2$. Hence v_i is for $i \geq n - l$ not connected to at least two of the vertices v_j where $j < n - l$. The number of missing edges is at least $2(l + 1)$. This is at least $n - 1$ iff

$$l \geq (n - 3)/2\tag{7.17}$$

is satisfied. It is easy to see that always either (7.16) or (7.17) is satisfied.

Case 2 : G^* is equal to the complete graph on $n - l$ vertices, K_{n-l}, together with l isolated vertices.

This minimum satisfying graph has, for $r = n - l$, $\binom{r}{2}$ edges. It follows from our assumption that

$$\binom{r}{2} \leq n - 2 .\tag{7.18}$$

Until now we have not counted the missing edges within the vertex set $v_{n-l}, \ldots, v_n$. Since $m \geq 1$, at least $l + 1 = n - r + 1$ edges are missing between the two vertex sets. Let z be the number of vertices

v_i $(i \geq n-l)$ which are not connected to at least two vertices v_j where $j < n-l$. Then we may count at least $n-r+1+z$ missing edges between the two vertex sets. Furthermore there are $n-r+1-z$ vertices v_i $(i \geq n-l)$ for which only one edge to the other vertex set is missing. If $z \geq r-2$, we have already counted enough missing edges. Otherwise we partition the $n-r+1-z$ vertices v_i $(i \geq n-l)$ with one missing edge to $r-1$ equivalence classes. v_i and v_j are equivalent if they have the same missing neighbor v_k $(1 \leq k \leq n-l-1 = r-1)$. If v_i and v_j are in the k-th equivalence class the edge between v_i and v_j is missing. Otherwise v_i, v_j and all v_l $(1 \leq l \leq r-1, l \neq k)$ build an r-clique and G is a satisfying graph.

Let $N(k)$ be the size of the k-th equivalence class. Altogether we have proved the existence of

$$n - r + 1 + z + \sum_{1 \leq k \leq r-1} \binom{N(k)}{2} \qquad (7.19)$$

missing edges. The parameters $N(k)$ satisfy the condition

$$\sum_{1 \leq k \leq r-1} N(k) = n - r + 1 - z. \qquad (7.20)$$

The sum of all $\binom{N(k)}{2}$ where the parameters $N(k)$ satisfy (7.20) is minimal (because of the convexity of $x \to \binom{x}{2}$) if $\{ N(1), ..., N(r-1) \}$ consists of at most two numbers M and $M+1$. If the sum of all $N(k)$ is $2(r-2-z) + (z+1)$, the sum of all $\binom{N(k)}{2}$ is minimal if $N(k) = 2$ for $r-2-z$ terms and $N(k) = 1$ for $z+1$ terms. Then the sum of all $\binom{N(k)}{2}$ is at least $r-2-z$ and the number of missing edges is at least $n-1$. Hence we are done if

$$n - r + 1 - z \geq 2(r - 2 - z) + (z + 1) = 2r - 3 - z \qquad (7.21)$$

is satisfied. (7.21) is equivalent to

$$r \leq (n + 4)/3. \qquad (7.22)$$

It is easy to prove that (7.18) implies (7.22).

$\square$

It follows from Theorem 7.7 and Theorem 4.3 that the PRAM time complexity of all graph properties is $\Omega(\log N)$ and from Theorem 7.7 and Theorem 5.3 that the time complexity of all graph properties with respect to PRAMs of communication width m is $\Omega((n/m)^{1/3}) = \Omega(N^{1/6}/m^{1/3})$. The last lower bound can be improved to $\Omega((N/m)^{1/3})$ for most of the fundamental graph properties $f \in G_N$ by proving that $l_{\max}(f) = \Theta(N)$ for these graph properties. Nearly all fundamental graph properties are monotone. Schürfeld and Wegener (86) present conditions which can be tested efficiently and which lead for most of the fundamental graph properties to the assertion that these graph properties are $\Theta(N)$-critical.

We have seen that some functions have small critical and small maximal sensitive complexity, that several functions have small minimal sensitive complexity and that many functions have a large complexity with respect to the complexity measures. We present tight bounds for the complexity of almost all functions in B_n, M_n or S_n. These results have already been applied in Ch. 11, § 4, and Ch. 13, § 6, and they generalize all lower bounds of Ch. 11 and Ch. 13.

THEOREM 7.8 : i) The fraction of $f \in B_n$ where $c(f) = n-1$ or $c(f) = n$ tends to e^{-1} or $1 - e^{-1}$ resp., hence $c(f) \geq n-1$ for almost all $f \in B_n$.

ii) $c(f) = l_{\max}(f)$ for almost all $f \in B_n$.

iii) Let $\alpha(n)$ be any function tending to ∞ as $n \to \infty$. Then

$$n - \lceil \log(n + \log^2 n - \log n + \alpha(n)) \rceil < l_{\min}(f) \qquad (7.23)$$

$$\leq n - \lfloor \log(n - \log n - \alpha(n)) \rfloor$$

for almost all $f \in B_n$, in particular $l_{\min}(f) \in I_n$ for almost all $f \in B_n$ and some intervals I_n containing $n - \lfloor \log n \rfloor$ and at most one further positive integer.

Proof : i) We motivate the result. Consider a random Boolean function, i.e. all 2^{2^n} $f \in B_n$ have the same probability. Then for all

$a \in \{0,1\}^n$

$$Pr(c(f,a) = n) = 2^{-n} \quad \text{and} \quad Pr(c(f,a) = n-1) = n\,2^{-n}. \qquad (7.24)$$

Let us assume for a moment that $c(f,a)$ and $c(f,b)$ are independent, which is only satisfied if $d(a,b) \geq 3$ for the Hamming distance d. Then

$$Pr(c(f) = n) = 1 - (1 - 2^{-n})^{2^n} \qquad \to 1 - e^{-1} \quad \text{and} \qquad (7.25)$$

$$Pr(c(f) \geq n-1) = 1 - (1 - (n+1)2^{-n})^{2^n} \to 1 \quad \text{as } n \to \infty. \qquad (7.26)$$

The critical complexity $c(f,a)$ is not independent from the critical complexity of only $n + \binom{n}{2}$ of the other $2^n - 1$ inputs. Thus we suggest that (7.25) and (7.26) are almost correct.

Let $X_a(f) = 1$ if $c(f,a) = n-1$ and $X_a(f) = 0$ otherwise. Let $X(f)$ be the sum of all $X_a(f)$, then $X(f)$ is the number of $(n-1)$-critical inputs. Since

$$Pr(c(f) \geq n-1) \geq Pr(X > 0), \qquad (7.27)$$

it is sufficient to prove that $Pr(X=0) \to 0$ as $n \to \infty$. From Chebyshev's inequality follows that

$$Pr(X = 0) \leq V(X) / E^2(X) = E(X^2) / E^2(X) - 1. \qquad (7.28)$$

Obviously $E(X_a) = n\,2^{-n}$ and $E(X) = n$. By definition

$$X^2 = \sum_a X_a^2 + \sum_{a \neq b} X_a X_b = \sum_a X_a + \sum_{a \neq b} X_a X_b. \qquad (7.29)$$

By case inspection, we prove that

$$E(X_a X_b) = O(n^2 2^{-2n}) \quad \text{if} \quad d(a,b) \leq 2. \qquad (7.30)$$

If $d(a,b) \geq 3$, $c(f,a)$ and $c(f,b)$ are independent and

$$E(X_a X_b) = E(X_a) E(X_b) = n^2 2^{-2n}. \qquad (7.31)$$

Altogether

$$E(X^2) \leq E(X) + E^2(X) + O(n^4 2^{-n}) \quad \text{and} \qquad (7.32)$$

$$Pr(X = 0) \leq \frac{1}{n} + 1 + O(n^2 2^{-n}) - 1 \qquad (7.33)$$

tends to 0 as $n \to \infty$.

By a more complicated calculation, using the method of factorial moments, one proves that the number of n-critical inputs is asymptotically Poisson distributed with parameter $\lambda = 1$. In particular

$$\Pr(c(f) = n) \to 1 - e^{-1} \quad \text{as} \quad n \to \infty. \tag{7.34}$$

For a detailed proof of these claims we refer to Bublitz, Schürfeld, Voigt and Wegener (86). (7.34) together with the fact that $\Pr(c(f) \geq n-1) \to 1$ as $n \to \infty$ implies the assertions of Part i.

ii) follows from i, Theorem 7.1 i and Theorem 7.1 v.

iii) Again we investigate random Boolean functions $f \in B_n$. For f we color the vertex a of the input cube $\{0,1\}^n$ by $f(a)$. We want to prove that

$$\Pr(l_{\min}(f) \leq n - c(n)) \to 1 \tag{7.35}$$

$$\text{for} \quad c(n) = \lfloor \log(n - \log n - \alpha(n)) \rfloor \quad \text{and}$$

$$\Pr(l_{\min}(f) \leq n - d(n)) \to 0 \tag{7.36}$$

$$\text{for} \quad d(n) = \lceil \log(n + \log^2 n - \log n + \alpha(n)) \rceil.$$

To prove (7.35) we observe that $l_{\min}(f) \leq n - c(n)$ iff there exists a $c(n)$-dimensional subcube of $\{0,1\}^n$ colored by one color. We partition $\{0,1\}^n$ to $2^{n-c(n)}$ disjoint $c(n)$-dimensional subcubes C_i $(1 \leq i \leq 2^{n-c(n)})$. Then the events E_i: "not all vertices of C_i have the same color" are independent. Obviously the probability of E_i is $1 - 2^{-2^{c(n)}+1}$. Hence

$$\Pr(l_{\min}(f) \leq n - c(n)) \geq 1 - \Pr(\forall i : E_i) \tag{7.37}$$

$$\geq 1 - (1 - 2^{-2^{c(n)}})^{2^{n-c(n)}}$$

$$= 1 - ((1 - 2^{-2^{c(n)}})^{2^{2^{c(n)}}})^{2^{n-c(n)-2^{c(n)}}}.$$

The right-hand side of this inequality tends to 1 if $n - c(n) - 2^{c(n)}$ tends to infinity. This property is fulfilled for $c(n) = \lfloor \log(n - \log n - \alpha(n)) \rfloor$.

For the second assertion we observe that a function f where $l_{min}(f) \leq n-d(n)$ has to possess an implicant or a clause of length $n-d(n)$. An implicant or a clause of length $n-d(n)$ determines the value of f on $2^{d(n)}$ inputs. Therefore there are $2^{2^n - 2^{d(n)}}$ functions $f \in B_n$ with the same fixed implicant or clause of length $n-d(n)$. Furthermore there are $2 \binom{n}{n-d(n)} 2^{n-d(n)}$ different implicants and clauses of length $n-d(n)$. Thus

$$\Pr(l_{min}(f) \leq n-d(n)) \leq 2^{-2^n} 2 \binom{n}{n-d(n)} 2^{n-d(n)} 2^{2^n - 2^{d(n)}}$$
$$\leq 2^{n + 1 + d(n)(\log n - 1) - 2^{d(n)}} . \tag{7.38}$$

The right-hand side of this inequality tends to zero if $2^{d(n)} - (n + 1 + d(n)(\log n - 1))$ tends to infinity. This happens if

$$d(n) = \lceil \log(n + \log^2 n - \log n + \alpha(n)) \rceil . \tag{7.39}$$

□

THEOREM 7.9 : i) $c(f) = l_{max}(f) = \lceil n/2 \rceil + 1$ for almost all $f \in M_n$.

ii) $l_{min}(f) = \lfloor n/2 \rfloor - 1$ for almost all $f \in M_n$.

Proof : The proof is based on the characterization of almost all $f \in M_n$ due to Korshunov (81 a) , see Theorem 5.1, Ch. 4 . His result implies that for almost all $f \in M_n$

$$a_1 + \cdots + a_n \leq \lfloor n/2 \rfloor - 2 \Rightarrow f(a) = 0 \quad \text{and} \tag{7.40}$$

$$a_1 + \cdots + a_n \geq \lceil n/2 \rceil + 2 \Rightarrow f(a) = 1 . \tag{7.41}$$

Since prime implicants correspond to minimal ones and prime clauses correspond to maximal zeros, we know that for almost all $f \in M_n$ the length of any prime implicant or prime clause may take only the values $\lfloor n/2 \rfloor - 1 , \ldots , \lceil n/2 \rceil + 2$. Hence

$$\lfloor n/2 \rfloor - 1 \leq l_{min}(f) \leq l_{max}(f) = c(f) \leq \lceil n/2 \rceil + 2 \tag{7.42}$$

for almost all $f \in M_n$. For the proof of the exact bounds of the theorem we refer to Bublitz, Schürfeld, Voigt and Wegener (86) . Here we are satisfied with the weaker result (7.42). □

THEOREM 7.10 : i) $c(f) = l_{max}(f) = n$ for almost all $f \in S_n$.

ii) Let $\alpha(n)$ be any function tending to ∞ as $n \to \infty$. Then

$$n - \log n - \alpha(n) \leq l_{min}(f) \leq n - \log n + \alpha(n) \tag{7.43}$$

for almost all $f \in S_n$.

Proof : i) $c(f) = n$ if the value vector $v(f)$ contains $0\,1\,0$ or $1\,0\,1$ as a substring. Obviously almost all $v \in \{0,1\}^{n+1}$ contain $0\,1\,0$ or $1\,0\,1$ as a substring.

ii) By Theorem 7.3 i $l_{min}(f) = n + 1 - v_{max}(f)$ for $f \in S_n$. The claim (7.43) is equivalent to

$$\log n - \alpha(n) \leq v_{max}(f) \leq \log n + \alpha(n) \tag{7.44}$$

for almost all $f \in S_n$. This is a well-known result about the longest constant substring of a random $0 - 1$-string of length $n + 1$ (see e.g. Feller (68)). □

EXERCISES

1. (Cook, Dwork and Reischuk (86)). A PRAM is called almost oblivious if the number of the memory cell into which the i-th processor writes at time step t is allowed to depend on the input length but not on the input itself. A PRAM is called oblivious if also the decision whether the i-th processor writes at time step t may depend on the input length and not on the input itself. The time complexity of oblivious PRAMs computing f is not smaller than $\lceil \log c(f) \rceil + 1$. Hint: $K_{t+1} = L_{t+1}$, $L_{t+1} = K_t + L_t$.

2. The time complexity of almost oblivious PRAMs computing f is not smaller than t if $c(f) \geq F_{2t+1}$, the $(2t+1)$-st Fibonacci

number. Hint: $K_{t+1} = K_t + L_t$, $L_{t+1} = K_{t+1} + L_t$.

3. Prove Theorem 7.5 ii .

4. The graph property "no vertex is isolated" can be decided by a PRAM with $O(N)$ realistic processors in time $\log N + O(1)$.

5. Estimate the size and the depth of the circuit designed in the proof of Theorem 3.1 .

6. The processors of a non deterministic WRAM (N-WRAM) may flip during one computation step independent unbiased coins. An N-WRAM accepts a $\in \{0,1\}^n$ iff there is an accepting computation path. There is an N-WRAM with $O(n)$ processors and communication width 1 computing T_2^n in $O(1)$ steps.

7. Prove Lemma 4.2 .

8. Let $f \in B_n$ be defined by a set of clauses or implicants and $k \in \{1,\ldots,n\}$. It is NP-hard to decide whether $c(f) \geq k$. The same holds for l_{min} and l_{max} .

9. Investigate the complexity of the outputs of
    a) the binary addition ,
    b) the binary multiplication ,
    c) the Boolean matrix product ,
    d) the Boolean convolution
    with respect to c , l_{min} and l_{max} .

10. How long are the prime implicants and prime clauses of the monotone storage access functions ?

11. How long are the prime implicants and prime clauses of $f_n^t \in B_n$ where $f_n^t(a) = 1$ iff $a_i = \cdots = a_{i+t-1}$ (indices mod n) for some i ?

12. Each non constant graph property depends on all N variables.

13. The graph properties
    a) G contains a k-clique ,
    b) G contains a Hamiltonian circuit ,
    c) G contains an Eulerian circuit ,
    d) G contains a perfect matching
    are $\Theta(N)$-critical.

14. The graph property " G contains a vertex whose degree is at least $\lceil d n \rceil$ " is $\Theta(N)$-critical, if $0 < d < 1$.

15. The graph property " G contains no isolated vertex" has minimal sensitive complexity $\lceil n/2 \rceil$.

16. $l_{min}(f) = \min \{ l(f,0), l(f,1) \}$ for $f \in M_n$ and the constant inputs 0 and 1 .

17. Determine the number of $f \in M_n$ where $l_{min}(f) \geq \lfloor n/2 \rfloor + 1$.

18. Let M be the complexity measure of Def. 5.1 . Then $M(f) \leq l_{max}(f)$ for all $f \in B_n$ and $M(f) = O(1)$ for almost all $f \in B_n$.

19. The number of $f \in S_n$ where $c(f) < n$ or $l_{max}(f) < n$ is $2 F_{n-1}$ for the $(n-1)$st Fibonacci number F_{n-1} .

14. BRANCHING PROGRAMS

14.1 The comparison of branching programs with other models of computation

DEFINITION 1.1 : A branching program (BP) is a directed acyclic graph consisting of one source (no predecessor), inner nodes of fan-out 2 labelled by Boolean variables and sinks of fan-out 0 labelled by Boolean constants. The computation starts at the source which also is an inner node. If one reaches an inner node labelled by x_i , one proceeds to the left successor, if the i-th input bit a_i equals 0 , and one proceeds to the right successor, if $a_i = 1$. The BP computes $f \in B_n$ if one reaches for the input a a sink labelled by $f(a)$.

A branching program may be understood as a single processor of arbitrary computation resources which can read at most one input bit per time unit.

DEFINITION 1.2 : The size of a BP is equal to the number of inner nodes (computation nodes), and the depth of a BP is equal to the length of a longest path. The corresponding complexity measures for $f \in B_n$ are denoted by $BP(f)$ and $BPD(f)$.

The branching program depth is a measure for the computation time. What is the meaning of the branching program size ? Obviously, a BP of size c can be written as a (non uniform) program of GO TO's depending on if-tests on the Boolean variables. Then c is the number of GO TO's , i.e. the program size. The following relations between the branching program size $BP(f)$ and the space complexity $S(f)$ of non uniform Turing machines (see Def. 4.1, Ch. 9) for f have been proved by Cobham (66) and Pudlák and Zák (83) .

THEOREM 1.1 : If $f_n \in B_n$, then

$$S(f_n) \quad = \quad O(\log(\max\{BP(f_n), n\})) \quad \text{and} \tag{1.1}$$

$$BP(f_n) = 2^{O(h(n))} \quad \text{where} \quad h(n) = \max\{S(f_n), \log n\}. \tag{1.2}$$

Proof : Let G_n be a BP for f_n of size $BP(f_n)$. We simulate G_n by a non uniform Turing machine whose oracle is an encoding of G_n . We encode each node of G_n by its number ($O(\log BP(f_n))$ bits) , the number of its direct successors ($O(\log BP(f_n))$ bits) and the index of its label ($O(\log n)$ bits) .

The encoding of G_n has length $O(BP(f_n)(\log BP(f_n) + \log n))$. G_n can be simulated step-by-step. We store on the working tape the encoding of the node we have reached, look on the input tape for the input bit tested at this node and copy the encoding of the successor node. Hence the space complexity of the Turing machine is bounded by (1.1) .

Let M be a non uniform Turing machine for f_n with space complexity $S(f_n)$. The number of configurations of M is bounded by $2^{O(h(n))}$ (see (3.3) and § 4, Ch. 9). We simulate M by a BP G_n . Each configuration of M is simulated by a node, the initial configuration is the source, accepting configurations are 1-sinks, and rejecting configurations are 0-sinks. The successors of a node v simulating the configuration c are the nodes for the configurations c_0 and c_1 which are the successor configurations of c if M reads on the input tape 0 and 1 resp. The label of v is x_i if c is neither accepting nor rejecting and the head of the input tape reads x_i . Hence (1.2) is proved. $\qquad\square$

Moreover, there are tight relations between branching programs and circuits (see e.g. Wegener (84 b)).

THEOREM 1.2 : i) $C(f) \le 3\,BP(f)$ for all $f \in B_n$.

ii) $D(f) \leq 2 \, BPD(f)$ for all $f \in B_n$.

iii) $BP(f) \leq L_\Omega(f) + 1$ for all $f \in B_n$ and $\Omega = \{\wedge, \vee, \neg\}$.

Proof : i) Let G be a BP for f of size $BP(f)$. At an inner node labelled by x_i we select the left successor if $x_i = 0$ and the right successor if $x_i = 1$. The selection function $sel(x,y,z) = \bar{x}\,y \vee x\,z$ selects y
if $x = 0$ or z if $x = 1$. Hence we obtain a circuit over the basis $\{sel\}$
with $BP(f)$ gates for f if we reverse the direction of the edges, all
inner nodes are sel-gates with the following inputs: x_i , the former
label of the node, v_0 , the former left successor of the node, and v_1 ,
the former right successor of the node. The assertion follows since
$C(sel) = 3$.

ii) can be proved in a similar way starting with a depth optimal BP .
$D(sel) = 2$.

iii) is proved by induction on $l = L_\Omega(f)$. The assertion is obvious for
$l = 0$. Let $l = L_\Omega(f) > 0$, and let the assertion be proved for functions
of smaller formula size. Let F be an optimal formula for f . If the
last gate of F is a $\neg$-gate, the assertion follows from the induction
hypothesis, since f and $\neg f$ have the same BP size. If the last gate
of F is an $\wedge$-gate , $f = g \wedge h$ for some functions g and h , where
$L_\Omega(g) + L_\Omega(h) = l - 1$. By induction hypothesis, $BP(g) + BP(h) \leq l + 1$.
Hence it is sufficient to prove that $BP(f) \leq BP(g) + BP(h)$. We use optimal BPs $G(g)$ for g and $G(h)$ for h . We obtain a BP $G(f)$ for f of
size $BP(g) + BP(h)$ in the following way. The source of $G(f)$ is the
source of $G(g)$ and all 1-sinks of $G(g)$ are identified with the source
of $G(h)$. Similar arguments work for an $\vee$-gate.

□

The branching program complexity of f lies in the interval
$[C(f)/3, L_\Omega(f) + 1]$. For almost all $f \in B_n$, $BP(f)$ is close to the left
end of the interval.

THEOREM 1.3 : i) $BP(f) \geq (1/3) \, 2^n \, n^{-1}$ for almost all $f \in B_n$.

ii) $BP(f) = O(2^n \, n^{-1})$ for all $f \in B_n$.

Proof : i) follows from Theorem 2.1 , Ch. 4 , and Theorem 1.2 i .

ii) follows from a simple simulation of the improved decoding circuit in § 2 , Ch. 4 . □

DEFINITION 1.3 : A BP G is synchronous if for all nodes v in G all paths from the source to v have the same length $d(v)$. The width $w(l)$ of level l is the number of nodes v with $d(v) = l$. The width of G is the maximum $w(l)$.

Bounded-depth circuits with gates of unbounded fan-in can be simulated efficiently by branching programs of small width.

THEOREM 1.4 : If $f \in B_n$ can be computed by a circuit with c gates of unbounded fan-in ($\wedge$- , $\vee$-gates) and k logical levels, then f can be computed by a BP G of depth $c^{k-1}n$ and width max $\{2, k\}$. Hence the size of G is at most $c^{k-1} \, n \, \max\{2, k\}$.

Proof : Induction on k . For $k = 1$ we can compute the conjunction or disjunction of at most n literals. This can be done by a BP of depth n and width 2 . The BP can be constructed in such a way that it has only two sinks, both on the same level.
If $k > 1$, let $g_1, \ldots, g_m$ be the functions computed in $k-1$ logical levels. By the induction hypothesis there are BPs $G_1, \ldots, G_m$ of depth $c^{k-2}n$ and width max $\{2, k-1\}$ for $g_1, \ldots, g_m$. If the last gate of the circuit is a conjunction (similar arguments work for a disjunction) , we join the BPs $G_1, \ldots, G_m$ in the same way as $G(g)$ and $G(h)$ in the proof of Theorem 1.2 . We have to ensure that the new BP is synchronous. Therefore we gather the 1-sinks of each G_i on a new path which increases the width by 1 . If $k = 2$, the new path is not necessary, since G_i has only one 1-sink at its bottom. Since $m \leq c$, we obtain a BP for f of depth $c^{k-1}n$ and width k . □

This theorem implies that functions with c prime implicants can be computed by a BP of depth cn and width 2 . The theorem also implies that lower bounds on the complexity of width-bounded BPs are harder to achieve than lower bounds on depth-bounded circuits. For instance, the parity function is not in SIZE - DEPTH(poly,const) but has width-2 BPs of depth n . At the computation nodes on level i $(0 \le i \le n-1)$ we test x_{i+1} . If $x_1 \oplus \cdots \oplus x_{i+1} = 0$, we proceed to the first node on level $i+1$, otherwise to the second node on level $i+1$. On level n the first node is a 0-sink, the second one a 1-sink. We discuss width-bounded BPs more detailed in § 5 .

14.2 The depth of branching programs

DEFINITION 2.1 : A function $f \in B_n$ with $BPD(f) = n$ is called elusive.

This notation has been introduced by Bollobás (76) . Kahn, Saks and Sturtevant (84) used the notion evasive instead of elusive. The elusiveness of many functions can be proved by the following relation (Bublitz, Schürfeld, Voigt and Wegener (86)) and results of Ch. 13 .

THEOREM 2.1 : $BPD(f) \ge l_{max}(f) \ge c(f)$ for all $f \in B_n$.

Proof : The second inequality has been proved in Proposition 4.1 , Ch. 13 . For the first inequality we consider an input $a \in \{0,1\}^n$ where $k := l(f,a) = l_{max}(f)$. If $BPD(f) < k$, the computation path for a in some depth-optimal BP for f has length $l < k$. We have tested at most l variables and f is constant on some $(n-l)$-dimensional cube containing a . Since $n-l \ge n-k+1$, this contradicts the definition of k . $\qquad\Box$

This result indicates that many functions are elusive. This fact is also underlined by the following asymptotic results.

THEOREM 2.2 : i) Almost all $f \in B_n$ are elusive.

ii) Almost all $f \in M_n$ are elusive.

iii) All non constant $f \in S_n$ are elusive.

Proof : i) (Rivest and Vuillemin (76)). If $BPD(f) \leq n-1$, we consider a depth-optimal decision tree for f. A decision tree is a BP whose nodes have fan-in bounded by 1. This restriction does not increase the depth. We add computation nodes such that all leaves (sinks) are lying on level $n-1$. Since the BP is a tree, we assume w.l.o.g. that no variable is tested twice on any computation path. Hence each of the 2^{n-1} leaves is reached for 2 inputs a and b with Hamming distance $d(a,b) = 1$. Each 1-leaf is reached by one input a where $|a|$, the number of ones in a, is even and one input b where $|b|$ is odd. We conclude that the sets $\{a \in f^{-1}(1) \mid |a|$ even$\}$ and $\{a \in f^{-1}(1) \mid |a|$ odd$\}$ have the same size $k \in \{0,...,2^{n-1}\}$ if $BPD(f) \leq n-1$.

For fixed k, there are $\binom{2^{n-1}}{k}$ possibilities of choosing k inputs out of the 2^{n-1} inputs with $|a|$ even. The same holds for $|a|$ odd. Therefore $N(n)$, the number of non elusive $f \in B_n$, can be estimated by

$$N(n) \leq \sum_{0 \leq k \leq 2^{n-1}} \binom{2^{n-1}}{k}\binom{2^{n-1}}{k} \tag{2.1}$$

$$= \sum_{0 \leq k \leq 2^{n-1}} \binom{2^{n-1}}{k}\binom{2^{n-1}}{2^{n-1}-k} = \binom{2^n}{2^{n-1}}.$$

The number of all $f \in B_n$ is 2^{2^n}. Hence the assertion i follows from a simple application of the Stirling formula.

ii) has been proved by Bublitz, Schürfeld, Voigt and Wegener (86) using results of Rivest and Vuillemin (76) and Korshunov (81 a). We do not present the proof here.

iii) If $f \in S_n$ is not constant, then $v(f)$, the value vector of f, is not constant either. Let $v_i \neq v_{i+1}$. We consider a depth-optimal decision tree for f. We follow that path where the first i tested variables have value 1 and the next $n-1-i$ tested variables have value 0. Afterwards it might be possible that the number of ones in the input is i or $i+1$. Since $v_i \neq v_{i+1}$, we have to test the last variable and the depth of the tree is n. $\qquad\square$

It is easy to describe functions with the minimum BP depth.

THEOREM 2.3 : i) If f depends essentially on n variables, then
$\quad$ BPD$(f) \geq \lceil \log(n+1) \rceil$.

ii) There are functions $f \in B_n$ depending essentially on n variables where BPD$(f) = \lceil \log(n+1) \rceil$.

Proof : i) If f depends essentially on x_i, each BP for f contains at least one inner node labelled by x_i. Since the fan-out in a BP is bounded by 2, the lower bound follows.

ii) Consider a binary tree with n inner nodes and depth $\lceil \log(n+1) \rceil$ and label exactly one inner node by x_i $(1 \leq i \leq n)$. The leaves are labelled in such a way that brothers have different labels. The function f, computed by this BP, depends essentially on $x_1, \ldots, x_n$ and its BP depth is $\lceil \log(n+1) \rceil$. $\qquad\square$

Another example of a simple function with respect to BP depth is the storage access function $SA_n \in B_{n+k}$ where $n = 2^k$ (see Def. 5.1, Ch. 3). First of all, we test the k address variables $a_{k-1}, \ldots, a_0$ and then $x_{|a|}$. Hence

$$BPD(SA_n) = k + 1 = \lceil \log(n+k+1) \rceil. \qquad (2.2)$$

It is often difficult to decide whether f is elusive. Elusiveness proofs follow, in general, the pattern of the proof of Theorem 2.2 iii. For each BP for f one tries to define an input a whose computation path has length n .

The input size for graph properties is $N = \binom{n}{2}$. The results of Ch. 13 imply that $BPD(f) \geq n/4$ for all $f \in G_N$, $BPD(f) \geq n-1$ for all $f \in MG_N$ and $BPD(f) = \Omega(N)$ for most of the fundamental graph properties. Best, van Emde Boas and Lenstra (74) described a graph property (scorpion graphs) whose BP depth is small, namely at most 6 n . Aanderaa and Rosenberg conjectured that there is some $\varepsilon > 0$ such that $BPD(f) \geq \varepsilon N$ for all $f \in MG_N$. This conjecture has been proved by Rivest and Vuillemin (76) for $\varepsilon = 1/16$ and by Kleitman and Kwiatkowski (80) for $\varepsilon = 1/9$. Kahn, Saks and Sturtevant (84) achieved the best result which is

$$BPD(f) \geq (1/4)N - o(N) \quad \text{for all n and } f \in MG_N \text{ and} \tag{2.3}$$

$$BPD(f) = N \quad \text{for } n = 6 \text{ or } n = p^k \text{ (p prime) and } f \in MG_N . \tag{2.4}$$

The extended conjecture of Karp that all $f \in MG_N$ are elusive is still open. Further examples of elusive graph properties are "the graph contains a k -clique" and "the graph is k -colorable" (Bollobás (76)). For additional results on elusiveness we refer to Bollobás (78) and Hedtstück (85).

14.3 The size of branching programs

There is no theory on design methods for size optimal BPs. What is known about lower bounds ? We cannot expect $\omega(n^2)$ -bounds, since $BP(f) \leq L_{\{\wedge,\vee,\neg\}}(f) + 1$ (Theorem 1.2 i). The Krapchenko method cannot be translated to BPs , since this method yields its largest bound for the parity function, and the parity function has linear BPs . But the idea of the Nechiporuk method (Ch. 8, § 7) works also for BPs .

THEOREM 3.1 : Let $f \in B_n$ depend essentially on all its variables, let $S_1, \ldots, S_k \subseteq X$ be disjoint sets of variables and let s_i be the number of S_i-subfunctions of f . Then

$$BP(f) = \Omega \left(\sum_{1 \le i \le k} (\log s_i) / (\log \log s_i) \right).\tag{3.1}$$

Proof : We estimate $N(r,t)$, the number of BPs of size t on r variables. The number of edges is $2t$, since each inner node has fan-out 2 . Each edge leaving v_i may select its end out of $v_{i+1}, \ldots, v_t$ and the two sinks. There are r possible labellings for each inner node. Hence

$$N(r,t) \le r^t ((t+1)!)^2 \le r^t t^{2t} , \text{ if } t \ge 3.\tag{3.2}$$

Let $r(i) = |S_i|$ and let $t(i)$ be the number of nodes in an optimal BP for f labelled with some $x_j \in S_i$. Each S_i-subfunction of f can be computed by a BP of size $t(i)$. We only have to replace the other variables by the appropriate constants. Hence

$$s_i \le N(r(i),t(i)) \le r(i)^{t(i)} (t(i))^{2t(i)} , \text{ if } t(i) \ge 3.\tag{3.3}$$

Since f depends essentially on all variables, $r(i) \le t(i)$. Therefore

$$s_i \le t(i)^{3t(i)} , \text{ if } t(i) \ge 3 \text{ and}\tag{3.4}$$

$$t(i) = \Omega((\log s_i) / (\log \log s_i)).\tag{3.5}$$

Since, by definition, $BP(f)$ is the sum of all $t(i)$, we have proved the theorem. $\square$

From the arguments used in Ch. 8, § 7, we obtain the following results. By Theorem 3.1 one cannot prove larger lower bounds than bounds of size $n^2 \log^{-2} n$. $BP(ISA_n) = \Omega(n^2 \log^{-2} n)$ but $C(ISA_n) = O(n)$ for the storage access function for indirect addressing, $BP(det_n) = \Omega(n^3 \log^{-1} n)$ for the determinant and $BP(cl_{n,m}) = \Omega((n-m)^3 \log^{-1} n)$ for clique functions.

Pudlák (84 b) translated the Hodes and Specker method (Ch. 8, § 5) to BPs and proved $\Omega(n(\log\log n)/(\log\log\log n))$ lower bounds on the BP complexity of threshold functions T_k^n where k and n−k are not too small. Budach (84) applied topological methods, but he obtained only bounds for decision trees.

14.4 Read-once-only branching programs

DEFINITION 4.1 : A read-k-times-only branching program (BPk) is a branching program where each variable is tested on each computation path at most k times. The minimum size of a BPk for f is denoted by BPk(f) .

A BP1 is called read-once-only branching program. This computation model was introduced by Masek (76). The corresponding machine model is the non uniform eraser Turing machine, i.e. a Turing machine that erases each input bit after having read it. For BPk s each input bit is given k times. Theorem 1.1 holds also for read-once-only BPs and eraser Turing machines. Hence lower bounds on the BP1 complexity lead to lower bounds on the space complexity of eraser Turing machines. The same holds for upper bounds.

For read-k-times-only BPs and $k \geq 2$ no lower bounds are known which are essentially larger than lower bounds for general BPs . Hence we consider in this section only read-once-only BPs .

At first we show that optimal BP1s for symmetric functions $f \in S_n$ can be designed by an efficient algorithm working on the value vector $v(f)$ of f (Wegener (84 b)). In the following we denote by S_n the class of all non constant symmetric functions $f \in B_n$.

THEOREM 4.1 : For all $f \in S_n$ there is an optimal BP1 which is synchronous and where all computation nodes on level l are labelled by x_{l+1} .

Proof : The following claim holds for all BP1s but in general not for

BPs . If p is a path in a BP1 , then there is an input a(p) for which p is part of the computation path. Let f_p be the subfunction of f where we have replaced the variables read on p by the proper constants.

Now we consider an optimal BP1 G for $f \in S_n$. Let p' and p'' be paths from the source to the computation node v . We claim, that $l(p') = l(p'')$, where $l(p)$ is the length of p , that we read the same input variables on p' and p'' (perhaps with different results) and that $f_{p'} = f_{p''}$.

If v is followed for some $b \in \{0,1\}$ by b-sinks only, v can be replaced by a b-sink. Hence we assume that $f_{p'}$ and $f_{p''}$ are not constant. $f_{p'}$ is a symmetric function on $n - l(p')$ variables. By Theorem 2.2 iii the longest path p starting in v has length $n - l(p')$. The same holds for p'' . Hence $l(p') = l(p'')$. On p' and p'' we read all variables that have not been read on p . In particular, we read on p' and p'' the same set of variables. The BP1 with source v computes $f_{p'}$ and $f_{p''}$. Hence $f_{p'} = f_{p''}$.

Now we relabel the computation nodes such that the nodes on level l (the BP is synchronous by the claim above) are labelled by x_{l+1} . We claim that the new BP1 G' computes f . Let p be a path in G from the source to a b-sink. If we have chosen m_0 times the left successor and m_1 times the right successor on p , then $f(a) = b$ for all inputs a with at least m_0 zeros and at least m_1 ones. If the same path is used in G' , the input contains at least m_0 zeros and at least m_1 ones. The output b is computed correctly. $\square$

By this theorem on the structure of optimal BP1s for symmetric functions f , we can design optimal BP1s efficiently. The level 0 consists of the source labelled by x_1 . At each node v on level l we still have to compute a symmetric function f_v on $n - l$ variables. The node v gets a second label i indicating that $(v_i, \ldots, v_{i+n-l})$ is the value vector of f_v . This additional label is $i = 0$ for the source. For a node v on level l labelled by x_{l+1} and i we need two successors

v^0 and v^1 on level $l+1$ with labels x_{l+2} (if $l+2 \leq n$) and i or i+1 resp. The only problem is now to decide which nodes on level $l+1$ can be merged or replaced by sinks. A node can be replaced by a constant iff the proper value vector is constant. Two nodes can be merged iff the proper value vectors coincide.

The number of nodes constructed on level $l+1$ is at most $2 N(l)$ where $N(l)$ is the minimum number of nodes on level l in an optimal BP1 for f. This consequence results from the fact that all nodes on level l for which we have constructed successors belong to an optimal BP1 for f. We know the value vectors which belong to the nodes on level $l+1$. By a generalized bucket sort we sort these value vectors in time $O(n N(l))$ according to the lexicographical order. In time $O(n N(l))$ it can be decided which nodes can be replaced by sinks and which nodes can be merged. We continue until all nodes are replaced by sinks on level n. Altogether we have constructed an optimal BP1 for $f \in S_n$ in time $O(n \, BP1(f))$. If we can handle also large numbers in one unit of time, we can decrease the running time of the algorithm to $O(BP1(f))$. But then the space complexity is large, namely $O(2^n)$. The original algorithm can be performed with linear space.

THEOREM 4.2 : There is an $O(n \, BP1(f))$ - time and $O(n)$ - space algorithm for the computation of an optimal BP1 for $f \in S_n$ given by its value vector.

Together with this algorithm we obtain the following characterization of the BP1 - complexity of symmetric functions.

THEOREM 4.3 : For $f \in S_n$ let $r_l(f)$ $(0 \leq l \leq n-1)$ be the number of different non constant subvectors $(v_i, \ldots, v_{i+n-l})$ $(0 \leq i \leq l)$ of the value vector $v(f)$.

i) $BP1(f) = \sum\limits_{0 \leq l \leq n-1} r_l(f)$.

ii) $BP1(f) \leq \sum\limits_{0 \leq l \leq n-1} \min\{l+1, 2^{n-l+1}-2\}$

$= n^2/2 - n \log n + O(n)$.

Proof : i) follows from Theorem 4.1 and the algorithm from Theorem 4.2 . For ii) we state that $r_l(f) \leq l+1$ (we consider only $l+1$ subvectors) and that $r_l(f) \leq 2^{n-l+1}-2$ (we consider non constant vectors of length $n-l+1$). $\qquad \square$

If the value vector of $f \in S_n$ is a de Bruijn sequence (see Exercises), we obtain a symmetric function of maximum BP1 - complexity. The proofs of the following results on the majority function $T^n_{\lceil n/2 \rceil}$ and the exactly - $\lceil n/2 \rceil$ function $E^n_{\lceil n/2 \rceil}$ are left as an exercise.

THEOREM 4.4 : i) $BP1(T^n_{\lceil n/2 \rceil}) = n^2/4 + \Theta(n)$.

ii) $BP1(E^n_{\lceil n/2 \rceil}) = n^2/4 + \Theta(n)$.

iii) $BPk(E^n_{\lceil n/2 \rceil}) = O(n^{(k+1)/k})$.

iv) $BP(E^n_{\lceil n/2 \rceil}) = O(n \log^2 n / \log\log n)$.

All symmetric functions have BP1-complexity bounded by $O(n^2)$ (Theorem 4.3 ii). Because of the small number of subfunctions many computation paths can be merged after a short time. For many other functions f one can prove that paths, whose lengths are at most d , cannot end in a sink and cannot be merged with other computation paths. Then each BP1 for f contains at its top a complete binary tree of d levels and therefore at least 2^d-1 computation nodes. This lower bound method has been introduced by Wegener (84 c) for the proof of lower bounds on the BP1-complexity of clique functions $cl_{n,k}$ (see Def. 11.1, Ch. 6). Dunne (85) applied this method to the logical permanent PM_n (perfect matching, see Def. 12.2, Ch. 6) and to the Hamiltonian circuit functions (see Exercise 32 b, Ch. 6).

THEOREM 4.5 : Let G be a BP1 for the clique function $cl_{n,k}$. Let p and q be different paths in G starting at the source and ending in $v(p)$ and $v(q)$ resp. If at most $k(1) = \binom{k}{2} - 1$ ones and at most $k(0) = n - k^2 + 2$ zeros have been read on p and q, then neither $v(p)$ nor $v(q)$ is a sink and $v(p) \neq v(q)$. In particular

$$BP1(cl_{n,k}) \geq \sum_{0 \leq m \leq k(0)+k(1)} \sum_{m-k(0) \leq j \leq k(1)} \binom{m}{j}. \qquad (4.1)$$

Proof : (4.1) follows easily from the first part of the theorem. For each 0-1-sequence $a_1, \ldots, a_m$ with at most $k(0)$ zeros and $k(1)$ ones there is a computation node in G. The lower bound in (4.1) is equal to the number of these sequences.

We turn to the proof of the structural results. Before we have not tested all variables of a prime implicant or a prime clause with the right result we do not reach a sink. $cl_{n,k}$ is monotone. Consequently, the variables of a prime implicant have to be ones. All prime implicants of $cl_{n,k}$ have length $\binom{k}{2} > k(1)$, they correspond to a minimal graph with a k-clique. According to the results of Ch. 13 prime clauses correspond to maximal graphs without any k-clique. The largest maximal graphs are by Turán's theorem (see e.g. Bollobás (78)) complete $(k-1)$-partite graphs where the size of all parts is $\lfloor n/(k-1) \rfloor$ or $\lceil n/(k-1) \rceil$. We have to estimate the number of missing edges. This number is underestimated if we assume that all parts have size $n/(k-1)$ and each vertex is not connected to $n/(k-1)-1$ other vertices. Hence $l(0) \geq (1/2)n(n/(k-1)-1)$ for the length $l(0)$ of the shortest prime clause. Since $l(0) > k(0)$, neither $v(p)$ nor $v(q)$ is a sink.

Let us assume that $w = v(p) = v(q)$. Since p and q are different paths, there is a first node w' where the paths separate. W.l.o.g. w' is labelled by $x_{1,2}$. Let G_p and G_q be the partially specified graphs specified by the computation paths p and q resp. Edges tested positively are called existing, whereas edges tested negatively are called forbidden, all other edges are called variable. W.l.o.g. the edge $(1,2)$ exists in G_p and is forbidden in G_q. Let G' be the part of G

whose source is w. We shall prove the existence of a path r from w to some sink such that we have to reach a 1-sink on the compound path (p,r) and a 0-sink on (q,r). This will contradict the assumption that $v(p) = v(q)$.

Let A be the set of vertices $i \notin \{1,2\}$ such that i lies on some existing edge in G_q. Since G_q contains at most $k(1)$ edges,

$$|A| \leq 2\,k(1) = k^2 - k - 2. \tag{4.2}$$

Let B be a set of vertices $j \notin \{1,2\}$ such that for each edge $e = (i,i')$ forbidden in G_p, $i \in B$ or $i' \in B$. It is possible to choose B such that

$$|B| \leq k(0) = n - k^2 + 2. \tag{4.3}$$

The set $C := \{1,...,n\} - A - B$ contains at least k vertices, among them the vertices 1 and 2. Let $D \subseteq C$ be chosen such that $|D| = k$ and $1,2 \in D$. Let r be the path from w to a sink where we choose the right successor, the 1-successor, iff $i,j \in D$ for the label x_{ij} of the computation node. The path (p,r) leads to a 1-sink, since no edge on D has been tested negatively. Let $G_{q,r}$ be the graph specified on (q,r). Only vertices in $D \cup A$ may have positive degree. Since G_q does not contain any k-clique and only edges on D are tested positively on r, a k-clique in $G_{q,r}$ has to contain two vertices of D. Since the edge $(1,2)$ is forbidden, a k-clique in $G_{q,r}$ has to contain a vertex $i \in D - \{1,2\}$ and a vertex $j \in A$. The edge (i,j) is not tested positively on (q,r). Hence $G_{q,r}$ does not contain any k-clique, and the path (q,r) leads to a 0-sink. $\qquad\Box$

COROLLARY 4.1 : i) $BP1(cl_{n,k}) = \Omega(n^{k(k-1)/2-1})$ for constant k.

ii) $BP1(cl_{n,m(n)}) \geq 2^{n/3-o(n)}$ for $m(n) = \lceil (2n/3)^{1/2} \rceil$.

iii) $BP1(cl_{n,n/2}) \geq 2^{n/6-o(n)}$.

iv) The space complexity of eraser Turing machines for $cl_{n,n/2}$ is $\Omega(n) = \Omega(N^{1/2})$ where $N = \binom{n}{2}$ is the input size.

Proof : i) follows from (4.1) where $\binom{k(0)+k(1)}{k(1)}$ is the largest term.

ii) By definition of $m(n)$, $k(0)$ and $k(1)$ are of size $n/3 - o(n)$. Each BP1 for $cl_{n,m(n)}$ contains at the top a complete binary tree of depth $n/3 - o(n)$.

iii) $cl_{n-m(n),n/2-m(n)}$ is a subfunction of $cl_{n,n/2}$. Let $m(n) = n/2 - \lceil (n/3)^{1/2} \rceil$. Then $k(0)$ and $k(1)$ are of size $n/6 - o(n)$.

iv) is a corollary to iii. $\qquad\square$

Larger lower bounds have been proved by Ajtai, Babai, Hajnal, Komlós, Pudlák, Rödl, Szemerédi and Turán (86).

THEOREM 4.6 : Let $\oplus cl_{n,3}$ be the graph property computing 1 if the number of triangles (3-cliques) in the graph specified by x is odd. Then $BP1(\oplus cl_{n,3}) = 2^{\Omega(N)}$ and the space complexity of eraser Turing machines for $\oplus cl_{n,3}$ is $\Omega(n^2) = \Omega(N)$.

Recently Kriegel and Waack (86) gave an easier proof of a $2^{\Omega(N)}$-bound for another function. We do not prove these theorems. We prove two results which we shall apply in § 6. The first one is due to Wegener (86 a).

DEFINITION 4.2 : $cl_{n,k}^* \in MG_N$ is the graph property which tests whether a graph contains a k-clique of special type, these are k-cliques where at least $k-2$ vertices $i_1, \ldots, i_{k-2}$ build a consecutive sequence $i, i+1, \cdots, i+k-3 \mod n$.

THEOREM 4.7 : $BP1(cl_{n,k(n)}^*) = 2^{m(n)}$ if $k(n) = \lfloor n^{1/3} \rfloor$ and $m(n) = (1/4) n^{2/3} - o(n^{2/3})$.

Proof : After $m(n)$ positive tests we still have not found a k-clique of special type. After $m(n)$ negative tests at most $(1/2) n^{2/3}$ vertices lie on a forbidden edge. Hence there is a consecutive sequence of $k(n)$ vertices which may still build a $k(n)$-clique of special type. The depth of all sinks is larger than $m(n)$.

It is now sufficient to prove that two paths p and q whose lengths are bounded by $m(n)$ and which start at the source of a BP1 for $cl_{n,k(n)}^{*}$ cannot stop at the same node. Again w.l.o.g. $(1,2)$ exists in G_p but is forbidden in G_q. There is a set of vertices D such that $|D| = k(n)$, D contains the vertices 1 and 2, D contains a consecutive sequence of $k(n) - 2$ vertices, and no edge incident to some $i \in D - \{1,2\}$ has been tested on p or q. The proof is completed on the pattern of the proof of Theorem 4.5.

$\square$

DEFINITION 4.3 : $clo_n \in G_N$ (n even) is the graph property which tests whether a graph contains an $n/2$-clique but no edge outside of this clique.

This so-called clique-only function has been investigated by Pudlák and Zák (83) and Zák (84). The function has short prime clauses. If the edges $(1,2)$ and $(1,3)$ exist, but $(2,3)$ is forbidden, we know that $clo_n(x) = 0$. But all prime implicants have length $N = \binom{n}{2}$. It is possible to prove that the "width" of a BP1 for clo_n is somewhere not too small.

THEOREM 4.8 : $BP1(clo_n) \geq 2^{n/3 - o(n)}$.

Proof : W.l.o.g. n can be divided by 6. Let G be a BP1 for clo_n. For a vertex set H of size $n/2$ let $p(H)$ be the computation path for the graph that contains only the clique on H. Let $v(H)$ be the first computation node on $p(H)$ where at least $n/2 - 2$ vertices lie on an existing edge. We claim that $v(H) \neq v(H')$ if $|H \cap H'| \leq n/2 - 3$. We conclude the theorem from our claim before we prove the claim. We partition the vertex set $\{1,...,n\}$ to three sets M_1, M_2 and M_3 each of size $n/3$. The number of subsets of M_i of size $n/6$ is $a = \binom{n/3}{n/6}$. Let $M_{i,j}$ $(1 \leq j \leq a)$ be these sets. We consider H_j, the union of $M_{1,j}$, $M_{2,j}$ and $M_{3,j}$ for $1 \leq j \leq a$. Then $|H_j \cap H_{j'}| \leq n/2 - 3$ if $j \neq j'$.

The computation nodes $v(H_1), \ldots, v(H_a)$ are different due to the claim above. Hence G contains at least $a = 2^{n/3 - o(n)}$ computation nodes.

For the proof of the claim we assume that $v(H) = v(H')$ although $|H \cap H'| \leq n/2 - 3$. Let $p^*(H)$ and $p^*(H')$ be those parts of $p(H)$ and $p(H')$ resp. that lead from the source to $v(H)$. On $p^*(H)$ and $p^*(H')$ we have tested the same set of variables. Otherwise some path, where not all variables are tested, would lead from the source to a 1-sink although all prime implicants have length N.

We investigate the computation path leading from the source via $p(H)$ to $v(H)$ and then via $p(H')$ to a 1-sink. The computation path is the path $p(H'')$ for some set H'' of size $n/2$. $|H \cap H''| \geq n/2 - 2$ by definition of $v(H)$. In particular, H'' contains some vertex $i \notin H'$. We prove the claim by proving that $H' = H''$. Each positive test increases the number of vertices lying on existing edges at most by 2. Hence there is some $j \in H'$ such that no edge $(j, \cdot)$ has been tested positively on $p^*(H')$. For all $k \in H' - \{j\}$, the edge (j, k) is tested positively on the second part of $p(H')$ and therefore on $p(H'')$. All these vertices $k \in H'$ and j have to belong to H'' because of the definition of clo_n.

□

We have proved exponential lower bounds on the BP1-complexity of NP-complete functions like $cl_{n, n/2}$ but also on the BP1-complexity of functions in P like clo_n, $cl^*_{n, k(n)}$ and $\oplus cl_{n, 3}$.

14.5 Bounded-width branching programs

We have defined the width of BPs in Definition 1.3. By Theorem 1.4 all $f \in B_n$ can be computed by a width-2 BP. Therefore w-k-BP(f), the minimum size of a width-k BP for f, is well-defined for

$k \geq 2$. We have already proved in Theorem 1.4 that depth-bounded circuits can be simulated efficiently by width-bounded branching programs. But the converse is false. The parity function has linear width-2 complexity but exponential size in circuits of constant depth (see Ch. 11, § 3). Later we present a complete characterization of BPs of bounded width and polynomial size.

Before that we report the history of lower bounds. Borodin, Dolev, Fich and Paul (83) proved that width-2 BPs for the majority function have size $\Omega(n^2 \log^{-1} n)$. By probabilistic methods Yao (83) improved this result. Width-2 BPs for the majority function cannot have polynomial size. Shearer (pers. comm.) proved an exponential lower bound on the width-2 BP complexity of the counting function $C_{1,3}^n$ computing 1 iff $x_1 + \cdots + x_n \equiv 1 \mod 3$.

For $k \geq 3$ no large lower bounds on the width-k BP complexity of explicitly defined Boolean functions are known. Using the Ramsey theory (see e.g. Graham, Rothschild and Spencer (80)) Chandra, Fortune and Lipton (83) proved that there is no constant k such that the majority function can be computed in width-k BPs of linear size. Ajtai et al. (86) could prove non trivial lower bounds for BPs whose width is not larger than $(\log n)^{O(1)}$ (poly log). Almost all symmetric functions, and in particular the following explicitly defined function "$x_1 + \cdots + x_n$ is a quadratic residue mod p for a fixed prime p between $n^{1/4}$ and $n^{1/3}$", cannot be computed by polylog−width BPs of size $o(n(\log n)/\log\log n)$.

All these results are motivated by the conjecture that the majority function cannot be computed by BPs of constant width and polynomial size. But this conjecture has been proved false by Barrington (86).

THEOREM 5.1 : Let $f_n \in B_n$. There is for some constant k a sequence of width-k BPs G_n computing f_n with polynomial size iff there is a sequence S_n of circuits with binary gates computing f_n with polynomial size and depth $O(\log n)$.

Each symmetric function $f_n \in S_n$ can be computed by a circuit of linear size and logarithmic depth (Theorem 4.1, Ch. 3). Hence Theorem 5.1 implies the existence of polynomial BPs of constant width for all symmetric functions, among them the majority function. We prove Theorem 5.1 in several steps.

Proof of Theorem 5.1 , only-if-part : Let G_n be BPs computing f_n in constant width k and polynomial size $p(n)$. The nodes of G_n are denoted in the following way: $v_{i,j}$ ($1 \leq i \leq k$, $0 \leq j \leq p(n)$) is the i-th node on level j , $v_{1,0}$ is the source, w.l.o.g. we have only two sinks both on level $p(n)$, $v_{1,p(n)}$ is the 1-sink, $v_{2,p(n)}$ the 0-sink. Let $g_{i,j,i',j'}(x) = 1$ if starting at the node $v_{i,j}$ on input x we reach $v_{i',j'}$. Then $f_n = g_{1,0,1,p(n)}$.

The functions $g_{i,j,i',j+1}$ depend essentially at most on one input variable, namely the label of $v_{i,j}$. These functions can be computed at a single gate. Let $j < j' < j''$. Each path from level j to level j'' has to pass through level j' . Hence

$$g_{i,j,i'',j''}(x) = \bigvee_{1 \leq i' \leq k} g_{i,j,i',j'}(x) \wedge g_{i',j',i'',j''}(x) . \tag{5.1}$$

This leads to a divide-and-conquer approach. W.l.o.g. $p(n) = 2^{m(n)}$. Then $m(n) = O(\log n)$. We proceed in $m(n)$ steps. In Step 0 we compute in parallel all $g_{i,j,i',j+1}(x)$. In Step r we apply (5.1) and compute in parallel all $g_{i,j,i'',j''}$ where j is a multiple of 2^r , $j'' = j + 2^r$ and $j' = j + 2^{r-1}$. The functions on the right-hand side of (5.1) are computed in Step $r-1$. In Step $m(n)$ we compute $g_{1,0,1,p(n)} = f_n$. Altogether we apply (5.1) not more than $2k^2 p(n)$ times. (5.1) can be realized by a circuit of size $2k$ and depth $\lceil \log k \rceil + 1$. Hence there is a circuit for f_n of size $4k^3 p(n)$ and depth $(\lceil \log k \rceil + 1)\lceil \log p(n) \rceil = O(\log n)$. $\square$

For the if-part Barrington introduced a new type of BPs .

DEFINITION 5.1 : A permutation $\sigma \in \Sigma_5$ is called a 5-cycle if $\sigma^i(j) \neq j$ for $i \in \{1,2,3,4\}$ and $j \in \{1,...,5\}$. We present a 5-cycle σ by the string $(a_1 a_2 a_3 a_4 a_5)$ where $\sigma(a_i) = a_{i+1}$ for $i \le 4$ and $\sigma(a_5) = a_1$.

DEFINITION 5.2 : A permutation branching program (PBP) of width k and length (or depth) l is given by a sequence of instructions $(j(i), g_i, h_i)$ for $0 \le i < l$, where $1 \le j(i) \le n$ and $g_i, h_i \in \Sigma_k$. A PBP has on each level $0 \le i \le l$ k nodes $v_{1,i}, \ldots, v_{k,i}$. On level i we realize $\sigma_i(x) = g_i$ if $x_{j(i)} = 0$ and $\sigma_i(x) = h_i$ if $x_{j(i)} = 1$. The PBP computes $\sigma(x) = \sigma_{l-1}(x) \cdots \sigma_0(x) \in \Sigma_k$ on input x . The PBP computes $f_n \in B_n$ via τ if $\sigma(x) = $ id for $x \in f_n^{-1}(0)$ and $\sigma(x) = \tau \ne$ id for $x \in f_n^{-1}(1)$.

LEMMA 5.1 : A PBP for f of width k and length l can be simulated by a BP of width k and length kl .

Proof : The PBP has k "sources" on level 0 . We obtain k BPs of width k and length l (one for each source). The nodes $v_{m,i}$ $(1 \le m \le k)$ are labelled by $x_{j(i)}$, and the wires from level i to level $i+1$ correspond to g_i and h_i . The nodes on the last level are replaced by sinks. In the r-th BP the $\tau(r)$-th node on the last level is replaced by a 1-sink, all other sinks are 0-sinks. This BP computes 1 iff $\sigma(x)(r) = \tau(r)$. Hence $f(x) = 1$ iff all BPs compute 1 . Similarly to the proof of Theorem 1.4 we combine the k BPs to a BP for f . We do not have to increase the width since all sinks lie on the last level.
□

Hence it is sufficient to design PBPs of width 5 . We restrict ourselves to 5-cycles τ which have properties that serve our purposes.

LEMMA 5.2 : If the PBP G computes f via the 5-cycle τ and ρ is another 5-cycle, then there is a PBP G' of the same length computing f via ρ .

Proof : The existence of $\vartheta \in \Sigma_5$ where $\rho = \vartheta \tau \vartheta^{-1}$ follows from elementary group theory (or by case inspection). In G' we simply replace the permutations g_i and h_i in the sequence of instructions by

$\vartheta g_i \vartheta^{-1}$ and $\vartheta h_i \vartheta^{-1}$ resp. Then the output permutations id and τ are replaced by $\vartheta \operatorname{id} \vartheta^{-1} = \operatorname{id}$ and $\vartheta \tau \vartheta^{-1} = \rho$.

□

LEMMA 5.3 : If the PBP G computes f via the 5-cycle τ, then there is a PBP G' of the same length computing ¬f via a 5-cycle.

Proof : Obviously τ^{-1} is a 5-cycle. We only change the last instruction : g_{l-1} is replaced by $\tau^{-1} g_{l-1}$ and h_{l-1} is replaced by $\tau^{-1} h_{l-1}$. Then $\sigma'(x) = \tau^{-1} \sigma(x)$. Hence $\sigma'(x) = \tau^{-1}$ for $x \in f^{-1}(0)$ and $\sigma'(x) = \operatorname{id}$ for $x \in f^{-1}(1)$. G' computes ¬f via τ^{-1}.

□

LEMMA 5.4 : There are 5-cycles τ_1 and τ_2 such that $\tau_1 \tau_2 \tau_1^{-1} \tau_2^{-1}$ is a 5-cycle.

Proof : $(12345)(13542)(54321)(24531) = (13254)$. □

THEOREM 5.2 : Let f be computed by a depth-d circuit S over the basis U_2. Then there is a PBP G computing f in width 5 and length 4^d.

Proof : The proof is by induction on d. For $d = 0$ the assertion is obvious. For the induction step we assume (by Lemma 5.3 w.l.o.g.) that the last gate of S is an ∧-gate where f is computed as $f = f_1 \wedge f_2$. Hence, by induction hypothesis, for f_1 and f_2 there are PBPs G_1 and G_2 of length 4^{d-1} each computing f_1 and f_2 via the 5-cycles ρ_1 and ρ_2 resp. By Lemma 5.2 and Lemma 5.4 we replace ρ_1 and ρ_2 by τ_1 and τ_2 resp. such that $\tau_1 \tau_2 \tau_1^{-1} \tau_2^{-1}$ is a 5-cycle. Furthermore there are PBPs G_3 and G_4 of length 4^{d-1} each computing f_1 and f_2 via the 5-cycles τ_1^{-1} and τ_2^{-1} resp. (see Lemma 5.2). If we concatenate the PBPs G_1, G_2, G_3 and G_4, we obtain a PBP G of length 4^d. Let $\sigma(x) = \sigma_1(x) \sigma_2(x) \sigma_3(x) \sigma_4(x) \in \Sigma_5$ be the permutation computed by G.

1. $f_1(x) = f_2(x) = 0 \Rightarrow \sigma_1(x) = \cdots = \sigma_4(x) = \text{id} \Rightarrow \sigma(x) = \text{id}$.

2. $f_1(x) = 0$, $f_2(x) = 1 \Rightarrow \sigma_1(x) = \sigma_3(x) = \text{id}$, $\sigma_2(x) = \tau_2$, $\sigma_4(x) = \tau_2^{-1} \Rightarrow \sigma(x) = \text{id}$.

3. $f_1(x) = 1$, $f_2(x) = 0 \Rightarrow \sigma(x) = \text{id}$ (similarly to Case 2).

4. $f_1(x) = f_2(x) = 1 \Rightarrow \sigma(x) = \tau_1 \tau_2 \tau_1^{-1} \tau_2^{-1}$, a 5-cycle and therefore unequal to id .

Hence G computes $f = f_1 \wedge f_2$ in width 5 and length 4^d .

$\square$

Proof of Theorem 5.1 , if-part : We only have to concatenate the constructions of Theorem 5.2 and Lemma 5.1 .

$\square$

This result explains also why one was not able to prove non polynomial lower bounds on the width- k BP complexity of explicitly defined functions if $k \geq 5$.

14.6 Hierarchies

We have proved implicitly that certain functions are hard in some models and simple in other models. We summarize these results.

THEOREM 6.1 : The majority function has non polynomial complexity with respect to circuits of constant depth and BPs of width 2 , but it has polynomial complexity with respect to monotone circuits, monotone formulas, BP1s and BPs of width 5 .

THEOREM 6.2 : The clique function $cl_{n,k(n)}^*$ for cliques of special type and size $k(n) = \lfloor n^{1/3} \rfloor$ has exponential complexity with respect to BP1s, but it has polynomial complexity with respect to width-2 BPs, depth-2 circuits, monotone circuits, and monotone formulas.

Proof : The number of prime implicants of $cl^*_{n,k(n)}$ can easily be estimated by $O(n^3)$.

$\square$

THEOREM 6.3 : $\oplus cl_{n,3}$ has exponential complexity with respect to BP1s , but it has polynomial complexity with respect to BPs of constant width and circuits.

Proof : We only have to prove the upper bound. In constant depth we decide with $O(n^3)$ binary gates for each 3-clique whether it exists. Then we compute the parity of these results in logarithmic depth and size $O(n^3)$. Finally we apply Theorem 5.1 .

$\square$

In Ch. 11, § 5, we have seen that the classes $\Sigma_k(P)$ build a proper hierarchy.

DEFINITION 6.1 : Let w-k-BP(P) be the class of sequences $f = (f_n)$ of functions $f_n \in B_n$ which can be computed by width-k BPs of polynomial size.

Obviously w-k-BP(P) $\subseteq$ w-(k+1)-BP(P) for $k \geq 2$. The results of Barrington (86) (see § 5) imply that this hierarchy collapses at the fifth level. But, from the results on the majority function, we know that w-2-BP(P) $\subsetneq$ w-5-BP(P) .

DEFINITION 6.2 : Let BPk(P) be the class of sequences $f = (f_n)$ of functions $f_n \in B_n$ which can be computed by read-k-times-only BPs of polynomial size.

Obviously $BPk(P) \subseteq BP(k+1)(P)$ for all k. We conjecture that the classes $BPk(P)$ build a proper hierarchy. But we only know that the first step of the hierarchy is proper (Wegener (84 c)).

THEOREM 6.4 : $BP1(P) \subsetneq BP2(P)$.

Proof : By Theorem 4.8, $(clo_n) \notin BP1(P)$. We design BP2s of polynomial size for clo_n. We use the following simple characterization of the clique-only function. $clo_n(x) = 1$ iff in $G(x)$, the graph specified by x, the degree of each vertex is 0 or $n/2-1$, and there is some vertex i^* of degree $n/2-1$ such that all vertices $i < i^*$ have degree 0 and all vertices of positive degree are connected to i^*.

It is easy to design a BP1 on m variables which has size $O(m^2)$ and $m+1$ sinks and where all inputs with exactly i ones reach the i-th sink $(0 \le i \le m)$. Let T_l $(1 \le l \le n)$ be such a BP1 for all variables representing edges $(l,\cdot)$. The source of T_1 is the source of the BP2 we construct. For $l < n$, the sink 0 of T_l is the source of T_{l+1}, and the sink $n/2-1$ of T_l is the source of H_l which we define later. All other sinks including those of T_n are 0-sinks. If we reach such a sink, $clo_n(x) = 0$. If we reach the source of H_l, we know that the vertices $1,\ldots,l-1$ are isolated in $G(x)$ and that the vertex l equals the vertex i^* in the characterization above.

H_l is the concatenation of $H_{l,l+1}, \ldots, H_{l,n}$. In $H_{l,j}$ we test whether the vertex j has the right degree and whether it is, if necessary, connected to $i^* = l$. At first we "compute" (similar to the BP1 T_l) $d^*(j)$, the number of vertices $j' \neq l$ connected by an edge to the vertex j. If $d^*(j) \notin \{0, n/2-2\}$ we reach 0-sinks. If $d^*(j) = 0$ and the edge (l,j) exists (does not exist), we reach a 0-sink (the source of $H_{l,j+1}$). If $d^*(j) = n/2-2$ and the edge (l,j) exists (does not exist), we reach the source of $H_{l,j+1}$ (a 0-sink). If $j = n$, the source of $H_{l,n+1}$ is replaced by a 1-sink. The so defined BP computes clo_n, if $n \ge 6$.

The size of each T_l and $H_{l,j}$ is $O(n^2)$. Hence the total size is $O(n^4)$. The BP is a read-twice-only BP. Each path leads for some l at most through the BP1s $T_1, \ldots, T_l$, $H_{l,l+1}, \ldots, H_{l,n}$. The edge (i,j) is tested in T_i, if $i \leq l$, in T_j, if $j \leq l$, in $H_{l,i}$, if $l < i$, and in $H_{l,j}$, if $l < j$. Hence each edge is tested at most twice. $\quad\square$

We present a candidate which is in BPk(P) and probably not in BP(k-1)(P). An edge in an undirected graph is a two-element subset of the set of vertices. A k-hyperedge in a hypergraph is a k-element vertex set.

DEFINITION 6.3 : The k-hyperclique-only function $kclo_n$ is defined on $\binom{n}{k}$ variables representing the possible k-hyperedges of a hypergraph. $kclo_n(x) = 1$ iff the hypergraph $H(x)$ specified by the variables contains exactly all k-hyperedges on an $n/2$ vertex set.

EXERCISES

1. The number of 1-leaves in a decision tree for $f \in B_n$ is not smaller than the number of gates on level 1 in a Σ_2-circuit for f.

2. Let $DT(f)$ be the decision tree complexity of f. Then $D(f) \leq c \log(DT(f) + 1)$ for some constant c.

3. Estimate the time complexity of the Turing machine we used for the proof of (1.1).

4. Let $f \in B_n$ be not elusive. Let $f' \in B_n$ be a function differing from f on exactly one input. Then f' is elusive.

5. $BP(PAR_n) = 2n - 1$.

6. Determine $BP1(E_k^n)$ and $BP1(T_k^n)$ exactly.

7. The upper bound in Theorem 4.3 ii is optimal. Hint: Consider de Bruijn sequences (see e.g. Knuth (81)) as value vectors.

8. Prove Theorem 4.4. Hint: Chinese Remainder Theorem.

9. Design an efficient algorithm for the construction of optimal decision trees for symmetric functions.

10. Prove a counterpart of Theorem 4.3 for decision trees.

11. Determine $DT(PAR_n)$.

12. $BP1(clo_n) = 2^{O(n)}$.

13. There is a BP1 for $cl_{n,k}$ where two paths, on which at most $k(1)+1$ variables are tested positively and at most $O(k(0))$ variables are tested negatively, lead to the same node.

14. (Dunne (85), just as 15.). Assume that for $f \in B_n$, all sets $V \subseteq \{x_1, \ldots, x_n\}$ of size bounded by m, and all $x_i \notin V$ there is a restriction $\rho : \{x_1, \ldots, x_n\} - (V \cup \{x_i\}) \to \{0,1\}$ such that $f_\rho(V, x_i) \in \{x_i, \bar{x}_i\}$. Then $BP1(f) \geq 2^{m-1} - 1$.

15. The BP1-complexity of the Hamiltonian circuit function and the BP1-complexity of the logical permanent are exponential.

16. Prove an upper bound (as small as possible) on the constant-width BP complexity of the majority function.

17. $(kclo_n) \in BPk(P)$.

442

References

Adleman(78): Two theorems on random polynomial time. 19.FOCS,75-83.

Adleman;Booth;Preparata;Ruzzo(78): Improved time and space bounds for Boolean matrix multiplication. Acta Informatica 11, 61-70.

Ahlswede;Wegener(86): Search problems. Wiley (in press).

Aho;Hopcroft;Ullman(74): The design and analysis of computer algorithms. Addison-Wesley.

Ajtai(83): Σ_1^1-formulae on finite structures. Ann.Pure and Appl.Logic 24, 1-48.

Ajtai;Babai;Hajnal;Komlós;Pudlák;Rödl;Szemerédi;Turán(86): Two lower bounds for branching problems. 18.STOC, 30-38.

Ajtai;Ben-Or(84): A theorem on probabilistic constant depth computations. 16.STOC, 471-474.

Ajtai;Komlós;Szemerédi(83): An O(n log n) sorting network. 15. STOC, 1-9.

Alekseev(73): On the number of k-valued monotonic functions. Sov. Math.Dokl.14,87-91.

Alt(84): Comparison of arithmetic functions with respect to Boolean circuit depth. 16.STOC, 466-470.

Alt;Hagerup;Mehlhorn;Preparata(86): Simulation of idealized parallel computers on more realistic ones. 12.MFCS, LNCS 233, 199-208.

Alon;Boppana(85): The monotone circuit complexity of Boolean functions. Preprint.

Anderson;Earle;Goldschmidt;Powers(67): The IBM system/360 model 91: floating-point execution unit. IBM J.Res.Dev.11, 34-53.

Andreev(85): On a method for obtaining lower bounds for the complexity of individual monotone functions. Sov.Math.Dokl. 31, 530-534.

Arlazarov;Dinic;Kronrod;Faradzev(70): On economical construction of the transitive closure of a directed graph. Sov.Math.Dokl.11, 1209-1210.

Ashenhurst(57): The decomposition of switching functions. Symp. Theory of Switching, 74-116.

Ayoub(63): An introduction to the analytical theory of numbers. Amer.Math.Soc.

Balcázar;Book;Schöning(84): Sparse oracles, lowness and highness. 11.MFCS, LNCS 176, 185-193.

Barrington(86):Bounded-width polynomial-size branching programs recognize exactly those languages in NC^1. 18.STOC, 1-5.

Barth(80): Monotone Bilinearformen. TR Univ. Saarbrücken.

Bassalygo(82): Asymptotically optimal switching circuits. Probl.Inf.Transm.17, 206-211.

Batcher(68): Sorting networks and their applications. AFIPS 32, 307-314.

Beame(86a): Limits on the power of concurrent-write parallel machines. 18.STOC, 169-176.

Beame(86b): Lower bounds in parallel machine computation. Ph.D.Thesis, Univ. Toronto.

Beame;Cook;Hoover(84): Log depth circuits for division and related problems. 25.FOCS, 1-6.

Bennet;Gill(81): Relative to a random oracle A, $P^A \neq NP^A \neq coNP^A$ with probability 1. SIAM J.on Comp.10, 96-113.

Berkowitz(82): On some relationship between monotone and non-monotone circuit complexity. TR Univ. Toronto.

Best;van Emde Boas;Lenstra(74): A sharpened version of the Aanderaa-Rosenberg conjecture. TR Univ.Amsterdam.

Bloniarz(79): The complexity of monotone Boolean functions and an algorithm for finding shortest paths in a graph. Ph.D.Th., MIT.

Blum(84): A Boolean function requiring 3n network size. TCS 28, 337-345.

Blum(85): An $\Omega(n^{4/3})$ lower bound on the monotone network complexity of the n-th degree convolution. TCS 36, 59-70.

Blum;Seysen(84): Characterization of all optimal networks for a simultaneous computation of AND and NOR. Acta Inform.21, 171-182.

Bollobás(76): Complete subgraphs are elusive. J.on Comb.Th.21, 1-7.

Bollobás(78): Extremal graph theory. Academic Press.

Boppana(84): Threshold functions and bounded depth monotone circuits. 16.STOC, 475-479.

Borodin(77): On relating time and space to size and depth. SIAM J.on Comp.6, 733-744.

Borodin;Dolev;Fich;Paul(83): Bounds for width two branching programs. 15.STOC, 87-93.

Brent(70): On the addition of binary numbers. IEEE Trans.on Comp.19, 758-759.

Brent;Kuck;Maruyama(73): The parallel evaluation of arithmetic expressions without division. IEEE Trans.on Comp.22, 532-534.

Brent;Kung(80): The chip complexity of binary arithmetic. 12.STOC, 190-200.

Brown(66): On graphs that do not contain a Thompsen graph. Can.Math.Bull.9, 281-285.

Brustmann;Wegener(86): The complexity of symmetric functions in bounded-depth circuits. TR Univ.Frankfurt.

Bublitz(86): Decomposition of graphs and monotone formula size of homogeneous functions. Acta Inform. (in press).

Bublitz;Schürfeld;Voigt;Wegener(86): Properties of complexity measures for PRAMs and WRAMs. TCS (in press).

Budach(84): A lower bound for the number of nodes in a decision tree. TR Univ.Berlin (GDR).

Caldwell(64): Der logische Entwurf von Schaltkreisen. Oldenbourg.

Carlson;Savage(83): Size-space tradeoffs for oblivious computations. JCSS 26, 65-81.

Chandra;Fortune;Lipton(83): Lower bounds for constant depth circuits for prefix functions. 10.ICALP, 109-117.

Chandra;Fortune;Lipton(85): Unbounded fan-in circuits and associative functions. JCSS 30; 222-234.

Chandra;Furst;Lipton(83): Multiparty protocols. 15.STOC, 94-99.

Chandra;Kozen;Stockmeyer(81): Alternation. JACM 28, 114-133.

Chandra;Stockmeyer;Vishkin(82): A complexity theory for unbounded fan-in parallelism. 23.FOCS, 1-13.

Chandra;Stockmeyer;Vishkin(84): Constant depth reducibility. SIAM J.on Comp.13, 423-439.

444

Cobham(66): The recognition problem for the set of perfect squares. 7.SWAT, 78-87.

Commentz-Walter(79): Size-depth tradeoff in monotone Boolean formulae. Acta Inform.12, 227-243.

Commentz-Walter;Sattler(80): Size-depth tradeoff in non-monotone Boolean formulae. Acta Inform.14, 257-269.

Cook(71): The complexity of theorem proving. 3.STOC, 151-158.

Cook(79): Deterministic CFL's are accepted simultaneously in polynomial time and log squared space. 11.STOC, 338-345.

Cook(80): Towards a complexity theory of synchronous parallel computation. Symp.on Logic and Algorithmic, 75-100.

Cook(83): The classification of problems which have fast parallel algorithms. FCT, LNCS 158, 78-93.

Cook;Dwork;Reischuk(86): Upper and lower time bounds for parallel random access machines without simultaneous writes. SIAM J.on Comp. 15, 87-97.

Cook;Hoover(85): A depth-universal circuit. SIAM J.on Comp.14, 833-839.

Cooley;Tukey(65): An algorithm for the machine calculation of complex Fourier series. Math.Comp.19, 297-301.

Coppersmith;Winograd(82): On the asymptotic complexity of matrix multiplication. SIAM J.on Comp.11, 472-492.

Denenberg;Gurevich;Shelah(83): Cardinalities definable by constant depth polynomial size circuits. TR Univ. Harvard.

Dunne(84): Techniques for the analysis of monotone Boolean networks. Ph.D.Th., Univ. Warwick.

Dunne(85): Lower bounds on the complexity of 1-time only branching programs. FCT, LNCS 199, 90-99.

Edwards(73): The principles of switching circuits. MIT Press.

Ehrenfeucht(72): Practical decidability. TR Univ.of Colorado.

Fagin;Klawe;Pippenger;Stockmeyer(85): Bounded depth, polynomial-size circuits for symmetric functions. TCS 36, 239-250.

Feller(68): An introduction to probability theory and its applications. Wiley.

Finikov(57): On a family of classes of functions in the logic algebra and their realization in the class of π-schemes. Dokl.Akad.Nauk.115, 247-248.

Fischer(74): Lectures on network complexity. TR Univ. Frankfurt.

Fischer;Meyer(71): Boolean matrix multiplication and transitive closure. 12.SWAT, 129-131.

Fischer;Meyer;Paterson(82): $\Omega(n \log n)$ lower bounds on length of Boolean formulas. SIAM J.on Comp.11, 416-427.

Friedman(84): Constructing $O(n \log n)$ size monotone formulae for the k-th elementary symmetric polynomial of n Boolean variables. 25.FOCS, 506-515.

Furst;Saxe;Sipser(84): Parity, circuits and the polynomial time hierarchy. Math.Syst.Th.17, 13-27.

Gabber;Galil(79): Explicit constructions of linear size superconcentrators. 20.FOCS, 364-370.

Galbiati;Fischer(81): On the complexity of 2-output Boolean networks. TCS 16, 177-185.

Galil;Paul(83): An efficient general purpose parallel computer. JACM 30, 360-387.

Garey;Johnson(79): Computers and intractability: A guide to the theory of NP-completeness. W.H.Freeman.

Gaskov(78): The depth of Boolean functions. Probl.Kibernet. 34, 265-268.

Gilbert(54): Lattice theoretic properties of frontal switching functions. J.Math.Phys.33, 57-97.

Glassey;Karp(72): On the optimality of Huffman trees. SIAM J.on Comp.1, 31-39.

Goldschlager(78): A unified approach to models of synchronous parallel machines. 10.STOC, 89-94.

Graham;Rothschild;Spencer(80): Ramsey theory. John Wiley.

Gumm;Poguntke(81): Boolesche Algebra. BI.

Hansel(64): Nombre minimal de contacts de fermeture nécessaire pour réaliser une fonction Booléenne symmétriques de n variables. C.R.Acad.Sci.Paris 258, 6037-6040.

Hansel(66): Sur le nombre de fonctions Booléennes monotones de n variables. C.R.Acad.Sci.Paris 262, 1088-1090.

Harper(77): An n log n lower bound on synchronous combinational complexity. Proc.AMS 64, 300-306.

Harper;Hsieh;Savage(75): A class of Boolean functions with linear combinational complexity. TCS 1, 161-183.

Harper;Savage(72): On the complexity of the marriage problem. Adv.Math.9, 299-312.

Harper;Savage(73): Complexity made simple. Symp.on Comb.Th., 2-15.

Harper;Savage(79): Lower bounds on synchronous combinational complexity. SIAM J.on Comp.8, 115-119.

Hastad(86): Almost optimal lower bounds for small depth circuits. 18.STOC, 6-20.

Hedtstück(85): Über die Argumentkomplexität Boolescher Funktionen. Diss. Univ. Stuttgart.

Henno(79): The depth of monotone functions in multivalued logic. IPL 8, 176-177.

Hill;Peterson(81): Switching theory & logical design. John Wiley.

Hodes(70): The logic complexity of geometric properties in the plane. JACM 17, 339-347.

Hodes;Specker(68): Length of formulas and elimination of quantifiers. Contr.to Math.Logic. North-Holland.

Hoover;Klawe;Pippenger(84): Bounding fan-out in logical networks. JACM 31, 13-18.

Hopcroft;Karp(73): An $n^{5/2}$ algorithm for maximum matching in bipartite graphs. SIAM J.on Comp.2, 225-231.

Hotz(74): Schaltkreistheorie. de Gruyter.

Hromkovic(85): Linear lower bounds on unbounded fan-in Boolean circuits. IPL 21, 71-74.

Hsieh(74): Intersection theorems for systems of finite vector spaces and other combinatorial results. Ph.D.Th., MIT.

Huppert(67): Finite groups I. Springer.

Johnson;Savage;Welch(72): Combinational complexity measures as a function of fan-out. TR.

Kahn;Saks;Sturtevant(84): A topological approach to evasiveness. Combinatorica 4, 297-306.

Kannan(82): Circuit-size lower bounds and non-reducibility to sparse sets. IC 55, 40-56.

Karatsuba;Ofman(63): Multiplication of multidigit numbers on automata. Sov.Phys.Dokl.7, 595-596.

Karnaugh(53): The map method for synthesis of combinational logic circuits. AIEE Trans.Comm.Elect.72, 593-598.

Karp(72): Reducibility among combinatorial problems. Complexity of computer computations. Plenum Press. 85-104.

Karp;Lipton(80): Some connections between non uniform and uniform complexity classes. 12.STOC, 302-309.

Khasin(69): On realizations of monotonic symmetric functions by formulas in the basis +,•,-. Syst.Th.Res.21, 254-259.

Khasin(70): Complexity bounds for the realization of monotone symmetrical functions by means of formulas in the basis +,•,-. Sov.Phys.Dokl.14, 1149-1151.

Klawe;Paul;Pippenger;Yannakakis(84): On monotone formulae with restricted depth. 16.STOC, 480-487.

Kleiman;Pippenger(78): An explicit construction of short monotone formulae for the symmetric functions. TCS 7, 325-332.

Klein;Paterson(80): Asymptotically optimal circuit for a storage access function. IEEE Trans.of Comp.29, 737-738.

Kleitman(69): On Dedekind's problem: The number of monotone Boolean functions. Proc.AMS 21, 677-682.

Kleitman(73): The number of Sperner families of subsets of an n element set. Colloq.Math.Soc. János Bolyai 10, 989-1001.

Kleitman;Kwiatkowski(80): Further results on the Aanderaa-Rosenberg conjecture. J.on Comb.Th.(B) 28, 85-95.

Kleitman;Markowsky(75): On Dedekind's problem: the number of isotone Boolean functions II. Trans.AMS 213, 373-390.

Kloss(66): Estimates of the complexity of solutions of systems of linear equations. Sov.Math.Dokl.7, 1537-1540.

Kloss;Malyshev(65): Estimates of the complexity of certain classes of functions. Vestn.Moskov.Univ.Ser.1 4, 44-51.

Knuth(81): The art of computer programming. Addison Wesley.

Ko;Schöning(85): On circuit-size complexity and the low hierarchy in NP. SIAM J.on Comp.14, 41-51.

Korobkov(56): The realization of symmetric functions in the class of π-schemes. Dokl.Akad.Nauk.109, 260-263.

Korshunov(77): The solution to a problem of Dedekind on the number of monotone Boolean functions. Dokl.Akad.Nauk.233, 543-546.

Korshunov(81a): On the number of monotone Boolean functions. Probl.Kibern.38, 5-108.

Korshunov(81b): On the complexity of the shortest disjunctive normal forms of Boolean functions. Met.Diskr.Anal.37, 9-41.

Kovari;Sós;Turán(54): On a problem of K. Zarankiewicz. Coll.Math. 3, 50-57.

Kramer;van Leeuwen(82): The complexity of VLSI circuits for arbitrary Boolean functions. TR Univ. Utrecht.

Krapchenko(70): Asymptotic estimation of addition time of parallel adder. Syst.Th.Res.19, 105-122.

Krapchenko(71): Complexity of the realization of a linear function in the class of π-circuits. Math.Notes Acad.Sci.USSR 10, 21-23.

Krapchenko(72a): The complexity of the realization of symmetrical functions by formulae. Math.Notes.Acad.Sci.USSR 11, 70-76.

Krapchenko(72b): A method of obtaining lower bounds for the complexity of π-schemes. Math.Notes Acad.Sci.USSR 11, 474-479.

Krichevskii(64): Complexity of contact circuits realizing a function of logical algebra. Sov.Phys.Dokl.8, 770-772.

Kriegel;Waack(86): Lower bounds on the complexity of real-time branching programs. TR AdW Berlin (GDR).

Kucera(82): Parallel computation and conflicts in memory access. IPL 14, 93-96.

Kuznetsov(83a): On the complexity of the realization of a sequence of Boolean functions by formulas of depth 3 in the basis {∨,&,-}. Ver.Met.Kibern.19, 40-43.

Kuznetsov(83b): On the lower estimate of the length of the shortest disjunctive normal form for almost all Boolean functions. Ver.Met. Kibern.19, 44-47.

Ladner;Fischer(80): Parallel prefix computation. JACM 27, 831-838.

Lamagna(75): The complexity of monotone functions. Ph.D.Th., Brown Univ.

Lamagna(79): The complexity of monotone networks for certain bilinear forms, routing problems, sorting and merging. IEEE Trans.on Comp.28, 773-782.

Lamagna;Savage(73): On the logical complexity of symmetric switching functions in monotone and complete bases. TR Brown Univ.

Lamagna;Savage(74): Combinational complexity of some monotone functions. 15.SWAT, 140-144.

Lee(78): Modern switching theory and digital design. Prentice Hall.

Lipton;Tarjan(79): A separator theorem for planar graphs. SIAM J.on Appl.Math.36, 177-189.

Lipton;Tarjan(80): Applications of a planar separator theorem. SIAM J.on Comp.9, 615-627.

Lotti;Romani(80): Application of approximating algorithms to Boolean matrix multiplication. IEEE Trans.on Comp.29, 927-928.

Lupanov(58): A method of circuit synthesis. Izv.VUZ Radiofiz 1, 120-140.

Lupanov(61): Implementing the algebra of logic functions in terms of bounded depth formulas in the basis &,∨,- . Sov.Phys.Dokl.6, 107-108.

Lupanov(62a): On the principle of local coding and the realization of functions of certain classes of networks composed of functional elements. Sov.Phys.Dokl.6, 750-752.

Lupanov(62b): Complexity of formula realization of functions of logical algebra. Probl.Kibern.3, 782-811.

Lupanov(65a): On the realization of functions of logical algebra by formulae of finite classes (formulae of limited depth) in the basis •,+,- . Probl.Kibern.6, 1-14.

Lupanov(65b): A method of synthesis of control systems - the principle of local coding. Probl.Kibern.14, 31-110.

Lupanov(70): On circuits of functional elements with delay. Probl.Kibern.23, 43-81.

Mac Lane;Birkhoff(67): Algebra. Mac Millan.

Margulis(75): Explicit construction of concentrators. Probl.of Inform.Transm., Plenum Press.

Masek(76): A fast algorithm for the string editing problem and decision graph complexity. M.Sc.Th. MIT.

McCluskey(56): Minimization of Boolean functions. Bell Syst.Techn.J.35, 1417-1444.

McColl(76): Some results on circuit depth. Ph.D.Th., Univ. Warwick.

McColl(78a): Complexity hierarchies for Boolean functions. Acta Inform.11, 71-77.

McColl(78b): The maximum depth of monotone formulae. IPL 7, 65.

McColl(78c): The circuit depth of symmetric Boolean funtions. JCSS 17, 108-115.

McColl(81): Planar crossovers. IEEE Trans.on Comp.30, 223-225.

McColl(85a): On the planar monotone computation of threshold functions. 2.STACS, LNCS 182, 219-230.

McColl(85b): Planar circuits have short specifications. 2.STACS, LNCS 182, 231-242.

McColl;Paterson(77): The depth of all Boolean functions. SIAM J.on Comp.6, 373-380.

McColl;Paterson(84): The planar realization of Boolean functions. TR Univ. Warwick.

McKenzie;Cook(84): The parallel complexity of some Abelian permutation group. TR Univ. Toronto.

Mead;Conway(80): Introduction to VLSI systems. Addison Wesley.

Mead;Rem(79): Cost and performance of VLSI computing structures. IEEE J.Solid State Circuits 14, 455-462.

Mehlhorn(77): Effiziente Algorithmen. Teubner.

Mehlhorn(79): Some remarks on Boolean sums. Acta Inform.12, 371-375.

Mehlhorn;Galil(76): Monotone switching circuits and Boolean matrix product. Computing 16, 99-111.

Mehlhorn;Preparata(83): Area-time optimal VLSI integer multiplier with minimum computation time. IC 58, 137-156.

Mehlhorn;Vishkin(84): Randomized and deterministic simulations of PRAMs by parallel machines with restricted granularity of parallel memories. Acta Inform.21, 339-374.

Mendelson(82): Boolesche Algebra und logische Schaltungen. McGraw-Hill.

Meyer;Stockmeyer(72): The equivalence problem for regular expressions with squaring requires exponential time. 13.SWAT, 125-129.

Meyer auf der Heide(84): A polynomial linear search algorithm for the n-dimensional knapsack problem. JACM 31, 668-676.

Meyer auf der Heide(86): Efficient simulations among several models of parallel computers. SIAM J.on Comp.15, 106-119.

Mileto;Putzolu(64): Average values of quantities appearing in Boolean function minimization. IEEE Trans.El.Comp.13, 87-92.

Mileto;Putzolu(65): Statistical complexity of algorithms for Boolean function minimization. JACM 12, 364-375.

Miller,R.E.(79): Switching theory. Robert E.Krieger Publ.Comp.

Miller,W.(75): Computer search for numerical instability. JACM 22, 512-521.

Muller;Preparata(75): Bounds to complexities of networks for sorting and switching. JACM 22, 195-201.

Muller;Preparata(76): Restructing of arithmetic expressions for parallel evaluation. JACM 23, 534-543.

Muroga(79): Logic design and switching theory. John Wiley.

Nechiporuk(66): A Boolean function. Sov.Math.Dokl.7, 999-1000.

Nechiporuk(71): On a Boolean matrix. Syst.Th.Res.21, 236-239.

Nigmatullin(67a): Certain metric relations in the unit cube. Discr.Anal.9, 47-58.

Nigmatullin(67b): A variational principle in an algebra of logic. Discr.Anal.10, 69-89.

Nurmeev(81): On circuit complexity of the realization of almost all monotone Boolean functions. Iz.VUZ Mat.25, 64-70.

Oberschelp(84): Fast parallel algorithms for finding all prime implicants for discrete functions. LNCS 171, 408-420.

Ofman(63): On the algorithmic complexity of discrete functions. Sov.Phys.Dokl.7, 589-591.

Okol'nishnikova(82): On the influence of negations on the complexity of a realization of monotone Boolean functions by formulas of bounded depth. Met.Diskr.Anal.38, 74-80.

Pan(84): How can we speed up matrix multiplication? SIAM Rev.26, 393-415.

Paterson(73): New bounds on formula size. 3.TCS-GI, 17-26.

Paterson(75): Complexity of monotone networks for Boolean matrix product. TCS 1, 13-20.

Paterson(76): An introduction to Boolean function complexity. Astérisque 38-39, 183-201.

Paterson(83): An improved depth O(log n) comparator network for sorting. Oberwolfach Conf.on Compl.Th.

Paterson;Hewitt(80): Comparative schematology. Proj.MAC Conf.on Conc.Syst.and Par.Comp., 119-127.

Paterson;Valiant(76): Circuit size is nonlinear in depth. TCS 2, 397-400.

Paterson;Wegener(86): Nearly optimal hierarchies for network and formula size. Acta Inform.23, 217-221.

Paul(75): Boolesche Minimalpolynome und Überdeckungsprobleme. Acta Inform.4, 321-336.

Paul(76): Realizing Boolean functions on disjoint sets of variables. TCS 2, 383-396.

Paul(77): A 2.5 n lower bound on the combinational complexity of Boolean functions. SIAM J.on Comp.6, 427-443.

Paul(78): Komplexitätstheorie. Teubner.

Picard(65): Théorie des questionnaires. Gauthier-Villars.

Pippenger(76): The realization of monotone Boolean functions. 8. STOC, 204-210.

Pippenger(77a): Superconcentrators. SIAM J.on Comp.6, 298-304.

Pippenger(77b): Fast simulation of combinatorial logic networks by machines without random-access storage. 15.Allerton Conf.on Comm.,Contr.and Comp.

Pippenger(77c): On another Boolean matrix. TR IBM Yorktown Heights.

Pippenger(78): The complexity of monotone Boolean functions. Math.Syst.Th.11, 289-316.

Pippenger(79): On simultaneous resource bounds. 20.FOCS, 307-311.

Pippenger;Fischer (73): Relations among complexity measures. TR IBM Yorktown Heights.

Pippenger;Fischer(79): Relations among complexity measures. JACM 26, 361-381.

Pippenger;Valiant(76): Shifting graphs and their applications. JACM 23, 423-432.

Pratt(75a): The power of negative thinking in multiplying Boolean matrices. SIAM J.on Comp.4, 326-330.

Pratt(75b): The effect of basis on size of Boolean expressions. 16.FOCS, 119-121.

Preparata;Muller(71): On the delay required to realize Boolean functions. IEEE Trans.on Comp.20, 459-461.

Preparata;Muller(76): Efficient parallel evaluation of Boolean expressions. IEEE Trans.on Comp.25, 548-549.

Pudlák(83): Boolean complexity and Ramsey theorems. TR Univ. Prague.

Pudlák(84a): Bounds for Hodes-Specker theorem. LNCS 171, 421-445.

Pudlák(84b): A lower bound on complexity of branching programs. 11.MFCS, LNCS 176, 480-489.

Pudlák;Zák(83): Space complexity of computations. TR Univ. Prague.

Quine(52): The problem of simplifying truth functions. Am.Math.Soc.61, 521-531.

Quine(53): Two theorems about truth functions. Bol.Soc.Math.Mex.10, 64-70.

Quine(55): A way to simplify truth functions. Am.Math.Monthly 62, 627-631.

Razborov(85a): A lower bound on the monotone network complexity of the logical permanent. Matemat.Zametki 37, 887-900.

Razborov(85b): Lower bounds on the monotone complexity of some Boolean functions. Dokl.Akad.Nauk.281, 798-801.

Razborov(86): Lower bounds on the size of bounded-depth networks over the basis $\{\wedge,\oplus\}$. Preprint.

Red'kin(73): Proof of minimality of circuits consisting of functional elements. Syst.Th.Res.23, 85-103.

Red'kin(79): On the realization of monotone Boolean functions by contact circuits. Probl.Kibern.35, 87-110.

Red'kin(81): Minimal realization of a binary adder. Probl.Kibern.38, 181-216,272.

Reif(83): Logarithmic depth circuits for algebraic functions. 24.FOCS, 138-145.

Reznik(62): The realization of monotonic functions by means of networks consisting of functional elements. Sov.Phys.Dokl.6, 558-561.

Riordan;Shannon(42): The number of two-terminal series-parallel networks. J.on Math.Phys.21, 83-93.

Rivest;Vuillemin(76): On recognizing graph properties from adjacency matrices. TCS 3, 371-384.

Runge;König(24): Die Grundlehre der mathematischen Wissenschaften 11. Springer.

Ruzzo(81): On uniform circuit complexity. JCSS 22, 365-383.

Sattler(81): Netzwerke zur simultanen Berechnung Boolescher Funktionen. 5.TCS-GI, LNCS 104, 32-40.

Savage(72): Computational work and time on finite machines. JACM 19, 660-674.

Savage(74): An algorithm for the computation of linear forms. SIAM J.on Comp.3, 150-158.

Savage(76): The complexity of computing. John Wiley.

Savage(81): Planar circuit complexity and the performance of VLSI algorithms. VLSI Syst.and Comp., Comp.Sc.Press.

Savage(82): Bounds on the performance of multilective VLSI algorithms. TR Brown Univ.

Scarpellini(85): Complex Boolean functions obtained by diagonalization. TCS 36, 119-126.

Schnorr(74): Zwei lineare untere Schranken für die Komplexität Boolescher Funktionen. Computing 13, 155-171.

Schnorr(76a): The network complexity and the Turing machine complexity of finite functions. Acta Inform.7, 95-107.

Schnorr(76b): The combinational complexity of equivalence. TCS 1, 289-295.

Schnorr(76c): A lower bound on the number of additions in monotone computations. TCS 2, 305-315.

Schnorr(77): The network complexity and the breadth of Boolean functions. Stud.Logic Found.Math.87, 491-504.

Schnorr(80): A 3-n lower bound on the network complexity of Boolean functions. TCS 10, 83-92.

Schönhage;Strassen(71): Schnelle Multiplikation großer Zahlen. Computing 7, 281-292.

Schöning(83): A low and a high hierarchy within NP. JCSS 27, 14-28.

Schöning(84): On small generators. TCS 34, 337-341.

Schürfeld(83): New lower bounds on the formula size of Boolean functions. Acta Inform.19, 183-194.

Schürfeld;Wegener(86): On the CREW PRAM complexity of Boolean functions. Parallel Computing 85, Eds.Feilmeier, Joubert, Schendel; Elsevier Publ., 247-252.

Shannon(38): A symbolic analysis of relay and switching circuits. Trans.AIEE 57, 713-723.

452

Shannon(49): The synthesis of two-terminal switching circuits. Bell Syst.Techn.J.28, 59-98.

Simon,H.U.(83): A tight $\Omega(\log\log n)$ bound on the time for parallel RAM's to compute nondegenerate Boolean functions. FCT, LNCS 158, 439-444.

Simon,J.(77): Physical limits on the speed of computing. TR Univ. Campinas.

Sipser(83): Borel sets and circuit complexity. 15. STOC, 61-69.

Sklansky(60a): An evaluation of several two-sum and binary adders. IRE Trans.Elect.Comp.9, 213-226.

Sklansky(60b): Conditional-sum addition logic. IRE Trans.Elect.Comp. 9, 226-231.

Skyum(83): A measure in which Boolean negation is exponentially powerful. IPL 17, 125-128.

Skyum;Valiant(85): A complexity theory based on Boolean algebra. JACM 32, 484-502.

Soprunenko(65): Minimal realizations of functions by circuits using functional elements. Probl.Kibern.15, 117-134.

Spaniol(76): Arithmetik in Rechenanlagen. Teubner.

Specker;Strassen(76): Komplexität von Entscheidungsproblemen. LNCS 43.

Spira(71a): On time-hardware complexity tradeoffs for Boolean functions. 4.Hawaii Symp.on Syst.Sc., 525-527.

Spira(71b): On the time necessary to compute switching functions. IEEE Trans.on Comp.20, 104-105.

Stockmeyer(74): The complexity of decision problems in automata and logic. TR MIT.

Stockmeyer(76): The polynomial-time hierarchy. TCS 3, 1-22.

Stockmeyer(77): On the combinational complexity of certain symmetric Boolean functions. Math.Syst.Th.10, 323-326.

Stockmeyer(83): The complexity of approximate counting. 15.STOC, 118-126.

Stockmeyer;Vishkin(84): Simulation of parallel random access machines by circuits. SIAM J.on Comp.13, 409-422.

Strassen(69): Gaussian elimination is not optimal. Num.Math.13, 354-356.

Strassen(86): Relative bilinear complexity and matrix multiplication. TR Univ. Zürich.

Tarjan(78): Complexity of monotone networks for computing conjunctions. Ann.Discr.Math.2, 121-133.

Thompson(79): Area time complexity for VLSI. 11.STOC, 81-88.

Thompson(80): A complexity theory for VLSI. Ph.D.Th., Carnegie-Mellon Univ.

Tiekenheinrich(83): Verallgemeinerungen des Tiefenhierarchiesatzes für Boolesche Funktionen. Dipl.arb. Univ. Bielefeld.

Tiekenheinrich(84): A 4n-lower bound on the monotone network complexity of a one-output Boolean function. IPL 18, 201-202.

Tkachev(80): On the complexity of realizations of a sequence of Boolean functions by Boolean circuits and π-schemes under some additional restrictions on the construction of the schemes. Comb.and Alg.Meth.in Appl.Math., 161-207.

Turán(84): The critical complexity of graph properties, IPL 18, 151-153.

Ugolnikov(76): On the realizations of monotone functions by circuits of functional elements. Probl.Kibern.31, 167-185.

Uhlig(74): On the synthesis of self-correcting schemes from functional elements with a small number of reliable elements. Math.Notes Acad.Sci.USSR 15, 558-562.

Uhlig(84): Zur Parallelberechnung Boolescher Funktionen. TR Ing.hochsch. Mittweida.

Ullman(84): Computational aspects of VLSI. Comp.Sc.Press.

Valiant(76a): Graph-theoretic properties in computational complexity. JCSS 13, 278-285.

Valiant(76b): Universal circuits. 8.STOC, 196-203.

Valiant(79): Completeness classes in algebra. 11.STOC, 249-261.

Valiant(80): Negation can be exponentially powerful. TCS 12, 303-314.

Valiant(83): Exponential lower bounds for restricted monotone circuits. 15.STOC, 110-117.

Valiant(84): Short monotone formulae for the majority function. J.of Algorithms 5, 363-366.

Valiant(86): Negation is powerless for Boolean slice functions. SIAM J.on Comp.15, 531-535.

van Leeuwen(83): Parallel computers and algorithms. Coll.on Par.Comp.and Alg.

van Voorhis(72): An improved lower bound for sorting networks. IEEE Trans.on Comp.21, 612-613.

Veitch(52): A chart method for simplifying truth functions. Proc.Ass. Comput.Mach., 127-133.

Vilfan(72): The complexity of finite functions. Ph.D.Th., MIT.

Vishkin;Wigderson(85): Trade-offs between depth and width in parallel computation. SIAM J.on Comp.14, 303-314.

Vuillemin(83): A combinatorial limit to the computing power of VLSI circuits. IEEE Trans.on Comp.32, 294-300.

Wallace(64): A suggestion for a fast multiplier. IEEE Trans.on Comp.13, 14-17.

Wegener(79a): Switching functions whose monotone complexity is nearly quadratic. TCS 9, 83-97.

Wegener(79b): A counterexample to a conjecture of Schnorr referring to monotone networks. TCS 9, 147-150.

Wegener(80): A new lower bound on the monotone network complexity of Boolean sums. Acta Inform.13, 109-114.

Wegener(81): An improved complexity hierarchy on the depth of Boolean functions. Acta Inform.15, 147-152.

Wegener(82a): Boolean functions whose monotone complexity is of size $n^2/\log n$. TCS 21, 213-224.

Wegener(82b): Best possible asymptotic bounds on the depth of monotone functions in multivalued logic. IPL 15, 81-83.

Wegener(83): Relating monotone formula size and monotone depth of Boolean functions. IPL 16, 41-42.

454

Wegener(84a): Proving lower bounds on the monotone complexity of Boolean functions. LNCS 171, 446-456.

Wegener(84b): Optimal decision trees and one-time-only branching programs for symmetric Boolean functions. IC 62, 129-143.

Wegener(84c): On the complexity of branching programs and decision trees for clique functions. TR Univ. Frankfurt.

Wegener(85a): On the complexity of slice functions. TCS 38, 55-68.

Wegener(85b): The critical complexity of all (monotone) Boolean functions and monotone graph properties. IC 67, 212-222.

Wegener(86a): Time-space trade-offs for branching programs. JCSS 32, 91-96.

Wegener(86b): More on the complexity of slice functions. TCS 43, 201-211.

Weiß(83): An $\Omega(n^{3/2})$ lower bound on the monotone complexity of Boolean convolution. IC 59, 184-188.

Weyh(72): Elemente der Schaltungsalgebra. Oldenbourg.

Wilson(83): Relativized circuit complexity. 24.FOCS, 329-334.

Wippersteg(82): Einige Ergebnisse für synchrone Schaltkreise. Dipl.arb. Univ. Bielefeld.

Yablonskii(57): On the impossibility of eliminating trial of all functions from P_2 in solving some problems on circuit theory. Dokl.Akad.Nauk.USSR 124, 44-47.

Yao(83): Lower bounds by probabilistic arguments. 24.FOCS, 420-428.

Yao(85): Separating the polynomial-time hierarchy by oracles. 26.FOCS, 1-10.

Yap(83): Some consequences of non-uniform conditions of uniform classes. TCS 26, 287-300.

Zák(84): An exponential lower bound for one-time-only branching programs. 11.MFCS, LNCS 176, 562-566.

FCT	- Fundamentals of Computation Theory
FOCS	- Symp. on Foundations of Computer Science
IC	- Information and Control
ICALP	- Int.Colloquium on Automata, Languages and Programming
IPL	- Information Processing Letters
JACM	- Journal of the Association for Computing Machinery
JCSS	- Journal of Computer and System Sciences
LNCS	- Lecture Notes in Computer Science
MFCS	- Mathematical Foundations of Computer Science
STACS	- Symp. on Theoretical Aspects of Computer Science
STOC	- Symp. on Theory of Computing
SWAT	- Symp. on Switching and Automata Theory
TCS	- Theoretical Computer Science
TCS-GI	- GI Conf. Theoretical Computer Science
TR	- Technical Report

Index

addition 7,39,124,313,322,341,348
affine function 251
Ajtai, Komlós and Szemerédi sorting network 152
almost all 87
arithmetic circuit 64
Ashenhurst decomposition 304

basis 7
Batcher sorting network 149
bilinear function 169
bipartite matching 310
Boolean convolution 58,168,209,350
Boolean matrix product 78,107,170, 350
Boolean sum 36,107,163,213
BPP 286
branching program 414

canonical slice 203
carry function 39,226,341
carry-look-ahead-adder 83
carry save adder 51
cell partition 388
central slice 204
Chinese Remainder Theorem 61
circuit 7
circuit size 9
circuit value problem 310
clause 36
clique function 107,184,189,192,203, 204,257,270,384,421,422,427,436
clique-only function 430,438
communication width 363
comparison function 143,322
complete basis 9
conditional sum adder 40
configuration 278
conjunctive normal form 5
connectivity 85,309
constant depth reducibility 312
counting function 74,123,127,252,314
CO WRAM 363
CRCW PRAM 363
CREW PRAM 362
critical complexity 379

data rate 348
de Morgan laws 4
decision tree 419

decoding circuit 90
depth 9
determinant 81,256,262,343,422
direct product 301
Discrete Fourier Transform 63
disjoint bilinear form 215
disjunctive normal form 5
division 67,308
dual function 148

elimination method 121
elusive function 418
equality test 126
EREW PRAM 362
essential dependence 19,120
Eulerian cycle 309
evasive function 418
exactly - k - function 74,426
explicitly defined function 119,139
exponential growth 17
EXP TAPE HARD 139

fan-in 11
fan-out 10
Fast Fourier Transform 62
Fischer, Meyer and Paterson method 251
formula 12
formula size 12

gate 7
generating circuit 283
graded set of Boolean functions 389
graph property 402

Hamiltonian circuit 217,426
hierarchy 296,337,394,436
(h,k)-disjoint Boolean sum 163
Hodes and Specker method 249
homogeneous function 107
Horner scheme 227

implicant 24

Karnaugh diagram 30
Krapchenko method 258
(k,s) - Lupanov representation 91

Las Vegas algorithm 286
logical level 23,320

logical permanent 193,426

majority function 154,243,312,313,
    333,426,436
marriage problem 102
mass production 301
maxterm 5
merging function 149,151,158,322
minimal polynomial 23
minterm 5
monom 23
monotone basis 145
monotone circuit 145
monotone disjunctive normal form 32
monotone function 3
monotone representation 197
monotone storage access function
    399
Monte Carlo algorithm 285
multiplication 51,226,308,313,350

NC - Nick's class 292
NC_1 reducibility 307
Nechiporuk method 253,421
negative envelope of convolution 58
network flow problem 310
non degenerated function 19,120
non deterministic Turing machine
    269
non uniform computation model 19,
    279,363,414
NP 33,269
NP - completeness 33,184,203,270,288

oblivious Turing machine 271
odd-even merge 149
1 - fan-in 326
oracle 270,307

P 269
parity function 36,125,261,312,313,
    324,380,387
partially defined function 22
perfect matching 193,426
period 348
permutation branching program 434
Π_k-circuit 320
planar circuit 344
polynomial 23
polynomial growth 17
P / Poly 283
prefix problem 48
prime clause 36

prime implicant 24
probabilistic computation model 285,
    352
processor partition 388
programmable circuit 110
projection reducibility 146,309
pseudo complement 195

quadratic function 107
Quine and McCluskey algorithm 25

radix - 4 -representation 54
random restriction 326
read-once-only branching program
    423
replacement rule 160
ring sum expansion 6
root of identity 62

satisfiability problem 270,289
Schönhage and Strassen algorithm
    56
selection function 20,218
self reducibility 289
semi-disjoint bilinear form 169
sensitive complexity 374
set circuit 208
set cover problem 33
Shannon effect 88
Shannon's counting argument 87
Σ_k-circuit 320
single level 236
size 9
SIZE - DEPTH(poly,const) 312
slice function 195
sorting function 148,158,313
sorting network 74,148
space complexity 269
Stockmeyer hierarchy 270
storage access function 76,123,374,
    420
storage access function for indirect
    addressing 255,422
Strassen algorithm 79
strong connectivity 310
subtraction 50
symmetric function 74
synchronous circuit 340

table of prime implicants 27
threshold function 74,107,127,148,
    154,196,235,239,243,250,313,323,357,
    422

time complexity 269
trade-off 225
transitive function 349
Turing machine 268

uniform computation models 267,292
universal circuit 110
universal gate 112
universal graph 112

value function 176
value vector 74
variational principle 106
VLSI 226,347

weak Shannon effect 106
width of a branching program 417
WRAM 363